CHRISTIAN COCHINI, S.J.

Apostolic Origins
of Priestly Celibacy

CHRISTIAN COCHINI, S.J.

Apostolic Origins
of Priestly Celibacy

With a Preface by
Father Alfons M. Stickler

Translated by
Nelly Marans

IGNATIUS PRESS   SAN FRANCISCO

Title of the French original:
Origines apostoliques du célibat sacerdotal
Éditions Lethielleux, Paris
Le Sycomore
© 1981 Dessain et Tolra, Paris

Cover design by Roxanne Mei Lum

With ecclesiastical approval
© 1990 Ignatius Press, San Francisco
All rights reserved
ISBN 0-89870-951-2 (PB)
ISBN 0-89870-280-1 (HB)
Library of Congress catalogue number 89-81430
Printed in the United States of America ∞

For my Mother,

For the Society of Jesus

CONTENTS

PART TWO

Basic Patristic Records
on Priestly Celibacy-Continence

FOREWORD

The work of Father Cochini, S.J., about the origins of clerical celibacy in the Catholic Church has a history of its own: a first version was submitted, in May 1969, to the board of examiners of the Institut catholique de Paris presided over by Jean Cardinal Daniélou. The prominent churchman, who was also a universally recognized scholar, encouraged the author to proceed, i.e., to undertake an in-depth research and study beyond the first version and in line with it, for purposes of publication. Since he deemed the advice of such a master to be like a testament— as he explains in his Preface—Father Cochini devoted the following years, patiently and persistently, to rewriting his work. He was helped and encouraged by the advice of qualified specialists in the many fields that his research encompassed.

I was the last person involved in this great endeavor. From the start the texts, the research method, and its results drew my attention keenly because of a surprising identity of views I discovered in his work and in the results of my own research about the discipline of celibacy in the Western Church; my studies had been done before I knew anything about Father Cochini and his work. His thesis was all the more interesting to me in that I had been hoping for a long time to see a young researcher equipped with the necessary knowledge of history, linguistics, theology, and law embarking on an in-depth revision of our knowledge concerning the Eastern tradition in this matter. My wish was especially strong because of the late-nineteenth-century controversy between orientalist G. Bickell and historian F. X. Funk. The latter's final conclusion in 1897 had not been challenged by Bickell, which led people to think that the matter was settled according to Funk's views. Moreover, such views had become more widespread as the majority of historians had adopted them without offering any new or deeper reasons. In my humble opinion, the controversy could not be taken as settled for three main reasons: first of all, because the debate had become too polemic to enable a calm appreciation of both sides' arguments; next, because not enough of a distinction had been made in the *Anordnung* (arrangement) under study between written norm and oral tradition, with all the implications of the latter, especially during the Church's early centuries; and last, because the concept of celibacy as it was understood during those early centuries (and not only then) had not sufficiently developed. Celibacy is not only, as most laymen tend to think, an interdict against marriage, but it is also continence, i.e., a relinquishing of the use of marital rights by those who had been married before ordination, which was very frequently, if not commonly, the case in the early Church.

Reading this work of Father Cochini, I immediately realized that my wish had been fulfilled because the study had been solidly done and included the Eastern Church; it needed only some additions, some changes, and more of a specific emphasis. The author wanted to enlarge on the results he had already obtained and undertook a deep and exacting research, listing all the instances of married clerics during the first centuries, both in the East and in the West, on whom we have some data. He worked for weeks on his inquiry at the Vatican Apostolic Library, where the abundant resources of that pontifical institution were graciously made available to him.

If I may take the liberty of commenting on the work such as it is today in its final version, I will first of all express the satisfaction I feel in being able to join in highly qualified opinions such as those of Cardinal Daniélou and other historians of the early Church who specialized in various fields of her doctrinal and disciplinary life, and not least among them, Father Henri de Lubac.

The method chosen for the external criticism deserves to be mentioned from the outset: the author spared neither time nor strength in taking stock of all the sources that could, in any way, help him find out what had been, in fact as in law, the tradition in the questions to be studied and clarified. He made sure of the sources and integrity of his documents by using modern methods of historical research and, above all, by reading those documents in the light of contemporary patristic literature. As far as internal criticism is concerned, he took into account all evaluative criteria in the fields of general and specialized history, as well as those of theological, liturgical, philological, and juridical thought, giving special attention to scriptural and patristic interpretation. His method bestows on the whole interpretation a fullness and also a balance in which all the elements that tend to bring forth a precise understanding of text and context are objectively evaluated. Thus can the knowledgeable reader reach a calm judgment about the results of the research and, above all, of the arguments that are developed.

Father Cochini has a good knowledge of his topic's bibliography; moreover, he followed carefully the stages of its long historical development as interpretations and counter-interpretations down the centuries and until now have characterized the opinions of scholars and writers in the matter of clerical celibacy. The author did not limit himself to a determination of the various and frequently opposing positions; he made a criticism of their sources and their argumentations and took a careful account of it in working out his own position. The latter therefore reaches the scope of a global vision, a mirror of the centuries-old controversy, while succeeding in giving a first-class scientific retrospective. Father Cochini shows erudition and rigorous thought in his diagnoses; at the same time, his moderation is such that it excludes the slightest polemic; it even underevaluates, in my humble opinion, the strength of some of the arguments he developed himself in his general conclusions. A typical instance of his attitude is the way he handles the 3d canon of the Council of Nicaea and the narration of the Byzantine historian Socrates about the matter, in which the person and the action of one Bishop Paphnutius are mentioned. On that issue the author minimizes the impact of the result in favor of the celibacy tradition; moreover, he does not allow himself any sort of restatement that would have been fitting in the case of certain authors. The latter, though they use an extremely rigorous criticism with regard to any evidence in favor of celibacy, if it happens that such evidence lacks absolute certainty, are rather accommodating— indeed, show an inexplicable critical carelessness—in the face of such an argument, a principal one for the thesis that opposes celibacy, while that document, when seen in the light of modern criteria and tools of historical criticism, is only too clearly betraying its apocryphal origins.

There is another point on which I wish to comment: the interpretation of the famous Pauline passage about *unius uxoris virum*; to elucidate its meaning, one draws on both the patristic and pontifical tradition that is either neglected or ignored in modern biblical exegesis. Modern biblical study, very deeply involved in philological interpretation, is probably not enough so in historical interpretation even though such a tradition remained very much alive in medieval canonical literature, lending to the Pauline text the signification of a biblical argument in favor of celibacy as having been inspired by the apostles; indeed, the Pauline norm was interpreted as having the meaning of a guarantee ensuring the effective practice of continence by married ministers before they were ordained.

From a methodological viewpoint the greatest merit of this work seems to be found in the adequate way with which historical evaluation is related to all the phenomena of the early Church's doctrinal and disciplinary development, a field often lacking the explicit and written evidence that leads to the truth. However, one cannot refuse to admit the existence of what happens not to have been explicitly affirmed or go so far as to feel bound to deny such a reality. To use a comparison, would one deny the past existence of a tree simply because it was impossible to identify and recognize one in the seed or the fragile plant it barely managed to bring forth? On the contrary: the correct method is to posit that from the present tree, which needed time to evolve to the shape enabling us to know it well, we can assume the original existence of the very same tree nature in the seed and in the little plant. This is precisely the point that Father Cochini attempted to stress and elucidate in his study on ecclesiastical celibacy, as had already been done for a long time with regard to other topics, such as Christology's doctrinal assertions, the awareness of the distinction of the sacraments in themselves, the development of the Bishop of Rome's primacy of jurisdiction, and so forth.

In such a light it would not be possible to describe as antihistorical or antiscientific what Pope Pius XI affirmed in his encyclical on the priesthood, when he said that the legislation enacted in the early 4th century about celibacy presupposed an older and similar tradition (AAS 28 [1936] 25), and what Pope John Paul II affirmed even more explicitly, as the author quotes in his Preface; these declarations connect priestly celibacy with "the example of Our Lord Jesus Christ himself, the teaching of the apostles, and the whole of tradition" (AAS 71 [1979] 406). Thus, while the written law of celibacy was promulgated in the early 4th century, one should not talk about a break or an innovation but about a continuity.

To conclude, I believe that I am entitled to stress that there is a twofold merit in Father Cochini's work. First of all, on a level I would describe as quantitative, it has the scope of a most intensive scientific inquiry concerning facts and evidences about the universal Church in her early days and during the patristic era. To this are added, on the qualitative level, the features of a deep, clear, and balanced critical evaluation using all the tools of historical verification undertaken and led to fruition in accordance with the method that is suitable to the Church's history during those early centuries of her organic development. Thus the results acquired in such a way have become a milestone of sorts on the road paved by all the rich scientific works concerning priestly celibacy. This authoritative work is fully in accordance with the tradition of the Society of Jesus in the area of high-level scientific apostolate and adds to it a valid element of renewal. It will likely become a decisive contribution to the painstaking research on the history of celibacy's origins and its first developments in the Church, both in the East and in the West, when she was still undivided, the history of a practice that was to become slowly more precise and diversified along two lines branching out of one common root.

ALFONS M. STICKLER
The Vatican Apostolic Library
January 24, 1981

PREFACE

Ut quod apostoli docuerunt, et ipsa
servavit antiquitas nos quoque custodiamus.

This work is based on my dissertation for a doctorate of theology, submitted in May 1969 at the Institut catholique de Paris. The late and lamented Jean Cardinal Daniélou, who had honored me by agreeing to preside over the board of examiners, was kind enough to encourage me to publish the results of my humble work while taking into account, of course, legitimate criticisms. "I do wish it very much", he wrote to me the following year, "since you would be rendering a true service to the Church." That was more than an invitation; it has become since then a testament of sorts, and as such it was binding to me in spite of what I felt about my limitations. During the past eleven years numerous professors and friends have also expressed the same wish. I was also encouraged by the Reverend Father Prefect of the Vatican Library, Father Alfons M. Stickler, who was kind enough to show an interest in my thesis; his great proficiency in the field of the history of canon law was priceless to me.

There have been many studies about the historical origins of the law on clerical celibacy, and it is sufficient to open any of the big dictionaries of religious sciences to perceive the essential outlines. It never would have occurred to me to take my own turn at such a well-documented topic had I not been led to it through fortuitous circumstances. Quite a long time ago, as I was compiling some documentation about the priesthood in the early African Church, my attention was drawn to a canonical decree promulgated in the year 390 by a council held in Carthage. It stipulated that married clerics had to observe continence with their wives, on the basis of a tradition originating with the apostles. My curiosity was soon replaced by a passion for the truth after I had read other late-fourth-century documents in which there was the same claim of apostolicity. This claim, tested by means of historical facts and questions encountered in the course of the same inquiry, progressively appeared to me as being a coherent principle of explanation. Moreover, my research was stimulated by some reflections aroused in my mind by the history of the history. The thesis of a compulsory clerical celibacy rooted in the very origins of the Church had been defended throughout the centuries by more than one serious theologian on grounds that frequently seemed to me to maintain their entire validity.

I became convinced, and this is why I chose to express it from the outset in a title echoing the voice of the Fathers at Carthage: "What the apostles taught". May the specialists be willing to accept this book as a modest contribution to contemporary research about clerical celibacy, and may they point out to me the shortcomings and faults they will discover in it, so that should there be a new edition I would be able to improve it accordingly. To my brother priests and to all who will read this book, I will quite simply confess the joy I felt when reading the words of Pope John Paul II, who wrote to all the priests of the Church on Holy Thursday 1979:

> The Latin Church has wished, and continues to wish, referring to the example of Christ the Lord Himself, to the apostolic teaching and to the whole Tradition that is proper to her, that all those who receive the sacrament of Orders should embrace this renunciation "for the sake of the kingdom of heaven".

Paris, June 29, 1980   CHRISTIAN COCHINI, S.J.
Feast of the Holy Apostles   Doctor of Theology
Peter and Paul

ACKNOWLEDGMENTS

I wish to add to the expressions of thankfulness already embodied in my Preface a few words of deep gratitude toward Father Henri de Lubac. His friendship and intellectual goodwill have shone like the sun on the slow genesis of this work, which owes much more to him than I could say. I also owe a great debt of gratitude to Fathers Marc Fang and Henri Madelin, provincials of China and France, respectively, of the Society of Jesus, whose help made this publication possible. Father André Manaranche, in spite of his heavy schedule, was kind enough to take upon himself the thankless though indispensable chore of carefully reviewing the proofs: may each page of this book be a cordial thank-you to him. Having enjoyed the services of many libraries, I want to express my particular gratitude to the librarians and devoted staff of the Cultural Center "Les Fontaines" (Chantilly), the Center for Studies and Research of the Society of Jesus (Paris), the French National Library, Loyola University of Chicago, the Catholic University of America (Washington, D.C.), the Center for Christian Oriental Studies (Washington, D.C.), the Universitätbibliothek Heidelberg, and above all the Vatican Apostolic Library. I also have the pleasant duty to give thanks for the brotherly support I received during my long research sessions in the Jesuit communities of CERAS (Action Populaire) in Vanves, of Stimmen der Zeit in Munich, of Loyola University in Chicago, and of the Collegio Bellarmino and Casa dei Scrittori in Rome. Lastly, to Father Georges Chantraine, who honored me by welcoming this book in his new, vigorous collection "Le Sycomore", I wish to express my deepest thanks.

CHRISTIAN COCHINI, S.J.
Taipei, October 1981

ABBREVIATIONS

In citing works in the footnotes, short titles have often been used. Works frequently cited have been identified by the following abbreviations.

AAS   *Acta Apostolicae Sedis* (Acts of the Holy See).

BLE   *Bulletin de litterature écclésiastique.*

Bruns   *Canones apostolorum et conciliorum saeculorum IV, V, VI, VII recognovit atque insignioris lectionum varietatis notationes subiunxit* Herm. Theod. Bruns, 2 vols. Berlin, 1839.

CC   *Corpus Christianorum.*

CIG   *Corpus inscriptionum Graecarum.* Berlin, 1825–77.

CJC   *Codex Juris Canonici.*

CPG   *Corpus Patrum Graecorum.*

CPL   *Corpus Patrum Latinorum.*

CSCO   *Corpus scriptorum christianorum orientalium.*

CSEL   *Corpus scriptorum Ecclesiasticorum Latinorum.*

CTh   *Codex Theodosianus*, 2 fasc. Berlin, 1923–26.

DACL   *Dictionnaire d'archéologie chrétienne et de liturgie.*

DDC   *Dictionnaire de Droit Canonique.*

DHGE   *Dictionnaire d'Histoire et de Géographie Ecclésiastiques.*

Diehl   *Inscriptiones Latinae Christianae veteres*, Berolini, I (1925), II (1927), III (1931). 2d edition by J. Moreau, Berolini, 1961. Reproduced by Weidmann Editions. Dublin and Zurich, 1970. Volume IV, *Supplementum*, published by J. Moreau and H. I. Marrou. Dublin and Turici, 1967.

DSp   *Dictionnaire de Spiritualité.*

DTC   *Dictionnaire de Théologie Catholique.*

DZ   H. Denzinger and A. Schonmetzer. *Enchiridion sym-*
                  bolorum definitionum et declarationum de rebus fidei et morum.
                  Barcelona-Freiburg-Rome, 1979.

Ep.   *Epistolae.*

GCS   *Greischische Christliche Schriftsteller der ersten drei Jahr-*
                  hunderte.

Hefele-Leclercq   *Histoire des conciles d'après les documents originaux* by
                  Charles Joseph Hefele, New French trans. made from
                  the second German edition corrected and supplemented
                  by critical notes and a bibliography by a Benedictine
                  religious of Saint-Michel de Farnborough Abbey. 9 vol-
                  umes. Paris, 1907–31.

Hist. Eccl.   *Historia Ecclesiastica.*

ICUR, NS   *Inscriptiones Christianea Urbis Romanae septimo saeculo anti-*
                  quiores. Nova Series. I. A. Silvagni, Inscriptiones incer-
                  tae originis, Rome, 1932. II. A. Silvagni, Coemeteria in
                  viis Cornelia, Aurelia Portuensi et Ostiensi, Rome, 1956.
                  III. A. Silvagni and A. Ferrua, Coemeteria in via Ardea-
                  tina cum duabus appendicibus, Rome, 1956. IV. A. Fer-
                  rua, Coemeteria inter vias Appiam et Ardeatinam,
                  Rome, 1964. V. A. Ferrua, Coemeteria reliqua via
                  Appiae, Rome, 1971. VI. A. Ferrua, Coemeteria in viis
                  Latina, Labicana et Praenestina, Rome, 1975. VII. A.
                  Ferrua, Coemeteria in via Tiburtina, Rome, 198?.

Joannou   P. P. Joannou, *Discipline generale antique,* 2d–9th cen-
                  turies. Grottaferrata, 1962.

JTS   *Journal of Theological Studies.*

JW   *Regesta Pontificum Romanorum ab condita Ecclesia ad a.*
                  1198, by P. Jaffe and G. Wattenbach. Leipzig, 1885–88.
                  2d ed. by S. Lowenfeld, F. Kaltenbrunner, and P. Ewald.
                  2 vols. Leipzig, 1885–88. Reed. Graz, 1956.

Latouche   Gregory of Tours, *Histoire des Francs,* trans. R. Latouche
                  (Coll. Classiques de l'histoire de France au Moyen-âge),
                  2 vols., 1963–65.

LTK   *Lexikon für Theologie und Kirche.*

Maassen   *Geshichte des Quellen und der Literature des canonischen*
                  Rechtes im Abendland. I. Die Rechtssammlungen bis zur
                  Mitte des 9. Jahrhunderts. Graz, 1870. Reprinted 1956.

Mansi	*Sacrorum conciliorum nova et amplissa collectio.* 31 vol. (Florence-Venice, 1759–98). Reprinted and continued by L. Petit and J. P. Martin, 53 vols. in 60 (Paris, 1901–27). Reprinted by Graz, 1960–61.
MGH	*Monumenta Germaniae Historica*: auct. ant. = Auctores antiquissimi; epist. = Epistolae; scr. mer. = Scriptores rerum Merovingicarum; script. = Scriptores.
NRT	*Nouvelle Revue Théologique.*
PG	J. G. Migne. *Patrologia Cursus Completus*, Series Graeca.
PL	J. G. Migne. *Patrologia Cursus Completus*, Series Latina.
PO	J. G. Migne. *Patrologia Cursus Completus*, Series Orientalia.
RICG	*Recueil des Inscriptiones Chrétiennes de la Gaule antérieures à la Renaissance carolingienne*, published under the direction of Henri Irenée Marrou. I. Première Belgique by Nancy Gauthier, Paris, 1975.
SCh	*Sources Chrétiennes.*
ThRev	*Theologische Revue.*
ThW	G. Kittel, *Theologisches Wörterbuch zum Neuen Testament*, 1933–58.
TThQ	*Theologische Quartalschrift.*
TU	*Text und Untersuchungen zur Geschichte der altchristlichen Literatur.*
ZKTh	*Zeitschrift für Katholische Theologie.*
ZntW	*Zeitschrift für neutestamentliche Wissenschaft und die Kunde der älteren Kirche.*

PART ONE

Historical and
Methodological Approaches

CHAPTER ONE

Defining the Problem: Does Clerical Celibacy Go back to the Apostles?

I. THE COUNCIL OF CARTHAGE IN 390

On June 16, 390, several bishops met in Carthage.[1] Presided over by one Genethlius, metropolitan of the Proconsular province,[2] they were primarily going to discuss disciplinary matters. With the exception of the first one, the thirteen canons, which enable us today to know the nature of the debates, were all concerned with practical matters: Who should have the exclusive right to prepare the holy chrism and handle the penitents' reconciliation (can. 3)? Should it be proper to multiply over easily the number of dioceses (can. 5)? Is everyone free to apply or not apply the common decisions of the synod (can. 13)? All the questions had rather limited importance. Having modest objectives, the African meeting was also modest in the number and qualification of its members. The preface mentions, besides Genethlius of Carthage, the presence of two of his colleagues (Victor of Abzir and Victor of Pupput) and other co-bishops of various provinces, but there is ground for thinking that empty seats were not rare; as to the participants, their names will remain unknown.[3]

---

[1] Concerning the African Councils, we have had available for several years the excellent critical edition of C. Munier's *Concilia Africae ca. 345–525* (Turnholti, 1974), = CC 149. For a historical presentation of the Council of Carthage of 390, one can consult Hefele and Leclercq, *Histoire des Conciles* II, 1 (Paris, 1908), pp. 76–78. See the study of the problems relative to the manuscript tradition in C. Munier, "La tradition du IIe concile de Carthage", in *Revue des sciences religieuses* 46 (1972): pp. 193–214.

[2] This bishop, whose biography is unknown to us, was one of the most prominent men in the African episcopate. St. Augustine mentions him. The spelling of his name varies from one manuscript to the next; the most common is *Genethlius*.

[3] Genethlius makes a special reference to those who did not come: "Ut qui corpore sunt absentes, nobiscum in spiritu videantur esse conjuncti" (can. 1). Hefele and Leclercq point

Yet these Carthage meetings were to take a position on one of the problems that would give rise, throughout history, to the most violent controversies. Among the twelve disciplinary canons is a decree relative to clerical continence. The very scarcity of such documents in the early Church is itself a reason to feel that the text has some interest. And the feeling, little by little, gives way to certainty. The law that was promulgated during the modest synod of 390 would remain valid and be officially inserted in the great legislative record of the African Church, the *Codex canonum Ecclesiae africanae*, compiled and promulgated in 419 (in the time of St. Augustine). Moreover, it would be made known through the collection of Denys the Minor in all the dioceses of the Roman Church;[4] and the Quinisext Council itself (691), rightly famous in Byzantine tradition because of its decisions regarding clerical marriage and celibacy, would refer to it explicitly as a sure link to Tradition.[5] Is this an exceptional destiny? The fact is that in the 11th century, for instance, when the secular structure of clerical celibacy was attacked and shaken, the promoters of the Gregorian Reform were to borrow more than once from the Carthage canon of 390 for their most solid historical argument.[6] Let us next open the archives of the Council of Trent, at the page recording the discussions of the theological commission studying the theses relative to clerical marriage: here is the African document, standing out, in the files of the experts.[7] And when, after hesitating for a long time, Pius IV finally decided to give his answer to the German princes asking Rome to authorize the marriage of priests, his first word on the matter would be a quotation from the decree of Carthage.[8]

---

out that all the bishops whose names are mentioned, a total of six, belonged to the Proconsular province. It seems quite likely that the representatives of the other provinces were not numerous (*Histoire des Conciles*, I, 2, p. 17).

[4] In his collection of synodal canons of the East and West, Denys the Minor (ca. 500–545) gives an important place to the Carthaginian archives. With the full *Codex canonum Ecclesiae africanae*, the canon of 390 would become an integral part of the *Dionysiana* collection and, as such, enjoy widespread credit in the Latin Church.

[5] We will have the opportunity to speak more at length about this council; the text can be found either in Mansi 13, c. 219ff., or in the critical edition of P. P. Joannou, *Pontificia Commissione per la redazione del Codice di Dirrito canonico orientale*, Fontes Series I, fasc. IX, General ancient discipline (4th–9th centuries), vol. I, 1, Canons of the ecumenical councils (Grottaferrata, 1962), pp. 120ff.

[6] MGH, *Libelli de lite imperatorum et pontificum saeculis XI et XII*, II (Hanover, 1892), pp. 7ff. See below, pp. 18ff.

[7] *Concilium Tridentinum Diariorum, Actorum, Epistolarum, Tractatuum Nova Collectio*, Ed. Societas Goerresiana, vol. IX, pt. 6 (Freiburg im Breisgau, 1965), pp. 380–82 and 425–70. See below, pp. 19ff.

[8] "Responsum a Pio IV datum consiliariis electorum et principum imperii, qui sacerdotum conjugia petebant", in J. Leplat, *Monumentorum ad historiam concilii Tridentini amplissima collectio*, VI (Louvain, 1876), p. 336.

Here then is the document that was to play such a part in the history of ecclesiastical celibacy:[9]

> Epigonius, Bishop of the Royal Region of Bulla, says: The rule of continence and chastity had been discussed in a previous council. Let it [now] be taught with more emphasis what are the three ranks that, by virtue of their consecration, are under the same obligation of chastity, i.e., the bishop, the priest, and the deacon, and let them be instructed to keep their purity.
>
> Bishop Genethlius says: As was previously said, it is fitting that the holy bishops and priests of God as well as the Levites, i.e., those who are in the service of the divine sacraments, observe perfect continence, so that they may obtain in all simplicity what they are asking from God; what the apostles taught and what antiquity itself observed, let us also endeavor to keep.
>
> The bishops declared unanimously: It pleases us all that bishop, priest, and deacon, guardians of purity, abstain from [conjugal intercourse] with their wives, so that those who serve at the altar may keep a perfect chastity.

This text is interesting in many respects. Mention is made of the clerics' wives, and particularly, the wives of the hierarchy's high-ranking members: bishops, priests, and deacons. Most of those—or at least a large number—were thus bound by marriage. Such men are being asked by the African synod to give up no less than all conjugal intercourse and to observe perfect chastity. Because they are ministers at the service of the divine sacraments, it is deemed that marital life would prevent them from carrying out *simpliciter* (in all simplicity) their intercessory function. Moreover, we are assured that such a discipline is not a new one: the Fathers of Carthage are only stressing the obligation of something that was "taught by the apostles and observed by antiquity itself". Such arguments might at first surprise our modern minds because we are accustomed to have a different conception of the law of ecclesiastical celibacy (or continence). And the unanimity of the assembly in accepting the proposition of one of their members in favor of this regulation, and

---

[9] "Epigonius episcopus Bullensium Regionum dixit: Cum praeterito concilio de continentia et castitate tractaretur, gradus isti tres qui constrictione quadam castitatis per consecrationem annexi sunt, episcopus inquam, presbyter et diaconus, tractatu pleniori, ut pudicitiam custodiant, doceantur.

"Genethlius episcopus dixit: Ut superius dictum est, decet sacros antistites ac Dei sacerdotes nec non et levitas vel qui sacramentis divinis inserviunt, continentes esse in omnibus, quo possint simpliciter quod a Domino postulant impetrare, ut quod apostoli docuerunt et ipsa servavit antiquitas, nos quoque custodiamus.

"Ab universis episcopis dictum est: Omnibus placet ut episcopus, presbyter et diaconus, pudicitiae custodes, etiam ab uxoribus se abstineant ut in omnibus et ab omnibus pudicitia custodiatur qui altario inserviunt" (CC 149, p. 13).

of the motivations on which it is based, increases the mixture of surprise and curiosity aroused by this old text.

Let us look at some of its points in more detail. Those whom the canon explicitly named as subjects to the law are the members of the three higher ranks of the clergy to which they rose through their *consecrationes*. These have in common the fact of associating the three classes of clerics by the same bond of chastity. In this connection between the consecration of the bishop, the priest, the deacon and the obligation of continence, there is already a desire to highlight one of the profound reasons for the required purity: consecration, as the name itself expresses it, is an act through which man is raised to the rank of sacred persons, set apart to carry out functions of a divine nature. Those who receive it must manifest in their lives that they have been introduced to an order of realities that is different from the one in which they were previously involved. The most obvious sign of this passage is that of putting an end to conjugal intercourse, a bond that would be holding the minister outside the sacred sphere where he must now live. This close connection between the service of divine mysteries and perfect chastity is explicitly stressed three times in circumlocution: "*qui sacramentis inserviunt*" (those who are at the service of the divine sacraments); "*qui sacramenta contrectant*" (those who touch the sacred mysteries); "*qui altari deserviunt*" (those who serve at the altar). In thus qualifying bishops, priests, and deacons without distinction, the text stresses the common feature they have, thus the common obligation that is theirs, and also the fact that serving the *sacramenta* and the altar, i.e., serving the Eucharist, is the specific foundation of the continence they are asked to observe.

To this first motivation the Council of Carthage adds another that is somehow more central because it expresses the finality of the obligation imposed upon the ministers of the altar: "*Quo possint simpliciter quod a Domino postulant impetrare*" (so that they may obtain in all simplicity what they are asking from God). If one is so demanding when it comes to bishops, priests, and deacons, the reason is that they have to address God with a conscience fulfilling the conditions required in a mediator. The adverb *simpliciter* can be understood in several ways: pertaining to an attitude devoid of any hesitation or fear, to innocence close to original justice, to simplicity of soul, or to gift of an exclusive love—but no matter what shade of translation is chosen, the word highlights the original environment in which the intercessory dialogue between God and his minister must take place. Without chastity the minister would lack an essential quality when presenting to God the petitions of his human brothers and would thus deprive himself of freedom of speech. With it he enters into very "simple" communication with the Lord, a guarantee of prayers being granted. Byzantine commentators,[10] in particular, have emphasized the close bond thus created between the clerics' continence and their preferential role in the service of the Kingdom of God:

> These, Zonaras wrote about this Carthage canon, are indeed intercessors between God and men; setting up a link between the divinity and the rest of the faithful, they are asking for salvation and peace on behalf of the whole world. Therefore, if they practice, he went on, all the virtues and converse in full trust with God, they will obtain right away all that they are asking for. But if these same men deprive themselves, through their own fault, of their freedom of speech, how could they fulfill their role as intercessors for the good of others?

Lastly, and here is the important point in the history of clerical celibacy's origins, the African canon of 390 defines itself as a faithful echo of a tradition that would have started during the apostolic era: "Ut quod apostoli docuerunt et ipsa servavit antiquitas, nos quoque custodiamus." (What the apostles taught and what antiquity itself observed, let us also endeavor to keep.) It would be wrong, though some did it, to underestimate a priori the importance of this reference to a remote past. As the Byzantine Zonaras rightly pointed out, there is in it a desire to be anchored in a well-founded custom or law and to show that the African Church had always been concerned with the need to preserve it carefully.[11] We, for our part, also believe that it should be taken into consideration and that we should study the historical period of the early centuries in attempting to answer the question: What is the value of this claim to apostolicity? Is it possible that the discipline of clerical celibacy did indeed go back to the time of the apostles?

Three other documents issued by the Church hierarchy at the end of that 4th century claim an apostolic origin for clerical celibacy and the perpetual continence required of the ministers of the altar.

---

[10] These are great Byzantine canonists of the 12th century—Alexis, Aristenes, John Zonaras, and Theodore Blasamon—whose commentaries, still authoritative on many points, were edited and translated into Latin in 1672 by William Beveridge. That edition was reprinted in PG 137–38. The passage of Zonaras quoted here is in PG 138, 32c.

[11] PG 138, 32c–d.

II. THE "DIRECTA" AND "CUM IN UNUM" DECRETALS
OF POPE SIRICIUS

On February 10, 385, Pope Siricius sent to the Spanish bishop Himerius, metropolitan of the province of Tarragona, a long letter in reply to the bishop's written request with regard to various subjects sent several months earlier to Pope Damasus († 384).[12]

Siricius answered in the name of his late predecessor because the questions had not been asked to the person of Damasus but to the representative of Peter. Before studying the questions, the *Directa* decretal begins with the affirmation of the permanent presence and action of the Apostle Peter on the Roman See in the person of his successors: "We carry the burdens of all those who are laden: rather, Blessed Apostle Peter is carrying them in us, and we firmly trust that he protects and guards us in all things, as we are heirs to his functions." [13]

Fifteen points are studied. With regard to the clerics, two of these points unveil a background of numerous married deacons, priests, and bishops. One recalls in this respect that remarried men were not permitted to receive major Orders (VIII, 12) a fact that confirms indirectly the compatibility of monogamous marriage and the priesthood. On the other hand, we are going to read a long text devoted to the duty of continence that presupposes as normal and legitimate many matrimonial situations in the ranks of the clergy. This was also attested, as we have seen, by the Council of Carthage in 390. One must keep such a background in mind when studying the matter of clerical celibacy's origins. It was with the best and most honorable intentions that some men, married before ordination, were carrying out priestly functions and even received episcopal dignity. However, they were expected to live in a state of perfect chastity, of perpetual continence with regard to their wives, even if the latter were still alive.

It was against violations committed by some men that Pope Siricius took a firm position in chapter 7 of his *Directa* decretal when answering a question of Bishop Himerius:

---

[12] PL 13, 1131b–47a (= P. Coustant, *Epistolae Romanorum Pontificum* [Paris, 1721], pp. 623–38).

[13] "Portamus onera omnium qui gravantur: quin immo haec portat in nobis beatus apostolus Petrus, qui nos in omnibus, ut confidimus, administrationis suae protegit et tuetur heredes" (PL 13, 1133a. P. Coustant, *Epistolae*, p. 624).

Let us talk now about the very holy clerical Orders. As your Charity advises us, we see that in your provinces they are trampled underfoot and confused, with great prejudice to the honor due to religion. It has come to the point where we must say with Jeremiah: "Who will turn my head into a fountain, and my eyes into a spring for tears, so that I may weep all day, all night for all the dead out of the daughter of my people?" (Jer 8:23). If the blessed prophet declares that tears are not enough to lament the sins of the people, how much more can we be grief stricken when we have to bemoan the crimes of those in our own body? We especially, because as Blessed Paul put it, we must constantly be preoccupied daily, anxious for all the Churches. "When any man has had scruples, I have had scruples with him; when any man is made to fall, I am tortured" (2 Cor 11:29). We have indeed discovered that many priests and deacons of Christ brought children into the world, either through union with their wives or through shameful intercourse. And they used as an excuse the fact that in the Old Testament—as we can read—priests and ministers were permitted to beget children.

Whatever the case may be, if one of these disciples of the passions and tutors of vices thinks that the Lord—in the law of Moses—gives an indistinct license to those in sacred Orders so that they may satisfy their passions, let him tell me now: why does [the Lord] warn those who had the custody of the most holy things in the following way: "You must make yourselves holy, for I am Yahweh your God" (Lev 20:7). Likewise, why were the priests ordered, during the year of their tour of duty, to live in the temple, away from their homes? Quite obviously so that they would not be able to have carnal knowledge of any woman, even their wives, and, thus, having a conscience radiating integrity, they could offer to God offerings worthy of his acceptance. Those men, once they had fulfilled their time of service, were permitted to have marital intercourse for the sole purpose of ensuring their descent, because no one except [the members] of the tribe of Levi could be admitted to the divine ministry.

This is why, after having enlightened us by his coming, the Lord Jesus formally stipulated in the Gospel that he had not come to abolish the law, but to bring it to perfection; this is also why he wanted the beauty of the Church whose Bridegroom he is to shine with the splendor of chastity, so that when he returns, on the Day of Judgment, he will find her without stain or wrinkle, as his Apostle taught. It is through the indissoluble law of these decisions that all of us, priests and deacons, are bound together from the day of our ordination, and [held to] put our hearts and our bodies to the service of sobriety and purity; may we be pleasing to our God in all things, in the sacrifices we offer daily. "People who are interested only in unspiritual things can never be pleasing to God", says the Chosen Vessel. "Your interests, however, are not in the unspiritual, but in the spiritual, since the Spirit of God has made his home in you" (Rom 8:8–9).[14]

[14]PL 13, 1138a–39a. P. Coustant, *Epistolae*, pp. 629–31.

The circumstance leading the Roman Pontiff to write about clerical continence, as this document shows, was the news coming from Spain: many clerics belonging to major Orders in those provinces went on living with their wives and having children. He was distraught by such news because they were grave violations of what he saw as an indisputable discipline. Hence his intervention, the purpose of which was not to promulgate new regulations, but to reinstate those that should never have been broken. Siricius also learned from Himerius that those clerics were attempting to justify their behavior through Scripture, which is why he also uses Scripture. Some people are saying that the Old Testament, in particular the rules of Leviticus, authorized marriage for the Levites. Yes, indeed, he retorts, but married priests were under the obligation of temporary continence when serving in the temple. Now the priesthood of Christ brought the old priesthood to perfection. And by this very fact the obligation of continence became an obligation to perpetual continence. If the ministers had to abstain periodically from intercourse with their wives "so that, with a conscience radiating integrity, they could present to God offerings worthy of his acceptance", the conclusion, as far as Siricius is concerned, is that the ministers of Jesus Christ who offer sacrifice daily, a sacrifice far superior to that of Jerusalem, must be pleasing to God through perfect chastity.

In his eyes there is thus a deep continuity between the present law and the Old Testament interdicts. The latter cannot be used against the former because this is the same law perfected in its demands by the transformation of the entire priestly institution realized through Christ. The basis of the obligation of perpetual continence is to be sought in the Gospel. Thus Siricius declares this law to be "indissoluble" ("*insolubili lege constringimur*"); it is derived from the new order brought about by the Lord himself who, when fulfilling the law, gave to his bride the splendor of chastity and transfigured the priesthood. The *Directa* decretal does not make any explicit reference to an apostolic tradition; however, it makes the beginnings of the law of continence imposed on the priests of Jesus Christ coincide with the very origins of the Church.

A year later another document was written in the same vein. It was the *Cum in unum* decretal that Siricius sent to the sees of various provinces in order to advise them of the decisions made in Rome in January 386 by a council of eighty bishops.[15] The circumstances leading to the meeting of such a synod are unknown. And it was only thanks to the

---

[15] PL 13, 1155b–62a. P. Coustant, *Epistolae*, pp. 651–58.

archives of the African Church that we still have Siricius' letter.[16] It includes an introduction followed by eight canons of ecclesiastical discipline, a long exhortation about the observance of clerical continence, and a conclusion in which the Roman Pontiff, by enacting sanctions against the guilty parties, calls for a temperance of justice through mercy. Here is the passage related to compulsory continence for the higher ranks of the clergy:

> Moreover, as it is worthy, chaste, and honest to do so, this is what we advise: let the priests and Levites have no intercourse with their wives, inasmuch as they are absorbed in the daily duties of their ministries. Paul, when writing to the Corinthians, told them: "Leave yourself free for prayer" (1 Cor 7:5). If lay people are asked to be continent so that their prayers are granted, all the more so a priest who should be ready at any moment, thanks to an immaculate purity, and not fearing the obligation of offering the sacrifice or baptizing. Were he soiled by carnal concupiscence, what could he do? Would he excuse himself? With what shame, in what state of mind would he carry out his functions? What testimony of conscience, what merit would give him the trust to have his prayers granted, when it is said: "To all who are pure themselves, everything is pure; but to those who have been corrupted and lack faith, nothing can be pure" (Titus 1:15). Which is why I am exhorting, warning, supplicating: let us do away with this opprobrium that even the pagans can rightly hold against us. Perhaps does one believe that this [is permitted] because it is written: "He must not have been married more than once" (1 Tim 3:2). But [Paul] was not talking about [a man] persisting in his desire to beget; he spoke about the continence that one should observe [*propter continentiam futuram*]. He did not accept those who were not beyond reproach [in this matter], and he said: "I should like everyone to be like me" (1 Cor 7:7). And he stated even more clearly: "People who are interested only in unspiritual things can never be pleasing to God. Your interests, however, are not in the unspiritual, but in the spiritual" (Rom 8:8–9).[17]

While the *Directa* decretal drew its argumentation from the Old Testament interdicts of Leviticus, in order to answer the objections of the Spanish clerics, Siricius and the eighty bishops of the Roman Synod were now using the epistles of St. Paul as scriptural foundation. Using an argument a fortiori, they show that if continence is at times necessary for lay people who want to dedicate themselves to prayer, as explained in the first epistle to the Corinthians, it becomes a permanent necessity

---

[16] See Hefele-Leclercq, *Histoire des Conciles*, II, 1 (Paris, 1908), pp. 68ff. On the whole issue, one could also find it useful to consult P. Coustant's historico-critical introduction (PL 13, 1149b–55a; *Epistolae*, pp. 643–52).

[17] PL 13, 1160a–61a. P. Coustant, *Epistolae*, pp. 655–57.

for those who have the permanent duty of addressing themselves to God in their ministries. Moreover, the Pauline instruction regarding the choice of candidates for bishops and deacons was probably invoked by certain clerics in order to justify the matrimonial relations they had retained. To answer such an objection, the *Cum in unum* decretal elaborates an exegesis of the *unius uxoris virum*, claiming to be and stating it is the only one faithful to St. Paul's thought: if the apostle has asked Timothy and Titus to choose bishops, priests, or deacons among "men married only once", this does not mean that he permitted these husbands, once ordained, to go on with their conjugal life and have more children, but *propter continentiam futuram*. Monogamy is a condition for receiving Orders because fidelity to one woman is a guarantee that the candidate will be able to practice the perfect continence that will be required of him after ordination. This exegesis of St. Paul's instruction to Timothy and Titus is an essential link by which the bishops of the Roman Synod in 386 and Pope Siricius place themselves in continuity with the apostolic period.[18]

The conviction that they are not introducing anything new but are faithful to the traditions coming from the apostles is expressed openly by the Fathers of the Roman Council in the introduction to the synodal document:

> For the special instruction of those who, for reasons of health or fatigue due to old age, were unable to take part in the present synod, it seemed appropriate to write this letter so as to preserve its acts definitively. The question is not one of ordering new precepts, but we wish through this letter to have people observe those that either through apathy or laziness on the part of some have been neglected. They are, however, matters that

---

[18] The same interpretation is found in several patristic writers of the same era. St. Ambrose writes to the Church of Verecelli: "The apostle is a master of virtue; he teaches how to convince the contradictors patiently; he orders that [the bishop] be the husband of only one wife, not in order to exclude in such a way one who would not have been married (this is indeed above the law), but so that, through conjugal chastity, he keeps the grace of his baptism; on the other hand, the apostolic authority is not an invitation to beget children during his priesthood; [the apostle] spoke about a man who [already] had children, but not about one who is begetting them or who contracts a new marriage" (*Epistolae*, hereafter cited as *Ep.*, 63:62. PL 16, 1205b–c). Epiphanius of Salamis is just as affirmative: "Since the Incarnation of Christ, the holy Word of God doesn't admit to the priesthood monogamists who, after the death of their wives, have remarried; (this is so) because of the exceptional honor of the priesthood. This is observed with great exactitude, without failing, by the holy Church of God. But the man who goes on living with his wife and begetting children is not admitted by [the Church] as deacon, priest, bishop, and subdeacon, even if he married only once, but [only the one] who, being monogamous, observes continence or is a widower; above all in those places where the ecclesiastical canons are very precise" (*Panarion* [*Adversus Haereses*], Haer. 79, 4. CGS 31, 367. See also Ambrosiaster, *In Epistolam B. Pauli ad Timotheum primam*, III, 12–13. PL 17, 470b–71b).

have been established by an apostolic constitution and by a constitution of the Fathers, as is written: "Stand firm, then, brothers and keep the traditions that we taught you, whether by word of mouth or by letter" (2 Th 2:15).[19]

The reference to the "matters that have been established by an apostolic constitution and by a constitution of the Fathers" covers all the points studied in the document. There is no reason to restrict it to one point or another. The obligation of perfect continence for higher clerics is, like all the rest, considered by the authors of the *Cum in unum* decretal as having its origins in a positive will of the apostles.

III. THE "DOMINUS INTER" DECRETAL OF THE ROMAN SYNOD TO THE BISHOPS OF GAUL

At about the same time, there was a Roman synod whose acts have been listed in several conciliar collections among the letters of Pope Siricius and credited by some critics either to that Pontiff or to Innocent I (401?–17), or even with less probability to Pope Damasus (366–84).[20] It also deals with the problem of clerical continence and stresses fidelity to the tradition of the Fathers. In reply to the questions of the bishops of Gaul, the *Dominus inter* decretal begins with a declaration of intention to explain the traditions that have to be followed:

We know, very dear brothers, that in various Churches many bishops [have let themselves be led] by a most human presumption and hastened to alter the tradition of the Fathers with great prejudice to the reputation

---

[19] PL 13, 1156a. P. Coustant, *Epistolae*, p. 652.

[20] PL 13, 1181a–94c. P. Coustant, *Epistolae*, pp. 685–700. E. C. Babut, *La plus ancienne décrétale* (Paris, 1904), pp. 69–87. Babut attempted to prove that the *Dominus inter* decretal was the work of Pope Damasus (366–84). His views were adopted, particularly by the *Clavis Patrum latinorum*, no. 1632, and by R. Gryson, *Les origines du célibat ecclésiastique du premier au septième siècle*, hereafter cited as *Les origines du célibat ecclésiastique* (Gembloux, 1970), pp. 127ff., though Gryson admitted at a later date that "the issue deserved a deeper study" (R. Gryson, *Aux origines du célibat ecclésiastique: la continence cultuelle des clercs majeurs dans l'ancienne église d'Occident. Corona gratiarum. Miscellanea E. Dekkers o.s.b.*, II [Bruges, 1975], p. 12). E. Caspar opines that Babut's thesis is an unfruitful attempt (*Geschichte des Papsttums*, I [Tübingen, 1950], p. 216, n. 1, and p. 594). In order not to prejudge the attribution of that *Dominus inter* decretal, we mention it here separately while admitting to being more sensitive to the reasons given by P. Coustant to see it as the work of Siricius (P. Coustant, *Epistolae*, pp. 683–86).

attached to their dignity; they thus fell into the darkness of heresy while taking pleasure in the plaudits of men instead of endeavoring to receive their reward from God. And this is how your Holiness condescended to consult with the Apostolic See about the science of law and traditions, not in order to find out [our opinion] indiscreetly, but with the benevolent intention of affirming your faith; you want us to explain clearly and freely all the questions you submitted to us. God grant that our words be enriched in the very measure you sincerely desire it and will listen to them with goodwill. No matter how mediocre my discourse may be, its meaning is legitimate, and I am going to explain what has to be followed if one wants to remedy the clashing dissidences that were brought about only by the presumption of arrogance, according to what is written in divine Scripture: "In this way you have made God's word null and void by means of your tradition" (Mt 15:6). If you want to know, with the integrity of faith, what the true observances are, kindly give a welcoming attention to what I am going to say. First of all, what is proposed concerns modesty and chastity. Then there is a complexity of very many questions. This is why we must reply to the questions that were asked in their proper order, by explaining the traditions ("Singulis itaque propositionibus suo ordine reddendae sunt traditiones").[21]

The third of the sixteen canons promulgated by the Roman Synod—in this spirit of fidelity to Tradition—follows two decrees concerning the chastity of virgins. Here are the main passages of this long document:

Indeed, we have already frequently touched upon these matters—and our word has been spread in many churches—especially when it comes to priests whose dignity demands that they be the very rule of their good works for the people. . . . [Indeed,] when one does not observe what has been the object of useful warnings, the apostolic commandments are held in contempt and ignored as it were; [but] judgment with respect to those who have committed [these violations] cannot be changed. Here is what has been decided, first of all, with regard to bishops, priests, and deacons: those who have the responsibility of the divine sacrifice, and whose hands give the grace of baptism and consecrate the Body of Christ, are ordered by divine Scripture, and not only ourselves, to be very chaste; the Fathers themselves had ordered them to observe bodily continence. Let us not omit this point but explain the reason for it: how would a bishop or a priest dare preach continence and integrity to a widow or a virgin, or yet [how would he dare] exhort [spouses] to the chastity of the conjugal bed, if he himself is more concerned about begetting children for the world than begetting them for God? This is why we read in Scripture regarding these three ranks that the ministers of God are under the obligation to

[21] PL 13, 1182a–c. P. Coustant, *Epistolae*, pp. 687–88.

observe purity; it is obvious that this is always a necessity for them; they must either give baptism or offer the sacrifice. Would an impure man dare soil what is holy when holy things are for holy people? It was thus that [the priests of the Old Testament] who offered sacrifices in the temple rightly stayed there without going out during the entire year they were on duty and had nothing more to do with their homes. As to the idolaters, when they dedicate themselves to their impieties and immolate [sacrifices] to the demons, they impose on themselves continence with regard to women and also endeavor to keep themselves pure from [certain] foods; and you would ask me if the priest of the living God, who must offer spiritual sacrifices, must be constantly purified, if he must, in his whole flesh, be concerned about flesh? If commixture is defiling, it is obvious that the priest must be ready to carry out his celestial functions—he who has to supplicate on behalf of the sins of the others—so that he himself not be found impure. If the lay people are told: "Leave yourselves free for prayer" (1 Cor 7:5), these men who put themselves first at the service of human procreation might have the title of priests, but they cannot have that dignity. . . .[22]

The argumentation is akin to that of the *Directa* (to Himerius of Tarragona) and the *Cum in unum* (to the African bishops and sees of various provinces) decretals. It is to Scripture and apostolic tradition that clerical continence is linked, as is stressed in the formulae "apostolica mandata quasi ignota contemnuntur" (the apostolic commandments are held in contempt and ignored as it were) and "statutum est de episcopis, presbyteris et diaconibus . . . quos non solum nos sed et scriptura divina compellit esse castissimos" ([here is what] has been decided . . . with regard to bishops, priests, and deacons . . . on whom divine Scriptures, and not only us, impose the obligation to be most chaste).

In this perspective, it is interesting to read, in addition to this canon related to ecclesiastical continence, what the Pontiff says a little later in the same *Dominus inter* decretal about the unity of faith and discipline that must prevail among Catholic bishops:

There must be only one profession of faith for the Catholic bishops: this was decreed by the apostolic rule. Therefore, if there is one faith, there should also be one tradition. If there is one tradition, there must be one discipline observed by all the Churches. Indeed, the Churches were established in very diverse regions, but throughout the whole world [the Church] is called "one" thanks to the unity of the Catholic faith. Thus we read:

---

[22] PL 13, 1184a–86a. P. Coustant, *Epistolae*, pp. 689–91.

"My dove is unique, mine, unique and perfect. She is the darling of her mother" (Song 6:9).[23]

The four documents of the late 4th century we have studied pose the problem that started our research: does the discipline of ecclesiastical celibacy, such as that expressed in the first legislative texts making it known to us, go back to the time of the apostles? The second canon of the Council of Carthage in 390 and the three decretals (*Directa, Cum in unum,* and *Dominus inter*) originated from the highest men in the Church using their authority in a collegial framework. Three of these documents come from episcopal synods gathering the representatives of many dioceses; the decisions they made are in communion with the Bishop of Rome and thus partake of the authority that is proper to the college of apostles united to its head.[24] Though they do not have the authority of an ecumenical council's decisions, they are nonetheless an act of government committing the Magisterium of the Church in its highest forms. One should not underestimate a priori the value of such documents. As for the *Directa* decretal sent by Siricius to Himerius of Tarragona, it was also the object of a common deliberation between the Roman Pontiff and some of his colleagues in the episcopate.[25] Above all, it is the position adopted by Peter's successors, in whom are expressed and summarized the collective teaching of the apostolic college. The decretal's affirmations regarding the apostolicity of tradition concerning clerical continence and its scriptural origins cannot fail to be taken into account, because the question is to find out what the apostles taught. For the historian of the early Church as well as for the theologian, they are a call to research, indeed a guide for the proper undertaking of an inquiry into the origins.

We will therefore choose the late 4th century as our chronological basis for inquiry on the birth and development of the law on clerical celibacy rather than the year 325, the date of the First Ecumenical Council of Nicaea. This was a watershed in the life of the Church granted from then on Constantinian peace and the possibility of overt organization; however, it does not represent—in our field of study—a sufficiently clear landmark. The documents of the years 380 and 390 clarify for the first

---

[23] "Catholicorum episcoporum unam confessionem esse debere apostolica disciplina composuit. Si ergo una fides est, manere debet et una traditio. Si una traditio est, una debet disciplina per omnes ecclesias custodiri. Diversis in regionibus quidem ecclesiae sunt conditae: sed per omnem mundum unitate fidei catholicae una est appellata. Nam et sic legimus, *Una est columba mea, una est perfecta mea, una est genitrici suae*" (PL 13, 1187b–88a. P. Coustant, *Epistolae*, p. 692).

[24] Cf. Vatican II, Dogmatic Constitution *Lumen Gentium*, III, 22.

[25] PL 13, 1132b. P. Coustant, *Epistolae*, p. 624.

time in the history of the Church, as far as we are concerned, the Church's precise discipline with respect to clerical continence by simultaneously showing its scriptural and traditional motivations. Is such a discipline, as we are told, as old as the Church? In his research about the development of doctrine, Newman did not hesitate to lay down as a principle: "The whole question boils down to whether we can faithfully be guided by the strong light coming from the 4th and 5th centuries in order to explore the still pale, though sharp, outlines of the previous centuries." [26] It seems to us that we too can attempt to look into time with the help of that light.

---

[26] *An Essay on the Development of Christian Doctrine* (London: Longmans Green, 1885), p. 165.

CHAPTER TWO

The State of the Issue

To embark on a study of the origins of clerical celibacy is also to accept
a dialogue. There have been many studies—some of which are quite
important—on this topic at various times in Church history, and their
influence reaching us through several channels still bears upon contemporary research. To know them is useful and can help us, as it were, to
enter into a critical discussion with their authors so as not to miss a
potentially fruitful contribution. Moreover, history is man's memory,
and it needs at certain times and in certain fields all the past as food for
thought on the conditions of its progress.

In the voluminous literature dedicated to clerical celibacy,[1] the books
or articles dealing *ex professo* with the issue under study—i.e., can the
discipline of clerical celibacy claim an apostolic origin—are relatively few
in number. The selection we are offering in this chapter includes those
that seem to have had a more determining role, either from the viewpoint
of historical research or in the life of the Church, the latter being used
to return periodically to her origins so as to gain a better self-knowledge
and a surer orientation for the future.

BERNOLD OF CONSTANCE, "De prohibenda sacerdotum incontinentia",
MGH, "Libelli de lite imperatorum et pontificum saeculis XI et XII",
II, Hanover, 1892, pp. 4–26.

This first historical retrospective on the origins of priestly celibacy is
written as a correspondence between two twelfth-century clerics with
regard to the Gregorian reform. Bernold of Constance, a papal theologian
(ca. 1050–1100) embarks on a fierce polemic against a friend of his named
Alboinus, who was a canon. Alboinus had become the spokesman for

---

[1] A. de Roskovany, at the end of the 19th century, had already counted more than seven
thousand titles! See below, pp. 31ff.

18

a large number of clerics opposing the decisions of the 1074 Roman Synod against clerical incontinence. Six letters, three from Bernold and three from Alboinus, are milestones in this controversy from 1074 to 1076. The letters are essentially concerned with the interpretation to be given to the 3d canon of the Council of Nicaea (325) regarding the cohabitation of clerics with women not belonging to their families,[2] and with the problem that arose when Paphnutius allegedly intervened at the same Council;[3] they thus provide an interesting illustration of the interest aroused by the history of the controversy's origins, both among the promoters of the Gregorian Reform and among its opponents. The main argument of Bernold of Constance is that of the basic incompatibility between the 3d canon of Nicaea on the one hand and the story of the intervention of Paphnutius on the other. That correspondence was also published by Migne (PL 148, 1079–1104).

THE COMMISSION OF THEOLOGIANS OF THE COUNCIL OF TRENT, report of the debates in Concilium Tridentinum Diariorum, Actorum, Epistularum, Tractatuum Nova Collectio, Societas Goerresiana, ed., vol. IX, pt. 6, Freiburg im Breisgau, 1965, pp. 380–82 and 425–70.

Since the publication of the Jugement de Martin Luther sur les voeux monastiques (Martin Luther's Judgment about Monastic Vows) in 1521, there had been a revival of criticism against ecclesiastical celibacy. These criticisms became rapidly more serious, to such a degree that within a few decades it was deemed necessary to entrust a commission of experts with the task of studying the objections brought forth by the Reformers.

The Council of Trent asked seventeen theologi minores[4] to give their opinions about the two Protestant propositions: (1) Marriage should not

---

[2] Here is the text of this 3d canon of the Council of Nicaea, of which more later: "The great council has absolutely forbidden the bishops, priests, and deacons, in a word all the clergy members, to have with them a sister companion, unless she be a mother, sister, aunt, or other persons who are above all suspicion" (P. P. Joannou, Discipline générale antique, 2d–9th centuries, hereafter cited as Joannou, I, 1 [Grottaferrata, 1962], pp. 25–26).

[3] In his Historia Ecclesiastica (completed around the year 440), Socrates tells that at the Council of Nicaea one Paphnutius, bishop of Upper Thebaid, would have intervened to prevent the enactment of a law aiming to forbid married bishops, priests, and deacons from having conjugal intercourse with their wives. In every period and especially during the Protestant Reformation that anecdote provoked heated controversies, about which more later.

[4] The committee included five diocesan priests (Jean Peletier, Antonio Solisius, Richard du Pré, Lazare Brochot, Ferdinand Tricus), three Franciscans (Miguel of Medina, Jean Lubera, Francis Orantes), five Dominicans (Francis Ferrer, Jean Gallo, Jean de Ludenna, Basil of Pisis, Sanctus Cithius), two hermits of St. Augustine (Simon Florentinus, Anthony of Modulpho), one Carmelite (Désiré de St. Martin), and one regular canon of St. Augustine

be relegated to second rank; it is, on the contrary, superior to chastity. God gives married couples a greater grace than other people ("Matrimonium non postponendum, sed anteferendum castitati, et Deum dare coniugibus maiorem gratiam quam aliis"). (2) Western priests can marry licitly notwithstanding ecclesiastic vows or law; to affirm the contrary is nothing less than a condemnation of marriage. All those who are not aware of having received the gift of chastity can freely enter into marriage ("Licite contrahere posse matrimonium sacerdotes occidentales, non obstante voto vel lege ecclesiastica, et oppositum nihil aliud esse quam damnare matrimonium, posseque omnes contrahere matrimonium, qui non sentiunt se habere donum castitatis").

The discussions opened on March 4, 1563, in Trent, and went on for thirteen sessions. It was mainly the second of the two propositions that brought forth historical considerations because people asked themselves whether the prohibition of marriage for priests was not in contradiction with either Holy Writ or written and oral apostolic tradition. A distinction was made between the case of celibates who became priests and that of married men accepted for ordination. As far as the former were concerned, there had never been in the Church any exception to the prohibition of marriage: its origin was apostolic (Jean Peletier, Miguel of Medina, Jean Lubera, Jean de Ludenna, Francis Orantes, Didacus of Paiva). Some theologians went so far as to conclude that it was of divine law (Richard du Pré, Miguel of Medina, Francis Orantes), while others deemed to the contrary that this was only a point of ecclesiastical law (Francis Ferrer, Didacus of Paiva). As to married men accepted for Orders (a historical fact that no one ever contested), Claude de Saintes argued that the obligation of perfect continence imposed on them from the moment of ordination was of apostolic origin; he even deemed it, because of this very fact, as being *de jure divino primario*. More numerous were the *theologi minores* who saw in this obligation the result of an ecclesiastical decision (Miguel of Medina, Lucius Anguisciola, Didacus of Paiva). Lastly, it is notable that all the advisers who studied the question of the apostles' marriages affirmed unhesitatingly that those apostles who could have been married before Christ called them to follow him practiced continence thereafter in conformity with their own declaration: "Ecce nos reliquimus omnia et secuti sumus te . . ." (Mt 19:27). If the apostles left *everything* to follow Christ, it is obvious that they also gave up conjugal life with their wives (see in particular the argumentation of Désiré de St. Martin).

(Claude de Saintes, future bishop of Evreux). Moreover, other experts were at times invited to take the floor during one session or another. That was in particular the case for Lucius Anguisciola, a Conventual Franciscan, and for Didacus of Paiva, a diocesan priest.

The discussions of the theological commission led to the writing of a canon that, after a few amendments, was approved by the Fathers of the Council:

> Can. 9. Si quis dixerit, clericos in sacris ordinibus constitutos, vel regulares castitatem solemniter professos, posse matrimonium contrahere, contractumque validum esse, non obstante lege Ecclesiastica vel voto, et oppositum nil aliud esse, quam damnare matrimonium, qui non sentiunt se castitatis (etiamsi eam voverint) habere donum: an.s. Cum Deus id recte petentibus non deneget, "nec patiatur, nos supra id, quod possumus, tentari" (1 Cor 10:13). (Sess. XXIV, Dz. 1809 [= 979].)

Though they bear the mark of their time, these expositions of the theologians at the Council of Trent remain valid today insofar as they review practically all the classical objections that have been formulated throughout history against ecclesiastical celibacy (and continence).

GEORG CALIXTUS, *De conjugio clericorum liber. Quo et libertas hujus conjugii adversus pontificias leges, Hildebrandinam haeresin, Baronium, Bellarminum et socios, ex jure divino et humano vindicatur et praecipue quidquid umquam in Ecclesia tentatum gestumque est ad hanc libertatem vel conservandam vel infringendam ac denique abrogandam ex historiae fontibus ordine suo accurate narratur.* Helmstadt, 1631; 2d ed.: Frankfurt, 1651, xxiv–624–xxxii p. in quarto.

As indicated in the title, the work is presented as a plea in favor of clerical marriage and a refutation of the laws on clerical celibacy in the Roman Church. It is also directed against contemporary Catholic historians and theologians such as Cardinals Baronius and Bellarmine who had recently defended in their writings the apostolic origins of the celibacy-continence discipline.[5] Calixtus, whose real name was Callisen (1586–1656), was a Lutheran theologian and a professor at Helmstadt. In favor of a

---

[5] Robert Bellarmine, *Disputationes de Controversiis Christianae fidei adversus hujus temporis Haereticos*, 3 vols. (Ingolstadt, 1586–93). New ed.: 4 vols. (Venice, 1596). Ed. Vivès, 12 vols. (Paris, 1870), vol. II, *Quinta controversia generalis. De membris Ecclesiae, lib.I. De clericis. cap. XVIII, De coelibatu Sacerdotum: sit de jure divino annexus sacris ordinibus coelibatus, an non? cap. XIX, Coelibatum jure Apostolico rectissime annexum ordinibus sacris, cap. XX, Solvuntur argumenta Calvini. cap. XXI, Solvuntur argumenta Philippi. cap. XXII, Solvuntur argumenta Magdeburgensium. cap. XXIII, De Bigamia. cap. XXIV, Solvuntur objectiones Lutheri* (pp. 453–78).

Caesar Baronius, *Annales Ecclesiastici*, 12 vols. in folio, 1588–1607. The Lucques edition published by J. D. Mansi, 28 vols. in folio, is considered to be the best. See, in particular, vol. 1, an. 58, nn. xiv to xxix, pp. 495–501.

Stanislas Hosius, *Confessio catholicae fidei christiana: vel potius explicatio quaedam confessionis, in synodo petricoviensi, a patribus provinciarum Gnesnensis et Leopoliensis in regno Poloniae factae, Anno Domini MDLI.* The Vienna edition, 1651, is the best. See, especially, chap. LVI,

rapprochement with the Catholic Church, he was seen at times by his brothers in religion as a "cryptopapist". When it came to clerical marriage, however, his intentions left no room for doubt, as can be seen in his letter to the Senate of Hildesheim, used as a preface to his work. He intended to demonstrate the frailty of the scriptural, historical, and doctrinal foundations on which, in his views, the legislation relative to clerical celibacy was based, and to prove, with Martin Luther, and by such an example, that the Roman pontiff was no longer *"supremus catholicae ecclesiae princeps, dogmatum infallibilis judex et conditor. . . ."* The work is extremely well researched and documented and studies with a care equal to its manifestly tendentious bias all the elements of the scriptural and patristic works that were known at the time. In this respect it can be seen as the most solid work produced by the Protestant Reformation against ecclesiastical celibacy. Many are those who would resort to it later, often at great lengths. It was reprinted in 1783 by Heinrich Henke[6] and thus continued to have a strong influence at the time of the *Aufklärung* (Enlightenment) and until the end of the 19th century.

LOUIS THOMASSIN, "Du célibat des Bénéficiers dans l'Église Orientale pendant les cinq premiers siècles" (ca. 885–94), bk. II, chap. LXI; "Du célibat des Bénéficiers dans l'Église Latine pendant les cinq premiers siècles" (ca. 894–901), bk. II, chap. LXI, in *Ancienne et nouvelle discipline de l'Église touchant les Bénéfices et les Bénéficiers*, Paris, 1678–79, 3 vols. in folio; newly revised and amended edition, Paris, 1725.

Louis d'Eynac Thomassin (1619–95) was a priest, a member of the Oratory, and one of the best Catholic theologians of the 17th century. Henri Bremond described him as "an eternal honor to the Oratory, to French erudition, and to the Church". He published many works that remain monuments of ecclesiastical science. *L'Ancienne et nouvelle discipline de l'Église . . .* is generally considered his masterpiece. "The documents gathered in this work are countless", A. Molien wrote, "and remain very valuable, even after the progress achieved in modern scholarship; it is difficult to find fault with Thomassin, and one can still refer to him."[7] Our quotations are taken from the new French edition, published in Paris in 1725, in which chapters covering the same subject are gathered together in a more systematic way.

De impedimentis matrimonii, pp. 154–75. There is a good presentation of Hosius' ideas on clerical celibacy in Franciscus Zaorski, *Doctrina Card. Stanislai Hosii de coelibatu ecclesiastico adversus haereses saec. XVI*, XI (Rome, 1957), 57 p.

[6] See below, pp. 28ff.

[7] DTC XV, c. 816.

Thomassin deals with the history of clerical celibacy's origins in the first volume of book II, devoted to "the second Order of clergy". He was perfectly acquainted with the documents on the issue—as they were known in his time—and studied each element with great freedom of judgment and a very knowledgeable critical sense. A modern historian will always be able to profit from Thomassin's chapters on the celibacy of the *Bénéficiers* (those were major clerics, i.e., clerics whose functions entitled them to an ecclesiastical benefice or living) in the East and West, even if he does not share all of Thomassin's conclusions. The following quotation will give an idea of the way the author understood the origins of the law:

> This law [of celibacy] for the Major Orders' clerics is as ancient as the Church; the eternal Pontiff, who had wanted to be born of a Virgin and was himself a virginal Host wanting it to be eternally immolated in his Church by those he called to his divine priesthood, also wanted those who offered his sacrifice to imitate him, to offer their bodies together with his as a chaste, pure, and innocent victim. This is why he chose apostles or virgins forever, or those who would be continent in the future: for this reason, the apostles chose as keepers and successors of their priestly kingship only virgins, or in the absence of virgins, people vowed to eternal celibacy; lastly, this is why the divine disciples banned forever from the virginal priesthood of the Church those whose incontinence had been manifested through a double marriage (p. 886).

The French edition of 1725 was reprinted by Migne in 1858, in volumes XXV and XXVI of its *Dictionnaires*. In 1854–67, M. André published "a new edition, revised, amended, and enlarged" of the *Ancienne et nouvelle discipline de l'Église* (Bar-le-Duc), 7 vols. in quarto. Thomassin's chapters on the history of the *Bénéficiers'* celibacy in the East and West are, in that edition, in vol. II, pp. 128–40.

Noël Alexandre, *Dissertationum ecclesiasticarum trias. Prima de divina episcoporum supra presbyteros eminentia adversus Blondellum. Altera de sacrorum ministrorum coelibatu, sive de historia Paphnutii cum Nicaeno canone concilianda. Tertia de vulgata Scripturae sacrae versione*, Paris, 1678, 1 vol. in octavo.

The Dominican Noël Alexandre (1639–1724) was a doctor from the Sorbonne and rector of theology at the convent of Saint-Jacques. He had a very strong influence on the ecclesiastical issues of his time. Author of many books on theology, history, and Holy Scripture, as well as a very prolific polemist, he remains rightly famous for the twenty-six volumes in octavo of his *Histoire Ecclésiastique*, written for the instruction of Colbert's son and future archbishop of Rouen. His Gallican tendencies prompted the listing of that work on the Index in 1684–87 (he wrote a new and amended edition in Paris, 1699), and while it would be excessive to see him as leaning toward Jansenism, it remains true that he "objected" to the bull *Unigenitus* and recanted only a few days before his death.

His dissertation on the history of celibacy's origins appears in the framework of a small in octavo, in which he put together three polemic booklets. It is titled, "On the celibate of the holy ministries, or the agreement of Paphnutius' story with a Nicaean canon", and it centers the problem, as Bernold of Constance had already done, in the relationship between those two testimonies of the early centuries. His exposition is divided into three "propositions" that are a good summary of the author's opinions:

Proposition 1: The 3d canon of Nicaea does not order the major clerics to observe continence with the wives they had married before holy ordination and thus is not incompatible with the story of Paphnutius as related by ecclesiastical writers (Nicaenae Synodi Canon 3. Continentiam ab uxoribus ante sacram Ordinationem ductis majoribus Clericis non praecipit, nec proinde Historiae Paphnutii ab Auctoribus Ecclesiasticis relatae repugnat).

Proposition 2: Even though the Council of Nicaea had no statutes about clerical celibacy, at that time bishops, priests, and deacons did observe continence because of an ancient usage derived from apostolic times; that discipline was corroborated by the decrees and canons of Siricius and other pontiffs after him, as well as by the councils. It was the sanctity of that discipline and of that law that the heretics attempted to defeat, to no avail (Quamvis Nicaena Synodus de Clericorum coelibatu nihil statuerit, ejus tamen temporibus Episcopi, Presbyteri, et Diaconi, perpetuam continentiam servabant ex Ecclesiae Disciplina, diuturno usu et ab Apostolicis temporibus derivato firmata, quam Siricius, et alii deinde Pontifices, Conciliaque, Decretis suis, atque Canonibus roborarunt. Cujus Disciplinae, legisque sanctimoniam irrito conatu impugnant Heterodoxi).

Proposition 3: The law of perpetual continence was not imposed on the sacred ministers either by Christ or by the apostles (Perpetuae lex continentiae nec a Christo, nec ab Apostolis, Sacris Ministris imposita fuit).

The authority of Noël Alexandre on the one hand and the serious nature of his dissertation on the other made him among the Catholic circles of his time the best representative of a historical line of interpretation that was to be adopted by certain authors up to our time.

Noël Alexandre's dissertation was reprinted by F. A. Zaccaria in his *Thesaurus theologicus*, vol. XII (Venice, 1783), pp. 565–601, under the title "De Historia Paphnutii cum Nicaeno Canone III, concilianda et de Sacrorum Ministrorum Coelibatu".

JAN STILTINCK, "An veresimile sit, S. Paphnutium se in Concilio Nicaeno opposuisse legi de continentia Sacerdotum et Diaconorum", in *Acta Sanctorum Septembris*, vol. III, Venice, 1761, pp. 784–87.

This critical study is included in a dissertation published in the *Acta Sanctorum* under the title "De S. Paphnutio episc. conf. in Aegypto Commentarius historico-criticus".[8] Its author, Jan Stiltinck—or Stilting (1703–62)—was one of the more prominent members of the Bollandist Society. He worked for twenty-five years at editing the *Acta Sanctorum*. We owe to him most of the five volumes of August, all those of September, and the first volume of October. When asking the question "Is it likely that St. Paphnutius, at the Council of Nicaea, did oppose a law on priests' and deacons' continence?" the scholarly Jesuit meant to refute the opinion defended more than a century earlier by Noël Alexandre. In his view, the interpretation that is most faithful to historical truth is that of Baronius and Bellarmine: it is not only in accordance with a custom but with a genuine law that perpetual continence has been observed by deacons, priests, and bishops since the time of the apostles. The anecdote of Paphnutius, as related by Socrates and Sozomenus, is a forgery. There might have been a basic historical element, but what might have happened at the Council of Nicaea was quite different from what we read in Byzantine works. In conclusion Stiltinck wrote: "I tend to believe that this is a purely fictitious work. But what I cannot doubt in any way is this: it is false that the Council of Nicaea let everyone freely decide for himself that he could either have conjugal intercourse or separate from his wife."

The author returned to the question of clerical celibacy's origins in another dissertation, studying at length and with great sagacity the objection drawn from the birthdate of Gregory Nazianzen. Did Gregory the Elder, a bishop, sire Gregory Nazianzen while he was a bishop or before he received Orders? Stiltinck is in favor of the latter opinion, thus confirming the conclusions of his dissertation about Paphnutius.[9] These two studies of Jan Stiltinck, which for a long time drew the attention of scholars, still remain very useful today.

---

[8] It was reprinted by F.A. Zaccaria, *Thesaurus theologicus*, vol. XII (Venice, 1783), pp. 602–7.

[9] Jan Stiltinck, "Dissertatio de tempore natali S. Gregorii Nazianzeni", in *Acta Sanctorum Septembris*, vol. III (Venice, 1761), pp. xxiii–xl.

FRANCIS ANTHONY ZACCARIA, *Storia polemica del celibato sacro da contrapporsi ad alcune detestabili opere uscite a questi tempi*, Rome, 1774.

The "Storia polemica" was brought about by the publishing in Tuscany of a book against clerical celibacy, in which—in spite of the author's precautions—it was not difficult to recognize the translation of a work by Abbé Pierre Desforges that had been secretly published in France a few years earlier.[10] Francis Anthony Zaccaria (1714–95), an Italian Jesuit famous in the scholarly circles of the 18th century for his numerous publications in the most diverse fields,[11] had become, after the Society of Jesus had been suppressed, a professor of ecclesiastical history at the College of Sapience in Rome. Through Desforges, all the anticelibate movement aroused in Europe by the philosophers of the "Century of Enlightenment" is gathered on Zaccaria's desk, and he is moved to write.

Even though it had originated in polemical needs, if we take its time into account, Zaccaria's work does remain highly scientific. There are three parts: the first is devoted to the history of ecclesiastical celibacy in the Eastern Church; the second, to the history of ecclesiastical celibacy in the Western Church; and the third, to the study of the objections against celibacy as voiced by the "Moderns", and especially Abbé Desforges. Here are the tables of contents of the first two books, dealing in greater details with the history of the origins:

Book I. History of Sacred Celibacy
in the Eastern Church

1: The apostles' celibacy. 2: Did the apostles promulgate laws about priestly celibacy, and if so, which ones? 3: History of celibacy from apostolic times until the Council of Nicaea. 4: Was there any decree relative to celibacy at the Council of Nicaea? 5: What credit can we give to a certain story of Paphnutius told by Socrates? 6: More on the history of celibacy from the Council of Nicaea until the death of St. Gregory Nazianzen. 7: Death of St. Gregory Nazianzen: had he been born while his father was already a bishop? 8: Discipline in the Greek Church from the death of St. Gregory Nazianzen to the Trullan Council. 9: New discipline established for the Greeks at the Trullan Council. Short history of that Council. Comments on the canons. 10: Attitude of the Latin Church with respect

---

[10] *Advantages du mariage, et combien il est nécessaire et salutaire aux prêtres et aux évêques de ce temps-ci d'épouser une fille chrétienne*, 2 vols. (Brussels, 1760 = Paris, 1758 and 1760), 208 and 197 p.

[11] "F. A. Zaccaria is one of the greatest scholars and one of the most universal minds of his time" (J. P. Grausem, DTC XV, 3644).

to the Greeks, and of the Greeks with respect to the Latin Church after the Trullan Council about the issue of celibacy.

Book II. History of Celibacy in the Western Church

1: Documents concerning ecclesiastical celibacy in the West before the time of Pope Siricius. 2: Report on Pope Siricius' decrees on celibacy, with a few important observations. 3: More on the history of celibacy until the end of the pontificate of St. Leo. 4: Sacred celibacy becomes stronger and stronger from the time of St. Leo to the end of the pontificate of St. Gregory the Great. 5: Ups and downs in the history of celibacy from the pontificate of St. Gregory until the end of the 10th century. 6: Detestable war waged on all sides during the 11th century by incontinent clerics against the laws of the Church; firm stance of the popes, especially of St. Gregory VII, to maintain and strengthen them in the face of prevaricators. 7: Chronology of other events related to clerical continence from the death of St. Gregory VII until today.

Eleven years later, when he became director of sacred history studies in the Roman Academy of noble clerics, F. A. Zaccaria published a new work on clerical celibacy titled *Nuova giustificazione del celibato sacro dagli inconvenienti oppostogli anche ultimamente in alcuni infamissimi libri dissertazioni quattro* (Fuligno, 1785), xxxi + 280 pp. in quarto.

In his introduction the author declares that it would never have occurred to him, when he published his first book, that he would have to take up his pen again on the subject of clerical celibacy, but that he was compelled to do so because of the very relentlessness with which people, on all sides, went on struggling against "such a holy discipline that came to us from the apostles, and that was perpetuated until our time in the most solemn fashion by the Fathers, the councils, and the pontiffs of the Roman Church". Among the books that he undertook to refute, Zaccaria enumerated the following works: *Les inconvénients du Célibat des Prêtres, prouvés par des Recherches historiques* (Geneva, 1781) (anonymous);[12] Stanislas Orzechowski, *Premurose rappresentanze alla umanità, ed alla ragione per*

---

[12] The author of this anonymous work is a former member of the Oratory, judge and librarian of La Rochelle, named Jacques Maurice Gaudin (1740–1810). His book, republished in Paris (Lejay) in 1790, inspired F. A. Zaccaria to start a new refutation that probably his death, in 1795, prevented him from completing and publishing. Two manuscripts of the Vatican Apostolic Library written by Zaccaria himself and bearing respectively the numbers *Vat. lat.* 8395 and *Vat. lat.* 8396 contain reflections that still remain unpublished and are pertinent to our topic.

ottenere l'abolizione del Celibato del Clero Cattolico (rev. ed., 1782);[13] Jean Schalli, *Fervens desiderium Cleri soecularis, quo justissime sibi expostulat, mediantibus Catholicis Principibus susceptionem Sacramenti Matrimonii indulgeri* (Augusta, 1783). This "new justification of sacred celibacy" gave to Zaccaria the opportunity to strengthen his arguments and to add other proofs for the defense of his thesis.

Seen as a whole, the two works of the (ex-)Jesuit scholar of the 18th century constitute a *Summa* of sorts on the history of ecclesiastical celibacy that is far from having lost all its interest in contemporary research. In fact, today they are still the most satisfactory product of Catholic science in this field: once freed from the polemical content of their time, they can still render tremendous service to theology and history; any new history of clerical celibacy has to take them into account.

GEORG CALIXTUS, *De conjugio clericorum liber, emendatius edidit in capita sua divisum, indicibus locupletatum, addita praefatione et appendice Henr. Phil. Conr. Henke,* Helmstadt, 1783, xvi–662 pp. in quarto.

This work is a reprint of Georg Calixtus' book published for the first time in 1631.[14] Conrad Henke, professor of theology at the University of Helmstadt as had been Calixtus, deems his predecessor to be capable still of bringing, after more than one hundred and fifty years, a solid refutation to the recently published work of Zaccaria and, by the same token, of accelerating the German movement which, favored by Josephism, seemed to lead infallibly to the abolition of celibacy. In a dithyrambic preface he declares:

> Neither before nor after Georg Calixtus was anyone capable of writing in such a deep and scholarly way in favor of the marriage of clerics, forbidden until now in the Roman Church, as everybody knows, by laws that are declared inviolable. All men of heart and right judgment recognize this. No one has ever refuted—or, as far as I know, attempted to refute it—in the past one hundred and fifty years yet; it has not been read enough, and it is difficult to find it today in the bookstores. Which is why it seemed to me not unreasonable, but rather quite opportune for our time, to prepare a revision and a reprint.

A little later we are told that the revised book is above all meant to demolish Zaccaria's work (*Storia polemica del celibato sacro*), of which an

---

[13] The author is a Polish canon who had married after his ordination and had been excommunicated. His book, published in 1551, was translated into Latin in 1782. It was that last edition that Zaccaria commented upon here.

[14] See above, pp. 21f.

abbreviated German translation had just been published in Bamberg and Würzburg (1781). It is likely that Zaccaria himself was not aware of this reprint of Calixtus' book (no more than he knew the original) because otherwise he would have mentioned it in his *Nuova giustificazione*.

Henke's edition did not obtain the results expected by its author, i.e., the abolition of celibacy, yet it had a very strong influence on historical research in Germany at the end of the 18th and during the 19th centuries. Franz Xaver Funk made several references to it in his articles for the *Theologische Quartalschrift*,[15] and he did not hesitate to list it first in the bibliography given at the end of his "Cölibat" in the *Real-Encyclopädie der christlichen Alterthümer* of Kraus (vol. I, p. 307).

JOHANN ANTON THEINER and AUGUSTINE THEINER, *Die Einführung der erzwungenen Ehelosigkeit bei den christlichen Geistlichen und ihre Folgen. Ein Beitrag zur Kirchengeschichte*, 3 vol. (= vol. I, vol. II/1 and 2), Altenburg, 1828, X and 580 pp., VI and 1039 pp. in octavo.

This work of more than sixteen hundred pages, still well known among historians today, was written by the two Theiner brothers of Breslau. Augustine, the younger (1804–74), was the first to have the idea of this "introduction of forced celibacy among Christian clerics and its consequences", which he brought to completion, barely past his twenty-fourth birthday, with the help of his older brother, Johann Anton (1799–1860). The destinies of the two men were very different after that. The elder, compelled to leave his exegesis and canon law chair at the University of Breslau after the publication of the *Einführung*, was condemned by the Church authorities and joined the "German Catholic Church" of Ronge; then he gave up the priesthood and died excommunicated. Augustine, on the other hand, had a deep conversion, joined the Oratory, and pursued a scientific and ecclesiastical career in Rome where he enjoyed the favor of the sovereign pontiffs for a long time. Appointed prefect of the Vatican Archives in 1855, he brought forth many unpublished documents about the history of the Church. However, his sympathies for Döllinger and the anti–infallibilist movement caused him to fall into disgrace at the time of the Vatican Council. One cannot affirm with absolute certainty that he died in union with the Catholic Church.

The work of the two brothers, in spite of its imposing volume of compiled documents, is far less impressive as far as serious argumentation goes. It is a huge compilation of texts and histories—often little stories— linked by the thread of a clearly expressed intention that never varies from one end to the other of the three volumes: to show that the holy

[15] See below, pp. 32ff.

doctrine of the New Testament on marriage was perverted early in time under the influence of external causes and currents of ideas alien to the true faith. Having confused motivations, the law on ecclesiastical celibacy could have been enacted and could have developed only long after apostolic times. It was, throughout the centuries, the cause of countless disorders and errors among the clergy, and "it would therefore be one of the greatest services one could render to mankind to dry up once and forever the source of so many moral evils."

Reprinted by R. Nippolt in 1897, the book of the Theiner brothers was published again in an abbreviated edition in 1932 by W. Mehnert. It is still one of the most frequently used reference books, especially by the opponents of priestly celibacy.

HENRY CHARLES LEA, *The History of Sacerdotal Celibacy in the Christian Church*, London, 1867; many editions.

This book of pseudoscholarly vulgarization, *The History of Sacerdotal Celibacy in the Christian Church*, deserves mention in these pages only because it is widely read in the United States and other English-speaking countries.[16] It is for the general public what the works of Georg Calixtus and the Theiner brothers are for the learned. The thesis of the author, who was a successful American writer of the late 19th century, is as simple as it is clearly enunciated: the mysterious and irresistible moral power of the Catholic Church, which has survived and spread her influence throughout the centuries, is to be credited mostly to the law of priestly celibacy:

> Here is not, by far, the least of the causes contributing to the victorious march of the Church: the demands she imposed on all those who received from her the supernatural powers conferred by Holy Orders; they have to surrender themselves to her without any reservation and irrevocably, to break off all human attachments, to aspire only to serve her, and not to be led astray from their loyalty to her by any familial affection, by any family obligation that might cause them to alienate ecclesiastical property from her, or by any ambitions, save the rewards that only she can offer them.

As an instrument of domination, celibacy is not rooted in the Gospel. It is the dangerous fruit of currents of thought that came from outside, progressively penetrated genuine Christian spirituality, and led it to excesses; here the author is pointing the finger at Buddhism, Neoplatonism,

---

[16] Among the recent editions, let us indicate here that of New York, 1957 (Russel and Russel), without notes or bibliography, and that of University Books, USA, 1966.

and Manichaeism. Once it became institutionalized, compulsory celibacy was shored up by laws and sanctions, numerous scandals giving the proof that it is nothing but an inhuman burden. The author ends his book, which mixes history with polemics, just as he began it: a priestly caste whose privileges and influence are derived from celibacy is a dangerous element in the social body.

AUGUSTINO DE ROSKOVANY, *Coelibatus, et Breviarium: duo gravissima clericorum officia, e monumentis omnium seculorum demonstrata. Accessit completa literatura*, vols. I–IV, Pestini, 1861; vols. V–VIII, Nitrae, 1877; vols. IX–X, Nitrae, 1881; *Supplementa ad collectiones monumentorum et literaturae*, vols. III–IV, Nitrae, 1888.

The author of this huge compilation, which has become indispensable in spite of its shortcomings, was a Hungarian theologian of the 19th century (1807–92). As first rector of the Eger Seminary, he was appointed auxiliary bishop in the same town (1847), then bishop of Waitsen (1851), and, finally, bishop of Neutra in Slovakia (1859). A tireless man, he labored at collecting documents about the religious sciences on a variety of topics: primacy of the Roman pontiff, mixed marriages, independence of ecclesiastical power, the Immaculate Conception, marriages in the Catholic Church, celibacy, and the breviary. The compilation on the latter, though it is not the largest, includes no less than fourteen volumes, of which three are supplements.[17] There are two broad categories of documents: the sources themselves (*monumenta*)—Holy Scripture, testimonies of the Fathers of the Church, decrees of the councils and sovereign pontiffs, letters and pastoral communications, and so on—and the texts of various authors related to the topics under study (*literatura*).[18] They are presented in chronological order, but account must be taken of the supplements added by the author in volumes of the collection he published later. This peculiarity, together with the fact that the same series of works contains works and documents about topics that are as distinct as celibacy and the breviary (even if these two obligations do have a connection) does not make things easy for the reader. Some practice is needed to overcome the obstacle and to familiarize oneself with a valuable instrument of study. With regard to celibacy and the

---

[17] The volumes dealing with celibacy are I–IV, VI, VII, X, and XII. The others deal with the breviary.

[18] The sources are generally given *in extenso* or are at least abundantly quoted. Their value is that of the editions from which they were borrowed, but the references are solid enough that one can find them quickly in the modern critical editions. The Greek documents are given in Latin translation, which must, needless to say, be checked.

period we are studying (from the origins to the end of the 7th century), the sources reprinted by Roskovany are to be found in vol. I, pp. 1–171 (301 texts);[19] in vol. IV, pp. 1–13; in vol. VI, pp. i–iii and 1–3; and in vol. IX, p. 1.

The author, who wanted to write a work of apologetics, thinks that letting the texts speak for themselves is the best way to refute the opponents of ecclesiastical celibacy or those who believe in a late origin of this discipline in the Church:

> These texts will shed a strong light on the error of those who claim that the law of sacred celibacy had been unknown during the first four centuries of the church and was introduced by Pope Siricius, saying as they do that such a law is intrinsically unjust and not founded in right in the least. The documents we are publishing will clearly prove that the law of clerical continence existed long before Pope Siricius, and even long before the Council of Nicaea, and that not only those who were single when they received Sacred Orders, i.e., promoted to the ministry of the altar, but also those who might already have been married had to abstain from conjugal intercourse: indeed, this law is very rightly described as "apostolic", if not for its origin itself, at least for the one it claims to have.[20]

Roskovany's work remained too imperfect, when seen in the light of contemporary scholarship, to achieve the desired result. Such as it is, however, it offers an unequaled collection of texts and documents that can be very useful. The Hungarian bishop might one day inspire a specialist to undertake a genuinely scientific *Enchiridion*, gathering documents on the history of clerical celibacy in the early Church. Until that time, we will always need the "Roskovany".

GUSTAV BICKELL, "Der Cölibat eine apostolische Anordnung", in *Zeitschrift für katholische Theologie*, 1878, pp. 26–64.

FRANZ XAVER FUNK, "Der Cölibat keine apostolische Anordnung", in *Theologische Quartalschrift*, 1879, pp. 208–47.

GUSTAV BICKEL, "Der Cölibat dennoch eine apostolische Anordnung", in *Zeitschrift für katholische Theologie*, 1879, pp. 792–99.

FRANZ XAVER FUNK, "Der Cölibat noch lange keine apostolische Anordnung", in *Theologische Quartalschrift*, 1880, pp. 202–21.

---

[19] It would be good to consult also the notes of the Historical Introduction to this series of texts, vol. 1, pp. i–lvii.

[20] Roskovany, *Coelibatus et Breviarium*, "Monitum", I, p. ii.

These four articles constitute two opposing sides of a controversy about the origins of priestly celibacy that pitted one German scholar against another during the last years of the 19th century, a century rich in polemics for or against clerical marriage in the Germanic lands of the *Aufklärungszeit*.

Professor Gustav Bickell (1838–1906) was the son of a famous Protestant canonist, Johann Wilhelm Bickell, author of important works on the sources of canon law. Converted to Catholicism, he chose the priesthood and pursued, first in Münster and then in Innsbrück and Vienna, a long career as an orientalist that was made particularly fruitful by his knowledge of the Syriac and Hebrew languages. The printing of certain unpublished Syriac works seems to have incited him to write his first article on clerical celibacy in 1878. Taking into account the fact that many theologians, at various times in the history of the Church and up to modern times, had opined in favor of the apostolic origin of the higher clerics' compulsory continence, he expressed his intention to take his turn in trying to justify such a viewpoint, relying especially on the Syriac documents. His long article, substantial and documented, thus attempted to prove two complementary theses:

1. In the West, the obligation of continence, including that for priests and deacons, did not start with Siricius; it goes back to the apostles.
2. In the East, the same obligation existed at the time of the apostles, but in these areas it has been progressively neglected since the 4th century.

The response came very promptly. As early as the following year of 1879, the *Theologische Quartalschrift* of Tübingen published an article with an incisive title ("Celibacy Is Not an Apostolic Constitution") bearing the signature of another authority among the patristic disciplines: Franz Xaver Funk (1821–1907). Ordained a priest in 1864, Funk had succeeded Hefele in the chair of history and theology at Tübingen in 1870. Thirty-seven years of highly scholarly works earned him a long-lasting international reputation. Relying on conclusions accepted, he assures us, by "the most eminent German theologians of modern times", he rejects the idea of celibacy rooted in a law coming from the apostles. Contrary to Bickell, he holds that if celibacy had in fact been practiced by quite a few clerics since the days of the early Church, it was only because they chose to do so on a truly individual and free basis. It was only in the 4th century that the West witnessed a true and valid legislation. On the other hand, the East had remained "firmly faithful to the origins".

Entrenched in their positions, the two scholars exchanged in their respective reviews two other polemic articles: "Yes, Celibacy Is an Apostolic Constitution" (Bickell); "Celibacy Is Not, Far from It, an Apostolic

Constitution" (Funk). While the Innsbrück professor used the opportunity to add a few new pieces to the record, Funk, for his part, worried about the favorable response already given to the theories of his adversary. Was Bickell's reputation as an orientalist going to give him an advantage in the controversy? Funk feels duty-bound to demolish a historical cause that he deems unacceptable. "Whoever has a correct view of scholarship", he protests in the conclusion of his article,

> and takes seriously to heart the future of Catholic scholarship, could not help but be saddened during these past years by the publication of an abundant literature serving neither scholarship nor edification. Matters were questioned that, for an unprejudiced mind, had been settled for a long time. One got lost in speculations that should be described as dreams rather than scholarly research. . . . I am very far from putting on the same plane these phenomena and the work of my adversary. But it remains to be seen whether I was not right in assuming, were it only in a certain way, a parallel between them. This will be settled by the conclusion of our controversy.[21]

But the controversy went no further because matters remained as they were on the part of Bickell though he lived until 1906. Undoubtedly not because in "this joust of ecclesiastical history and archeology" he had been forced "to lay down his weapons", but for the sake of peace and convinced both that his viewpoint was correct and that Funk was intransigent, he preferred to remain silent rather than pursue this dialogue of two deaf men. This can be regretted. Under the stimulation of the controversy he could have built a synthesis—interesting in many respects—on more solid foundations without too easily risking being forgotten by posterity. As for Funk, he would not hesitate seventeen years later to revise his two articles and use them in a new publication.

FRANZ XAVER FUNK, "Cölibat und Priesterehe im christlichen Altertum", in *Kirchengeschichtliche Abhandlungen und Untersuchungen*, vol. 1, Paderborn, 1897, pp. 121–55.

This article revived and combined in one text Funk's two articles published in 1879 and 1880 in the *Theologische Quartalschrift* of Tübingen. The author made few changes, but his tone was less polemic. It still remains a controversial work essentially directed against Bickell's theses. Funk declares himself concerned about the favorable responses Bickell continued to receive in certain scholarly circles and among the general public. The note added by Kraus at the end of his article "Cölibat" in

---

[21] Art. of 1880, pp. 220–21.

the *Real-Encyclopädie der christlichen Altertürmer*[22] compelled him, he said, to break his silence.

The starting point of Funk's theory is the historical watershed seen by him in the Council of Elvira:

> The most eminent German theologians of modern times studied the question of the early Church's discipline in the field of clerogamy. Möhler, Hefele, and Probst, in particular, are unanimous in the result of their research: The Synod of Elvira in the year 300 is a watershed. Canon 33 of that synod did impose to the higher clerics, *episcopis, presbyteris, et diaconibus vel omnibus clericis positis in ministerio,* absolute continence, while until then it had been permitted to lead a matrimonial life even after ordination on condition that the marriage had taken place before it (pp. 121–22).

The article is divided into two parts. In the first (pp. 123–41), Funk reviews the testimonies of Eastern and Western authors that Bickell used in favor of the apostolic origin of the law relative to clerical continence and endeavors to refute them, notably on grounds of philology. Not a single text brought forth by his old adversary seems acceptable to him. Moreover, he proves to be insensitive to the argument of Tradition, which he discards once and for all:

> It is true that Epiphanius refers to the apostles. But even though he goes back to them, he has nothing but generalities to offer. Nowhere does he say in a clear and unmistakable way that the apostles had formally prescribed continence. And even if he had done so, we would not be compelled to believe him without further ado. Whoever is thoroughly acquainted with ancient Christian literature is aware that the Fathers spoke only too easily about apostolic decrees and were always quick to claim an apostolic origin for institutions whose late origin can be proven with certainty (p. 131).

In the second part of the article (pp. 142–55), the author studies in particular the documents that are favorable to clerogamy and that had been rejected by Bickell, claiming them for his thesis—for instance, the intervention of Paphnutius at the Council of Nicaea whose authenticity Funk defends.

---

[22] Kraus wrote in that note, which can still be read in the 1880 edition of the *Real-Encyclopädie,* p. 307: "The publisher cannot entirely agree with the ideas put forth by the author (i.e., F. X. Funk). He thinks that Bickell's arguments proving the apostolic institution of celibacy deserve, in part, a more favorable judgment. . . . The declaration of Origen (Hom. 6 in Levit.), of Eusebius (*Dem. ev.* I, 9), of Cyril of Jerusalem (*Catech.* XII, 29) appear to him in a light that permits tracing celibacy—that of the priests as well as that of the bishops—to a much higher antiquity than Mr. Funk is inclined to admit. Nothing prevents one from supposing that the *principle* of celibacy had already been expressed by the apostles, while in practice it was able to develop only in a progressive way."

As a conclusion, the professor emeritus of Tübingen University, then seventy-six years old, pronounced a judgment that he wished to be definitive: "At the end of this study, the interpretation that prevailed in modern times, is proven, without the shadow of a doubt, to be the right one. The future is therefore also in its favor" (p. 154).

ELPHÈGE-FLORENT VACANDARD, "Les origines du célibat ecclésiastique", in *Études de critique et d'histoire religieuse*, 1st ser., Paris, 1905; 5th ed., Paris, 1913, pp. 71–120.

E. Vacandard (1849–1927), chaplain of the Corneille *lycée* in Rouen, was a scholar well known for his many and important works in the field of ecclesiastical sciences. He was one of the first contributors to the *Dictionnaire de Théologie Catholique*, in which many articles bear his signature. From 1905 to 1923 he published on various topics four volumes of *Études de critique et d'histoire religieuse*. It is in the first volume that we find the dissertation related to the origins of ecclesiastical celibacy. In fact, it is a reprint of an article published on January 1 of the same year (1905) in the *Revue du clergé français* (vol. XLI, pp. 252–89); the author would also publish it in the second volume of the *Dictionnaire de Théologie Catholique*, also printed in Paris in 1905 (DTC, II [Paris, 1905], s.v. *Célibat*, pp. 2068–88).

After a brief introduction, in which he declares that he is in favor of Funk's theories, Vacandard divides his exposition into two parts corresponding to the two periods that are easily distinguishable in the history of clerical celibacy: "The first [from the 1st to the 4th centuries], during which it [the practice of celibacy] is honored without being truly compulsory, both in the Latin and in the Greek Churches; the second, when it is subject to precise laws that are much more rigorous in the West than in the East" (pp. 72–73). While his plan is slightly different from Funk's, Vacandard does, however, follow very closely the article that the professor of Tübingen had published eight years earlier, to the extent that he is often content with summing it up or even copying it as is.[23] For the period between the origins and the end of the 7th century, the article of Vacandard does not really bring anything new in comparison with Funk's, being nothing more than its vulgarization in the French language.

---

[23] Compare, for instance, the criticism of the testimonies of Tertullian (Vacandard, pp. 82–83 = Funk, "Cölibat und Priesterehe im christlichen Altertum", p. 139), of John Chrysostom (Vacandard, pp. 84–85 = Funk, ibid., pp. 134–35), of Epiphanius (Vacandard, pp. 85–88 = Funk, ibid., pp. 129–34), of Siricius and of the Council of Carthage of 390 (Vacandard, p. 90 = Funk, ibid., pp. 14–41); etc.

HENRI (DOM) LECLERCQ, "La législation conciliaire relative au célibat ecclésiastique", in Charles Joseph Hefele, *Histoire des conciles d'après les documents
originaux*. New French translation by Dom H. Leclercq, vol. II, pt. 2, Paris,
1908, Appendix VI, pp. 1321–48. Article republished by the author in
DACL 2, pp. 2802–32 (with a complement on "clerogamy in epigraphy").

Scholar and critic Henri Leclercq d'Orlancourt (1869–1945) wrote many
imposingly erudite publications. The main contributor to the *Dictionnaire
d'archéologie chrétienne et de liturgie* (DACL), whose co-director he rapidly
became, and in fact, the only editor after the fifth volume, he is mostly
known today for his monumental *Histoire des Conciles* of Hefele, which
he translated into French with amendments and critical and bibliographical notes (eight parts, sixteen volumes, from the origins to the Council
of Trent). [This book is cited hereafter as Hefele-Leclercq.]

The study of Dom Leclercq on "La législation conciliaire relative au
célibat ecclésiastique" constitutes Appendix VI of the second part of the
second volume of the *Histoire des Conciles*. From the start the author
declares himself against a possible apostolic origin of the law on celibacy:
"What can be said with quasi-certainty is that the practice of celibacy
became more prevalent from the 1st to the 4th centuries without being
subjected to canonical laws. Starting with the 4th century, the practice
became the institution but the latter was not imposed with the same rigor
in the West and the East" (p. 1322). Then the article is divided into six
points: (1) *The celibacy of the apostles* (pp. 1322–26): Neither Scripture
nor patristic testimonies allow one to say with certainty whether the
apostles were married. With the exception of Peter, "we declare that we
know absolutely nothing about the other members of the apostolic college, including St. John", and "we do not know any more about the
example of continence that the apostles would have set when starting
their apostolate". (2) *Priestly monogamy* (pp. 1326–29): St. Paul's instructions to Timothy and Titus about the qualities required for a candidate
bishop (1 Tim 3:2; Titus 1:6) very quickly brought about an interpretation
leading to the choice of monogamists. Thus "monogamy is the first
stage on the way to celibacy". (3) *Spontaneous celibacy* (pp. 1329–32):
However, people went further under the influence of "certain souls aspiring to perfection". From monogamy they went to celibacy. The concern
of being distinct from Judaism (in which marriage is an obligation), some
traces of Gnosticism or Manichaeism, the discredit with which marriage
was often regarded because of an excessive exaltation of virginity—
these various factors also helped spread the practice of celibacy. Nevertheless, it was wholly spontaneous and "waited several centuries before being elevated to the rank of an institution". (4) *The law of celibacy*

(pp. 1332–39): A study of the texts allows us to conclude that "save local and unknown exceptions that were probably few, the right of marriage was recognized for the clergy in the East as well as in the West, at least until the 4th century, and from then on the concession became narrower and narrower as the obligation of celibacy prevailed and the institution was established, imposing and regulating it." In that part of the article, Leclercq follows Funk very closely and rejects Bickell's interpretation, which he, too, describes as "tendentious". (5) *The intervention of Bishop Paphnutius at the Council of Nicaea* (pp. 1339–41): Those who, like Bickell, deem the anecdote to have been apocryphal have "no reason to say so other than the impossibility to reconcile Paphnutius' motion with a compulsory law of celibacy going back to the apostolic time". (6) *Canonical legislation in the West* (pp. 1341–48): It was during the 4th century that an evolution started, leading rapidly enough to the regulation of ecclesiastical celibacy. The 33d canon of the Council of Elvira, around the year 300, was the first attempt in the West to turn the practice of celibacy into an institution. Later councils and popes would bring this process to completion. (The author studies only the Western councils and does not mention the Eastern legislation.)

Generally speaking, this study of Dom Leclercq is in line with Funk's theories. It is, together with the work of Vacandard, one of the main channels through which the ideas of the Tübingen patrologist were spread during the 20th century in French scholarly circles and then among the general public.

ROGER GRYSON, *Les origines du célibat ecclésiastique du premier au septième siècle*, Gembloux, 1970, pp. xi and 228.

A professor at the Louvain University, Roger Gryson attempts in this work to "study the question of the origins of priestly celibacy in itself, from a strictly historical viewpoint" (p. x). Starting from the conclusions of Funk that he does not deem necessary to question (p. vii), he elaborates in three long chapters a view of the matter that is in line with that of the nineteenth-century ideas of the Tübingen patrologist: until the 4th century there is nothing to indicate the existence of a law on celibacy or the continence of clerics. Some clerics were freely giving up marriage or their marital rights. The instances of married clerics, as the author stresses, during that three centuries' period were "more numerous than those of celibate ones" (p. 42). If a legislation was decided, it was mostly due to influences going against the spirit of the New Testament:

> The movement in favor of celibacy or continence of clerics started in a
> general climate of marriage discredit and enthusiasm for virginity that

spread among Christian circles during the 3d century under the pressure of multiple and convergent influences: certain pagan philosophies (Stoicism, Pythagoreanism, Neoplatonism), certain Jewish sects, and the Encratite and Gnostic heresies of the 2d century, all of which seemed to be anchored in Paul's first epistle to the Corinthians, people having quite forgotten that it had been written with the concept of an early end of the world.

Worse even was a factor destined to play a determining role, i.e., "the feeling of repulsion between sexual activity and prayer or a contact with sacred things, a feeling connected with the perception of sexual activity as something 'impure', 'indecent', 'dirty', a source of 'blemish', discrediting the prayer of whoever practiced it" (p. 43). Mr. Gryson adopts as his the explanation proposed in 1916 by the (Lutheran) professor of Church history Heinrich Böhmer in a study for the Albert Hauck Memorial.[24]

Throughout the work one can discern the two keys of interpretation adopted by the author: on the one hand, the late origin of the law, and on the other, the principle of ritual purity, a decisive factor in the evolution leading to the canonical regulations and ensuring their practice down the centuries. Though the research is done with method and based on an ample documentation, Mr. Gryson's stance led him to minimize the scope of certain documents (for instance, Pope Siricius' decretals and the Council of Carthage in the 4th century), and to overestimate some others (such as the Persian Councils of the 5th century in particular, which were, as we know, bodies of legislation for the Nestorian Church, which was openly dissident from Rome and cut off from the rest of the Christian world). We will have the opportunity to give more precision to these criticisms in this work. It is to be said, though, that the author had the merit to stress one of the essential motivations at the basis of the law relative to celibacy-continence, i.e., the major liturgical function of ministerial priesthood. Having accepted the entirety of Funk's conclusions on the late origin of that law, however, he was led to establish a discontinuity between the New Testament theology and the thought of the legislators and theologians who, especially from the 4th century on, contributed to the practice and strengthening of the obligation, and he somehow blurred an essential aspect of the priesthood. While the liturgical function of

---

[24]Heinrich Böhmer, "Die Entstehung des Zölibates", in *Geschichtliche Studien Albert Hauck zum 70. Geburtstage dargebracht* (Leipzig, 1916), pp. 6–24. Böhmer sums up his position in the following way: "I reach the following conclusion: the concept serving as the basis and determining motivation to a movement in favor of continence, and according to which sexual intercourse makes one unfit for worship, comes neither from the New Testament nor from the Old one (though, indirectly, from the latter), but from paganism" (p. 18).

the Christian priest makes him a minister identified with Christ the mediator, and thus one who is led with Christ the priest into a type of relationship with God that relativizes the value of marriage and sexuality, the principle of ritual purity enunciated by Gryson has in itself nothing to do with the Gospel:[25] it could only be a resurgence of Judaic formalism or the fruit of a mentality alien to Christianity.

Basically, we find here the thesis of the Theiner brothers: confused in its motivations, the law relative to ecclesiastical celibacy was born and evolved at a time and in a theologico-spiritual context that were far removed from apostolic times. It is not surprising that it was contested.

GEORG DENZLER, *Das Papsttum und der Amtszölibat. Erster Teil: Die Zeit bis zur Reformation; Zweiter Teil: Von der Reformation bis in die Gegenwart* (Päpste und Papsttum, Band 5, I, II), Stuttgart, 1973, 1976, pp. xii and 180; pp. vi and 181–482.

The author of these two volumes on the papacy and clerical celibacy notes in his introduction that the law of celibacy poses today a problem that is more and more crucial for the Roman Catholic Church. Added to the many departures from the priesthood during these last years is a worrisome drop in vocations. The main cause of this crisis would be compulsory celibacy: whoever pays careful attention to this must therefore "be interested in the historical origins and development of this law in force since 1139, but contested again in our time" (p. x). In order to respond to this need to question history, which is all the more imperative because previous attempts in this direction, we are told, remained tainted with partiality (the Theiners and Lea on the one hand, Roskovany on the other), G. Denzler wants to offer the public an annotated list of the Holy See's documents and of the history of the papacy—from the origins until Paul VI—relative to the issue of ecclesiastical celibacy. The reader himself is to form an opinion with the help of these texts "with regard to the value or uselessness of a law imposing strict celibacy on all priests" (p. xii).

It is in the first part, devoted to the period extending from the origins to the Protestant Reformation, that we find the chapters corresponding to the first seven centuries of the Church under study in this book. In a first chapter the author studies the concepts of sexuality and marriage in Scripture. Neither the Old nor the New Testament establishes a direct and necessary link between celibacy and priestly functions. The leaders of the first Christian communities were married, as was Peter. This is

---

[25] "The Christians didn't discover it in the Gospel, but in a pagan environment and in the Old Testament" (p. 203).

obvious in the pastoral epistles asking that the bishop, deacon, and priest be chosen among "husbands of an only wife". During the first two centuries there was a change in the genuine evangelical spirit under the combined influence of Judaic and Hellenic currents. As a consequence, there was an excessive increase in the importance of virginity, the corollary being a discredit of marriage and sexuality. A further step was taken when priestly celibacy was imposed. Denzler adopts the opinion of J. P. Audet:[26] "With the progressive sacralization of the ecclesiastical function, the celibacy of those responsible became an indispensable presupposition" (p. 7). The fourth-century synods (Ancyra, Elvira, Nicaea) enacted the first regulations. Let us note that here Denzler mentions F. Winkelmann's recent critical study establishing the legendary character of the anecdote on Paphnutius' intervention at the Council of Nicaea, and seems to agree with it.[27]

The second chapter, titled "The obligation of continence for married priests", covers the period from the pontificate of Damasus (366–84) to that of Gregory the Great (590–604), inclusive. The various decretals and papal decisions illustrate the decisive role played by the Roman pontiffs, who shared the ideas of their times about the negative value of sexuality and the ideal of celibate priests. (St. Jerome had, in this, a great influence on Pope Damasus, as we are assured.) They were the ones who, presenting the discipline of the Roman Church as a more or less compulsory model, contributed to spread it to all the West.

Further on the author studies in a third chapter the "countless infractions of clerics in all Orders against the obligation of continence" (from the 7th to the 11th centuries). The fact that it was necessary to reinforce continually the obligation of continence for clerics and threaten violators with rigorous sanctions does indicate that the situation was far from desirable in many places and at many times.

Our reading of Denzler's work stops with the pontificate of Sergius I (687–701) and the Council in Trullo (691). Altogether it is a collection of texts and information that are useful as references in spite of serious shortcomings. An obvious lack of impartiality, the vagueness of the concepts (for instance, the author affirms that the law of clerical celibacy only goes back to the second Council of Lateran [1139], while the measure enacted by the 7th canon of that Council is of a completely different

[26] J. P. Audet, *Mariage et célibat dans le service pastoral de l'Église* (Paris, 1967).

[27] F. Winkelmann, "Paphnutios, der Bekenner und Bishof", in *Probleme der koptischen Literatur*. Published by the Institut für Byzantinstik der Martin-Luther-Universität Halle-Wittenberg. Bearbeitet von Peter Nagel. Wissenschaftliche Beiträge der Martin-Luther-Universität Halle-Wittenberg (Halle [Saale], 1968/1 [K2]), pp. 145–53.

nature), and the many contradictions he brings to his text are calling for serious reservations.[28] As to the issue of the origins of clerical celibacy, the author adopts, as we have seen, the interpretation of Funk, Vacandard, and Leclercq that was later accepted by Gryson: the law compelling the high clerics to perfect continence was of late origin. After Böhmer and Gryson, the explanation of the phenomenon is presented as the result of Judaic and pagan influences that contaminated the genuine spirituality of the Gospel and apostolic times. It was only later, with great labor and at the cost of laws that became stricter and stricter, that the leaders of the Church and especially the popes managed to maintain an obligation that is as contestable in its motivations as it is in its historical origins.

Funk's theories, favorably accepted until today by a large sector of public opinion, are beginning to be questioned in the light of contemporary historical studies, especially those brought about by Vatican II. Becoming aware of the fact that the late nineteenth-century controversy between Bickell and Funk did not put an end to research, but that the attainments as well as the limitations of the two German scholars are a call to restudy the issue, several Catholic authors have, in different manners, drawn attention recently to the patristic and conciliar testimonies of the 4th century claiming an apostolic origin for the law of clerical celibacy-continence.

In this vein, the work of HENRI DEEN, *Le célibat des prêtres dans les premiers siècles de l'Église* (Paris, 1969), 67 pp., deserves to be mentioned. This modest work, devoid of any scholarly tools or pretensions, has the courage to outline a criticism of Vacandard's study and thus of Funk's thesis. More than one judicious comment and several pertinent questions asked of Vacandard make this a valuable contribution to the history of the origins of priestly celibacy.

ALFONS M. STICKLER, "La continenza dei diaconi specialmente nel primo millenio della chiesa", in *Selasianum* 26, 1964, pp. 275–302. "Tratti salienti nella storia del celibato", in *Sacra Doctrina* 15, 1970, pp. 585–620. "Nota storica sul celibato dei chierici *in sacris*", in *L'Osservatore Romano*, March 2–3/4, 1970. "Il celibato ecclesiastico", in *L'Osservatore della Domenica*, supplements to nos. 103, 109, 115 of *L'Osservatore Romano*, May 6, 13, 20, 1979.

The author of this series of articles, history professor of canon law and then rector of the Pontifical Salesian University, is now prefect of the Vatican Apostolic Library. Among other scholarly publications mention

---

[28] See the critical review of A. M. Stickler, "A New History of Papal Legislation on Celibacy", in *The Catholic Historical Review* 65 (1979), pp. 76–84. Cardinal Stickler is now Librarian and Archivist of the Roman Catholic Church.—*Ed.*

must be made of his *Historia juris canonici latini. I. Historia Fontium* (Pas-Verlag, 1950; new ed., 1974), which has become a classic.

Father Stickler was an expert at the Second Vatican Council, which decided, as we recall, the restoration of the permanent diaconate in the Church. His study "The Continence of the Deacons Especially during the First Millennium of the Church", published in 1964, was written as part of studies aiming to bring to the Council Fathers elements of reflection borrowed from history. The author points out that one must understand celibacy in the early Church not only as meaning a prohibition of marriage, but also in the sense of perfect continence for those who were already married. The Western Church Tradition is studied in the light of the teachings of the councils, of the Fathers, and of the Roman pontiffs who always preserved (or restored) its essential features. The author opines it is on the basis of motivations inherent in the very nature of the Order and sacred ministry that this uninterrupted Tradition demands a perfect continence on the part of those who had been married before receiving sacred Orders.

In "Outstanding Features in the History of Celibacy" (1970), the author undertakes, also in the light of the history, to clarify several fundamental points. A first observation must be made: the documents of the first three centuries relative to discipline and the life of the Church were generally written in response to doubts and contestations. Above all, the legislators were inspired by a desire to remain faithful to the tradition of "the elders" and to apostolic tradition in order to oppose suspicious innovations. This having been said, one must guard against an anachronistic attitude that would give to priestly celibacy in early Christianity a connection with written laws in proper form. The testimonies of later centuries reflect an older practice and must be understood as such. On the other hand, it is extremely important to make a distinction between celibacy–prohibition of marriage after ordination and celibacy-continence, i.e., celibacy understood as the obligation to observe a perfect continence by those who had been married before receiving major Orders. In this full sense, celibacy finds its scriptural foundation in the example of Jesus Christ himself, "the only priest of the New Testament who is to be taken as a model by any priest or sacred minister of his Church" (p. 587), and in the example of the apostles "who left *everything* to follow Jesus" including a possible wife. When St. Paul asks Timothy and Titus to choose as leaders of the Church "husbands of an only wife", he is stipulating conditions guaranteeing that the candidates have the aptitude to practice the perfect continence that will be required of them at ordination. The exegesis of this key passage in the Pauline epistles was authenticated by the popes and the councils from the 4th century on. It is therefore not surprising to find very ancient patristic testimonies crediting the apostles themselves with the introduction of compulsory celibacy.

The second "outstanding feature" is the normative activity of the Church exercised since the end of the era of persecutions. Functioning openly, the Church then witnessed a phase of numerical expansion with an inescapable diminishing of fervor. Local, regional, and universal councils on the one hand, and the Roman pontiffs, successors of Peter, on the other, promulgated disciplinary measures adapted to the needs of the times. Ecclesiastical Fathers and writers also added their voices to the official ones. It must be remembered that many of the sacred ministers then were married men and that the issue of celibacy meant for them perfect continence, as the use of intercourse in a marriage contracted before the reception of Orders was forbidden. It is in the West that the legislative and patristic testimonies constitute the more coherent collection, under the leadership of the Church of Rome which, according to St. Irenaeus, *"habet ab apostolis traditionem"* and *"in qua semper . . . conservata est ea quae ab apostolis traditio"* (p. 592). When one studies the Eastern texts, things are more obscure and changing. As a result of many causes (influence of heresies, notably Arianism; lack of sufficient action on the part of the local and regional hierarchy; lack of an effective exercise of government on the part of the Roman pontiffs), the East was to experience a weakening of the primitive discipline that was institutionalized at the Trullan Council—Quinisext—of 691. The other "outstanding features" more rapidly studied in the last pages of the article are the period of decadence that was to be corrected in the 11th century by the Gregorian Reform, the advent of canonical science and the great juridical collections (Decree of Gratian, *Corpus Juris Canonici*), the agitation following the Protestant Reformation and the reaffirmation of the law of celibacy at the Council of Trent, the movements of various origins and tendencies that from the 17th to the 20th centuries militated for the abolition of a discipline that the Catholic Church never ceased to keep and restore in her fidelity to an uninterrupted Tradition and on grounds that are inseparable from the idea she has about ministerial priesthood.

In "Historical Note on Clerical Celibacy *'in sacris'*" (March 1970), one finds again most of the ideas already developed by A. M. Stickler in the two preceding articles. Let us mention in particular his position with regard to the anecdote of the intervention of Paphnutius at the Council of Nicaea:

No serious scholarly criticism can accept that fact as a proof. . . . How could men of solid scholarship [such as Hefele, Funk, and Vacandard] recently support the historicity of that episode in spite of many serious obstacles pointed out by scholars such as Baronius, the Bollandists, Zaccaria, and even Bickell—and in spite of all the modern rules of historical criticism? This is rather surprising. One must rather consider the story of Paphnutius as a historical fable—even if, unfortunately, it has had an excessive weight on the entire history of the celibacy controversy—as long as its historicity cannot be proven in the face of sure historical testimonies (p. 8).

Lastly, in interviews granted to *Osservatore della Domenica*, Father Stickler had the opportunity to reiterate his views about the history of the origins of clerical celibacy. Following the "Letter of the Sovereign Pontiff John Paul II to all the Priests of the Church on the Occasion of Holy Thursday 1979" (April 8, 1979), his reflections appear as a historico-theological commentary on the Pope's words about the link between priestly celibacy and the language and the very spirit of the Gospel. "Far from being a discipline of purely ecclesiastical origin, i.e., human and capable of derogation, celibacy is in fact a practice going back to Jesus himself and his apostles, even before it was made into a formal law. Thus does celibacy belong to the Tradition of the early Church as were many other articles of faith or discipline that became explicit and progressively took definite form as they were needed in accordance with the development of doctrine and Christian life, in which there have been frequent contestations and infractions." [29] Then the author develops, in the course of three interviews, the ideas we know and concludes by answering a question about possible ordinations of married men in today's Church:

> In the light of Tradition, I must say that it would not be impossible in itself, as long as continence is preserved, such as it was largely practiced during the first millenary of the Latin Church. When people talk today about the ordination of married men, however, it is generally implied that they should retain, after ordination to the priesthood, the possibility of continuing to practice conjugal life, because people generally do not know that such a concession was never granted when married men were ordained. . . . Whether there is a chance that the Church might go back to such practices—demanding celibacy-continence as a condition—I could not say. When one thinks that she tried little by little to decrease this kind of ordination because of its inconvenience, and to ordain only single men, excluding from the priesthood those who married after having received minor Orders, I do not think that one would want to restore a practice that is obsolete now, at least under the present circumstances. But there is nothing to prevent the ordination of older bachelors or widowers or even married men in the case of a couple deciding to opt on both sides for consecrated life and therefore continence (art. cit., n. 115, p. 2).

[29] Art. cit., n. 103, p. 1.

One could benefit greatly from reading these articles of A. M. Stickler, which explain and stress principles of historico-critical methodology, projecting a useful light on the complexity of the problems surrounding the origins of clerical celibacy. They are timely and helpful in the orientation of those, more and more numerous today, who refuse to let themselves be locked into the problematic of Funk and his successors.[30]

---

[30] I will take the liberty of mentioning also, in the same vein, the thesis of theology that I defended in 1969 at the Institut catholique de Paris: Christian Cochini, "Le célibat des clercs aux premiers siècles de l'Église" (mimeographed thesis, Paris, 1969), 3 vols., vii–561 pages and 141 pages of notes.

The reader should also be aware of the important work *Clerical Celibacy in East and West*, by Roman Cholij (Herefordshire: Fowler Wright Books, 1988).

CHAPTER THREE

Methodological Precisions

It is first of all important to keep in mind the concept of clerical celibacy corresponding to the discipline of the early centuries.

Nowadays, almost all candidates to the priesthood are recruited among young men or older bachelors. The clerics in minor Orders who get married are automatically excluded from the clergy,[1] and a man who has already been married cannot be ordained without a special dispensation from the Apostolic See.[2] With the institution of seminaries by the Council of Trent,[3] the Church had enough celibate candidates to the Orders to cover the needs of the dioceses. Consequently, instances of married men admitted to the clergy through a dispensation of the Holy See became more and more infrequent. To talk about ecclesiastical celibacy today means, in fact, to talk about a situation in which only bachelors have the qualifications required to be ordained.

It is also necessary to make a conceptual readjustment if we do not want to risk confusion when we refer to the discipline before the Council of Trent, and even more when we refer to that prevailing during the first seven centuries of the Church. What today has become an extremely rare exception was then common practice: a large number of the higher members of the hierarchy (bishops, priests, and deacons) were married men. This fact, which is of capital importance in the history of the origins, is attested without the shadow of a doubt by both the legislation of those days and patristic testimonies as well as by many concrete situations which narrations of the times or epigraphy have preserved for us.[4] Along with these married clerics, and in proportions that varied with the times, we also meet many clerics who had never been married.

---

[1] CIC, 132 § 2.
[2] CIC, 132 § 3.
[3] Sess. XXIII, c. 18, *de Reform.*
[4] See below, pp. 87ff.

There were thus two large "circles" from which were recruited candidates to the Orders: Christians living in marriage, on the one hand, and on the other, those who had remained celibate, whether their celibacy was the result of a simple factual situation (including widowers) or they had consecrated themselves to celibacy through an explicit profession. The early centuries of the Church had no law on celibacy as it is understood in modern times, i.e., a law stating as a primary condition for admission to the Orders the obligation to renounce marriage. However, the unmarried higher clerics were forbidden to contract a marriage once they had crossed the threshold of ordination; as to the married man who had become a deacon, priest, or bishop, he could not remarry if he lost his wife. Thus, celibacy, in the early Church, was understood as a prohibition to marry (or to remarry) *after* the reception of major Orders.

Here we must add a new conceptual precision of great importance. If married men could be chosen for the priesthood, numerous legislative texts, from the 4th century on, stress this is only on the condition that they live in perfect continence with their wives. The question is to know to what date such an obligation goes back and in what areas of the Christian world it was enforced. This is precisely the purpose of our study. But we should not forget that the canonical norms of that period had as a main object not only the prohibition of marriage after ordination but also perfect continence. It is all the more necessary to stress this point because our thinking habits do not prepare us for such a distinction, though perfect continence was familiar in the early Christian communities. Marriage and conjugal intercourse do not necessarily go hand in hand for married clerics. On the contrary, abstinence from conjugal intercourse, continence lived within the framework of a matrimonial situation, was characteristic of these men who, with the agreement of their wives, accepted the call to receive the imposition of hands conferring the priesthood upon them.

In order to make this distinction easier on the level of vocabulary, we shall instead use the phrase "the law of celibacy in the strict sense" to describe the present legislation, and the phrase "the law of celibacy in the broad sense" to talk about the discipline during the early centuries of the Church, one of whose characteristics was, as we just recalled it, the *lex continentiae*. We also propose to use for this period of the origins the term "law of celibacy-continence" unless the context enables us to talk simply and without any possibility of equivocation about "the law of celibacy".

The question we will attempt to answer in the course of this study is that of knowing whether the law of celibacy-continence, or continence in the broad sense, can claim to have ancient origins, even an apostolic origin. The documents of the late 4th century, especially the 2d canon of the Council of Carthage of 390 and the decretals of Pope Siricius, claim this apostolicity. It is good method to take note of this because such affirmations came not from mere individuals but from hierarchical leaders who took on the responsibility of many leaders of the Church. In Carthage it was the whole African episcopate, in the person of its representatives at the synod, that took upon itself the declaration of one of its members: "Ut quod apostoli docuerunt, et ipsa servavit antiquitas nos quoque custodiamus."[5] In Rome the successor of Peter, Siricius, is conscious of expressing himself in the name of a tradition placing him in living continuity with his predecessors, and to be, through the action of the Spirit, the very voice of the chief of the apostles, transmitting, as it were, what he has received from himself, according to the exact formula of Pope Sixtus III (432–40): "Beatus Petrus apostolus in successoribus suis quod tradidit hoc accepit."[6]

We have seen that this issue of the apostolicity of the law of celibacy-continence is not a new one. It was raised several times in the course of history, especially during the major crises that have questioned the traditional institutions. Until a relatively recent time (the late 19th century), a good majority of Catholic theologians have been of the opinion that it would be historically correct to link to the apostles the discipline known in the early centuries. The issue did not become a dead one after the works of F. X. Funk, notwithstanding what some people might think. Even when Funk was still alive, erudite scholars opined that the ideas of Bickell had not been completely refuted by the Tübingen professor. Nowadays, the limitations of the theory represented by Funk, Vacandard, and Leclercq seem even more visible, especially in the light of Vatican II's documents restoring the role of "the Tradition coming from the apostles" in the development of the life of God's people.[7] It is therefore not only legitimate, but also very desirable, to return to the issue, taking into account the data acquired by modern science in order to try to test the

---

[5] We have already had the occasion to stress that this 2d canon of the Council of Carthage of 390 presents itself as an archival piece, a document that had already been adopted by a previous council whose date and place are not given. It will later be fully assumed, still as an expression of fidelity to an apostolic tradition, by the African conciliar legislation during the following centuries, and especially by the plenary synod of 419 held in Carthage, presided over by Aurelius and with the participation of the pontifical legate Faustinus (one must also note the presence of St. Augustine), in which were renewed a whole series of ordinances of ancient African councils.

[6] Sixtus III, letter to John of Antioch, in *Acta Romanorum Pontificum a S. Clemente I (an. c. 90 ad Coelestinum III* [† *1198*], I, Fontes Series III [1943], p. 171).

[7] Vatican II, Dogmatic Constitution *Dei Verbum*, II, 8.

validity of the testimonies that, from the 4th century on, linked celibacy-continence to a positive will of the apostles.

It must be stressed that we do not have the slightest intention of searching for a written law in the proper form, which would have been preserved either in Scripture or in the documents of apostolic times. Had such a text ever existed, historical criticism would have brought it to our attention long ago. But there is a difference between brushing aside the idea of a written text and asking oneself if there had not been, insofar as this issue is concerned, a "teaching" of the apostles that, on account of the exceptional authority of these men who had been chosen by Christ to found the Church, was granted a normative character from the outset. Here we must stress a point that has been forgotten at times today, but whose consequences were felt as early as the end of the apostolic age in the development of dogmas and Church organization and still unfold in rhythm with its secular growth.

Next to the written Tradition that set in book form the preaching of the apostles and closely linked to it through a network of communications guaranteed by the gift of the Spirit on Pentecost, there is an oral Tradition—transmitted by the apostles to their successors and entrusted by the latter to men who were just as honorable—which was at times embodied in institutions remaining as its permanent memory, came down to us, and will be heard until the end of history. This unwritten word coming from the apostles has a multiple content enabling us to talk about "oral Traditions" (plural). St. Paul exhorts the Thessalonians not to forget it: "Stand firm, then, brothers, and keep the traditions that we taught you, whether by word of mouth or by letter" (2 Th 2:15); he praises the Christians of Corinth who remained faithful to them: "You have done well in remembering me so constantly and in maintaining the traditions just as I passed them on to you" (1 Cor 11:2).[8] The patristic literature of the early centuries echoes in many ways these words of St. Paul; every author comments on them and adds his personal touch,[9] but they all agree in their conviction that one remains in the apostolic order by remaining attached to unwritten Traditions. The letters of Ignatius of Antioch, *Adversus Haereses* of Irenaeus of Lyon (book III), *De praescriptione haereticorum* of the then-Catholic Tertullian, the correspondence of Cyprian, among other eminent testimonies, point to the existence of this oral teaching coming from the apostles and to the vital concern that the first Christian communities and their leaders had to remain in

---

[8] Cf. also 2 Tim 2:2; and 2 Jn 12.

[9] In this respect, see the excellent issue of *L'Année Canonique* 23 (1979) devoted to "la Tradition Apostolique régulatrice de la Communauté ecclésiale aux premiers siècles".

conformity with it. We will simply refer to a frequently quoted text by St. Basil:

> Among the "doctrines" and the "definitions" [δόγματα καὶ κηρύγματα] kept in the Church, we have received some from the written teaching and we have obtained the other ones, secretly transmitted, from the apostolic Tradition. They all have the same validity with regard to piety, as no one would doubt if he has any experience of ecclesiastical institutions; because if we attempt to do away with unwritten customs, by claiming that they have no great validity, we would unknowingly hurt the Gospel on its very essential points. . . .[10]

Again, a little further on:

> People claim that the doxology "with the Spirit" is not attested and is not to be found in Scripture. Here is our answer: If we receive only what is in Scripture, let us not accept it either, but if most of the rites surrounding the mysteries are accepted by us without their being in Scripture, let us also accept this doxology, together with many other things. Moreover, I believe that it is "apostolic" to be attached even to unwritten traditions [and here St. Basil quotes the two Pauline texts 1 Cor 11:2 and 2 Th 2:15] . . . traditions of which the present doxology is a part. Those who established it in the beginning transmitted it to their successors; and usage spreading with time, they anchored it in the Churches through a long custom. In addition, if we should bring forth a crowd of witnesses, as is done in court, when there are no written proofs, would we not obtain an acquittal from you? I think so, for "the evidence of two witnesses or three is required to sustain the charge" (Dt 19:15). . . . Ancient doctrines are rather moving because they have the venerable character of a remote antiquity.[11]

If the domain of unwritten traditions is, above all, that of the truths of faith progressively clarified throughout the centuries by theological reflection and the process of dogmatic elaboration through the great councils which stand as milestones, then the part given to customs relative to discipline and liturgical life in this apostolic deposit that was orally transmitted remains considerable.[12] One may say that, "The concept of

---

[10] *Traité du Saint-Esprit*, 28. SCh 17, 232–33.

[11] Ibid., 29. SCh 17, 245–46. P. P. Joannou, *Discipline générale antique*, II, pp. 186–87, translates in a picturesque manner: "For the ancient beliefs enjoy a favorable bias, drawing their respectability from their white-haired antiquity".

[12] Cf. Vatican II, Dogmatic Constitution *Dei Verbum*, II, 8: "Now what was handed on by the apostles includes everything which contributes to the holiness of life and the increase in faith of the People of God; and so the Church, in her teaching, life, and worship,

unwritten traditions seems to have been born, above all, from a reflection on ecclesiastical discipline and cult".[13] For instance, we can recall how St. Irenaeus connected with the apostles the custom of Paschal fast, the Easter celebration, and the custom of standing during the liturgical celebrations of Easter and Pentecost. Origen would mention the practice of praying on one's knees while facing the East, the rites surrounding the confection and receiving of the Eucharist, those followed in administering baptism, and still others.[14] Certain usages remained limited to a specific region or a particular community, while others were observed in the universal Church.[15] Some would have a relatively short span of life,[16] while several others would see their compulsory character strengthened by time. This phenomenon is especially visible in all disciplinary usages or liturgical rites involving doctrinal positions. The baptismal controversy opposing Cyprian and Pope Stephen is the best illustration. The custom not to baptize anew heretics converting to the Catholic faith has remained out of fidelity to a tradition that the Roman Church claimed as coming from the apostles, but more deeply so, as Augustine stressed it, because the traditional practice not to baptize anew those who came from heresy was in itself teaching the dogma of the efficacy of baptism given in the name of the Father, the Son, and the Holy Spirit. Another instance of the same type is given by the baptism of infants, a usage so closely linked in the mind of the Fathers to the belief in original sin that Augustine argued against Julian of Eclana and the Pelagians in proving dogma through practice. If the Church has remained attached to this traditional custom, he basically states, is it not sufficient to make us believe in the reality of this original sin of which man has to be washed clean as early as birth? The same goes for the custom of praying for the dead, as ancient as the Church, which contains an implicit though formal teaching relative to the dogma of Purgatory.[17]

---

perpetuates and hands on to all generations all that she herself is, all that she believes" (Walter M. Abbot, ed., *The Documents of Vatican II*, p. 116).

[13] D. Van den Eynde, *Les Normes de l'Enseignement Chrétien dans la littérature patristique des trois premiers siècles* (Gembloux-Paris, 1933), p. 275.

[14] Ibid., pp. 274–80.

[15] Cf. St. Augustine, *Ep.* 54, 1–2. CSEL, 34–2, 160.

[16] This was the case, for instance, for baptism in the name of Jesus and for prayer uttered while facing east.

[17] (On the baptism of infants) *De baptismo contra Donatistas l. VII*, IV, 30. CSEL 51; *Contra Julianum l. VI*, I, 22. PL 44; ibid., *VI*, II, 22. PL 44, 655; et passim (On prayer for the deceased) *Sermones*, 173, 2. PL 38, 936–37.

It would be such an apostolic tradition, if there is a tradition, that confronts us with respect to the law of celibacy-continence of the early centuries. Indeed, the reasons invoked by the legislators to justify the discipline imposed on the higher clerics of the hierarchy are, besides fidelity to tradition proper, considerations relative to doctrine: superiority of virginity and continence over marriage, intercessory function of the priestly ministry (especially linked to the celebration of the eucharistic mysteries), connection between continence and the efficacy of prayer. This point will deserve attention in the course of our study, because this doctrinal "component" of celibacy's discipline (in the broad sense of the term) is directly based on Scripture and thus constitutes a common good of the ecclesiastical communities since their foundation, a patrimony of truths that one does not question as long as one shares the same faith. Heinrich Böhmer rightly pointed out that the spiritual and theological context revealed in the writings of St. Cyprian offers all the conditions enabling us to suppose the existence of a law on celibacy-continence, even though no document that has come to us from that time mentions it.[18] Whatever the case may be, let us note that certain points of ecclesial discipline are part of a deposit orally transmitted by the apostles, just like the Creed, and that from this viewpoint it is legitimate to ask ourselves, as the texts call for it, whether the discipline of celibacy-continence, attested since the 4th century, did not also have its origin in this early deposit.

What are the conditions that are necessary to determine whether a tradition is of apostolic origins?

A principle that remains fundamental is the one enunciated by St. Augustine in his controversy with the Donatists: "What is kept by the whole Church and was always maintained, without having been enacted by the councils, is very rightly considered as having been transmitted solely through apostolic authority."[19]

---

[18] "Es ist sonach bloss als ein Zufall zu betrachten, dass uns in den Fragmenten, die wir von der kirchlichen Literatur des 3. Jahrhunderts noch besitzen, keine direkte Aüsserung über die Kontinenz der Altardiener erhalten ist. Die Vorstellungen, aus denen jene Forderung sich mit logischer Notwendigkeit ergab, waren jedenfalls damals alle schon vorhanden und die Stellen, die sie zu beglaubigen und zu rechtfertigen schienen, Leuten wie Cyprian schon ebenso geläufig und präsent, wie die allbekannten messianischen Sprüche" (H. Böhmer, "Die Entstehung des Zölibats", in *Geschichtliche Studien Albert Hauck zum 70. Geburtstage dargebracht* [Leipzig, 1916], p. 17). Though we cannot share the general thesis of the article (see above, p. 39, n. 24), we agree with the author on this point: the context at the time of Cyprian does seem to "reveal" the existence of a law on celibacy-continence in the 3d century.

[19] "Quod universa tenet Ecclesia nec conciliis institutum, sed semper retentum est, nonnisi auctoritate apostolica traditum rectissime creditur" (*De Baptismo contra Donatistas l. VII*, IV, 31. CSEL 51, 259). Similar principles were formulated by Tertullian: "Quod apud

There is a well-established historical fact: fidelity to the tradition inherited from the origins is the rule of the ecclesial life in the early centuries. The constant reflex of writers and churchmen of the patristic times is to have recourse to this root authority in order to prove how solid the position they defend is. One can, for instance, discern a sign of such a strategy in the fabrication of the "pseudoapostolic constitutions".[20] Their authors, most of whom remain unknown, wanted to respond to the need for collecting and establishing written norms of Christian life and ecclesiastical discipline that were, until then, only part of various traditions. With the numerical growth of the Church, it became necessary to put the pen at the service of oral transmission in order to avoid the risk of distortion, a risk that was all the more real as sects and heresies rapidly proliferated. These compilations, falsely credited to the apostles, include errors that are due either to the editors themselves or to later interpolations; yet they offer a very interesting outline of the discipline that prevailed at the time they were written, especially in the Eastern Churches.[21] The reason for their wide and rapid spread and for their general acceptance in conformity with the claims about them—namely that they were collections of norms set by the apostles—without being generally disapproved by the hierarchical authorities,[22] is that they reflected the usages that had been known and observed since the most

---

multos unum invenitur, non est erratum sed traditum" (*De praescriptione haereticorum*, 28, 3. SCh 46, 125; CC I, 209); and by Vincentius of Lérins: "In ipsa item catholica Ecclesia magnopere curandum est ut id teneamus quod ubique, quod semper, quod ab omnibus creditum est" (*Commonitorum* 2. PL 50, 640b).

[20] The main pseudo-apostolic collections are the following:

—*Doctrine of the Twelve Apostles* (Didaché): late 1st century–early 2d century (or late 2d–early 3d century); Syria or Palestine; author unknown.

—*Didascalia of the Apostles*: 2d half of the 2d century; Syria or Palestine; author unknown.

—*Apostolic Tradition*: ca. 218; Rome; author: Hippolytus of Rome.

—*Ecclesiastical Canons of the Holy Apostles*: ca. 300; Egypt or Syria; author unknown.

—*Apostolic Constitutions*: late 4th century–early 5th century; Syria or Palestine; author unknown. Attributed to Clement of Rome.

—*85 Apostolic Canons*: same as forty-seven canons of book VIII of the *Apostolic Constitutions*.

—*Testamentum Domini Nostri Jesu Christi*: late 5th century; Syria; author unknown.

[21] There is a good presentation of the pseudo-apostolic collections in A. M. Stickler, *Historia Juris canonici latini. I Historia fontium* (Turin, 1950, reprinted 1974), pp. 22–28.

[22] *The Apostolic Constitutions*, published in Syria or Palestine around the late 4th century or early 5th century, enjoyed a great authority in the East until the Council in Trullo (691), which declared them contaminated by the heretics and rejected them, with the exception of the apostolic canons.

The *85 Apostolic Canons* were rejected as being apocryphal in the Western Church by a decree attributed to Pope Gelasius (written probably during the 6th century). The Easterners accepted them and officially canonized them at the Council in Trullo (691).

remote antiquity. The general tendency during patristic times was therefore to keep, to preserve the deposit that had been transmitted, and not
to innovate.[23] The heretics themselves were led to cover their novelties
with the mantle of apostolic authority, proving in their own ways the
importance of such a reference to the apostles in the life and organization
of the first Christian communities.[24] The principle of St. Augustine
mentioned above enjoyed the full weight of history, at a time when so
much value was granted to what had been transmitted, and when nothing
could be transmitted with the guarantee of authority except what came
from the apostles. So that, insofar as we can note that a point of doctrine
or discipline is effectively "kept by the whole Church" and "had always
been maintained", we are justified in thinking that it originated in the
apostolic age, even if it is not possible to point to a proof in documents
preceding those in which such a point appeared for the first time in
written form. The unanimity of the Fathers regarding this important
issue therefore allowed St. Augustine to formulate the following conclusion in one of his works: "They had preserved what they had found,
taught what they had learned, and transmitted to their sons what they
had received from their fathers."[25]

One should attempt to be more precise. What do "kept by the whole
Church" and "had always been maintained" mean?

When one talks about a point "kept by the whole Church", it can only
and obviously mean a moral universality that does not exclude exceptions
and enables the Church to reach a sufficient degree of certainty in the
field of historical research. The main conditions for reaching a conclusion
of moral universality seem to be the following ones:

1. A point of doctrine or of discipline can be considered as "kept by
the whole Church" at a given time in its history if the majority of men
who enjoy a great moral and intellectual authority in the Church during
that period share the same feelings about it. For the early centuries we
are talking about the most influential Fathers, the most famous doctors,

---

[23] The famous recommendation of Pope Stephen in his letter to Cyprian of Carthage is
well known: "Nihil innovetur, nisi quod traditum est" (Ep. 74: 1. CSEL 3–2, 799).

[24] It is thus, for instance, that the leaders of the Artemon heresy—according to Eusebius—
claimed to be the heirs of the genuine tradition coming from the apostles: "They say that
all the ancients and the apostles themselves received by tradition and taught what they are
saying now, and that the truth of the preaching had been kept until the time of Victor,
who was the 13th bishop of Rome after Peter; but that starting with his successor
Zephyrinus, the truth had been altered" (Eusebius, Historia Ecclesiastica [hereafter cited as
Hist. Eccl.], V, XXVIII, 3. SCh 41, 75).

[25] "Quod invenerunt in Ecclesia, tenuerunt; quod didicerunt, docuerunt; quod a patribus
acceperunt hoc filiis tradiderunt" (Contra Julianum l. VI, II, 34. PL 44, 698b).

the most renowned bishops credited by their contemporaries as well as posterity with an exceptional value. It is not necessary to have the totality of their testimonies; one can be content with the agreement expressed by those who had the most important role among them, as being the spokesmen for many others.[26]

2. A point of doctrine or discipline can be considered as "kept by the whole Church" at a given time in its history if it is "kept" by the apostolic Churches, i.e., above all, the Churches personally founded by the apostles,[27] or even by Churches that, without having been founded by the

---

[26] It could happen that a Father, enjoying a great authority among his contemporaries, supported a viewpoint that was contrary to theirs. It happened with St. Cyprian in the case of the baptismal controversy. The development and the solution of the problem show that, if the Church of Africa could indeed claim a long tradition enabling her to rebaptize heretics, such a tradition did not have the guarantee of apostolicity. As early as the Council of Arles in 314, the Africans rallied to the common position without any difficulty (can. 8), and St. Augustine did not hesitate to affirm that St. Cyprian had fallen into error on this issue of heretics' rebaptism, while stressing that it had not prevented the great bishop of Carthage from remaining firmly attached to Catholic unity. (Augustine, *De baptismo contra Donatistas l. VII*, 5, 27–29; II, 9. CSEL 51, 170–73, 183–84. *Contra Cresconium*, II, 42. CSEL 52, 401–2. *De unico baptismo contra Petilianum*, 23. CSEL, 53, 23–24). Cf. J. Tixeront, *Histoire des dogmes dans l'antiquité chrétienne. I. La théologie anténicéenne* [Paris, 1930], pp. 380–89). This example sheds an interesting light on the importance that the Christian communities of the early centuries attached to the Fathers' consensus. It was not conceivable that a lasting dissension could persist on an important issue among the most qualified representatives of the Church. It went so far that every effort had to be made, according to St. Augustine, to interpret in a sense favorable to the common opinion possible ambiguous assertions found under the pen of such and such author. About a passage of St. John Chrysostom in which Julian of Eclana wanted to find a confirmation for his Pelagian ideas Augustine grew indignant: "By quoting these words of St. John Chrysostom, would your purpose be to put him in contradiction with his colleagues, to separate him from their communion, to make him their adversary? God forbid that the bishop of Constantinople, on the important issue of the infants' baptism and their salvation in Jesus Christ, would put himself in opposition to his many illustrious colleagues: Pope Innocent, Cyprian of Carthage, Basil of Cappadocia, Gregory Nazianzen, Hilarius of Gaul, Ambrose of Milan! There are such or other particular points on which the most illustrious defenders of the Catholic rule can find themselves in disagreement, and more or less in the truth, without the faith being damaged in any way. But as to the truth that we are discussing, it belongs directly to the very foundations of the faith" (*Contra Julianum l. VI*, I, 22. PL 44, 655a–b).

[27] St. Irenaeus, for whom "it is in any Church that it [the Tradition of the apostles] can be perceived by those who want to see the truth" (*Adversus Haereses*, III, 2, 1. SCh 211, 31), mentions in particular: "the very great, very ancient, and universally known Church, that the two very glorious Apostles Peter and Paul founded and established in Rome" (ibid., III, 2, 2. SCh 211, 33), the Church of Smyrna where lived Polycarp, "he who always taught the doctrine that he had received from the apostles, the doctrine which is also that which the Church transmits and is the only true one" (ibid., III, 4. SCh 211, 39–41), and the Church of Ephesus "founded by Paul and where John lived until the time

apostles, had been originated by the apostles either as direct or indirect foundations or by those that manifested "a consanguinity of doctrine"[28] keeping themselves in communion with the Churches founded by the apostles. It was about them that Bellarmine formulated the principle according to which "one must believe without the shadow of a doubt that something comes from an apostolic tradition if it is so deemed in the Churches where there is an unbroken tradition since the apostles."[29] Here too it is not necessary to undertake an exhaustive inquiry. It suffices to know the feelings of some of them, among the most representative, in order to suppose with enough reasons, unless there is a formal proof to the contrary, that the others agree with them. For on important points of doctrine or discipline one finds it difficult to believe that important divergences existed between apostolic Churches as long as they kept their bond of unity, as was the case during the early centuries of the Church. Now unity of faith and "consanguinity of doctrine" binding all the

---

of Trajanus" (ibid., III, 4. SCh 211, 45). Tertullian talks about Smyrna, "where Polycarp was installed by John", and about the Church of Rome "showing that Clement was ordained by Peter" (*De praescriptione haereticorum*, XXXII, 2. SCh 46, 131), and he invites his readers "[to visit] the apostolic Churches where the very cathedrae of the apostles are still presiding at their place, where their genuine letters are read. . . . If you are close to Achaia: you have Corinth. If you are near to Macedonia: you have Philippi; if you can go to the Asian side: you have Ephesus; and if you are in the Italian boundaries, you have Rome, whose authority brings us also her support. Blessed Church! The apostles poured all their doctrine into her together with their blood" (ibid., XXXVI, 1–3. SCh 46, 137–38).

It was because of their apostolic origin that certain Churches, in conformity with the custom prevailing in Rome, were officially recognized by the ecumenical councils. Canon 6 of the Council of Nicaea (325) recognizes and confirms the preeminence of the bishop of Alexandria in Egypt, Pentapolis, and Lybia as well as that of the bishop of Antioch and the bishops "of other dioceses", i.e., the metropolitans of Caesarea (Pontus), Ephesus (Asia), and Heraclea (Thracia). Canon 7of the same Council acknowledges to the bishop of Aelia-Jerusalem an honor of precedence in virtue of "custom and ancient tradition". Constantinople was also rapidly granted a precedence of honor, superior even to the other metropoles, since it placed the bishop of the imperial capital as second "after the bishop of Rome", but the preamble of the Council could not invoke for that recently founded town an ancient tradition (Council of Constantinople in 381, can. 3).

The "New Rome", Constantinople, had its privileges increased and confirmed by the Council of Chalcedon (can. 28); not only did it continue to enjoy a precedence of honor, but it obtained jurisdiction over the dioceses of Pontus, Asia, and Thracia, whose administrative autonomy had been eclipsed to Byzantium's benefit during the 5th century. (On the whole issue, see P. P. Joannou, *Discipline générale antique*, I, 2, Appendix II, "Pape, concile et patriarches dans la tradition canonique de l'Église orientale jusqu'au IXᵉ siècle", pp. 489ff.).

[28] Tertullian, *De praescriptione haereticorum*, XXXII, 6. SCh 46, 132.

[29] Bellarmine, *Prima Controversia generalis de Verbo Dei*, lib. IV, cap. IX, in *Opera omnia*, I (Paris, 1870), p. 218.

apostolic Churches do not have as a necessary corollary uniformity of religious practice; when it comes to secondary matters, such a communion easily puts up with, and is even enriched by, a diversity of usages.[30] But such is not the case for important matters. This is the case, for the celibacy-continence discipline in particular, considered by the legislators and Fathers of the 4th century and thereafter as an issue leading to commitments on scriptural and doctrinal matters.

3. A point of doctrine or discipline can be confirmed as "kept by the whole Church" at a given time of its history if it is found to be "kept" by all the bishops, i.e., by all those who, in the Church, were established as the successors of the apostles and hold, by the grace of the Spirit, what we could call the cutting of the apostolic seed.[31] The unanimity of the bishops on a specific point is confirmed in the synods and episcopal assemblies meeting to deal with it and where common decisions deemed to be in conformity with Tradition are made.[32] It is especially verified in general or ecumenical councils that have "the character of infallibility

[30] In his answer to the questions of Januarius, St. Augustine wrote: "There are things that vary according to place and country; thus, some fast on Saturday, others do not, some receive communion every day with the Body and Blood of the Lord, the others on certain days only; here not a single day passes without offering the holy sacrifice; elsewhere it is on Saturday and Sunday; in other places, only on Sunday. Observances of this kind leave you perfectly free; and for a serious and prudent Christian, there is nothing better to do in such a case than to conform to the usage of the Church where he happens to be. What is not contrary to faith or good mores must be held as indifferent and observed out of deference for all among whom one lives" (*Ep.* 54, 1–2. CSEL, 34–2, 160).

The testimony of the writer Socrates, who mentions the different customs concerning celibacy-continence in Thessalonika and the East (*Hist. Eccl.*, V, 22. PG 67, 637a–39a), calls for reservations. See below, pp. 321–22. Let us note that it was precisely in a decretal elaborating at length on the scriptural and theological reasons establishing, in the eyes of the Roman Pontiff, the necessity of priestly continence that we find a principle enunciated very clearly: "Catholicorum episcoporum unam confessionem esse debere apostolica disciplina composuit. Si ergo una fides est, manere debet et una traditio. Si una traditio est, una debet disciplina per omnes ecclesias custodiri" (Siricius, *Ep.* 10, 9, in P. Coustant, *Epistolae Romanorum Pontificum* [Paris, 1721], p. 692 = Bruns, II, 278. See also E. Babut, *La plus ancienne décrétale* [Paris, 1904], pp. 78–79).

[31] Cf. Vatican II, Dogmatic Constitution *Lumen Gentium*, III, 20.

[32] Cf. Eusebius, *Hist. Eccl.*, V, XXIII. SCh 41, 66–67. The gathering of synods is a custom going back to the very origins of the Church, according to the example given by the Council of Jerusalem (between 50 and 52), where the apostles solved the issue of the obligations to be imposed upon the new converts from gentiles (Acts 15:1–35). The testimony of Tertullian confirms this (*De Jejunio*, 13, 6. CC II, 1272). Certain synods were held during the 2d century, but it is mostly with the 3d century that the custom was formed, both in the West and in the East (cf. Hefele and Leclercq, *Histoire des Conciles*, I, pp. 125ff.). They all aimed to keep the deposit transmitted by the apostles, in the domain of faith as well as in those of morality and ecclesiastical discipline. The Council of Nicaea (325) would prescribe a biannual meeting of provincial synods (can. 5).

in dogmatic decisions and of sovereignty without appeal in disciplinary decisions".[33] The authority of an ecumenical council being at the same time universal and beyond compare, one must give the greatest attention to the manner in which the bishops, either individually or gathered in synods, later interpret the doctrinal or disciplinary decisions of such councils, for it could hardly happen that the members of the apostolic college, in communion with the successor of Peter, make on important points decisions that do not take into account the decrees of an ecumenical council, go against them, or distort their meaning through arbitrary interpretations. The way they apply what has been ordered by an ecumenical council is in itself an authorized commentary and can be useful in trying to elucidate certain doubtful cases.

This is all the more true if we add that the essential factor giving the college of bishops its authority is the bond of unity with the Roman pontiff.[34] The pontiff enjoys a special rank and power as chief of the Church founded by "the two very glorious Apostles Peter and Paul",[35] the Church into which the apostles "poured out all their doctrine together with their blood".[36] It is above all as the successor of Peter, who received from Christ the promise that he would not fail in his faith and the mission to confirm his brothers, that the Bishop of Rome is recognized as the keeper par excellence of the apostolic tradition. Not only "has there never been an ecumenical council that was not confirmed as such or at least received by the successor of Peter",[37] but as a matter of fact, there has never been an important issue concerning the life of the Churches that was decided without his advice.[38] The history of the many recourses

---

[33] P. P. Joannou, I, 2, p. 525: "The ecumenical council of the first nine centuries was a religious assembly gathering, in principle, the leaders of all the orthodox Christian Churches in order to deal with the matters concerning the religious life of Christianity; gathered by order of the civil authorities, responsible for the maintenance of order in Christendom, in agreement with the religious authorities; with the actual participation of the bishop of Rome or with his subsequent approval if the meeting had taken place without his being present, having the character of infallibility in its dogmatic decisions and sovereignty without appeal in its disciplinary decisions, thanks to the guarantee conferred to it by the concomitant or subsequent approval of its acts by the bishop of Rome, considered the supreme judge of the faith."

[34] Cf. Vatican II, Dogmatic Constitution *Lumen Gentium*, III, 22.

[35] Irenaeus, *Adversus Haereses*, III, 2. SCh 211, 33.

[36] Tertullian, *De praescriptione haereticorum*, XXXVI, 3. SCh 46, 137–38.

[37] Vatican II, *Lumen Gentium*, III, 22.

[38] According to Socrates, ecclesiastical rule forbids that "praeter sententiam Romani pontifici quidquam ab Ecclesiis decernatur" (*Hist. Eccl.*, II, 17. PG 67, 217a). The same assertion is made by Sozomenes: "Legem enim esse pontificiam, ut pro irritis habeantur quae praeter sententiam episcopi Romani fuerint gesta" (*Hist. Eccl.*, III, 10. PG 67, 1058a). In his letter to the Antiochian bishops about the matter of Athanasius of Alexandria, Pope

to the "Apostolic See"—a title that, without any other determination, was used very early for the city where Peter had reigned—on the part of the Eastern as well as of the Western Churches during the early centuries of the Church, illustrates the prominence accorded to the Bishop of Rome and the unique role he played in deciding what the true traditions were.[39] Therefore it is for all these reasons that one attaches a particular value to the declarations of the bishops gathered as a college united to the Bishop of Rome, as well as those of the Apostolic See itself, when they claim a tradition going back to the apostles.

One can then consider that a point of doctrine or of discipline "has always been maintained" in the Church when we witness the following conditions:

1. If, between the time when one can observe with sufficient certainty that this point is "kept by the whole Church" (in the meaning we have just made explicit) and the Christian origins, no decision coming from an authorized hierarchical authority proves the previous existence of a contrary belief or practice. Such a hierarchical authority could only be, in such a case, an ecumenical council whose "decisions have a character of infallibility in dogmatic issues and of sovereignty without appeal in disciplinary issues",[40] or for the same reasons, the Apostolic See. The decisions

---

Julius I writes in 341: "An ignoratis hanc esse consuetudinem, ut primum nobis scribatur, et hinc, quod justum est, decernatur? Sane si qua hujusmodi suspicio in illius urbis episcopum cadebat ad hanc Ecclesiam illud rescribendum fuit" (*Acta Romanorum Pontificum a S. Clemente I (an. c. 90 ad Coelestinum III [† 1198], I, Fontes Series III [1943], p. 60).

[39] St. Jerome testifies that at the time he was in Rome, as secretary to Pope Damasus, he answered on his behalf "to the synodal consultations from the East and from the West" (*Ep.* 123, 9. CSEL 56, 82). Several important instances of these recourses to the Bishop of Rome and to the interventions of the Roman pontiffs in the affairs of the Eastern Churches during the first three centuries are to be found in P. P. Joannou, I, 2, p. 528, who mentions in particular:

— The intervention of Rome in the province of Asia about the Paschal quarrel under Anicetus (157–68);
— The intervention in Egypt in the Sabellian quarrel of Denys (259–68) and the letter of apology of Denys of Alexandria;
— The profession of faith, together with a recantation of his error, handed to Pope Fabian by Origen;
— The intervention of Stephen in 253, with threat of excommunication against the synod of Iconium, on the rebaptism of the heretics.

"These are significant facts", Joannou notes, "not only because of the high antiquity of the right of intervention's exercise, but also because this intervention is accepted without protest on the part of the Orthodox East" (p. 528).

For a more complete study of the issue, one would benefit from reading *Acta Romanorum Pontificum* . . . (= Fontes Series III).

[40] P. P. Joannou, I, 2, p. 525.

of specific councils that would be contrary to this point of doctrine or of discipline are not enough to affirm that it was not "always maintained" in the whole Church, since such synods have only a limited scope in time and space.

2. If, during the same period, the point in question was never contested in the name of a contrary tradition on the part of apostolic Churches. If there has been a contestation, it is necessary to examine it to find out whether this led to the recognition of two parallel traditions, as was the case in the Quartodeciman Quarrel starting in 154 between Polycarp of Smyrna and Pope Anicetus about the determination of Easter's date,[41] or to a rejection of one of the two traditions, as was the case in the baptismal controversy resolved in favor of Pope Stephen against Cyprian of Carthage on the issue of rebaptizing the heretics.[42] When the point in question is contested only by individuals or by groups of people separated from the apostolic Churches, the possibility of a tradition that remained unbroken since the origins is not questioned. There have always been, since the beginning of Christianity, people who refused this or that point of the deposit received from the apostles in the name of another so-called apostolic tradition, though their assertions have never committed anyone but themselves. Helvidius and Jovinian contested the validity of celibacy-continence, but it is only in the case of a contestation initiated by an apostolic Church, during the first four centuries, that we would have to raise serious doubts about testimonies enabling us to say that this discipline "was always maintained". A similar reasoning is to be used in the case of Churches that fell into heresy or dissidence and, in a historically verifiable way, became autonomous in doctrine as well as in discipline (Novatian, Arian, Nestorian, and other Churches).

3. If the point in question is not in formal contradiction with a Scriptural text, for there could not be an apostolic tradition where there is a disagreement with God's written Word. The traditions that were entrusted orally by the apostles to their successors and the early Christians, even though they are not included in one form or another in Holy Scripture, are nevertheless deeply in tune with the teachings of the Old and the New Testaments. It would be unthinkable for the apostles to ask for the observance of something going against Scripture, especially when we deal with Scriptures that determined part of the preaching of these

---

[41] Disagreement flared up again at the end of the 2d century between Pope Victor and the Asian bishops led by Polycratus of Ephesus and was peacefully settled thanks to the intervention of Irenaeus of Lyon, who brought out the precedent established by Anicetus (Eusebius, *Hist. Eccl.*, V, 24. SCh 41, 67–71).

[42] This issue has an abundant bibliography. J. Tixeront devoted a good chapter to it in his *Histoire des dogmes dans l'antiquité chrétienne*, I (Paris, 1930), pp. 378–89.

same apostles, as for instance the Gospels and the Epistles of the New Testament. In other words, if a practice were discredited by Scripture, it would be contradicted by the apostles themselves. It would be futile to think that "it had always been maintained" and to try to find for it alleged claims to apostolicity. It is also important to remember that the genuine interpretation of Scripture takes place within the context of the living Tradition,[43] and that in particular, the meaning of certain texts that are in themselves apt to have various and at times contradictory explanations can only be determined with certainty by the Magisterium of the Church, exercised by men who, as heirs to the entire teaching of the apostles, are capable of "reading and interpreting Holy Scripture with the same Spirit that caused it to be written",[44] and to say without any ambiguity what the inspired authors, especially the apostles, meant to say.

These various conditions would enable us to apply, in a prudent yet fruitful way, St. Augustine's principle to the particular case of the celibacy-continence law. This principle, which will guide our research, might be entitled, for convenience's sake, "principle of spatio-temporal universality".

Our work of historical reconstitution will also be helped by two other methodological principles:

1. The first is based on the fact that quite a few points related to doctrine and discipline were not, in the beginning, the object of an explanation. Yet they are actually included in Scripture or in the oral teaching of the apostles, and as such they are part of the things that had been accepted and practiced by the early Christian communities. It was only with the passage of time and under the pressure of new circumstances that truths of faith adhered to until then without question would become debated, then dogmatically defined, and that customs observed without discussion from the outset—because they were held to be compulsory by the apostles and their successors—would take on a juridical form and be turned into explicit norms.[45] This "principle of progressive

---

[43] "Written testimonial of the unique apostles' kerygma, Holy Scripture cannot be read correctly outside of the living Tradition of the apostolic Churches." C. Munier, "La Tradition apostolique chez Tertullien", in *l'Année Canonique* 23 (1979), p. 183.

[44] Cf. Vatican II, Dogmatic Constitution *Dei Verbum*, II, 10, 12. Cf. Jerome, *Commentariorum in epistolam ad Galatas*, III, 5. PL 26, 417a.

[45] The circumstances leading to the progressive explication of these points of doctrine or discipline can be: The distance from the apostolic era, causing one to question the origin of certain traditions. The Churches are wondering either about what they themselves observe or about the different traditions of another Church. This was the case in particular for the quarrel about the Paschal date (see above, p. 61, n. 41). Unforeseen historical situations: appearance of the heresies and conversion to the Catholic faith of members of

explicitation" enables us to keep in mind, in particular, that certain points of ecclesial discipline existed before their canonical expression. It would be a serious mistake of historical perspective to equate the origin of an obligation with the date of the document in which it is formulated for the first time, whether it be a council decree or a papal letter. How could we be certain that the texts we have today were the first ones, as chronology goes, to have addressed the issue? During the first three centuries, times of persecution, very many writings were lost and Church archives frequently disappeared in fires or systematic destructions (we know that the archives of the Church of Rome were destroyed during the Diocletian persecution). Even supposing that the documents we have were the first, nothing permits us to infer that the law we find in them does express a new obligation, even if the text itself does not stipulate this. And even less so when the legislators refer explicitly to a previous tradition, as is the case for the celibate-continence law (Council of Carthage in 390, decretals of Siricius, Innocent I, and so on). A corollary of this "principle of progressive explicitation" is that it is not only legitimate, but in many cases indispensable, to explain obscure things with the help of clear ones. Otherwise, one runs the risk of misunderstandings and one can be led to fly in the face of evidence.[46]

2. A second principle of methodology, also necessary for any scientific research, consists of interpreting the facts by inserting them as much as possible into the whole context to which they belong. This means that it is important to try to perceive the many connections linking the phenomena or different aspects of a phenomenon one to the other so as to grasp them in their complex reality. Such a principle, which we could call "principle of comprehensive interpretation", will invite us to take into account all the data converging on a single moment of history or a difficult text to be clarified by using particular points to shed light on

---

heretical sects, a phenomenon that led to the controversy about baptism (see above, p. 56, n. 26). Lastly, and this is the most frequent case, a particular point is contested by people who dispute its grounds. Many infractions are committed. While contestation and the number of infractions spread and threaten the faith or the peace of the Churches, the leaders decide to intervene (with synods, ecumenical councils, papal decretals) and to stipulate officially the beliefs or points of discipline.

[46] "These testimonies (i.e., those of the 4th century) must be weighed and evaluated according to the scientifically sure methodical principle, and above all of an extreme importance in order to reach with some certainty a proper knowledge of the ecclesiastical institutions of the early Church, such principle being an interpretation of the circumstances and phenomena wrapped in obscurity in the light of later testimonies referring and constantly conforming, with a keen sense of attachment to tradition, to all that was transmitted since the first era of the Church" (A. M. Stickler, "Nota storica sul celibato dei chierici *in sacris*", in *L'Osservatore Romano* [March 2/3, 1970], p. 2).

the others, and all of them together to shed as much light as possible on the issue. Holy Scripture, conciliar and patristic documents, historical sources, Roman pontiffs' decretals, vocabulary study—nothing can be neglected in trying to do away with a doubt or to go ahead with more certainty.

CHAPTER FOUR

The Issue of the Apostles' Marriages

The issue of the apostles' marriages is at the forefront of any inquiry into the origins of clerical celibacy. When the African Fathers of 390 affirmed that they wanted to observe "what the apostles taught us", they referred not only to an oral teaching of the Twelve (and of St. Paul), but above all to the example that Peter and other members of the apostolic college left to posterity. For it is unquestionable that their example played a decisive role in the life of the Church and in the organization of its discipline. Two problems are raised with regard to the apostles, corresponding to the necessary distinction between "celibacy in the strict sense of the term" and "celibacy in the broad sense of the term" that we evoked above.[1] The first one concerns the state of life that the apostles were in when the Lord called them: were they married or single? The second deals with the kind of life they led after they followed Christ, in a definitive way: were the married ones among them still living as husbands with their wives, or when leaving everything to follow their vocation, did they also leave their wives and practice perfect continence from then on? To attempt to shed all possible light on these two points is to gather the fundamental data of Scripture and to determine the value of the patristic testimonies that history has left us.

I. WERE THE APOSTLES MARRIED WHEN JESUS CALLED THEM TO FOLLOW HIM?

We will study separately the case of each of the apostles, following the nominal order in St. Matthew's Gospel,[2] adding to that list the names of Matthias (who replaced Judas Iscariot) and Paul.

[1] See above, p. 48.

[2] Mt 10:2–4: "These are the names of the twelve apostles: first, Simon who is called Peter, and his brother Andrew; James, the son of Zebedee, and his brother John; Philip

1. PETER (Simon). We know, from the Synoptics, that Simon was married because Jesus cured his mother-in-law, who, in his house at Capharnaum, "was in bed with a fever".[3] Let us note, however, that nowhere in the texts of the New Testament is there any explicit mention of Peter's wife, a silence that caused St. Jerome to suggest that she may already have been dead when Peter was called by the Lord.[4] Nor is there mention of any children that Simon might have had before his conversion.

A fact so clearly attested by Scripture was of course accepted and confirmed by the entire patristic tradition. Here are the main testimonies:

Clement of Alexandria († ca. 215): "Will they [the Encratites, who maligned marriage] also reject the apostles? Peter and Philip had children. Philip even gave his daughters [in marriage] to men. And Paul does not hesitate, in an epistle, to greet a woman companion whom he had not taken along, for the good of his ministry.[5] Peter's wife would have died a martyr: It is said that Blessed Peter, seeing his wife led to death, felt joy because of her call and her return home and that he encouraged her and consoled her, calling her by name and saying: 'So-and-so, remember the Lord!' Such was the marriage of the blessed ones and the perfect disposition of those who loved each other so much."[6]

St. Basil of Caesarea († 379) quotes Abraham and other upright married men of the Old Testament as examples of a perfect fidelity to God, and he adds: "Peter and the other apostles, in the New Testament, were of the same caliber."[7]

Ambrosiaster (ca. 366–84) points out that being married did not prevent Peter from being chosen as leader of the apostles.[8]

For *St. John Chrysostom* († 407), the exceptional sanctity of the apostles must not make us forget that they were men like us: "What does it mean: 'Ah, but he was Paul, but he was Peter?' Tell me, did they not have the same nature we do? . . . Were not some of them married and family men? . . . "[9] And elsewhere he says, "What can we say about Peter, the foundation of the Church, the passionate lover of Christ. . . . Did he not

---

and Bartholomew; Thomas and Matthew the tax collector; James, the son of Alphaeus, and Thaddaeus; Simon the Zealot and Judas Iscariot, the one who was to betray him."

[3] Mk 1:29–31; Mt 8:14–15; Lk 4:38–39.

[4] *Adversus Jovinianum*, I, 26. PL 23, 246b.

[5] *Stromata*, III, 6, 52–53. Related by Eusebius, *Hist. Eccl.*, III, 30, 1. SCh 31, 140.

[6] *Stromata*, VII, 63–64. Related by Eusebius, *Hist. Eccl.*, III, 30, 2. SCh 31, 141.

[7] *Sermo de renuntiatione mundi*, 1. PG 31, 628c.

[8] *Quaestiones Veteris et Novi Testamenti*, 127, 33. CSEL 50, 414.

[9] *Ad Demetrium de compunctione*, liber I, 8. PG 47, 407c.

also have a wife? Of course he had one. Listen to the testimony of the Evangelist. What does he say? Jesus entered the house of Peter's mother-in-law who was ill with a fever.[10] Where there is a mother-in-law, there is a wife; where there is a wife, there is a marriage."[11]

Epiphanius († 403) says that if Jesus, nailed on the Cross, entrusted his virgin mother to John, it was because the latter was a virgin: "Why did he not entrust her rather to Peter, or Andrew, or Matthew, or Bartholomew? It is undoubtedly because of his virginity that John was granted [this privilege]. . . ."[12]

St. Jerome († 419 or 420) comments: "We can say about Peter that he had a mother-in-law at the time he believed [in Christ] and that he did not have a wife anymore."[13] And he writes to Julian, who had lost his wife and two daughters: "Would you too be perfect? Would you not, you who are first in the world, also be first in the service of Christ? Is it because you had a wife? So did Peter: he left her when he left his nets and his boat. . . ."[14]

Some of these patristic testimonies also talk about the children that Peter would have had (*Clement of Alexandria; Ambrosiaster*), though without giving any details. On the other hand, apocryphal works have more data and credit Peter with a daughter, whom some even call Petronilla.[15]

2. ANDREW. Scripture is silent about a possible marriage of Andrew, the brother of Simon Peter.

[10] Mk 1:30.

[11] *In Illud: Vidi Dominum (Is 6:1), homiliae 1–6*, 4, 3. PG 56, 123c.

[12] *Panarion (Adversus Haereses)*, Haer. 78, 10. PG 42, 714c.

[13] *Adversus Jovinianum*, I, 26. PL 23, 246b.

[14] *Ep.* 118, 4. Trans. J. Labourt, Coll. "Budé", VI, p. 93. We note a passage from the *Pseudo-Ignatius*, of lesser interest because it has been proven that it is an Apollinarist forgery of the 5th century but one that is still sometimes quoted. The author praises virginity and adds: "I don't blame the other blessed ones who were bound by marriage and whom I remember now. I do wish to be found worthy of God in his Kingdom for having followed in the footsteps of those such as Abraham, Isaac, and Jacob, Joseph, Isaiah and the other prophets, those such as Peter and Paul and the other apostles, who were bound to a wife. That they married was not out of love for pleasure but to have a posterity" (*Ignatii epistula ad Philadelphienses*, IV, 5, in Funk and Diekamp, *Patres apostolici*, II [Tübingen, 1913], pp. 176–79). See the discussion about the authenticity of this "long lesson" of the letters of Ignatius of Antioch by P. T. Camelot in SCh 10 at p. 11).

[15] These are the Coptic fragments in *The Acts of Peter* (French trans. by L. Vouaux, *Les Actes de Pierre* [Paris, 1922], pp. 221–27), *The Acts of Philip* (142 [ed. Lipsius and Bonnet], 2–2, 81), and *The Acts of Saints Nereus and Achilleus*, 4, 15 (*Acta Sanctorum Maii*, 3d ed., III, pp. 10–15). There is a good presentation of the apocryphal narratives concerning the daughter of Peter in R. Gryson, *Les origines du célibat ecclésiastique du premier au septième siècle* (Gembloux, 1970), pp. 9–10.

Commenting on the verses of St. Luke about the cure of Peter's mother-in-law, *St. Ambrose* († 397) writes: "It may be that under the symbolic figure of that woman, mother-in-law of Simon and Andrew, it was our flesh that was ill, suffering from the fever of various crimes." [16] Ambrose seems to imply here that Peter and Andrew had married two sisters, daughters of the woman cured by Jesus and thus mother-in-law to both of them. As far as Ambrose is concerned, Andrew then would also have been married.

Epiphanius († 403) lists him among the apostles who had wives. [17]

As far as we know, no other patristic author named Andrew among the apostles who had been married.

3. JAMES (brother of John). There is no scriptural information about whether James was married or single.

Two patristic writers specify that he lived, as did his brother, in a state of virginity:

Epiphanius gives two brief but clear references in his *Panarion*. [18]

Proclus of Constantinople († 446) explains that this gift [of virginity] was the reason for the two sons of Zebedee, James and his brother John, to have been called "sons of thunder". [19]

4. JOHN. Jesus' special love for the apostle John is frequently attested in the Gospels and other texts of the New Testament. Tradition was unanimous in crediting this preference on the part of the Lord to his beloved apostle's state of perpetual virginity.

Among the main patristic testimonies, we can quote in particular:

Epiphanius: "If Jesus, as he was dying on the Cross, entrusted his mother to John and not to Peter or any other apostle, it was because John was a virgin." [20] He and his brother had embraced the same kind of life (i.e., virginity) and persevered in it. [21]

---

[16] *Expositio evangelii secundum Lucam*, 4. CC 14, 128.

[17] *Panarion (Adversus Haereses)*, Haer. 78, 10. PG 42, 714c.

[18] *Adversus Haereses*, Haer. 58, 4. PG 41, 1016a. Ibid., Haer. 78, 13. PG 42, 720a.

[19] *Homilia VI. Laudatio S. Dei genitricis Mariae*, V. PG 65, 730b. On the problem of this homily's authenticity, see CPG, n. 5805.

[20] *Panarion (Adversus Haereses)*, Haer. 78, 10. PG 42, 714c.

[21] *Panarion (Adversus Haereses)*, Haer. 58, 4. PG 41, 1016a. *Panarion (Adversus Haereses)*, Haer. 78, 13. PG 42, 720a.

Ambrosiaster (ca. 366–84): "All the apostles, with the exception of John and Paul, were married." [22]

St. Jerome: "Yet John, one of the disciples who was said to be the youngest among the apostles [*qui minimus traditur fuisse inter Apostolos*], and whose faith in Christ started when he was a virgin, remained a virgin, and this is the reason that he was preferred by the Lord and leaned on Jesus' breast." [23]

St. Augustine († 430): "Among the commentators of the holy word, several—and those were not men whose opinions we can hold in contempt—think that if Christ loved the Apostle John with a special love, it was because he had never been married and that from his earliest childhood he practiced the most delicate purity. There are no conclusive proofs in canonical Scripture; nevertheless, what seems to support such a feeling and demonstrate its aptness is that John was a figure of the heavenly life, during which no wedding would be celebrated." [24]

St. Paulinus of Nola († 431): "Among his disciples he chose the youngest one so as to entrust his mother, as was fit, to a virgin apostle." [25]

Proclus of Constantinople († 446): "The Apostle John received 'the principal and most eminent gift from God', i.e., virginity. And this is why the two sons of Zebedee were called 'sons of thunder'." [26]

5. PHILIP. There are, in the New Testament, two men bearing the name of Philip. The first is one of the Twelve chosen by Jesus, the one who hastened to find Nathanael and announce, "We have found the one Moses wrote about in the law, the one about whom the prophets wrote: he is Jesus, son of Joseph, from Nazareth." [27] Nothing in Scripture enables us to affirm that he was married. The second Philip is one of the seven deacons appointed by the apostles after Pentecost "to serve at the tables". [28] St. Luke tells us that he was married and a family man: "The next day,

---

[22] *In epistolam B. Pauli ad Corinthios secundam*, XI, 2. PL 17, 320a. See also *Quaestiones Veteris et Novi Testamentum*, 127, 33: "Certe sanctus Johannes sanctimonii fuit custos" (CSEL 50, 414).

[23] *Adversus Jovinianum*, I, 26. PL 23, 246b–c.

[24] *Tractatus in Evangelium Joannis*, 124, 7. CC 36, 687. See also *De bono conjugali*, 21. CSEL 41, 221; *Contra Faustum Manichaeum*, 30, 4. CSEL 25, 751.

[25] *Ep.* 50. PL 61, 416a. CSEL 29, 421.

[26] *Homilia IV. Laudatio S. Dei genetricis Mariae*, V. PG 65, 730b.

[27] Jn 1:45.

[28] Acts 6:5.

we left [Ptolemais] and came to Caesarea. Here we called on Philip the evangelist, one of the Seven, and stayed with him. He had four virgin daughters who were prophets." [29]

Some patristic texts seemed at times to have confused the two men. Before making any judgment, we will note their testimonies:

The oldest one was given by *Papias*, bishop of Hierapolis, in Phrygia, who was writing around the year 130. Eusebius of Caesarea, in his *Historia Ecclesiastica*, preserved that testimony: "It has already been recalled . . . that the Apostle Philip had stayed in Hierapolis with his daughters. [30] We must now indicate how Papias, who lived at that time, related a wonderful story about Philip's daughters." [31] Here we are truly dealing with Philip the Apostle, one of the Twelve, and with his daughters (no number is given for them).

It is again Eusebius who preserved the testimony of another second-century bishop, *Polycratus of Ephesus* (ca. 189–98). In a letter to Pope Victor, Polycratus also mentions the Apostle Philip and his daughters in these words: "Great stars have indeed set in Asia, and they will rise again on the last day at the Lord's Parousia, when he will come in glory from heaven and look for all his saints—Philip, one of the twelve apostles who rests in Hierapolis; as well as two of his daughters, who grew old in a state of virginity; and his other daughter, who after living in the Holy Spirit, is buried at Ephesus." [32] Here too we are dealing with the Apostle Philip and his daughters, who, we are told, were three in number.

A third piece of information, also found in the *Historia Ecclesiastica* of Eusebius, finds its source in a sentence of the Roman priest Caius' *Dialogue*. *Caius*, who lived at the time of Pope Zephyrinus (199–217), refutes in it the arguments of one *Proclus*, head of the Cataphrygian sect. Well that Proclus, Eusebius stresses, "agrees with what we have explained regarding the death of Philip and his daughters when he says: 'After this one there were four prophetesses, the daughters of Philip, in Hierapolis, of Asia: there stands their tomb as well as that of their father. Here is what he says.'" [33] One must note that Eusebius relates these words of Proclus to confirm the testimony of Polycratus of Ephesus, whom he had just mentioned. Though Proclus does not explicitly say that the

[29] Acts 21:8–9.

[30] This is a testimony from Polycratus of Ephesus, related by Eusebius in a previous chapter of the *Historia Ecclesiastica*, though it chronologically follows that of Papias.

[31] *Hist. Eccl.*, III, 39, 8–9. SCh 31, 155.

[32] *Hist. Eccl.*, III, 31, 2–3. SCh 31, 141–42. Eusebius quotes *in extenso* this passage from the letter of Polycrates a second time in another chapter of his *Historia* (V, 24, 2).

[33] *Hist. Eccl.*, III, 31, 4. SCh 31, 142.

Philip he mentions is the Apostle Philip, one of the Twelve, Eusebius' process of reasoning does not permit us to doubt it. There are two contradictory indications, however: whereas Polycratus of Ephesus seems to know only three daughters of the Apostle Philip, Proclus himself mentions four of them, and they are prophetesses (as were those of the Deacon Philip, mentioned in the Acts). Moreover, immediately after having quoted the words of Proclus, Eusebius writes, without any transition: "On the other hand, Luke, in the Acts of the Apostles, mentions the daughters of Philip, who lived then in Caesarea of Judaea at the time of their father and had been honored with the prophetic charism." He states in his own words: "We came to Caesarea. There we called on Philip the evangelist, one of the Seven, and stayed with him. He had four virgin daughters who were prophets."[34] Why did Eusebius want to quote here this passage of the Acts? Was it a mere association of ideas, provoked by the homonym, or an intentional connection to draw attention to a possible confusion in the minds of Papias and Polycratus, who had confused one Philip for the other and given to the Apostle the daughters of the deacon evangelist?

Insofar as *St. John Chrysostom* († 407) is concerned, biblical examples prove that marriage is not an obstacle to holy life. After having spoken about Peter,[35] he comes to Philip: "And what should we say about Philip? Did he not have four daughters? Where there are four daughters, there is a wife, there is a marriage."[36] It is not possible to say with certainty if John Chrysostom is speaking here about the Apostle Philip or about the deacon of the same name mentioned in the book of Acts. Undoubtedly it is more logical to choose this second probability because of its scriptural support.

St. Jerome, in a note in *De viris inlustribus*, reproduces the letter of Polycratus of Ephesus to Pope Victor about the issue of Easter.[37] The passage related to the Apostle Philip and his daughters is, with a few differences, identical to the one we read in Eusebius.[38]

---

[34] Ibid., III, 31, 5. SCh 31, 142.

[35] See above, p. 66.

[36] *In illud: Vidi Dominum (Is 6:1), homiliae 1–6,* 4, 3. PG 56, 123c.

[37] *De viris inlustribus,* 45. PL 23, 659a.

[38] See above, p. 70.

Isidore of Pelusium († ca. 435) explains in a letter to one Antiochus that it was not the Apostle Philip, but a deacon of the same name, one of the Seven, who baptized the eunuch of Queen Candace, instructed Simon in the Christian faith in Samaria, and then went to live in Caesarea. He does not say anything about the possible matrimonial situation of either of the two Philips. But we can note that the memory of deacon Philip was tied, for Isidore, to the town of Caesarea (as in the Acts of the Apostles) and not to Hierapolis (*Ep.* III, 447. PG 78, 428c–29a.).

What can one conclude from these patristic themes? Some did, at times, try to explain the contradictions they contain with a confusion of names, of which Papias and Polycratus would have been guilty. They say that it was the Apostle Philip who stayed in Hierapolis and was buried there with his daughters while in fact it would only be his homonymous deacon, Philip the Evangelist. Indeed, the name "Evangelist" was what caused the mistake of the two second-century writers. Eusebius, according to the same explanation, had reestablished the truth by bringing in the testimony of Caius. We have seen that St. John Chrysostom does not help to resolve the matter, and that St. Jerome only reproduces the letter of Polycratus that he probably found in Eusebius' writings. It would therefore have been the Deacon Philip who had four daughters, not the Apostle; and the tomb that Polycratus of Ephesus said was in Hierapolis would have been his.

Nevertheless, if such a solution has the advantage of being simple, it does have the disadvantage of minimizing the importance of Papias' and Polycratus' testimonies, both very ancient and coming from men who had lived in Asia. Papias was the bishop of Hierapolis, and thus in quite a good position to know whether the Apostle or the Deacon Philip was buried in his town. It is hard to see that on a point of that nature and importance he could have committed such a gross mistake. Polycratus, on the other hand, lived in Ephesus, not far from Hierapolis. Moreover, we have already noted that the purpose of Caius' *Dialogue* quoted by Eusebius does not necessarily concern the Deacon Philip, and that in fact Eusebius seems rather to see in it a confirmation of Polycratus' testimony about the death of the Apostle Philip and his daughters in Hierapolis.

All this being considered, we think that the tradition represented by Papias, Polycratus, and undoubtedly also by Caius (Proclus) must be taken into account. According to that tradition, the Apostle Philip would have been married and the father of several daughters (three in all likelihood, as Polycratus writes).[39] He would have lived in Hierapolis and been buried there with two of his daughters, while the third had her tomb in Ephesus. For his part, the Deacon Philip, the one who baptized the eunuch of Queen Candace and evangelized Samaria, was also married and the father of four daughters, as attested to in the Acts of the Apostles. He resided in Caesarea, where Paul and Luke called on him.[40]

---

[39] The *Dialogue* of Caius mentions four of them, probably from assimilation with the four daughters of Deacon Philip mentioned in the Acts.

[40] We can see, in support of this opinion: F. Vigouroux, "Philippe l'Évangeliste", in *Dictionnaire de la Bible*, V, c. 271–72; and J. B. Lightfoot, *St. Paul's Epistles to the Colossians and to Philemon* (London, 1875), pp. 44–47.

6. BARTHOLOMEW. There is no scriptural information about him.

Epiphanius, among the Fathers, seems to be the only one explicitly alluding to the marriage of the Apostle Bartholomew.[41]

7. THOMAS. Neither Scripture nor the patristic writers gives us any information about a possible marriage of the Apostle Thomas.

8. MATTHEW. There is no reference to a marriage of Levi Matthew in the New Testament.

Epiphanius, in the passage already quoted, also mentions Matthew among the married apostles, together with Peter, Andrew, and Bartholomew.[42]

9. JAMES, son of Alpheus. The Gospels, which give to this apostle the name of James, son of Alpheus, to distinguish him from James, brother of John and son of Zebedee, do not tell us whether he was married; nor are there indications in other texts of the New Testament.

The only patristic testimony we have seems to be that of *Epiphanius*: "That one [James, brother of the Lord]," he writes, "died at the age of ninety-six, having kept his virginity. . . . James and John, as well as our James, had embraced the same kind of life. . . ."[43]

10. THADDEUS (Jude). There is no scriptural information about him.

At times passages of the *Historia Ecclesiastica* by *Eusebius* have been evoked in which he, quoting the words of Hegesippus, mentions descendants and grandsons of Jude[44] in order to affirm that the Apostle Thaddeus, alias Jude, had been married and a family man. But the Jude Eusebius refers to is one of "the brothers of the Lord" (cf. Mt 13:55) and has nothing to do with the apostle of the same name.[45]

11. SIMON THE ZEALOT. We have no scriptural indication or patristic testimony related to the apostle Simon on the question under study.

---

[41] See the passage of Epiphanius concerning the Apostle Peter, above, p. 67.

[42] See above, p. 67.

[43] *Panarion (Adversus Haereses)*, Haer. 78, 13. PG 42, 720a.

[44] *Hist. Eccl.*, III, 19–20, 32. SCh 31, 122–23.

[45] See, about this point, J. Stiltinck's dissertation "De fratribus Domini Jacobo, Josepho, Juda et Simone", *Acta Sanctorum Septembris*, VI (Antwerp, 1757), p. xv, n. 51; and F. A. Zaccaria, *Storia polemica del celibato sacro de contrapporsi ad alcune detestabili opere uscite a questi tempi* (Rome, 1774), p. 20.

12. JUDAS ISCARIOT. The New Testament does not say whether that apostle was married or not.

However, there is a passage of Scripture that certain Fathers quote when talking about Judas, the apostle who betrayed Jesus, as having been a man with a wife and children. Interpreting the curses of Psalm 108 (JB Ps 109), *Eusebius of Caesarea* writes: "You will understand the other passages of the psalm in the same vein: what follows—and seemed to be said about the certain sons of Judas, 'May his children be orphaned' (Ps 108:9) and other such things—is above all meant for Judas himself, then, after him, for all those who betray the Saving Word. In the same way you will understand also [what is said] about his wife. . . ." [46]

The same kind of reasoning is found in *St. Augustine* in his commentary on Psalm 108: "May his children be orphaned and his wife widowed! And indeed, when he died, his sons were orphans and his wife a widow." [47]

It goes without saying that such scriptural interpretations are not sources of historical information. Let us remember, however, that in the Fathers' eyes, the fulfillment of the Old Testament's prophecies was an essential key to understanding the events in the life of Christ. The prophetic argument had for them, as for their audiences, a very great weight. For our part, we can note that if Eusebius and Augustine did not cast doubt—on the weight of a scriptural prophecy—on the marriage and children of Judas Iscariot, they only could have done so because no unquestionable tradition in the opposite direction contradicted them. Their commentaries were thus indicative of an opinion about Judas that was quite common in those days. [48]

13. MATTHIAS. Neither Scripture nor patristic tradition stipulates whether the man who was chosen after Pentecost to take the place of Judas in the group of Twelve was a married man or single.

14. PAUL (Saul). The scriptural texts do not say directly whether Paul had a wife or if, on the contrary, he was single. Two passages of the Pauline epistles do, however, contain an indirect reference that brought about various interpretations:

[46] *Demonstratio evangelica*, 10. PG 22, 740b–c.

[47] *Enarrationes in psalmos*, 108, 11. CC 40, 1590.

[48] A commentary on the Psalms, wrongly credited to St. Jerome and probably written in Gaul during the 5th century, declares not to find in Scripture that Judas had a wife and children. *Breviarium in psalmos*, 108. PL 26, 1158b.

In 1 Cor 7:7–8, Paul asks Christian couples not to refuse themselves to one another, unless it is for a while in order to free themselves for prayer; then he adds:

> I should like everyone to be like me, but everybody has his own particular gifts from God, one with a gift for one thing and another with a gift for the opposite. There is something I want to add for the sake of widows and those who are not married: it is a good thing for them to stay as they are, like me, but if they cannot control the sexual urges, they should get married, since it is better to be married than to be tortured.

In Phil 4:3, the Apostle exhorts someone he greets with the name γνήσιε σύζυγε to come to the assistance of Evodia and Syntyche and to the other collaborators who worked with him for the cause of the Gospel. The word σύζυγος (literally, yoke mate) is used at times in the Greek language to describe the wife; certain authors during the patristic times deduced from this that Paul had been married.

Clement of Alexandria († ca. 215) seems to be the first to have adopted such an interpretation. He does not doubt that Paul had been married and sees a proof of it in Phil 4:3: "Will they [the Encratites] also reject the apostles? Indeed, Peter and Philip had children. Philip even gave his daughters [in marriage] to men. And Paul does not hesitate in an epistle to greet his woman companion, whom he did not take along with him for the good of his ministry." [49]

Methodius of Olympia (ca. 240) sees in 1 Cor 7:7–8 a clear reference to Paul's widowhood: "Here, too, he [Paul] stresses his preference for continence; he gave himself as a signal example to invite all his listeners to follow him in this state of life, by teaching them that it is better for one who had been married to an only wife then to remain alone, as he bound himself to do." [50]

According to *Ambrosiaster* (ca. 366–84), "all the apostles, with the exception of John and Paul, were married".[51] For this fourth-century author, Paul was therefore single.

In his treatise *De Virginitate*, *St. Ambrose* († 397) quotes the example of Paul: "Let Paul strengthen you, he who ordered that one should be

---

[49] *Stromata*, III, 6. GCS 52, 220.

[50] *Le Banquet*, XII, 82–83. PG 18, 80a. Trans. SCh 95, 119. It is strange that V. H. Debidour, its translator in *Sources Chrétiennes*, could have written the following note about the passage of Methodius of Olympia: ". . . it does not seem that St. Paul was ever a widower."

[51] *In epistolam B. Pauli ad Corinthios secundam*, 11, 2. PL 17, 320a.

considerate to widows (1 Tim 5:3): it is good for you to remain in this state, as I do (1 Cor 7:8). He calls for consideration, teaches as a master, and invites through his example." [52] The bishop of Milan wrote his treatise for the intention of virgins. In the passage we have quoted, however, he seems instead to be interested in widows and to suggest the example of Paul, not as a model of virginity but as the model of a widower who kept continence, Indeed, the reference to 1 Tim 5:3, in which St. Paul asks for "consideration for those who are truly widows", is explicit. On the one hand, 1 Cor 7:8 ("It is a good thing for you to remain in this state, as I do") indicates without ambiguity that Paul lived in perfect chastity. Lastly, in concluding that "he [Paul] invites through his example", Ambrose seems to imply that Paul was indeed a widower and a continent one.

For *St. John Chrysostom* († 407), the words γνήσιε σύζυγε do not indicate in any way a wife but any woman, unless it refers to a man, because the term σύζυγος is also masculine. [53] John Chrysostom thus rejects the idea of a married Paul.

The *Letter to Eustochium*, of *St. Jerome* († 419 or 420), clearly indicates that one should not listen to those who claim that Paul had been married: "Let us not lend an ear to those who pretend that he had a wife, because when he writes about continence and advises perpetual chastity, he argues from his own case: 'I should like everyone to be like me.' and later, 'I say to those who are not married and to the widowers: it is better to remain so as I myself do', and in another passage: 'Do we not have the right to take along our wives as the other apostles do?'" [54]

For *St. Augustine* († 430), it is obvious that Paul proclaimed his own chastity when he said: 'I should like everyone to be like me" (1 Cor 7:7). [55] Augustine therefore believed that Paul had lived in perfect chastity, but it must be noted that he does not thereby state whether Paul was married or single. Perfect chastity can be observed not only by a single man but also by a widower or a married man living in continence.

As to *Theodoret of Cyrus* († 466), he does not hesitate to describe as silly the interpretation of those who see in the σύζυγε of Phil 4:3 a wife of the Apostle Paul:

---

[52] "Vivificet vos Paulus, qui vos praecepit honorari, qui ait: Bonum est si sic maneant sicut et ego. Honore provocat, magisterio docet, invitat exemplo" (PL 16, 315a).

[53] *In epistulam ad Philippenses argumentum et homiliae 1–15*, 13, 3. PG 62, 279d.

[54] *Ep.* 22, 20. CSEL 54, 170–71. Trans. J. Labourt, Coll. "Budé", I, p. 129. See also *Adversus Jovinianum*, I, 34. PL 23, 258a.

[55] *De opere monachorum*, 32, 40. PL 40, 579b. CSEL 41, 592.

Some have stupidly deemed that the σύζυγε was the wife of the Apostle. They paid no attention to what was written in the epistle to the Corinthians, to wit, that he counted himself among the single men: " . . . for the sake of widows and those who are not married: it is a good thing for them to stay as they are, like me." And, to be sure, it is evident that he had no wife, either because he had never been married or because he had been widowed. It is more likely that he had never had a wife because he had been called [by the Lord] as an adolescent. He therefore calls her σύζυγε (i.e., yoke mate) because she wears with him the yoke of piety; and he exhorts her to assist the good women and to make concord rule among them. [56]

Thus, one can group these patristic testimonies into three categories: The first is tradition represented by Clement of Alexandria, according to which Paul had been married and his wife still alive when he was writing to the Philippians, though Clement stresses that Paul did not take her with him in his travels. A second group, along with Methodius of Olympia and Ambrose of Milan, think that Paul was a widower at the time of his conversion. Finally, the largest group rejects the idea of marriage for the apostle and affirms that Paul was single before believing in Christ and remained so (Ambrosiaster, John Chrysostom, Jerome, Theodoret of Cyrus). The testimony of Augustine is a case in itself insofar as the "perfect chastity" of St. Paul, about which the bishop of Hippo speaks, can be reconciled with the opinion of each of the three groups. These divergences among the Fathers can be explained by the vagueness of the term γνήσιε σύζυγε used by Paul in Phil 4:3.[57] Nevertheless, all—including Clement of Alexandria—agree in affirming that the apostle Paul led a life of perfect chastity (either in continence if he was a widower or still had a wife, or in celibacy in the strict meaning of the word).[58]

In addition to these patristic opinions regarding the situation of each individual apostle, we find in the literature of the early centuries testimonies concerning, in an overall way, either all the apostles or a group among them.

---

[56] *Interpretatio epist. ad Philip.*, 4, 3. PG 82, 585a–b.

[57] One must, however, note that the interpretation of γνήσιε σύζυγε by Clement of Alexandria cannot easily be justified from the philological viewpoint. See in particular, Delling, Σύζυγος, in ThW 7, pp. 749–50.

[58] Clement of Alexandria, in the previously quoted passage, p. 66, stressed that the apostles "took everywhere with them women, not as wives, but with the title of sisters. . . ." (*Stromata*, III, 6. GCS 52, 220). See also below, pp. 79–80.

It is thus that *St. Basil of Caesarea* († 379), in a text we already saw regarding Peter, affirms that the latter "and all the other apostles, in the New Testament, were of the same caliber" as the just who were married in the Old Covenant and who had given an example of a singular fidelity to God.[59] Basil thus deems that all the apostles, without exception it seems, were married men.

This is also the opinion of the Apollinarist author of the *Pseudo-Ignatius*: "I do wish to be found worthy of God in his Kingdom for having walked in the footsteps [i.e., of these blessed ones who live in holy matrimony] of Abraham, Isaac, and Jacob, Joseph, Isaiah, and the other prophets, Peter and Paul and the other apostles, who were all tied to a wife."[60]

For *Tertullian* († ca. 220), all the apostles, with the exception of Peter, were either celibates [eunuchs] or continent: "Peter is the only one I found [in Scripture] to have been married, because of his mother-in-law; I presume that he was monogamous, since the Church would have had to establish upon him [as upon a foundation] all the degrees of her hierarchy amid monogamous men. The others, whom I did not find to be married, were perforce either celibate [eunuchs] or continent."[61]

This is also the opinion of *St. Jerome* († 419 or 420), who, like Tertullian, declares himself in favor of scriptural proofs: if the apostles were taking their wives with them, he replies to Jovinian, they were like "sisters" and not "spouses". "Though", he adds immediately, "it is not clearly stated about the apostles, with the exception of Peter, that they had wives; and since only one is mentioned and silence is kept about the others, we must understand that the latter, about whose spouses Scripture said nothing, did not have wives."[62] In a more general way, St. Jerome writes to Pammachium: "The apostles were either virginal men or married men who became continent afterward."[63]

Ambrosiaster (ca. 366–84) thinks he knows "that all the apostles, with the exception of John and Peter, were married".[64]

---

[59] *Sermo de renuntiatione mundi*, I. PG 31, 628c.

[60] *Ignatii epistula ad Philadelphienses*, VI, 5, in Funk and Diekamp, *Patres apostolici*, II (Tübingen, 1913), pp. 176–79.

[61] "Petrum solum invenio maritum, per socrum; monogamum praesumo per ecclesiam, qua super illum omnem gradum ordinis sui de monogamis erat collocaturus. Ceteros cum maritos non invenio, aut spadones intellegam necesse est aut continentes" (*De monogamia*, 8, 4. CC II, 1239).

[62] *Adversus Jovinianum*, I, 26. PL 23, 246a.

[63] "Apostoli vel virgines vel post nuptis continentes" (*Apologeticum ad Pammachium, ep.* 49 [48], 2, 21. CSEL 54, 386–87).

[64] *In epistolam B. Pauli ad Corinthios secundam*, XI, 2. PL 17, 320a.

As to *Proclus of Constantinople* (ca. 434–46), he thinks that only John and James, out of the whole apostolic group, had received the gift of virginity, a gift that earned them the name "sons of thunder".[65] Therefore, Proclus seems to imply that all the other apostles were married.

Lastly we see some Fathers thinking that some apostles were married but they do not give names or numbers (Origen [† 253][66] and St. John Chrysostom [† 407]).[67]

II. WHAT MANNER OF LIFE DID THE APOSTLES LEAD WHEN FOLLOWING CHRIST?

Did those among the apostles who were married at the time of their call by the Lord go on living with their wives, or did they put an end to their conjugal lives, either through separation or by treating their wives as sisters? A passage of the first epistle to the Corinthians poses a problem of exegesis in this respect. In his apology following certain criticisms aimed directly at him, Paul writes: "My answer to those who want to interrogate me is this: 'Have we not every right to eat and drink? And the right to take a Christian woman [ἀδελφὴν γυναῖκα] around with us, like all the other apostles and the brothers of the Lord and Cephas?'"[68] How are we to understand this reference to the ἀδελφαι γυναῖκες, whom the other apostles took around with them in their apostolic rounds? Were they wives, sisters in faith (i.e., Christians)? Or wives whom the apostles considered now as sisters, living with them in continence? Or, more simply, "believing women", who accompanied the apostles to take care of their material needs, like the holy women who followed the Lord in Palestine (Lk 8:2–3)? Without going into more detail than is necessary here, let us note that the majority of contemporary exegetes have accepted, especially for linguistic reasons, the last hypothesis. Those women who followed the apostles were Christians who helped them in material as well as spiritual matters. One tends to think that an apostle who had a wife took her along rather than someone else, but in that case lived with her as "with a sister".[69]

---

[65] *Homilia VI. Laudatio S. Dei genetricis Mariae*, V. PG 65, 730b.

[66] *Commentariorum in epistulam b. Pauli ad Romanos*, 9. PG 14, 1205a.

[67] *Ad Demetrium de compunctione liber I*, 8. PG 47, 407a.

[68] 1 Cor 9:4–5.

[69] See, for instance, E. B. Allo, *Saint Paul, Première épître aux Corinthiens* (Paris: Etudes Bibliques, 1934), p. 214.

The main patristic commentaries on this passage of the first epistle to the Corinthians are those of Clement of Alexandria, Tertullian, St. Jerome, and Isidore of Pelusium.

Clement of Alexandria († ca. 215), who, as we have seen, was the only one to think that Paul was married and still had his wife during his apostolic ministry, does, however, exclude categorically the idea that married apostles could practice conjugal intercourse with their wives. If they took women with them, the women "were not treated as wives but as sisters, to serve as interpreters with women whose duties kept them within their homes, and in order that, through these intermediaries, the doctrine of the Lord could penetrate the women's quarters without the apostles being blamed or unjustly suspected by people of ill will." [70]

Tertullian († ca. 220) eliminates, by studying its context, an interpretation of 1 Cor 9:5 that would tend to prove that all the apostles, and not only Peter, had wives: "If, among the Greeks, a single word is used for women and for wives because of an easy custom (but in fact the word applies properly to wives), we will not interpret Paul as if he had said that the apostles were married. For if he were talking about married women as he does later, [in a passage] where the Apostle could have more easily given some example, we would be quite right in understanding his sentence in the following way: '[Have we not] the right to take a wife around with us, like all the other apostles . . . and Cephas?' But he adds a comment showing his abstinence in matters of food: 'Have we not every right to eat and drink?' Those women taken along by the apostles are not described by him as wives (even those who do not have wives still have the right to eat and drink), but simply as women who were at their service, just like those who followed the Lord." [71]

The same idea is encountered in *St. Jerome* († 419 or 420): "Even if, to prove that all the apostles had wives, he [Jovinian] would oppose to us [the sentence] 'Have we not the right to take a Christian woman or a wife [the Greek word γυνή has both meanings] around with us, like all the other apostles and the brothers of the Lord and Cephas?' Let him add also what is found in the Greek codices: Have we not the right to

---

[70] *Stromata*, III, 6. GCS 52, 220. It might be interesting to reread here the portrait of the true Gnostic as depicted by Clement of Alexandria in another book of the *Stromata*: "When his wife [that of the true Gnostic] has given him children, she is no more than a sister in his eyes, begotten by the same father, and remembering her husband only at the sight of her children. For she will truly be his sister one day when she will have done away with that garment of flesh distinguishing the sexes one from the other and preventing them from being united through knowledge" (*Stromata*, VI, 12).

[71] *De monogamia*, 8. CC II, 1239–40.

take around with us sister-women? Thus it is proven that the Apostle was talking about the other holy women who, according to Judaic custom, assisted their masters with their goods, as was done, we can read, for the Lord himself. Indeed, even the order of the words indicates this: 'Have we not every right to eat and drink? And the right to take sister-women around with us?' (1 Cor 9:4–5). For he speaks first about eating and drinking and of the responsibility for the cost of living and then about the sister-women. It is clear that [they] must not be seen as wives but, as we have said, as women who assisted them with their goods." [72]

Isidore of Pelusium († ca. 435) devoted his letter to Deacon Isidore to an explanation of 1 Cor 9:5. If women accompanied the apostles, "it was not in order to procreate children or to lead with them a common life but, in truth, to assist them with their goods, to take care of feeding the heralds of poverty". If Paul called them sister-women, it is "because by the word *sister* he wanted to show that they were chaste, while describing their nature with the word *women*". [73]

There is, therefore, as we have just seen, a consensus among the Fathers about the interpretation of the Pauline passage relative to ἀδελφαί γυναῖκες. This would not mean, in their minds, women with whom the apostles went on living a conjugal life, but persons of the feminine sex who were attached to their service for the needs of the ministry. In the case where one of these women was indeed the wife of an apostle, it is to be understood that she then lived with her husband "as a sister".

This conviction, according to which the apostles who could have been married before the call of Christ had led thereafter a life of perfect chastity, observing continence with their wives, is found still in other patristic texts, independently of the commentaries on 1 Cor 9:5 that we have studied.

In his *Demonstratio Evangelica, Eusebius of Caesarea* († 339) described the life of detachment that the disciples led in the footsteps of Christ as the best testimony of the Gospel's truth: "Why not believe this multitude of men who embraced this austere religion and abandoned their goods and what they held to be dearest to them—their wives, their children, their families—to practice poverty, and who gathered to give with a common voice, in view of the whole universe, the same testimony about their master?" [74] This sentence of Eusebius describes all the disciples, but

---

[72] *Adversus Jovinianum*, I, 26. PL 23, 245c–d.
[73] *Ep.* III, 176. PG 78, 865d–68c.
[74] *Demonstratio evangelica*, III, 4, 37. GCS 23, 117.

it is obvious that the first ones to give the example of such total detachment—including with regard to their wives and children, when they had
any—were the apostles.

Ambrosiaster (ca. 366-84), after reminding us that having a wife and children did not prevent Peter from being chosen as chief of the apostles,
and after confirming by this example that a married man can very well
be admitted to the priesthood, explains why the ministers of God are
no longer permitted conjugal intercourse.[75] Indirectly but unequivocally
he implies that the apostles, as far as he is concerned, lived in perfect
continence with their possible wives.

As far as *St. Jerome* († ca. 419 or 420) is concerned, the only apostle
whom Scripture says was married is Peter. With such a certainty Jerome
then affirms in his letter to Julian that if Peter had a wife, "he left her
when he gave up his nets and his boat".[76]

The issue of the apostles' marriages, studied on the basis of scriptural
data and with the help of patristic testimonies, leads us then to a twofold
conclusion:
  1. With the exception of Peter, whose matrimonial status is confirmed
by the Synoptics, nothing certain can be said about the apostles. The
variety of patristic testimonies confirms that there was no oral tradition
of a sufficiently general and constant nature to support that one had had
a wife and children while another had been single. There are two exceptions, though: the case of the Apostle John, whom a quasi-unanimous
majority recognized as having been a virgin; and that of Paul, of whom
a majority of Fathers say that he had never been married or in any case
was a widower.
  2. On the other hand, if the scriptural texts themselves do not enable
us to know what kind of lives the apostles led after their call, the Fathers,
on their part, are unanimous in declaring that those who might have
been married then gave up their marital lives and practiced perfect continence. On this point their common opinion constitutes an authoritative hermeneutics of the scriptural texts in which reference is made to
the detachment practiced by Christ's disciples, especially Mt 19:27 and

---

[75] *Quaestiones Veteris et Novi Testamenti*, 127, 33–36. CSEL 50, 414–16.

[76] *Ep.* 118, 4. Trans. J. Labourt, Coll. "Budé", VI, p. 93. See also *Adversus Jovinianum*,
I, 26: Jerome concedes momentarily to Jovinian that certain apostles might have been
married, but he immediately adds: "Raised then to the apostolate, they abandoned the
obligations of conjugal life [Qui assumptit postea in Apostolatum, relinquunt officium
conjugale]" (PL 23, 245b).

Lk 18:28–30.[77] This opinion echoes the official preaching of the early centuries in the great Christian centers (as early as the end of the 2d century and the beginning of the 3d in Alexandria with Clement, for instance, and in Africa with Tertullian). As such it is the expression of the collective memory of the apostolic Churches with regard to the example left by the apostles for future generations. It is, to be sure, an argument from Tradition that cannot be overlooked.

---

[77] "Then Peter spoke: 'What about us?' he said to him. 'We have left *everything* and followed you . . .'" (Mt 19:27). "Then Peter said: 'What about us? We left all we had to follow you.' He said to them: 'I tell you solemnly, there is no one who has left house, *wife*, brothers, parents, or *children* for the sake of the kingdom of God, who will not be given repayment many times over in this present time, and in the world to come, eternal life'" (Lk 18:28–30) (emphasis added).

J. P. Audet claimed that the Twelve, and Paul himself, did not "leave everything" (and certainly not their wives) to live immediately their apostolic existence in freedom, but that they arranged for long periods of time during which they continued to handle their family obligations. "Among such considerations of necessity and motives of propriety", he assures us, "there was certainly room for a just attention to family situations already in place. Everything leads us to think that, in fact, such an attention was not lacking. Our narratives did not say anything about this because at the time, and in that environment, people understood one another well, and it was self-understood, so to speak. Nothing more" (J. P. Audet, *Mariage et célibat dans le service pastoral de l'Église* [Paris, 1967], p. 75). Such an opinion does not seem exact to us. Whether they had left or not left the conjugal home, the apostles might very well have adopted detachment in their lives, as the Fathers suggest, and abstained from sexual intercourse, with an inner freedom that did not exclude visiting their wives and even living in the same house. Would the apostles have been incapable of living what generations of priests lived later?

CHAPTER FIVE

Instances of Clerics Who Were Married and Family Men during the First Seven Centuries of the Church

The Christian communities of the early centuries, living as they did with the memory of the apostles still fresh in their minds, considered the presence of married bishops, priests, and deacons in their midst to be a normal condition. With the exception of sects such as the Encratites, all the Churches, whether in the East or in the West, saw the elevation of monogamous men to the ranks of the priestly hierarchy as consistent with a proper regard for the dignity of the sacrament of marriage, as well as with the Lord's decision to call Simon Peter, and very likely one or more other family men, to leave everything to follow him and to make up the apostolic group.

The fact is generally attested, as we have seen, by the first legislative documents relative to celibacy-continence, which presuppose a background of many concrete instances of sacred ministers bound by marriage. This general certainty is corroborated by the examples found in contemporary history. The studies on the origins of priestly celibacy always gave married clerics a certain place, inviting, as it were, those ordained husbands of the early centuries to come forth and testify about how they really lived. Such testimonies were unfortunately too often invoked for polemical purposes that did not favor any objective inquiry. Today's common conviction is that history and truth can only gain from as exact as possible a knowledge of reality. In this spirit, we have therefore attempted, using all available sources, to make a list of married clerics so as to obtain a broad enough basis for reflection.

Nowadays, historians have better tools than their predecessors for this kind of research, thanks to the critical editions and remarkable apparatus available to them. We think that the moment has come for an inventory, which would be, if not exhaustive, at least systematic. We would like to offer in the following catalog a modest contribution to such a project, though a complete inventory would demand more time and means than we were able to devote to it. We consulted some of the ecclesiastical histories of the early centuries,[1] the main works of the patristic authors, and, in a certain measure, epigraphy.[2] There remains, especially in epigraphy, a rather large field for additional research. We apologize for the involuntary omissions that certainly occurred in our text, and thank all those who will be kind enough to share with us their criticisms and suggestions.

The biographical notices are grouped into four main categories, suggested by the data we were able to collect: (I) Catholic Church (East and West); (II) Nestorian Church (Persia); (III) Novatian Church; (IV) Pelagian Church. The first category is, of course, the most important. For each century we give in alphabetical order the names of the married bishops (if there were any); then those of the priests, deacons, and deaconesses; and, last, those of the subdeacons. There is no reason to be surprised that the bishops' lists are generally longer, since the documents of those days stressed the most important figures. Each biographical notice gives the name of the cleric, then the place where he exercised his functions, a date (generally that of his death or of his ordination), and his matrimonial and family status as the sources indicate it.[3] For convenience we have given after each notice the bibliographical references

---

[1] With regard to the Greek writers, we are speaking in particular of the ecclesiastical histories by Eusebius of Caesarea, Socrates, Sozomenes, and Theodoret of Cyrus; and the fragments still remaining from the works of Philostorges, Theodore the Lector, and Evagrius the Scholastic. The *Collection of Ancient Historians of Armenia*, translated into French and published under the title *Collection des Historiens anciens et modernes de l'Arménie* by Victor Langlois, and the modern critical editions of the *Narratio rerum Armeniae* and of *The Book of Agathangelo* were used for the Armenian Church. As to the Syriac sphere, the *Chronicon Ecclesiasticum* of Bar Hebraeus and the historico-chronological commentary of J. A. Assemani were our main sources of information. As far as the Latin authors go, we have especially studied the histories or chronicles of Rufinus of Aquilea, Sulpicius Severus, Paulus Orosius, Prosper of Aquitaine, Idacius d'Aquae Flaviae, Victor of Vita, Victor of Tunnunum, Gregory of Tours, Isidore of Seville, and Bede the Venerable.

[2] We think that we have collected all the epigraphic data on married clerics included in the works of E. Diehl, *Inscriptiones latinae christianae veteres*, Berolini, I (1925), II (1927), III (1931), reprinted by J. Moreau (Berolini, 1961), and in the very useful *Appendice prosopographique à la Roma Christiana (311–440)*, by Charles Pietri. On the other hand, we were able to conduct only a few researches in the huge bodies of Greek and Latin inscriptions (CIG, CIL, ICUR, NS), which certainly include other inscriptions bearing upon our study.

[3] If we happen to omit the notation "married" when talking about a cleric who was a family man, it is because the sources themselves have no indication of a wife, but it goes without saying that the cleric had his children from a legitimate marriage.

that yielded the information. We have to stress that these references are limited to passages or texts informing us with certainty that the cleric in question had a wife or children, though, of course, they do not give all the biographical information about the person. Here and there a note brings forth some details and precisions that seemed to us useful in better bringing out the person we were studying and perhaps facilitating a better knowledge of his conjugal status. We mention especially in these notes all the cases of married clerics who were publicly known as having lived in continence and for whom the fact has been historically attested. The notices that have no biographical information are those of clerics about whom there is no sufficiently precise biographical data to affirm directly that they observed continence with their wives or that they continued having intercourse. It is indirectly that we can, at least in certain cases, clarify the matter.

I
CATHOLIC CHURCH
(East and West)

IST CENTURY

Married bishops

1. Anonymous bishop. Of Sinopus (Pontus, late 1st century), father of Marcion. [Epiphanius, *Panarion* (*Adversus Haereses*), Haer. 42, 1, 3–4 (GCS 31, 94).]

Married deacons

2. NICOLAS. Deacon of Jerusalem (1st century), married.[4] [Acts of the Apostles, 6:5. Clement of Alexandria, *Stromata* III, 52–53.]

---

[4] This Nicolas, proselyte of Antioch, is one of the seven deacons installed by the apostles for the "service at the tables". A tradition says that he had a pretty wife and that, in order to vindicate himself from the reproach of jealousy with regard to her, he "surrendered her to whoever would want to marry her". That action seems to be the origin of the narrative crediting Deacon Nicolas with the start of the heresy referred to as of the "Nicolaitans", whose initiates, among other things, were known for their great moral laxity. This is probably a confusion caused by a misinterpreted legend. Clement of Alexandria sets things straight in the following way: "He [Nicolas] had, it is said, a wife in the prime of life. After the Savior's Ascension, the apostles reproached Nicolas for being jealous; then he brought his wife to the midst [of the assembly] and surrendered her to whoever would want to marry her. It is said that his action was in conformity with the formula 'one must not pay much attention to the flesh'. And when they imitate his action and words simply and without studying them, those who follow his heresy prostitute themselves in a shameful way. As for myself, I know from hearsay that Nicolas never knew another woman but the one he married, and his daughters grew old as virgins, his son also remaining chaste. If these things were true, then the surrender in the midst of the apostles of the wife who was an object of jealousy was a renunciation of passion, and continence with regard to seeking pleasures, once pursued with the keenest alacrity, showed that he had learned to pay little attention to the flesh. He did not want, as far as I can tell, to serve two masters—the Lord and pleasure—conforming himself to the Savior's commandment" (*Stromata*, III, 52–53, related by Eusebius, *Hist. Eccl.*, III, 29, 2–3. SCh 31, 139–40. Theodoret of Cyrus agrees with Clement; see *Haereticarum fabularum compendium*, III, 1. PG 83, 402b–c). However, we must also make note of the testimony of Irenaeus of Lyon, who links the heresy of the Nicolaitans to Deacon Nicolas: "The Nicolaitans had

2D CENTURY

Married priests

3. VALENS. Priest of Philippi (2d century), married.[5] [Polycarp of Smyrna, *Letter to the Philippians XI*, 1, 4 (SCh 10, 189, 191).]

Married deacons

4. Anonymous deacon (Asia, 2d century), married.[6] [Irenaeus of Lyon, *Adversus Haereses*, I, 5 (PG 7, 588a–b).]

---

their master in Nicolas, one of the first seven deacons installed by the apostles. They live without restraints. The Revelation of John plainly shows who they are: they teach that fornication and eating the flesh offered to idols are indifferent matters. Thus Scripture says about them: 'It is in your favor, nevertheless, that you loathe as I do what the Nicolaitans are doing' (Rev 2:6)" (*Adversus Haereses*, I, 26, 3. SCh 264, 349). The *Philosophoumena* of Hippolytus of Rome also deem that Deacon Nicolas was a heresiarch (VII, 36, 2–3. GCS 26, 223). Whatever the actual facts were, we can retain the information that Deacon Nicolas was married and made, albeit in a singular fashion, a public profession of continence. Did he remain faithful to his plan of life, as Clement testifies, or did he fall later on into license? This cannot be answered with certainty, but in any event it is not explicitly said that he separated from his wife after having been chosen as deacon and in consequence of the choice. The story related by Clement might well have been anterior to the institution of the Seven by the apostles.

[5] Here is the passage of Polycarp's letter about this Valens: XI, 1—"I was quite sad about Valens, who had been a priest with you for some time, [to see] that he misunderstands to such a degree the responsibility you gave him. I therefore warn you to abstain from greed and to be pure, chaste, and true. Abstain from all that is evil. . . .

"Thus, I am quite sad for him and his wife; may the Lord grant them true repentance" (4). Of what fault had priest Valens been guilty? P. T. Camelot points out, in a note to his translation in *Sources Chrétiennes*: "The context and the repeated allusions to greed lead us to believe that this priest, about whom we know nothing, was carried away by love of money to the extent of doing some prevarications that made him lose his dignity" (*Letter to the Philippians*, XI, 1).

[6] We learn from St. Irenaeus that the wife of that deacon let herself be seduced by Mark the magician:

"That selfsame Mark also uses potions and charms, if not with all women, at least with some of them, in order to dishonor their bodies. . . . A deacon, one of ours who are in Asia, received him in his house and fell into the following mishap: his wife, who was beautiful, was corrupted in spirit and body by that magician and followed him for a long time; then she was converted with great difficulty by the brothers and spent the rest of her life in penance, weeping and lamenting over the corruption that she had undergone because of that magician" (*Adversus Haereses*, I, 13, 5. SCh 264, 201).

3D CENTURY

Married bishops

5. CHEREMON. Bishop of Nilopolis (3d century), married.[7] [Eusebius of Caesarea, *Historia Ecclesiastica* VI, XLII, 3 (SCh 41, 151–52).]

6. DEMETRIAN. Bishop of Antioch (3d century), father of Bishop Domnus, who succeeded him.[8] [Eusebius of Caesarea, *Historia Ecclesiastica* VII, XXX, 17 (SCh 41, 219).]

7. DEMETRIUS. Patriarch of Alexandria († 231), married.[9] [B. Evetts, ed., trans., *History of the Patriarchs of the Coptic Church of Alexandria, I. Saint Mark to Thomas (300)*. Arabic text with notes by B. Evetts (PO I, pp. 154ff.).]

[7] It was about the martyrs of the Decian persecution in Alexandria that Eusebius relates the story of this bishop Cheremon: "What should one say about the multitude of those who arrived in the deserts and mountains, suffering from hunger and thirst, frost, sickness, brigands, and wild beasts? Those who survived are bearing witness to their election and victory. I will relate, to prove it, a fact about one of them. Cheremon was very old and the bishop of a town called Nilopolis. Having fled to the mountain of Arabia with his woman companion (ἅμα τῇ συμβίῳ ἑαυτοῦ), he had not come back, and the brothers, though they looked for a long time, could never find them or their bodies."

[8] This bishop is mentioned in the letter that members of the Council of Antioch sent to Pope Denys (255–68), to Maximus of Alexandria, and "to all the provinces" to advise them of the sentence of excommunication that they had decided to pronounce against the leader of the Antioch heresy, Paul of Samosata. At the end of their letter, which has been passed on to us by Eusebius, we read: "We have thus been compelled, after having excommunicated this adversary of God [Paul of Samosata], in spite of his resistance, to replace him in the Catholic Church with another bishop (and this, we are convinced, through God's Providence): the son of Blessed Demetrian who presided gloriously before him over the same Christian community, Domnus, [a man] gifted with all the qualities fitting a bishop; and we are advising you of this so that you will write to him and receive from him letters of communion" (Eusebius, *Hist. Eccl.*, VII, XXX, 17).

[9] Demetrius was the first bishop of Alexandria (189–231) mentioned in history (see, in particular, Eusebius, *Hist. Eccl.*, V, V, 22; VI, 2, 3, 8, 19, 26). He was at first Origen's protector, but his feelings changed later on and he had Origen deposed by a council gathered for that purpose. *The History of the Patriarchs of Alexandria*, compiled toward the end of the 10th century by Severus of El-Eschmounein (Upper Egypt), relates a tradition mixed with legends, according to which Demetrius, married at the age of fifteen by his parents, had always been continent with his wife, in mutual agreement with her. Such a circumstance, once known, would have put an end to the suspicions of the local Christian community who, hearing about his election, had been upset that for the first time in the Church of Alexandria's history a married man had been chosen to succeed Mark the Evangelist. It is not possible to trust the *History* of Severus of El-Eschmounein fully, because he likes wonder stories too much, but that *Liber Pontificalis* of the Coptic Church, as it is sometimes called, may have retained a historical foundation beneath the legend.

8. IRENAEUS. Bishop of Sirmium (3d century), married, with children.[10] [*Acta Sanctorum Martii*, III (1668), pp. 555–57; *Acta graeca*, p. 23].

9. MARTIAL. Bishop of Merida (ca. 254), father of several sons. [Cyprian, *Ep.* 67, 6 (CSEL III, 2 740. Trans. Bayard, Coll. "Budé", II, pp. 231–32).]

Married priests

10. CECILIAN. Priest (Carthage, middle 3d century), married, with children.[11] [Pontius the Deacon, *Vita Caecilii Cypriani*, 4 (CSEL 3–3, XCIV, 21–XCV, 6).]

11. NOVATUS. Priest of Carthage (3d century), married.[12] [Cyprian, *Ep.* 52, 2, 5 (CSEL 3–2, 619. Trans. Bayard, Coll. "Budé", II, p. 127).]

[10] The *Acts* of the martyrdom of Irenaeus, bishop of Sirmium, in lower Pannonia, were published by the Bollandists using a famous martyrology of the Bodecennis convent, then owned by the Canons Regular of the diocese of Paderborn. They would go back to great antiquity and relate, almost word for word, the original account of the martyrdom. Here are the passages related to the wife and children of Bishop Irenaeus: "At that point his parents arrived and, seeing him thus tortured, threw themselves at his feet and begged him to take pity on his young age and to obey the orders of the emperor. His father, on one side, his wife and children on the other, clung to him, weeping; the servants also voiced their grief and moanings; the cries of his neighbors' affliction were heard, the lamentations of his friends; all cried with one voice: 'Have pity on your tender youth. . . .' [Several days later,] Probus [the governor] asked him: 'Do you have a wife?' St. Irenaeus answered: 'I do not have one.' Probus asked: 'Do you have sons or daughters?' St. Irenaeus replied: 'I do not have any.' Probus asked: 'Do you have parents?' St. Irenaeus answered: 'I do not.' Probus asked: 'What about those who were here and beseeched you with their tears during the last interrogatory?' St. Irenaeus replied: 'I have fulfilled the precept of my Lord Jesus Christ: "He who does not deny his parents and does not renounce all that he owns cannot be my disciple; and he who loves his father or his mother or his wife or his children, his brothers, and relatives more than he loves me is not worthy of me." This is why he who truly loves God and directs his heart perfectly toward his promise despises all earthly things and confesses that he has no parents besides him' " (*Acta Sanctorum Martii*, III, p. 556).

[11] Here is the passage from his life of St. Cyprian, in which Pontius the Deacon tells us about the priest Cecilian:
"He was still very close to Cecilian, one of ours, a just man whose memory is worthy of praise, then a priest as much in age as in dignity. It was he who had led Cyprian away from the error of the world and toward the knowledge of true divinity. Cyprian had for him an affection full of respect and homage, considering him with deference and veneration, not as his equal or friend of his soul, but as the father of his new life. Finally, many signs of esteem and a very great and well-deserved affection so moved him [Cecilian] that when he was about to leave this world and die, he entrusted his wife and children to Cyprian. To the one who was his companion through the sharing of a same way of life he bequeathed all his family affections."

[12] Writing to Pope Cornelius, Cyprian paints a portrait of Novatus, which is a genuine indictment: "Always thirsty for novelties, carried away by unquenchable greed and rapacity, full of extreme arrogance, inflated with an insane pride, always seen in an unfavorable

12. NUMIDICUS. Priest of Carthage (3d century), married and father of a daughter.[13] [Cyprian, *Ep.* 40, 1, 1 (CSEL 3–2, 585–86. Trans. Bayard, Coll. "Budé", II, p. 101).]

13. SATURNINUS. Priest of Abitina (Africa, 3d century), father of four children, two of whom were the lectors Saturninus and Felix. They all suffered martyrdom. [*Acta Sanctorum Februarii*, II (1658), pp. 515–19.]

14. TERTULLIAN. Priest(?) (Africa, † after 220), married. [Jerome, *De viris inlustribus*, 53. Ed. E. Richardson, TU XIV, 31–32. Tertullian, *Ad uxorem* I–II. CC 1, 373ff.]

4TH CENTURY

Married bishops

15. AJAX. Bishop of Botolius (Syria, 4th century), married and father of three children.[14] [Sozomenus, *Historia Ecclesiastica*, VII, 28 (GCS 50, 344).]

---

light by the bishops, always condemned by the voice of all the pontiffs as a heretic and pervert, always eager to betray, flattering [people] to dupe them, never faithful in love, he is a torch, a firebrand setting the fires of seditious discords, a whirlwind, a storm causing shipwrecks in the faith, a troublemaker, an adversary of tranquility, an enemy of peace" (Bayard, Coll. "Budé", II, p. 126).

That dangerous individual did not hesitate to commit any crime: "[He] robbed orphans, fleeced widows, and even denied the Church her rightful dues: all of these victims cry out for his excesses to be punished. He let his father starve in his house and did not even give him a burial. He kicked his wife in the belly with his heel and made her lose a child before its term, causing an abortion and a parricide. And now he dares condemn the hands of those who sacrifice, while his feet are more criminal because he used them to kill the son who was going to be born to him!" (Bayard, Coll. "Budé", II, p. 127). In this way, we find out that Novatus was married.

[13] Cyprian praises the priest Numidicus in a letter to his clergy and announces the reason for enrolling him with the priests of Carthage: "He exhorted a glorious phalanx of martyrs who have left before him, stoned to death or set on fire; and while his faithful wife was being consumed—or, rather, preserved—with the others, he looked at her in the flames with joy. He himself was half-burnt, stoned, and left for dead. It is only later that his daughter, looking in tears for the body of her father, found him barely breathing. Pulled out from among the other victims, he stayed regretfully behind the companions he had sent to heaven before him. The reason was, as we see it, that God wanted to add him to our clergy and to give to our group, heartbroken by the fall of certain priests, the adornment of glorious priests."

[14] Ajax had a very beautiful wife. She gave him three children; then he practiced continence and led a monastic life before being elected bishop of Botolius.

16. ANASTASIUS I. Pope (399–402), father of Pope Innocent I(?), his successor.[15] [Jerome, *Ep.* 130, 16 (PL 22, 1120a. Trans. J. Labourt, Coll. "Budé", VII, p. 187).]

17. Anonymous bishop (Italy, 4th century), father of the Deacon Florentius. [A. Ferrua, *Epigrammata Damasiana*, 68, 5 (1942), p. 242. C. Pietri, *Appendice prosopographique*, p. 387. Deacons attested in Rome at the time of Pope Damasus (366–84).]
(N.B.: This is perhaps the same person as in no. 30.)

18. Anonymous bishops (six) (Ephesus area, 4th century), married. [Palladius, *Dialogus historicus de vita et conversatione Beati Joanni Chrysostomi*, XV (PG 47, 51b. Ed. P. R. Coleman-Norton [Cambridge, 1928], p. 90).]

19. ANTONINUS. Bishop of Ephesus (4th century), married with children.[16] [Palladius, *Dialogus historicus de vita et conversatione Beati Joanni Chrysostomi*, XIII (PG 47, 47d–49a. Ed. P. R. Coleman-Norton [Cambridge, 1928], pp. 83–84).]

20. ANTONIUS. Bishop (*sacerdos*) of a suburban diocese of Rome. Husband of Laurentia; father of Pope Damasus (366–84).[17] [O. Marucchi, "Osservatione storiche ed epigrafiche sulla iscrizione recentemente scoperta della madre del papa Damaso", *Nuovo Bulletino di archeologia cristiana*, nos. 1–3 (Rome, 1903), pp. 59ff. A. Ferrua, *Epigrammata Damasiana*, 57 (1942), p. 210. L. Duchesne, *Liber Pontificalis*, I, p. 212. C. Pietri, *Appendice prosopographique à la Roma Christiana* (311–440), MEFRA, 89, 1 (1977), p. 385.]

---

[15] It was in a letter to the virgin Demetrius that Jerome wrote: "Keep the faith of St. Innocent, who is the son and successor in the apostolic chain of the man about whom I just spoke [i.e., Anastasius I], and do not receive any outside doctrine no matter how learned and ingenious it appears to you." The Christian literature of antiquity frequently uses the words *father* and *son* in order to express bonds of spiritual kinship and filiation. It is not impossible that such would be the case here, in this passage of St. Jerome, who is, moreover, the only one to mention these bonds of kinship between Anastasius I and Innocent. But the possibility of a carnal kinship is not to be excluded and would not be surprising in itself.

[16] In the year 400, Bishop Antoninus, metropolitan of Ephesus, was denounced before a council held in Constantinople by Eusebius, bishop of Valentinopolis. Seven counts were leveled against Antoninus. The sixth accused him "of having resumed common life with his wife, after separating from her, and sired children [ἕκτον, ὅτι ἀποταξάμενος τῆς οἰκείας γαμετῆς, πάλιν αὐτῇ συνῆλθεν, καὶ ἐπαιδοποίησεν ἐξ αὐτῆς]". The bishops of the synod, presided over by St. John Chrysostom, judged at the close of their deliberations that each of the counts (leveled against Antoninus) was absolutely in opposition to the holy laws (ἐν τοῦ ἑρὸς κεφαλαίου δυσσεβές ἐστι, καὶ ἀπηγορευμένον πανταξόθεν τοῖς ἱεροῖς νόμοις).

[17] The inscription informs us that the mother of Damasus lived to the age of eighty-nine and perhaps even to ninety-two years. She lived in continence for sixty years.

21. ARTEMIUS. Bishop of Auvergne (ca. 400), married.[18] [Gregory of Tours, *Libri Historiarum decem*, I, 46 (MGH, *scr. mer.* I, 1, ed. 2a [1951], p. 30. Gregory of Tours, *Histoire des Francs*, trans. R. Latouche [Coll. Classiques de l'histoire de France au Moyen-âge] 2 vols., 1963–65 [hereafter cited as Latouche], I, p. 64).]

22. ASRUG. Bishop of Pakravant (Armenia, 4th century), married, son-in-law of Bishop Khat, his predecessor. [Faustus of Byzantium, IV, 12 (Victor Langlois, *Collection des Historiens anciens et modernes de l'Arménie*, I [= *Fragmenta Historicorum Graecorum*, V, 2], [Paris, n.d. (1867)], p. 248).]

23. CARTERIUS. Spanish bishop (late 4th century), married once before his baptism and a second time after.[19] [Jerome, *Ep.* 69, 2 (CSEL 54, 680).]

24. EULALIUS. Bishop of Caesarea (Cappadocia, early 4th century), father of Eusthatius of Sebastus. [Socrates, *Historia Ecclesiastica*, II, 43 (PG 67, 352b). Sozomenus, *Historia Ecclesiastica*, IV, 24 (GCS 50, 180).]

25. GREGORY. Bishop of Nyssa († 379), married(?). Husband of Theosebia(?).[20] [Gregory Nazianzen, *Ep.* 197 (PG 37, 321a–24b). Gregory of Nyssa, *De Virginitate*, III, 1 (SCh 119, 273–77).]

---

[18] Artemius, ambassador to Spain, was cured by St. Nepotian, bishop of Auvergne. Later, St. Gregory of Tours writes, "Forgetting his earthly wife as well as his personal goods, he united himself to the Church and became a cleric; his sanctity was such that he was called to succeed blessed Nepotian to lead the folds of the Lord's flock."

[19] Oceanus, friend of St. Jerome, had been surprised to see that a man remarried after his baptism was admitted to the episcopate. Jerome answered that there was nothing contrary in that to the commandments of St. Paul, adding: "I am surprised that you named only one, while the whole world is full of such ordinations. I am not talking about priests or lower ministers: I am thinking about the bishops; if I wanted to make a list of their names, the total would be so high as to surpass the multitude gathered at the Synod of Rimini." In his *Apologia adversus libros Rufini*, St. Jerome tempered that affirmation and spoke only about several bishops: "*istiusmodi sacerdotes in Ecclesiis esse nonnullos*" (PL 23, 424c). The council held during the spring of 359 in Rimini (a suburb of Rome) by order of Emperor Constantius gathered four hundred Western bishops.

[20] It does seem that Gregory of Nyssa was married before he reached the episcopate, as can be understood in a passage of his treatise on virginity: "Why am I not myself capable of benefiting from such a zeal! . . . But in fact my knowledge of the beauties of virginity is, as it were, vain and useless, as are the ears of wheat for the muzzled ox circling around the threshing floor or as water running at the bottom of an abyss is for a thirsty man. Blessed are those to whom the choice of the superior goods is still possible and who have not been walled in by having been first caught in the common life; this is the case for us, who are separated as if by a chasm from this title of glory of virginity, to which no one can return once he has set foot in the life of the world. We are thus reduced to contemplate beauties that are alien and to witness the beatitude of others" (III, I. SCh 119, 273–75). M. Aubineau, the translator in *Sources Chrétiennes*, thinks, quite rightly, that this confession is self-explanatory (ibid., p. 66). That was also the opinion of the Bollandists Henchius and Papebroch (*Acta Sanctorum Martii*, II [1668], p. 5). Gregory Nazianzen, in a letter of

26. GREGORY THE ELDER. Bishop of Nazianzen (373), husband of Nonna, father of Gregory Nazianzen, Gorgonia and Cesarius of Nazianzen.[21] [Gregory Nazianzen, *Oratio* XVIII (PG 35, 985b); *Epitaphia* LV–LXV (PG 38, 37–44).]

27. GREGORY THE ILLUMINATOR. First Armenian Katholikos († ca. 328). Husband of Mary and father of two sons: the younger, Aristakes, was the first successor of his father; the eldest, Verthanes, succeeded Aristakes and was the third Katholikos.[22] [Agathangelo, *Histoire du règne de Tiridate et de la prédication de saint Grégoire l'Illuminateur traduite pour la première fois en français sur le texte arménien accompagné de la version grecque* (V. Langlois, *Collection*, I [= C. Muller, *Fragmenta Historicorum graecorum*, V, *pars altera*], CXXIII [159], CXXIV [160–61], CXXVII [169], [Paris, 1867], pp. 183–85, 190). G. Garitte, *Documents pour l'étude du livre d'Agathange* (Rome, 1946), pp. 71 and 307–8. G. Lafontaine, *La version grecque ancienne du livre arménien d'Agathange*, critical edition (1973), (158–59), pp. 329–31; (168), pp. 339–40. G. Garitte, *La narratio de rebus Armeniae*, critical edition with commentary, CSCO 132, Subsidia vol. 4 (1952), pp. 27, 55, 415. Moses of Khorene, II, 80 (V. Langlois, *Collection*, II [1869], p. 121). Faustus of Byzantium, III, 2 (V. Langlois, *Collection*, I [1867], pp. 210–11). *Généaologie de la famille du saint Grégoire*, I (V. Langlois, *Collection*, II [1869], p. 21). Zenobius of Glag, *Histoire de Daron* (V. Langlois, *Collection*, I [1867], p. 343).]

---

sympathy to his friend Gregory of Nyssa, praises one Theosebia, described as "woman companion of a priest" (ἱερέως σύζυγον) (Gregory Nazianzen, *Ep.* 197. PG 37, 321c–324a). What meaning can we give here to the word σύζυγος? We have seen the various interpretations that the term used by St. Paul in his epistle to the Philippians received (see above, pp. 75ff.). It is not certain that it should be translated here as *wife*. If such were the case, we would still have to find out what kind of a life the couple was leading after Gregory's election to the episcopate (371) and until the death of Theosebia (385). In our opinion, M. Aubineau dismisses too quickly the idea that they could have lived in perfect continence; we have more than one example of married clerics who lived in such a way during the early centuries of the Church.

[21] For discussion of the problems concerning Gregory the Elder, already a bishop when he sired Gregory Nazianzen, the reader should refer to pp. 242ff. of this work.

[22] The book of Agathangelo relates that King Tiridates, converted to the Christian faith, was looking for men capable of one day succeeding Gregory the Illuminator as Katholikos of Armenia. Then, proceeds the narrative, "some of those who knew him warned the king that St. Gregory, when he was a youth, had been married and had had two sons, the first called Verthanes [a secular and also a priest] and the second Rhesdagues [Aristakès], who had been raised since childhood in God's service. The latter had entered an order of solitary monks . . ." (Agathangelo, *Histoire du règne de Tiridate*, p. 183). The narrative leads to the conclusion that Gregory had not lived with his wife for a long time; she might even already have been dead. A new Greek recension of the book of Agathangelo, published by G. Garitte, includes an episode relating that Gregory, freed after a reclusion of fifteen years in a dungeon of the castle of Artaschat and then elected bishop, did not want to resume conjugal life and proposed that his wife, because she could not live with him, be responsible for the service of the holy virgins in the churches of the kingdom (G. Garitte, *Documents pour l'étude du livre d'Agathange* [1946], pp. 307–8).

28. HILARY. Bishop of Poitiers († 367), married and father of a daughter named Apra.[23] [Venantius Fortunatus, *Vita Sancti Hilarii* III, VI, XIII (MGH, *auct. ant.*, IV, 2 [1881], pp. 2–3, 6).]

29. KHAT. Bishop of Pakravant (Armenia, 4th century), father of two daughters, father-in-law of his successor, Bishop Asrug. [Faustus of Byzantium, IV, 12 (V. Langlois, *Collection*, I [1867], pp. 247–48).]

30. LEO. Bishop (Italy, 4th century), husband of Laurentia, father of the Deacon Florentius. [G. B. de Rossi, "Il monumento d'un ignoto S. Leone vescovo e martire, nell'agro Verano", *Bulletino di Archeologia cristiana* (Rome, 1864), pp. 54f. Diehl 997, 13; 1231, 5f. Undated, but Pope Damasus could be the author of the inscription (366–84).]
(N.B.: This is perhaps the same person as in no. 17).

31. LEONTIUS. Bishop of Tripoli (deposed in 359), father of a son. [Ada Adler, ed., *Suidae Lexicon*, pt. III (1933), p. 245.]

32. MARCELLUS. Bishop of Apamea, Syria (4th century), with children. [Sozomenus, *Historia Ecclesiastica*, VII, 15, 15 (GCS 50, 322).]

33. MEMORIUS. Bishop of Southern Italy (late 4th century), husband of Juliana; father of Julian, future bishop of Eclanus, and of two daughters. [Paulinus of Nola, *Carmina* 25, 199, 201, 213, 215, 219, 222, 225, 239, 241 (CSEL 30, 244–45). Marius Mercator, *Commonitorium adversum haeresim Pelagii et Caelestii vel etiam scripta Juliani*, 7 (E. Schwartz, ACO, I, V [1924–26], pp. 9, 26–36). Augustine, *Contra Julianum I*, VI, 1, 12 (PL 44, 647c).]

34. NERSES THE GREAT. Armenian Katholikos († 374). Grandson of Yusik and great-grandson of Gregory the Illuminator. Husband of Santukhd, and father of the Katholikos Sahak the Great (Isaac).[24] [G. Garitte, *La narratio de rebus Armeniae*, pp. 61–62, 417. Moses of Khorene, III, 16, 20 (V. Langlois, *Collection* II [1869], pp. 141–43). Faustus of Byzantium, IV, 3 (ibid., I, p. 236). *Généalogie*, I (ibid., II, p. 22).]

---

[23] A passage in the life of St. Hilary by Venantius Fortunatus clearly implies that the bishop of Poitiers had separated from his wife: "Now, in those days, it was known by a revelation of the Holy Spirit that a young man of high nobility, extremely rich and handsome, was seeking to marry his blessed daughter Apra, whom he had left with her mother in Aquitaine" (MGH, *auct. ant.*, IV, 2, p. 3).

[24] Nerses had first been the chamberlain of the king. His wife died after three years of marriage, leaving him an only son, the future Sahak the Great. It was only a few years later that Nerses was elected Katholikos of Armenia and consecrated by Eusebius of Caesarea.

35. PACIAN. Bishop of Barcelona († between 379 and 392), father of the pretorium prefect Dexterus.[25] [Jerome, *De viris inlustribus*, 106, 132 (PL 23, 742b, 755a). Ed. E. Richardson, TU XIV, 1a (1896), pp. 49, 55).]

36. PELAGIUS. Bishop of Laodicea (4th century), married.[26] [Theodoret of Cyrus, *Historia Ecclesiastica*, IV, 12 2–3 (GCS 44, 233).]

37. PETRONIUS DEXTRUS. Bishop († 322), father of five sons. [Diehl 1027. Clusii, *Inscr.*: ca. 322.]

38. PHÂREN. Armenian patriarch (early 4th century), father of the bishop John. [Faustus of Byzantium, III, 16; VI, 8, 10 (V. Langlois, *Collection*, I, [1867], pp. 308–9).]

39. PHILEAS. Bishop of Thmuis (Egypt † ca. 304, 307), married with children.[27] [Eusebius of Caesarea, *Historia Ecclesiastica*, VIII, 9, 7–8 (SCh 55, 19).]

40. PHILOGONIUS. Bishop of Antioch (ca. 386), married and father of a daughter. [John Chrysostom, *De beato Philogonio* (PG 48, 751b).]

41. RETICIUS. Bishop of Autun (ca. 314), married.[28] [Gregory of Tours, *Libri in gloria Confessorum*, n. 74 (MGH, *scr. mer.*, I, 2 [1885], pp. 791–92).]

42. SEVERUS. Archbishop of Ravenna († 348), husband of Vincentia, father of a daughter called Innocentia.[29] [*Acta Sanctorum Februarii*, I (1658), pp. 79, 86. *Vita et translatio S. Severi auctore Liutolfo presbytero* (MGH, *script.*,

---

[25] At n. 106 of his *De viris inlustribus*, St. Jerome talks about Bishop Pacian as a man "castitate et eloquentia, et tam vita quam sermone clarus". The fact that St. Jerome, ardent advocate of priestly continence, praised the chastity of Pacian leads us reasonably to suppose that he was already a widower or separated from his wife.

[26] Pelagius persuaded his young wife, during their wedding night, to accept living together as brother and sister.

[27] After having evoked the admirable faith of the martyr Phílomoros, high functionary of Alexandria, Eusebius goes on: "Such also was Phileas, bishop of the Church of Thmuis, a man who had won renown through his public functions and responsibilities in his country as well as through his knowledge of philosophy. When a great number of their kin or friends, as well as the magistrates in office and even the judge himself, begged them to have pity on themselves and to spare their children and their wives, they were not at all convinced by such reasons to choose love of life and to despise the rules set by our Lord about confession and denial. With a courageous reflection, worthy of the philosophers, or, rather, with a religious soul and friendship for God, they resisted all the threats and insults of the judge, and both were beheaded."

[28] This Reticius, who attended the Council of Arles in 314, was elected bishop after the death of his wife.

[29] The *Vita et translatio S. Severi*, by the priest Ludolfo, relates that in learning the news of Severus' election to the archbishopric of Ravenna, his wife and daughter ran to the church where the unexpected had just taken place; and the narrative adds: "Both took the holy veil on the spot and persevered in a pious life, the one in widowhood and the other in virginity" (*Vita et translatio S. Severi*, MGH, *script.*, XV, 1, p. 289). *Widowhood* must

XV, 1 [1887], pp. 289–93). U. Chevalier, *Répertoire des sources historiques du Moyen-Âge. Bio-bibliothèque*, II (1907), col. 4222.]

43. SIMPLICIUS. Bishop of Autun (ca. 364), married.[30] [Gregory of Tours, *Libri in gloria Confessorum*, n. 75 (MGH, *scr. mer.*, I, 2 [1885], pp. 792–93).]

44. SPIRIDON. Bishop of Trimithus (Cyprus, ca. 325), father of several children, including a daughter called Irene. [Rufinus of Aquilea, *Eusebii Historiarum continuatio*, X, 5 (GCS 9–2, 964). Socrates, *Historia Ecclesiastica*, I, 12 (PG 67, 105a–b). Sozomenus, *Historia Ecclesiastica*, I, 11 (GCS 50, 21–22).]

45. SYMPOSIUS. Bishop of Astorga (Spain, ca. 380, 400), father of Bishop Dictinius, his successor († ca. 420). [*Concilium Toletanum I. Exemplaria professionum in concilio Toletano, contra secta Priscilliani*, Mansi, 3, 1006c–d.]

46. URBICUS. Bishop of Clermont (4th century), married and father of a daughter.[31] [Gregory of Tours, *Libri Historiarum decem*, I, 44 (MGH, *scr. mer.*, I, 1, ed. 2a [1951], pp. 28–29. Latouche, pp. 62–63).]

47. VERTHANES. Armenian Katholikos (early 4th century). Eldest son of Gregory the Illuminator, married and father of twin sons: Yusik, who succeeded him and would be the fourth Armenian Katholikos, and Gregory, future bishop of Iberia and Albania.[32] [G. Garitte, *La narratio de rebus Armeniae*, p. 416. Moses of Khorene, II, 80 (V. Langlois, *Collection*, II [1869], p. 121). Faustus of Byzantium, III, 3, 5 (V. Langlois, *Collection*, I [1867], pp. 211–13). *Généalogie*, I (V. Langlois, *Collection*, II [1869], p. 21).]

---

obviously be understood as a separation of that woman from her husband, now called by the episcopate to a life of continence.

[30] Simplicius had kept his wife with him in the episcopal residence. In order to disarm the suspicions that were caused by such a cohabitation, he obtained from heaven a miracle proving his perfect chastity and led more than a thousand persons to ask for baptism. Gregory of Tours, who relates the event, stresses that the couple had led a life of perfect continence, though that was unknown to their entourage, even before Simplicius was elected to the episcopate: "His fuit castissima, obtegente saeculo, vita, soli Deo cognita, mortalibus tamen ignota."

[31] That bishop was, according to Gregory of Tours, the first successor to Austremonius, founder of the Church of Auvergne (ca. 300). He came from a senatorial family and had converted. The narrative adds: "He had a wife who, according to ecclesiastical custom, had given up any conjugal relations with the bishop and lived in a religious manner" (Quae juxta consuetudinem ecclesiasticam, remota a consortio sacerdotis, religiose vivebat). She, however, did not persevere and managed to persuade her husband to resume conjugal life. A daughter was born, and the bishop went to do penance in a monastery.

[32] According to a chronology that seems to have been established with enough exactitude, Verthanes, oldest son of Gregory the Illuminator, would have been elected to the office of Katholikos of Armenia in 327, i.e., a year before the death of his father (Paul Ananian, "La date et les circonstances du sacre de saint Grégoire l'Illuminateur" [Ital. trans.], in *Le Museon* [1961], pp. 352–54). Now, Gregory the Illuminator would have been born between 253 and 255 (cf. Fr. Tournebize, *Histoire politique et religieuse de l'Arménie*, I [Paris, n.d.],

48. VICTOR. Bishop of Ucresium (Numidia), father of Victor. [ICUR, NS II, 4499. Basilica Ss. Nazari et Naboris. *Inscr.*: a. 404.]

49. YUSIK. Armenian Katholikos (early 4th century). Son of Verthanes, grandson of Gregory the Illuminator. Married and father of twin sons: Pap (Bab) and Athanagines, who would be ordained deacons. Grandfather of Nerses the Great.[33][G. Garitte, *La narration de rebus Armeniae*, pp. 58–59, 416. Moses of Khorene, III, 16 (V. Langlois, *Collection*, II [1869], p. 141). Faustus of Byzantium, III, 5, 15, 19 (V. Langlois, *Collection*, I [1867], pp. 212–13, 227, 229). *Généalogie*, I (V. Langlois, *Collection*, II [1869], pp. 21–22).]

Married priests

50. Anonymous priests (two) (Italy, 4th century), married. [Diehl 994.]

51. ANYSIUS. Priest of Borilla (Cappadocia, middle 4th century), married and father of four sons and a daughter. The latter, called Eulampia, was the mother of the Greek historian Philostorges (born ca. 370). [Philostorges, *Historia Ecclesiastica*, IX, 9 (GCS 21, 119).]

52. APER. Priest (Gaul or Aquitaine, late 4th century), husband of Amanda, with children.[34] [Paulinus of Nola, *Ep*. 39, 1 (CSEL 29, 334); *Ep*. 44 (CSEL 29, 372–77).]

53. APOLLINARIS. Priest (Laodicea, 4th century), father of Bishop Apollinaris, of Laodicea. [Socrates, *Historia Ecclesiastica*, II, 46 (PG 67, 361c–63a). Sozomenus, *Historia Ecclesiastica*, VI, 25 (PG 67, 1362a). Bar Hebraeus, *Chronicon Ecclesiasticum*, edited and translated by J. B. Abbeloos and T. J. Lamy, I (1872), pp. 101–2.]

---

p. 49, n. 1). Supposing that he had married around the age of twenty and his eldest son, Verthanes, would have been born the following year, the birth of the latter would have taken place between 254 and 276. In 327, date of his elevation to the episcopate, Verthanes would then have been between fifty-one and seventy-three years old. His twin sons, Gregory and Yusik, were therefore very certainly already born, even if one wants to take into account the narrative of Faustus of Byzantium, who said, "Though married, Verthanes had no posterity. During many years, he prayed God. . . . In his old age, the Lord rewarded his prayers; his wife conceived and gave birth to twin sons" (V. Langlois, *Collection*, I, p. 212).

[33] Faustus of Byzantium relates that Yusik, "after the first night [of his wedding], did not touch his wife." Yusik's wife was dead when, several years later, he was chosen to succeed his father, Verthanes, to the See of the Katholikos.

[34] That former lawyer who had converted to Christianity was the friend of St. Paulinus of Nola. Having become a priest, he led with his wife, Amanda, a life of continence, as attested by letter 44 of St. Paulinus of Nola. This remarkable letter sheds an interesting light on the role of the *presbyterae*, wives of priests, during that time in the history of the Church.

54. GAUDENTIUS. Priest (Rome), husband of Severa. [ICUR, NS II, 4823. Via Ostiensi. Basilica Beati Pauli Apostoli. C. Pietri, *Appendice prosopographique*, p. 376. Presbyteri attested at the time of Damasus (366–84).]

55. LEONTIUS. Priest (Rome, late 4th century), grandfather of a child of same name who died at the age of eight. [ICUR, NS I, 729. In S. Martini in montibus. Inscription of unknown origin. C. Pietri, *Appendice prosopographique*, p. 378. Presbyteri attested under the pontificates of Siricius and Anastasius (384–401).]

56. LIMENIUS. Priest (Rome), father of a daughter called Victoria. [ICUR, NS III, 8161. Via Ardeatina. Coemeterium Domitillae. C. Pietri, *Appendice prosopographique*, p. 378. Date of the deposition: 395. Presbyteri attested under the pontificates of Siricius and Anastasius (384–401).]

57. MELON. Priest (Melos, in Illyria), married and family man. [CIG IV, 9289. *Meli* (Illyricum) in catacombis Christianorum anno 1844 repertis. *Inscr.*: 3d or 4th century.]

58. PAC. PATROCLUS. Priest (ca. 347), husband of Val. Severa. [Diehl 272a–b (cf. III, p. 392).]

59. POTITUS. Priest (early 4th century), father of the Deacon Calpornius (Kalfurnus). Grandfather of St. Patrick. [*Confessio S. Patricii*, I (PL 53, 801b. L. Bieler, "Liber epistolarum Sancti Patricii Episcopi", *Classica et Mediaevalia*, XI [1950], p. 56).]

Married deacons

60. Anonymous deacon (*altaris minister*) (Florence, late 4th century). Husband of Juliana, father of a son who became a lector and of three daughters, who consecrated their virginity to God.[35] [Ambrose of Milan, *Exhortatio virginitatis*, II, 12; III, 13; IV, 24 (PL 16, 339d, 340b, 343b).]

61. Anonymous deacon (Italy), husband of Nunita. [ICUR, NS V, 13355, Via Appia. Inscriptio coemeterii Subdialis: a. 389. Unknown origin.]

---

[35] The *Exhortatio virginitatis* was pronounced around 393 by St. Ambrose at Florence for the consecration of a church dedicated to the martyrs Vital and Agricola. In chapters 2 to 9, the orator lets speak a widow called Juliana. She had been the wife of a man who, toward the end of his life, had been called to the clergy (probably as a deacon). When he died, Juliana turned to her four children—one son and three daughters—exhorting them to consecrate themselves to God in a life of perfect chastity. She stressed the advantages of consecrated celibacy and, in strong contrast, the inconveniences of married life. Incidentally, we learn that once he had become a cleric her husband had to live with her in continence ("Fecit [Dominus] altaris ministrum, continuoque et mihi et vobis raptus est" [PL 16, 343b]).

62. Anonymous deacon (Rome), married. [ICUR, NS II, 4839. Via Ostiensi. Basilica Beati Pauli Apostoli. *Inscr.*: a. 402.]

63. CALPORNIUS (Kalfurnus). Deacon (late 4th century), husband of Concessa and father of St. Patrick. [*Confessio S. Patricii*, 1 (PL 53, 801b. L. Bieler, "Liber epistolarum Sancti Patricii Episcopi", *Classica et Mediaevalia*, XI [1950], *Confessio*, 1, p. 56). L. Bieler, ibid., *Epistularum deperditarum fragmenta et testimonia*, 2, p. 103.]

64. FL. JULIUS. Deacon (Salonis), husband of Aurel. Ianuaria. [Diehl 1223. Salonis. *Inscr.*: a. 358.]

65. SEVERUS. Deacon (Rome), father of a daughter named Severa. [ICUR, NS IV, 10183. Inter vias Appiam et Ardeatinam. Coemeterium inferius. C. Pietri, *Appendice prosopographique*, p. 385. Deacons attested at the time of Miltiades and Sylvester (311–35).]

5TH CENTURY

Married bishops

66. AMATOR. Bishop of Auxerre († 418), husband of Martha.[36] [Vita S. Amatoris, I (L. M. Duru, *Bibliothèque historique de l'Yonne*, I [Auxerre, 1850], pp. 136–41).]

67. Anonymous bishop (Gaul, early 5th century), father of Senator Germanicus. [Apollinaris Sidonius, *Ep.* IV, 13 (MGH, *scr. mer.*, VIII [1887], p. 65. Trans. A. Loyen, Coll. "Budé", II, p. 142).]

68. Anonymous bishop (Gaul, early 5th century), married.[37] [Pseudo-Jerome, *De septem ordinibus Ecclesiae* (PL 30, 159c–60a. Ed. A. W. Kalff [1938], pp. 62–63, 66). G. Morin, "Pages inédites de deux Pseudo-Jérômes des environs de l'an 400", *Revue Bénédictine* 40 (1928), pp. 310–18: II. "Portion inédite de l'apocryphe hiéronymien de septem ordinibus Ecclesiae". Cf. p. 314.]

69. Anonymous bishop (Gaul, 5th century), grandfather of Projectus "vir clarissimus". [Apollinaris Sidonius, *Ep.* II, 4 (MGH, *auct. ant.*, VIII [1887], p. 27. Trans. A. Loyen, Coll. "Budé", II, p. 55).]

---

[36] If one is to believe the *Vita S. Amatoris*, published by the Bollandists and Father Duru, Amator kept continence with his young wife, Martha, as early as their wedding day.

[37] The addressee of the long letter titled *De septem ordinibus Ecclesiae* was, in all likelihood, a married layman who had been suddenly elevated to the episcopate. By reminding him of the duties of his functions, his correspondent (probably a priest) stresses in particular the continence he must now observe with his wife (who had in fact explicitly agreed to his election): "Because of the ancient custom, and the damage [that could result] for the priesthood, do not give your wife power over your soul. . . . You must love her, of course, but as the Church or temple of God; pray with her, read [with her], observe continence, be in communion [with her] at the altar, but not in the work [of the flesh]. . . . You surely know very well that the use of marriage is forbidden to you as soon as

70. Anonymous bishop (Italy, late 5th century or early 6th), married. [Diehl 1121 + add., vol. II, p. 512. *Inscr.*: a. 491 or 526.]

71. Anonymous bishop (late 5th century), maternal grandfather of Chronopius, bishop of Périgueux. [Venantius Fortunatus, *Carmina* IV, 8 (MGH, *auct. ant.* IV [1881], p. 84). L. Duchesne, *Fastes épiscopaux*, II (1900), p. 87.]

72. Anonymous bishop (late 5th century), father of Chronopius, bishop of Périgueux. [Venantius Fortunatus, *Carmina*, IV, 8 (MGH, *auct. ant.*, IV [1881], p. 84). L. Duchesne, *Fastes épiscopaux*, II (1900) p. 87.]

73. Anonymous bishop. Of Zura (Proconsular province of Africa, 5th century), father of a daughter. [Victor of Vita, *Historia persecutionis Africanae provinciae*, II, 30 (MGH, *auct. ant.*, III, 1 [1879], pp. 19–20. CSEL 7, 35).]

74. APOLLINARIS SIDONIUS. Bishop of Clermont († between 487 and 489); husband of Papianilla (daughter of Emperor Avitus); father of Apollinaris, the future bishop of Auvergne, and of a daughter (or of three?).[38] [Apollinaris Sidonius, *Ep.* II, 12; III, 13; IV,12; V, 5, 16 (MGH, *auct. ant.*, VIII [1887], pp. 35–36, 49, 64, 80, 88. Trans. A. Loyen, Coll. "Budé", pp. 73, 104, 139, 180, 199. Gregory of Tours, *Libri Historiarum decem*, II, 21–22; III, 2, 12 (MGH, *scr. mer.*, 1, ed. 2a [1951], pp. 67–68. Trans. R. Latouche, I, pp. 109–10; 142; 153).]

---

you learn that you will become a bishop" (PL 30, 159c–d). And in another passage of the letter that anonymous bishop could further read: "For the man who has repudiated [his] God and is a prisoner of his wife's love is guilty of adultery; he makes use less of the ancient law of marriage than he shows himself ready to violate the new one, the one that compels him to keep purity" (G. Morin, "Portion inédite de l'apocryphe", p. 314). The problem of dating this anonymous booklet has not yet been completely solved. G. Morin opines that it should be attributed to a Pelagian author who was writing around the year 417 to Patrocles of Arles (G. Morin, "Le destinataire de l'apocryphe hiéronymien 'De septem ordinibus Ecclesiae'", RHE, 34 [1938], pp. 229–44). E. Griffe, in his article "L'apocryphe hiéronymien 'De septem ordinibus Ecclesiae'" (Bull. Lit. eccl. 57 [1956], pp. 213–24), agrees with G. Morin about the place and the date (though he goes back to the year 400), but thinks that the author of "De septem ordinibus Ecclesiae" was a Gallic bishop, even a metropolitan, while the addressee would have been a Gallic bishop other than Metropolitan Patrocles. D. Vallarsi, the publisher of St. Jerome's works reprinted by Migne, thinks that this was a seventh-century writing posterior to Isidore of Seville († 636) (PL 30, 147c–48a). He was followed in modern times by J. Lechner ("Der Schlussegen des Priesters in der heiligen Messe", *Festschrift Eduard Eichmann zum 70 Geburstag*, ed. by Martin Grabmann and Karl Hofmann [Wien-Zürich, 1940], pp. 666–70); and by R. Gryson, *Les origines du célibat ecclésiastique*, pp. 186–87. The reasons given by G. Morin and E. Griffe are the most convincing.

[38] Son-in-law of Emperor Avit, count of Emperor Majorian, prefect of Rome under Emperor Anthemius, Appolinaris Sidonius went directly from the state of layman to the episcopate. Nevertheless, three years before he was elected against his will to the seat of Clermont, he had completely changed his life, detaching himself from the affairs of the world and spending his days in retreat, silence, and study. It is quite likely that he started

75. AVITUS (Eparchius). Bishop of Plaisance (ordained in 456, died the same year), father of a daughter named Papilliana and father-in-law of Apollinaris Sidonius.[39] [Gregory of Tours, *Liber Historiarum decem* II, 11 (MGH, *scr. mer.*, I, 1, ed. 2a [1951]. Latouche, I, p. 102). Victor of Tunnunum, *Chronica* (MGH, *auct. ant.*, XI, *Chronicorum minorum saec. IV, V, VI, VII* [Berlin, 1894], p. 186).]

76. BONOSUS. Bishop (Narbonne), father of Bishop Rusticus of Narbonne. [Diehl 1806a. Narbonne. *Inscr.*: a. 441.]

77. CELIDONIUS (Chélidoine). Bishop of Besançon (ca. 445), married.[40] [*Vita S. Hilarii Arelatensis vita*, XVI, 21 (PL 50, 1236cd–37a). St. Leo, *Ep. X, ad episcopos per provinciam Viennensem constitutos* (Mansi, 5, 1243).]

78. DIOGENES. Bishop of the Antioch area (early 5th century), married twice.[41] [Theodoret of Cyrus, *Lettres*, 110 (SCh 111, 40–42).]

---

at that time to lead a life of continence with his wife, before ecclesiastical law made it compulsory for him (cf. P. Allard, *St. Sidoine Apollinaire*, 2d ed. [Paris, 1910], pp. 127–28). The exact number of his children is difficult to establish. The identity of his son Apollinaris is certain (*Ep.* III, 13; IV, 12), but we can wonder whether the three feminine first names given to his daughters (Roscia [*Ep.* V, 5, 16], Severiana [*Ep.* II, 12], and Alcima [Gregory of Tours, *Liber Historiarum decem*, III, 2, 12]) do not in fact refer to a single person.

[39] That senator, the former prefect of the Gaul praetorium, then *magister militum per Gallias* (general at the head of the troops stationed in Gaul), was raised to imperial dignity on July 9, 455. As early as the following year, he was defeated by the patrician Ricimerius, who, wishing to spare his life, had him consecrated bishop of Plaisance. "Avitus did not keep a good reputation and saved himself by becoming a bishop", as Bossuet would say in a biting witticism (*Discours sur l'histoire universelle*, pt. 1, 11th epoch). Avitus did not stay long in Plaisance. "Having discovered that the Senate was still hostile and wanted to do away with him, as Gregory of Tours related, he went to the basilica of St. Julian, the martyr of Auvergne, bringing many gifts; but the course of his life ran out while he was still on his way. He died, and his body was carried to the village of Brioude [Haute-Loire], where he was buried at the feet of St. Julian."

[40] Celidonius was deposed by a council over which Hilary of Arles presided. St. Leo annulled the sentence because it could not be proved that the woman whom Celidonius married when he was a layman was a widow.

[41] The letter of Theodoret of Cyrus to Domnus of Antioch attests that in the East instances of remarried men who became bishops were not rare. "I was pushed by the votes of the bishops of Phoenicia, very dear to God, to ordain as bishop Irenaeus, very dear to God, and it was because I knew his zeal, the greatness of his soul, his love for the poor, and other virtues, to which has to be added the orthodoxy of his faith. . . . As to the issue of his second marriage, we followed in the footsteps of our predecessors. Thus Alexander, of happy and holy memory, who ruled this Apostolic See, together with blessed Acacius of Berea, ordained Diogenes of happy memory in spite of a double marriage; this was also the case with blessed Praylius, who ordained Domninus of Caesarea in spite of his double marriage. All we did was follow the custom and example of illustrious and famous men known for both their knowledge and their lives. Because he knew many such cases, Proclus

79. DOMNINUS. Bishop of Caesarea (early 5th century), married twice.[42] [Ibid.]

80. EUCHERUS. Bishop of Lyon († 449 or 450); husband of Galla; father of Salonius, bishop of Geneva, and of Veranus, bishop of Vence.[43] [Gennade, *De viris inlustribus*, 63 (PL 58, 1096b–97a). Ed. E. Richardson, TU, XIV, 1 (1896), p. 83. Eucherus of Lyon, *Formularum Spiritalis intelligentiae ad Uranium liber unus* (PL 50, 727a. CSEL, 31, 3); *Instructionum ad Salonium Libri duo—Prefatio ad Salonium* (PL 50, 773a–b. CSEL 31, 65–66). Salvian of Marseilles, *Ep.* 8 (MGH, *auct. ant.*, I, 1, p. 116). Paulinus of Nola, *Ep.* 51 (PL 61, 417b–18a. CSEL 29, 423–25).]

81. EULOGIUS. Bishop of Bourges (5th century), father of Simplicius, bishop of Bourges. [L. Duchesne, *Fastes épiscopaux de l'ancienne Gaule*, II (1900), p. 27. Apollinaris Sidonius, *Ep.* VII, 9 (MGH, *auct. ant.*, VIII [1887], pp. 115–17. Trans. A. Loyen, Coll. "Budé", III, pp. 58–59.]

82. EUTROPUS. Bishop of Orange († 475), married.[44] [P. Varin, "Vita Eutropi", *Bulletin du Comité historique des monuments écrits de l'histoire de France*, I (1949), p. 54. Albanes-Chevalier, *Gallia christiana novissima*, VI (1916), chap. 11.]

83. FELIX III. Pope (483–92). Husband of Petronia; father of two children (Paula and Gordianus), and perhaps of another girl (Aemiliana); great-great-grandfather of St. Gregory the Great. [ICUR, NS I, n. 843, p. 321f. F. Buecheler, *Carmina latina epigraphica*, n. 1358. ICUR, NS II, 4964. Via Ostiensi. Basilica Beati Pauli Apostoli. *Inscr.*: a. 472, 484, 485, and 489. Gregory the Great, *Homiliae XI in Evangelio*, II, 38, 15 (PL 76, 1291b); *Dialogorum libri IV*, IV, 16 (PL 77, 348a).]

84. GERMANUS. Bishop of Auxerre († ca. 448), husband of Eustacia.[45] [Constance of Lyon, *Vie de saint Germain d'Auxerre*, I, 1–2 (SCh 112, 124–25). L. M. Duru, *Bibliothèque historique de l'Yonne*, I, 18 (1850), p. 316.]

---

of happy memory, bishop of Constantinople, also accepted the election and sent a letter of praise and congratulations."

[42] See note above.

[43] At a date that must be set before 426, Eucherus and his wife, Galla, of whom he had two sons, retired to the monastery of Lérins to lead there a life of prayer and study. A few years later, between 432 and 441, Eucherus was raised to the episcopal See of Lyon. In addition to the above-mentioned sources, see R. Étaix, *Eucher de Lyon*, DHGE, XV, c. 1315–17.

[44] After the death of his wife, Eutropius entered the clergy. He became a deacon in Marseilles, then was elected to the episcopal See of Orange. See also E. Griffe, *Eutrope d'Orange*, DHGE, XVI, c. 82–83.

[45] Here is the passage in which Constance of Lyon relates the election of the young aristocrat Germanus to the episcopate and the radical change in his life that ensued: "He [Germanus] was surely formed by a hidden design of the divinity so that nothing would

85. GERMANUS. African bishop (5th century), father of a daughter named Leontia. [Victor of Vita, *Historia*, III, 24 (MGH, *auct. ant.*, III, 1 [1879], p. 46. CSEL 7, 83).]

86. HESYCHIUS. Bishop of Vienna (5th century), husband of Audentia, father of four children, including Apollinaris, future bishop of Valence, and Avitus, future bishop of Vienna.[46] [Alcimi Ecdicii Aviti, *Homilia in Rogationibus* (MGH, *auct. ant.*, VI, 2 [1883], p. 110. U. Chevalier, *Œuvres complètes de Saint Avit* [1890], p. 295; *Poematum libri VI*, VI, 19, and *Prologus ad Apollinarem episcopum* (MGH, *auct. ant.*, VI, 2 [1883], pp. 274–76. U. Chevalier, *Œuvres complètes*, pp. 90–91, 93). *Vita Beati Aviti episcopi Viennensis*, I (MGH, *auct. ant.*, VI, 2, p. 177. U. Chevalier, *Œuvres complètes*, p. xxi).]

87. IRENAEUS. Bishop of Tyre († before 451), married twice(?), father of a daughter (perhaps Alexandra?).[47] [Theodoret of Cyrus, *Lettres*, 12 (SCh 98, 43) and 110 (SCh 111, 40–42).]

---

be lacking in the perfection of one fated to become a pontiff successor to the apostles. Eloquence prepared him for preaching, knowledge of the law for justice, the company of one spouse for a testimonial of chastity. Then the divine will was suddenly manifested and endorsed by general agreement. For all the clerics, the entire nobility, the population of the town and country came to a unanimous conclusion: with one voice, they all asked for Germanus as bishop. . . . He received the priesthood against his will, constrained, forced; but all of a sudden he was completely transformed. He abandoned the service of the world; he trampled on the vanities of the world, chose humility as his style of life; his wife changed from being his companion to being his sister [*uxor in sororem mutatur ex conjuge*]; he distributed his wealth to the poor and sought poverty."

[46] A poem by St. Avitus alludes to the continence that by common agreement Hesychius and his wife decided to observe after the birth of their fourth child:

Fourth of the children that she brought into the world, your mother Audentia gave you, by a happy confinement, to the noblest of families. She immediately consecrated herself to a humble life; then, through the same promises, your dear parents decided, in their love, to observe a perfect chastity. And as you were to be the principle of such a holy covenant, you bear at the same time your limbs of an infant in the cradle of Christ, who receives them immediately from this consecrated [couple].

[Edidit ut quartam genitrix Audentia prolem
Teque dedit generi partu fecunda supremo
Confestim parcam promittit ducere vitam
At deinceps paribus castum servare cubile
Constituit votis carorum cura parentum.
Et quia principium tam sancti foederis esses,
Tu simul efferis Christo, qui protenus ipsis
Accipit in cunis lactantia membra decatis.]
(*Poematum libri VI*, VI, 19)

[47] Theodoret of Cyrus does not say explicitly in letter 110 that this Irenaeus, bishop of Tyre, was married (and then remarried), but it seems to be understood quite clearly from the context. See the passage of that letter already quoted about bishop Diogenes (pp. 102–3).

88. JULIAN. Deacon of Benevento, then bishop of Eclanum († ca. 454), husband of Ia.[48] [Paulinus of Nola, *Carmina* 25 (CSEL 30, 238ff.). Augustine, *Contra Julianum 1. VI*, III, XIV, 28, 49–50 (PL 44, 716c–d). Marius Mercator, *Commonitorium adversum haeresim Pelagii et Caelestii vel etiam scripta Juliani*, 7 (E. Schwartz, ACO, I, V [1924–26], pp. 9, 26–36).]

89. LUPUS. Bishop of Troyes († 478 or 479), husband of Pimeniole, sister of St. Hilary of Arles.[49] [*Vita Lupi episcopi Trecensis*, 1 (MGH, *scr. mer.*, VII [1919], pp. 295–96).]

90. NAMATIUS. Bishop of Auvergne (ca. 450), married. [Gregory of Tours, *Libri Historiarum decem*, II, 16–17 (MGH, *scr. mer.*, I, 1, ed. 2a [1951], pp. 64–65. Latouche, I, pp. 105–6).]

91. PALLADIUS. Bishop of Bourges (5th century), father-in-law of Simplicius, bishop of Bourges. [L. Duchesne, *Fastes épiscopaux* II (1900), p. 27. Apollinaris Sidonius, *Ep.* VII, 9 (MGH, *auct. ant.*, VIII [1887], p. 116. Trans. A. Loyen, Coll. "Budé", III, p. 60).]

92. PANCRATIUS. Bishop of Umbria († 455), father of bishops Pancratius and Herculus. [Diehl 1030. Narniae. *Inscr.* a. 493.]

93. PAULINUS. Bishop of Nola († 431), husband of Therasia, father of a child, Celsus, who died in infancy.[50] [Idatius Episcopus Aquae Flaviae, *Continuatio Chronicorum Hieronymianorum (a) ad a. 468*, 80, XXX (MGH, *auct. ant.*, XI, 1. *Chronica minora s. IV–VII* [1894], p. 20). Gregory of Tours, *Libri in gloria Confessorum*, n. 108 (MGH, *scr. mer.*, I, 2 [1885], pp. 817–18).]

Letter 12 alludes to the son-in-law of Irenaeus ("Accept courageously the death of him who was your son-in-law and my truest friend"). It is by comparing letter 12 to Irenaeus and letter 14 to a person of high position in society bearing the name of Alexander that Yvan Azéma, translator of *Sources Chrétiennes*, proposed identifying Irenaeus' son-in-law with the husband of Alexandra (SCh 40, 55).

[48] Julian, future bishop of Eclanum, had married while still young, around the year 403. Thereafter there is no more reference to his wife. Was she already dead, or did the two separate when Julian was ordained deacon of Benevento in 408 and then, soon after, bishop of Eclanum? Several passages in St. Augustine's *Contra Julianum* attest in any case that at the time of his episcopate, Julian had made a profession of continence.

[49] The *Vita* of St. Lupus informs us that after seven years of marriage, Pimeniole and her husband decided, by common agreement, to lead a life of perfect chastity (that change of lifestyle was then called *conversio*): "Septimo conjugii anno, instigante Domino, se ad conversionem hortatu mutuo contulerunt." Pimeniole took the veil, and Lupus went to Lérins; but against his will he was raised to the episcopal See of Troyes, which he occupied for fifty-two years.

[50] Here is the notice that Idatius of Aquae Flaviae devotes to St. Paulinus: "Paulinus, of high nobility and consummate eloquence, was even more ennobled recently by his conversion to God, an apostolic man, bishop of Nola in Campania. He is deemed to be a remarkable man: Therasia, who was once his wife and is now his sister, is equal to him in bearing witness to a blessed and meritorious life."

94. PRINCE (or PRINCIPE). Bishop of Soissons († ca. 505), father of a son called Lupus, who succeeded him.[51] [*Flodoardi Historiae Remensis Ecclesiae*, I, 10 (PL 135, 44a. MGH, *script.*, XIII [1881], p. 421).]

95. RURICIUS. Bishop of Limoges († ca. 507); husband of Iberia; father of several children, including Eparchius, a cleric in Auvergne, and Omnatius, bishop of Tours. Grandfather of Bishop Ruricius, his successor. [Apollinaris Sidonius, *Carmina* 10 (MGH, *auct. ant.*, VIII [1887], pp. 226–27. Trans. A. Loyen, Coll. "Budé", pp. 95–96). Ruricius, *Ep.* I, 18; II, 4, 24, 28, 43, 56, 57 (MGH, *auct. ant.*, VIII [1887], pp. 309, 313, 332, 333, 342, 347–48).]

96. SAHAK THE GREAT (Isaac). Armenian Katholikos († 437 or 438). Son of Nerses the Great and last Katholikos of the Gregorian dynasty. Married and father of a daughter called Anovisch.[52] [G. Garitte, *La narratio de rebus Armeniae*, pp. 92–94, 421. Moses of Khorene, III, 49, 51 (V. Langlois, *Collection*, II [1869], pp. 159–60). Lazarus of Pharbe, nn. 15, 16, 17, 18 (ibid., pp. 273–78).]

97. SIMPLICIUS. Bishop of Bourges (elected ca. 472), married with children.[53] [Apollinaris Sidonius, *Ep.* VII, 9 (MGH, *auct. ant.*, VIII [1887], p. 116. Trans. A. Loyen, Coll. "Budé", III, p. 60).]

---

[51] Lupus of Soissons was truly the son of Bishop Principius, and not his nephew, contrary to what P. Viard affirms in *Catholicisme*, VII, c. 1192. In the brief version of the will of St. Remi—the brother of Bishop Principius—Lupus is mentioned several times; three times, St. Remi addresses him as follows: "O Lupus, bishop, son of my brother [Principius]" (cf. H. Leclercq, DACL, XIV, 2, 2233–36). It was of course because of absentmindedness that in another article of the DACL, H. Leclercq has Hincmar of Reims say that Lupus was the nephew of Principius (DACL, XV, 2, c. 1562). In his *Vita sancti Remigii*, Hincmar says clearly that Lupus was the son (and not the nephew) of Principius; he only copies the quoted passage of Flodoard (PL 125, 1133b).

[52] It was after the death of his wife that Sahak became a monk. "He lived as a true religious, surrounded by about sixty disciples, going barefoot, wearing a hairshirt, an iron chain around his loins, and following the rule of the great convent of Spoudées, also called Acoemètes" (Fr. Tournebize, *Histoire politique et religieuse de l'Arménie*, I [Paris, n.d.], p. 610).

[53] Around 472, Apollinaris Sidonius was called to preside over the election of the new bishop of Bourges. He used all his influence to make the people accept the only candidate who, after investigation, had seemed to him to possess the best qualities for the episcopate: Simplicius, whose father-in-law, Palladius, and father, Eulogius, had been bishops of Bourges. Simplicius was married, and it is interesting to note here the praise given by Sidonius to the wife of Simplicius in a sermon he gave for the occasion: "She is worthy of having had a father and father-in-law who both were bishops, raised by one and chosen as a daughter by the other." This is to be compared with the law of Honorius of May 8, 420, bearing witness to the importance paid to the qualities of the wife in the choice of a candidate to the priesthood ("Neque enim clericis incompetenter adjunctae sunt, quae dignos sacerdotio viros sui conversatione fecerunt" [CTh 16, 2, 44. CJC II, p. 20]).

98. SYNESIUS OF CYRENE. Bishop of Ptolemais († ca. 414), married and father of three sons.[54] [Synesius of Cyrene, Ep. 105 (PG 66, 1485a). R. Hercher, Epistolographi graeci (1873), p. 705.]

99. VOLUSIAN. Bishop of Tours (late 5th century), married. [Ruricius, Ep. II, 64 (MGH, auct. ant., VIII [1887], p. 350. CSEL 21, 441–42 = Ep. 65).]

Married priests

100. Anonymous priest. Of Belley (early 5th century), father of St. Eugendus (or Oyand), abbot of Condat. [Acta Sanctorum Januarii, I, pp. 49–54.]

101. Anonymous priest. Of Cyzicus (Propontis, early 5th century), father of the historian Gelasius of Cyzicus. [Gelasius of Cyzicus, Historia concilii Nicaeni, Proem. PG 85, 1193a. GCS 28, 2.]

102. Anonymous priest. Of Bethlehem (early 5th century), married and family man. [Jerome, Ep. 130, 6 (CSEL 56, 182. Trans. J. Labourt, Coll. "Budé", VII, p. 173).]

103. FAUSTINUS. Priest of Auvergne (late 5th century), family man. [Apollinaris Sidonius, Ep. IV, 4 (MGH, auct. ant., VIII [1887], pp. 56–57. Trans. A. Loyen, Coll. "Budé", pp. 121, 124).]

104. FELIX. Priest (Rome), father of Pope Felix III (483–92). [L. Duchesne, Liber Pontificalis, I, pp. 252–53.]

105. HILARY. Priest (Gaul, 5th century), married. [Venantius Fortunatus, Carmina, IV, 12 (MGH, auct. ant., IV, 1, p. 88).]

106. IOCUNDUS. Priest (Rome), father of Pope Boniface I (418–22). [L. Duchesne, Liber Pontificalis, I, p. 227.]

107. JANUARIUS. Priest of Hippo († 424), father of a daughter and a son.[55] [Augustine, Sermo CCCLV, II, 3; Sermo CCCLVI, 11 (PL 39, 1570cd–71ab, 1579a).]

---

[54] During the summer of 410, a plebiscite acclaimed the philosopher Synesius and appointed him successor to the recently deceased archbishop metropolitan of Ptolemais. Caught by surprise, Synesius refused the appointment and declared, among other things, that he did not want to separate from his wife. One cannot say with any certainty what happened to the conjugal life of Synesius, who finally resigned himself to accept the episcopate. C. Lacombrade rightly pointed out that the bishop of Ptolemais never talks about his wife or his hope for other children in his correspondence: "It is more than probable that he renounced his conjugal life" (Synesius of Cyrene, Hymnes, Coll. "Budé" [1978], p. xxxvii). For a more detailed discussion of Synesius' case, see below, pp. 303–7.

[55] That Januarius was a member of the monastic community of priests of the Hippo diocese and therefore observed perfect continence. His daughter lived in a monastery

108. LEO. Priest (Rome). Father of a daughter. [Diehl 1132, a. 445.]

109. MARCIAN. Priest (Constantinople, late 5th century), husband of Leoncia and brother-in-law of Emperor Zeno.[56] [Theodore the Lector, *Historia Ecclesiastica* (excerpts from the *Ecclesiastical History* of Nicephorus Callistus (PG 86, 184a).]

110. PETRUS. Priest (Rome), father of Pope Anastasius II (496–98). [L. Duchesne, *Liber Pontificalis*, I, p. 258. ICUR, NS II, 4149. Via Cornelia. Basilica Beati Petri Apostoli. *Epitaphia Anastasii Pontificis II (a. 498)*.]

111. SALVIAN. Priest of Marseilles († ca. 480), husband of Palladia, father of a daughter named Auspiciola.[57] [Salvian, *Ep.* 4 (SCh 176, 89ff.).]

112. SENATORUS. Priest of Alesia (early 5th century), husband of Nectariola. [Constance of Lyon, *Vie de Saint Germain d'Auxerre*, 22 (SCh 112, 165).]

113. SILVIUS. Archpriest (Gaul, end of 5th century or beginning of 6th century), father of the priest Papulus. [*Vita Eptadii presbyteri Cervidunensis* (MGH, *scr. mer.*, III [1896], pp. 191–92).]

114. SULPICIUS SEVERUS. Priest(?) (Aquitaine † ca. 420), married.[58] [Paulinus of Nola, *Ep.* V, 5–6 (CSEL 29, 28). Gennadius, *De viris inlustribus*, c. 19 (PL 58, 1072a–73a). Ed. E. Richardson, TU, XIV, 1 (1896), p. 69.]

Married deacons

115. ADEODATUS. Deacon (Rome), husband of Maria. [ICUR, NS II, 4926. Basilica Beati Pauli Apostoli, Via Ostiensi. *Inscr.*: a. 474.]

---

for women, and his son in a monastery for men. Nothing is said about his wife in the two sermons of St. Augustine in which he is mentioned.

[56] Following a conspiracy against his brother-in-law, the emperor, Marcian was enrolled forcibly in the clergy. The plot having failed, Zeno the Isaurian ordered that Marcian be ordained priest by Acacius, the patriarch of Constantinople, and incarcerated at the fort of Papyrius.

[57] At a young age Salvian had married Palladia, daughter of pagan parents. After having converted his wife to Christianity, he decided to lead an ascetic life with her; and both, taking along their little girl, Auspiciola, went to live in the monastery of Lérins (ca. 424). It is not known whether Palladia was still alive when, several years later, Salvian was ordained a priest.

[58] A brilliant lawyer, Sulpicius Severus had the grief of losing his young wife very early. The trial drew him to God. He was not yet thirty when, newly "converted", he retired in solitude to live in prayer and asceticism. It is certain that Sulpicius Severus did not marry again. Was he ordained a priest, as Gennadius avers? Nothing prevents us from thinking so, though we have no other testimony than that of Gennadius.

116. Anonymous deacon (Rome). Husband of Maria and father of a family. [Diehl 1196. *Subscr.*: a. 474.]

117. CRISCIENTIANUS. Deacon (Salonis), husband of Ursacia. [Diehl 1225a–b. In sarcophago Salonitano. *Inscr.*: early 5th century.]

118. DIONYSIUS. Deacon (Rome), likely to have been married to a woman called Rhodina. [C. Pietri, *Appendice prosopographique*, p. 388. Deacons attested at the time of Zozimus and Boniface (401–22).]

119. JANUARIUS. Deacon (Rome), husband of Lupercilla and father of a daughter called Marturia. [ICUR, NS VI, 15710. Via Latina. C. Pietri, "Appendice prosopographique", p. 391. Deacons attested between the pontificate of Damasus and that of Sixtus (366–440).]

120. TETTIUS. Deacon (Spoleta), husband of Marcia Decentia. [Diehl 1209. Materillae prope Spoletum. *Inscr.*: a. 424.]

121. TINOUTOS. Deacon (Lycaonia), husband of Aurelia Domna. [CIG IV, 9268. *Kadun Khana* Lycaoniae prope *Laodiceam combustam* (Ladik), in coemeterio. *Inscr.*: 4th or 5th century.]

Married deaconesses

122. AXIA. Deaconess (Tyre[?], early 5th century), married and mother of a daughter named Susan. [Theodoret of Cyrus, *Lettres*, 17 (SCh 98, 63–64).]

123. CASIANA. Deaconess (Tyre[?], early 5th century), mother of a son. [Theodoret of Cyrus, *Lettres*, 17 (SCh 98, 63–64).]

Married subdeacons

124. BASIL. Subdeacon (Trier), father of a daughter named Bonosa. [RICG, I, 109. Trier, necropolis of St. Paulinus–St. Maximinus. Inscription found in 1901 in front of St. Paulinus' church. Could not go back earlier than second half of 5th century.]

6TH CENTURY

Married bishops

125. Anonymous bishop. Of Nantes (early or middle 6th century), married.[59] [Gregory of Tours, *Libri in gloria Confessorum*, n. 77 (MGH, *scr. mer.*, I, 2 [1885, p. 794).]

[59] Gregory of Tours relates that this bishop of Nantes, whose name is not known, was separated from his wife. The latter became jealous, suspecting her husband of having an affair with another woman. She started to spy on him and was then witness to a miracle

126. Anonymous bishop. Of Syracuse (middle 6th century), married and a family man.[60] [Pelagius I, *Ep.* 33 (P. M. Grasso and C. M. Battle, *Pelagii I Papae espistulae quae supersunt* [Montserrat, 1956], pp. 89–92).]

127. APOLLINARIS. Bishop of Auvergne († 516), husband of Placidina and father of Archadius. [Gregory of Tours, *Libri Historiarum decem*, III, 2, 12 (MGH, *scr. mer.*, I, 1, ed. 2a [1951], pp. 98, 108. Latouche, I, pp. 142–43, 153).]

128. ARTEMIUS. Bishop of Sens (late 6th century), father of a daughter called Verosia. [*Vita Lupi episcopi Senonici*, 8 (MGH, *scr. mer.*, IV [1902], p. 181).]

129. ASTIDIUS. Bishop of Limoges (6th century), husband of Tecla and father of five children. [*Vita aridii Abbatis Lemovicini, Appendix* (MGH, *scr. mer.*, III [1896], pp. 611–12).]

130. AVITUS. Bishop of Vienna († 518), married and a family man. [Alcimi Ecdicii Aviti, *Ep.* 55 (49) (MGH, *auct. ant.*, VI, 2 [1883], pp. 84–85. U. Chevalier, *Œuvres complètes de saint Avit, évêque de Vienne* [1890], p. 209).]

131. BADEGISIL. Bishop of Le Mans († 586), husband of Magnatrude and father of a daughter.[61] [Gregory of Tours, *Libri Historiarum decem*, VIII, 39; X, 5 (MGH *scr. mer.*, I, 1, ed. 2a [1951], pp. 405, 488. Latouche, II, pp. 171–72, 266).]

132. BAUDIN. Bishop of Tours (early 6th century), family man. [Gregory of Tours, *Libri Historiarum decem*, X, 31, 16 (MGH, *scr. mer.*, I, 1, ed. 2a. [1951], p. 533. Latouche, II, p. 322).]

133. BLANDUS. Bishop of Ortona († 594), father of Scholasticus, lord of Ortona. [Gregory the Great, *Registrum epistularum*, IX, 194 (MGH, *epist.*, II [1899], p. 182).]

---

that convinced her of her error: a lamb of radiant whiteness kept company with the bishop! This wondrous narrative attests indirectly to the law of continence for the higher ranks of the clergy.

[60] During the month of February 559, Pope Pelagius I wrote to the patrician Cathegus to explain the reasons for having waited a year before approving the election of the new bishop of Syracuse. The new bishop was married and had children: now a *principalis constitutio* prohibited the promotion of that kind of candidate to the episcopate. The imperial law to which Pelagius I is referring here is that of Justinian's Code (*Codex Justiniani*, I, 3, 41, 2–4; I, 3, 47; *Novellae* 6, 1; *Novellae* 123, 1). See below, pp. 352–54; 358–59; 361–63.

[61] Mayor of King Clotarius' palace, Badegisil had ascended in forty days all the degrees of the clergy. Having become the bishop of Le Mans, he left, according to Gregory of Tours, a detestable reputation: "[During that year died] Badegisil, bishop of Le Mans, a man of great cruelty toward the people and who looted without any right the goods of many people. Besides that man whose heart was harsh and cruel, there was his wife, even more cruel than he was, pushing him with the detestable stimulant of her advice in committing his crimes" (R. Latouche, trans., II, pp. 171–72).

134. CASSIUS. Bishop (Narni, Province of Perusia), husband of Fausta. [Diehl 1031. Narniae, in Umbria. *Inscr.*: a. 558.]

135. DESIDERATUS. Bishop of Verdun (early 6th century), father of Syagrus. [Gregory of Tours, *Libri Historiarum decem*, III, 35 (MGH, *scr. mer.*, I, 1, ed. 2a [1951], p. 130. Latouche, I, p. 175).]

136. ENNODIUS (Magnus Felix). Bishop of Pavie (473–521), married. [Ennodius, *Eucharisticon de Vita sua* (MGH, *auct. ant.*, VII [1885], pp. 300–304).][62]

137. EUPHRONIUS (Eufronius). Bishop of Tours (556–73), father of a son named Aventius. [Venantius Fortunatus, *Carmina*, III, 2, 6 (MGH, *auct. ant.*, IV, 1, pp. 50–51).]

138. EUSANIUS. Bishop of Agrigentia (Sicily, ca. 594), father of Euplus. [Gregory the Great, *Registrum epistularum*, IV, 36 (MGH, *epist.*, I [1891], p. 271).]

139. FIRMINUS. Bishop of Viviers (6th century), husband of Aula. [L. Duchesne, *Fastes épiscopaux*, I (1894), p. 230.]

140. FRANÇILLON. Bishop of Tours (early 6th century), husband of Clara. [Gregory of Tours, *Libri Historiarum decem*, X, 31, 14 (MGH, *scr. mer.*, I, 1, ed. 2a [1951], pp. 532–33. Latouche, II, p. 321).]

141. GALLOMAGNUS. Bishop of Troyes (late 6th century), father of a daughter named Palatina, wife of Duke Bodegisilus. [Venantius Fortunatus, *Carmina*, VII, 6, 23 (MGH, *auct. ant.*, IV, 1, p. 158).]

142. GENEBAUD. Bishop of Laon (5th–6th centuries), married, father of a daughter named Vulpecula and of a bishop, Latro, his successor.[63] [*Flodoardi Historiae Remensis Ecclesiae*, I, 14 (MGH, *script.*, XIII [1881], p. 425). *Vita Remigii episcopi Remensis auctore Hincmaro* (MGH, *scr. mer.*, III [1896], pp. 256, 300–305).]

[62] Ennodius himself mentions that he was married: "Hoc amplius suffragator meus emeruit, quam poposci, ut illa quae mecum matrimonii habuit parilitatem religiosae mecum habitudinis decora partiretur, et fieret praeclari dux femina tituli" (*Eucharisticon de Vita sua*, MGH, 304). It is hard to see on what G. Bardy was basing himself when, in *Catholicisme* IV, 206, he affirmed that Ennodius had only been engaged.

[63] This Genebaud was the first bishop installed by St. Remi. *L'Histoire de l'Église de Reims*, composed in the 10th century by Canon Flodoard, relates that after having been raised to the episcopal See of Laon, he was imprudent enough to see frequently the wife from whom he had separated. Two children were born! The bishop gave a symbolic name to each: the boy was called Latro (thief) and the girl Vulpecula (she-fox); then he went to do penance in solitude. After seven years of reclusion, he was reinstalled on the See of Laon and led an exemplary life until his death. His son, Latro, succeeded him and left a reputation of sanctity. This legendary narrative probably has a kernel of truth.

143. GREGORY. Bishop of Langres († ca. 539), husband of Armentaria, father of two children, one of whom was Bishop Tetricus, his successor. Grandfather of Gregory of Tours.[64] [Gregory of Tours, *Vitae Patrum*, VII (MGH, *scr. mer.*, I, 2 [1885], p. 687).]

144. GREGORY. Spanish bishop (of Osma? late 6th century), father of five children: Braulio, bishop of Saragossa; John, bishop of Saragossa; Fronimian, abbot; Pomponia, abbess; Basilla, mother of Eugene, bishop of Toledo (646–57). [Eugenii Toletani Episcopi, *Carmina, carmen 21*, v. 17–18 (MGH, *auct. ant.*, XIV, p. 248, note p. 301). A. Lambert, "The Family of St. Braulio and the Expansion of the Rule of John of Biclar", *Universidad*, X (1933), pp. 65–80.]

145. HORMISDAS. Pope (514–23), father of Silverius, who would become his sixth successor to the throne of Peter (536–38).[65] [L. Duchesne, *Liber Pontificalis*, I, p. 290. Diehl 984, *Hormisdae pontificis elogium a Silverio filio papa romano conditum*.]

146. LEONTIUS. Bishop of Bordeaux († between 557 and 574), husband of Placidina, the great-granddaughter of Apollinaris Sidonius.[66] [Venantius Fortunatus, *Carmina*, I, 6, 14, 15; IV, 10 (MGH, *auct. ant.*, IV, 1 [1881], pp. 10–11, 15–18, 86–87).]

---

[64] It was after the death of his wife that Senator Gregory "converted" to a life of prayer and asceticism and was elected by plebiscite as bishop of Langres.

[65] The *Liber Pontificalis* notes, about Pope Silverius: "Silverius, natione Campanus, ex patre Hormisda episcopo Romano . . . ."

Here is also the text of Pope Hormisda's epitaph, which was composed by his son and successor Silverius:

> Quamvit digna tuis non sint pater ista sepulchris
> Nec titulis egeat clarificata fides
> Sume tamen laudes quas Petri captus amore
> Extremo veniens hospes ab orbe legat
> Sanasti patriae laceratum scismate corpus
> Restituens propriis membra revulsa locis
> Imperio devicta pro tibi Graecia cessit
> Amissam gaudens se reparasse fidem
> Africa laetatur multos captiva per annos
> Pontifices precivus promeruisse tuis
> Haec ego Silverius quamvis mihi dura notavi
> Ut possent tumulis fixa manere diu.

[66] A poem by Venantius Fortunatus contains an allusion to the life of perfect chastity led by Leontius of Bordeaux and his wife: "Affection impels me to say something about Placidina, who was once your wife and is now a very dear sister to you" (Cogor amore etiam Placidinae pauca referre, quae tibi tunc coniux, est modo cara soror) (MGH, *auct. ant.*, IV, 1, p. 18).

147. LUCILLUS. Bishop of Malta (deposed in 599), father of Peter. [Gregory the Great, *Registrum epistularum*, X, I (MGH, *epist.*, II [1899], p. 236).]

148. MACLOU. Bishop of Vannes (middle 6th century), married.[67] [Gregory of Tours, *Libri Historiarum decem*, IV, 4 (MGH, *scr. mer.*, I, 1, ed. 2a [1951], pp. 137–38. Latouche, I, pp. 182–83).]

149. NAMATIUS. Bishop of Vienna († 522), husband of Euphrasia. [Venantius Fortunatus, *Carmina*, IV, 27 (MGH, *auct. ant.*, IV, 1, p. 99).]

150. NONNICHIUS. Bishop of Nantes (middle 6th century), father of a son. [Gregory of Tours, *Libri Historiarum decem*, VIII, 43 (MGH, *scr. mer.*, I, 1, ed. 2a [1951], p. 409. Latouche, II, p. 176).]

151. PANTAGATHE. Bishop of Vienna († 541?), father of two children. [Ed. Le Blant, *Inscriptions chrétiennes de la Gaule antérieures au VIIIe siècle*, II (1865), n. 429.]

152. PASSIVUS. Bishop of Fermo (Picenum, ca. 598), father of the clerics Demetrianus and Valerianus. [Gregory the Great, *Registrum epistularum*, IX, 52 (MGH, *epist.*, I, 2 [1899], p. 77).]

153. PAUL. Bishop of Trois Châteaux (6th or 4th century?), married. [*Gallia christiana*, I, Paris (1715), p. 706. "Vita sancti Pauli Tricastinensis episcopi ex codice Gratianopolitano", *Analecta Bollandiana*, XI, pp. 375–76. L. Duchesne, *Fastes épiscopaux*, I, p. 256.]

154. PRISCUS. Bishop of Lyon († ca. 586), husband of Susanna and father of a son. [Gregory of Tours, *Libri Historiarum decem*, IV, 36 (MGH, *scr. mer.*, I, 1, ed. 2a [1951], pp. 168–69. Latouche, I, pp. 221–22).]

155. SALVIUS. Bishop of Albi († 584), husband of Herchenefreda, father of five children, including Desiderius and Rusticus, future bishops of Cahors. [*Vita Desiderii Cadurcae urbis episcopi* (MGH, *scr. mer.*, IV [1902], pp. 563–69). Herchenefreda. *Epistulae ad Desiderium filium* (MGH, *scr. mer.*, pp. 569–71).]

156. VICTEUR. Bishop of Rennes (late 6th century), father of a daughter called Domnola. [Gregory of Tours, *Libri Historiarum decem*, VIII, 32 (MGH, *scr. mer.*, I, 1, ed. 2a [1951], p. 400. Latouche, II, p. 166).]

---

[67] Maclou was the brother of the Breton count Chanao. Chanao attempted to kill him, and Maclou was saved by a stratagem. After which, Gregory of Tours relates, "He went to the town of Vannes, where he was tonsured and ordained bishop. After the death of Chanao, however, he apostatized, and, having let his hair grow, he took back both the wife he had left after joining the clergy and the kingdom of his brother, but he was excommunicated by the bishops."

Married priests

157. ANASTASIUS. Priest (Auvergne, middle 6th century), family man. [Gregory of Tours, *Libri Historiarum decem*, IV, 12 (MGH, *scr. mer.*, I, 1, ed. 2a [1951]. Latouche, I, pp. 190–93).]

158. Anonymous priest (Arles?, 6th century), married, father of a daughter. ["Sancti Caesarii vita ab ejus familiaribus scripta", *Sancti Caesarii episcopi Arelatensis opera omnia*, ed. D. G. Morin, II (1942), p. 337.]

159. Anonymous priest (Nursia, late 6th century), married.[68] [Gregory the Great, *Dialogorum libri IV*, IV, 11 (PL 77, 336b–37b. Ed. U. Moricca [1924], pp. 243–44).]

160. BASIL. Priest (Rome), husband of Felicity. [ICUR, NS II, 5155. Basilica Beati Pauli Apostoli. Via Ostiensi. *Inscr.*: early 6th century.]

161. EUNOMIUS. Priest of Auvergne (6th century), father of Fedamius. [Gregory of Tours, *Liber in gloria Martyrum*, n. 52 (MGH, *scr. mer.*, I, 2 [1885], p. 525).]

162. EVODIUS. Priest of Auvergne (early 6th century), father of the priest Eufrasius and of another son. [Gregory of Tours, *Libri Historiarum decem*, IV, 13, 35 (MGH, *scr. mer.*, I, 1, ed. 2a [1951], pp. 144, 167. Latouche, I, pp. 193, 219). *Liber Vitae Patrum*, VI, 4 (MGH, *scr. mer.*, I, 2 [1885], p. 683).]

163. FLORENTIUS. Priest (region of Rome, early 6th century), grandfather of the Roman subdeacon Florentius. [Gregory the Great, *Dialogorum libri IV*, II, 8, 1 (SCh 260, 161).]

164. GORDIANUS. Priest (Rome early 6th century), father of Pope Agapetus I (535–36). [L. Duchesne, *Liber Pontificalis*, I, p. 287.]

165. SILVESTER. Priest of Langres († ca. 572), married; elected bishop of Langres, but died before receiving the episcopal consecration. [Gregory of Tours, *Libri Historiarum decem*, V, 5 (MGH, *scr. mer.*, I, 1, ed. 2a [1951], pp. 201–2. Latouche, I, pp. 253–54).]

---

[68] The story of that priest of Nursia, whose name is unknown, is related by Gregory the Great, who said that he had heard it from a certain Abbot Stephen, "*vir venerabilis*", who had recently died in Rome. The author of *Dialogorum libri IV* tells how that cleric was concerned with chastity to the extent of refusing the presence of his wife at his deathbed. The point to be noted here is the reference to the continence practiced by the priest of Nursia from the day of his ordination: "Qui ex tempore ordinationis acceptae presbyteram suam ut sororem diligens, sed quasi hostem cavens, ad se proprius accedere nunquam sinabat . . ." (PL 77, 336b–c).

166. TRANSOBAD. Archdeacon, priest of Rodez (late 6th century), father of a son. [Gregory of Tours, *Libri Historiarum decem*, V, 46 (MGH, *scr. mer.*, I, 1, ed. 2a [1951], p. 256. Latouche, I, p. 313).]

167. VALENS. Priest (Villeneuve-les-Avignon), husband of Césarie. [Diehl 1689. Propre Avennionem. *Inscr.*: a. 586.]

168. VICTORIANUS. Priest (Italy, late 6th century), family man. [Gregory the Great, *Registrum epistularum*, X, 2 (MGH, *epist.*, II [1899], p. 238).]

Married deacons

169. Anonymous deacon (Chiusi, middle 6th century), married with children.[69] [Pelagius I, *Ep.* 47 (P. M. Gasso and C. M. Battle, *Pelagii I Papae epistulae quae supersunt* [Montserrat, 1956], pp. 127–28).]

170. Anonymous deacon (Italy), married and a family man. [ICUR, NS I, 175. In S. Celsi *Inscr.*: a. 533. Uncertain origin.]

171. EVANGELUS. Deacon of Siponto (ca. 593), father of a daughter. [Gregory the Great, *Registrum epistularum*, III, 40 (MGH, *epist.*, I [1891], p. 197).]

172. PETRUS. Deacon (Arles, 6th century), father of a daughter. ["Sancti Caesarii vita ab ejus familiaribus scripta", *Sancti Caesarii episcopi Arelatensis opera omnia*, ed. D. G. Morin, II (1942), p. 324.]

173. QUIRILLUS. Roman deacon, father of a daughter called Caretosa. [Diehl 1205. Capuae. *Inscr.*: a. 565.]

Married deaconesses

174. THEODORA. Deaconess (Rome), or wife of a deacon. [Diehl 1238 (49). a. 539.]

Married subdeacons

175. MARCELLUS. Subdeacon (Rome), family man. [ICUR, NS II, 4186. Via Cornelia. Basilica Beati Petri Apostoli. *Inscr.*: a. 563.]

---

[69] Responding to a request from Bishop Florentinus of Chiusi, Pope Pelagius I consented to the ordination to the diaconate of a widower who, if he did not marry a second time after the death of his wife, had not, however, observed chastity and had had children by his female servant. The Roman Pontiff agreed to make an exception in his favor, on the one hand because of the dearth of clerics in the diocese of Bishop Florentinus, and on the other hand because of the old age of the candidate, which allowed one to be quite sure of his future continence. But one condition was set: the servant had to retire to a monastery and make a profession of continence in order to put an end to suspicions.

176. STEPHEN. Subdeacon (Rome, late 6th century, early 7th century), father of Pope Adeodatus I (Deusdedit) (615–18). [L. Duchesne, *Liber Pontificalis*, I, p. 319.]

7TH CENTURY
Married bishops

177. AETHERIUS. Bishop of Vienna (early 7th century), married and father of a child. [*Vitae Desiderii episcopi Viennensis*, II, 19 (MGH, *scr. mer.*, III [1896], p. 645).]

178. AQUILINUS. Bishop of Évreux (620–ca. 695), married with children.[70] [Baronius, *Annales Ecclesiastici*, XII (1867), p. 51, n. 9. L. Duchesne, *Fastes épiscopaux*, II, (1900) 225.]

179. ARNULFUS. Bishop of Metz (early 7th century), father of two sons: Chlodulfus, future bishop of Metz, and Anseghiselus, father of Pepin of Herstal (called Pepin the Young). [*Chronicarum quae dicuntur Fredegarii Scholastici libri IV cum continuationibus* (MGH, *scr. mer.*, II [1888], pp. 170–74). *Vita sancti Arnulfi*, 5 (MGH, *scr. mer.*, II [1888], p. 433).]

180. FARON. Bishop of Meaux (7th century), husband of Blidechilde.[71] [*Vita Faronis episcopi Meldensis* 106, 107 (J. Mabillon, *Acta sanctorum O.S.B. saec. II* [1669], p. 618. MGH, *scr. mer.*, V [1910], pp. 188, 195). Dom Toussaints Du Plessis, *Histoire de l'église de Meaux*, I (1731), pp. 32, 652–53.]

181. FILIBAUD. Bishop of Aire-sur-l'Adour (Landes, early 7th century?), father of St. Philibert de Jumièges. ["Vita Sancti Filiberti, II", *Monuments de l'histoire des abbayes de Saint-Philibert*, ed. René Poupardin (1905), p. 3.]

182. JOHN THE ALMONER. Patriarch of Alexandria († 616), married with children.[72] [Simon Metaphrastes, *Vita et conversatio S. Patris nostri Joannis Alexandriae Archiepiscopi cognomine eleemosynarii* (PG 114, 896bc–97b). Leontius Neapolitanus Episcopus, *Vita sancti Joannis eleemosynarii* (PG 93, 1652ab; PL 73, 376ab).]

---

[70] Aquilinus had made a perpetual vow of continence with his wife before being called from the lay state to the episcopate.

[71] The *Vie de Faron évêque de Meaux* relates that Blidechilde shaved her head in order to remove all temptation to resume the common life with her husband. It is certain that they were already separated when Faron entered the service of the Church, though it is not known whether Blidechilde had retired to a monastery or was simply living as a widow. In addition to the above-mentioned references, one can find others in J. Guérout, *Faron*, DHGE, XVI, c. 643–66.

[72] The wife and children of John the Almoner had been dead for a long time when he was elected to the episcopate. We have to note that in such a way he fulfilled the conditions set by the imperial laws of Justinian forbidding the elevation to the episcopate of men having children or grandchildren and still bound to a wife (see below, pp. 352ff.).

183. LEUDINUS (also called Bodon). Bishop of Toul († ca. 680), husband of Odile, who became a nun in Loudun.[73] [*Vita Sadalbergae abbatissae Laudunensis*, 4, 18 (MGH, *scr. mer.*, V [1910], pp. 53, 60).]

184. MAGNUS. Bishop of Avignon (644–60), husband of Gandaltruda, father of the bishop Agricola who would be his successor (660–700). [*Gallia christiana*, I, Paris (1715), p. 800. L. Duchesne, *Fastes épiscopaux*, I, p. 261.]

185. MEDOALD. Bishop of Trier (627–39), father of several children. [Desiderii Episcopi Cadurcensis, *Epistolae*, I, 7 (MGH, *Epistolae Merowingi et Karolini aevi*, vol. I, p. 197).]

186. PALLADIUS. Bishop of Eauze (7th century), father of the bishop Sidocus, his successor. [Pseudo-Fredegarius, *Chronicon libri IV cum continuationibus*, IV, 54 (MGH, *scr. mer.*, II, p. 148). L. Duchesne, *Fastes épiscopaux*, II (1900), p. 95.]

187. REOLUS. Bishop of Rheims († ca. 692); husband of the daughter of King Chilperic; father of several children, including a son called Gideon, who became a monk in Hautvilliers (Marne), and a daughter called Odile, who became a nun in Soissons. [*Vita Nivardi episcopi Remensis*, 1, 8, 10 (MGH, *scr. mer.*, V [1910], pp. 160, 167–68). *Flodoardi Historiae Remensis Ecclesiae*, II, 10 (MGH, *script.*, XIII [1881], p. 458).]

188. SIGILAICUS. Bishop of Tours (early 7th century), father of St. Cyran of Brenne. [*Vita Sigiramni abbatis Longoretensis*, 3 (MGH, *scr. mer.*, IV [1902], p. 608). L. Duchesne, *Fastes épiscopaux*, II (1900), p. 305.]

189. THEODORUS. Bishop born in Jerusalem (See unknown, late 7th century), father of Pope Theodore I (642–49). [L. Duchesne, *Liber Pontificalis*, I, p. 331.]

Married priests

190. Anonymous priest (Alexandria, early 7th century), married with children. [Leontius Neapolitanus Episcopus, *Vita sancti Joannis eleemosynarii* (PG 93, 1654bc; PL 73, 378bc).]

191. GEREMARUS. Priest, abbot of the monastery of Flay (Flaviacus) in the Oise († ca. 660), husband of Domana, father of St. Amalbert and of two daughters. [*Vita Geremari abbatis Flaviacensis*, 4, 5, 9, 12, 13 (MGH, *scr. mer.*, IV [1902], pp. 629–31).]

---

[73] When he was a layman, Leudinus and his wife, Odile, lived the life of "converts". When Leudinus was raised to the episcopate, Odile became a nun at Loudun.

Married subdeacons

192. BAVON (Allowinus). Tonsured cleric, monk (perhaps bishop?) at Ganda (Belgium † ca. 659), husband of the daughter of the Merovingian count Adilion, father of a daughter called Aggletrude.[74] [*Vita Bavonis Confessoris Gandavensis*, 2–3 (MGH, *scr. mer.*, IV [1902], pp. 535–36).]

NO DATE AVAILABLE

Married bishops

193. CRESIMUS. Bishop (Italy), father of the lector Primigenius. [ICUR, NS VI, 17297. Via Praenestina. No date.]

194. JULIANUS. Bishop (Calabria), husband of Feliciana, family man. [Diehl 1010. G. B. de Rossi, *Bulletino di Archeologia cristiana* (1876), p. 92. Inscr. of Aieta, province of Consenza, near Policastro in Calabria. Antecedent to the Constantinian era?]

Married priests

195. ALOUPIOS. Priest (Galatia), father of a son. [ICUR, NS II, 4441. Coemeterium Octavillae ad S. Pancratium. Via Aurelia. No date.]

196. Anonymous priest (Calabria), husband of Leta. [Diehl 1192. Tropeae in Calabria. No date.]

197. Anonymous priest (Italy). Husband of Martia. [Diehl 1191. No date.]

198. Anonymous priest (Rome), married. [Diehl 1139. A. Romae, e coemeterio Valentini via Flaminia. No date.]

199. AUFIDIUS. Priest (Trier), husband of Augurina and father of the deacon Augurius. [RICG, I, 214. Trier. Inscription found in 1781 "in a garden not far from the bridge of the Mosel". However, it might be as late as the 8th century.]

200. EUSEBIUS. Priest (Catania, in Sicily), perhaps with children. [G. Kaibel, ed., *Inscriptiones Graecae*, vol. XIV (Berolini, 1890), n. 534. Sicilia. Catanae apud priorem Coco. No date.]

---

[74] At the death of his wife, Bavon, who until then had led a dissolute life, resolved to convert. Under the influence of St. Amand he decided to enter the clergy, then became a monk and recluse in the monastery of Ganida. Rabanus Maurus, who calls Bavon a bishop, is not generally followed by the historians (PL 110, 1171d).

201. EVAGRIUS. Priest (Iconium), grandfather of Evagrius. [CIG III, 3998. Iconii, in lapide moenibus urbis incerto. Christian inscription? No date.]

202. GABINUS. Priest (Rome), father of a daughter called Susanna. [Aringhi, *Roma subterranea*, II (1651), p. 228. De coemeterio Chrysanti et Dariae. No date.]

203. JOHN. Priest (Laodicea in Lycaonia), father of Aur. Domna. [CIG III, 3989d. *Kadun Chana*, prope *Laodiceam combustam* (Ladik). No date.]

204. MARTIUS FIRMISSIMUS. Priest (Italy), husband of Decimia Apronianeta. [Diehl 1154. E coemeterio christiano inter Morlupo et Leprignano sito. No date.]

205. MONSIS. Priest (Calabria), family man. [G. B. de Rossi, *Bulletino di Archeologia cristiana*, 3d ser., 2d year (Roma, 1877), pp. 88–95. (Inscription would be prior to the year 498.) Diehl 1150. Tropeae in Calabria. No date.]

206. RUSTICUS. Priest (Vercelli), husband of Maxentia. [Diehl 1163. Vercelli. No date.]

207. STEPHEN. Priest (Salonis), husband of Martana. [Diehl 1172. In operculo sarcophagi Salonitani. No date.]

208. TURRIANUS LEONTIUS. Priest (Mesia), husband of Aurelia Marcellina. [Diehl 393. Nicopoli in Moesia in dextro latere putei Turcici. No date.]

Married deacons

209. AFUSIUS CECILIUS. Deacon (Rome), husband of Licinia Victoria. [L. Perret, *Catacombes de Rome* (Paris, 1851), vol. V, pl. XLI, n. 14. No date.]

210. Anonymous deacon (Corcyrius in Cilicia), father of the subdeacon John and of another son, Paul. [CIG IV, 9192. Coryci Ciliciae (Korghos) in coemeterio Christianorum. No date.]

211. Anonymous deacon (Rome), married. [Diehl 3332 adn. Romae e Soteridis coemeterio ad s. Callistum. No date.]

212. AUR. MARCELLINUS. Deacon (Rome), father of the subdeacon Aur. Zinzius. [Diehl 1202. In Portu Ostiensi. No date.]

213. AUR. SATURNINUS. Deacon (Rome), husband of Aura Veneriae. [Diehl 3832. Altini. No date.]

214. CRESCENTIUS. Deacon (Algeria), father of Bruttanicus. [Diehl 1229. Opere musivo in basilicae christianae pavimento. No date.]

215. FELIX. Deacon (Rome), husband of Aurelia Geminia. [Diehl 1201. In Portu Ostiensi. No date.]

216. SULPICIUS. Deacon (Chiusi), married and family man. [Diehl 1208. Clusii e Coemeterio Mustiolae. No date.]

217. THEODOTOS. Deacon (Rome), husband of Licinia and family man. [ICUR, NS I, 3148. Veronae. Inscription of uncertain origin. No date.]

Married deaconesses

218. AUSONIA. Deaconess (Italy) or wife of a deacon. Mother of several children. [Diehl 1239. No date.]

Married subdeacons

219. POLYCARP. Subdeacon (Smyrna), husband of Palladia. [CIG IV, 9281. Prope *Smyrnam* Ephesus versus in acra sepulcrali. No date.]

220. URSINIANUS. Subdeacon (Trier), husband of Ludula. [RICG, I, 170. Trier, necropolis of St. Paulinus and St. Maximinus. Found in 1824 in the cemetery of St. Paulinus. 4th or 5th century, or perhaps 8th century.]

II

NESTORIAN CHURCH OF PERSIA

Married bishops

221. BABAEUS (Mar Babai). Bishop of Seleucia-Ctesiphon, Katholikos of the Nestorians († 503). Married and family man.[75] [J. A. Assemani, *De Catholicis seu Patriarchis Chaldeorum et Nestorianorum Commentarius Historico-chronologicus* (1775), p. 22. Bar Hebraeus, *Chronicon Ecclesiasticum*, edited and translated by J. B. Abbeloos and T. J. Lamy, III (1877), p. 81. Ortiz de Urbina, *Patrologia Syriaca* (1958), p. 114.]

222. BARSUMAS (Bar Sauma, Bar Cauma). Bishop of Nisibe († between 492 and 495), married (illegitimately) to the nun Mamoe.[76] [Bar Hebraeus, *Chronicon Ecclesiasticum*, III (1877), pp. 62–66. H. Gismondi, *Maris Amri et Slibae de Patriarchis Nestorianorum commentaria, pars prior* (1899), pp. 37–40.]

[75] It was under that Nestorian Katholikos that the Synod of Mar Babai was held, during which it was authorized that "from the patriarch to the least in the hierarchy, anyone could openly contract a chaste marriage with an only wife, in order to beget children and use marital rights" (J. B. Chabot, *Synodicon orientale* [Paris, 1902], p. 312). Bar Hebraeus even assures that the clerics were compelled to marry under penalty of sanctions: "Hic [Babaeus] synodum celebravit, atque sub poena suspensionis ut omnes catholici posthac constituendi mulieres in uxores acciperent, similiter et episcopi: presbyter vero, quotiescumque ejus uxor decederet, aliam duceret" (*Chronicon ecclesiasticum*, III, p. 80).

[76] Barsumas studied at the Edessa school, from which he was expelled at the death of Ibas (457). He settled in Nisibe and became its bishop, thanks to the favor of King Perôz. In a spirit of rivalry with Patriarch Baboui (Babowai), he held in April 484 a synod of opponents at Beth-Lafath. Monks and priests who "could not keep continence" were authorized to marry. Later Barsumas repudiated that synod and annulled all its decisions (J. B. Chabot, *Synodicon orientale*, pp. 308–9). Nevertheless, the measures relative to marriage of clerics were approved and renewed by the Synod of Mar Acacius (486), then by that of Mar Babai (497) (ibid., pp. 303–6, 312). Once he was a bishop, Barsamas himself married a nun called Mamoe.

6TH CENTURY

Married bishops

223. ELISAEUS. Bishop of Seleucia-Ctesiphon. Katholikos of the Nestorians (Rival of Narses. Ordained in 520 or 523). Married, son-in-law of the Katholikos Silas, his predecessor. [J. A. Assemani, *De Catholicis*, p. 23. Bar Hebraeus, *Chronicon Ecclesiasticum*, III, p. 82.]

224. EZECHIEL. Bishop of Zabe. Katholikos of the Nestorians (ordained ca. 570), married, son-in-law of the Katholikos Paulus.[77] [J. A. Assemani, *De Catholicis*, p. 31. Bar Hebraeus, *Chronicon Ecclesiasticum*, III, p. 98.]

225. PAULUS. Bishop of Seleucia-Ctesiphon. Katholikos of the Nestorians (early 6th century), married and family man. [Bar Hebraeus, *Chronicon Ecclesiasticum*, III, pp. 88–90.]

226. SILAS. Bishop of Seleucia-Ctesiphon. Katholikos of the Nestorians († 520 or 525), married and father of a daughter. Father-in-law of the Katholikos Elisaeus. [J. A. Assemani, *De Catholicis*, p. 23. Bar Hebraeus, *Chronicon Ecclesiasticum*, III, p. 82.]

7TH CENTURY

Married bishops

227. JESUJABUS (Isô Yahb II). Bishop of Balada, Patriarch of the Nestorians († 647), married. [J. B. Chabot, *Chronique de Michel le Syrien Patriarche Jacobite d'Antioche (1166–99) éditée pour la première fois et traduite en français*, III (1905), p. 521.]

---

[77] The *Liber turris* of Mare ibn Sulaiman (12th century) relates that a synod gathered by the Katholikos Mar Aba (540–52) decreed that in the future no married man would be ordained as a bishop or patriarch (H. Gismondi, *Maris Amri et Slibae de Patriarchis Nestorianorum commentaria*, pars altera [1897], p. 24. Cf. J. S. Assemani, *Bibliotheca Orientalis Clementino-Vaticana*, II [Rome, 1721], p. 412b). In fact, the election of Katholikos Ezechiel (ca. 570), who was married to the daughter of his predecessor, Paul, seems somehow to weaken such an assertion. J. Labourt points out, quite rightly, that the works of Mar Aba we have do not allow us to check the value of these affirmations (those of Mare) (J. Labourt, *Le christianisme dans l'empire perse sous la dynastie sassanide, 224–632* [Paris, 1904], p. 191, n. 3).

III
NOVATIAN CHURCH

Married bishops

228. MARCIAN. Novatian bishop of Constantinople (4th century), father of the bishop Chrysantus, his successor. [Socrates, *Historia Ecclesiastica*, VII, 12 (PG 67, 757c).]

IV
PELAGIAN CHURCH

5TH CENTURY

229. JULIAN. Deacon of Benevento, then bishop of Eclanum († ca. 454), husband of Ia. [See also the list of bishops of the Catholic Church, no. 88 above.]

230. SEVARIANUS. Pelagian bishop (unknown See, ca. 429), father of Agricola, Pelagian. [Prosper of Aquitaine, *Epitoma Chronicon* (MGH, *auct. ant.*, IX, XI, and XIII. *Chronica minora saec. IV–V–VI–VII*, 1 [Berlin, 1891], p. 472, n. 1301).]

Now we can make a few quick observations based upon this list.

During the *1st century*, other than the case of the apostles studied in the previous chapter, we know of only two married men who received the imposition of hands. One is the deacon Nicolas [2], and the other is an anonymous bishop of Pontus [1], remembered by Epiphanius because he had been the father of the heretic Marcion. Did those two men continue to have a marital life after their ordinations, or did they then live in continence? History does not say anything about this.[78] We must therefore be careful not to draw any conclusion, one way or the other. One is at times tempted to say, "It goes without saying" that being married, those men consecrated to the service of the Church continued to use their conjugal rights because there was no obligation of continence for the clergy as yet. But this is precisely what we are trying to find out. On the one hand, the unanimous consensus of the Fathers relative to continence observed by those of the apostles who could have been married, and on the other hand, the claim to apostolicity of the legislative documents at the end of the 4th century with respect to clerical continence compel us to be cautious. One must beware of hasty generalizations: all in all, two cases of married sacred ministers, for a period of several decades (in the second half of the 1st century), give us a numerical basis that is not sufficient to form a conclusion about what could have been the rule of practice in the whole Church. It is only in an indirect way, in the light of the following centuries, that the issue can be clarified.

The only two instances of married clerics that we know of in the *2d century* call for the same reflection. Neither the story of the priest Valens and his wife [3] nor that of the anonymous deacon of Asia whose wife had let herself be seduced by a magician [4] can in themselves lead us to a conclusion regarding the ways these consecrated couples led their conjugal lives and, even less, to a conclusion about the general discipline at that time.

As to the *3d century*, we know of five bishops and five priests who were (or had been) bound by marriage. The case of Irenaeus of Sirmium [8] in Dalmatia is interesting because of the spirit of total detachment attested to by this martyr bishop, confessing at the point of death that "he had

---

[78] The fact that Nicolas separated from his wife is not tied to his reception of the diaconate; it may be that the event happened before his election to the group of Seven and had even been a reason for the choice made by the apostles; but it is also possible that Nicolas did not abandon his wife until he became a deacon.

no" wife, sons, or daughters and that he had "obeyed the precept of [his] Lord Jesus Christ: 'He who does not leave his parents and give up all that he possesses cannot be my disciple.'" A bishop who was animated by such feelings had surely been capable of practicing the form of renunciation that is conjugal continence if the Church had then made it an obligation. Whether that had actually been the case, or if, to the contrary, he still had had intercourse with his wife after ordination, it is a question that the narrative in the *Acts of the Martyrs* does not permit us to solve. The story of the patriarch Demetrius of Alexandria [7] cannot supply us with sure information because it is mixed with legend. Did he live in continence with his wife, as the narrative attests, or is it true that before he came, all the patriarchs of Alexandria were single? It would be prudent not to be too positive, *The History of the Patriarchs of Alexandria* by Severus of El-Eschmounein, our only source, having been written at a late date.[79] As to Demetrian of Antioch [6], the passage of Eusebius that mentions him has no information regarding his practice of marital rights or continence. In the case of Cheremon of Nilopolis [5], the fact that he kept his wife with him and fled together with her during the persecution of Deces does not imply that he did not live with her in perfect chastity.

The five married priests of the 3d century belong to the African Church. Numidicus [12] and Saturninus [13] were martyrs; their heroic behavior suggests the same reflections as for Irenaeus of Sirmium. Did the old priest Cecilian [10] have conjugal intercourse with his wife? Here too the narrative of Pontius the Deacon leaves us in the dark. Nevertheless, the fact that Cecilian was capable of thinking that he should entrust his wife to a celibate bishop seems rather to indicate that he and Cyprian already led, as far as perfect chastity is concerned, the same kind of life. Lastly, we come to Novatus [11], and we can think either that the crime of parricide perpetrated by a man who was altogether a scoundrel caused St. Cyprian to keep silence on the (relatively minor) infraction that could have been conjugal activity on the part of that priest, or that the heinous crime had been committed before Novatus became a member of the clergy (as deacon and as priest). These two hypotheses are sufficiently plausible to prevent us from a black-and-white conclusion such as: since Novatus was married, there was no obligation of continence for the African clergy during the 3d century. As to Tertullian [14], one cannot

[79] An indication in this direction is contained in the *Annals* of Eutychius of Alexandria (ca. 876): until the Council of Nicaea, married men could become bishops and keep their wives with them; only the patriarchs were the exception: they had to be bachelors (PG 111, 1008c). Though of unequal value, the *Annals* of Eutychius have been derived from sources of which some have vanished, and they are generally considered of real interest because of this very fact.

entirely trust the testimony of St. Jerome affirming that he had been a priest.

The *4th century* offers us more numerous examples of married clerics, thanks especially to the Greek ecclesiastical histories (Eusebius of Caesarea, Socrates, Sozomenus, and Theodoret of Cyrus), the works of Gregory of Tours, the ancient historians of Armenia, and information collected from epigraphy.

For some of them, historical data attest that they lived in continence after ordination, either because they were already widowers or because they had decided to consider their wives as sisters. Such are, in Italy, Bishop Antonius, father of Pope Damasus [20]; Bishop Severus of Ravenna [42]; and an anonymous deacon of Florence [60]; in Spain, Pacian of Barcelona [35]; in Gaul, the bishops Artemius of Auvergne [21], Hilary of Poitiers [28], Reticius of Autun [41], Simplicius of Autun [43], and Urbicus of Clermont [46], as well as the priest Aper [52]. In the East we know: in Phrygia, Pelagius of Laodicea [36]; in Syria, Ajax of Botolius [15]; and in Armenia, the Katholikos Gregory the Illuminator [27], Verthanes [47], Yusik [49], and Nerses the Great [34].

As far as the others are concerned, the data we have do not allow us to give a direct answer to the question of their living or not living in continence with their wives. Very often we do not even know whether the wife was still alive when the husband became a deacon, priest, or bishop. In this group we include, in Italy, the bishop Anastasius I of Rome [16];[80] an anonymous bishop [17]; Leo [30]; Memorius, father of Julian of Eclanus [33]; the bishop Petronius Dextrus [37]; four priests: Pac. Patroclus [58], Gaudentius [54], Leontius [55], and Limenius [56]; and three deacons: two anonymous, [61] and [62], and Severus [65]. In Spain we have the bigamous bishop Carterius [23] and Symposius, bishop of Astorga [45]. In Britain(?) the priest Potitus [59] and the deacon Calpornius [63], respectively grandfather and father of St. Patrick. In Africa, the bishop Victor of Ucresium in Numidia [48]. In Illyria, the priest Melon [57] and the deacon F. Julius [64]. In the East, the married bishops belonging to the same category are the following: Eulalius of Caesarea of Cappadocia [24], Gregory of Nyssa [25], Gregory the Elder of Nazianzen [26], Philogonius of Antioch [40], Marcellus of Apamea [32],

---

[80] Suppose that it were necessary to take in the proper sense the affirmation of St. Jerome, according to whom Pope Innocent had been "the son" of Anastasius. If such were indeed the case, there is a strong presumption for thinking that the author of the *Adversus Jovinianum* would not have evoked such a kinship if Pope Anastasius had not been, on the throne of Peter, an example of perfect continence.

Antoninus of Ephesus [19], the six anonymous bishops of the Ephesus area mentioned in the Life of St. John Chrysostom [18]: Leontius of Tripoli in Lydia [31], Spiridon of Trimithus in Cyprus [44], Phileas of Thmuis in Egypt [39],[81] and the Armenians Khat of Pakravant [29], Asrug of Pakravant [22], and Phâren [38]. Finally, two oriental priests: Apollinaris of Laodicea in Phrygia [53] and Anysius of Borilla in Cappadocia [51].

Three cases of Western bishops, among those whom history directly informs us were living in continence, suggest some observations. We are referring to Urbicus of Clermont [46], Simplicius of Autun [43], and Severus of Ravenna [42]. Gregory of Tours tells us that the wife of Urbicus, once her husband had been elevated to the episcopal dignity, "juxta consuetudinem ecclesiasticam, remota a consortio sacerdotis, religiose vivebat."

It is note worthy that the author of *Histoire des Francs* does not say that "in conformity with ecclesiastical custom", the wife of Urbicus lived in perfect chastity with her husband, but that in conformity with that custom she had left the conjugal home ("*remota a consortio sacerdotis*") and lived religiously. Thus, it is not the practice of continence that Gregory of Tours describes as an ecclesiastical custom, but the departure from the bishop's home.[82] Such a custom had undoubtedly not spread to all the Churches of Gaul, if we look at the case of Simplicius of Autun (about whom more later), who deemed it licit to keep his wife at home. If the successor of Austremonius to the See of Clermont separated from his wife, it is because there was a custom (*consuetudo*) in that province, i.e., an unwritten law that was established for quite a long time, that was approved by competent authorities, and on which one could reasonably base oneself in adopting a certain attitude, though this custom was not formally prescribed by law. But the important point to discern is that the existence of such a custom presupposed the obligation of continence, since it was obviously in order to put the married bishop and his wife in a better position to observe it that the Church of Auvergne had adopted a practice of asking for the separation of the couple. In other words, the "*consuetudo ecclesiastica*" to which Gregory of Tours refers in the case of Urbicus was a practical application of a formal obligation of

---

[81] About this married bishop, who was one of the most remarkable men of his generation, one should make the same remarks as those about Irenaeus of Sirmium and the priests Numidicus and Saturninus. See above, p. 125.

[82] The translation of R. Latouche, I, p. 62, does not sufficiently emphasize this point and may lead to confusion.

perfect continence.[83] It bears witness to that obligation as also does the penance that the bishop imposed on himself by retiring temporarily to a monastery.[84] With Simplicius of Autun, the existence of a compulsory discipline of continence for the high clergy appears even with more clarity because the fact of seeing a bishop and his wife in the same house provoked suspicion, which would not have been the case if married clerics had then been free to observe or not to observe perfect chastity with their wives. It was not only because Simplicius and his wife had spontaneously chosen to live in continence that the people of Autun were scandalized to see them living under the same roof, but because they were compelled to do so according to a universally known rule. The story of Severus of Ravenna sheds light on the same disciplinary background. The life of continence to which her husband, suddenly elevated to the rank of bishop, is henceforth bound, compels Vincentia, his wife, to put on immediately the widows' veil. Equating this new mode of life with widowhood also seems to indicate that the wife was separating from her husband according to a custom similar to that which was observed in Clermont.

If we can thus establish with sufficient certainty that an obligation of perfect continence for the higher clerics was the rule in the 4th century in the dioceses of Clermont, Autun, and Ravenna, there is no great risk in affirming that such an obligation was not limited to those dioceses but had spread to larger areas. It would be rather strange for the clerics of Clermont to be compelled to observe continence while those of Lyon, for example, would have been free to practice or not practice conjugal intercourse, in which case it would have been enough to change one's residence in order to change one's morals. In the case of Gaul, we would then have an additional indication in favor of the authenticity of canon 29 of the Council of Arles in 314, which enjoined continence on the higher members of the clergy.[85] In the case of Italy, it is quite likely that the discipline followed by Severus of Ravenna and the anonymous deacon of Florence in the first half of the 4th century was customary in all of northern Italy and reflected the practices of Rome.

---

[83] One could wonder whether this was a custom in conformity with the law (*juxta legem, secundum jus*), about which the Roman jurist Julius Paulus said in the 3d century, "optima [enim] est legum interpres consuetudo", or whether it was a custom *praeter legem*, in the direction of the law, but adding an extra demand. The issue is a secondary one here.

[84] Urbicus seems to have voluntarily gone to a monastery, without waiting for his fault to be known (through the birth of his daughter) and so bring him ecclesiastical punishment. His repentance was his judge. It might also be that, at one time, no official sanction had yet been foreseen for faults against continence, though the obligation was no less real.

[85] See below, pp. 161–69.

In the East, the history of the Armenian Katholikos of the Gregorian lineage deserves special attention. Those who had been married were all consecrated bishops at a period in their lives when they had no more matrimonial activity. Gregory, the first of the lineage, was separated for a long time from his wife, who had given him two sons when he was young, and while a bishop he did not live with her (she might perhaps have been dead then). His eldest son Verthanes, who succeeded the younger and single Aristakes, was elected Katholikos at an advanced age. Yusik, grandson of Gregory, and Nerses the Great, grandson of Yusik, were both widowers when they were called to the episcopate. Thus, if it is true that "in the early days of the Armenian Church, bishops or even Katholikos were not required to be celibate, since for six generations from Gregory to Sahak the Great, patriarchal dignity was transmitted from father to son in the lineage of the Illuminator",[86] it must be stressed at the same time that those married patriarchs lived in continence from the time of their consecrations (if it had not in fact been long before that). In other words, the quasi-hereditary dynasty of the first Armenian Katholikos is an illustration of the principle of distinction between celibacy in the strict sense and celibacy in the broad sense of the term (or celibacy-continence), a principle that we have already enunciated, affirming its utility for the study of the apostolic origins of priestly celibacy.[87] Did those leaders of the Armenian Church observe continence simply because of circumstances and by virtue of a completely personal option, or did they respond to the demands of an objective discipline? History is silent about this. But the question is a legitimate one when we see continence associated so regularly for several generations with the choice of Katholikos.[88] It does appear that this is more than a coincidence.

We know also that during the first century of its existence, the Church of Armenia remained organizationally attached to Caesarea of Cappadocia, her mother Church. Was it not from this apostolic Church[89] that Armenia received, together with its hierarchy, the discipline of celibacy-continence observed in such an exemplary way during that period of its history? Moreover, if we remember that Caesarea was then in close communion with Rome, and that the Church of Armenia partook, through her intervention, as through her particular life, of the same "consanguinity of doctrine" with the See of Peter, we are normally

---

[86] G. Garitte, *Documents pour l'étude du livre d'Agathange* (Rome, 1946), p. 309.

[87] See above, pp. 48ff.

[88] Let us note that what we know about the other married Armenian bishops in the 4th century (Khat, Asrug, and Pharen) does not weaken the possibility of a rule of continence in these areas, because it is not said they lived maritally.

[89] In the meaning we have seen above, pp. 56–57.

led to ask ourselves whether the Armenian Katholikos of the 4th century are not, from the historical viewpoint, privileged witnesses to the fact that there was then in the East a rule of continence identical to that which was observed, as we have seen, in certain Western Churches.[90]

The following are married clerics of the *5th century* who are known historically as having lived in continence. *In the West*: Italy—the bishops Julian of Eclanum [88] and Paulinus of Nola [93]; Gaul—the bishops Amator of Auxerre [66], Apollinaris Sidonius [74], Eucherus of Lyon [80], Eutropus of Orange [82], an anonymous one [68], Germanus of Auxerre [84], Hesychius of Vienna [86], and Lupus of Troyes [89]; the priests Salvian of Marseilles [111] and Sulpicius Severus(?) [114]. *In the East*: Armenia—the Katholikos Sahak the Great [96]; Egypt—quite likely, Synesius of Cyrene [98].

The following are married clerics about whom we have no biographical data enabling us to state whether or not they lived in continence. *In the West*: Italy—Pope Felix III [83]; bishops Avitus of Plaisance [75] and Pancratius [92] and an anonymous bishop [70]; the priests Leo [108], Felix [104], Iocundus [106], and Petrus [110], the last three of whom were fathers of future popes; and the deacons Adeodatus [115], an anonymous one [116], Dionysius [118], Januarius [119], and Tettius [120]; Gaul—bishops Bonosus of Narbonne [76], Eulogius of Bourges [81], four anonymous bishops [67], [69], [71], [72], Namatius of Auvergne [90], Palladius of Bourges [91], Prince of Soissons [94], Ruricius of Limoges [95], Simplicius of Bourges [97], and Volusian of Tours [99]; the priests Faustinus [103], Hilary [105], Senatorus [112], and Silvius [113]; and the subdeacon Basil [124]; Illyria—Deacon Criscientianus [117];

---

[90]Gregory the Illuminator went to Caesarea of Cappadocia to receive from the hands of the exarch Leontius the sacerdotal and episcopal consecration (285–305), and by that fact found himself in a hierarchical framework that made him dependant on the Roman pontiff; on the other hand, the participation of Katholikos Aristakes, son of Gregory, in the Council of Nicaea (325), where he went with Leontius of Caesarea, was probably an opportunity to strengthen ties with the Apostolic See through the intermediary of pontifical legates present at the First Ecumenical Council. Later, and through Patriarch Nerses the Great inclusive († 374), all the Armenian Katholikos were consecrated by the archbishop of Caesarea (Gelasius of Cyzicus avers that Leontius of Caesarea presided over the Churches of Cappadocia of Small and Great Armenia. *Historia Ecclesiastica*, II, c. 28. GCS 28, 105). Even after political events had put an end to that tradition, and the exarchate of Caesarea had ceased being a point of organizational unity of the Armenian Church with the Universal Church, the Armenians still remained in communion with Rome, until the Synod of Vagharchapat (491) and especially the one of Dvin, which, during the first years of the 6th century, solemnly approved the Henotica of Zenon, leaning toward Monophysitism (about the issue as a whole, see Fr. Tournebize, *Arménie*, DHGE IV, c. 290ff.).

Africa—Bishop Germanus [85] and an anonymous one of Zura, in the Proconsular province [73]. *In the East*: bishops Diogenes of Antioch [78], Domninus of Caesarea in Palestine [79], and Irenaeus of Tyre [87]; an anonymous priest of Cyzicus [101], father of the historian Gelasius of Cyzicus, and another anonymous priest, of Bethlehem [102], as well as the priest Marcian in Constantinople [109]; Tinoutos, a deacon of Lycaonia [121]; and two deaconesses of the Tyre area [122], [123].

The lack of direct information about this second group, in the West, is counterbalanced by the situation that we know through the legislation expressed at the Council of Carthage and in the decretals of Pope Siricius[91] as early as the 4th century, a legislation that would be repeated and confirmed many times during the 5th century, in particular by Innocent I and Leo the Great, by the Gallic Councils, and by the *Codex Canonum Ecclesiae Africanae*. Taking only the case of Gaul, we can affirm with certainty that bishops such as Bonosus of Narbonne, Eulogius of Bourges, and the others were subject to the law of celibacy–continence, and, insofar as we do not know of any canonical sanctions against them, we can conclude that they observed it faithfully. The same reasoning applies to the bishops, priests, and deacons of the other Western provinces. This leads us to an important note, since one cannot fail to observe on the basis of these examples that certain situations of married clerics can only be correctly interpreted in the framework of the general context at that time. Simply to note in the *Liber Pontificalis* that Pope Felix III was the son of a priest of Rome called Felix [104] and to conclude from this without any other study that the law of celibacy–continence did not exist in fifth-century Italy would be an obviously gross historical mistake, because it would not take into account what we have learned from the legislation of that time. We encountered bishops, priests, and deacons from the first three centuries of the Church whose matrimonial situations were revealed to us through historical narratives and certain references in contemporary literature. Are we permitted to base ourselves on this sole fact and to infer that those married clerics were not subject to an obligation to continence? It would be prudent not to form a conclusion too hastily, even in the absence of any explicit legislation, because the general context is not sufficiently known to us. Under such conditions, it is legitimate to try to find out what could have been the actual conjugal life of the third-century married clerics in the retrospective light shed by the following centuries.

Worthy of note is the fifth-century case of two married Persian bishops, for the reason that their situation is placed within a particular legal context

---

[91] See above, pp. 3–17.

created by the Persian Church that around the year 480 officially allied itself with Nestorianism. The synod called by Barsumas at Beth-Lafath in 484 promulgated special laws having to do with the marriage of the clergy, as the synods of Mar Acacius (486) and Mar Babai (497) did also. Those synods ruled, namely, that "from the patriarch down to the lowest member of the hierarchy, any cleric may openly contract a chaste marriage to one wife, for the procreation of children and for mutual comfort".[92] From this we may conclude that in all probability Bishop Barsumas of Nisibe [222] and Katholikos Babaeus (Mar Babai) [221] were both married and continued to live, each with his own wife, in the married state, their right to do so having been confirmed by their own legislation. At the same time, we learn by implication something about the other Eastern Churches that had remained in communion with Rome, because the Nestorian Church of Persia, by passing its own laws authorizing all members of its hierarchy to be married and to enjoy all the rights and privileges pertaining to marriage, gave a clear impression that it was declaring itself to be autonomous at the level of Church discipline, as it had already done at the doctrinal level. If one places this direct evidence for the existence of a discipline of celibate continence in the East alongside the evidence furnished by the Armenian Church of the 4th and 5th centuries (at least until the time of Sahak the Great), one cannot fail to ponder seriously on the matter.

In the *6th century*, our list shows only five married bishops, one married priest, and one married deacon whom history tells us lived in continence. These are the Gallic bishops Gregory of Langres [143], Leontius of Bordeaux [146], an anonymous bishop of Nantes [125], Genebaud of Laon [142], and Maclou of Vannes [148]; an anonymous priest of Nursia [159]; and the anonymous deacon of Chiusi [169]. The bad fortunes of Genebaud and the infidelities of Maclou attest, in their own way, to the existence of the law of celibacy-continence, on which, moreover, the legislation of the 6th century and other testimonies of that time are quite clear. We are also sure that all the other married Western bishops, priests, and deacons of that time were subject to the obligation of continence. In Gaul, bishops Apollinaris of Auvergne [127], Artemius of Sens [128], Astidius of Limoges [129], Avitus of Vienna [130], Badegisil of Le Mans [131], Baudin of Tours [132], Desideratus of Verdun [135], Euphronius of Tours [137], Firminus of Viviers [139], Françillon of Tours [140], Gallomagnus of Troyes [141], Namatius of Vienna [149], Nonnichius of

---

[92] *Synode de Mar Babai*, in J. B. Chabot, *Synodicon Orientale* (Paris, 1902), p. 312. See also below, pp. 283–87, the complete text of the 3d canon of the Synod of Mar Acacius.

Nantes [150], Pantagathe of Vienna [151], Paul of Trois Châteaux [153], Priscus of Lyon [154], Salvius of Albi [155], and Victeur of Rennes [156]; the priests Anastasius [157], Eunomius [161], Evodius [162], Silvester [165], Transobad [166], and Valens [167], an anonymous priest [158], and Petrus, a deacon of Arles [172]; in Italy, bishops Blandus of Ortona [133], Cassius, of the area of Perusia [134], Eusanius of Agrigentia [138], an anonymous bishop of Syracuse [126], Pope Hormisdas [145], and Passivus of Fermo [152]; the priests Basil [160] and Florentius [163], the priest Gordianus [164], father of Pope Agapetus I, and the priest Victorianus [168]; an anonymous deacon [170] and the deacons Evangelus [171] and Quirillus [173]; the subdeacon Stephen [176], father of Pope Adeodatus I, and the subdeacon Marcellus [175]. In Malta, Bishop Lucillus [147] and in Rome a deaconess Theodora [174].

The three Nestorian Katholikos of Seleucia-Ctesiphon—Elisaeus [223], Paulus [225], and Silas [226]—were elected and exercised their pontificates at a time when the clergy of the Persian Church was still ruled by the legislation of the synod of Mar Babai (497). Not only was marriage not an obstacle to their election, but it is very likely that they went on using their marital rights even during the time of their patriarchate, as their laws permitted them to do. One can think that the case was the same for Katholikos Ezechiel [224], even though he had been elevated to the episcopate under the recent legislation of Mar Aba (540–52) that would have forbidden a married man to be chosen as bishop or patriarch. In any event, the rule of Mar Babai remained valid for priests and deacons. All through the 6th century, as was the case in the following centuries, the Persian Nestorian clergy (with the exception of its bishops and patriarchs who, after Mar Aba, were generally single) were free to marry and to use their conjugal rights normally.

If we found no instances of married bishops in other provinces of the Christian East that were still loyal to the faith of Chalcedon, the main reason—taking into account the limitations of our data—is to be found in the imperial laws of Justinian formally prohibiting the elevation to the episcopate men who had children or grandchildren or were still bound to wives.[93] From that time on, the Eastern bishops were mostly, even exclusively, recruited among monks and single clerics.

---

[93] These are the laws of March 1, 528, and July 29, 531 (*Codex Justinianus* 1, 3, 41, 2–4; 1, 3, 47), and of the 6th, 123d, and 137th *Novellae*, respectively dated March 16, 535, May 1, 546, and March 26, 565. For a detailed presentation of these Justinian laws, see below, pp. 352ff.

It is for the same reasons that in the *7th century*, we do not find in the Eastern historiographies any example of married bishops.[94] One must also take into account the great political upheavals that followed Islam's conquests in Egypt, Syria, Mesopotamia, and Armenia (as well as in Africa) and brought darkness on the ecclesiastical history of these provinces during that tragic century.

In the West, we find the names of two married bishops whose biographies mention that they were separated from their wives: Faron of Meaux [180] and Leudinus of Toul [183]. As to the others, the legislation that we know and is strengthened with the passage of time leaves no doubt about the kinds of lives they led: they obviously gave up any conjugal life, supposing that their wives were still alive when they were ordained bishops. We list the following bishops: Aetherius of Vienna [177], Arnulfus of Metz [179], Filibaud of Aire-sur-l'Adour, in the Landes [181], Magnus of Avignon [184], Medoald of Trier [185], Palladius of Eauze [186], Reolus of Rheims [187], and Sigilaicus of Tours [188]. Next to these bishops who, as it happens, were all in the provinces of Gaul, we also know of Bishop Theodorus [189], born in Jerusalem but whose See is unknown,[95] father of Pope Theodore I. The priest Geremarus [191] and the subdeacon Bavon [192], among many others certainly, were also examples of that period's Western married clerics who were subject to the law of celibacy-continence.

Finally, let us note that the list of married bishops, priests, deacons, and deaconesses whose dates we do not know ([193] to [220]) was composed on the basis of information obtained from epigraphy. It is likely that they were clerics who lived during the early centuries of the Church, but the lack of precise dates calls for prudence as to possible conclusions regarding the nature of their conjugal lives. One must remember that if an epitaph or an inscription enables us to know the state of life of the deceased (married or single), it does not say anything about the concrete existence he led with his wife after ordination.

[94] One can refer particularly for that period to the *Chronographie* of Theophanius the Confessor (PG 108, 63ff.), the *Chronographicon syntomon* and the *Breviarium* of Nicephores Callistus (PG 145–47), the *Chronique* of Michael the Syrian (J. B. Chabot, trans., 3 vols. [Paris, 1900–10]), *The History of the Patriarchs of Alexandria* by Severus of El-Eschmounein (PO 1, pp. 103ff.), the *Chronique* of John of Nikou (*Notices et Extraits des manuscrits de la Bibliothèque Nationale*, vol. 24 [Paris, 1883], pp. 125ff.), and the *Histoire d'Héraclius* by Sebeos (F. Macler, trans. [Paris, 1904]).

[95] What we know about the Byzantine legislation, forbidding to raise family men to the episcopate, leads us to think that this Theodorus was already in the West when he was elected bishop.

PART TWO

Basic Patristic Records on
Priestly Celibacy–Continence

In addition to the testimonies pertaining to the marriages of the apostles and the instances of clerics who were married and had children, the patristic records on the celibacy-continence of clergy members in the early centuries of the Church include a certain number of documents of various kinds (conciliar texts, papal decretals, and so forth) whose study is indispensable for the knowledge of history. They will be introduced and analyzed in the following sections. As was the case for the list of married clerics, we have set as *terminus ad quem* the late 7th century, the Quinisext Council of 691, determining in a clear and decisive way the Eastern (Byzantine) legislation at that time on the issue under study. The point of departure is indicated by a text of St. Ignatius of Antioch († ca. 107), which happens to be the first nonscriptural document having something to say about the topic. We will pause at the end of the 4th century, after the Council of Carthage, to take a retrospective glance at the first four centuries and to check in what measure the claim to apostolicity expressed by Siricius and the African Fathers can be understood. In this first part of the records we will read the documents in their chronological order, which, because of the relatively small number of testimonies, seems to be more appropriate to research needs. From the 4th century on and until the Quinisext Council we will regroup the texts by affinity of literary genre, both in order to avoid repetitions and to highlight better the hierarchy of merit in the documents we introduce.

The preparation of these patristic records has a long history. As early as the time of the Council of Trent, the commission of theologians in charge of studying Protestant theses regarding the marriage of clerics had gathered a certain portion of writings drawn from the works of the Fathers and the councils. It seems that the first truly systematic catalog was compiled by the Lutheran Georg Calixtus, in his book *De conjugio clericorum liber* published in 1631. On the Catholic side the works of L. Thomassin drew attention, but it was thanks to the work of F. A. Zaccaria (in the 18th century) that a very complete—for that time—and remarkably analyzed record was made available to the public. In the 19th century the Theiner brothers and then Monsignor A. de Roskovany enriched the collection. The voluminous catalog of Roskovany still remains, in spite of its shortcomings, a mine of information for researchers. G. Bickell, on his part, brought an original contribution with his translation of Syriac texts. Lastly, modern times have witnessed reports prepared with the care and the rigor enabled by contemporary critical editions of the Fathers and councils of the Church's works, progress in historical science, and the priceless work tools now available to scholars (Index, dictionaries, *Claves Patrum*, and so forth).[1]

---

[1] See chapter 2, "The State of the Issue", p. 18.

The work of text collection was generally accompanied by the necessary effort of discernment to select authentic documents and reject apocryphal ones. It was thus that one was able to dismiss with certainty the testimonies borrowed from the Pseudo-Clementines (wrongly credited for a long time to Bishop Clement of Rome) and to mention a famous example in the history of the controversies, the pseudo-rescript of Ulric of Imola forged in 1060 in an attempt to bring the Church to a canonical recognition of priestly marriage.[2]

A similar effort of discernment is still indispensable today when it comes to such and such a document of doubtful origin, or when one must reject documents that, under study, prove to be alien to the issue. The main thrust, however, remains the interpretation of certain more difficult texts, which must be approached with the resources of philology, but even more important, and at the same time, with attention to the total historical context of the period.

---

[2] This pamphlet can be read in MGH, *Libelli de lite*, I, pp. 254–60. For several centuries it obstructed the records on priestly celibacy. G. Calixtus quotes it in his work, and F. A. Zaccaria also felt duty-bound in the 18th century to prove its apocryphal nature.

From the Origins to the Year 390

1st and 2d Centuries

St. Ignatius of Antioch († ca. 107)

According to Eusebius, Ignatius became bishop of Antioch around the year 69. He was probably a disciple of the apostles, and St. John Chrysostom, for one, is convinced that he was ordained bishop by Peter himself. Nothing is known about him until the time when he was condemned to the beasts and led to Rome by ten soldiers ("ten leopards") and used the stopovers to visit and encourage the Christian communities. Seven genuine letters from "that man of fire" have been kept. They have crossed the centuries, communicating to their readers something of the mystical flame of the great spiritual man of the Church the bishop of Antioch had been. In particular, the famous letter to the Romans, which he wrote in Smyrna, remains one of the gems of Christian literature. In Rome—and very likely in the Coliseum—he became what he had wished for so ardently: to be "the wheat of Christ . . . ground by the teeth of the beasts".

Letter to Polycarp

The letter of Ignatius of Antioch to Polycarp, "bishop over the Smyrnaean Church—or rather, who has God the Father for bishop over him, together with the Lord Jesus Christ" includes, among other advice, a warning to embrace humility and chastity so as not to lose, out of pride, the benefit of a difficult virtue. On his way to martyrdom, the bishop recommends that his colleague enlighten the Christians on that point: "If somebody is capable of passing all his days in chastity, in honor of the Lord's body, let him do so without boasting; for if he boasts of it, he is lost, and if the news gets beyond the bishop's ears it is all over with his chastity." [1]

The Greek text of this last sentence can be read in two ways. Certain manuscripts give us Ἐὰν καυχήσηται, ἀπώλετο, καὶ ἐὰν γνωσθῇ πλὴν τοῦ ἐπισκόπου, ἔφθαρται, which is the lesson adopted by the translation used in *Sources chrétiennes*. But one can also read πλέον, instead of πλὴν, as the Codex Mediceus, for instance, does in the 11th century, and thus understand: The chaste man loses himself not "if the news gets beyond the bishop's ears", but if, in his pride, "he believes himself to be superior to the bishop". [2] The interest in this variation is obvious. If one considers the possibility of a contemptuous attitude toward the bishop on the part of the "nonmarried" class, it is because there were many men bound by marriage at the heads of the Christian communities. At a time when virginity was crowned with honor, there was a strong temptation for those who had made a profession of chastity to compare themselves advantageously to others, their bishops included. The 4th canon of the Synod of Gangres in 340 would react against a similar tendency, pushed then to extremes on the part of the "Cathar" sects. [3] The πλέον variant, in the meaning we just indicated, therefore seems quite likely. [4]

As to the πλὴν lesson, it is not very satisfactory. How could or should a man or a woman who has made a vow of chastity be known only by the bishop? Though it is true that discretion is desirable in such matters, a good reputation and the necessities of social life still require that, without any fanfare, one should be known for what he is. [5] Let us rather

---

[1] *Lettre à Polycarpe*, V, 2. SCh 10, 4th ed. (1969), 150–51. English translation from *Early Christian Writings: The Apostolic Fathers*, trans. Maxwell Staniforth (Middlesex, Eng.: Penguin Books, 1968), p. 129.

[2] SCh 10, 151, n. 4. See also, on the issue of the manuscripts, the introduction of P. T. Camelot, pp. 14–15.

[3] The "Cathars" refused communion from the hands of married priests. See below, pp. 201–2.

[4] J. B. Lightfoot deems that πλέον does not modify the general meaning of the passage, which is to be understood, in his opinion, exactly as if one were reading πλὴν (*The Apostolic Fathers*, 2d ed. [London, 1889], II, 2, p. 349, n. 5). However, it does seem, as Bihlmeyer and P. T. Camelot think, that πλέον implies the idea of some superiority (SCh 10, 151, n. 4).

[5] The virginal state always enjoyed an official public recognition in the Church, as attested by the first patristic writings on virginity. For instance, the *Apostolic Tradition* of Hippolytus (n. 13) deals with virgins. Under such conditions, it is difficult to see how Ignatius of Antioch could have blamed those who were able to remain chaste (ἁγνεία) for making themselves known to others besides the bishop, for the category of virgins was at least known by everyone in the Church. The opinion of A. d'Alès (ΕΑΝ ΓΝΩΣΘΗΙ ΠΛΕΟΝ ΤΟΥ ΕΠΙΣΚΟΠΟΥ ΕΦΘΑΡΤΑΙ), in *Recherches de science religieuse*, 25 (1935), pp. 489–92, who agrees with J. B. Lightfoot, does not therefore seem sufficiently convincing. Here, it is the interpretation of F. X. Funk (*Opera Patrum Apostolicorum* [Tübingen, 1878],

adopt, at least as a hypothesis, the πλέον variant confirming the existence of married bishops in the Eastern Church during the 1st century. There is nothing surprising here, St. Paul having foreseen that one could elect to the episcopate *unius uxoris virum*; other documents attest to the same state of affairs. Should one go further and understand that the colleagues of Ignatius of Antioch and of Polycarp of Smyrna were targets of the criticisms of the "pure" not only because they once had been married, but also because they went on living their conjugal lives? Some think so or very likely do not think that it could have been otherwise.[6] The general context of the early centuries teaches us, however, that a distinction should be made between married clerics and clerics using their marital rights. On the other hand, the Encratists, Eusthacians, and other sectarians hostile to marriage were against the married clergy because they were married, notwithstanding the fact that they may have been living in a state of continence since their ordination. To be sure, we are here only at the threshold of the 2d century. But was it not a similar state of mind that appeared here and there in the dioceses of Asia Minor and worried the friend of Polycarp? Such questions invite us to be prudent in using the reference of St. Ignatius of Antioch in his letter to Polycarp.

Polycratus of Ephesus (late 2d century)

Polycratus, bishop of Ephesus, was sixty-five years old when he wrote to Pope Victor (189–ca. 199) about the Paschal date. It was in that letter, preserved by Eusebius, that we hear about him. The Quartodeciman Quarrel opposed the Churches of Asia Minor, which celebrated the Resurrection of the Lord on the very day of the Jewish Passover (i.e., the eve of the fourteenth day of the month of Nisan), and the Churches that, like Rome, celebrated the feast on a Sunday, to honor the day of the week on which Christ had risen from the dead. Around the year 155, Polycarp of Smyrna had already visited Pope Anicetus concerning the matter. At the end of the 2d century the dispute experienced an acute phase because Pope Victor had excommunicated "the Christian

---

p. 250) and of W. Bauer (*Die Apostolischen Väter*, II [Tübingen, 1920], p. 278), among others, which must be retained; this letter of Ignatius to Polycarp describes those who, practicing chastity, believe themselves to be superior to the bishop.

[6] Cf. J. Colson, *Les fonctions ecclésiales aux deux premiers siècles*, p. 228, n. 2: "The bishop is, however, not necessarily a continent, as can be understood from *Pol.*, 5, 2, where Ignatius recommends to those who practice chastity, for the honor of the Savior's flesh, to remain humble and not to despise married people, and especially the bishop if he happens to be one of them."

communities of all Asia as well as the neighboring Churches" and had agreed to retract his sentence only through the pacifying intervention of Irenaeus of Lyon.

The letter to Pope Victor
(late 2d century)

A passage from the letter of Polycratus of Ephesus to Pope Victor was invoked at times as a testimony about the freedom to use marital rights as it had been granted, some said, to the bishops of the early Christian communities of Asia. After naming all those who, since the apostolic times, had "kept the fourteenth day of the month [of Nisan] as according to the Gospel", the bishop of Ephesus adds: "And I myself, the least among you, Polycratus, [live] according to the tradition of my family, some of whom I followed. Seven of my kin were bishops, and I am the eighth; and my parents always kept the day when people abstain from leavened bread. As to me, brothers, I am sixty-five years old in the Lord. . . ." [7]

Commenting on this testimony, J. P. Audet explains that "among other things, Polycratus stresses the traditions of his own family [συγγενεῖς]. At the age of sixty-five, he is the eighth in an episcopal line that allows him, it seems, to link his liturgical traditions until the beginning of the 2d century. Polycratus even seems to stress that he is a direct descendant of some of those bishops whose succession he ensured." Now all this is said, J. P. Audet concludes, "for the sake of Rome, not only without the slightest trace of embarrassment, but also with a proud feeling that there was in such a situation, for the great Church of Ephesus, an important factor of continuity and stability." [8]

All of this might be convincing if Polycratus had actually spoken about his parents and direct ascendants. Now the word συγγενεῖς (repeated three times) indicates, in common parlance, kin in a collateral lineage. [9] Frequently used in Greek of the New Testament, it is always used with the same meaning, moreover stressed by the prefix συν. [10] The exact

---

[7] Eusebius of Caesarea, *Hist. Eccl.*, V, XXIV, 6. SCh 41, 68.

[8] J. P. Audet, *Mariage et célibat dans le service pastoral de l'Église* (Paris, 1967), pp. 20–21.

[9] Cf. A. Bailly, *Dictionnaire grec-français*, rev. ed. by L. Sechan and P. Chantraine (Paris, 1950), p. 1806: συγγενής: I. born with, i.e., (1) innate, natural . . . (2) of same origin, same family, parent . . . : the parents, *but not when speaking of the children in relation to the father and the mother*. . . . Cf. also G. Muller, *Lexicon Athanasianum* (Berlin, 1952), c. 1356: συγγενής = *cognatus, natura et genere*.

[10] Cf. Lk 1:58; 2:44; 14:12; 21:16; Jn 17:26; Acts 10:24; Rom 9:3; 16:7; 11:21.

term indicating father or mother is γονεύς, as we can still see in the unvarying use in the writings in the New Testament.[11]

Polycratus' pride in the liturgical traditions inherited from seven members of his family who belonged to the episcopate is of interest as far as the history of the Paschal controversy is concerned, but it does not give us any information on the issue under study: these uncles, cousins, or ancestors in the collateral line did not constitute a priestly dynasty. Thus there is no need to place undue emphasis on this document from Eusebius' *Historia Ecclesiastica*; those who attempted to use it in the past were basing their references on an inaccurate translation.[12]

3d Century

Tertullian (ca. 150/60–after 220)

Quintus Septimius Florens Tertullianus was born in Carthage between 150 and 160 and had a solid background, especially in philosophy and law, when he converted to Christianity (ca. 195). He immediately put his exceptional talents at the service of apologetics. The works he wrote during this first period of his Christian life (fourteen have been preserved) bear witness to the vigor of his thought as well as to the orthodoxy of his doctrine. Tertullian was married and, according to the testimony of St. Jerome, had been ordained a priest. Around the year 206, he started to lean toward the Montanist heresy, which he fully embraced in 213, thus breaking from the Catholic Church, which became the target of his sharp criticisms. He finally founded his own sect and died in obscurity, probably at an advanced age. The shadows of his Montanist period cannot make us forget the irreplaceable contribution of his genius to Catholic theology. St. Cyprian used to read Tertullian every day.

De exhortatione castitatis (before 207)

In this text, which belongs to the second period of his life, Tertullian undertakes to change the mind of a widower friend who is thinking about remarriage. At the end of his plea in favor of continence, in which the rigorism of the Montanist with regard to second marriage is fully displayed, the writer refers to the models of pagan antiquity. Those are

[11] Cf. Mt 10:21; Mk 13:12; Lk 2:27, 41, 43; 8:56; 21:16; Jn 9:2–3, 18, 20, 22, 23; Rom 1:30; 2 Cor 12:14; Eph 6:1; Col 3:20; 2 Tim 3:2.

[12] It is also the opinion of R. Gryson, *Les origines du célibat ecclésiastique*, p. 5.

well known, he says; they are the virgins of Vesta and of Juno in Achaia, those of Apollo at Delphes, of Minerva and Diana in other places. Also continent are the priests of the bull of Egypt, but also women: the priestesses of Ceres, in whose service they grow old after having given up marriage, turning away from contact with men and even refusing the kisses of their sons. Let the friend of Tertullian now look into Christianity: the examples are more numerous and of a much higher quality: "How many men and women [from] among the continent are to be found in the ecclesiastical orders; [men and women] who reestablished [their] flesh in its dignity, and who already proclaimed themselves sons of eternity, killing in themselves the concupiscence of the passions and all that could not have access to paradise."[13]

Such a sentence is a rather controversial part of the records on priestly continence. Does not Tertullian seem to make us believe that all the members (male or female) who belonged to ecclesiastical orders practiced perfect continence? This is Bickell's view; he notes about the word *quantae* (how many women) that all the women admitted to the official service of the Church—widows, deaconesses, and virgins—were so only on the express condition of having made a profession of continence.[14] The word *quanti* (how many men) could thus have the same impact. Such a rigorous logic was quite rightly rejected by pointing out, in particular, that the relative *quantus* could not refer to all the people (or things) of whom the author speaks. Does it mean that by evoking a large number, and only a large number, of men and women involved in ecclesiastical orders who practiced continence, the writer of Carthage recognized by the same token that some of them (be it even a small number) did not practice it? This is the opinion of Funk, adopted by Vacandard and Leclercq and several others.[15] It does not seem to be well justified, for if Tertullian does at times use excessive rhetoric, he is generally careful about the efficacy of his argumentation. Now how could he manage to change his friend's mind about remarriage if he demonstrates to him that even in ecclesiastical orders there are men and women who do not live this ideal of continence to which he is inviting his friend? On the other hand, from

---

[13] "Quanti igitur et quantae in ecclesiasticis ordinibus de continentia consentur, qui deo nubere maluerunt, qui carnis suae honorem restituerunt—quique se iam illius aevi filios dicaverunt, occidentes in se concupiscentiam libidinis et totum illud, quod intra paradisum non potuit admitti" (*De exhort. cast.*, XIII, 4. CC 2, 1035).

[14] G. Bickell, "Der Cölibat eine apostolische Anordnung", ZkTh 2 (1878), pp. 38–39.

[15] Cf. F. X. Funk, "Cölibat und Priesterehe im christlichen Altertum", in *Kirchengeschichtliche Abhandlungen und Untersuchungen*, I (Paderborn, 1897), p. 139; J. P. Audet, *Mariage et célibat dans le service pastoral de l'Église* (Paris, 1967), p. 22. R. Gryson, *Les origines du célibat ecclésiastique*, pp. 22–23.

the viewpoint of syntax, the phrase *de continentia censentur* used by Tertullian appears to indicate not so much the present situation of the men and women he discusses as the way they lived originally. It seems to us that his phrase does not refer to the men and women who, being in the orders, do observe continence, but to the men and women who have been admitted to the orders because they practiced continence, the generic term qualifying all the lay Christians who, in one way or another, made a profession of perfect chastity. We find a similar grammatical construction in another passage of *De exhortatione castitatis*, when Tertullian writes about an only marriage: "De uno matrimonio censemur utrobique et carnaliter in Adam et spiritaliter in Christo" (We draw our double origin from an only marriage, carnally in Adam and spiritually in Christ).[16]

This is why we suggest the following translation of the sentence in question: "How many men and women, coming from continence (i.e., recruited from among the continent) are counted in the ecclesiastical orders! . . ." Tertullian's thought thus seems clarified in a more satisfactory way when we remember that it was not only in the ranks of the clergy but throughout the whole Church that one met people who had chosen continence, men and women who had decided to consecrate themselves to perfect chastity because they had always been celibate (or virgins), because they voluntarily became continent while married, or because they decided not to remarry after having lost their spouses, and this out of an evangelical ideal.[17] Tertullian reminds his friend who is tempted by a second marriage of the great number of lay people practicing voluntary continence who were chosen as members of the ecclesiastical orders, thus giving him an additional reason for not remarrying and also observing perfect chastity. If he follows the example of those men and women, could he not also one day be chosen for the clergy?[18] Beyond

---

[16] *De exhort. cast.*, V, 22. CC 2, 1023. Cf. A. Blaise, *Dictionnaire latin-française des auteurs chrétiens* (Strasbourg, 1954), p. 143.

[17] The word *continentia* in Tertullian's vocabulary includes those several different meanings (cf. *De exhort. cast.*, IX, 5; XIII, 2 [CC 2, 1029–30; 1034]). A passage of the *Ad uxorem* tells about the many who took a vow of virginity as soon as they were baptized, and of the great number of those who committed themselves to continence in marriage "for the Kingdom of Heaven": "Quot enim sunt, qui statim a lavacro carnem suam obsignant? Quot item, qui consensu pari inter se matrimonii debitum tollunt, voluntarii spadones pro cupiditate regni caelestis?" (I, 6. CC 1, 380). The number of widows and widowers who renounced remarriage must also have been quite important, if we base ourselves on the fact that early Christian preaching generally advised against remarriage (cf. for instance, Origen, *Com. in Lucam*, hom. 17, 10–11. SCh 87, 261–62).

[18] Even though the profession of continence (in each of the above-mentioned categories) did not itself lead to ecclesiastical Orders, and though the "continent" were not seen as candidates for hierarchical functions, it is likely that a life of perfect chastity was considered

this sort of "reserve" of voluntarily continent people, the ecclesiastical orders also recruited either among the lower ranks in Church service[19] or among the single people who had not made a profession of continence but were pressed into the clergy.[20] Tertullian knows this wider circle of recruitment, and this is why he does not say that "all" in the ecclesiastical orders are coming from continence, but only a large number (*quanti et quantae*). What remains to be known is if all of them, not only those who had been recruited among the voluntary "continent" but also the others, were compelled to observe perfect continence after joining the ecclesiastical orders; Tertullian does not deal with the issue. However, we can note that when talking to his friend about the state of continence as a favorable condition for election to the ecclesiastical orders, Tertullian does seem to indicate that orders demanded from all their members the observance of perfect chastity.

Clement of Alexandria (ca. 150–211/16)

Titus Flavius Clemens was born around the year 150, probably in Athens. Converted to Christianity, he undertook a long voyage in the East, seeking Christian masters until he finally settled in Alexandria after having discovered Pantaeus, the famous master of the Didascalia, of whom he said one day in a moving confession: "Him whom I met last and who

---

a preparation of sorts for ecclesiastical life. It would more clearly become the case during the 5th and 6th centuries in many Western Churches (see below, pp. 274–77). The sentence of the *De exhortatione castitatis* in the sense we proposed would let us think that such was already the case at the time of Tertullian.

[19] The existence of what we today call minor Orders is attested, in the early 3d century, for the Church of Rome, by the *Apostolic Tradition* (lectors and subdeacons: n. 12 and 14. SCh 44, 43) and by a letter of Pope Cornelius to Fabius of Antioch that mentions seven subdeacons, forty-two acolytes, and fifty-two exorcists, lectors, and porters (Eusebius, *Hist Eccl.*, VI, 43, 11. SCh 41, 156). It is likely that all those lower Orders also appeared at the same time in other Western Churches, especially in Africa. Tertullian alludes to lectors (*De praescriptione haereticorum*, 41, 8. SCh 46, 148). It is noteworthy that, according to the *Apostolic Tradition*, the lectors and subdeacons did not receive the imposition of hands; they were not "ordained" and therefore were not part of the "ecclesiastical Orders" (deacons, priests, and bishops).

[20] St. Augustine seems to have known quite a few cases of men recruited against their will to the clergy, and on whom continence was imposed (a proof that they had not made a profession before that): *De conjugiis adulterinis*, II, 22. CSEL 41, 409. See below, pp. 288–91. It is probable that the custom attested by St. Augustine originated in a previous era, and that in Tertullian's age, the Churches of Africa called from time to time upon laymen who had not consecrated themselves to continence and ordained them as priests or bishops.

was the first in worth I found in Egypt and did not look for anyone else." Ordained a priest, he succeeded Pantaeus at the head of the catechetical school and Origen was one of his students. The Septimus Severus persecution compelled Clement to take refuge in Cappadocia, where he died between 211 and 216. A tremendous scholar, he was the first to make a full study of the relation between philosophy and Christianity. His lofty moral and mystical doctrine makes him above all "an educator and a wonderful awakener of souls". The intellectual movement that he and Origen inspired is called the School of Alexandria. Thanks to those two men, Christian Egypt played a major role in the Church at the beginning of the 3d century. It has been beautifully expressed: "If, at that time, Rome was the heart of the Catholic universe, Alexandria was its brains" (Prat).

The 3d book of the Stromata

While encouraging absolute continence for the clergy "the Church nevertheless permitted, according to certain historians, those who did not feel they had a vocation to celibacy to use their marital rights".[21] A passage of the third book of the *Stromata* by Clement of Alexandria would be "one of the most ancient witnesses to this priestly freedom".[22] After having quoted St. Paul's recommendation to Timothy—"I think it is best for young widows to marry again and have children and a home to look after, and not to give the enemy any chance to raise a scandal about them"[23]—the master of Alexandria adds:

> Truly the Apostle accepts easily the husband of an only wife, whether he be priest, deacon, or layman; if he uses his marriage irreproachably, he will be saved by begetting children.

> ναὶ μὴν καὶ τὸν τῆς μιᾶς γυναικὸς ἄνδρα πάνυ ἀποδέχεται, κἂν πρεσβύτερος ᾖ κἂν λαϊκός, ἀνεπιλήπτως γάμῳ χρώμενος· σωθήσεται δὲ διὰ τῆς τεκνογονίας[24]

This sentence of Clement's had various and quite different translations. Following Funk, Vacandard links the participle χρώμενος not only to λαϊκὸς but just as well to πρεσβύτερος and to διάκονος; from a grammatical viewpoint the singular might well be meant for each of the terms in the list. Others are for a dissociation of the three words: on the one

[21] E. F. Vacandard, *Les origines du célibat ecclésiastique* (Paris, 1913), p. 92.
[22] Ibid.
[23] 1 Tim 5:14.
[24] *Stromata*, III, 12, 90. GCS 15, 237.

hand πρεσβύτερος and διάκονος, and on the other λαικὸς; according to them, the apposition ἀνεπιλήπτως γάμῳ would exclusively refer to the last of the three, i.e., λαικὸς. The sentence should therefore be understood as follows: Paul accepts the husband of an only wife, whether he is a priest, a deacon, or even a layman using his marital rights in an irreproachable way; indeed, he (the layman) will be saved by begetting children.[25]

Is this second reading of the text "tendentious", as Vacandard reproaches it with being?[26] When it is read without an a priori interpretation, nothing could be less obvious. Though it is true that the singular χρώμενος can be applied simultaneously to the three words *priest, deacon,* and *layman*, its position at the end of the list still entitles us, with all grammatical rigor, to isolate the logical grouping καὶ λαικὸς ἀνεπιλήπτως γάμῳ χρώμενος, thus distinguishing it from the priests and deacons. Through an underlying meaning that Clement's listeners were able to understand, the master of Alexandria would then have evoked the continence observed by married clerics following their ordinations. It is not the possibility of this second reading that is surprising, but rather the fact that people were ready to reject it without appeal. Indeed, Vacandard invites us to judge for ourselves and to weigh Funk's reasons, which are, according to him, decisive. As far as grammar is concerned, Funk points out that the participle χρώμενος did not have to be made plural to apply to the three terms in the list, and one must agree with him.[27] But such as it is, it can also have been directly opposed to the word λαικὸς so as to qualify it in an exclusive way. This first reason does not therefore have the demonstrative force it is supposed to have.[28] Funk then says that one would attribute to Clement unbelievable thoughts if only the laymen were described as ἀνεπιλήπτως γάμῳ χρώμενοι, because the author of the *Stromata* would let us suppose that the priests

---

[25] This is the opinion of G. Bickell and also of N. Le Nourry, in the dissertation that Le Nourry devotes to the commentary of the *Stromata*: "Paulus unius uxoris virum admittit, seu sit presbyter, seu diaconus, sive etiam laicus: servabitur autem ille scilicet laicus, per filiorum generationem" (*Dissertationes de omnibus Clementis Alexandrini operibus*, PG 9, 1167a).

[26] E. F. Vacandard, *Les origines*, p. 92.

[27] "First of all, the relation of *chrômenos* to all three persons does not create any grammatical or linguistic difficulty. While one might perhaps concede that Clement could well have written *chrômenoi*, it is, however, impossible to deny that the singular form is just as correct, and even better in such a case" (F. X. Funk, "Cölibat und Priesterehe im christlichen Altertum", p. 148).

[28] From a grammatical viewpoint, it seems even more probable that χρώμενος relates only to the third word. If the contrary were true, one would have a rather more analytical construction such as *provided that* or *since*.

and deacons, for their parts, were using their marital rights in a reprehensible way.[29] But the alternative is not so clear. If Clement uses the adverb ἀνεπιλήπτως to specify under what conditions the apostle accepted married people, he certainly alludes to a category of persons behaving in marriage in a way that goes against morals worthy of the Gospel. We could quote here numerous patristic texts censuring the thinly disguised fornication of certain couples forgetful of their duties. That priests and deacons could belong to such a category is an idea that did not even occur to the Gnostic master of Alexandria, and Funk is right in this case. But Clement might very well have contrasted priests and deacons to the lay people using marital rights in a whole different sense. Among the monogamous men accepted by St. Paul some quite properly use their marital rights, and they are the lay people; the others—priests and deacons—have quite simply cut off the legitimate relations with their wives that an honest marriage permitted them in the past. Nothing is more natural than such a contrast, in the mind of a Father of the early Church; and here too examples are not rare. The third reason Funk invokes does not seem to be any more solid than the previous ones. If the text of Clement deals with husbands (of an only wife), it goes without saying—in the mind of the German patrologist—that the persons listed together in that category—priests, deacons, and lay people—did practice conjugal intercourse; it is then of little importance to know whether the ending of the sentence (καὶ λαικὸς ἀνεπιλήπτως γάμῳ χρώμενος) applies or does not apply to the single word λαικὸς. In any case, the meaning does not change.[30] But to reason in such a way implies that the problem has been solved. Now the question is whether those monogamous people were all couples continuing to live as husband and wife, and there is doubt with regard to the behavior of the priests and deacons of Alexandria in those first years of the 3d century: did they or did they not abandon the conjugal bed in order to lead a life of perfect continence?

All in all, the three reasons we have studied are not as weighty as people have made them out to be, and we do not see why they should not be questioned. We shall take another, closer look at Clement's

---

[29] "Secondly, my interpretation is absolutely logical within the context. Indeed, if the words were only related to *laikos*, the meaning would be as follows: The Church does not admit the layman unless he uses marriage in an irreproachable way, but as to the priest and the deacon, they are admitted even in case they abuse it; a thought that is quite difficult to credit to the Alexandrian" ("Cölibat und Priesterehe im christlichen Altertum").

[30] "Third, the three words in question have in fact no importance for the issue under study, for it has been already spoken, without any ambiguity, of marriage and conjugal intercourse for the husband of an only wife, i.e., the priest, deacon, and layman. Therefore we can, if we wish, leave them aside; things remain the same" (ibid.).

passage. Wishing to fight against the theories of the heretics who turned their backs in horror on marriage (Valentinians, Encratites, and so forth), the doctor of Alexandria ties his argumentation around scriptural texts honoring the sanctity of marriage. In this vein he quotes St. Paul:

> This is why the Apostle himself [says]: "I think it is best for young widows to marry again and have children and a home to look after, and not give the enemy any chance to raise a scandal about them. There are already some who have left us to follow Satan" (1 Tim 5:14–15). Indeed, he does accept the husband of an only wife, whether he be a priest, a deacon, or a layman using his marital rights in an irreproachable way: "because he will be saved by begetting children".[31]

Two comments can be made about this passage:

1. The real subject of the sentence ναὶ μὴν καὶ τὸν τῆς μιᾶς γυναικὸς ἄνδρα πάνυ ἀποδέχεται is not "the Church", contrary to what Funk, and Vacandard[32] after him, supposed, but "ὁ ἀπόστολος"; it is indeed the same subject governing the previous quotation on young widows (1 Tim 5:14–15) and the verb ἀποδέχεται. We are thus dealing in this second case with a precise reference to a word of St. Paul's regarding the admission of monogamous men. Now the Pauline epistles mention only twice the case of a "man married to an only wife" (μιᾶς γυναικὸς ἀνήρ), a first time with regard to choosing bishops (1 Tim 3:2) and a second time with regard to choosing deacons (1 Tim 3:12). Clement's reference to a thought of St. Paul's was undoubtedly made in connection with one or the other of these rules. The monogamous people he mentions are not, generally speaking, those whom the Church admits into the Christian community, but more likely those whom the Apostle means to recruit either for the episcopate or for the diaconate. Between these two possibilities, the enumeration κἂν πρεσβύτερος ἦ κἂν διάκονος κἂν λαικὸς invites us naturally to opt for the first one. Clement does not refer to the monogamous men chosen for the diaconate, since he mentions the deacons among those who are "admitted" to something, but rather to the monogamous men chosen for the episcopate, "priests, deacons, or laymen using their marital rights in an irreproachable way". The use of the quotation "σωθήσεται δὲ διὰ τῆς τεκνογονίας" from the first epistle to Timothy (2:15), where it comes immediately before the passage concerning the selection of bishops, in our opinion, corroborates this hypothesis. Toward the end of this same third book of the

---

[31] GCS 15, 237.

[32] Vacandard translates: "Indeed the *Church* admits quite well the husband of an only wife . . ." (E. F. Vacandard, *Les origines*, p. 92).

Stromata, the bishop of Alexandria will speak explicitly about the bishop and will use again, in this respect, the phrase μιᾶς γυναικὸς.[33]

2. On the other hand, if this were simply a case of admitting people to the Christian community, it would seem strange for Clement to limit the group of admissible persons to monogamous people only. The early Church's reticence with regard to second marriages did not go so far as to exclude from communion those who had contracted a second marriage. As to St. Paul, he was never such a rigorist, and he even urged young widows to marry again, as is attested in the quotation given in this passage by Clement of Alexandria.

Taking these observations into account, we tend to think that here Clement is referring directly to the passage of the first epistle to Timothy regarding the admission of a candidate to episcopal responsibility. To show how much esteem the Church bestows upon the union of husband and wife, he would have wanted to bring forward the testimony of St. Paul, in which he accepts the election of men who had had the experience of marriage to the highest pastoral functions. In his list of persons thus "admitted", he will therefore not talk about bishops, an omission that would have been surprising in the hypothesis (a rather incoherent one) of a general admission into the ecclesiastical community, but only of the various categories potentially able to reach the episcopate: priests, deacons, and monogamous laymen. Under such conditions, we would be ready to understand Clement's passage in the following way: the Apostle also admits precisely (to the episcopate) the husbands of single wives, be they priests, deacons, or laymen using marriage in an irreproachable way: "for they will be saved by procreating children." Nothing prevents us from thinking that in this hierarchy of candidates admissible to the episcopate priests and deacons are contrasted with laymen because they have given up the use, even the irreproachable use, of their marital rights. What we know from other sources inclines us strongly to believe that such was indeed the meaning of the sentence of the master of the School of Alexandria.[34]

---

[33] GCS 15, 246.

[34] To support his argumentation, Funk also quotes a passage from the 7th book of the *Stromata*, in which Clement of Alexandria seems to propose the example of apostles to the people who want to marry (VII, 12, 70. GCS 17-2, 51). But that example of the apostles, to judge by another text of the very same Clement, was rather such as to invite the Gnostic to the path of renouncing marriage; for the author of the *Stromata*, there was indeed no doubt that the apostles, in their ministry, were not bound to wives but were accompanied by women they treated like sisters. See above, pp. 79–80. Cf. also N. Le Nourry, art. cit.; PG 9, 1165c–66c.

Hippolytus of Rome (170/75–235)

Visitors to the Apostolic Vatican Library are greeted today by the marble statue of a man in the garb of a philosopher seated on a *cathedra*. Discovered in 1551, this work of sculpture was first exhibited in the Lateran Museum, where it remained until Pope John XXIII had it transferred to its present site. The list of works engraved on the sides and back of the statue led to the identification of the man as Hippolytus of Rome. In 1842, another discovery, that of the "Refutation of All Heresies" (*Philosophoumena*), enabled people to find out more about the man whose work and personality are still shrouded in mystery. Priest of Rome, Hippolytus was a talented exegete (comparable in certain ways to Origen) and a vigorous apologist who had no intention of sparing any of the heresies of his time. Regrettable excesses made him oppose Pope Zephyrinus, but it was mostly against Callistus, elected pope around 217, that he had a solid rancor feeding on frustrated ambitions. "He did not cease to attack with the most extreme injustice even the most reasonable acts of his rival" (E. Amann). The first antipope in the history of the Church, he was reconciled with Pope Pontian, his companion in deportation to Sardinia during the persecution of Maximinus the Thracian. He died on that island (235) and was very soon honored as a martyr.

The Philosophoumena

In order to discredit Pope Callistus, who gets the spotlight in the "Refutation of All Heresies", Hippolytus goes so far as to ascribe to him unforgivable innovations in the field of ecclesiastical discipline. If one is to believe him, the regulations then defining the matrimonial situation of clerics were then relaxed, through the fault of the Bishop of Rome, in a singular way:

> Under his [Callistus'] government, people who had been married two or even three times began to be accepted in the clergy as bishops, priests, and deacons. And even if a member of the clergy got married, he could, as far as Callistus was concerned, remain a cleric, as if he had not sinned. It was about such an issue, Callistus used to repeat, that the Apostle had said: "It is not for you to condemn someone else's servant" (Rom 14:4). Again, according to Callistus, the parable of the darnel applies here: "Let them both [the darnel and the wheat] grow till the harvest" (Mt 13:30), i.e., "Let the sinners stay in the Church." [35]

---

[35] *Refutatio omnium haeresium*, IX, 12, 22. GCS 26, 249–50. A. Siouville, trans., I (Paris, 1928), p. 193.

The situation described by Hippolytus seems to be, according to him, a break in the traditional discipline. Indirectly the testimony of this antipope informs us about his concept of the tradition: married men could be admitted to the higher ranks of the hierarchy only if they were monogamous. Widowers who married a second or third time were excluded. On the other hand, whether he was a widower or still single after his ordination, the cleric was bound to give up marriage forever under penalty of dismissal from his functions.

As far as the first point is concerned, we cannot fully trust Hippolytus. The Pauline recommendation of *unius uxoris virum* was certainly the norm during the early centuries. But not everyone agreed on the meaning of the phrase. While some saw as monogamous those who had never remarried, others chose a broader interpretation: St. Paul had wanted to eliminate, of course, bigamous and debauched men, but he had no objection, in their opinion, to widowers who had remarried.[36] Therefore, nothing prevents us from thinking that, in Callistus' time, remarried widowers were deemed perfectly qualified for the Roman clergy; nobody saw in that a denial of the Pauline precept. Or, if such was not the practice in the Roman Church, Callistus could have introduced it without appearing to be an innovator. The rigorist tendencies of Hippolytus rather lead us to think that, judging remarriage severely, he wanted his opinion to be a general rule. Whatever the case may be, there is still an unanswered question: were the married (or remarried) clerics compelled to observe continence after their ordinations, or did they remain free to use their marital rights? Hippolytus' text has nothing to say about the matter.

When it comes to members of the clergy who, according to Callistus' adversary, would have been permitted to retain their functions even if they had married, it seems difficult not to agree with Hippolytus when he saw a disciplinary novelty in this. All that we know about the ecclesiastical regulations of those early centuries, in the East as well as in the West, shows us an unbroken continuity in the legislation regarding the prohibition against marriage for the sacred ministers after ordination.[37] If he did authorize it, Callistus likely permitted the clerics married under such conditions to remain in the clergy by taking it upon himself to modify the prevailing laws. But here we must remember the bias of the

---

[36] Once he became a Montanist, Tertullian would specifically reproach Catholics for admitting remarried men to the episcopate: "How many are the bigamists among you, presiding, and thus insulting the Apostle, incapable of blushing when these texts are read in their presence!" (*De monogamia*, XII, 3. CC 2, 1247).

[37] With perhaps the exception of the Council of Ancyra (314) for the deacons who had asked for it before ordination. See below, pp. 169ff.

antipope, which could have—on this point as on others—led him to distort facts. Or still, as A. Siouville[38] suggests, was Hippolytus making no distinction in his own mind between lower clerics on the one hand, and bishops, priests, and deacons on the other when it came to continence, and did he reproach his rival for not applying to all clerics the law that was in force for the three higher ranks? This last hypothesis does not seem solidly based, however. If he averted his eyes from the marriages of certain clerics, Pope Callistus did not, according to Hippolytus himself, cease to see them as sinners: "This is where the parable of the darnel applies, according to Callistus: 'Let them both [the darnel and the wheat] grow till the harvest', i.e., let the sinners stay in the Church." The comment is enlightening. If it had been only a matter of the lower clergy, Callistus would not have called a sin what was accepted in usage and law. The cases judged as reprehensible were quite likely those of deacons, priests, and bishops. But it must be noted that Hippolytus reproaches the Roman Pontiff, not for legalizing the infractions that had been committed but for not punishing them, an important difference. It is one thing "to let the sinners stay in the Church", as he puts it, and not to chastise them, and quite another to declare officially that their behavior was legitimate. It might be that Callistus found it opportune not to punish the guilty parties; it does not mean that he modified the discipline itself. The fact that Hippolytus puts in Callistus' mouth the words we have quoted confirms, quite to the contrary, the strong impression we get from later documents; the marriage of clerics, from the deacons up, was never authorized by the Church. If he tolerated it—which is far from certain, given the reserve that is necessary when it comes to Hippolytus' testimony—Callistus was nevertheless indirectly testifying to its illegality. Hippolytus and Callistus inform us, each in his own way, about what the disciplinary tradition was at that time, one by raging and the other by closing his eyes while both agreed on the essential point—the obligation for the higher clerics to remain in the state they had been at ordination.[39]

Origen (ca. 185–253/55)

While still a child, Origen was exhorting his father to embrace martyrdom: "Take care not to change your mind because of us", he wrote to

---

[38] *Refutatio omnium haeresium*, I, pp. 75–76.

[39] Not taking the context into account, J. P. Audet thought that he could affirm that "Pope Callistus did not hesitate to keep clerics who got married in their functions" (*Mariage et célibat dans le service pastoral de l'Église* [Paris, 1967], p. 21).

him. This character trait describes the man. Born around 185, probably
in Alexandria, the passionate lover of Christ and the Church, the son of
St. Leonides, Origen was quickly entrusted by his bishop with the administration of the Didascalia, a school that had been made famous in earlier
days by Pantaeus and Clement of Alexandria. A brilliant teacher of
various disciplines, he led a highly ascetic life that included some excesses.
Having made himself a eunuch, he was refused priestly ordination by
Demetrius. The bishops of Caesarea of Palestine and of Jerusalem had
no such scruples. Origen was ordained a priest and was consequently
deposed by the bishop of Alexandria who, moreover, had taken umbrage
at the great reputation acquired by the head of his catechetical school.
Origen retired to Caesarea, where he founded a theological school that
he administered for twenty years and that was, in many respects, far
superior to the one in Alexandria. Confessor of the faith during the
persecution of Decius, he died from the consequences of tortures at Tyre
in 253–55. His written works, most of which are lost, were wide-ranging,
covering the various fields of exegesis, theology, and ascetic spirituality.
Origenism (a system stressing certain weak points of Origen's works)
was condemned, but the influence of "the one who pleases all who are
wise" (Jerome) was tremendous and beneficent. "His thought was, together with that of St. Augustine, the most powerful and rich in influence
in all Christian antiquity" (H. Crouzel).

23d homily on Numbers
6th homily on Leviticus

In his 23d homily on Numbers, Origen suggests that his listeners meditate
on the Christian feast days, those feast days that God gave to himself in
his joy of man's salvation and in which we are all invited to participate.
Sabbath, New Moon, the Pasch . . . but above all, the feast of feasts
that knows no interruption, the perpetual sacrifice, the morning and
evening prayer, the day of eternity. If it was the first one instituted by
God, "it is because he desires to teach the one who is striving for perfection
that there are no feast days or days without a feast consecrated to God,
but that the just must celebrate a perpetual feast." [40] From this celebration
no disciple of the Gospel can be exempted because the duty to "pray
constantly" (1 Th 5:17) is an obligation for all. But let not the sinner be
misled: whoever celebrates the "day of sin" turns the feast into mourning.
Perpetual sacrifice "can only be offered by him who perpetually practices
justice and guards himself from sin. The day he stops and commits sin,
he does not offer perpetual sacrifice to God." [41]

[40] *Homélies sur les Nombres*, XXIII, 3. SCh 29, 440.   [41] Ibid., 441.

Impossible for those who do evil, the perpetual divine feast also seems off limits, in a certain measure, for a category of faithful who are otherwise pleasing to God, but whose condition compels them to fulfill other duties than unceasing prayer. Here the preacher apologizes: "I will express what the words of the Apostle mean, but I am afraid that some will be saddened." The Apostle tells married people: "Do not refuse yourselves to each other, unless through a mutual agreement for a given occasion, so as to free yourselves for prayer, and then come together again; it is therefore certain that perpetual sacrifice is impossible for those who are subject to the obligations of marriage." [42] Origen, like St. Paul, does not fall into a contempt for the flesh that would make him see sin where there is none; but one must abstain at times from sexual relations, even if they are legitimate, says the Apostle, so as to have the freedom to pray, and the husband who owes himself to his wife, like the wife who owes herself to her husband, cannot always enjoy such a freedom. "I therefore conclude", the orator continues, "that only the one vowed to perpetual chastity can offer the perpetual sacrifice." But, he hastens to add: "There are other feasts for those who cannot offer the perpetual sacrifice of chastity", [43] meaning that if it is an obstacle to perpetual prayer, the act of the flesh sanctified by marriage is not an obstacle to prayer as such. [44]

What does such a homily mean to us? Origen indicates clearly that only those men, married or not, who have professed perpetual continence are authorized to offer the sacrifice of uninterrupted prayer. In itself this comment is meant for the category of the continent, ascetics or virgins whose place was so important in the early Church; and if we remain within the text, we see that Origen did not think about including clergy members in this group (no more than he excluded them). Yet another sermon by the master of Alexandria can help us complete on this point a question that had been omitted here. We are talking about the 6th homily on Leviticus, in which Origen explains that the priest of the New Covenant must be a man of unceasing prayer, following the example of the great leaders of God's people, who never left the tent of sacrifice and who untiringly supported with their intercessions the struggles of Israel. Moses and Aaron, he points out, needed at all times to learn from God what they had to teach the people, and this is why they always

[42] Ibid., 441–42.

[43] Ibid., 442.

[44] Origen develops the same thought in a commentary on the first epistle to the Corinthians, stressing, in conformity with the advice of St. Paul, that the practice of continence creates a climate that is more favorable to prayer (*Fragments sur la première aux Corinthiens*, 34, JTS 9, 501–2).

remained in his presence. "There was yet another task for Moses", he says. "He did not go to the battlefield and did not fight [personally] with the enemy. What did he do? He prayed, and while he prayed, his people won the victory. When he let go and his hands fell down, his people was vanquished and put to flight."

Such is the behavior that the new leaders of the people of God, the priests of the Church, have to imitate: "Therefore, let the priest of the Church also pray without cease, so that the people he leads [literally, the people under him] can win the victory over these invisible Amalekites, the demons hot in pursuit of those who want to live piously in Christ." [45] In Origen's mind, the duty of continuous prayer is first of all that of priests. If this idea is juxtaposed with the relationship established in the homily on Numbers between perpetual sacrifice and continence, one can reasonably think that as far as the head of the Alexandrian school was concerned, one identical obligation of prayer and ceaseless chastity was binding on the priests of the New Covenant. From another angle, the 6th homily on Leviticus again confirms this viewpoint. Pointing out that the Levites were obliged to observe continence only within certain limits, since they had to ensure their descent, Origen stresses: "But as far as the priests of the Church are concerned I would not venture into such an explanation. For I see something that agrees with the mystery. Begetting sons can also be done by priests and doctors of the Church, just as he who said: 'little children, whom I am begetting anew, until Christ be formed in you'." [46]

If Origen was thus, on his own account, in favor of an obligation of continence, does that mean the obligation was already inscribed in the ecclesiastical discipline of that time? To say so without any reservation

---

[45] *In Leviticum Homilia VI*, 6. GCS 29, 369–70.

[46] GCS 29, 368–69. H. Leclercq points out about the passage: "Origen . . . offers us a useful testimony when, after having noted that the priests of the Old Testament were not bound by the observance of perpetual chastity, he adds, 'I would be careful not to apply such an explanation to the priests of the New Law', from which one can conclude that the Christian priests observed perpetual continence" (Hefele-Leclercq, II, 2, 1331). The edition of the *Histoire des Conciles* by Hefele, in which Leclercq wrote the comment we have just read, dates from 1908. In his article "Célibat" published in DACL two years later, in 1910, H. Leclercq, commenting again on Origen's thinking about this text of Leviticus, concludes: "From which we can conclude that *some* Christian priests practiced perpetual continence" [emphasis added] (DACL, 2809). By replacing *the* with *some* we can see that H. Leclercq's conclusion is substantially modified. [The author stresses the difference between *les* (definite article) and *des* (indefinite article). This can only be translated as *the* vs. *some*, which is not as striking as the original French—*Trans.*] Is it intentional, after a lapse of two years, that the author preferred to give Origen's text a more restrictive interpretation than the one of 1908, or was it a printer's error? The article "Célibat" in DACL unfortunately has more than one!

would amount to inflating the importance of the text. However, when one rereads the 23d homily on Numbers in the light of the more general context of Origen's predication, in the way we have traced it back, the following comment can be made: By developing the idea that the sacrifice of an uninterrupted prayer is the privilege of men vowed to continence the doctor of Alexandria does not so much seek to give reasons for the practice of perfect chastity as to explain why, in fact, only one category of Christians can partake of the unceasing feast. If it was already understood by his listeners, as he himself thought, that priests were, by their very nature, specialists of prayer, the background of his argumentation would lead us to suppose that priestly continence was in a way a publicly known discipline. We might have there a testimony confirming that in the middle of the 3d century the head of the Alexandria school was not only in favor of imposing the obligation of perfect continence on sacred ministers, but that such a practice was already—at least in Egypt—a rule known by all and used by the preacher as a background against which he developed his ideas on the conditions for perpetual prayer.[47] We have seen that the story of the patriarch Demetrius, Origen's own bishop, related by Severus of El-Eschmounein, offers a testimony in the same vein.[48]

The Council of Elvira (ca. 305?)

That first council of Spain and also the first Church council that handed disciplinary canons down to us took place in Elvira in the province of Betica (the present Andalusia), not far from Granada. Nineteen bishops coming from the most diverse areas of the Iberian peninsula attended, among whom was Osius of Cordoba, one of the most influential men of his century, friend and adviser of Constantine, who also attended the Councils of Nicaea and Sardis.

The assembly also included twenty-four priests and a certain number of deacons and lay people who did not take part in the vote on decrees.

---

[47] The homilies of Origen were passed down to us thanks to a Latin translation by Rufinus, who confesses that he somewhat modified the original here and there. It is therefore not impossible that excerpts from the 23d homily on Numbers and from the 6th homily on Leviticus were revised by the monk of Aquilea. If such is the case, one would have to bring back the date of the documents to around 410. But because the modifications brought by Rufinus to the texts of Origen are essentially dealing with the passages related to the Trinitarian doctrine, we can think that the references to clerical continence are not those of the translator but in all likelihood those of Origen himself.

[48] See above, p. 89.

The date of the Council of Elvira is uncertain. Hefele suggests 305, the year in which the Emperor Constantius Chlorius, favorable to the Christians, became sovereign master of Spain.[49] The eighty-one disciplinary canons promulgated by the Spanish Fathers deal with the most diversified topics (such as *lapsi*, serious faults, admission to baptism, discipline of the clerics, and the liturgy).

Canon 33

The bishops of Elvira adopted several resolutions concerning clerics, specifically forbidding them to live with women not of their kin (can. 27) and to have sexual intercourse with their wives (can. 33). This 33d canon is chronologically the first of a long series of legislative measures on celibacy-continence that we know to have been enacted in the early Church. The text is as follows:

> It has seemed good absolutely to forbid the bishops, the priests, and the deacons, i.e., all the clerics in the service of the ministry, to have [sexual] relations with their wives and procreate children; should anyone do so, let him be excluded from the honor of the clergy.[50]

This document calls for several comments:

The prohibition concerns essentially the three higher ranks of the ecclesiastical hierarchy—bishops, priests, and deacons—that were bound by the same obligation. It is then extended to all the clerics "in the service of the ministry" without further stipulating at what point a member of the clergy has to be considered as belonging to that category. Perhaps one should see in the phrase *vel omnibus clericis positis in ministerio* a mere incidental clause seeking to clarify why bishops, priests, and deacons are especially bound by the obligation stipulated in the canon. *Vel* would thus be purely explicative and the word *ministerium* would have to be understood in its most restrictive meaning. The interpretation would be thus: It seems good absolutely to forbid the bishops, priests, and deacons, i.e., all the clerics at the service of the ministry, and so forth. If one prefers to translate *vel* as "and also", however, it does not seem that the Fathers of the Council of Elvira meant to extend the obligation of continence beyond the subdiaconate.

[49] Hefele-Leclercq, I, 1, 220.

[50] Bruns, II, 6. The original Latin has a double negative that causes the Spanish Fathers to say exactly the contrary of the obvious meaning ("Placuit in totum prohibere episcopis . . . abstinere se a conjugibus suis et non generare filios . . ."). It is obvious that we are dealing with a clumsiness of style or an error on the part of a copyist. Cf. E. Griffe, "A propos du canon 33 du concile d'Elvire", BLE 74 (1973), pp. 142–45; "Le concile d'Elvire et les origines du célibat ecclésiastique", BLE 77 (1976), pp. 123–27.

The law voted by the synod should not be confused with priestly celibacy as we understand it today. It is meant, not for single men, but for men who were married before receiving Orders and their request to observe continence. The way the decree reads lets one suppose that the number of such clerics was rather high. It does *not* say that the *married* bishops, priests, and deacons abstain from relations with their wives but that the bishops, priests, and deacons abstain. This way of expressing the prohibition sheds an interesting light on the general situation of the Spanish clergy in the early centuries of the Church.

If the law of the Council of Elvira is the first canonical document relative to priestly continence that has come down to us, it does not automatically mean that it inaugurated a new discipline. While they did not refer to a previous synod or, as the bishops of Carthage would later do, to a more ancient tradition, the members of the Spanish assembly also did not give the impression that they were aware of innovating. Nothing is said about a previous discipline, whereas so important a measure would have demanded such a reference so as to break free from it if that was the case and to explain for what reasons one had been led to do so. When one reflects on the magnitude of the canon's demands, the silence of the legislators is easier to explain if they were repeating and confirming a practice already common than if it were the opposite case. One does not brutally impose on married people, even if they are clerics, the harsh asceticism of continence without first telling why what had been permitted previously suddenly became forbidden. On the other hand, if the purpose was to correct infractions of an already ancient rule, and thus to address a current historical situation (as is the case with other canons of the same Council of Elvira, for instance, the canon regarding the *lapsi*), it is easier to see that the Spanish bishops did not feel the need to justify such a rigorous measure.

Though such comments do not amount to a certainty, they suggest at least that one should not fall too easily into the temptation of making the origins of the legislation on priestly celibacy coincide with the issuance of the first canonical document we happen to know.[51]

---

[51] This 33d canon of the Council of Elvira is one of the cases to which we must apply the "principle of progressive explicitation" that was described on pp. 62–63. Funk was wrong when he stated that the origin of the law on priestly celibacy coincided with the date of the first written law that we have inherited: "The Synod of Elvira of 300 constitutes a watershed. Canon 33 of that synod imposes on the higher clerics . . . an absolute continence, while until then they had been permitted to pursue marital life even after ordination if the marriage had been contracted before it" ("Cölibat und Priesterehe im christlichen Altertum", pp. 121–22).

The bishops who were present at the Synod of Elvira came from the most diverse regions of the peninsula. This did not mean, of course, that it was a truly national council, in the precise sense of the term, but one would be justified to "see the assembly as a council representing all of Spain".[52] Thus the whole of Spain was called, at the beginning of the 4th century, to live (or to continue to live) the experience of priestly celibacy. Taking into account the ties binding the various Churches of the Mediterranean world, one is entitled to think that the decisions of the Spanish council had some influence on the episcopates of the neighboring countries or vice versa.

The 1st Council of Arles (314)

Constantine had the intention of settling once and forever the Donatist controversy when he decided to gather the bishops of his empire at Arles on August 1, 314. The assembly did not limit itself to dealing with the African schismatics, however. The many bishops gathered in the Gallic city (certain traditions state that there were six hundred) were also concerned with several other points in dispute and enacted various disciplinary decrees. It seems that that synod, which was not an ecumenical council, could rightly be considered "a general council of the West".

Canon 29

Manuscripts generally reproduce a list of twenty-two canons voted by the 1st Council of Arles, but certain codices add to this list another six decrees numbered 24 to 29,[53] among which is a law on priestly continence akin to canon 33 of the Council of Elvira. Here are its terms:

> Can 29: Moreover, [concerned with] what is worthy, pure, and honest, we exhort our brothers [in the episcopate] to make sure that priests and deacons have no [sexual] relations with their wives, since they are serving the ministry every day. Whoever will act against this decision will be deposed from the honor of the clergy.[54]

Before we can discuss the matter of the canon's authenticity, we need to make a few comments suggested by the reading of this text:

---

[52] Hefele-Leclercq, I, 1, 215.

[53] One manuscript of the Novare collection and two manuscripts of the Dionysio-Hadriana collection, the *Parisiensis Lat. 12448* codex (fol. 124) and the *Bodl. 893* codex. Cf. CC 148, 25.

[54] CC 148, 25.

The decree, written in an exhortatory form, is nevertheless a proper law with sanctions. Whoever violates the obligation that is formulated will be "deposed from the honor of the clergy".

The prohibition is directed at the priests (*sacerdotes*) and at the Levites. Here too, as was the case at the Council of Elvira, one is dealing with bishops and priests, grouped under the generic name *sacerdotes*, and with deacons, the "Levites" of the New Covenant.

Contrary to the Spanish canon, it is not a question of extending the obligation to other categories of clerics. This may perhaps give us a clue helping us to decide the meaning of the *vel omnibus clericis positis in ministerio* incidental clause in the Elvira decree, and to see in it, as we suggested, a simple explanatory clause of the "bishops, priests, and deacons" grouping.

The motives of the law are somewhat more developed than was the case in the Spanish document. To abstain from conjugal intercourse is a matter of what is "worthy, pure, and honest"; it is required from priests and Levites because they have to devote themselves every day to the sacred ministry. Emphasis is placed here on the permanence of priestly functions tied to a permanence in sexual abstinence. The authors are probably referring implicitly to the prescriptions of Leviticus, calling for periodical chastity for the sons of Levi when they were serving in the temple. In all likelihood, it was in continuity with the law of the Old Testament that the bishops of Arles imposed on clerics the obligation of continence, as is shown in the use of the word *Levites*.

Here too the historical background is the same as in Spain. Bishops, priests, and deacons were mostly recruited from among married men. The comments we made with regard to the Council of Elvira apply with respect to the difficulties of the law and to the motivations that might have led the assembly of 314 to override those difficulties.

The absence of a reference to a prior discipline could not mean, once again, that the adopted position was absolutely new. The Fathers of the Council of Arles could have based themselves on the recent decision of the Spanish episcopate, of which they were certainly aware. One can think, of course, that they did not deem it necessary to do so, for reasons of expediency, for instance. But, on the other hand, they might have felt that it was not necessary to recall a tradition because in their minds it was not a matter of changing the discipline but of defending it against possible violations. In any event, we deem it necessary to make about this canon the point already stressed with regard to the law enacted in Elvira: one should not extrapolate the given of history by taking as the absolute starting point of legislation a canonical document that seems to have no ties to a prior tradition.[55]

[55] See above, p. 160.

The authenticity of this 29th canon of the 1st Council of Arles poses a problem on which the publishers take various positions. In his recent critical edition about the Gallic Councils, published in volume 148 of the *Corpus Christianorum*, C. Munier limits himself to indicating that the six canons of the Council of Arles, numbered from 24 to 29, are found only in a small number of manuscripts, for which he gives references. Hefele and Leclercq quote, without any criticism, the opinion of J. D. Mansi, who states that these additional canons were enacted by another Council of Arles.[56] This is also the feeling of Maassen, who declares more categorically: "The collection of the manuscript of Novare, the Sangem. Codex, Harlay 386, and the Bodl. Codex 893 add, after the last canon of the Vulgate, six other [decrees presented] as being canons of this same Council of Arles, but they undoubtedly were not part of that council."[57] However, the German critic does not justify his opinion in any way.

To help find some sort of a solution, let us first go quickly through the two lots of manuscripts:

1. Manuscripts that do not include the additional six canons:
   —Collection of the manuscript of Corbia, 6th–7th century
   —Collection of the manuscript of Cologne, 7th century
   —Collection of the manuscript of Lorsch, 9th century
   —Collection of the manuscript of Albi, 8th and 9th centuries
   —Collection of the manuscript of Saint-Maur, 9th century
   —Collection of the manuscript of Diessen, 9th century
   —Collection of the manuscript of Rheims, 8th century
   —Spanish Epitome, the most ancient codex of the 7th–8th century
   —Hispana (the most ancient codex is from the 8th century)
   —Collection of the manuscript of Lyon, 8th and 10th centuries
   —Collection of the manuscript of Saint-Amand, 9th and 10th centuries

2. Manuscripts including the six additional canons:
   —Collection of the manuscript of Novare, composed of six codices:
   • The Novar. Codex LXXXIV (54), 9th century
   • The Brix. Codex, B II 13, 10th century
   • The Modoec. Codex, h 3 151, 10th century
   • The Novar. Codex, XXX (66), 10th–11th century
   • The Lucan. Codex, 124, 11th century (according to Zaccaria) or 12th century (according to Mansi)
   • The Novar. Codex, XV (30), 12th century

[56] Hefele-Leclercq, I, 1, 295. Mansi, 2, 474.
[57] Maassen, n. 166.

—Lat. Codex, Paris, 3838, 10th century
—Sangem. Codex, Harlay 386, 10th century
—Bodl. Codex 893, 10th century[58]

The lot of the "minority" manuscripts (those including the six canons numbered 24 to 29) thus extends from the 9th to the 12th centuries; the lot of the "majority" extends from the 6th–7th to the 10th centuries. Thus the latter group offers the oldest collections, and in this respect is more likely to represent genuine tradition. However, the antiquity of a manuscript is not always a decisive criterion. The most ancient collection, that of the manuscript of Corbia, dates back to more than three centuries after the Council of Arles, a time span that implies a margin of uncertainty.

Moreover, the manuscripts containing the six additional canons are contemporary to several codices representing the "majority"; their independence with respect to these points to the existence of a different source. Whatever the case may be, neither the date nor the relative rarity of the manuscripts including the six additional canons could, in itself, be sufficient argument to reject the authenticity of these canons.

From the point of view of internal criticism, relations between the 1st Council of Arles and the Council of Elvira can, on the other hand, provide some material for an answer. The enactment of the twenty-two disciplinary canons—which are certainly genuine—by the episcopate of the Western world gathered in Gaul in 314 is directly inspired, on more than one point, by the decisions of the assembly that had taken place several years earlier in Spain. Without going into more details than necessary here, we have to point out that ten of these decrees reproduce, at times literally, texts voted at the Synod of Elvira, or else they manifest a clear intention of modifying them.[59] Now it so happens that the 29th canon of the Council of Arles shows analogies to the legislation of Elvira, as a synoptical reading of the two decrees enables us to see:

---

[58] These last three codices belong to the Dionysio-Hadriana collection. The two lists of manuscripts were established on the basis of Maassen's data, n. 166.

[59] Compare can. 2 of Arles and can. 77 of Elvira; can. 3 of Arles and can. 62 of Elvira; can. 6 of Arles and can. 39 of Elvira; can. 7 of Arles and can. 56 of Elvira; can. 9 of Arles and can. 25 of Elvira; can. 10 of Arles and can. 9 of Elvira; can. 11 of Arles and can. 15 of Elvira; can. 12 of Arles and can. 20 of Elvira; can. 14 of Arles and can. 75 of Elvira; can. 16 of Arles and can. 53 of Elvira.

29th can. of Arles: Moreover, [concerned with] what is worthy, pure, and honest, we exhort our brothers [in the episcopate] to make sure that priests and deacons have no [sexual] relations with their wives, since they are serving the ministry every day. Whoever will act against this decision will be deposed from the honor of the clergy.

33d can. of Elvira: It has seemed good absolutely to forbid the bishops, the priests, and the deacons, i.e., all the clerics in the service of the ministry, to have [sexual] relations with their wives and procreate children; should anyone do so, let him be excluded from the honor of the clergy.

The differences in terminology and the variations of style are secondary here. The meaning is not affected. The two canons have the same structure of composition: (1) who is affected by the law, (2) purpose of the prohibition, (3) motive of the law, (4) sanction. In both cases the same obligation of continence is required from the same members of the clergy for the same reasons, and the refusal to submit calls for the same penalty. One can normally think about a possible dependence of the Gallic canon in relation to its Spanish counterpart. Such a possible dependence, it has to be stressed, does not exclude the possibility of a much later date, but it would correspond with the spirit of fidelity to the recent decisions of the Council of Elvira, which seem to have guided the Fathers at the Council of Arles.[60]

If we now attempt to find another Council of Arles that would have enacted the six additional canons, as Mansi suggests, our inquiry will essentially concern two later Gallic assemblies:

1. The 2d Council of Arles, 442–506
2. The 3d (or 4th) Council of Arles, 524[61]

With regard to the 2d Council of Arles, two comments seem to be necessary:

[60] A certain relationship can also be discerned between can. 9 of the Synod of Elvira and can. 24 of the Synod of Arles (= first of the six additional canons): the latter can be related to can. 10, which has common points with can. 9 of Elvira, as was pointed out by Hefele and Leclercq (I, 1, 287). Two of the six additional canons of the Gallic council's acts can thus be understood to be in harmony with the Spanish decrees.

[61] Several other councils were gathered at Arles during the 4th and 5th centuries, but in general they do not seem to have promulgated disciplinary decrees. They are as follows: the council of 353, which should normally have been the 2d of Arles had it not been tainted with Arianism; the council of 451, during which the *epistola dogmatica* of St. Leo recently addressed to the Council of Chalcedon was approved; the council of 455, gathered to settle the conflict between the monastery of Lérins and the bishop of Fréjus (the practical decisions of that council were limited to the situation created by the dispute); the council held between 457 and 480, against the predestinationists with respect to the doctrine on grace.

Among the six additional canons that could possibly have been voted during that assembly there is one concerning the case of the Donatists (or "mountain dwellers") returning to the Catholic Church. It reads as follows:

> *Can. 28*: Let those who come [to us] from Donatism or from [the sect of] the "Mountain dwellers" be received through [the rite of] imposition of hands; it seems indeed that they baptize in a way that is contrary to the ecclesiastical rule.

Now the schism of Donatus, which was highly active during the entire 4th century, was solemnly condemned by the very large Carthaginian conference of 411 under the leadership of St. Augustine. Edicts of proscription, between the years 412 and 428, hunted down the dissident sect and silenced it. Under such conditions it is hard to imagine that a council held in the middle of the 5th century, several decades after the event, still had to concern itself with Donatism. It is likely that there were pockets of resistance here and there, but these very small groups survived mostly in Africa; why should a Gallic council have bothered with them? On the other hand, the acts of the Council of Arles in 314 let us know that the Donatist question was then on the agenda of the assembly: Cecilian, Donatus, and a group of their followers had been sent to the synod, and the synodal letter to Pope Silvester mentions drily that they had been "condemned and rejected". Moreover, canon 13 deals directly with the Donatist controversy by studying the central issue that had been at the origin of the schism, that of the validity of ordinations made by apostate bishops. In canon 8 we also read that it is forbidden to rebaptize heretics returning to the bosom of the Church—a measure aimed at the Africans—and that one should simply lay hands on them. Canon 28 could then appear as having been a corollary, applying to the particular case of the Donatists the general principle enunciated in canon 8. The comparison of historical contexts thus makes rather doubtful the ascribing of this canon 28—and consequently of the five other canons with which it is grouped—to the 2d Council of Arles of 442–506. On the other hand, it seems rightly to be connected with the decisions made in 314.

A second indication appears to reject the hypothesis of a link between the six additional canons and the 2d Council of Arles. There is, in the authentic acts of that synod, a decree relative to priestly continence, as follows:

> *Can. 44*: But if anyone, after having received the blessing of the diaconate, is found not to have observed continence with his wife, *cum uxore sua incontinens invenitur*, let him relinquish his office.

Canon 44 says exactly the same thing as canon 29, but in a more concise way. Those who have received the "Levitical blessing", i.e., all the sacred ministers from deacon up, must abstain from conjugal relations ("*incontinens*" describing here, in the very specific meaning of the term, the man who does not observe continence) or else they must be deposed from their office. If canon 29 had been an edict during the 2d Council of Arles, it would simply duplicate canon 44.

For these various reasons, we do not think that the additional six canons could have been promulgated by the 2d Council of Arles of 442–506.

Would it be more satisfactory to make the date still later and to ascribe them to the 3d (or 4th) Council of Arles, held in 524? It seems that nothing would be wrong with such a solution if it concerned only canon 29, which was related to priestly continence. In the 6th century, Church discipline on that point was already well developed in the Western world and brought forth in all Latin countries a large number of similar decrees.[62] It is only the formulation—depending very much on the Council of Elvira—that would pose a problem. Why should the legislators of 524 find their inspiration in the letter of a document more than two centuries old when many other texts, often more important,[63] could have given them richer material?

But the determining factor is the issue of the Donatist controversy. We have seen that, out of the six additional canons, there is one concerning the reintegration of Donatus' followers in the Catholic Church (can. 28). Now if the existence of some Donatists, well after the sect had been suppressed, could still preoccupy the bishops of Western Christendom in the middle of the 5th century (at the Council of Arles of 442–506), this would not have been the case in the 6th century, and it would be anachronistic to suppose that the assembly of 524 confronted the aftermath of Donatus' schism. We must therefore clearly eliminate the hypothesis of a possible attribution of canon 28—and of the five other canons on the same list—to the Council of Arles in 524.

To conclude this study on the problems of internal and external criticism posed by the six canons (24 to 29) of the 1st Council of Arles in 314, we do not see how it would be possible to verify with enough certainty Mansi's opinion regarding an elaboration of these canons by a later Council of Arles. On the other hand, several observations—when put together—tend to lean toward their authenticity, as we have just seen. The balance of the pros and cons leaning thus rather strongly toward the date given by the group of manuscripts that include them,

---

[62] See below, pp. 323ff.

[63] In particular, the decretals of Innocent I (401/2–17) and of St. Leo (440–61).

we think it to be of good method, for lack of contrary proof, not to reject the testimony of these documents. While retaining a question mark about them, we can think that these six additional canons have a sufficient guarantee of authenticity. This implies, as far as this study is concerned, that we must take into consideration a canon regarding priestly continence (can. 29) voted at the 1st Council of Arles in 314, in continuity with the similar decision made at the Synod of Elvira. This conclusion has some importance, and we shall obviously use it only while taking into account a coefficient of improbability. We believe, however, that it is sufficiently weighty to become part of our ongoing inquiry.[64] We must also remember the story of Bishop Urbicus, first successor of Austremonius to the See of Clermont.[65] It bears witness, as we saw, to the existence of an obligation of perfect continence for the bishops in certain parts of Gaul and thus provides us with an additional element of judgment favoring the authenticity of canon 29 of the Council of Arles.

If it turns out to be true that that Council did indeed promulgate a law forbidding bishops, priests, and deacons to have conjugal intercourse, one is entitled to think that such a decision must have had repercussions going far beyond the scope of the Synod of Elvira. We are not dealing with a mere nationwide assembly, as was the case in Spain at the dawn of the 4th century, but with a general meeting of the empire's bishops. Whatever the actual number of the attendees (certain traditions go so far as to mention six hundred bishops, while the letter addressed to Pope Silvester shows only thirty-three signatures), one thing is certain: "all the provinces of Constantine's empire were represented at the Council".[66] St. Augustine describes that assembly as a *"plenarium Ecclesiae universae concilium"*.[67] In fact, the absence of the Eastern patriarchs does not allow us to talk of an ecumenical council, but more correctly of a "general council of the West (or of the Roman patriarchate)".[68] Not only Gaul, but all the Western regions—Spain, Italy, Africa, Northern Europe—were affected by the decisions made during that council to which, Constantine rightly boasted, he had "called a considerable number of bishops from various places who are impossible to enumerate".[69]

The discipline of priestly continence, as expressed in canon 29, must have, under these conditions, extended, from the first years of the 4th

---

[64] R. Gryson limits himself to qualifying summarily as "apocryphal" these six additional canons, without justifying his affirmation (*Les origines du célibat ecclésiastique*, p. 190).

[65] See above, p. 97 and pp. 127–28.

[66] Hefele-Leclercq, I, 1, 276.

[67] *Ep.* 43, 7, 19. PL 33, 169a.

[68] Hefele-Leclercq, I, 1, 277.

[69] Eusebius of Caesarea, *Hist. Eccl.*, X, 5. PG 20, 889b. SCh 55, 110.

century, throughout the Western world, and one may judge what a contribution such a historical fact can bring to the study of the further development of this discipline.

Council of Ancyra (314)

Between twelve and eighteen bishops coming from Asia Minor and Syria met in 314 in Ancyra, the present Ankara, in order to solve various problems of discipline and particularly to determine the way to handle *lapsi* of the recent persecution. That synod was one of the many "bishops' assemblies", which, according to Eusebius, were held in the East after the death of Maximus. It was pointed out, quite rightly, that the disciplinary contents of the twenty-five (twenty-four) canons enacted there "are to be compared above all with the canons of Elvira but also those of Arles (314) dealing at about the same time with the same contemporary problems: the *lapsi* and the sins of the flesh".[70]

Canon 10

In Denys the Minor's version, which gives us one of the most ancient records of the Council of Ancyra,[71] there is a canon related to the deacons, granting them an exceptional authorization to marry if they asked for it at ordination:

> Can. *10*: Those who are promoted to deacons, if, at the time of their promotion, they protested and said that they had to marry and could not live in this way and then married later, can remain in the ministry because

[70] Joannou, I, 2, p. 55.

[71] For a brief presentation on the various versions of the canons of Ancyra's text, see Hefele-Leclercq, I, 1, 299, n. 1: "The canons of the Council of Ancyra are known to us principally through the Greek text whose most ancient manuscripts go back to the 10th century, and through the three Latin versions: one, called 'Isidorian', is dated from the first half of the 5th century; another from the second half of the same century is called by the name 'Prisca'; and the third is the work of Denys the Minor and is anterior to 525. The Syriac and Armenian versions are less ancient."

For more details on the Latin manuscripts and their dates, see Maassen, pp. 12–16 (for the "Isidorian" version); pp. 486–90 (for the Quesnel collection); pp. 425–26 (for the version of Denys the Minor). The Greek text was recently published in a new edition by P. P. Joannou, II, 2, p. 64. This is, as the author points out, the critical text developed by N. Benesevic, in his *Syntagma XIV titulorum sine scholiis secundum versionem palaeoslavicam adiecto textu graeco e vetustissimis codicibus manuscriptis (russ.)* (St. Petersburg, 1906). The excellent edition of R. B. Rackam, "The Text of the Canons of Ancyra", *Studia biblica et ecclesiastica* (essays chiefly in biblical and patristic criticism) (Oxford, 1891), 3, pp. 139ff., includes an inventory of the Greek manuscripts. The most ancient date back to the 10th century.

the bishop permitted them to do so. But those who have kept silence and were admitted to ordination [on the condition] that they persevere in this state [of celibacy], if they marry subsequently, they will be deprived of [the functions of] the diaconate.[72]

At first sight this text contrasts sharply with the 3d canon of the Council of Elvira, the 29th canon of the 1st Council of Arles, the Carthaginian synods—in other words, it contrasts with the Western laws. Certainly enough the Fathers of Ancyra meant to retain the general rule of celibacy imposed on deacons who were single before ordination, the ordinands' silence having a *de facto* commitment value. The exception they seem to make is, however, an important one, and in this respect it can be said that "this canon is very useful for the history of the origins of ecclesiastical celibacy".[73]

---

[72] "Quicumque Diaconi constituti, in ipsa constitutione testificati sunt et dixerunt, oportere se uxores ducere, cum non possint sic manere, ii si uxorem postea duxerint, sint in ministerio, eo quod hoc sit illis ab episcopo concessum. Si qui autem hoc silentio praeterito, et in ordinatione, ut ita manerent, suscepti sunt, postea autem ad matrimonium venerunt, ii a diaconatu cessent" (P. P. Joannou, I, 2, p. 64).

Here are also the texts of the "Isidorian" and of the "Prisca".

1—"Isidorian" recension, early 5th century:

  a. Original recension:

    "Diaconi quicumque constituuntur, si in ipsa ordinatione protestati sunt uxores se esse ducturos, quia non possunt contenere, hii postea, si in nuptias convenerint, maneant in ministerio propterea, quod his episcopus licentiam dederit. Quicunque sane tacuerint et susceperint manus impositionem professi continentiam et postea uxores sortiti sunt, a sacro ministerio cessare debebunt" (Maassen, p. 931).

  b. "Vulgate" recension:

    "Diaconi quicumque cum ordinantur, si in ipsa ordinatione protestati sunt dicentes velle se habere uxores nec posse se continere, hi postea, si ad nuptias convenerint, maneant in ministerio propterea quod his episcopus licentiam dederit: Quicumque sane tacuerunt et susceperunt manus impositionem professi continentiam, et postea ad nuptias convenerunt, a ministerio cessare debebunt" (PL 84, 106).

2—"Prisca" recension, late 5th century:

    "Diaconi qui sunt ordinandi, se contestati sunt ante ordinationem, et dixerunt oportere se nubere, non posse eos sic manere, hi post hoc nubentes, sint in ministerio pro quod praeceptum est eis ab Episcopo. Si autem aliqui non contestati tacuerunt et placuit eis in ordinatione perseverare innupti, et postmodum venerunt ad nuptias, cessare eos omnino a ministerio diaconi" (Mansi 6, 1116d–17a).

Unfortunately, there is not as yet a critical edition of these different Latin versions. On the other hand, as was pointed out by R. B. Rackam, "the early authors of the fifth-century translations seemed to have had only a mediocre knowledge of the Greek language; at the very least, they were often incapable of understanding the meaning of the canons of Ancyra. . . . Even Denys, in spite of his concern for exactitude, made some errors" ("The Text of the Canons of Ancyre", p. 160). One cannot therefore put a blind trust in these Latin versions in order to know the true meaning of the original Greek texts.

[73] Hefele-Leclercq, I, 1, 312, n. 1.

Nevertheless, certain things draw attention to a problem of interpretation. In 572, Martin of Duma, archbishop of Braga, sent to his colleague Nitigisius of Lugo his Latin translation of eighty-four Greek canons.[74] Included was canon 10 of Ancyra, though the version was quite different from that given by Denys the Minor. Here is the translation:

> If someone is chosen for the ministry of the diaconate but does raise a protest beforehand [to claim the right of] taking a wife, declaring that he cannot persevere in chastity, let him not be ordained. If at the time of ordination he kept silent and was [actually] ordained and later seeks to marry, let him be rejected from the ministry and eliminated from the clergy.[75]

Here the man chosen for the service of the diaconate is free to express his desire to marry, but if he does so he will not be ordained. The exception formulated in Denys the Minor's text has disappeared. There remains only a law quite in harmony with what we know of the Western discipline at that time. For this reason Martin of Braga was not free from a suspicion that he wanted to alter the Eastern canon in order to put it in line with the Latin tradition; moreover, he congratulates himself, in his preface, for having amended obscure passages included in previous translations.[76] But this leads us, in all objectivity, to ask ourselves whether

---

[74] In Bruns, II, 43, this collection has the following title: *Capitula sive canones ex orientalium antiquorum Patrum synodis a venerabili Martino episcopo vel ab omni Bracarensi synodo excerpti vel emendati tituli, ubi clericorum seorsum et laicorum sententias restauravit, ut quod translatores a Graeco in Latinum obscurius dixerunt, vel scriptorum ignavia depravaverat aut immutaverat simplicius et emendatius omnia uno hoc contineantur in loco, ut de quo capitulo quis scire voluerit, possit celerius invenire.*

[75] 2ᵉ *concile de Braga, can. 39*. Bruns, II, 52.

[76] "In ipsis canonibus aliqua apud simpliciores videantur obscura: ideoque visum est, ut cum omni diligentia et ea quae per translatores obscurius dicta sunt, et ea quae per scriptores sunt immutata, simplicius et emendatius restaurem . . . " (Bruns, II, 43).

One should not forget that Martin of Braga, who originally came from Pannonia, had a good knowledge of the East, where he had stayed for a long time before unknown circumstances brought him to Spain around the year 560. That monk, who had traveled a great deal, is perhaps a sure witness of Eastern customs, which he knew better than his Spanish colleagues did. One must also note the way he expresses himself in the above-mentioned preface. He does not say that he took it upon himself to amend *the original text* of the Greek canons, but, on the contrary, he affirms that his true aim was to correct *the translations*, which at times obscure the original, as well as the modifications because of unintelligent or absentminded copyists ("*aut non intelligentes aut dormitantes*"). This he did in order to restore faithfully the true meaning of the Greek canons for Latin readers. It thus seems that he could not be suspected of having intentionally modified the original text of canon 10 of Ancyra in order to adapt it to the Western discipline unless his word is to be doubted. Would he have misunderstood the original Greek text? As far as his knowledge of the Greek language is concerned, one can refer to the praise given to him

we would not have to do, in the original Greek text of the 10th canon of Ancyra, with a document that is less easy to understand than it first seemed, and whether the correction of Martin of Braga—who knew his Greek quite well—could not be an invitation of sorts to reread the text with greater attention.

First, we have to note that the 10th canon of Ancyra was never confirmed by the later Byzantine legislation in the sense that Denys the Minor gave to it: neither Justinian nor the Eastern Fathers of the Quinisext Council of 691 put their signatures at the bottom of a law authorizing anyone to marry after the diaconate. There is even in the *Corpus juris civilis* of Justinian a new law, dated 546, that seems quite close to the version of the 10th canon of Ancyra given by Martin of Braga. The text is as follows:

> But if the deacon who is about to receive the imposition of hands does not have a woman united to him [in marriage] as was stipulated above, let no one impose hands on him before the ordaining [bishop] has questioned him and before he has promised to be able to live worthily and without a legitimate wife after ordination; the ordaining [bishop] does not have the power, at the time of the imposition of hands, to authorize the deacon to take a wife after the imposition of hands; should such a thing occur, the bishop who would have granted such an authorization would be rejected from the episcopate; if, after the imposition of hands, a priest, a deacon, or even a subdeacon enters into a marriage contract, let him be rejected from the clergy and delivered, body and goods, to the council of the town where he had been a cleric.[77]

The exception stipulated by the version of Denys the Minor in favor of candidates who would have applied for it at the time of ordination is not taken into account here. The emperor could surely have taken it

---

by Gregory of Tours: "In tantum se litteris inbuit, ut nulli secundus suis temporibus haberetur" (*Libri Historiarum decem*, V, 37. MGH, *scr. mer.*, I, 1, 2d ed. [1951], p. 243). If it is true that Martin of Braga had no rivals in the field of letters—an education that certainly included the study of Greek—we can consider his translation of the Greek canons as being quite likely more faithful to the original than that of Westerners who wrote the other Latin versions ("Isidorian", "Prisca", "Dionysian", and so forth. See above, n. 72, p. 170). In any case, if the Greek texts that we have today do not always correspond exactly to the Latin of Martin of Braga—as might be the case for canon 10 of the Council of Ancyra—one must perhaps conjecture that the Spanish bishop had in hand a different Greek original. This is the opinion of C. W. Barlow: "His methods of translation have previously been shown to be quite literal, and if our Greek text does not correspond to his Latin, then it must be conjectured that he had a different Greek original" (*Martini episcopi Bracarensis opera omnia* [New Haven, Conn., 1950], p. 85).

[77] *Novella* 123, cap. 14. CJC (J), III, 605.

upon himself to modify the early canon of Ancyra in a way that suited him, but we can also ask ourselves, here too, whether the Code of Justinian does not suggest an interpretation of the canon that was closer to the historical truth than the Dionysian interpretation.

The Fathers of the Council in Trullo, in their turn, while confirming as a whole with their authority the canons of the Council of Ancyra, still formulated a law forbidding marriage to all clerics, an exception being made only for lectors and cantors: "As is said in the apostolic canons, that 'among the single men promoted to the ranks of the clergy, only lectors and precantors can be married', we too, obeying this regulation, order that from now on no subdeacon, deacon, or priest be permitted, once ordained, to contract a marriage; should he dare do so, let him be deposed." [78]

The decision had not been inspired by the Council of Ancyra but, in particular, by the 26th apostolic canon. Nothing can therefore be deduced as to the meaning that the Byzantines saw in the text of the Greek synod of 314, though it must be stressed that they felt no need to justify themselves, as though they had rejected the Council of Ancyra, while they would do so later when it came to the bishops. These various indications thus invite us to take a closer look at the Greek text of the 10th canon from the Council of Ancyra. [79] Several points are to be noted:

1. The canon deals first with the case of deacons at the time they present themselves for ordination: we are not talking here about *deacons* about to receive the diaconate, which would be nonsensical, but of lower clerics proposed for the imposition of hands—in other words, "those who are promoted to deacons", according to Joannou's good translation. [80] This precision is important in order to situate the viewpoint of the legislators: they are studying the case of candidates to the diaconate—

---

[78] The twelfth-century Byzantine commentators would understand the canon of Ancyra as did Denys the Minor. They would then apply themselves to deny any legislative value to them by sending their readers back to canon 6 of the Quinisext Council, which forbids to priests, deacons, and subdeacons marriage after ordination (PG 137, 1151).

[79] Here is the Greek text, as edited by Joannou, I, 2, p. 64:

Περὶ διακόνων ἐν τῷ χειροτονεῖσθαι περὶ
γάμου μαρτυρουμένων.

Διάκονοι ὅσοι καθίστανται, παρ᾽ αὐτὴν τὴν κατάστασιν εἰ ἐμαρτύραντο καὶ ἔφησαν χρῆναι γαμῆσαι, μὴ δυνάμενοι οὕτως μένειν, οὗτοι μετὰ ταῦτα γαμήσαντες ἔστωσαν ἐν τῇ ὑπηρεσίᾳ διὰ τὸ ἐπιτραπῆναι αὐτοὺς ὑπὸ τοῦ ἐπισκόπου τοῦτο. Εἰ δέ τινες σιωπήσαντες καὶ καταδεξάμενοι ἐν τῇ χειροτονίᾳ μένειν οὕτως, μετὰ ταῦτα ἦλθον ἐπὶ γάμον, πεπαῦσθαι αὐτοὺς τῆς διακονίας.

[80] Ibid.

cantors, lectors, or, more likely, subdeacons *at the time they are preparing to receive the imposition of hands*—and are facing two hypotheses: either the candidate, supposedly single, declares that he intends to marry, "not being able to remain as he is"; or he remains silent and thus tacitly agrees to remain single.

2. In the first instance, if he marries at a later date, he will be able to retain his functions (ἔστωσαν ἐν τῇ ὑπηρεσίᾳ), provided the bishop gives his authorization. In the second instance, if he violates his commitment and takes a wife, he will be deposed from his functions in the diaconate (πεπαῦσθαι αὐτοὺς τῆς διακονίας). It must first be noted that the mention of imposition of hands, the χειροτονία, appears only in the second part of the canon, precisely with respect to those who accepted remaining single (σιωπήσαντες καὶ καταδεξάμενοι ἐν τῇ χειροτονίᾳ μένειν οὕτως). As to the first group, nothing is explicitly said about them. It is simply declared with respect to them that if, having asserted their desire to marry, they actually take a wife,[81] they will be able to retain their functions, without specifying whether this means the diaconate, as in the case of the second group, or other ecclesiastical functions. The Greek word that is used here is ὑπηρεσία, which implies a service "subordinate" (ὑπὸ-εἰρεσία) to other functions that are superior to it. Borrowed from maritime vocabulary, its etymological meaning is the service or duty of a rower or sailor, a man in a low position. By extension it expresses any idea of service and assistance, of help given to higher-class people, and in its concrete sense the term is applied to the category of craftsmen, laborers, and servants.[82] The Church adopted that word, keeping its original meaning, to describe the totality of the staff "at the service of the Church".[83] This was a collective description, covering various categories of clerics, or defining their functions with respect to clerics holding a higher rank in the hierarchy. Thus the canons of the Council of Laodicea (late 4th century) regularly use the word ὑπηρέτης, which is the exact equivalent of ὑπηρεσία, when talking about sub-deacons.[84] Elsewhere the word applies to various hierarchical functions

---

[81] μετὰ ταῦτα is grammatically applicable to the preceding phrase, i.e., to the candidates' possible declaration regarding their marriages, and not to ordination.

[82] Cf. A. Bailly, *Dictionnaire grec-français*, rev. ed. by L. Sechan and P. Chantraine (Paris, 1950), p. 2012.

[83] The translation of ὑπηρεσία as "service of the Church" seems to be the most fitting one. Cf. Joannou, I, 2, p. 78.

[84] Cf. can. 20: The deacon must not sit in the presence of the priest or must do so only by invitation of the latter, in the same way the deacons will be honored (τοὺς διακόνους) by the subdeacons (ὑπὸ τῶν ὑπηρετῶν) and all the clerics; can. 21: the subdeacons (ὑπηρέται) must not take their place in the diakonikon nor touch the sacred vessels;

leading to the summit of the episcopate, a rank that is obviously not part of the ὑπηρεσία, since it is not subordinate to any other one.[85] And the Council of Nicaea (325) reminds the deacons that they are servants (ὑπηρέται) of the bishops and inferior to the priests.[86]

In this way the concept of ὑπηρεσία in canonical language seems to be essentially relative, applying to the various ranks of the clergy insofar as they are subordinate to others, and all together to the episcopate. Its most frequent use seems reserved for the category of subdeacons, as is evident in the Council of Laodicea.[87] This relative characteristic of the phrase suggests the idea that, while using two different words (ὑπηρεσία for the first group and διακονία for the second), the legislators of Ancyra might have intended precisely to distinguish the functions of the candidates who wanted to marry from the functions of those who had tacitly committed themselves to remain single. While the latter, coming forward in silence to receive the imposition of hands and thus manifesting their profession of continence (καταδεξάμενοι ἐν τῇ χειροτονίᾳ μένειν οὕτως) were elevated to the diaconate, the others, about whom the χειροτονία precisely is not mentioned, would have been authorized to remain in the service of the Church in that ὑπηρεσία that had been theirs until then, in all likelihood the subdiaconate. Being free to marry because they had expressed their desire to do so, they could not forcibly be constrained

---

can. 22: the subdeacon (ὑπηρέτης) must not wear the orarion nor leave his place at the door; can. 24: the clerics, from priests to deacons and the other ecclesiastical ranks, down to the subdeacons (ὑπηρέται), the lectors, the cantors, the exorcists, or the porters, must not enter a tavern; can. 25: the subdeacons (ὑπηρέται) must not distribute the bread nor bless the chalice; can. 43: the subdeacons (ὑπηρέται) must not, even for a short time, leave the doors to take part in the prayer (ibid., p. 139).

Another use for the word ὑπηρέται in the meaning of "subdeacons" is found in the *Apostolic Constitutions* VI, 17, 3 (F. X. Funk, *Didascalia et Constitutiones apostolorum*, I [Paderborn, 1905], p. 341). It is rightly pointed out by R. Gryson, *Les origines du célibat ecclésiastique*, p. 99, n. 1.

[85] Council of Sardiquius (343–44), can. 10: "That if a rich man or a jurist of the forum wanted to become a bishop, he should not be ordained before having fulfilled the duties of lector, deacon, and priest (ἐὰν μὴ καὶ ἀναγνώστου καὶ διακόνου καὶ πρεσβυτέρου ὑπηρεσίαν ἐκτελέσῃ), so that, from one promotion to the other, if he is judged worthy, he could go on to the summit of the episcopate" (Joannou, I, 2, p. 173).

[86] Can. 18: "The deacons must remain within the limits of their attributions, remembering that they are the servants of the bishops and lower than the priests" (Joannou, I, 1, p. 39). "It is also the diaconate that was probably meant by the word ὑπηρεσία in canon 8 of the Council of Neocaesarea" (ibid.).

[87] Referring to the Council of Laodicea, Du Cange translates ὑπηρέται as *subdiaconi* (*Glossarium Mediae et Infimae Graecitatis*, col. 1641). See also a letter of Basil of Caesarea to the choirbishops, in which 'ϲπηρέτης means a cleric at the service of the Church who is not yet part of the ἱερατικοί (ibid., II, 173–75).

to receive an ordination that would have compelled them to continence,[88] but they did not lose the right to remain in that subordinate service of the subdiaconate (or in the other functions of lectors, cantors, and porters that became theirs in the Church).

Reread from such a perspective, the Greek text of the 10th canon from the Council of Ancyra could be translated as follows:

> If those who are elevated to the diaconate declare and protest, at the moment of the rite of ordination ($\pi\alpha\rho'\ \alpha\mathring{v}\tau\mathring{\eta}\nu\ \tau\mathring{\eta}\nu\ \kappa\alpha\tau\acute{\alpha}\sigma\tau\alpha\sigma\iota\nu$), that not being able to continue living in this way [i.e., as single men], they have to marry, and later do marry, they may retain their functions [as subdeacons or minor clerics] pending the bishop's authorization. But if any keep silent, thereby undertaking at the time of the laying-on-of-hands to remain in that state of life [i.e., the celibate state], and later get married, they shall be dismissed from the functions of the diaconate.

This reading, which remains a hypothesis, has the advantage, in our eyes, of accounting for certain terms and certain peculiarities of style that need to be elucidated. Moreover, it thus harmonizes with Martin of Braga's version and with the later Byzantine tradition, particularly with the 123d novella of Justinian. At the same time, if it is only a conjecture, it seems to us that it is offering sufficient grammatical supports and internal coherence to define the so-called classical translation of any absolute value. The latter should be used with a little more caution than is ordinarily done,[89]

---

[88] The case is not fictitious. St. Augustine gives the example of many clerics who had been forced to accept "this burden". See below, pp. 289–90.

[89] To us this interpretation seems to be supported by another terminological particularity in the canon of Ancyra, to wit, the distinction between the $\kappa\alpha\tau\acute{\alpha}\sigma\tau\alpha\sigma\iota\varsigma$ and the $\chi\epsilon\iota\rho\sigma\tau\sigma\nu\acute{\iota}\alpha$. The first of these two words is used at the beginning of the canon, to refer to the entirety of the ceremony during which the candidate is to be ordained a deacon, while the word $\chi\epsilon\iota\rho\sigma\tau\sigma\nu\acute{\iota}\alpha$ does not appear until the end of the text. As G. Dix points out about the ritual of the Apostolic Tradition, "the 'installation' ($\kappa\alpha\tau\acute{\alpha}\sigma\tau\alpha\sigma\iota\varsigma$) in a function recognized by the Church is not identical to the 'ordination' ($\chi\epsilon\iota\rho\sigma\tau\sigma\nu\acute{\iota}\alpha$) by the imposition of hands. . . . Since the time of Solon at least, $\kappa\alpha\tau\acute{\alpha}\sigma\tau\alpha\sigma\iota\varsigma$ was the usual Greek term describing the installation of all civil functionaries. . . . It confers 'the entrance in function' and 'the power of function'; it constitutes 'an official testimonial' according to which such a man is at the service of the community in a particular function. But the major Orders—episcopate, priesthood, and diaconate—need, in addition to the katastasis, the cheirotonia, the sacramental imposition of hands" (G. Dix, Le ministère dans l'Église ancienne [Paris, 1955], p. 27). One can therefore conceive that the possible declaration of the candidate happened during the ceremony of installation (katastasis), which did not include the consecrating imposition of hands (cheirotonia) except for the candidates who, by their silence, had made the equivalent of a profession of continence. The others, who had declared their intention to marry, did not receive the cheirotonia conferring the diaconate but were permitted to remain in the service of the Church that had been theirs previously.

for it is not certain that it is totally faithful to the intentions of the legislators of Ancyra.[90] In the comprehensive study, we therefore propose to keep in mind the two possibilities of translation. While we do prefer the meaning that we have just proposed, we will of course keep the "traditional" interpretation in the place that belongs to it by right.[91]

Council of Neocaesarea (314–325)

Between the Council of Ancyra (314) and the Council of Nicaea there was held in Neocaesarea of Cappadocia a synod whose president, Vitalis of Antioch, and several other members had attended the assembly of Ancyra before. Similar problems were studied without, however, returning to the question of the *lapsi*.[92]

Canon 1

The first of the fifteen disciplinary canons promulgated by the Synod of Neocaesarea states as follows: "If a priest marries, he will be excluded from the ranks of the clergy; if he commits fornication or adultery, he will in addition be excommunicated and subject to penance."[93]

This canon does not call for a long commentary, but one can wonder why the priest is the only one subject to the law. Does it mean that the deacons were free to marry? Not likely. If the Synod of Ancyra gave such a permission, it did not grant an indiscriminate authorization of marriage to the deacons. The Fathers of Neocaesarea, some of whom had already attended the Council of Ancyra, seemingly had no reason to be more liberal and to turn an exception into a general rule. It therefore appears difficult to read in this canon an implicit confirmation of the possible legislation in Ancyra. In the hypothesis that we have suggested with regard to canon 10 of Ancyra, the two other canons—the one of

[90] Cf. also J. B. Pitra: "Qualis sit X canonis sensus vix affirmari potest, cum aliter omnino referatur a Martino Bracarensi, sane orientalis disciplinae studioso" (*Juris ecclesiastici Graecorum historia et monumenta*, I [Rome, 1864], p. 449).

[91] At the end of this analysis, it is obvious that we cannot agree with the judgment of Vacandard to which H. Leclercq subscribes: "Canon 10 of Ancyra obviously shows that if the Fathers of the council authorized the deacons to marry after their ordinations when they had kept that right for themselves, all the more so did they grant to those who had already married the authorization to continue to use their conjugal rights" (E. Vacandard, "Les origines du célibat ecclésiastique", pp. 92–93).

[92] For the date of this council, see Hefele-Leclercq, I, 1, 326–27, and Joannou, I, 2, p. 74.

[93] Joannou, I, 2, p. 75.

Ancyra and that of Neocaesarea—do, however, complete each other. Following sanctions against deacons who marry after ordination we have now penalties—harsher because they concern a higher rank of the clergy—directed at priests who have committed the same offense. The fact that several bishops who were present at Ancyra also took part in the Council of Neocaesarea makes even more plausible the idea of a continuity of legislation in this pattern.

Also noteworthy is the fact that the Council of Neocaesarea does not mention the conjugal life of priests who would have been married before their ordinations. Was it understood that they could freely continue to use their marital rights? It is possible to think so if one did not already know that this problem is precisely the point on which the discipline of that time was applied in several regions of Christendom, and one that would be the object, throughout the first seven centuries, of many regulations. It therefore seems that prudence is necessary in order to avoid assuming that the problem has been already solved. Being always difficult to use, the *a silentio* argument would run the risk of distorting the interpretation of the canon of Cappadocia, by making it say more than what it contains.[94]

Eusebius of Caesarea (ca. 265–339/40)

Born around 265 in Palestine (perhaps in Caesarea), Eusebius was ordained a priest and studied under the scholar Pamphilus, head of the school of Caesarea, whose close friend as well as faithful collaborator he became. In 313 he became the bishop of Caesarea, which did not prevent him from completing his monumental ecclesiastical history, thereby

---

[94] The rule enunciated by canon 8 of the Council of Neocaesarea was invoked sometimes as an indirect testimony of the freedom that the clerics would have had to use the marriage contracted before ordination. Here is the exact text of this canon: "If the wife of a layman has committed adultery, and the fact has been clearly established, the man cannot join the ministry. If she committed adultery after the ordination of her husband, he must send her away. If he continues to live with her, he cannot exercise the ministry entrusted to him" (ibid., 78–79).

In fact, this canon proves only that the behavior of a high cleric's wife reflected on his reputation; to send away from the conjugal home the wife who had committed adultery was, for the cleric, a way of disapproving publicly the guilty woman and of disassociating himself from her acts against chastity. It did not necessarily imply that the cleric and his wife were free to live as husband and wife, as is well shown by the Council of Elvira, which voted simultaneously a canon on the compulsory continence of clerics (can. 33) and a canon demanding the eviction of the adulterous wife of a cleric (can. 65), which was similar to the one voted by the Council of Neocaesarea. See below, p. 192, n. 145.

earning posterity's gratitude: "If Eusebius had not, with unequaled diligence, searched the Palestinian library where Origen the doctor and Alexander the bishop had collected all the Christian literature of ancient times, our knowledge on the first three centuries of the Church would amount to very little" (L. Duchesne). He was one of the most prominent bishops at the first ecumenical council, but his Arian sympathies rapidly put him on the side of the adversaries of Nicaea. He took part in the synods that deposed the main defenders of the Council and even in "that banditry of Tyre" (335), sadly famous for the condemnation of Athanasius. He died in 339 or 340, leaving his episcopal See to the Arian Acaces, his disciple. It was said about him: "Lacking the vigor of spirit and the firmness of conscience corresponding to his tremendous erudition, Eusebius, in spite of the fecundity of his pen and the exceptional value of some of his works, left only a doubtful memory and an obscured name" (O. Bardenhewer).

The Demonstratio Evangelica

In the first book of this work, written between 315 and 325, Eusebius elaborates on the dignity of the priests of the New Covenant, called to give birth to a numerous divine and spiritual posterity. While the patriarchs of the Old Testament were responsible for ensuring the propagation of the human race and the increase of the Chosen People, which explains why they had wives and children, the doctors and preachers of the Gospel have a higher mission exempting them from the works of carnal generation. And Eusebius continues, commenting on St. Paul:

> "It is fitting", according to Scripture, "that a bishop be the husband of an only wife." But this being understood, it behooves consecrated men, and those who are at the service of God's cult, to abstain thereafter from conjugal intercourse with their wives. As to those who were not judged worthy of such a holy ministry, Scripture grants them [conjugal intercourse] while saying quite clearly to all that "marriage is honorable and the nuptial bed is without stain, [and that] God judges profligates and adulterers".[95]

It does not seem that in the mind of the *Demonstratio Evangelica*'s author, the continence required from clerics be a corollary having, strictly speaking, force of law. The Apostle said that the bishop must be the husband of an only wife; but later (i.e., after ordination) it is fitting that the sacred minister busy at the duties of the cult and divine service abstain from any intercourse with his wife. "It is fitting", προσήκει, but only

---

[95] Eusebius of Caesarea, *De Demonstratione Evangelica*, I, 9. GCS, 23, 43.

"fitting". When we take a closer look, however, this manner of speaking seems to point to a certain obligation. The verb προσήκει, generally translated in Latin as *decet*, expresses several shades of meaning;[96] it is often rendered in English as "it belongs to" or "it is the duty of", formulae that suppose more than a simple suitability. Moreover, the sentence is introduced by the conjunction πλὴν ("except", "with the difference that", "however"), showing that there is a restriction in the idea that will be enunciated in the main proposition. These grammatical reasons lead us to think that the meaning of this passage of Eusebius could be the following: "It is fitting, says the logos, that the bishop be the husband of only one wife, but this being understood, the sacred ministers and those who are busy with the divine service must now abstain from conjugal intercourse." [97]

Another passage of the same work seems to show quite clearly that the bishop of Caesarea put the ministers of the cult in the category of the faithful who had to lead a "heavenly" life: two states of life, he says, are offered to the disciples of Christ: the one going beyond the ordinary human condition, renouncing the joys of marriage and paternity, despising riches and "exclusively devoted to the cult of God, because of a tremendous love of heaven"; the other, closer to man's level, defined by

---

[96] For instance: προσήκει μοι ποιεῖν ταῦτα = "Pertinet ad me haec facere, consentaneum mihi est, haec facere" (H. Stephano, *Thesaurus Graecae linguae*, 6 [Paris, 1842–47], c. 1922).

[97] The phrase γαμικὴ ὁμιλία generally describes sexual relations and not marriage as such. It would therefore seem that Eusebius aims here at showing the incompatibility between conjugal intercourse and the priestly functions and did not content himself with the exclusion of a second marriage. The reference to what is "conceded" to laymen is probably an echo of the first letter to the Corinthians, in which St. Paul truly seems to talk about conjugal relations when he says to the couples: "What I am saying now is a concession, not an order." See, for instance, the commentary of X. Léon-Dufour: "Paul does not talk about the state of marriage without immediately evoking another state: voluntary nonmarriage. Thus, he just gave judicious counsels about agreement in sexual relations—continence for the sake of prayer, then a resumption of normal relations, but he does not go on to study in depth the mystery of this new life of the couple; he stops abruptly and adds immediately: 'What I am saying now is a concession, not an order' " (VII, 6–7). "One must not mistake the advice he just gave with an order on his part. What does he concede? To look closely at the context, it seems that one can see exactly what the concession is: it is not the state of marriage as such that would be a last resort; it is not periodical continence that would be part of the truth contained in the Encratism of the Corinthians: it is the resumption of conjugal relations. I am conceding to you a resumption of normal relations in marriage, but let us be clear about this, I am not compelling you because, deep down, I would like all of you to be like me, in solitude with the Lord. Paul does not criticize the institution of marriage, but, evoking the exercise of its rights, he is embarrassed and cannot help but oppose his charism of solitude to married people . . . " (X. Léon-Dufour, "Mariage et Virginité", in *Christus* 42 [1964], pp. 185–86).

the choice of an honest marriage and concern for temporal things, though of course not neglecting the duties of piety but occupying a secondary rank area: "To those [disciples] times have been assigned [to practice asceticism] and days to receive instruction and listen to divine words. They have been granted this second degree of piety. . . ."[98]

If the members of the clergy are not the only ones to consecrate themselves to the exclusive service of the divine cult—virgins, widows, and other faithful equally animated by "a tremendous love for heavenly things" can also devote themselves to it—at least there is no doubt that, in Eusebius' mind, all clerics belong to that first class and cannot, on account of this fact, fail to opt for a quasi-heavenly life (*"cogitatione, vero atque animo in ipso coelo degentes, quasi quidam coelites"*), something that he delights in contemplating.

The fact that, in this privileged group, the clergy has the most important part, the part which he seems to consider primary, is expressed rather clearly in the following sentence:

> Consecrated by the Most High God for [the service] of the whole human race, it is not through animal sacrifices, bloody ceremonies, libations, fat taken from the victims, or smoke [from the sacrifices], the devouring fire, or the consumed flesh, but through righteous intentions of a genuine piety, the disposition of a purified soul, and, in addition, deeds and words in conformity with virtue that the priests render the divinity propitious, and they fulfill the liturgy for themselves and for mankind.[99]

This reminder of animal sacrifices, practiced in the past by the Levites, this evocation of a mediating role, and, finally, the choice of the word ἱερουργία, frequently used by Eusebius himself to depict the ministerial priesthood—all contribute to support a practical certainty that the author of the *Demonstratio* is thinking here about the ministers of the liturgy.[100] The readers of the bishop of Caesarea will certainly place them in the category of the "heavenly host", and if they had any doubts, the portrait of the faithful belonging to the second category would be enough to remove those doubts, because the latter are the audience and not the preachers of God's word.

---

[98] *De Demonstratione Evangelica*, I, 8. GCS, 23, 29.

[99] Ibid.

[100] R. Gryson sees in this passage of *De Demonstratione Evangelica* only a description of the monastic ideal. The consecrated men of whom Eusebius is speaking here would only be monks, and the holy function (ἱερουργία) they exercise thus to their own profit and that of all their brothers in mankind would be the sacrifice of their own lives (*Les origines du célibat ecclésiastique*, pp. 56–57). Such an interpretation does not, however, take enough into account the fact that that passage is introduced by the verse of the first epistle to Timothy relative to the choice of bishops.

Historia Ecclesiastica, Book X

This description of the states of life in which Christians find themselves enables us to clarify another page of Eusebius, whose symbolism remains partly mysterious. We are talking about a passage of the tenth book of the *Historia Ecclesiastica*.

The rededication of the Tyre basilica, restored thanks to the Constantinian peace, provided a brilliant orator—quite likely, Eusebius himself—with the opportunity to give one of those lengthy discourses that seem to be the specialty of Oriental people. He speaks at length about the beauty of the reconstructed edifice and then soars to mystical heights: "What is even more wonderful than these wonders are the archetypes and their intelligible prototypes, their divine models; I mean the renewal of the divine and reasonable edifice in souls." [101] Playing on the parallel, the bishop of Caesarea contemplates the various parts of the souls' edifice, arranged according to the architectural order of the temple before his eyes. "Yes, it is in justice that he builds, and it is according to the merit of the whole people that he apportions spiritual gifts. Some he surrounds only with an outer wall, which is a faith without error. . . . Others are entrusted with the gates of the house and ordered to watch over the doors and guide those who go in. . . . Others yet are strictly kept lined up along each side of the basilica; they are still catechumens. . . ." [102]

Little by little, men come from the outer wall, defined as faith, toward the house of God, where the faithful regenerated by baptism will enter: "Among the latter [the faithful] he chose the pure souls refined like gold by a divine washing; and here he supports some on pillars that are much stronger than the ones outside, on the most mystical doctrines at the heart of Scripture; the others are instructed through windows opened toward the light." [103]

And here is the temple, adorned with the triple portal to the glory of the Father, the Son, and the Holy Spirit: "Throughout the whole Church, God shows without jealousy and in many diversified ways the clarity and light of truth in details. Everywhere and on all sides he chose the living, solid, well-adjusted stones of the souls. . . ." [104]

The orator enjoys the spectacle of the community proper, the assembly purified by baptism who have crossed the threshold in order to glorify God. Now (and here is the page that is of interest to us) it does seem that

[101] *Hist. Eccl.*, X, 4, 55. SCh 55, 99.
[102] Ibid., X, 4, 63. SCh 55, 101.
[103] Ibid., X, 4, 64. SCh 55, 101–2.
[104] Ibid., X, 4, 65. SCh 55, 102.

inside the temple Eusebius distinguishes two categories of "living stones". Indeed, after the first general glance, he directs his eyes toward the basilica itself where priceless stones are glittering: "Everywhere, and on all sides, the orator said, God had chosen the living, solid, well-adjusted stones of the souls"; and now he adds: "With all of them he prepares the great royal house, radiant, full of light inside and outside, because not only the soul and the thought but also the body radiates in them with the multiple flowery beauty of chastity (ἁγνεία) and sobriety." [105]

The fact that he is speaking of a well-defined category among the baptized is clearly indicated at the end of the sentence by the choice of the word ἁγνεία, meaning generally and throughout Eusebius' work either virginity or perfect continence. [106]

Again we seem to find here the distinction established in the *Demonstratio Evangelica* between the married Christians, who lead a "human" life, and those who, through renunciation of the joys given to common mortals, become "quasi-heavenly", totally consecrated to the divine cult. The "great royal house . . . full of light inside and outside" is not the whole church, but is this sanctuary at the heart of the church, this portion chosen by the divine architect, made of stones shining with the radiance of the ἁγνεία. Does the preacher also see this invisible border projected in the assembly before him? One could not answer this, of course. The fact remains that while evoking the splendor of the "royal basilica" he seems to identify it with the sanctuary, and pursuing his description, he comes to those who sit there, in the seat of the elect, the central place, i.e., the members of the clergy: "There are also in this sanctuary thrones and countless benches and seats; and upon as many souls as rest upon them descend the gifts of the Holy Spirit, such as they were once seen in the holy apostles and their companions as 'cloven tongues as of fire, resting on each of them'." [107]

Just as the text of the *Demonstratio Evangelica* gave priority, even within the first class of the faithful, to those who exercise the office of the priesthood, the sermon of the preacher of Tyre proceeds to place at the heart of the heavenly sanctuary, made of living stones adorned with the ἁγνεία, those who preside over the liturgical functions, both passages clearly indicating that the clergy was at the summit of the Christian assembly, not only by virtue of its ministry but also by reason of the splendor of the ἁγνεία.

---

[105] Ibid.

[106] Cf., in particular, *Hist. Eccl.*, II, 17, 19 (SCh 31, 76); IV, 23, 6–7 (SCh 31, 204); V, 5, 1 (SCh 41, 91), etc.

[107] *Hist. Eccl.*, X, 4, 66. SCh 55, 102, et passim.

After having carefully read this discourse, we think that we can sub-scribe to the comment of Valois, in a note to his Latin translation repro-duced by Migne: "This is a famous passage on priestly chastity and continence; it had, however, remained in the darkness until now because of a defective translation." [108]

The Council of Nicaea (325)
1st Ecumenical Council

By May 20, 325, at the opening in the hall of the imperial palace of Nicaea of the Council that was to inaugurate in history a long series of ecumenical councils, the Arian heresy had already burst forth some time before. A priest of Alexandria, Arius had had problems with his bishop Alexander since 318 because his theories led him to deny the eternal divinity of the Word. Excommunicated, then compelled to flee, that adroit and deductive dialectician was able to win over a large group of people, among whom were influential bishops. The polemic took on such proportions that the unity of the Church was severely threatened, at the very time when the conversion of the emperor had given it back liberty and peace. Constantine, who saw himself as "the bishop chosen by God to handle external affairs", decided to settle the matter by calling for a universal synod. Thus there gathered in Nicaea, near Nicomedia, capital of the empire, a large number of bishops (250 according to Eusebius, up to 318 according to Athanasius), to whom were added a multitude of priests and deacons, as well as some laymen. This "great crown of hierarchs made of beautiful and diverse flowers" (Eusebius) was presided over by bishop Osius of Cordoba, probably representing Rome, which had also sent its own legates. We do not know how long the Council lasted. It was only after "having discussed at length and slowly" that the participants agreed on a Creed (our present Creed). Arius and two bishops of his party were excommunicated and exiled to Gaul. Soon, however, a group of semi-Arians, who had signed the acts of the Council out of mere expediency, circumvented the emperor and obtained a reversal of the situation: the most influential of the anti-Arius bishops were deposed one after the other, while Arius was back in grace. He was scheduled to be solemnly rehabilitated in Constantinople on Easter Sunday 336, but on Holy Saturday he was found dead of intes-tinal bleeding. After the death of Constantine (337), Arianism found a powerful protector in the person of Constantius II (337–61) and spread throughout the East. "The whole earth moaned and was surprised to

---

[108] PG 20, 876, n. 45.

find itself Arian", St. Jerome was to write about that time. The long and heroic resistance of St. Athanasius put the confusion to an end. In 362, a council called "of the confessors" gathered in Alexandria under his presidency and solemnly promulgated the acts of Nicaea while reestablishing communion with many Churches. It was, however, only with the second ecumenical Council of Constantinople (381) that Arianism knew its decisive decline.[109]

The 3d canon of Nicaea

In addition to the Creed, the Fathers of Nicaea promulgated a series of disciplinary canons.[110] The exact number of those that can rightly be deemed authentic was the object of various hypotheses.[111] It appears that there never were any others but those found on the already known list of Rufinus (345–411) and of Theodoret of Cyrus (ca. 393–458), and published by Gelasius of Cizycus in the second book of his "History of the Council of Nicaea".[112]

The majority of these decrees of a practical nature concern clerics.[113] One of them, the 3d, is titled "On the women who live with clerics" and deals with a topic of interest to the history of ecclesiastical celibacy:

> The great Council has absolutely forbidden bishops, priests, and deacons— in other words, all the members of the clergy—to have with them a sister-companion with the exception of a mother, a sister, an aunt, or, lastly, only those persons who are beyond any suspicion.[114]

Let us first note that the specific problem concerning the canon is not that of a spiritual marriage with a virgin consecrated to God, of whom certain patristic studies speak. The custom of living in the company of a sister (ironically) described as *agapete* (darling) seems to have been common enough in the early centuries of the Church, not only among the clergy but especially among laymen, and had always been severely stigmatized.[115] Here we have a regulation specifically meant for clergy

---

[109] For the history of the Council of Nicaea, cf. Hefele-Leclercq, I, 1, 335–632; I. Ortiz de Urbina, *Nicée et Constantinople* (History of the Ecumenical Councils), I (Paris, 1963).

[110] The minutes of the Council of Nicaea's deliberations, if there were any minutes, were not preserved. The documents we have are the Creed, the twenty disciplinary canons, a list of signing bishops, a synodal letter sent by the Fathers of the Council to the Church of Alexandria and to the bishops of Egypt, Lybia, and Pentapolis, and the decree on Easter.

[111] For a detailed study of the issue, cf. Hefele-Leclercq, I, 1, 503–28.

[112] PG 85, 1319–36; GCS 28, 112–18.

[113] Canons 1, 2, 3, 4, 8, 9, 10, 15, 16, 17, 18, 19.

[114] Joannou, I, 1, pp. 25–26.

[115] Cf. St. Cyprian, *Ep.* 4 (CSEL 3–2, 472–78); Council of Ancyra (314), can. 19 (Joannou, I, 2, p. 70); Council of Carthage under Gratus (345/48), can. 3 (CC 149, 5); St. John

members and referring to a quite different situation. The women with whom it is forbidden to live are called συνείσακτοι, a word that is derived from the verb συνεισάγειν (to introduce with, or at the same time).[116] A συνείσακτος is a person admitted to the company of another (in the home of or to intimacy with another). In this case, they are women and, moreover, women of whom it is not specified that they have made a profession of chastity. This is a generic term, embracing all the women who, in one way or the other, lived under the same roof as the clerics who have been mentioned. A mother, sister, and the other women for whom exceptions are also made are also literally συνείσακτοι.

But unlike the others, their presence with the clerics is recognized as legitimate. In the Latin documents we find the word habitually rendered by *subintroducta* or *extranea*.[117]

The main question posed by this 3d canon is what the Fathers of the First Ecumenical Council meant by the phrase "or, lastly, only persons who are beyond any suspicion". If there is mention of suspicion, it is obviously in connection with the chastity that was compulsory for the clerics and to which they had to give witness without any ambiguity. But what chastity are they talking about, and, therefore, who are these women—not next of kin—whose presence in the home of the bishop, priest, or deacon was considered by the Council as not being of prejudice to them? Were the wives of those who had been married before ordination also forbidden or, on the contrary, were they deemed "beyond any suspicion" and did they have a perfectly legitimate place near their husbands-turned-clerics? If such were the case, why did the Fathers of Nicaea deem normal the cohabitation of a clergy member with his wife? Was it because conjugal union, elevated to the dignity of a sacrament, continued to be for the married clerics the specific testimony of chastity expected by the ecclesiastical community? Or because one same profession of continence bound husband and wife, and that they, while still living together, could offer a public proof of their fidelity to such a commitment?

Chrysostom, *Contra eos qui subintroductas habent virgines* and *Quod regulares feminae viris cohabitare non debeant* (PG 47, 495–514 and 513–32). Cf. J. Dumortier, *Saint Jean Chrysostome. Les cohabitations suspectes* (Les Belles Lettres [Paris, 1955], pp. 44–137); St. Jerome, *Ep. 22 ad Eustochium* (CSEL 54, 143–211).

[116] Cf. G. W. H. Lampe, *A Patristic Greek Lexicon* (Oxford, 1965), pp. 1317–18; H. Stephano, *Thesaurus graeca linguae* (London, 1819–21), c. 866–67.

[117] The word *subintroduced* (from the Latin *subintroducta*) does not seem to be a very felicitous one. The translation "sister companion", adopted by Joannou, is already an interpretation.

In itself the text does not allow us to answer with certainty, and this explains the opposing commentaries that have been made.[118] But one must remember that "the canons of the first general synod were the fundamental rule that became a model for the later local and ecumenical councils in the measures they took."[119] As H. Leclercq rightly points out: "The Western Churches did not give less importance to the canons of Nicaea than the Eastern Churches did. It is enough to read the popes' letters, the canons of the councils held in Rome, Africa, Spain, Gaul, and so forth, to become convinced. The canons of Nicaea happen to be one of the sources of the later law and of ecclesiastical discipline. This explains the place almost always given to them at the beginning of the general canonical collections."[120] The authority of the First Ecumenical Council on matters of faith and also on matters of discipline was so great that it was used to support all the later decisions of the Roman pontiffs, of the councils, and even of the imperial legislation on the issue under study. One instance, the most remarkable of all, is provided by the case of Apiarius of Sicca, who in 419 put the African episcopate in opposition to Pope Boniface about a point of ecclesiastical jurisdiction. The Pope invoked a canon of Nicaea that in the last analysis turned out to have come from the Council of Sardicus; the Africans had to be given the last word.[121]

A general overview of the conciliar decisions and the declarations of the Roman pontiffs on the issue of the cohabitation of clerics with persons of the female sex during the centuries following the first ecumenical synod[122] will allow us not only to measure the importance given by the Church to the 3d canon of the Council of Nicaea, but also to provide a key for interpretation that we should rightly take into account.

Africa: At the council held in Hippo on October 8, 393—described by the biographer of St. Augustine as being *"plenarium totius Africae concilium"*—a first African canon was decreed that, to our knowledge, expresses a decision directly inspired by the 3d canon of Nicaea: "Let no 'outsider' woman live with a cleric, whoever he is; the only [authorized ones] are mothers, grandmothers, maternal and paternal aunts, sisters, nieces,

---

[118] As early as the 11th century, the controversy opposing Bernold of Constance and Canon Alboinus was precisely on the meaning to be given to the 3d canon of Nicaea. See above, pp. 18–19.

[119] Ortiz de Urbina, *Nicée et Constantinople* (Paris, 1963), p. 117.

[120] In Hefele-Leclercq, I, 2, *Appendice VI, Diverses rédactions des canons de Nicée*, 1139.

[121] See below, pp. 266f. Cf. H. Leclercq, in Hefele-Leclercq, I, 1, 504–7; and ibid., I, 2, 1143.

[122] We have to remember that our study has as a *terminus ad quem* the Quinisext Council of 691.

and all those who for reasons of familial [and] domestic necessity lived with him before his ordination." [123]

The legitimate wife is not explicitly mentioned in this canon of Hippo, but it is likely that the periphrase "and all those who for reasons of familial [and] domestic necessity lived with him before his ordination" includes her. The important point is that we are in the year 393, i.e., three years after the Council of Carthage demanded from the higher ranks of the clergy perfect continence (in the name of apostolic tradition). It is therefore reasonable to think that if the legislator of Hippo admitted the presence of the wife in the home of the cleric, it was with the condition that the couple respect the law of continence.

We find in the African collections two other canons on the same topic: the first in the *Breviatio Ferrandi* (ca. 546),[124] the other in the *Concordia Cresconii* (ca. 690).[125] Both, referring explicitly to the 3d canon of Nicaea, are to be read against the background of a compulsory continence for married clergy that was never changed in the Church of Africa.

Spain: In the Iberian peninsula they did not wait for the Council of Nicaea in order to legislate on the problem of the *subintroductae*. The Synod of Elvira (ca. 300–305) promulgated, at the same time as its famous decree on compulsory continence for the ministers of the altar, a canon excluding "outsider" women from the home of clerics: "Let no bishop or any other cleric have [a woman] with him, unless she be a sister or daughter, virgin [and] consecrated to God; it seemed good [to us] that he should have no 'outsider woman' [with him]." [126]

A hundred years later, before the episcopal assembly gathered in Toledo (400), Bishop Patruinus, president of the Council, started with a vote on a resolution of fidelity to the statutes of Nicaea:

> It seems good to me to continue observing, before all other things, the decrees of the Council of Nicaea, and not to deviate from them. The bishops said: This seems good to all [of us]: if anyone, knowingly, dares to act in a way that is different from that decided by the Council of Nicaea

---

[123] *Breviarium Hipponense*, can. 16. CC 149, 38. The Council of Carthage held between 345 and 348, presided over by Gratus, had already approached the issue of the *extranaea*, but in referring to all the faithful who had made a profession of chastity: "Nullus igitur"—it is there declared—"nullaque sanctimoniae et virginitati deserviens . . . in una domo cum extraneis penitus commorari debent" (can. 3. CC 149, 5). Clerics as such are not considered by this canon of Carthage, although the title, probably added later on, mentions them.

[124] N. 122. CC 149, 297.

[125] N. 110. PL 88, 883b–c.

[126] Can. 27. Bruns, II, 5.

and deems that one should not obey it anymore, let him be excommunicated, unless [he gives in to] the fraternal admonitions and corrects his
errors.[127]

The Spanish Fathers do not repeat the terms of the 3d canon of 325,
but limit themselves to prohibiting lectors from receiving at home young
girls other than a sister or a half-sister.[128] It is through an *a fortiori*
interpretation and the total adhesion to the Nicaean decisions given in
the preface that they clearly state that the prohibition relative to the
extraneae applies to the higher ranks of the clergy.

The Council of Girona, in 517, specifically authorizes the wife to
remain near her husband (from subdeacon to bishop) on condition that
she live with him as a sister with her brother.[129] Later, the Spanish
councils will periodically reiterate, under various forms, the prohibition
of the *extraneae*, while permitting under the roof of the cleric a wife
having made a profession of continence.[130]

The Spanish legislation, throughout the whole period under study,
ties the prohibition regarding the *extraneae* to the obligation of perfect
continence imposed on all the higher clerics, even on those who might
have been married before ordination.

Gaul: The question of the *subintroductae* is approached for the first time
in Gaul during the 2d Council of Arles, which took place between the
years 442 and 506: "If a cleric, starting from the order of the diaconate,
dares to take with him a woman for his consolation, let him be rejected
from communion; an exception is made for a grandmother, [a mother,]
a sister, a daughter, a niece, or a 'converted' wife."[131]

A "converted" wife means a wife who made a profession of chastity,
like her husband, as many documents give witness.[132] The Gallic councils
that will return later to the Nicaean prohibition about clerical cohabitation with "outsider" women will always recognize the legitimacy of

---

[127] Bruns, I, 203.
[128] Can. 6. Bruns, I, 204.
[129] Can. 6–7. Bruns, II, 19.
[130] Council of Lerida (523), can. 15 (Bruns, II, 23); 2d Council of Toledo (531), can. 3
(ibid., I, 208); Council of Braga (540), can. 15 (ibid., II, 32); 2d Council of Braga (572),
can. 32 (ibid., II, 50); 3d Council of Toledo (589), can. 5 (ibid., I, 214); Council of Seville
(590), can. 3 (ibid., II, 64); 4th Council of Toledo (633), can. 22–23 (ibid., I, 230–31); can.
42–43 (ibid., 234–35); 8th Council of Toledo (653), can. 5 (ibid., I, 279–80).
[131] Can. 3. CC 148, 114.
[132] See below, pp. 276–77.

a "converted" wife's presence at the side of her husband equally bound by his ordination to perfect continence.[133]

Roman Pontiffs: The Italian councils of that period do not contain any reference to the *extraneae*, but we find under the pen of Pope Siricius, St. Leo, and then Gregory the Great declarations recalling that the prohibition of Nicaea was still in force. It was in his *Directa* decretal to Bishop Himerius of Tarragona that Pope Siricius, after having recalled the motives that were, to his mind, the foundation for continence among priests and deacons,[134] firmly ordered not allowing the clerics to live with women other than those mentioned by the ecumenical Council: "We will not tolerate the presence of women in the homes of clerics, with the exception of those whom the Council of Nicaea authorized so as to [take care of] their needs, and only for that reason."[135]

Around 446, Pope St. Leo asked Anastasius of Thessalonika to see to it that the rule of continence was observed by all members of the clergy in Illyria, from the subdiaconate up inclusive.[136] It does not seem that he had the opportunity during his pontificate to make any direct statement on the issue of the *subintroductae*. However, his letter to Rusticus of Narbonne (458/59), reaffirming that "the law of continence is the same for the ministers of the altar, the bishops, and the priests", stipulates that these latter do not have to chase away their wives, but must live with them in perfect continence.[137] As to Gregory the Great, for whom the continence of subdeacons and other higher clerics was, as for all his predecessors, an obligation without the shadow of a doubt, we see him

---

[133] Council of Angers (453), can. 4 (CC 148, 137–38); Council of Tours (461), can. 3 (ibid., 145); *Statuta Ecclesiae antiqua* (late 5th century), can. 27 (46) (ed. C. Munier [Paris, 1960], p. 235); Council of Agde (506), can. 10 (CC 148, 199–200); Council of Orléans (511), can. 29 (CC 148A, 12); Council of Clermont (535), can. 13 and 16 (ibid., 108–10); Council of Orléans (538), can. 2 and 4 (ibid., 114–16); Council of Orléans (541), can. 17 (ibid., 136); Council of Orléans (549), can. 3–4 (ibid., 149); Synod of Bishop Aspasius (549), can. 1–2 (ibid., 163); Council of Tours (567), can. 10, 11, 13 (12), 16 (15), 20 (19) (ibid., 179–84); Council of Mâcon (581/3), can. 1 and 11 (ibid., 223 and 225); Council of Lyon (583), can. 1 (ibid., 232); council in an uncertain place (after 614), can. 8 (ibid. 287); Council of Châlons-sur-Saône (647–53), can. 3 (ibid., 303); Council of Bordeaux (662–75), can. 3 (ibid., 312); Council of Jean-de-Losne (673–75), can. 4 (ibid., 315); Council of Autun (663–80), can. 10 (ibid., 319).

[134] See above, pp. 8–11.

[135] Can. 12. PL 13, 1144a. P. Coustant, *Epistolae Romanorum Pontificum* (Paris, 1721), col. 635.

[136] PL 54, 672b–73a. See below, pp. 260–61.

[137] PL 54, 1204a. See below, pp. 261–63.

intervening several times to ask that the law of Nicaea regarding the *extraneae* be observed.[138]

The East: More than half a century before the Council of Nicaea, a synod held in Antioch to judge the bishop Paul of Samosata, accused of heresy and scandalous behavior, mentions the *subintroductae*.[139]

It is legitimate to ask oneself whether the decision made by this synod held in 268 (or 269) did not inspire the writers of the 3d canon of Nicaea, for we find in it the same preoccupation concerning suspicions liable to be aroused by the presence of women in the immediate environment of a bishop or priest. We will also note that criticism of Paul of Samosata's behavior was made by bishops gathered in Antioch in the name of the priestly model outlined in the Pauline epistles (1 Tim 4:12; 2 Tim 2:21, 3:17). The synod did not intend to innovate but rather to reprove an innovation, a manner of living that went against the accepted usages.[140] In 325, the universal Church took a position, but the precedent of Antioch lets us think that it was developed by bishops concerned with fidelity to a constant tradition.

---

[138] Letter to the defender Symmacus (June 591); to John of Cagliari (May 594); to the defenders Romanus and Fantinus, and others (February 599); to Syagrus, Aetherius, Virgil, and Desiderius, bishops of Gaul (July 599); to Gattulus, Romanus, and Vintarit (June 603); to Chrysanthes, bishop of Spoleta (June 603). These texts are to be found on pp. 371ff.

[139] Here is the passage from the letter that the bishops of Antioch sent to Rome and to "all the provinces" regarding Paul of Samosata:

"As to the *subintroductae* women, as they are called in Antioch, his women and those of the priests and deacons living around him, he hid them, as they did, together with other faults that are without remedy. . . . Why should we write these things? We know . . . that the bishop and all the priests must be for the people an example of all that is good, nor are we unaware of how they have fallen because they brought women to their homes; others were suspected, so that, even if it were agreed that he did not do anything dishonest, one should at least beware of suspicions that such an affair can arouse, lest some be scandalized and others stray and imitate him. How indeed could he admonish or warn another not to live anymore with a woman, and thus guard himself from falling, according to what is written, when he has already sent away a woman, but has brought in with him two others, in the prime of life and pleasant to look at. . . ." Eusebius of Caesarea, *Hist. Eccl.*, VII, 30, 12–14. SCh 41, 217–18.

[140] H. Achelis made himself the promoter of a thesis according to which the *virgines subintroductae* would have been quite numerous in Christian antiquity and encouraged for a long time (H. Achelis, *Virgines Subintroductae, Ein Beitrag Zur VII. Kapitel des Korintherbriefs* [Leipzig, 1902], viii–75 pp.). Among the texts that the author quotes to support his thesis is the page of Eusebius of Caesarea relating the condemnation of Paul of Samosata. We cannot see how one can find anything in that page except the idea of a scandal shocking to the Christians of the time who were obviously used to a clergy less familiar with women. No matter how attractive some of its aspects could be, the theory of H. Achelis is greeted today with more reserve. P. Ladeuze is not the only one to think, "We consider [therefore]

From the Council of Nicaea to the Quinisext Council (691), the East in communion with the West left us two conciliar texts regarding the problem of the *extraneae*.[141] The first was voted in 410 at the Persian Synod of Seleucia-Ctesiphon, which solemnly adopted "all the regulating canons established in the great synod held in the town of Nicaea".[142] The Persian bishops wrote a text in which the exception stipulated for close female relatives and women "beyond any suspicion" is no longer to be found:

> Concerning the *subintroductae*, we will do what was ruled at the synod [of Nicaea]: from now on, any bishop, priest, deacon, subdeacon, or cleric who brings in a woman to live in his house and does not live alone or in a monastic community in the chastity and sanctity that behoove the ministry of the Church, shall not be admitted to the ministry of the Church.[143]

The Persian Church of the early 5th century therefore knew the discipline of perfect continence for the higher members of the hierarchy and even seems to have extended it to all clerics without making any distinctions between ranks.

A second Eastern text about the *subintroductae* is found in the documents of the Armenian Synod of Chahabivan of 444: "If a bishop, priest, or deacon, either anyone belonging to the order of the ministers of the Church or a cleric, has in his home a woman 'introduced' as mistress of the household, as is the practice among those living with concubines, let him be demoted from his rank and held as a pervert and a publican. . . ."[144] The measure goes hand in hand with the recognition of the legitimate presence of the wife of a cleric at the conjugal home, but it is not specified whether or not she had to make a profession of continence.[145]

---

the thesis of H. Achelis to be an absolutely gratuitous one" (Review in *Revue d'Histoire Ecclésiastique* 6 [1905], pp. 58–62). See also Hefele-Leclercq, I, 1, p. 201, n. 2, and P. de Labriolle, "Le mariage spirituel dans l'Antiquité chrétienne", *Revue historique*, 46 [1921], pp. 204–25).

[141] Canon 19 of the Council of Ancyra does not deal with the issue of female cohabitation with clerics, but with that of the virgins living with laymen, as we have already seen.

[142] J. B. Chabot, *Synodicon orientale ou Recueil de synodes nestoriens* (*Notices et extraits des manuscrits de la Bibliothèque nationale et autres bibliothèques*, t. 37) (Paris, 1902), pp. 259–60.

[143] Ibid., p. 264.

[144] Can. 13. A. Mai, *Scriptorum veterum nova collectio*, X, 2 (Rome, 1838), p. 295.

[145] Can. 2. A. Mai, ibid., p. 292. See below, p. 280. The existence of such a canon ordering the eviction of the cleric's wife from the conjugal home if she is guilty of adultery does not imply in itself that those husbands and wives who were authorized to live together outside the case of adultery could legitimately use their conjugal rights. Canon 65 of the Council of Elvira (ca. 300–305) is an example in which we read: "If the wife of a cleric has committed adultery and if her husband, having found out about it, did not immediately

The quasi-general silence of the Eastern episcopates within the jurisdiction of Byzantium during the whole post-Nicaean period with respect to the question under study is balanced by the imperial constitutions of the Theodosian Code and the *Corpus juris civilis* of Justinian. Because the latter came from an authority outside the ecclesial Magisterium, we will simply note them here as a reminder.[146]

The Byzantine Fathers of the Quinisext Council (in Trullo) of 691 made their disciplinary decisions in a spirit of autonomy from the Western Church.[147] Canon 13 grants to the married clerics of all ranks, with the exception of the bishops, the right to live maritally with their wives save for the days when "they touch holy things".[148] In such a context it is obvious that the renewal of the Nicaean prescription regarding female cohabitations in canon 5 of the Quinisext synod[149] means to include the

---

send her away, he will never receive communion anymore, so that those who must be models of good behavior may not flaunt themselves as teachers of vices" (Bruns, II, 10).

Now, this same Council of Elvira also forbids clerics from conjugal intercourse. The meaning of canon 65 is therefore quite clear: the situation had to be avoided where the wife of the cleric who, like her husband, was bound to continence, would give an example of a behavior contrary to conjugal morality. To send her away from the conjugal home because of adultery shows that perfect chastity is a compulsory feature in the lives of married clerics and their spouses. Herbst rightly pointed out that the decision to send away the guilty wife was probably motivated by the fact that since men who had entered the Orders could not have conjugal relations with their wives, the latter must have been more easily exposed to the temptation of adultery ("Die Synode zu Elvira", TThQ 3 [1821], pp. 43–44). Other Spanish councils provided for the same sanction for the adulterous wife of a cleric, in particular the 2d Council of Braga (572), whose canon 28 is a textual copy of canon 8 of the Council of Neocaesarea (314–25) (Bruns, II, 50). Thus, one must be careful not to interpret canon 13 of the Synod of Chahabivan as an indirect recognition of conjugal rights for married clerics whose wives remained faithful. Here the sanction of eviction for the adulterous wife is, on the contrary, as in all the cases where it is found, a rather strong indication in favor of the concomitant existence of a discipline of compulsory continence as proven by the Spanish councils mentioned above.

[146] See the text of these various imperial laws on pp. 352ff. Cf. also pp. 318–19. They reiterate and reinforce the 3d canon of Nicaea, presenting it as an essential guarantee of chastity for single clerics and interpreting it in the more restrictive sense insofar as the bishop is concerned. As for the clerics who were already married before their ordinations, the same canon is recalled to them, but now it includes a clause permitting them to live in the same house with their wives.

[147] Cf. Joannou, I, 1, p. 98: "There is no doubt regarding the obvious particularist spirit of the Trullan legislation: it attempts to pass as Byzantine, which is why it opposes both the Latins and the Armenians, not on questions of principle, of course, but, orthodoxy having been safeguarded, on questions of clerical discipline and liturgy."

[148] Joannou, I, 1, p. 142.

[149] "Let none of those enrolled in the higher ranks of the clergy and living with non-suspect persons under a rule have in his home a woman or servant, in order that his reputation thereby remain irreproachable . . ." (Joannou, I, 1, pp. 130–31).

wives of clerics among the persons whose company cannot be suspicious. Only the wives of the bishops are forbidden to stay with their husbands, who are bound to perfect continence.[150] It was the first time since 325, as far as we know, that a disciplinary tradition affirmed in a council interpreted explicitly the 3d canon of Nicaea in a meaning that does not imply perfect continence for the clerics in question and their wives.[151]

This overview of the legislation generated by Nicaea about the cohabitation of clerics with *subintroductae* women shows, among the Roman pontiffs and the episcopates of Africa, Spain, and Gaul, the existence of a constant interpretation according to which the 3d Nicaean canon was meant to protect the higher members of the clergy, bound to perfect continence, against feminine temptations and to ensure them a reputation in conformity with their state of life. When the bishops of Rome or the regional synods evoke the case of the wife, it is generally in order to authorize her to live with her husband, promoted to a major Order, only under the explicit condition that she too make a profession of continence. She thereby enters the category of women "beyond any suspicion". This interpretation remains invariable until the end of the 7th century, and it is not contradicted by any other interpretation of the same nature (i.e., coming from hierarchical sources qualified to declare a Church tradition as authentic), which would be unequivocally claimed as going in a different direction.[152]

Coming from an important group of members of the order of bishops who were collegially in union with the Roman Pontiffs—throughout a long period of history when there was no sign of discontinuity but on the contrary a constant concern for faithfulness to the authority of an ecumenical council considered by all to be the supreme norm—this interpretation of the 3d canon of the Council of Nicaea exhibits all the traits to qualify it reasonably as "correct" and "authentic". In this instance we can apply the remark noted in this book, in the chapter on principles of methodology: the way the members of the college of apostles in union

---

[150] Can. 12. Joannou, ibid., pp. 138–39.

[151] The synods of the Church of Persia who had gone over to Nestorianism will authorize, starting in 484, the use of marriage for clerics, bishops and patriarchs included, but any reference to the Nicene canon is absent from their legislation. See below, pp. 281ff.

[152] The Council of Seleucia-Ctesiphon of 410, on the contrary, is going in the same direction as the "Western" interpretation (but with greater vigor), and the Council of Chahabivan of 444, although by itself it does not directly reveal whether the Armenian Church of the mid 5th century demanded from major clerics the observation of perfect continence, the sanction of eviction for the adulterous wife provided for in its 2d canon does constitute, for the reasons we have seen (p. 192), an important indication leading one to think that such was actually the discipline known by the clergy of those areas.

with Peter apply what is ordered by an ecumenical council constitutes an authorized commentary upon that council and can be easily used to resolve whatever questions may arise.[153]

This interpretation in itself, then, can be taken as a scientifically valid key to unlock the hidden ambiguities at the level of vocabulary in the Greek text of the 3d canon of the First Ecumenical Council, a key that will permit us to confirm with a satisfactory degree of certainty that the phrase used by the Nicene Fathers to refer to "the only persons who are above all suspicion" included, among others they had in mind, the possible wife of a cleric living with him in a state of perfect continence.[154]

The episode of Paphnutius' intervention at the Council of Nicaea

The Byzantine historian Socrates[155] relates the following in the first book of his *Historia Ecclesiastica*:

> We had promised earlier to mention Paphnutius and Spiridon, and the time has now come to speak of them. Now, in those days, Paphnutius was bishop of Upper Thebes, and he was such a friend of God that he was able to perform miracles. During the times of persecution, he had one of his eyes plucked out. The emperor had such a great devotion to this man that he often had him brought to the palace; so great was the reverence Constantine felt for this man, that the emperor would kiss Paphnutius' empty eye-socket.
>
> I will now relate what was decided thanks to his advice for the advantage of the Church and the honor of the clergy. It had seemed good to the bishops [of the Council of Nicaea] to introduce a new law in the Church:

---

[153] See above, pp. 58–59.

[154] It has at times been argued that canon 3 of Nicaea could not be compatible with a law on continence because the interdiction it contains concerns all members of the clergy, and therefore the lower clerics, who at that time had the right to marry and use their marital rights (cf. in particular Hefele-Leclercq, I, 1, 539). It must be noted that the conciliar decisions that we know authorizing lectors and cantors (even subdeacons) to marry and use their conjugal rights are all posterior to the Council of Nicaea: in the West, the first of those texts is from 393; in the East, it is the 14th canon of the Council of Chalcedon (451) which, for the first time, mentions the permission to marry granted to lectors and cantors "in several provinces". (See the section below regarding the "legislation on marriage and continence for the lower clerics" on pp. 411ff.)

[155] A lawyer in Constantinople, Socrates was born around 380 and died after 439. He wrote an ecclesiastical history in seven volumes, as a continuation of Eusebius of Caesarea's own, covering the period from Constantine's conversion to 439. His Novatian sympathies have sometimes led people to think that he himself was a member of the Novatian sect.

consecrated men—I mean bishops, priests, and deacons—should not sleep any more with the wives they had married while they were laymen. As the matter was under discussion, Paphnutius stood up in the middle of the episcopal assembly, and with a strong voice, protested that such a heavy yoke should not be imposed on consecrated men. The conjugal bed is honorable, and marriage has no stain, he said. One should fear lest, through an excess of severity, the bishops might bring harm to the Church. Not all are strong enough to live asceticism in total dispassion, and the chastity of the spouses would not be safeguarded with so many opportunities. It was by the name of chastity that Paphnutius did not hesitate to call a life in common with a legitimate wife. It is quite enough [he said] to require of these clerics that they not remarry [after ordination], in accordance with the ancient tradition of the Church; but let us not separate them from the wives whom, monogamous as they are, they once married when they were laymen.

Thus spoke Paphnutius, though he himself had nothing to do with marriage and, in fact, no experience with women. From childhood on, he had been raised in a monastery, and he was praised as a man of very great chastity if there ever was one. The college unanimously rallied to his proposal. They therefore remained silent on the issue and left it to the judgment of those who were ready to abstain from conjugal intercourse with their wives.[156]

The problem with this narrative is basically that it is not part of the authentic documents of the Council of Nicaea that we have, and Socrates is the first, and in fact the only one, to know it and to make it known.[157] Now, the Byzantine writer wrote his *Historia Ecclesiastica* in the mid 5th century, more than a hundred years after the first ecumenical council, a time farther from it that we are from Vatican I (1869–70); and, in addition, he is unable to provide the source of his information. Therefore, a healthy critical attitude calls for a careful screening of his claims to credibility.

In all eras, those who held the episode of Paphnutius' intervention at the Council of Nicaea to be true and those who rejected it as apocryphal have been opposed in controversies during which all the arguments

---

[156] Socrates, *Hist. Eccl.*, I, 11. PG 67, 101b–4b.

[157] Sozomenes, a contemporary of Socrates and also a lawyer in Constantinople, relates in his history, written between 439 and 450, many facts that he borrowed from Socrates. For the episode of Paphnutius it seems that he condensed and slightly revised the narrative of Socrates by adding subdeacons to the list of clerics affected by the draft on compulsory continence (*Hist. Eccl.*, I, 23. GCS 50, 44). Gelasius of Cyzicus, who, around 475–76, wrote a history of the Council of Nicaea, also depends very closely on Socrates with regard to the episode of Paphnutius (*Histoire du Concile de Nicée*, 2, 32–33. GCS 28, 118–19). Concerning the modifications brought by Gelasius to the narrative of Socrates, see R. Gryson, *Les origines du célibat ecclésiastique*, pp. 89–90.

pro and con were reviewed. If Socrates was telling the truth, the Fathers of Nicaea were against a draft aimed at imposing continence with their wives on bishops, priests, and deacons; the main authority of the Ecumenical Council of 325 would thus attest that the discipline of celibacy-continence had not been in force during the first three centuries of the Church, that in later making it an obligation for the higher clerics, the councils and Roman pontiffs moved away from a tradition that had had the highest antiquity in its favor. On the other hand, the doubts that rest upon Socrates' testimony and led more than one critic to deny the authenticity of the episode of Paphnutius' intervention are rooted first of all in the fact that this late story has against it the authority of many representatives of the patristic era[158] (not only certain Fathers taken individually, such as Ambrose, Epiphanius, Jerome, Siricius, and Innocent I, but also the episcopate of whole provinces, such as those of Africa, Spain, and Gaul) who, even though they were extremely concerned about staying in conformity with the decisions of the first ecumenical council, affirmed that the discipline of celibacy-continence was rooted in the tradition of the origins.

An important argument of external criticism was developed in our time, tending to demonstrate in a rather decisive way that the figure of Paphnutius highlighted by Socrates in his narrative is "the product of a progressive hagiographical confabulation". It was set forth in 1968 by Professor Friedhelm Winkelmann in a lecture published by the Institute of Byzantinology of the Martin-Luther University at Halle-Wittenberg,[159] the basic points of which are as follows:

1. All the testimonies regarding Paphnutius are contained in Greek sources. *Athanasius of Alexandria* knew several people, monks or bishops, called Paphnutius, but did not know any Paphnutius who would have been at the same time a confessor (of the faith during the persecution) and a bishop. The second witness, in chronological order, is *Epiphanius*, who, in a list of Melecian schismatics,[160] mentions a famous confessor and anchorite called Paphnutius.[161] The man was not a bishop. Twenty years later, *Gelasius of Caesarea* published an ecclesiastical history that

---

[158] This is, of course, the period from the Council of Nicaea (325) to the date that Socrates completed his ecclesiastical history (ca. 440).

[159] F. Winkelmann, "Paphnutios, der Bekenner und Bischof". *Probleme der koptischen Literatur*, = Wissenschaftliche Beiträge der Martin-Luther-Universität Halle-Wittenberg, 1968, 1 (K2), pp. 145–53.

[160] Those were the followers of Lycopolis, bishop of Upper Egypt, who initiated a rigorist schism and died shortly after 325. The sect survived him until the mid 4th century and was later absorbed into the Arian opposition.

[161] *Panarion (Adversus Haereses)*, 68, 5, 3.

has since been lost, but some of which has been reconstructed. For the first time there is a mention of the Orthodox confessor Paphnutius, who took part in the Council of Nicaea and is described as a man of God. He is one of the confessors who had their right eyes gouged at Emperor Maximinus' order and were condemned to the mines. As a thaumaturgist he was practically no less than the apostles. Gelasius described him as a confessor but not as an anchorite or a bishop. The materials used by Gelasius certainly did not refer to Paphnutius as having the episcopal dignity; otherwise, Gelasius would have mentioned it, as was his habit. It was in *Rufinus*, who, after 400, translated into Latin and edited the work of Gelasius, and then in *Gelasius of Cyzicus*, who for the most part utilized the work of his Caesarean namesake, that Paphnutius was promoted for the first time to the episcopate. That information is of no value and sprang from the idea that only bishops could have had any importance at the Synod of Nicaea. Lastly, *Socrates* knew the exact name of the diocese: it was Upper Thebaid (though the name of the episcopal See was not indicated). He also referred to an episode regarding the intervention of Paphnutius at the Council of Nicaea to prevent the prohibition against using marital rights. As to *Sozomenus*, he used the previous narratives, simplifying them, and all the historians and hagiographers who followed depended on the authors we have already mentioned. One can note, with the help of this chronological presentation, that the biographical data concerning Paphnutius were progressively enriched. What credit can we give to these stories?

2. The fact of Paphnutius' participation in the first ecumenical council is contradicted by the best list of contributors that has come down to us. The name of Paphnutius is missing from twenty-three of the twenty-five manuscripts of the Latin list, from the Coptic nomenclature, from the index of the monastery of Nitria, from the Ebediesu Sobensis index, and from the Armenian list. It is found in the sixteenth position in the index of Theodorus Anagnostes (the fourth and last bishop of the Theban group), in the third position in two manuscripts of the Latin list (immediately after Alexander of Alexandria), in the eighteenth position in the *Codex Vatic. Reg. gr. XLIV*, and in the seventh position in the Arab list. All these fluctuations reveal inauthenticity. E. Honigmann reaches the reverse conclusion by leaning on Rufinus' testimony,[162] but we have

---

[162] E. Honigmann is the author of several studies on the lists of the Fathers of Nicaea: "Recherches sur les listes des Pères de Nicée et de Constantinople", *Byzantion* 11 (1936), pp. 429–49; "Sur les listes des évêques participant aux conciles de Nicée, de Constantinople et de Chalcédoine", *Byzantion* 12 (1937), pp. 323–47; "La liste originale des Pères de Nicée", *Byzantion* 14 (1939), pp. 16–17; "The Original Lists of the Members of the Councils of

shown above, says Winkelmann, that that was not a proof. E. Schwartz
is right to consider the most ancient Syriac and Latin translations as being
the most faithful.[163] Under such conditions, all the narratives on the
intervention of Paphnutius at the Synod of Nicaea are to be questioned.

3. The most important feature of the man Paphnutius, a feature mentioned in all the fourth-century narratives, is that he was a confessor of
the faith. Beginning with this primitive nucleus, a legend was born and
grew, making of him a great thaumaturgist and a bishop who would
have taken part in the Synod of Nicaea. As to the episode that would
have taken place at the First Ecumenical Council, some voiced the hypothesis that Socrates had a rather good oral source, the Novatian priest
Auxanon. But this is impossible to prove because Socrates does not
disclose his source, contrary to the habit he had whenever he reported
an important fact. We must therefore conclude that the character of
Paphnutius, such as we know it today from the narratives of Rufinus
and Socrates, is the product of a progressive hagiographical confabulation
and that the critical examination of the best contributors' lists from the
Council of Nicaea leads us to deny any character of authenticity to the
famous episode of which Paphnutius would have been the hero.

Professor Winkelmann's conclusions are generally well accepted today
in scholarly circles.[164] They bring an additional and solid element to
judge better the value of Socrates' narrative.

Another element appears to be provided by a comparison between the
Eastern legislation on the marriage (and continence) of clerics and what
would have been decided in Nicaea about the intervention of Paphnutius.
At times people affirmed that there was no reason to reject Socrates'
anecdote as false because it would have been "quite in tune with the
practice of the Church, and in particular with the practice of the Greek
Church regarding clerical marriage".[165] Several points are in disagreement
with such an affirmation, however. No other council prior to Nicaea,
either in the East or in the West, ever authorized bishops and priests to
enter into marriage or to make use of the marriage into which they might
have entered before their ordinations.[166] The exception that might have

---

Nicaea, the Robber-Synod and the Council of Chalcedon", *Byzantion* 16 (1942/43), pp.
20–28; "Une liste inédite des Pères de Nicée", *Byzantion* 20 (1950), pp. 63–71.

[163] E. Schwartz, *Über die Bishofslisten der Synoden von Chalkedon, Nicaea und Konstantinopel*,
AAM, N.F., 13 (1937).

[164] Cf. the reviews of H. G. Beck, in *Byzantinische Zeitschrift* 62 (1969), p. 159, and of
W. Gessel in *Annuarium Historiae Conciliorum* 2 (1970), pp. 422–23. G. Denzler, *Das Papsttum
und der Amtszölibat*, I (Stuttgart, 1973), pp. 9–10.

[165] Hefele-Leclercq, I, 1, 624. Cf. also R. Gryson, *Les origines du célibat ecclésiastique*, p. 92.

[166] See, above, the sections related to the Councils of Ancyra (pp. 169ff.).

been provided for at Ancyra (314) in favor of a certain category of deacons attests and confirms the general rule. The Council's decision was, moreover, not endorsed by later Eastern councils. At the Council in Trullo of 691, which would determine decisively the legislation of the Eastern Churches that were separated from Rome and under the authority of Byzantium, the law of perfect continence was strictly maintained for the bishop, while the other higher members of the clergy (subdeacons, deacons, and priests), who were authorized to live with their wives, had the obligation of temporary continence.[167] Under such conditions, it is not surprising to see that the Council of 691, while quoting also the 3d canon of the First Ecumenical Council, did not refer in any way to the decision that the Fathers of Nicaea would have made at the proposal of Paphnutius, since that decision left the bishops free to use marital rights, just like priests and deacons, and did not impose temporary continence on any of these clerics. The famous episode of Socrates is therefore not quite "in tune" with the Eastern discipline.

We must also note that the story of Paphnutius seems not to have been known by the Eastern authors till long after the 7th century, or to have been deliberately rejected as a legend. The issue of priestly celibacy played an important part in the violent polemic placing the monk Nicetas Pectoratus in opposition to the Latins during the 11th century, but Paphnutius was not mentioned.[168] The same is true and even more remarkable in the main commentaries of the *Syntagma canonum* (composed in Byzantium in the 12th century) by the canonists Alexis Aristenes, John Zonaras, and Theodore Balsamon "whose decisions were the law for a long time and are still taken into consideration".[169] Even when they comment on the 13th canon of the Council in Trullo, referring to which, they say, some people wanted to correct: "*quod ea de causa fit in Romana Ecclesia*",[170] the three Byzantine scholars do not say a word about the story of Paphnutius that could have provided them with a useful argument. All this concurs in weakening the notion of a real agreement between the narrative of Socrates and Eastern tradition, and adds to the arguments against the authenticity of the alleged intervention of Paphnutius at the Council of Nicaea.

---

[167] See, below, the detailed presentation of the documents of the Council in Trullo (Quinisext), pp. 177ff.
[168] PG 120, 1019ff.
[169] E. Amann, "J. Zonaras", DTC 15, 3705ff.
[170] PG 137, 562.

Council of Gangres (ca. 340)

Around the middle of the 4th century, a council of thirteen bishops met in the city of Gangres in Paphlagonia (Asia Minor) "to deal with certain ecclesiastical matters, by investigating, among others, that of Eustathius [of Sebaste in Armenia]". The twenty canons promulgated by the synod are part of the synodal letter sent by the Fathers of Gangres to the bishop of Armenia; they are introduced by a prologue and followed by an epilogue.[171]

Canon 4

Among these twenty canons, one is formulated as follows: "If anyone affirms that one should not receive communion during the holy sacrifice celebrated by a married priest, let him be anathema."[172]

The Council of Gangres therefore attests that there were among the ranks of the clergy priests bound by marriage. Second observation: there were in the congregation faithful who were shocked, scandalized, even to the point of refusing to receive communion from the hands of those priests. Must one believe that these married priests were continuing to live as husbands with their wives and that the Council, by casting an anathema against their adversaries, was thereby legitimizing the usage that these priests were making of their marital rights? Some think so and see in this Synod of Gangres an ancestor of the Byzantine legislation that would clearly be formulated at the Quinisext Council. The matter is not that obvious, however. In the utmost accuracy of the term, the expression *uxorem duxit* (γεγαμηκότος) refers to a marriage contracted in the past. The scandal of these "weak ones" that the Council condemned seems to have been caused specifically by the fact that the ministers of the altar had been married; whether they were now widowers or known as practicing continence, they remained branded in the eyes of the Council with an indelible stigma. The general context of the Council of Gangres shows that the opponents were affected with an

---

[171] For a discussion about the date of that synod, see Joannou, I, 2, pp. 83, and Hefele-Leclercq, I, 2, 1029–30, n. 1. Eustathius of Sebaste was one of the first propagators of Monachism in Asia Minor. The singularities of his disciples' ascetic life remind us of the Encratists' excesses. He was for a while the friend of St. Basil the Great but separated from him to return to semi-Arianism. It is interesting to note that the synodal letter and the twenty canons of Gangres were sent to the bishops of Armenia at the time of Katholikos Nerses the Great († 374) (see above, p. 95).

[172] Can. 4. Joannou, I, 2, p. 91.

antimatrimonial fever that caused them to despise marriage wherever they saw it, and not only among priests. It seems that these "Eustathians"—as they were called—had strongly moved public opinion for a council to be called especially for them. The synodal letter of introduction to the canons declares: "Since the holy synod of the bishops gathered in the Church of Gangres to deal with certain ecclesiastical matters—investigating, for instance, the case of Eustathius—found many things done by the followers of Eustathius to be against the ecclesiastical rule, it was compelled to make decisions and hastened to make these decisions known to all in order to condemn that which had wrongly been done by them." [173]

Four of the charges deal with errors about marriage:

1. The Eustathians condemned marriage and affirmed that any hope in God was lost for the couples; as a result, many couples, fired by a fine zeal, separated. But by falling into adultery and license, they proved such a continence to be beyond their strength.

2. They refused to pray in the houses of married people.

3. They refused to take part in the eucharistic sacrifice in the same houses.

4. Married priests being, in their eyes, unworthy of the ministry, the Eustathians refused to receive communion from their hands. [174]

Seen in this context, the 4th canon appears essentially as an apology for men who, having been married, were admitted to the clergy; they are entitled to the respect of the faithful because marriage, far from being an object of contempt, is honorable. It would not be possible to infer, without doing violence to the text, that the Fathers of Gangres were talking about the married clerics who continued to have conjugal lives. Such a conclusion, in any event, is not attained with enough certainty, and it remains significant that the Easterners never referred later to the 4th canon of Gangres in order to support their discipline. [175]

---

[173] Ibid., pp. 85–86.

[174] It was quite rightly stressed that the attitude of the Eustathians with regard to married priests was the direct consequence of their contempt for marriage: "This sect, holding as it did that marriage debars from salvation, of course regarded it as incapacitating from the clerical office. Hence they refused to receive Holy Communion from a married priest, as though he ought not to minister" (C. Knetes, "Ordination and Matrimony in the Eastern Orthodox Church", JTS 11 [1910], p. 353).

[175] There are indeed no quotations or even any direct allusions to this canon in the acts of the Quinisext Council of 691. The measured conclusion of R. Gryson seems accurate to us: "One thus sees that there were married priests, but that certain Encratist sects despised them and refused to have recourse to their ministry" (Les origines du célibat ecclésiastique, p. 94).

Ecclesiastical Canons of
the Holy Apostles (ca. 300)

This pseudoapostolic collection was probably published around the year
300, in Egypt or Syria, and its author is unknown. Its first part depends
on the Didache (can. 1–14); the second part (can. 15–30) deals with the
election, obligations, and qualifications of the members belonging to the
various ranks of the ecclesiastical hierarchy. The *canones ecclesiastici Ss.
Apostolorum* are still known under the following names: *Ordo ecclesiasticus
apostolicus, Ordinatio ecclesiastica Apostolorum, Constitutio apostolica ecclesiastica, Canones Apostolici Aegyptiaci, Apostolische Kirchenordnung.*[176]
   The author of the canonical collection puts in the mouths of the apostles
the regulations dealing with the selection of bishops, priests, and deacons.
Here are the passages related to the conditions of chastity:

> Peter said: It would be better [for the bishop] not to be married; or else
> let him be the husband of only one wife . . . (καλὸν μὲν εἶναι ἀγύναιος,
> εἰ δὲ μή, ἀπὸ μιᾶς γυναικός); John said: There must therefore . . . be
> priests, who would have lived a long time in the world and would abstain
> (in a certain way) from relations with their wives . . . (Δεῖ οὖν εἶναι . . .
> τοὺς πρεσβυτέρους ἤδη κεχρονικότας ἐπὶ τῷ κόσμῳ, [τρόπῳ τινὶ]
> ἀπεχομένους τῆς πρὸς γυναῖκας συνελεύσεως . . .). Matthew said: Let
> there be deacons. . . . Let them be people experienced in all kinds of minis-
> tries and let them have a [good] testimony on the part of the whole people:
> let them be monogamous, raise their children . . . (μονόγαμοι, τεκ-
> νοτρόφοι).[177]

We must first note the literary genre of the work. This is not a question
of canon law, scriptural commentary, or a patristic homily. These are
logia credited to the apostles in order to show that the discipline of the
time was founded on their authority. The value of the *Ecclesiastical Canons
of the Holy Apostles* does not have anything to do with their so-called
apostolic origin, but with their date and with the prestige they enjoyed

---

[176] For the date of this collection, see F. X. Funk, *Didascaliae et Constitutiones Apostolorum*,
II (Paderborn, 1905), p. xliv. A. Van Hove, *Prolegomena*, 2d ed. (Rome, 1945), p. 128,
puts the writing of the work at the beginning of the 3d century or, at the latest, around
the year 300. This is also the opinion of A. Harnack, "Die Quellen der sogennanten
Apostolischen Kirchenordnung", TU II (Leipzig, 1886), p. 6. The Greek original was
published for the first time, under the title "Ecclesiastical Constitution of the Apostles"
(*Apostolischen Kirchenordnung*), by J. W. Bickell, *Geschichte des Kirchenrechts* (Giessen, 1843),
pp. 107–32.
[177] Pitra, *Juris ecclesiastici Graecorum historia et monumenta*, I (Rome, 1864), pp. 82–86.

very promptly in Egyptian and Eastern circles.[178] It is therefore as testimonies of the Egyptian (or Syriac) tradition in the first years of the 4th century that they deserve our attention. Though *Ecclesiastical Canons* do not determine the discipline, they probably tend to justify, through the intermediary of the apostolic authority, the legislation that was then in force or in the process of development. In this respect they give us indirect information on the content of this legislation, or at least of the legislative trends prevailing in Egypt or in Syria at the time they were written.[179]

The above passages concern the three higher ranks of the clergy—bishops, priests, and deacons. If we are to believe the rule that would have been established by Peter, the bishops had to fulfill one of the following two conditions: either have no wife (ἀγύναιος), or at least have had only one wife (ἀπὸ μιᾶς γυναικός). In the second case the rule seems to refer to a widower, because the phrase ἀπὸ μιᾶς γυναικός normally implies the idea of a situation that belonged to the past, of one state that led to another one. Indeed, if the author had wanted to talk only about monogamous men, without distinguishing between widowers and those whose wives were still alive, one does not see why he would not have taken up instead the Pauline phrase μιᾶς γυναικὸς ἄνδρα, rather than use ἀπὸ μιᾶς γυναικός. To be elected to the episcopate, a man therefore must either be single or free from conjugal obligations.[180] In other words, the bishop is bound to continence. It will be noted that a preference is given to those who had never been married, which is a novelty in comparison with the Pauline epistles to Titus and to Timothy, which deal only with the *unius uxoris viros*. It also marks an evolution with respect to what we know about Western contemporary discipline because the Councils of Elvira, Arles, and Carthage do not allude to such a preference. The choice of widowers—if this is actually the meaning

---

[178] The Greek text was rapidly translated into Latin, Coptic, Arabic, and Ethiopian.

[179] We have already had the opportunity of stressing that the apocryphal character of the pseudoapostolic writings of the early centuries did not take anything away from their historical testimonial value (see above, pp. 53–55). If they were able to be disseminated and accredited by the Christian communities and the Christian leaders of the time, it is because they reflected traditions that all knew.

[180] This is how J. B. Pitra understands it, quite rightly in our opinion, in his commentary on the edition of the *Constitution ecclésiastique des Apôtres*: "vel absona haec verba sunt, vel clare sonant oportere episcopum aut caelibem, aut unius uxoris viduum", ἀγύναιος, εἰ δὲ μή, ἀπὸ μιᾶς γυναικός (*Juris eccles. Graec.*, I, p. 87). A. Harnack does not seem to be free from bias himself here when he writes: "The explanation that Pitra gives of our passage—'oportere episcopum esse aut caelibem aut unius uxoris viduum'—is tendentious" ("Die Quellen der sogennanten Apostolischen Kirchenordnung", I, p. 9, n. 17).

of ἀπὸ μιᾶς γυναικός—denotes yet another appreciable difference in relation to these councils. The candidates to the episcopate are not only asked to abstain from conjugal relations; here they are chosen among those freed from their matrimonial status by being widowed.[181]

The alleged Johannine *logion* requires that priests abstain "to a certain extent" from relations with women (τρόπῳ τινὶ ἀπεχομένους τῆς πρὸς γυναῖκας συνελεύσεως). This τρόπῳ τινὶ can be understood in two ways: either priests are being required to observe continence for a limited interval, on the model of the ancient Levites—according to that interpretation, the canon is the only one of its kind in the literature of the first seven centuries, having nothing resembling it except in the Acts of the Council in Trullo (691)—or else it can be understood as conforming to the discipline of the West, where the priest would have to abstain from that aspect of relationship which is sexual intercourse, without, however, having to shun his wife altogether. The vague usage of τρόπῳ τινὶ leaves room for either interpretation, although the first comes more naturally to mind.[182] If it had to be understood in the sense of a temporary continence, we would have here a first testimony (or an echo?) of the discipline endorsed four centuries later in the Quinisext Council.

---

[181] R. Gryson (*Les origines du célibat ecclésiastique*, pp. 95–96) thinks that the idea expressed here by ἀπό is that of a separation. It seems to us that there is more to it, as we have suggested. Later on, when he will ask the priests to separate themselves from relations with their wives, the author of the *Constitution* will use a different expression, a more explicit one: ἀπεχομένους τῆς πρὸς γυναῖκας συνελεύσεως. If he uses another turn of phrase here, one that is more concise, it is without a doubt because the meaning of the instruction concerning the recruiting of bishops is different. While the *Constitution* asks priests to stay away, τρόπῳ τινὶ, from their wives, it demands from the candidates to the episcopate that they be at least ἀπὸ μιᾶς γυναικός, i.e., in the strong sense of the word ἀπό, men now deprived of their only wives (by death). On the other hand, when it comes to the degree of obligation implied in the sentence καλὸν μὲν εἶναι ἀγύναιον, εἰ δὲ μή, κτλ., it is not as certain as Funk would want to have us admit ("Cölibat und Priesterehe im christlichen Altertum", p. 124) that the word καλὸν is also applied to the two parts of the sentence. The preference for bachelors shown by the author of the *Constitution* is a measure with optional character; but the concession coming after (εἰ δὲ μή) logically has the same compulsory character (which, here, does not mean a juridical one) as the other required qualities either in the preceding sentence or in the part of the sentence that follows immediately. The meaning of the passage in question seems to be for us: "It is preferable [good] for the bishop to be a bachelor; otherwise let him be the widower of an only wife; let him know the doctrine, be capable of interpreting the Scripture, and so on . . . ".

[182] Funk thinks that the author of the *Constitution* is dealing here with temporary continence (*Doctrina duodecim apostolorum Canones Apostolorum Ecclesiastici ac Reliquiae Doctrinae de duabus viis expositiones veteres* [Tübingen, 1897], pp. 63–64, note). R. Gryson suggests that the phrase τρόπῳ τινὶ is to be understood as allusion to the advanced age of the priests (*Les origines du célibat ecclésiastique*, p. 97).

As to the deacons, the instruction credited to Matthew asks that they be married only once and that they raise their children (μονόγαμοι, τεκνοτρόφοι). The word μονόγαμοι is the very same used by St. Paul in his epistles to Titus and Timothy. We saw that it was the object, in the 4th century, of an official exegesis interpreting the thought of the Apostle as a prohibition of conjugal relations after monogamous men had been elevated to priestly functions. The same question is posed here again, and we have to leave it open. The fact that deacons were asked to take charge of the children's education, without any mention of their wives, leads one to think that being absent from the mind of the pseudo-Matthew, the wives might also have been out of the homes of the monogamous men chosen to be deacons. Were they also widowers like the bishops? Husbands separated from their wives so as to live in continence? It is not easy to say what the answer is.

In conclusion, the *Ecclesiastical Canons of the Holy Apostles* outline the features of a discipline of priestly recruitment in conformity with the Pauline epistles but including, in certain respects, original nuances: preferably the candidates to the episcopate must be selected from among single men; at the very least, the choice will be made from among those who had been monogamous, a word probably describing the category of widowers (who were formerly monogamous). As to the priests, one of the possible meanings of the Johannine *pseudo-logion* asks them to observe temporary continence, a nuance that is not found in St. Paul. Such a temporary continence departs from contemporary documents as a whole and is to be compared to the practice of the Eastern Churches codified, at the end of the 7th century, in the Council in Trullo. If this was really the form of discipline prevailing in the Egyptian and Syrian communities of the 300s, one can understand the interest in the testimony found in these apostolic pseudocanons in favor of the Eastern tradition; but one can also legitimately ask whether the Greek text of our anonymous document, found only in a twelfth-century codex,[183] had not purposely been harmonized with the decisions of the Quinisext Council. Finally, only the instructions concerning the deacons are formulated, when it comes to the subject of our study, in the same terms as the epistles to Titus and Timothy, and therefore pose the same questions.

---

[183] This is the *Codex vindobonensis hist. gr. olim 45, nunc 7*. It must be remembered that it was precisely in the 12th century that the great commentators of Byzantine law, Zonaras and Balsamon, published their studies on the Quinisext Council and the Eastern legislation.

The Canons of Hippolytus (4th century)

This is the title given to a collection of thirty-eight canons followed by a sermon that was known and used for a long time only by the Coptic Church. It depends on the *Apostolic Tradition* of Hippolytus of Rome, hence its title. The critics generally agree that this collection dates from the 4th century (between the Councils of Nicaea [325] and of Constantinople [381]); it was probably published in Egypt or Asia Minor and was written by an author (perhaps a priest) who is so far unknown. The *Canons of Hippolytus* presently exist only in an Arabic version dating from the 12th century at least, a translation of the Coptic version from the original Greek. Since the original Greek and the Coptic translation have both vanished, it is difficult to credit the twelfth-century Arabic version with absolute authenticity because of the risks of interpolations and alterations.[184] We cannot therefore take it into account.

Here, for strictly documentary purposes, is a translation of canons 7 and 8 regarding the issue of celibacy:

Canon 7
On the choice of lector and subdeacon

When one chooses a lector, let him have the virtues of a deacon. Let no one impose hands on him before he has received the Gospel from the bishop.

The subdeacon [will be admitted] according to this disposition. Let him not be ordained while still a single man without a wife, unless his neighbors testify in his favor that as a mature man he has stayed away from women.

Let no one impose hands on anyone who is a single man, unless he be already mature, about to enter maturity and be deemed [worthy] when people testify in his favor.

The subdeacon and the lector, when they pray alone, must stay in the background, and the subdeacon is to serve behind the deacon.

Canon 8
On healing gifts

If someone asks for ordination, saying: "I have received the gift of healing", let him not be ordained until the matter is clear, and if the healing he accomplished came from God.

As to the priest whose wife has a child, he will not be excluded.[185]

---

[184] See the critical introduction of R. G. Coquin in PO 31, fasc. 2, pp. 273ff. Cf. also B. Botte, "L'origine des canons d'Hippolyte", *Mélanges Andrieu* (Strasbourg, 1956), pp. 53–63.

[185] Trans. R. G. Coquin, PO 31, fasc. 2, pp. 359–61.

St. Cyril of Jerusalem (ca. 313–386)

A monk nourished by Scripture, Cyril of Jerusalem (who was probably born in that city around the year 313) was to take his place among the doctors of the Church thanks to his catecheses. In 348 he preached these homilies, a total of twenty-four, all meant for the instruction of the catechumens. An introductory *Procatechesis* is followed by eighteen catecheses called *ad illuminandos*, given during Lent of 348 and dealing essentially with the Creed. The last five, called *mystagogical* because they were meant exclusively for "the initiated" during the Paschal week imme-diately following the reception of baptism, elucidate the three sacraments of baptism, confirmation, and the Eucharist. The Eastern bishops of the Council of Constantinople (381) paid homage to Cyril in a letter to Pope Damasus: "We want [also] to let you know that the bishop of the Church of Jerusalem, that mother of all the Churches, is the reverend and most beloved of God, Cyril, who was once canonically ordained by the bishops of his province and fought many times and in several places against the Arians." He died around 386.

The 12th catechesis (ca. 350)

The 12th catechesis of Cyril of Jerusalem, given around 350, alludes to priestly continence briefly but in a way that remains of interest to our study. The instruction is addressed to candidates for baptism. Cyril, who already dealt at length with the spiritual disposition required for the sacrament, has now come to the theological outline of the mystery of the Incarnation, and this *De Verbo incarnato* brings him to an apologia of the Savior's birth. He preaches in Jerusalem; many among his listeners come from Judaism, and they are still concerned about objections against Jesus that are always feeding local polemics; beyond his listeners, the bishop knows that he is questioned by the entire Jewish priesthood and the crowd of the holy city's inhabitants. There is no need to follow all his reasonings, but here is the remark of interest to us: "To the Most Pure and the Master of Purity it was fitting to be born from a pure bed. For if the one who is a good priest for the sake of Jesus abstains from [relations with] women, how could Jesus himself be born of [the union] between a man and a woman?"[186]

---

[186] *Catechesis* 12, 25. PG 33, 757a. Ἔπρεπε γὰρ τῷ ἁγνοτάτῳ, καὶ διδασκάλῳ τῆς ἁγνείας, ἐξ ἁγνῶν ἐξεληλυθέναι παστάδων; εἰ γὰρ ὁ τῷ Ἰησοῦ καλῶς ἱερατεύων ἀπέχεται γυναικός, αὐτὸς ὁ Ἰησοῦς πῶς ἔμελλεν ἐξ ἀνδρὸς καὶ γυναικὸς ἔρχεσθαι.

It was fitting, said Cyril, that the Master of Purity, Jesus, be born of a completely pure nuptial chamber. We know of texts justifying priestly continence by the example of the Lord. The bishop of Jerusalem, for one, wants to prove the virginal conception of the Savior through the example of his priests. If he who is a priest for the sake of Christ—a beautiful priesthood—does abstain from relations with a woman, how could Jesus himself have been born from a carnal union?

One generally reads this text with an appropriate stress on the adverb καλῶς. Thus, as Vacandard points out: "He [Cyril] does not talk about a law of continence binding all priests, but about the practice of the priests concerned with their dignity: καλῶς ἱερατεύων."[187] It may be, indeed, that the bishop of Jerusalem wanted to make a distinction between two categories of priests: those who, abstaining from women, fulfill the ministry καλῶς, i.e., in a laudable way, and the others. The latter get, in passing, if not blame, at least a disavowal of which it would be too little to say that it would be hardly comprehensible if married clerics had been duly authorized to use their conjugal rights. To acknowledge this right to them and to discredit them in public by letting it be understood that they were not "good" priests would simply have been dishonest. If one wants to understand the sentence as does Funk or Vacandard, logic compels us to conclude that not exercising καλῶς their ministerial functions, clerics who would have been disavowed in such a way would place themselves in a marginal situation with respect to the official discipline. Epiphanius and others with him attest the existence of such situations known as παρὰ τὸν κανόνα.[188]

However, the general context of the 12th catechesis and the place of the adverb καλῶς in the body of the proposition suggest a reading that was probably more faithful to the orator's thought. This passage is part of a flight of oratory during which the bishop of Jerusalem aims to refute the objections of the Jews. The rhythm of his discourse thus plays on the contrast between the imperfection of the Old Covenant—to which

---

[187] Vacandard, *Les origines*, p. 84. It is also Funk's opinion that "Cyril does not speak purely and simply of a 'hierateuôn', but of a 'kalôs hierateuôn', and thereby he presupposes continence only for the latter, not for all priests. The objection according to which such an interpretation implies an unjust offense with regard to married priests is unfounded, no more than it would be deemed offending for all Christians to call perfect disciples of Jesus those who follow the evangelical counsels. In any event, this cannot prevent us from understanding the passage as the text wants it" ("Cölibat und Priesterehe im christlichen Altertum", p. 129). If it is not offensive to call perfect disciples of Jesus those who follow the evangelical counsels, it would be so to call them simply "good", which would be like calling all the others "bad".

[188] *Panarion (Adversus Haereses)*, Haer. 59, 4. PG 41, 1024a–b.

those who practice Judaism remain wrongly attached—and the marvelous novelty of the New Covenant. Having sensitized his public, Cyril then uses the opportunity to clarify with one word the superiority of the ministry that Christ inaugurated. If he adds the qualification καλῶς ἱερατεύων, it is not that he makes a distinction within the Catholic Church between "good" and "bad" priests. His thought is elsewhere: those who exercise the priesthood καλῶς are those who do so τῷ 'Ιησοῦ. As to the Jewish priesthood, it is misdirected, because it is not done for the One who is now the true mediator. More than a moral nuance, the adverb καλῶς seems to imply here the concept of something that one is right in doing because it is true, good, or, if one prefers, "beautiful", in the meaning that this adjective takes by summing up all the others and adding a note of admiration. The place of καλῶς, between τῷ 'Ιησοῦ and the verb ἱερατεύων, must also be noted, and the stress that some want to place on the adverb will naturally move in the eyes of the reader to τῷ 'Ιησοῦ, the important word in the sentence. To sum up our opinion, Cyril's idea would thus be the following: it was fitting that the sovereignly pure, totally pure master be born of a virginal conception: indeed, if he who is a priest—the true one, the one who exercises the priesthood for the sake of Jesus—abstains from relations with women, how could Jesus himself have been born from a carnal union?

This interpretation does not permit us to affirm directly that St. Cyril of Jerusalem was attesting the apostolic origin of priestly celibacy practiced in the New Covenant. However, by his linking priestly continence closely to the virginal birth of the Savior, to the extent of using it as a proof, this priestly continence seems to be based, in the mind of the bishop of Jerusalem, on a foundation going far beyond historical conjecture. This remains true, in fact, in the hypothesis—less justified by context and grammar but nonetheless acceptable—of the first reading: those who exercise the priesthood worthily abstain from women, Cyril would have told us, while the others, using illegal marital rights, are not καλῶς ἱερατεύων. Perfect continence appears here too as independent of contingent factors.

St. Athanasius (ca. 295–373)

A pillar of the Church, Athanasius was the man raised up by God to save the Christian faith from the Arian heresy. When he was a young deacon about thirty years old, he accompanied his bishop, Alexander of Alexandria, to the Council of Nicaea (325), where he was able to size up fully the danger that Arius brought to the Church. The following

fifty years of his life, until his death, are the history of the ceaseless fight
he led with a relentless energy to defend the doctrine of the Word's
divinity while "the entire world was moaning and discovered with surprise that it was Arian" and while the best were defecting. Out of the
forty-five years of his episcopate (he was elected in 328), the "immortal"
bishop of Alexandria spent more than seventeen years in exile, hiding
several times in the desert with the complicity of monks. He used the
years of relative calm that he was able to enjoy to affirm the hesitant,
practice a policy of fruitful conciliation, and gather around himself, in
communion, a great many bishops. The famous council called "of the
confessors", in 362, was his work. There is in the writings of Athanasius
"a powerful impression of faith and love for the Word made flesh" (F.
Cavallera). A passionate love for Christ is the principle explaining the
personality of this providential man in whom the entire orthodoxy
seemed to have gathered, in this time of trial, to forge her future. He
died peacefully on May 2, 373, when he was almost eighty years old.

Letter to Dracontius (354/55)

The letter to Dracontius, that monk pulled out of obscurity by a plebiscite
and driven to hide in the desert by a laudable fear of episcopal responsibilities, brought us from the pen of Athanasius, who knew how uncom-
fortable the throne was, a *pro episcopo* plea that remains a masterpiece of
its kind. We find slipped into it an allusion to bishops who were married
and family men.

Dracontius, out of an instinctive mistrust of "the world", a love of
asceticism not entirely devoid, perhaps, of a secret feeling of superiority,
dreaded the worst and needed to be told that by accepting the honor of
the episcopate, he was not going to fall into disaster but would find, like
Paul, Timothy, and many others, a life of austerity that the most monkish
of monks could envy. And the bishop of Alexandria set out to depict
the future for him with colors that could not fail to seduce him: you will
be free, as a bishop, to know hunger and thirst like St. Paul; you will
be free not to drink wine like Timothy; and also like the Apostle, to
practice a perpetual fast, so as to sate the crowd with your words; and
to mortify your thirst so as to quench the desires of those who want to
be taught. Are these apostolic examples overdone, too beautiful, perhaps,
for anyone to follow them? Let not the future bishop be misled: "We
indeed know bishops who fast and monks who eat to satiation. We know
bishops who drink no wine, and monks who drink it. . . ."

The parallel continues, and here are examples related to our study:

We know bishops who perform miracles and monks who do not. It is because many bishops never married, and it happened that some monks were family men; in the same way [we know] bishops who are family men and monks who have children of their own. And we know, on the other hand, clerics who drink wine and monks who fast. It is indeed permitted to act in this way and not forbidden to act in that way.[189]

Thus, Athanasius knew bishops who were family men, just as he knew monks who also had children.[190] Many bishops had never married, he stresses also, while monks who had begotten children were not rare. It seems, when one reads this text attentively, that the logical bond is not very rigorous. On the one hand we are told about single bishops, and they are opposed in a correct comparison to monks who had wives and children; on the other hand, we are shown bishops who are family men, and, in an abrupt break of the contrast, we see on the other side of the picture monks who have children, too.[191] There are other surprising peculiarities, for the passage is built around the verb οἴδαμεν, repeated

---

[189]PG 25, 532d–33b. Here is the text of this passage from the letter to Dracontius: Ἔξεστι γὰρ καὶ ἐπίσκοπον ὄντα σε πεινᾶν, καὶ διψῆν, ὡς ὁ Παῦλος; δύνασαι μὴ πιεῖν οἶνον, ὡς ὁ Τιμόθεος, καὶ νηστεύειν καὶ αὐτὸς συνεχῶς, ὡς ὁ Παῦλος ἐποίει; ἵνα κατ' ἐκεῖνον οὕτως νηστεύων, χορτάζῃς ἄλλους ἐν τοῖς λόγοις, καὶ διψῶν ἐν τῷ μὴ πιεῖν, ποτίζῃς ἄλλους διδάσκων. . . . Οἴδαμεν γὰρ καὶ ἐπισκόπους νηστεύοντας, καὶ μοναχοὺς ἐσθίοντας. Οἴδαμεν καὶ ἐπισκόπους μὴ πίνοντας οἶνον, μοναχοὺς δὲ πίνοντας. Οἴδαμεν καὶ σημεῖα ποιοῦντας ἐπισκόπους, μοναχοὺς δὲ μὴ ποιοῦντας. Πολλοὶ δὲ τῶν ἐπισκόπων οὐδὲ γεγαμήκασι, μοναχοὶ δὲ πατέρες τέκνων γεγόνασιν; ὥσπερ καὶ ἐπισκόπους πατέρας τέκνων, καὶ μοναχοὺς ἐξ ὁλοκλήρου γένους τυγχάνοντας. Καὶ πάλιν οἴδαμεν κληρικοὺς πεινῶντας, μοναχοὺς δὲ νηστεύοντας. Ἔξεστι γὰρ καὶ οὕτως, καὶ ἐκείνως οὐ κεκώλυται. Μὴ οὖν ταῦτα προβαλλέτωσαν οἱ συμβουλεύοντές σοι.

[190]Attention must be drawn to the exact meaning of μοναχοὺς ἐξ ὁλοκλήρου γένους τυγχάνοντας, often wrongly translated as "(cernimus) monachos vero nullam posteritatem habuisse" (we see monks who had no posterity). PG 25, 534a. Far from including a negation, the Greek sentence is, on the contrary, quite affirmative. The issue is truly that of monks who have "their own" children (ἐξ ὁλοκλήρου): cf. Guido Muller, Lexicon Athanasium (Berlin, 1952), p. 980: μοναχοὺς ἐξ ὁλοκλήρου γένους τυγχάνοντας = proprie sobolem habentes. Unfortunately, the misunderstanding of Migne's translation has often been accepted without checking it. Cf., for instance, Funk ("Cölibat und Priesterehe", p. 146): "There were still, among the bishops, many who had never married, while there were monks who were family men, as on the other hand there were family men among the bishops and one met monks without any progeny" (our emphasis). This led to many misunderstandings. The translation of R. Gryson (Les origines du célibat ecclésiastique, p. 46), "Just as we know bishops who are family men and monks who belong to the race of the perfect ones", does not seem either to take into account the shade of meaning expressed by ἐξ ὁλοκλήρου.

[191]One would expect so naturally a contrast that, trusting the Latin translation, some people believed, as we just saw, that the turn of phrase was negative and that it dealt with monks who had had no children.

four times; it is like a hinge where the various parts of the sentence are joined, and it calls each time for the accusative case: οἴδαμεν γὰρ καὶ ἐπισκόπους νηστεύοντας . . . οἴδαμεν καὶ ἐπισκόπους μὴ πίνοντας οἶνον . . . οἴδαμεν καὶ σημεῖα ποιοῦντας ἐπισκόπους . . . οἴδαμεν κληρικοὺς πεινῶντας. Now, in an unexpected way, there is in the course of the enumeration a line in the nominative case: πολλοὶ δὲ τῶν ἐπισκόπων οὐδὲ γεγαμήκασι, μοναχοὶ δὲ πατέρες τέκνων γεγόνασιν, which, and this is even more surprising, is immediately followed by the customary accusative: ὥσπερ καὶ ἐπισκόπους πατέρας τέκνων, καὶ μοναχοὺς ἐξ ὁλοκλήρου γένους τυγχάνοντας. On the other hand, these two parts of the sentence are partially repeated, at least about the monks. This is obviously a defective text. The break in parallelism, the incorrect passage from accusative to nominative, then from nominative to accusative (the latter without any verbal support), the duplicates from one line to the other—all these peculiarities of grammar and syntax reveal an alteration of the text. Some copyist who might have been absentminded or an editor who meant well but was clumsy left traces of his work; the alterations are not so invisible that we could not make a humble attempt at reconstruction. First, one would readily agree that the line ὥσπερ καὶ ἐπισκόπους πατέρας τέκνων, καὶ μοναχοὺς ἐξ ὁλοκλήρου γένους τυγχάνοντας must be directly reattached to a segment of sentence starting with οἴδαμεν, on top of the incidental clause in the nominative case. In all likelihood, it is the closest οἴδαμεν. We would then have the following sentence: "We know bishops who accomplish miracles and monks who do not; in the same way [we know] bishops who are family men and monks who have children of their own."

The line πολλοὶ δὲ τῶν ἐπισκόπων οὐδὲ γεγαμήκασι, μοναχοὶ δὲ πατέρες τέκνων γεγόνασιν could logically take its place after this sentence, before the last proposition also starting with an οἴδαμεν. Thus located, the nominative loses its unexpected character and appears to be an explanatory gloss. Athanasius has just explained, talking about bishops and monks, the case of family men; someone deemed it necessary to slip in a rapid commentary: πολλοὶ δὲ τῶν ἐπισκόπων οὐδὲ γεγαμήκασι, κτλ. ("many bishops indeed have never been married, while there are monks who have children"). Who thought it necessary to add the gloss? Athanasius himself? This is not impossible, but his correspondent very likely had no need of such a precision. It would be much more understandable if a copyist of a later time felt the need to inform the reader about the meaning of Athanasius' allusion. Put back to the place that seems normal to us, such a gloss will render us a service by shedding light, as if with a mirror, on the meaning of the sentence it was intended to comment upon. To be able to form a better judgment, the reader should view them side by side:

Athanasius' Text	*Copyist's Gloss (?)*
In the same way [we know] bishops who are family men and monks who have children of their own.	As it happens, many bishops never married, and it happens that monks were family men.

As the segments of the sentence correspond to each other, an anomaly appears. Indeed, while the reference to the monks who have children of their own finds a coherent explanation in the gloss, this is not the case as far as the bishops are concerned. "We know bishops who are family men", Athanasius said. "Indeed," the copyist comments, "many bishops never married." One would have to decide: either the gloss does not make any sense, or the original text of Athanasius is not the one we have in hand. In the first hypothesis it should have read: "We know bishops who are family men; indeed, many bishops were [then] married", which is a perfectly legitimate commentary at a later time when the memory of married bishops had faded. The meaning of the example thus proposed by Athanasius would, for its part, be very acceptable. However, the contrasted parallelism, through which the bishop of Alexandria wants to highlight the frequent superiority of the bishop in comparison with the monk, would be suddenly hanging in the air. We would just have an affirmation devoid of any argumentative value: "We know bishops who are family men and monks who have children of their own."

The second hypothesis, which we will take the liberty of suggesting, would provide a better solution. If the first part of the gloss responds logically to the first part of Athanasius' affirmation, the latter should say the contrary of what we read in the present text. Because we are told that "many bishops never married", this means the author of the letter to Dracontius spoke, not of bishops who were family men, but quite certainly of bishops who never had children. Instead of "in the same way [we know] bishops *who are family men* . . .", the original probably stated in the (approximate) following way: "in the same way [we know] bishops *having no children of their own*, and monks who have children of their own".[192] In this second hypothesis, the comparison started by Athanasius in the previous examples would thus go on more naturally.

---

[192] Replacing "family men" (πατέρας τέκνων) with "not having descendants" (γένους μὴ τυγχάνοντας) is suggested by the second part of the sentence "who have their own descendants" (ἐξ ὁλοκλήρου γένους τυγχάνοντας). In another of his examples, Athanasius uses the same verb twice, first for the bishops and then for the monks, adding only a negative sign: Οἴδαμεν καὶ σημεῖα ποιοῦντας ἐπισκόπους, μοναχοὺς δὲ μὴ ποιοῦντας. Our sentence could therefore have been built on the same pattern.

Let Dracontius not be afraid of accepting the episcopate: not only does one know bishops who fast, while more than one monk eats to satiation, but one knows bishops who have no children while certain professed ascetics are heads of families. We will stop briefly to read the text thus "reconstructed" so as to grasp better the train of thought:

Migne's Text

Μὴ οὖν ταῦτα προβαλλέτωσαν οἱ συμβουλεύοντές σοι. Οἴδαμεν γάρ καὶ ἐπισκόπους νηστεύοντας, καὶ μοναχοὺς ἐσθίοντας.

Οἴδαμεν καὶ ἐπισκόπους μὴ πίνοντας οἶνον, μοναχοὺς δὲ πίνοντας; Οἴδαμεν καὶ σημεῖα ποιοῦντας ἐπισκόπους, μοναχοὺς δὲ μὴ ποιοῦντας.

Πολλοὶ δὲ τῶν ἐπισκόπων οὐδὲ γεγαμήκασι, μοναχοὶ δὲ πατέρες τέκνων γεγόνασιν; ὥσπερ καὶ ἐπισκόπους πατέρας τέκνων, καὶ μοναχοὺς ἐξ ὁλοκλήρου γένους τυγχάνοντας; Καὶ πάλιν οἴδαμεν κληρικοὺς πεινῶντας, μοναχοὺς δὲ νηστεύοντας. Ἔξεστι γάρ καὶ οὕτως καὶ ἐκείνως οὐ κεκώλυται.

"Reconstructed" Text

(Same as Migne's text)

Ὥσπερ καὶ ἐπισκόπους γένους μὴ τυγχάνοντας, καὶ μοναχοὺς ἐξ ὁλοκλήρου γένους τυγχάνοντας. (Πολλοὶ δὲ τῶν ἐπισκόπων οὐδὲ γεγαμήκασι, μοναχοὶ δὲ πατέρες τέκνων γεγόνασιν). Καὶ πάλιν οἴδαμεν, κτλ.[193]

Let those who advise you, then, not advance such [arguments]. We indeed know bishops who fast and monks who eat to satiation. We know bishops who drink no wine, and monks who drink it. We know bishops who perform prodigies and monks who do not. There are indeed many bishops who never married, and it happened that monks were family men; just as [we know] bishops who are family men and monks who have their own children. And we know, on the other hand,

(Same as Migne's text)

. . . we [know] bishops who have no children of their own and monks who do. [There are indeed many bishops who

---

[193] As Father Paramelle, S.J., kindly pointed out to us, it would be easy to understand that at a later time, when the phrase γένους τυγχάνειν was no longer in use, a copyist would have substituted the more common form πατέρας τέκνων for it, thus causing the negative μὴ to vanish.

clerics who drink wine and monks who fast. It is indeed permitted to act in this way and not forbidden to act in that way. never married, and it happened that monks were heads of families.] And we know, on the other hand, clerics who drink wine and monks who fast.

When the author of the epistle reminds Dracontius of the existence of monks having children, does he refer to a category of ascetics who had become lax—concubinary? If this is the case, the oratorical contrast between bishop and monk would be quite awkward. Our monk might feel offended and poorly disposed to accept the reasoning of Athanasius. The meaning of the sentence should not be dubious. The monks did not have children from illegitimate unions, but having been married and family men before they took refuge in solitude, they were forever men who had children of their own. As to the bishops, if they were not always recruited from among experts of asceticism, there still were among them men who had neither wives nor children and were thus superior in their perpetual chastity to the late vocations to continence of the former family men turned monks.

What can we conclude from this analysis? The allusion to bishops who were married and family men has caused the letter to Dracontius to become a frequently quoted text. But a superficial reading (encouraged by the misinterpretation of the Latin translation with regard to $\mu o \nu \alpha \chi o \grave{\nu}s$ $\grave{\epsilon}\xi$ $\grave{\epsilon}\lambda o \kappa \lambda \acute{\eta}\rho o \nu$ $\gamma \acute{\epsilon}\nu o \nu s$ $\tau \nu \gamma \chi \acute{\alpha}\nu o \nu \tau \alpha s$) at times leads in a wrong direction. When Athanasius compares bishops to monks who are family men, he refers to the children that such monks had before their monastic profession; therefore, this is also applicable to bishops. Whatever version we adopt ($\grave{\epsilon}\pi \iota \sigma \kappa \acute{o}\pi o \nu s$ $\pi \alpha \tau \acute{\epsilon}\rho \alpha s$ $\tau \acute{\epsilon}\kappa \nu \omega \nu$ or $\grave{\epsilon}\pi \iota \sigma \kappa \acute{o}\pi o \nu s$ $\gamma \acute{\epsilon}\nu o \nu s$ $\mu \grave{\eta}$ $\tau \nu \gamma \chi \acute{\alpha}\nu o \nu \tau \alpha s$), we are talking about children that the latter had or could have had before their ordinations. Not only does the text not tell us that at the heads of dioceses were shepherds who went on procreating children, but we read rather an opposite meaning between the lines. On the one hand many bishops had never been married, but on the other, those who had been married are given as examples (if they are) on account of the children they once had, not of those they would have sired since they had become bishops. It would mean, as a matter of course, that as with the monastic profession, the threshold of ordination ushered in a life of perfect continence.[194]

---

[194] One could also read Athanasius' discourse by inserting the $\mu \acute{\eta}$ that is missing, in the following way: $\H{\omega}\sigma \pi \epsilon \rho$ $\kappa \alpha \grave{\iota}$ $\grave{\epsilon}\pi \iota \sigma \kappa \acute{o}\pi o \nu s$ $\pi \alpha \tau \acute{\epsilon}\rho \alpha s$ $\tau \acute{\epsilon}\kappa \nu \omega \nu$, $\kappa \alpha \grave{\iota}$ $\mu o \nu \alpha \chi o \grave{\nu}s$ $\grave{\epsilon}\xi$ $\grave{o}\lambda o \kappa \lambda \acute{\eta}\rho o \nu$ $\gamma \acute{\epsilon}\nu o \nu s$ $\mu \grave{\eta}$ $\tau \nu \gamma \chi \acute{\alpha}\nu o \nu \tau \alpha s$. The gloss thus could be well understood: Athanasius has just admitted that there are bishops who are family men and monks who did not want to have

St. Ephraem Syrus (ca. 306–373)

The man who was to become the great doctor of the Syrian Church was born around the year 306, probably in Nisibe (Mesopotamia). Not much is known about his life, except that he was the disciple of St. James of Nisibe, the bishop of the town where he was ordained a deacon. An ascetic who was also a mystic, he "sang God" and the Christian mysteries in a poetical language of great beauty, though not always with great rigor. Compelled to flee Nisibe when it was invaded by the Persians, he took refuge in Edessa, where, it seems, he founded the famous School of the Persians and taught during the last ten years of his life. A very prolific writer, St. Ephraem was translated into Greek, Armenian, and partially into Latin. The critical edition of his complete works remains to be done. The Syrians honor him with the most admiring titles: "Doctor of the Universe", "pillar of the Church", "harp of the Holy Spirit".

The Carmina Nisibena

In 1862, a chance finding in his researches put into the hands of Bickell, who was then at the British Museum of London, a previously unknown Syriac codex: the *Carmina Nisibena* of St. Ephraem. One of these songs, composed most likely in 363, is of interest to our inquiry: "It is not enough for the priest and his dignity—for it is the living body that he offers—to purify his soul, his tongue, and his hands and to make his whole body clear; he must at all times be absolutely pure, because he takes the place of mediator between God and mankind. Blessed be he who has purified his servants!" [195]

It is not enough for the priest to purify his soul and body since he offers the living body of the Lord, but he must—being the mediator between God and the human race—be of a total purity at all times (*omnino purus esse debet omni tempore*). It is obvious that this absolute purity does not directly allude to sexual continence but implies a limpidity of the whole being; what we know about the wealth of meaning implied in

---

children. The commentator voices a reservation: "Let us note, however, that among the bishops many never contracted marriage, and that among the monks some are family men." We owe this suggestion to the late Father Georges Courtade, S.J., who was a professor at the Institut Catholique of Paris.

[195] *S. Ephraemi Syri Carmina Nisibena*, ed. Gustavus Bickell, Carmen XVIII, 12 (Leipzig, 1866), p. 112. Cf. CSCO 218 (= Script. Syr. 92), p. 50; CSCO 219 (= Script. Syr. 93), p. 60 (= *Des Heiligen Ephraem des Syrers Carmina Nisibena* [*erster Teil*], ed. Edmund Beck [Louvain, 1961]).

the notion of purity throughout the Bible and the patristic literature does not, however, leave any doubt about abstention from conjugal relations, which, among other demands, is imposed here.[196] Besides, is it not presented in this passage as a degree of perfection that would be superior to the rites of liturgical purity, which already include continence? Continence is therefore requested permanently from the priest as a consequence of his permanent role as mediator, and we perceive here an echo, as it were, or, rather, a first expression of the motive that would be repeated by the councils of Africa: "Quo possint simpliciter quod a Deo postulant impetrare."

We have to ask whether St. Ephraem is outlining an ideal that is still to be achieved, or whether he is explaining the reasons for the absolute purity of a priest, that purity being required by well-known canonical regulations. By itself the text does not offer any answer, but it is interesting to note that through the conscience of one of the most representative Eastern writers of the 4th century, a conviction was expressed that perfect continence had to be, for reasons connected with something essential to the priesthood, the undisputable endowment of the clergy.[197]

---

[196] Bickell also points out here, and rightly so, that the following poem (19), whose first strophe is directly linked to the previous one, provides the proof that the purity evoked by St. Ephraem also includes abstention from conjugal relations. We read: "Respondes nomini tuo, Abraham, quia tu quoque factus es pater multorum. Sed quia tibi non est uxor, sicut Sara Abraham, ecce grex tuus est uxor tua. . . . Ecce, beate, surge et inspice gregem tuum, o sedule! Sicut Jacob ordinavit greges suos, ita tu quoque ordina oves loquentes et illustra ascetas pure et virgines caste, institue sacerdotes gloriose et praesules leniter et congregationem laicorum juste!" (S. Ephraemi, ed. G. Bickell, pp. 112–13).

Funk rejects the proof supplied by Bickell under the excuse that with poem 19 "we have a new chapter and a new thought" ("Cölibat und Priesterehe", p. 125). But in fact poem 19 simply continues the praises of Bishop Abraham begun in poem 18. There is thus no discontinuity from one to the other. Funk's criticism here is unfounded.

[197] A comment of St. Ephraem's on the epistles of St. Paul that was preserved in an Armenian manuscript of the late 10th century was translated into Latin by the Mekhitarist Fathers of Venice. About 1 Tim 3:2 one can read: "Unius uxoris vir (sit), ut uxoris suae loco occupatio quaedam nimia non sit ejus cum altera" (So that he not be absorbed by an excessive concern to find another woman to replace his wife) (S. Ephraem Syri commentarii in epistolas D. Pauli [Venice, 1893], p. 249).

According to that Latin translation, St. Ephraem is concerned here, in all likelihood, with the situation of a cleric after the death of his wife. He has no right to remarry, and thus is spared the preoccupation (excessive in his state) of finding another companion for his life. St. Ephraem's commentary does not tackle the following problem: while his wife was alive, did the cleric have to live with her in continence or not?

It must be noted that the Latin translation of St. Ephraem's commentary on the epistles of St. Paul is rather mediocre, as was stressed by J. Molitor, Der Paulus-text des Heiligen Ephräm (Rome, 1938), p. 24.

St. Basil the Great (ca. 329/30–379)

Born in Caesarea of Cappadocia, in a deeply Christian family that gave several saints to the Church, Basil was the brother of Gregory, the future bishop of Nyssa, and of Peter, the future bishop of Sebaste in Armenia. He received baptism as an adult, and after a trip inquiring about monastic life, he retired to solitude on the banks of the river Iris. Disciples soon followed him. He organized his communities of monks by composing rules (the "Great" and then the "Little" rules) that earned him the title of legislator of the Eastern world. Ordained by the bishop of Caesarea, he was chosen to succeed him in 370. He developed a prodigious activity during the nine years of his episcopate, as can be seen especially in his correspondence. A man of doctrine and of action, he deserved to be called "the Great" by his own contemporaries. He died on January 1, 379, two years before the final triumph of the Nicaean faith at the Council of Constantinople, for which he had fought with all the abundance of his gifts and an indomitable courage.

2d letter on the canons
addressed to Amphilochius, bishop of Iconium (374)

In the second of the three canonical letters that he wrote to Amphilochius, bishop of Iconium,[198] Basil of Caesarea defines how one should deal with a priest who is bound unknowingly in an illicit marriage:

> About the priest who was bound unknowingly in an illicit marriage (Περὶ πρεσβυτέρου ἀθέσμῳ γάμῳ περιπαρέντος). As to the priest who was bound unknowingly in an illicit marriage, I have already decided what has to be done, i.e., he would keep his place in the sanctuary but would abstain from any other function; a simple pardon would suffice for him. It would not be reasonable to let a man who has to bind his own wounds bless others; for blessing is a communication of grace, and he does not have it because of the fault he committed unknowingly. How then could he communicate it to another? Let him not bless therefore, neither publicly nor privately, nor distribute the Body of the Lord to others, nor fulfill any other ecclesiastical function; but let him be content with precedence and implore the Lord's pardon for the iniquity he committed in his ignorance.[199]

Let us first note that the illicit marriage mentioned here is, quite likely, a marriage preceding the priest's ordination. If it were a matrimonial

---

[198] For the date and text of these three letters, see Joannou, II, p. 86.
[199] Joannou, II, pp. 127–28.

union contracted after, the fact that Basil described it as illicit would seem to imply on his part an admission that there is a legal measure authorizing a priest—under certain conditions—to get married. Now in the first quarter of the 4th century, the Council of Neocaesarea of Cappadocia (in Basil's own diocese) had absolutely forbidden marriage to priests, under penalty of exclusion from the ranks of the clergy.[200] A churchman such as the bishop of Caesarea, concerned above all with the necessity to conform to "the canons of the Fathers",[201] would certainly not have taken it upon himself to modify on such an important point the decisions of an episcopal synod by admitting, even implicitly, the legality of certain marriages contracted by priests after their ordinations. It is all the more unthinkable that this would be the only instance, in all the period of the first centuries (until and including the Quinisext Council of 691), of a concession of that nature ever granted to priests.[202]

As to the conditions for admission to Orders, the canonical regulations of the early centuries stipulated particularly that the candidate to major Orders (diaconate, priesthood, episcopate) should have been married only once, and to a virgin. Bigamous men, not only simultaneous but successive ones, were generally considered as unacceptable to the clergy,[203] as well as men whose wives had been widows from a first marriage or, more, if it were a question of concubines or prostitutes.[204] Other irregularities made a marriage illicit and consequently were an obstacle to Orders, such as, for instance, marriage with a close family member.[205] Thus, if anyone found himself unwittingly branded with

---

[200] Can. 1. Joannou, I, 2, p. 75. See above, pp. 177ff.

[201] It was thus that he wrote to choirbishops at the start of his episcopate: "I am very grieved that the canons of the Fathers are now left aside and that all exactitude has been banished from the Churches; I fear that, little by little, this indifference is going to progress and that the affairs of the Church will reach a complete confusion." *Ep.* 54. Trans. Y. Courtonne, *Saint Basile, Lettres,* I (Paris, 1957), Coll. "Budé", p. 139.

[202] With the exception of the decisions made by the Persian synods of Beth-Lafath, Mar Acacius, and Mar Babai, in the 5th century, which come from a Nestorian Church that is completely autonomous as far as doctrine and discipline are concerned. See below, pp. 283ff.

[203] It does seem, however, that in the East, the instances of married men admitted to the priesthood and even the episcopate were not the exception if one judges by the testimonies of Theodoret of Cyrus (see above, p. 102).

[204] See, in particular, the *Directa* decretal of Pope Siricius to Himerius of Tarragona, nos. 12, 14, 15, and 19. PL 13, 1141a–42a, 1143a–44a, 1145a–46a, or P. Coustant, *Epistolae Romanorum Pontificum,* c. 632–37. There are good records on the issue in P. H. Lafontaine, *Les conditions positives de l'accession aux Ordres dans la première législation ecclésiastique (300–492)* (Ottawa, 1963), pp. 176–91.

[205] Cf. Basil of Caesarea, *Deuxième lettre sur les canons à Amphiloque d'Iconium,* c. 68, 87. Joannou, II, pp. 149, 167, 168.

any of these irregularities and was nevertheless admitted to Orders, he was in the situation described by Basil in the above-mentioned canon. His good faith considered an extenuating circumstance, he was not purely and simply deposed; but while he was then forbidden to exercise ecclesiastical functions, he was permitted "to keep his place in the sanctuary". This is exactly how the Byzantine canonist Aristenes understands it in his commentary on the letters of St. Basil:

> If anyone, before becoming a priest, married a woman without knowing that she was a widow, or a mentally ill woman, or an actress, or anyone of those who are forbidden by sacred canons [to future priests], and then is promoted to the rank of the priesthood and admits the illegitimacy of his marriage, he will be absolutely forbidden to exercise any ministry and will retain only his place of honor and precedence among the priests.[206]

There seems to be another possible interpretation of St. Basil's canon if we reread it in light of the historical context of that time, characterized by all sorts of upheavals in the regions dominated by Arianism. We have already seen how the bishop of Caesarea, writing to brother bishops, complained that there was now "a neglect of the Fathers' canons".[207] In a letter that is a true cry for help, Basil and thirty-one other Eastern bishops would also write in 372 to the bishops of Italy and Gaul, to advise them of the "terrible storm" that was shaking the Churches of Asia: "The dogmas of piety are ruined, and the laws of the Church overthrown . . . a strict observance of the canons is no longer seen; there is a great freedom to sin." [208] Because of those disorders, and in the oblivion that had been the fate of many Church canons, it was thus quite likely that certain priests could have been able, in rather good faith, to enter into marriage. It might be such a situation that Basil addresses when writing to Amphilochius: "As to the priest who was bound unknowingly by an illicit marriage, I have already decided. . . ." In such a context, it becomes clear that the bishop of Caesarea does not intend to recognize indirectly priests' marriages that would have been "licit" when they were compared to those he declares to be illicit. The marriage of a priest is in itself illicit; the ignorance of him who is bound by it is accepted here as an extenuating circumstance deriving from the perturbations in the field of dogma and discipline that here or there led to neglect of the canons. Hence the prudential and compassionate attitude of St. Basil,

---

[206] *Commentaria in S. Basilii archiepiscopi Caesarae Cappadociae ad Amphilochium Epistolam canonicam secundam*, Can. 27. PG 138, 680d–81a.

[207] See n. 201 above, p. 220.

[208] *Ep.* 92, 2. Trans. Y. Courtonne, I, p. 200.

who does not decide for a pure and simple deposition as was required, for instance, by the Council of Neocaesarea, but who finds a formula of compromise respecting the rights of the person while safeguarding the demands of the priestly function: the guilty party will be content with precedence but will be barred from any ministry.[209]

Ambrosiaster (366–384)

Since Erasmus this is the name that has been given to an unknown author from the patristic era whose works were generally published with those of St. Ambrose. The identification of the man poses one of the most difficult problems to be clarified in Christian antiquity. Specialists agree that he lived under the pontificate of Damasus (366–84).

Two passages of Ambrosiaster deal with the issue of priestly continence; the first is found in the commentary on the first epistle to Timothy, the other in a treatise titled *Quaestiones Veteris et Novi Testamenti*.

Commentary on the 1st epistle to Timothy

Having reached the third chapter of the first epistle to Timothy, Ambrosiaster explains his thought on the meaning that should be given to the Pauline instruction of *unius uxoris virum*:

> Deacons must not have married more than once . . . " (1 Tim 3:12–13). He [St. Paul] comments now on what he had briefly said before with regard to the ordination of deacons. He shows that deacons must also be husbands of only wives, so that one may choose for the service of God those who did not go beyond the limits set by God. For man, God wanted only one

---

[209]Three centuries later, the Quinisext Council (in Trullo) of 691 would take a direct inspiration from this canon of St. Basil's (can. 3 and 26. Joannou, I, 1, pp. 125–30 and 156–57). Now by illicit marriage, besides the cases of bigamy and marriage with a non-virgin, the Eastern Fathers of 691 mean, without any possible ambiguity, any marriage contracted by priests, deacons, and subdeacons after their ordinations (can. 6. Joannou, ibid., pp.131–32). If they authorize those who have contracted such a marriage to "have their share in the honor of their seat" and to keep precedence, it is on condition that they abstain from all priestly functions and do penance; and, they add, it is obvious that the illicit marriage will be dissolved and that the man will have no relations with the woman because of whom he was suspended from the holy ministry (ibid., 157). Their decision, which is meant to be expressly dictated by "the rule of humanity and condescendence" and the understanding that "the fault came from ignorance and concerned quite a great multitude of men" (ibid., 126–27), does not in any way equal an official recognition of the right to marry for the higher clerics.

woman with whom he would be blessed: no one, if he has a second wife, receives the blessing. If they have raised their children properly and taken good care of their households, i.e., of their slaves or servants, they will become worthy of the priesthood and have assurance in God's presence; let them know that they will obtain what they ask if they abstain also from the use of marriage. In the past, it was indeed permitted to the Levites or other priests to have relationships with their wives because they did not devote much time to their ministries or priestly functions. There were a multitude of priests and an abundance of Levites, and each one of them was on duty at the divine ceremonies for a given period of time, as had been determined by David (1 Chron 6:31–32), who instituted twenty-four classes of priests serving in shifts: thus Abia was given the eighth class, the one in which Zechariah was performing priestly duties when his turn came, as indicated in the book of the Paralipomenon (1 Chron 24). Consequently, during the periods when they did not have to serve at the altar, they took care of their households; but when the time of their ministry came, they purified themselves for several days, then went to the temple for the offering to the Lord. Now there should be seven deacons, several priests (two per church), and only one bishop for each city, which is why they must abstain from any conjugal relations: they have to be present in church every day, and they do not have the necessary time to purify themselves properly after conjugal union, as the priests of old used to do. They have to offer the sacrifice every week, and even if the liturgy is not offered every day in rural areas or in territories outside the empire, it is at least twice a week for the local people. And, moreover, there is no lack of sick people to baptize every day. Indeed, it was because they were not expected to go frequently to the temple and had a private life that the concession [to use their marital rights] was granted to the ancients [i.e., the Hebrew priests]. If [the Apostle] directs laymen to abstain temporarily [from conjugal union] in order to attend to prayer, how much more [would it be fitting] for deacons and priests, who must pray day and night for the people entrusted to them? Therefore, they must be purer than the others, because they are God's representatives (*actores Dei sunt*).[210]

The author develops here an exegesis that is also found in St. Ambrose, Siricius, and St. Jerome: by claiming to choose for the diaconate and the higher ranks of the clergy only men who have at least given proofs of their capacity for fidelity in a monogamous marriage, the Apostle did not for that reason grant to the husbands who became ministers of the altar the freedom to use their conjugal rights: once they have crossed the threshold of ordination, they are bound to observe perfect continence. This viewpoint is justified by Ambrosiaster through an *a fortiori* argument:

---

[210] PL 17, 497a–d.

what was demanded in the past from the Levites is demanded all the more from the mediators of the New Covenant; and if lay Christians must for a while be able to practice continence so as "to free themselves for prayer", the specialists of permanent prayer—deacons, priests, and bishops—must impose upon themselves permanently this condition for efficacious prayer.

Quaestiones Veteris et Novi Testamenti

We find again, under another form, the same idea in a passage of the work titled Quaestiones Veteris et Novi Testamenti:[211]

> But people might say: if it is permitted and good to marry, why should priests not be authorized to take wives? In other words, why should ordained men not be permitted to be united [to wives]? There are indeed things that are not permitted to anyone, without exception; on the other hand, there are some things that are permitted at certain times but not at others. Fornication is never permitted to anyone; to do business is at times licit and at times illicit. Indeed, before becoming a priest, one may do business; once he is a cleric, he is not permitted to do so. And for a Christian it is at times permitted, and at times not, for him to unite himself with his wife. Indeed it is not permitted to unite oneself [with one's wife] because of the days [when one takes part in] worship, since one must abstain even from licit things to obtain more easily what one is asking [from God]. Which is why the Apostle tells [the couples] that [they must] abstain for a while [from each other] so as to free themselves for prayer.
>
> Is everything that is permitted in the presence of other people also permitted in the presence of the emperor? All the more so [is it then] in God's matters. This is why the priest must be more pure than the others; indeed, he is seen as God's personal representative and is actually his vicar; so that what is permitted to others is not permitted to him; he must take every day the place of Christ, either by praying for the people or by offering [the sacrifice], or by administering baptism. It is not only to him that [conjugal relations] are forbidden, but also to his minister: he too must be all the more pure as the matters of his ministry are holy. Compared to the light of lamps, the darkness is not only obscure but sordid; compared to the stars, the light of a lamp is only fog; while compared to the sun, the stars are obscure; and compared to the radiance of God, the sun is only night. Thus, the things that for us are licit and pure, are, as it were, illicit and impure with regard to the dignity of God: no matter how good they

---

[211] "One can credit Ambrosiaster with certainty for the Quaestiones Veteris et Novi Testamenti, formerly attributed to St. Augustine and dealing, in a jumble, with 127 exegetic and dogmatic issues" (B. Altaner, Patrologie, 3d ed. [Freiburg in Breisgau, 1951], p. 548). Cf. also CPL, n. 185.

are, they are not fitting to the person of God. That is why the priests of
God must be purer than the others since they take the place of Christ and
why the ministers of God must be purer [than the others]. . . .[212]

This text takes up the essential argumentation already developed regarding the first epistle to Timothy. Let us stress only that it does not
intend to justify a custom, but rather to explain the reasons for an obligation already in force. The question posed at the beginning follows a
long plea in favor of marriage. In responding to his detractors, the
apologist stresses the dignity of conjugal union, a wonder of God's
design. It is not on the ruins of a condemned institution, but on the basis
of a most noble sacrament that he now approaches the objection: If it is
good to marry, why are priests not permitted to have wives? The background of the discussion therefore seems to be the existence of an obligation known by all, forbidding the priests to use a sacrament that is
excellent for the common faithful. This information is noteworthy: it
attests that the law voted at the Council of Elvira, and very likely at the
1st Council of Arles, had a corresponding law in Italy at the time when
our anonymous work was published (366–84). It is also of great value
for the knowledge of the theological climate in which the author's thought
is developing: it reveals nothing pessimistic in the style of Manichaeism
nor any Encratist distrust of "the carnal act", but rather a healthy vision
of sexuality ennobled by the Creator. The exceptional demands placed
on the priest are based on the equally exceptional nature of his functions.
It is "the cause of God" to which the minister is consecrated daily that
explains the necessity of a more total purification. We are not told why
the exercise of sexuality, recognized as good in other respects, constitutes
a kind of obstacle to prayer, but that point is supposedly admitted by
the readers who regulate their faith on the word of the Apostle: even
lay people are asked to abstain at times from conjugal life "to free themselves for prayer" (1 Cor 7:5). Ambrosiaster limits himself, as he did in
his commentary on the first epistle to Timothy, to drawing the conclusions from this principle. Since "the things that for us are licit and pure,
are, as it were, illicit and impure with regard to the dignity of God", it
follows that the representative of Christ and the ministers of God must
be "purer" than the rest of the faithful. Good in themselves, sexual
relations, however, "are not fitting to the person of God". Arguments
of suitability are based on a scriptural principle. The anthropology that
underlies the thought of this writer of the 4th century is completely
dominated by an acute sense of God's transcendence.

[212] 127. CSEL 50, 414–15.

To summarize, the data provided by Ambrosiaster can be expressed in a few sentences: marriage is good since it was wanted and sanctified by God. The use of conjugal relations is, however, forbidden to sacred ministers. This demand comes from the nature of priestly functions, especially the duty of continuous prayer. Because a certain "purity" is required from all in order to approach God, in conformity with St. Paul's teaching, it behooves priests to make themselves always worthy of this proximity through a continence superior to the normal.

Epiphanius of Constantia (ca. 315–403)

Uncertain biographical data inform us that Epiphanius was born around 315, near Gaza in Palestine. The influence of St. Hilary and the Egyptian monks directed him toward monastic life. He founded a monastery not far from his native land and there spent thirty years in prayer and study. He was then approached to be elevated to the episcopal See of Constantia (ancient Salamis) in Cyprus (367). His thirty-six-year episcopate was marked by a great concern to develop Christian and monastic life in his diocese and to promote orthodoxy everywhere. An excessive and poorly enlightened zeal caused him to be unfair toward Origen; he went so far as to suspect St. John Chrysostom himself of Origenist sympathies. It was said about him that "he had the excess of his virtues" (F. Cayré), and this judgment seems fair. His two main works, the *Ancoratus* (the anchor of faith) and the *Panarion* (a *Medicine Chest* against "eighty heresies"), are still of value to the history of Christian ideas. He died at sea, while returning from a voyage to Constantinople in 403, at the age of eighty-eight.

Panarion: Heresy 48

In two chapters of his *Medicine Chest*, Epiphanius approaches the problem of clerical chastity. At first it is a polemic against "the new prophecy of the Phrygians", alias the Montanists, that draws him into the field.[213] The new prophets, obsessed by the haunting thought of an imminent Parousia, went so far as to prohibit marriage and to condemn whoever refused to fast. Here was an opportunity for the bishop of Salamis to develop one of his favorite themes, the balance of Catholic sanctity, the rich gamut of states of life that God's spouse recognizes as being worthy of God. It is not only virginity but solitary life ($\mu o\nu\acute{o}\tau\eta\tau\alpha$), continence,

---

[213] *Adversus Haereses*, Haer. 48, 9. GCS 31, 219–41.

and widowhood; it is also the sanctity of marriage. All this is praised and approved by the Catholic Church, while, on the other hand, she says no to debauchery, adultery, dissolute mores. Approval of the various human situations, Epiphanius explains, is the distinctive mark (κἀρακ-τῆρα) of the Holy Catholic Church and the test for the detection of distortions. While heresy forbids what God has rightly established and dictates laws prohibiting marriage and condemning food, the Word of God on the one hand rejoices at virginity and on the other hand also honors monogamous marriage:

> And indeed, through a certain balance, the Word of God, who said in the Gospel "if you want to be perfect", condescending to the manner in which men were fashioned and to their frailty, assuredly rejoices with those who can manifest their piety by choosing to practice virginity, chastity, and continence, but [also] honors monogamy; and as if he prefigured precisely [μάλιστα] the charisms of the priesthood [by choice] of former monogamists practicing continence or of men living continually in virginity, it is in the same way that his apostles regulated, with wisdom and sanctity, the ecclesiastical canon of the priesthood [τὸν ἐκκλησιαστικὸν κανόνα].[214]

It is important to understand the general drift of the context in order to grasp Epiphanius' thought. His intention is to refute the error of the Cataphrygians, who condemned marriage. As a consequence, he has to show that the Lord, far from forbidding marriage, held it in high esteem. The Montanists base themselves on the preference for virgins expressed in the Gospel in order to discredit married people, but this is a distortion of divine wisdom's harmonious balance. If he rejoices with some, the Master of sanctity does not give less honor to the others. What better proof can be given than the choice of the apostles, who were going to be the first fruits of the new priesthood, by the Lord himself? Wanting to make known in advance, so to speak, the charisms that would distinguish his priests, Jesus recruited those who were to become priests not only among virgins, but also among monogamous men. This choice particularly (μάλιστα) reveals the esteem in which the Word of God held monogamy. And the apostles, following the line of behavior given to them by the rule of truth (ὁ κανὼν τῆς ἀληθείας), Jesus, set the norm—the standard—for the priesthood. Did Epiphanius conceive this standard after the manner of a regulation or a written, juridical law as the conciliar decrees would later be? The answer is only too clear. It would

---

[214]Ibid., 231.

be an anachronism to give to the word κανών a meaning that the fourth-century Fathers only rarely knew.[215]

But even though the word does not have a strictly juridical meaning, it still has a great strength stressed by the context. The deeds of the Lord—in this case the manner in which he honored virginity and monogamy in the choice of his apostles—are the norm, the legal precedent, unwritten but wholly effective, which henceforth would govern the priestly institution. From him who remains for the Church "the canon of the truth" (ὁ κανὼν τῆς ἀληθείας) the apostles will draw their inspiration for the choice of their assistants and successors, and, in turn, their example will serve as a "canon" for future ages. Participating in the normative power received from the Lord, this extra—or, rather, supra—juridical "canon" will from century to century direct the discipline relative to the priesthood. A close reading of this chapter leads us to shed all doubts about the thought of Epiphanius. His deep conviction is that the Church of the 4th century, like the Church of all times, decides the criteria of admission to the sacred ministry through obedience to the example of the Lord, an example that the apostles were the first to follow, establishing existentially the "canon" of the canon law that would have to be written out in detail one day because of the remoteness of apostolic times.[216]

---

[215] Cf. the right observation by Funk: "In ancient literature, the word *kanon* did not mean a canon as we understand it in modern times nor a prescription valid for the entire Church. It still meant 'line of behavior', 'standard', 'idea'; and this is the meaning given to it here, in all certainty, by the context" ("Cölibat und Priesterehe", p. 132).

[216] In his refutation of Bickell's opinion, Funk attempts to show that the word μάλιστα does not have an absolute meaning but only a relative one and that consequently one cannot make Epiphanius say more than he wanted to say. But having limited his exegesis to a single sentence—the one in which the word μάλιστα is found—Funk, without noticing, has misinterpreted the passage, as the context clearly manifests. We have seen that the point of the reasoning was to show that Christ had held monogamy in honor. In this respect, the opposition «χαίρει μὲν ἐπὶ τούς, κτλ. . . . τὴν δὲ μονογαμίαν τιμᾷ» is essential; this is why Epiphanius stresses the fact that "precisely", "rightly" (or even "quite especially": μάλιστα) the Lord chose his apostles among virgins and ex-monogamists. Therefore, the question, contrary to what Funk is discussing, is not whether the Lord has given the graces of the priesthood "mainly" through continence or virginity or if he did so "absolutely". The question is quite different, and the Bickell-Funk controversy on this point becomes futile. It will also be noted that the two particles εἰ καί are in correlation with ὡς καί. Consequently they do not have a meaning of concession here, as is generally the case when εἰ καί is seen as a whole, but they are exercising their values separately. To translate, as R. Gryson did (in *Les origines du célibat ecclésiastique*, p. 59), "But he honors an only marriage, *even* if he has, above all, shown in advance to the world the charisms of the priesthood for those who renounce the use of an only marriage and those who live in virginity" (our emphasis) does not render correctly the meaning of the correlation.

Heresy 59

The disciples of Novatian, like those of Montanus, were extremists, all-or-nothing people who also showed the greatest contempt for marriage. While the Phrygians wanted to make a precept out of the evangelical counsel of virginity, the "Cathars" drew their arguments from laws that were enforced for bishops, priests, and deacons. Why such a distinction between the members of the Church? they asked. Not only some but all must be "irreproachable", in conformity with St. Paul's order, and practice continence: "They deemed, in fact, that what was granted to the priesthood because of the imminent dignity of the liturgy should be equally applied to all; having heard that the bishop had to be irreproachable, husband of an only wife and continent, and having heard 'the same thing for the deacon and the priest', they did not understand the limit of these prescriptions." [217]

Such an excessive rigorism could not fail to be opposed by the bishop of Constantia in the very name of Tradition, for it shows a blindness with respect to the limits of the prescriptions that are invoked. Epiphanius then recalls the discipline of admission to the Orders, opening a digression of sorts that concerns our topic. Indeed, he observes, such is the situation:

> Since the Incarnation of Christ, the holy Word of God does not admit to the priesthood the monogamists who, after the death of their wives, have contracted a second marriage, [this] because of the exceptional honor of the priesthood. And it is observed by the Holy Church of God with great exactitude (μετὰ ἀκριβείας παραφυλάττεται) and without fail. But the man who continues to live with his wife and to sire children is not admitted by the Church as a deacon, priest, or bishop, even if he is the husband of an only wife; [only] he who, having been monogamous, observes continence or is a widower; [this is observed] especially where the ecclesiastical canons are exact (μάλιστα ὅπου ἀκριβεῖς κανόνες οἱ ἐκκλησιαστικοί). [218]

This last sentence deserves some thought. What exactly does the bishop of Cyprus mean? Does he limit himself to noting that there were regions

---

Moreover, it does not respect the punctuation of the text: there is a semicolon after τὴν δὲ μονογαμίαν τιμᾷ (GCS 31, 231, 13) and this part of the sentence is to be attached to what comes before, i.e., to συγγνωμόνων τῇ τῶν ἀνθρώπων πλάσει, κτλ. (condescending to the way men were molded, and so on . . .).

[217] *Adversus Haereses*, Haer. 59, 4. GCS 31, 367.
[218] Ibid.

where a rigorous canonical discipline forbade married clerics to continue having conjugal relations and other regions where the law was not as severe? That would be, we think, a misunderstanding about the meaning that the writer gives here to the word ἀκριβεῖς.

We should first note that Epiphanius already used the term ἀκριβεία a few lines above, in order to define the exactitude with which the Church of God observed what the Word of God had established for remarried widowers. Obviously, the choice of the adjective ἀκριβεῖς to indicate the canons forbidding the admission to the Orders of the new category of persons—i.e., monogamists who are not continent—corresponds to the word ἀκριβεία and leads us to the true thought of Epiphanius. On the first point, the Church of God always remained firm and precise, i.e., conformed herself exactly to the holy Word of God.[219] On the other hand, when it comes to the second point, the canons are not always ἀκριβεῖς, i.e., "exact"; they are not faithful everywhere to what had been established by the "holy Word of God". The meaning of the word ἀκριβεῖς is therefore not "rigorous", as if the Churches where one refused to ordain married men not ready to accept continence would have been more severe than was the norm, but "exact", i.e., corresponding exactly to the rule set by the Word of God. Where the canons are not "exact", one must therefore expect to encounter clergy members still living with their wives and continuing to have children. Let no one be too surprised, Epiphanius pleads; human weakness and a lack of vocations are the cause: "But you will surely ask me [and tell me]: in certain places there are priests, deacons, and subdeacons who are still begetting children. This is not done in conformity with the 'canon' but because men are now letting themselves go, and given the multitude [of the faithful], there are not [enough] ministers."[220] But this is not done in conformity with the "canon" (οὐ παρὰ τὸν κανόνα γίγεται). In other words, as the bishop of Constantia clearly suggests, if in these regions where such things are occurring the canons were more "exact", more in conformity with the "canon", it would put a rapid end to a practice that could perhaps be excused but that is contrary to the traditional norm.[221] The meaning

---

[219] It will be noted that "the Holy Word of God" (τό ἅγιον τοῦ θεοῦ κήρυγμα) is the subject of the verb "does not admit" (οὐ δέχεται). It is therefore this Holy Word that does not receive in the Orders remarried widowers, and again does not receive monogamists who are continent. As to the Church, she follows the decision of this Holy Word, more or less exactly.

[220] GCS 31, 367–68.

[221] It is quite likely that here Epiphanius is thinking about the areas troubled by Arianism. One can get an inkling of the upheavals in the areas of ecclesiastical discipline caused by the followers of Arius by reading the moving collective letter sent in 372 to the bishops

of the word κανών is not the same, as we can see, when it is used in the plural or in the singular form. In the first case, we are obviously dealing with particular regulations formulated by the law; in the other we again find the nuance already evoked with regard to the κανών ἐκκλησιαστικὸς established by the apostles,[222] a line of behavior imparting its direction and norm to the future development of discipline. Though it was not found in written form in the archives, that norm was nevertheless the general model according to which all the particular regulations had to be organized. In this respect the previous chapter shows very well the importance that the bishop of Cyprus gave to this "canon" of apostolic origins, and we believe that to deny him the conviction of an obligation imposed upon all would be a wrong interpretation of his thought.[223]

The Expositio Fidei

The *Expositio Fidei*, this "brief summary of the faith of the Catholic Church", which is the preface of the *Panarion*, includes a final text of Epiphanius regarding our topic. After having explained various articles of faith, the bishop of Cyprus undertakes to say something about the rites and law in force within the Church. In a hierarchical ordering, we then see, as if from the top of the episcopal cathedral, the harmonious arrangement of the various groups composing the Christian people.

First, and at the foundation of the building, is virginity, professed by a great many people and crowned by the greatest honors. Next to it, solitary life; a crowd of monks and contemplatives of both sexes have

---

of Italy and Gaul by St. Basil the Great and thirty-one other Eastern bishops calling on the West for help: "This is not a danger for one Church only, and there are not just two or three falling into this terrible storm. It is almost from the borders of Illyria all the way to the Thebaid that the scourge of heresy has spread its damage. The bad seed was first scattered by the infamous Arius. . . . The dogmas of piety are ruined and the laws of the Church overwhelmed. The ambitions of those who do not fear the Lord leap to the first places, and episcopal dignity is now openly offered as a price for impiety. . . . Priestly seriousness is gone; there are no more men who feed knowingly the flocks of the Lord because the resources of the poor are constantly wasted by the ambitious ones for their personal enjoyment or for their largesse. One no longer sees canons being observed; there is a great freedom to sin" (Ἠμαύρωται κανόνων ἀκριβεία, ἐξουσία τοῦ ἁμαρτάνειν πολλή). *Ep.*, 92, 2. Trans. Y. Courtonne, *Saint Basile, Lettres*, I, p. 200.

[222] See above, pp. 227–28.

[223] On this point we cannot share Funk's judgment: "Epiphanius does not speak of a perfect observation of the laws but of a perfection of the laws. Now his account shows that perfect laws did not exist everywhere, which leads us to understand by the same token that our author did not know the law in the sense that the adverse thesis (that of Bickell) gave to this word, i.e., universal law" ("Cölibat und Priesterehe", p. 132).

chosen it for themselves. Then, and step by step, continence, widowhood, marriage lived in sanctity. The vision of the Church, vivified by
the Spirit, leads to the crowning, or, as it were, the nurturing mother, the
priestly Order: "The crowning of all these [steps] or, if one wishes, the
mother and the one who gives them life, is the holy priesthood, whose
dynamic force comes in great part from the virgins [who compose it]." [224]

This contemplation being meant to recall the law regulating the discipline, Epiphanius lists here the conditions that are requested in order to
admit someone to the summit of the ecclesiastical building. Most of the
clerics come from groups of young men who have chosen virginity,
then one appeals to the monks; lacking qualified monks for the ministry,
one then recruits future priests from among the monogamous men, but
only monogamous men freed from conjugal duties either by widowhood
or a free profession of continence. As to the men who contracted a second
marriage, even if they henceforth would have no relations with their
wives, they can never be accepted to the episcopate, the priesthood, or
the diaconate:

> Lacking virgins, [priests are recruited] among the monks; if there are not
> enough monks for the ministry [they are recruited] among men who ob-
> serve continence with their wives or among the exmonogamists who are
> widowers; but in her [the Church], admitting a remarried man to the
> priesthood is not permitted; even if he observes continence or is a widower,
> [he is rejected] from the Order of the bishops, priests, deacons, and sub-
> deacons. [225]

Properly speaking, this summary does not teach us anything new
inasmuch as the chapter of the *Panarion* devoted to the Cathar heresy
had already provided Epiphanius with the opportunity to stress what the
discipline of the Church was. However, in addition to a confirmation
that should not be neglected, the page of the *Expositio Fidei* highlights
the degree to which continence was considered as a dominant quality of
the clergy. Through the hierarchical ordering of the possible candidates
to the priesthood—first the virgins, then the monks, and lastly the monogamists ready to observe continence—Epiphanius does indeed stress the
prevailing importance that the Church granted to it. The continence
demanded from the moment of ordination is thus placed within the large
movement gathering all the living forces of the Christian community
toward the ideal of virginity (a tendency which explains, for instance,
why widowhood is preferable to second marriage, and a strong reservation

---

[224] *Expositio fide*, 21. GCS 37, 522.
[225] Ibid.

with respect to a third marriage, to say nothing of subsequent marriages) and, beyond virginity, in truth, a tendency toward the order animating and fulfilling the entire body: sacred priesthood. It no longer appears as a strange demand that our twentieth-century minds at times discover in other texts with surprise, but as the luminous border of a zone lit at its center by virginity, a participation in a peerless, enviable state and in the privileged status reserved to it, rather than an arbitrary constraint imposed—and accepted—as a superhuman burden. Such at least was the discipline that Epiphanius knew—and advocated—in that 4th century. That the reality was not always in conformity with the ideal described by the bishop of Cyprus he himself testified by admitting that in certain regions there were still clerics continuing their matrimonial lives.[226] But the ideal, for him, posed no problem, and it was by such a "canon" that local practices had to regulate themselves and even reform themselves. Where the law enforced in the fourth-century Church came from, the author of the *Expositio Fidei* does not say. But the synthetic and normative character of his writing clearly bases itself on the fact that his was not, in his eyes, a new discipline motivated by conjecture. The priesthood is the "crowning and the mother" of all the categories of the faithful impelled in various ways by the same stream of chastity; it is not optional for the priesthood—starting point and fulfillment of this current—to be itself a source of superior limpidity. Based on this essential motive, the continence demanded of priests is thus linked, in the thought of Epiphanius, to the priestly institution itself. If he does not say so in this text, we know from elsewhere how he did not hesitate to link it to the time of the apostles.[227]

St. Ambrose (ca. 333–397)

"Ambrose, bishop!" The voice of the child was the voice of God, and the governor of Liguria-Emilia had to obey the plebiscite. Ambrose, who was only a catechumen, was immediately baptized and reached with one step the summit of the episcopal hierarchy. Likely born in Trier around 333, he had a brilliant administrative career. His first concern, as soon as he was appointed bishop of Milan, was to distribute his huge fortune to the poor and to acquire the scholarship he needed for his new functions. He studied Origen, Athanasius, Cyril of Jerusalem, Gregory Nazianzen, Hippolytus, and others, assimilating the Greeks with a

---

[226] See above, p. 231.
[227] *Adversus Haereses*, Haer. 48, 9. GCS 31, 230–32.

superior mind that stamped everything with a Roman mark. Bishop and shepherd of souls, he taught his people a practical and at the same time lofty doctrine that made him one of the four great doctors of the Latin Church, beside St. Augustine, St. Jerome, and St. Gregory. Adviser of Gratian (375–83) and of the regent Justina (383–88), he was respected by Theodosius (388–95), and was able "to be the bishop of the emperors but not their chaplain" (M. Jourjon). Confronting Justina, who wanted to restore Arianism in Milan, he uttered the famous phrase "Imperator intra Ecclesiam et non supra Ecclesiam est." As to Theodosius, he had to do public penance for the massacre at Thessalonika. Under those circumstances, "Ambrose personified not only the Catholic Church but human conscience, and never was he greater." He died on April 4, 397.

The letter to the Church of Vercelli

We first find the thought of St. Ambrose regarding our topic in a long letter that internal quarrels led him to write to the Church of Vercelli in order to reestablish calm there. The episcopal See was vacant; people who were disoriented by troublemakers had to be convinced to put a quick end to the situation and to choose someone worthily possessing qualities that one should expect from the shepherd of a diocese, to which the faithful of Vercelli should have felt all the more compelled than they had in the past, because their previous bishop had been Eusebius, a father and a doctor famous for his virtues. Thus, they were urged to be especially attentive to the patience and the purity of the future head of the community, in conformity with the portrait of a bishop outlined by the Pauline epistles:

> The Apostle is a master of virtue, and he teaches one to convince the opposition with patience; he orders that [the bishop] be the husband of an only wife, not in order to exclude the one who never took part in the marriage (which is in fact beyond the law), but so that, through conjugal chastity, he keep the grace of his baptism; and on the other hand, the apostolic authority does not ask him to beget children during his priestly [career]; [the Apostle] did talk about a man who [already] had children, but not about one who is begetting [others] or contracts a new marriage.[228]

It is quite obvious, St. Ambrose says, that the Apostle did not want to exclude single men from the priesthood. If the others are asked to be *unius uxoris (viros)*, it is to ensure that, through conjugal chastity, they have kept the grace of baptism ("*ut conjugali castimonia servet ablutionis suae gratiam*"). The monogamists are thus admitted to Orders, the bishop

---

[228] *Ep.* 63, 62–63. PL 16, 1257a.

of Milan goes on, but this does not mean that they are asked, once they have become priests, to beget new children. St. Paul's allusion to the children of the bishop concerns those that the married pastor had before and whose education he must continue to provide; it is not a matter of increasing their number: "habentem dixit filios, non facientem neque conjugium iterare."

Understood in such a way, the *unius uxoris virum* counsel determines the domain that extends beyond ordinations as solely ruled by the law of perfect continence. In all the rigor of the term, St. Ambrose uses the word *law* only to describe the obligation that Paul imposed to refuse candidates who would have contracted a second marriage to the priesthood or to the episcopate: "The Apostle proclaimed a law when he said . . . if someone is without fault the husband of an only wife. Consequently, if one is without fault, husband of an only wife, let him be bound by the law of the priesthood he is due to receive. . . . "[229]

But deriving from this fundamental law, or rather protected by it against the risks one would incur by admitting men who are not well prepared to obey it, the demands of clerical continence partake, in St. Paul's mind, of the law's regulatory character.

We will therefore note in this text the following two points: St. Ambrose is convinced that the Pauline recommendation implies for candidates, be they monogamous or single, a commitment to lead a life in which they would give up conjugal intercourse. This way of life, far from being optional, simply advised as an ideal of perfection that is desirable for some people, is part of the priestly state and imposed upon the Levites of the New Covenant, just as temporary continence was once imposed upon the ministers of the former temple. That it is for St. Ambrose a formal obligation we have an additional proof in the parallel he develops, in his manner, between the two priesthoods, in order to refute the objections of those who justified their illegal progeny through the example of the Old Testament: "Si in figura tanta observantia, quanta in veritate?" No more than those of Leviticus whose place they take, the prescriptions of the New Testament concerning the purity of the ministers could be, in his mind, considered mere counsels.

De officiis ministrorum

A passage from this treatise of St. Ambrose takes up again and completes the point of view developed in the letter of the Church of Vercelli:

[229] PL 16, 1257b.

You who have received the grace of the sacred ministry in an integral body and with an incorruptible purity and who are alien to the conjugal community itself know that the ministry must be immune from offense and stain and must not be subjected to any injuries from possible conjugal relations. I did not leave this issue aside for the following reason: in many places that are quite remote, some men who exercise the ministry, even the priesthood, have at times sired children; they try to justify [their behavior] by [the example] of what was done in the past, when the sacrifice was offered only from time to time; however, as we read in the Old Testament, even the people abstained, for two or three days, from carnal relations, so as to be pure when going to the sacrifice, and they washed their clothes. If such was the observance at the time of the prefiguration, how much more [it should be now for us who are] in the truth? Learn, O priest, O deacon, what the washing of your clothes means, so as to present your pure body to the celebration of the mysteries. If it was forbidden to the people to approach their victim without having purified their clothes, would you dare, without having purified your spirit and body even more, to offer supplications for the others; would you dare exercise your ministry for the others?[230]

This exhortation shows that the bishop of Milan saw the issue of clerical continence and the disciplinary variations of his time in the following way:

It is known that the purity of the ministry should not be violated by the exercise of conjugal relations (*ullo conjugali coitu violandum cognoscitis*). The notoriety of the demand obviously implies in the thought of St. Ambrose the existence of a solidly established discipline. Had it been optional, he would not have appealed to the experience of his readers in the same way. Also, everyone is aware that in a great many faraway places (*in plerisque abditioribus locis*) the discipline is not observed, even by men who have received the priestly Orders, bishops included. Moreover, this discipline is being disputed. The clerics of these remote regions are referring to the authority of the Old Testament: the Levites were compelled to continence only at the occasion of their periodic service in the temple; and the people, for their part, were bound to sexual purity only for brief periods of time. It is noteworthy that the Old Testament argumentation seems first to have been used by those who questioned the discipline recalled by Ambrose. We might have there an explanation of the importance granted to the law of Leviticus by the patristic authors of the late 4th century and of the concern they had in affirming the continuity between the discipline of their time and those

---

[230]PL 16, 104b–5a. Ed. J. G. Krabinger, *S. Ambrosii De officiis ministrorum libri III* (Tübingen, 1857), pp. 118–19.

ancient prescriptions.[231] To the objection the bishop of Milan answers in the same spirit as Ambrosiaster: *Si in figura tanta observantia, quanta in veritate?* We are no longer under the rule of the Old Covenant. The "figure" gave way to "the truth", and what was imperfect became perfect. Having lapsed, the ancient institutions were not suppressed but were fulfilled on a higher plane. Thus perfect continence is demanded of whoever is elevated to the dignity of the new priesthood.

This *a fortiori* argument implies a theology of the relationship between the Old and New Testaments and poses the question of the criteria of discernment that decided, among the Fathers such as St. Ambrose, the choice of the practices seen as definitively lapsed (the many Jewish rituals of bodily purification, for instance) and of the institutions that, on the other hand, found themselves reinforced by the new law.

St. Jerome (ca. 347–419)

Born in Strido, at the border of Pannonia and Dalmatia, around 347, Jerome came from a wealthy family and was able to pursue solid literary studies. He was attracted to monastic life: he went first to Aquilea, then to the "Syrian Thebaid" of the Chalcis wilderness, where he subjected himself to frightening austerities and also studied Scripture. Ordained a priest by Paulinus of Antioch, he accompanied the latter to Rome and was kept there by Pope Damasus, who made him his secretary and entrusted him with the preparation of an official and sole text of the Latin Bible. When Pope Siricius was elected (384), criticism and calumny made Jerome leave Rome. He settled in Bethlehem, followed by Paula and Eustochium, his two spiritual daughters, and founded two monasteries, one of which was for nuns. The thirty-five years he spent in Palestine were a period of intense literary activity. He completed the Vulgate Bible, a monument that would immortalize his memory. His studious peace was, however, troubled for twelve years by the Origenist

---

[231] R. Gryson writes about this passage: "The text shows clearly that the custom imposing continence on priests and deacons is a new practice, which is observed only in the important towns and which is tied, at least in part, to the daily celebration of the Eucharist" (*Les origines du célibat ecclésiastique*, p. 172). Indeed, the observation of perfect continence by the Christian priesthood is new, in the mind of St. Ambrose, but it is new in comparison with the prescriptions of the Old Covenant, and in comparison with customs that would have been legally kept until his time. The reasoning of Ambrose shows that by claiming to follow the laws of Leviticus, the clerics who went on living with their wives and having children went against what was being done and what had to be done by virtue of the transformation of the priesthood through the New Covenant.

quarrel: the vehemence of his discourses (particularly against Rufinus) saddened the Christian world. He made better use of his polemical talents against Helvidius, Jovinian, and Vigilantius, especially in the Pelagian controversy, which brought him close to St. Augustine. The soundness of his scholarship, his attachment to Tradition, and the clarity of his doctrine on the rule of the Catholic faith made of him one of the four great doctors of the Latin Church. But Jerome earned the gratitude of posterity mostly because of his translations and his scriptural commentaries. He died on September 30, 419.

Commentary on the epistle to Titus (387–389)

Among St. Jerome's works before 390 is the commentary on the epistle to Titus. It contains an interesting development about priestly continence.

Commenting on the words of recommendation given to the young bishop of Crete about the choice of priests, Jerome invites his readers to go back to the Book of Kings to peruse the passage about the shew bread and to keep in mind the demands of purity that prevailed at the time of David. Who would not then understand, he goes on, that, given the difference there is between shadow and bodies, image and truth, models of the things to come and the things themselves, the priesthood of the New Law must rise above the old prefiguration through the unadulterated radiance of the highest virtues, i.e., continence? This is the *a fortiori* argumentation developed at the same time by the *Directa* decretal of Pope Siricius to Himerius of Tarragona.[232] Like the Bishop of Rome, Jerome uses the comparison between priests and lay people: both have to attend to prayer, especially by practicing conjugal abstinence: but what is required from lay people for a while is imposed every day on clerics, because they have to fulfill prayer duties every day:

> But if laymen are asked to abstain from relations with their wives for the sake of prayer, what should one [then] think of the bishop, of him who must be able to present spotless offerings to God every day, for his own sins and for those of the people? . . . This is why, together with meekness, patience, sobriety, temperance, unselfishness, hospitality, and good will, the bishop especially—in a more pronounced way than lay people—must practice the chastity proper to his state, and, so to speak, priestly purity, so that not only will he abstain from impure acts, but his spirit, meant to consecrate the Body of Christ, will be freed from whims of the eye and wanderings of the mind. . . .
>
> Let the bishop also practice abstinence: not only, as some think, with respect to carnal desires and embraces with his wife, but also with respect

---

[232] See above, pp. 8–12.

to all the troubles [that can agitate] the soul; let him not be inclined to anger or crushed by sadness; let him not be tortured by fear, and let him not be exalted by an immoderate joy. . . .[233]

We must therefore read into the words of St. Paul a rule imposing perfect chastity. Chastity for people who had always observed continence or chastity for married men called to live as brother and sister with their wives—in Jerome's eyes, such is the normal condition of priestly life.

St. Gregory Nazianzen († 389/390)

A close friend of Basil of Caesarea, Gregory was the son of Gregory the Elder, bishop of Naziansus in Cappadocia. Ordained a priest against his will by his father, he left his father for solitude; when young Gregory's friend Basil forced him to accept the See of Sasima, he protested against the violence done to him by again fleeing to the desert. At the request of the Catholics of Constantinople, he settled in the imperial capital, where he endeavored to "resuscitate" the Church then oppressed by the Arians. During that period of his life he made the great speeches that earned him the title of "theologian". Acclaimed by the clergy and the people as bishop of Constantinople, he had his election confirmed by the ecumenical council of 381 that met in his city. But being too impressionable and sensitive, he wound up resigning to appease his opponents. After an interval of two years at the head of the diocese of Naziansus, he retired to his lands, where he died (in 389 or 390). It was said of Gregory that he was the great "theologian-orator". The forty-five speeches that have come down to us, his five famous theological discourses among them, are masterpieces of eloquence and doctrine. He linked his name to the dogma of the Most Holy Trinity.

Discourse 40

In this discourse about baptism, given in 381 at Constantinople, Gregory Nazianzen tackles an objection: does the validity of the sacrament, or at least its efficacity, depend on the qualities of the minister? Would a bishop born in Jerusalem not be more qualified than another, a celibate priest more than a married cleric? This passage is of interest for our study because of the historical background revealed through the worries of the catechumens:

---

[233] *Commentariorum in epistolam ad Titum* I (vv. 8–9). PL 26, 603b–4a.

Do not say: let the bishop baptize me, and let a metropolitan or the bishop of Jerusalem (since grace does not depend on a place but on the Spirit), and let him be of good birth, for fear that the nobility of my birth be offended by the one who confers baptism [on me]. Or, if he is a priest, let him be single or among those who observe continence and an angelic life, lest I be soiled during the [very] course of [baptismal] purification.[234]

Did the preference that certain neophytes had for bishops imply that the heads of dioceses normally belonged to the group of celibates? It is difficult to say because the emphasis is first on the hierarchical dignity of the bishop and not on the sanctity of his state or his family situation. As far as priests are concerned, we can easily guess that some of them were or had been married. This fact does, however, call for the following remark: the ἄγαμοι priests were those who had never been married, even when they were lay people. The preference shown to them might very well be explained by the special esteem then enjoyed by virginity—an esteem that, even though it did not always lead to the excesses of the Cathars, still ran the risk of distorting the judgment of simple people, making them believe that the ἄγαμοι administered the sacraments with a purer conscience and a greater efficacity. We have seen, in connection with the 4th canon of the Council of Gangres, that the instance was not imaginary. The reservations of the people with respect to married priests do not mean in any way that the latter continued to live with their wives.[235]

In asking that, in the absence of ἄγαμοι priests, baptism be administered to them by a minister "observing continence and the angelic life", the faithful of Gregory Nazianzen could have, it seems, two categories of people in mind: if the word ἐγκρατής is understood in the general meaning of "continent", it would apply here to married priests abstaining from conjugal relations. Thus we are indirectly informed that such was not the universal case. If the catechumens prefer the ἐγκρατεῖς in the absence of ἄγαμοι, this indicates that the clergy also had the noncontinent

---

[234]PG 36, 396b. Here is the Greek text of this passage of discourse 40: Μὴ εἴπης: Ἐπίσκοπος βαπτισάτω με, καὶ οὗτος μητροπολίτης, ἢ Ἱεροσολυμίτης (οὐ γὰρ τόπων ἡ χάρις, ἀλλὰ τοῦ Πνεύματος), καὶ οὗτος τῶν εὖ γεγονυιῶν. Δεινὸν γὰρ, εἰ τῷ βαπτιστῇ τὸ εὐγενές μου καθυβρισθήσεται· ἢ πρεσβύτερος μὲν, ἀλλὰ καὶ οὗτος τῶν ἀγάμων, καὶ οὗτος τῶν ἐγκρατῶν καὶ ἀγγελικῶν τὴν πολιτείαν· δεινὸν γὰρ, εἰ ἐν καιρῷ καθάρσεως ῥυπωθήσομαι.

[235]The hierarchy of values governing the election of future ministers of the altar, attested by Epiphanius' Expositio Fidei, likely had as a consequence a hierarchy of esteem on the part of the faithful with respect to priests. While having put an end to conjugal relations, married clerics were still different from those who had always kept perfect chastity; thus there was a possible preference for the latter. One could not, therefore, conclude from this passage that there was a regular lifestyle of priests using their conjugal rights.

among its ranks, that is, in the precise meaning of that word in the literature of the time, priests who continued having a married life. If we adopt this meaning, however, it does not necessarily follow that the situation of the latter was legal. Testimonies on the existence of clerics who did not practice continence are numerous—starting with that of Epiphanius, whom we could hardly suspect of having overemphasized the fact.[236] But those who relate them generally add that these instances were only regrettable abuses or at least the results of a temporary tolerance. It would not be unlikely that Gregory Nazianzen referred to such a situation; but to think that he would vouch for a legal disposition authorizing those married clerics to live as they did, remains, however, quite a step and one that objectivity does not permit us to take. When addressing catechumens, the shepherd in charge of teaching the faith is right to insist on the dissociation of the Sacrament's efficacity from the sanctity of the minister; even the priests behaving in ways of which the Church disapproves—the issue will be studied at length by St. Augustine with respect to the Donatist schism—are entitled to the sacramental trust of the faithful. Such could have been the background of Gregory of Nazianzen's thought.

Nevertheless, the association of ἐγκρατής with ἀγγελικός invites us to give a more precise meaning to the word. The "angelic" way of life generally denotes, in the early Church, the solitary or monastic life;[237] there are strong reasons to think that the word ἐγκρατής has that meaning here. Its apposition to ἀγγελικός makes it something of a synonym; on the other hand, the term πολιτεία also has a connotation of an official state of life, as was precisely that of ascetics and monks. Without excluding the first meaning that we evoked, we would be strongly inclined to read this passage in the following way: [Let a bishop baptize us . . .] or, if it is a priest, let him be at least someone belonging to the πολιτεία of the celibates (τῶν ἀγάμων) or to that of the continent and the angelicals (= ascetics or monks) (τῶν ἐγκρατῶν καὶ ἀγγελικῶν).

Now if we compare the hierarchy of values underlying this preference of St. Gregory Nazianzen's listeners with the hierarchy of criteria for election that rules the recruitment of priests, according to the *Expositio*

---

[236] See above, p. 232. Gregory, who came to Constantinople to help "resuscitate" the Church oppressed by Arians, also sees the decadence of the (Arian?) clergy. Cf. *Oratio 2*, 8. SCh 247, 98–100.

[237] Cf., for instance, Jean Moschus, *Le pré spirituel*, 168: Εἶπεν πάλιν ὁ γέρων (ὁ ἄββας Ἀλέξανδρος): Οὐαι μοί, τέκνα, πολιτείαν ἀγγελικὴν ἠφανίσαμεν (The old man [Abbot Alexander] said again: alas, my children, we have obscured the angelic life . . .). PG 87, 3036a. Other references are to be found in G. W. H. Lampe, *A Patristic Greek Lexicon*, I (Oxford, 1961), p. 9.

Fidei, we cannot help but be struck by the correspondence between the two texts. If it is true that one chose by priority the ἄγαμοι young men, then, in descending order, monks and solitaries, and, lastly, monogamists, it comes as no surprise that the initiates of the different catechumenates had expressed, with respect to the ministers of baptism, a hierarchical preference following this pattern.

The text of Gregory Nazianzen seems therefore to be in harmony with the testimony of Epiphanius, either because it contains traces of the various ecclesial groups among whom the candidates to the priesthood were chosen, or because it reveals the existence of priests who have not ceased to have conjugal relations (and provoking thereby a reticence on the part of the faithful), but without implying by this the legality of such a situation.

"De vita sua"

The perspective would be different if one thought that Gregory of Nazianzen had been born while his father was already a bishop. A passage of the poem "De vita sua" seems to authorize such a chronology. Evoking the moving encounter during which Gregory the Elder begged him to accept the priesthood, the bishop of Naziansus puts the following words in his father's mouth:

> I beg you as a father, O dearest of all sons,
> you [still] young and member of the family,
> [I beg] you as an aged father, master by nature and by a
>   double law.

> 505 I do not expect from you gold or precious stones,
>   silver, acres of land, my child,
> none of these delights.
> I ask you to take your place near Aaron and Samuel,
> and be a worthy assistant to God.
> He who gave, owns you; my child, do not shame me,

> 510 so that I can draw to me the favor of the only Father.
> This is a beautiful request, at least, a wholly paternal one.
> You have not spent such a long life yet
> for the time of sacrifices to have elapsed for me
> I beg you, do me this favor, or let another one lead me to my
>   tomb.

> 515 So harsh is the penalty I decree for disobedience.

Give to what is left to me [of my life] the brevity of your days,
and, with a good heart, the plans you have for your future.[238]

Verses 512–13 were translated into Latin by A. B. Caillau (in his edition
of the works of Gregory Nazianzen published by Migne) in the following
way:

Nondum tantam emensus es vitam
Quantum mihi effluxit sacrificiorum tempus.[239]
(You have not had as yet a life as long as the time of sacrifices
that has elapsed for me.)

It would seem, under these conditions, that Gregory the Elder was
already a bishop when he sired the one who was to succeed him. If this
is accepted as a fact, it becomes more difficult to credit Gregory Nazianzen
with the thoughts that we had suggested above with regard to the baptismal catechesis. Son of a bishop who would have had children after
episcopal ordination, he would have been in the wrong position to dis-
approve conjugal relations for married clerics.

However, the two verses quoted above have long been considered a
crux interpretorum. The Greek of Gregory Nazianzen's poems poses many
problems of translation because of the frequently allusive or symbolic
turn of phrases. Erasmus admitted that at times he had to give up trying
to give a faithful rendition of the author's thought. In this particular case
the meaning is difficult to grasp. In a dissertation of the *Acta Sanctorum*,
Bollandist Jan Stiltinck stresses in particular that the verb ἐκμετρέω
means generally "to measure", and in a figurative meaning "to estimate"

---

[238] PG 37, 1064a. Here is the Greek text of this poem:

Πατήρ σε λίσσεθ', υἱέων ὦ φίλτατε,
Πατήρ ὁ πρέσβυς τὸν νέον, τὸν οἰκέτην
Ὁ δεσπότης φύσει τε καὶ διπλῷ νόμῳ.
505 Οὐ χρυσὸν αἰτῶ σ', οὐ λίθους, οὐδ' ἄργυρον,
Οὐ γῆς ἀπούρας, τέκνον, οὐδ' ὅσα τρυφῆς.
Ζητῶ σ' Ἀαρὼν καὶ Σαμουὴλ πλησίον
Θεῖναι, Θεῷ τε τίμιον παραστάτην.
Ὁ δοὺς ἔχει σε; τέκνον, μή μ' ἀτιμάσῃς, . . .
510 Ὡς ἵλεώ γε τοῦ μόνου τύχῃς Πατρός;
Καλὸν τὸ αἴτημ', εἰ δὲ μή γε, πατρικόν.
Οὔπω τοσοῦτον ἐκμεμέτρηκας βίον,
Ὅσος διῆλθε θυσιῶν ἐμοὶ χρόνος.
Δὸς τὴν χάριν, δός; ἢ τάφῳ μ' ἄλλος δότω;
515 Ταύτην ὁρίζω τῆς ἀπειθείας δίκην.
Δὸς τάς βραχείας ἡμέρας τῷ λειφάνῳ
Τά δ' εἰσέπειτα σοί φίλως βουλευτέα.

[239] Ibid.

or "to consider".[240] In his opinion, the first verse thus would not refer to the life of young Gregory, but to that of the father himself. The old bishop would be inviting his son to consider well the great age of his father; the time for offering sacrifices has passed for him. Jan Stiltinck also proposes the following translation:

> Necdum tantam penitus considerasti vitam:
> Mihi praeteriit quodcumque tempus sacrificandi.[241]
> (You have not fully realized the length of my days;
> for me, the time of sacrifices is gone forever.)

With this call for a changing of the guard, Gregory the Elder would have touched the heart of his son at the sensitive point: where the other arguments had failed, the plea of an old father aspiring to rest would thus have succeeded. One would agree that the argument is a likely one. It remains to be seen which one of the two translations is truly in conformity with the thought of the author. We do not believe that the dispute can be resolved; it will probably remain a moot point for a long time to come. In the absence of a satisfactory solution, we think it best to leave the problem between brackets.

Which is why we take the liberty of proposing to the reader our commentary on the baptismal catechesis independently from the issue of Gregory Nazianzen's birth before or after his father's episcopal ordination.[242]

---

[240] J. Stiltinck, *Dissertatio de tempore natali S. Gregorii Nazianzeni* in *Acta Sanctorum Sept.* III (1820), pp. i–xviii. The dissertation aims to prove that Gregory was born before the ordination of his father. C. Knetes reaches the same conclusion ("Ordination and Matrimony in the Eastern Orthodox Church", JTS 11 [1910], pp. 484–85).

[241] J. Stiltinck, *Dissertatio*, p. xi B.

[242] About this passage of the poem *De vita sua*, Joannou points out that the word θυσιῶν, at verse 513, does not mean "sacrifices of the altar" but "my sacrifices", "my pains" (Joannou, II, p. 227, n. 1). Cf. also *Oratio* 16, 2, in which the word θυσιῶν also describes the sacrifice of the heart (PG 35, 936b).

If one accepts this meaning, the controversy aroused by verses 512–13 of the *De vita sua* seems to collapse by itself. It is on the basis of this remark by Joannou that we have suggested the following translation:

> You have not yet lived a life so long
> that the time of sacrifices should be over for me.

Thus, Gregory's father would have seen the gift of his son to the priestly ministry as a personal offering (sacrifice).

CONCLUSION OF SECTION A

With the Council of Carthage presided over by Genethlius in 390 the first part of our inquiry comes to an end. Sparse during the 2d and 3d centuries, the documents become more numerous as the Constantinian Church, living now in broad daylight, undertakes to structure her organization and to express to herself the riches of her patrimony. Of varying importance, these documents belong to the most variegated literary genres: scriptural commentaries, homilies or simple patristic references, *logia* credited to the apostles, conciliar texts and decretals of the Roman pontiffs. The last two categories of texts are obviously the only ones that can inform us with certainty on the state of the legislation regarding clerical continence in the various provinces of the Empire.

In this respect the Council of Elvira, around the year 300, inaugurated the series of Western laws, among which testimonies known by us are also again canon 29 of the Council of Arles (314), extending the discipline to the whole of the Roman patriarchate, the letters of Pope Siricius to Himerius of Tarragona as well as to the African bishops and the episcopates of the various provinces (*Directa* and *Cum in unum* decretals), the *Dominus inter* decretal of that time's Roman synod, and, lastly, canon 2 of the Council of Carthage. A great continuity of view is expressed in them, both in the indissociable grouping of the three higher ranks of the clergy and in the sanctions taken against the guilty parties, as well as in the theologico-scriptural motivations at the root of the prescribed demands. The canon voted in Africa at the proposal of Epigonius does somehow synthesize the heritage of at least a century of disciplinary development and summarizes this longstanding tradition in succinct formulas.

As far as the East is concerned, a difference appears with the law of the Council of Ancyra (314), which might have authorized deacons to make an express request at the time of ordination to get married. As we have said, however, this document can be interpreted in the same vein as can the ordinances in force in the prefectures of Italy and Gaul, and it can confirm the existence of a Western-type regulation in the Pontus diocese. Generally speaking, as mentioned previously, "the disciplinary content of the Ancyra canons is to be linked to that of the Elvira canons especially, but also to that of Arles".[243] Whatever the case may be, the

---

[243] Joannou, I, 2, p. 55.

exception stipulated in Ancyra concerned just the deacons—and only some of them—and left open the question of bishops and priests. The latter was tackled at the Council of Neocaesarea (314–25), which determined canonical penalties for the priests who violated the prohibition of marriage, but which also left open the problem whether married clerics were allowed to use their conjugal rights. These two Eastern canons, having the same date and the same geographical origin, are the only legislative documents of that period that give us data on the status of the discipline in the Greek-speaking provinces. One must give up, once and for all in our opinion, the so-called testimony of the Synod of Gangres (340), aimed at the Encratist heresy and shedding no direct light on research about clerical continence. As to the anecdote of Paphnutius' intervention at the Council of Nicaea, its fictional nature could not be doubted by any serious historian of our time. It did not play a role in the history of the early centuries in any case, neither in the East nor in the West, and would not be used as an argument in debates until the 11th century and later at the time of the Protestant Reformation. The totality of the conciliar documents is organized with a coherence going against the meaning indicated by the problematic Paphnutius. If we limit ourselves to the legislative sources, the East thus offers only two indications (Ancyra and Neocaesarea) opposed to well-developed Western texts. This is not much and is quite limited in time and space. Besides Pontus, what do we know about the canonical measures inside the great prefectures of the East and Illyria that, since, Diocletian, were under the administrative authority of the Greek world? Not Egypt or Asia, nor any one of their seven dioceses (except for Pontus), seem to have enacted laws on the issue under study. It would be a waste of time to go into conjectures, but it is important to point out that the decisions of Siricius and of the African and Roman councils had been the result of a defensive reaction against the attacks of Jovinian or of a need to remedy the disorder in the Christian communities recently issuing from paganism. Now, both of these phenomena were peculiar to the West. At the other end of the Mediterranean, the upheavals caused here and there by the Arian crisis in the discipline of clerical chastity did not seem to lead to specific conciliar decisions. It does seem that canon 3 of the Council of Nicaea (325) was deemed sufficient to serve as a norm of reference for the Easterners who had remained in communion with Rome.

However that may be, it goes without saying the scarcity of official documents does not mean that the matter was unknown in the law of those Churches. Quite to the contrary, patristic testimonies, more numerous there than in Italy or Africa, were frequently written in the context of a discipline similar to that prescribed by Siricius and his colleagues.

Origen in Egypt, Eusebius in Caesarea, the anonymous editor of the *canones ecclesiastici Ss. Apostolorum*, Ephraem the Syrian too, in his way, and also Epiphanius of Constantia, as well as Jerome of Bethlehem—all give the strong impression that not only customs but also genuine laws defined for deacons, priests, and bishops of their countries obligations similar to those of Western communities. And the discussion of the *Stromata* of Clement of Alexandria, of the 12th catechesis of St. Cyril of Jerusalem, of the letter of St. Athanasius to Dracontius, of the canon of St. Basil in his letter to Amphilochius, and of other controverted passages of St. Gregory Nazianzen, far from weakening this feeling, did, rather, lead us to the conclusion that each of those various authors brought a stone to the historical reconstruction suggested by their Eastern contemporaries. At the level of the concrete situations, the Armenian Katholikos of the 4th century seemed in their turn to have been privileged witnesses to a history able to confirm that there was then in the East a rule of continence identical to that obtained in the Western Churches.[244]

This body of convergences strongly inclines us to think that a rather broad consensus prevailed in the Christian world at that time and that the continence imposed on the ministers of the altar was seen as a duty, the infraction of which was illicit.

The contents of the documents that opine differently or indirectly for the discipline of continence imposed on clerics of the higher ranks of the hierarchy has provided us along the way with various information whose essence we will summarize.

Many deacons, priests, and bishops were men bound by marriage. That situation was undoubtedly created by the dearth of single vocations, but more so, it must be stressed, by the dignity of the sacrament binding Christian couples, the early Church being pleased to honor it in such a way as to oppose the errors of the Encratists and the Cathars. Quite far from deeming marriage incompatible with the priestly state, the religious leaders wanted, on the contrary, to emphasize the greatness of human marriage by recruiting ministers among married men.

Being firm on this principle, Constantinian Christianity was equally so when it came to establishing a distinction between marriage and the use of marital rights after ordination. The candidates were not required to be single, but if they were married, their rule of life from then on would be the observance of continence. We discover with no small admiration this great number of men and women renouncing the legitimate joys of home to answer the call of the Church. That was a difficult heroism, not frightening for survivors of the persecutions, but in our

---

[244] See above, pp. 129–30.

opinion it cannot be explained by mere considerations drawn from historical conjecture.

What the texts teach us is that the entire ecclesial organization in matters of priestly selection is meant to depend on the Pauline principle of *unius uxoris virum*. The apostolic criterion is variously interpreted as to the meaning of the phrase μιᾶς γυναικὸς. Ambrose and Epiphanius, for instance, deduce from it the inadmissibility of remarried widowers to the honors of the ministry, while others like Theodore of Mopsuestia and Theodoret of Cyrus hold the contrary opinion, coming to the defense of all men who had remained faithful to their wives, even if they had remarried [after being widowed]. All agree, however, on preference for single men, as well as on the admission [at least to the diaconate] of monogamists whose [first] wives were still alive—this basic criterion brings forth, each time the question arises, an exegesis tackling the obligations that follow the diaconate in the way we have seen. With the possible exception of the Council of Ancyra, and only for the order of deacons, legislators and various witnesses of the discipline at that time think that St. Paul linked, as early as the reception of the first major Orders, continence and service at the altar, the instruction of *unius uxoris virum* having as a purpose the elimination of candidates with little experience of chastity and not an authorization to have conjugal relations after ordination. According to the formula of Pope Siricius, it is "for the purpose of the continence that they would have to practice" (*propter continentiam futuram*) that the Apostle chose monogamists, but he is quite determined that these men enrolled in the new tribe of Levi would cease to have sexual relations.

Moreover, the epistle to Timothy is very much in tune with the prescriptions of the Old Testament, for the founder of the first Christian communities had brought to a state of perfection—and not suppressed in the least—the ancient Levitical law. Brought forth in response to the attempts at "free decision" on the part of a minority among the clergy who referred to the Jewish priesthood in order to reject the duty of total continence, this hermeneutics of the deep continuity between the two Covenants, stressing the *a fortiori* interpretation implied by the preeminence of the Gospel, is progressively asserting itself as a strength of the argumentation. For them the interpretation of the Pauline directives is not optional, but the only ones who discern it are those who are listening to the living voice of Tradition, echoed by the Apostolic See and the Churches who know themselves to be—and call themselves—its authentic representatives. And with the same awareness of being the authorized interpreters of Scripture, the successors of the apostles read in the first epistle to the Corinthians a foundation of the law they are defending that is just as incontestable in their eyes. Because the lay people are advised to abstain for a while from conjugal life in order to "free themselves for prayer", it is perforce understandable that perpetual prayer is synonymous with daily chastity for those who accept such a responsibility. This is a new *a fortiori* argument, indissociable from the first one and frequently used by the commentators of the 4th century. With the exception of the Johannine pseudologion in the *canones ecclesiastici Ss. Apostolorum*, which might have only instructed priests to observe temporary continence as in the Old Testament, all the authors who tackle this issue reason in the same way. Their perspective is not contingent but looks for a supportive point in the Word of God, the infallible norm of Christian and priestly behavior. For our part, such a reading of Scripture, which the Magisterium of the Church—in the person of those whose charism it is "to read and interpret Holy Scripture with the same Spirit that caused it to be written"[245]—answers for in the 4th century, is a fundamental point in the study of the conditions enabling us to judge whether the discipline of celibacy-continence in major Orders "has been observed by the whole Church and always kept", and, on this basis, it can effectively be regarded as an unwritten tradition of apostolic origin.[246]

All this explains that one does not find in the history of the early centuries any notion of evolution, according to which the discipline of clerical continence would have been accepted little by little under the pressure of currents favorable to virginity. If such had been the case, there would have been formulated a genuine law of celibacy in the strict sense of the term as we know it today, not a recruiting policy opening the doors to men bound by marriage. It is not the original nature of service at the altar, but the evangelical counsel inviting "some men to become eunuchs for the sake of the Kingdom of heaven" that would have been the determining motivation. And we cannot see what kind of ruling can have transformed such a counsel into a *precept* when numerous patristic writings on virginity conscientiously treasure that counsel's particular value as a virtue that can be pursued only through the exercise of a free will. It is still harder to see that the specific law of continence, supposing that it was promulgated at a later date, could immediately have been accompanied by severe canonical penalties, as was the case with the Council of Elvira. It would be at least a lack of wisdom not to allow for transitions in the case of obligations so difficult for human nature. And, finally, it is totally impossible to see the reasons for this

[245] Vatican II, Dogmatic Constitution *Dei verbum* II, 10, 12.
[246] See above, pp. 61–62.

insistence in linking the discipline to the very origins of the Christian priesthood if the general climate of the time, the increasing esteem for virginity, were enough to cross such a threshold.

The general climate of the legislative era in the 4th century, especially in the West, becomes clear, quite to the contrary—which is rather remarkable—as a violent crisis shaking the very foundations of religious life and the ecclesiastical organization. All the values connected with chastity are undermined by the Jovianist hurricane, convents are emptying, nuns and monks are getting married. Added to these unforeseen upheavals are difficulties for the young Churches of Gaul and Spain, more vulnerable to the solicitations of the surrounding paganism. While Italy sees most of her clergy remaining faithful, in spite of violent attacks of heresy, this is not the case in other areas, where the complaints of Pope Siricius show many grave faults. All in all, this is not the progression of a movement in favor of continence but rather a protest against it.

It is difficult to imagine, in such an atmosphere, that the first laws (known to us) imposing sexual abstinence on clerics could have been the fruit of a slow maturation, brought to term thanks to propitious conjectures. The opposite is true. The legislators want to contain a flood threatening a discipline that they see as a tradition, and they are concerned by the questioning of the principles at its origins. And the vigor of their vindication, the severity of the laws, is only equal to the conviction that these men have of being the guardians of an ancient patrimony; they would have been quite surprised had they been told that they had fathered a legislation they fought so hard to preserve. After all due consideration, what they explain themselves seems to be, in our eyes, the best explanation of the complex phenomenon characterizing that period. Those Fathers of a troubled era could not have imposed on clerics the heavy burden of continence if they had not had the conviction of being accountable to the apostles for the fidelity of their teaching. Neither Jovinian and his disciples nor the confusion of many minds, and not even the laxity of mores, could do anything against their certitude. Let us note that we see here an adequate application of the "principle of progressive explicitation", according to which certain points of ecclesial discipline existed before their canonical expression, the latter having occurred only with the passage of time and under the pressure of particular historical circumstances.[247]

Independent, though without exclusion, of course, of the motivations proper to monastic life, the obligations of clerics were justified at the time by the original function of the priestly ministry. The Old as

[247] See above, pp. 62–63.

well as the New Testament, and the passage from one to the other, sustains a reflection which discovers in the necessity of perpetual prayer the necessity of uninterrupted continence. The sixth homily of Origen on Leviticus regarding this topic is rather remarkable. It is the example of the great leaders of God's people that inspired the master of Alexandria; ambassadors of Yahweh, delegates of their brothers to the Almighty, Moses and Aaron fulfilled that double task, being responsible every day for Israel's destiny. Their lives, shared between divine audiences and prophecy, that sovereignly efficacious instrument of politico-religious education, are the prototypes of the priestly mission. The success of the Exodus depended on their intercession; the future of the Church now depends on the mediation of the priests of Jesus Christ. No more than Moses could afford to let his arms drop can the new leaders of the community let go. Should they weaken, "the invisible Amalekites who are the demons" would promptly win the victory. On the other hand, the priests' perseverance in prayer is the safe guarantee of the multitudes' salvation. One could not conceive a higher responsibility. The whole theology of the altar service will be governed by this principle. And the obligation of chastity appears as an indispensable corollary. Being permanently in God's presence, for the people he leads, the minister of the New Covenant does not have the leisure needed for married life, the freedom to be occupied with what would henceforth alienate his spiritual energies. Ephraem, Jerome, Ambrose, Siricius—all advocates of clerical continence—are only repeating, in different words, this leitmotiv borrowed from Scripture. The key to priestly discipline is this acute sense of the importance of prayer, praise, and adoration, of course, but also supreme politics in which are treated and decided all major human affairs.

It is important to stress that being ambassadors of the two parties face to face, the Almighty on the one hand and all men on the other, bishops, priests, and deacons must assume on their side the best possible opportunities for ensuring the right course of history. Even if it requires the resources of human intelligence and activity, the latter is essentially in the hands of God, and the leaders of the Church know that approaching the "Holy" is reserved for holiness. This is a demanding concept that taints with "defilement" activities that are otherwise excellent, worthy of honor and esteem, when they are seen from the simple human viewpoint.

Could the exercise of sexuality, even in marriage, be justified from such a perspective? The answer given by many Fathers of the early centuries is negative. In their eyes, it is not anthropology that decides the conditions for a dialogue with the divine, but the very Word of God. Or, to put it better, theology reveals its true nature to man and marks the limits separating him from the inaccessible.[248] This "total" anthropology puts its subject in contradiction with itself, affecting human values with an ambivalent sign; and the influence this has on language is not surprising. The marriage bed, ennobled by the sacrament (Heb 13:4), does not escape this ambivalent attitude, and the same ones who defend the dignity of marriage against Encratite errors do not hesitate to use words like "defilement" when referring to the sexual act. But it would be putting a grave error into their mouths were we to equate what the Fathers mean by "defilement" with the sort of bodily impurity the Levites referred to when they talked, for example, about the spilling of a man's seed. Suffice it to convince us to the contrary, were we to read the picturesque letter St. Athanasius wrote to the monk Ammun, where Athanasius realistically does not mince words.[249] When "defilement" is mentioned, it is because the sanctuary where the liturgy is celebrated is not, to the Fathers' minds, a suitable place to bring even the thought of activities whose whole value is merely earthly, and it would be difficult to find words that would express this idea in a genteel way. Both the nobility of the conjugal act and its unsuitability to be brought within the sanctuary are true things, and the Fathers believed both were true. Although they tried with all their might to explain the problem correctly, they were not always successful. Could they—or anyone—have been?

St. Jerome will be more fortunate, as we will see, when looking at the example of the Lord and his mother, to find in them the living principles of virginity and priestly recruitment, but the catechesis of St. Cyril of Jerusalem already shows that the discipline of clerical continence was anchored, without it always being explicit, in the model of the first priest, the living norm more expressive than all justifications. Beyond the apostles, and at the very moment of the change from the Old Covenant, Jesus himself justifies the new order by his very existence. If the chastity of his priests bears witness to his virginal conception, they cannot, on the other hand, not live in continence because they are closely linked to his mediator role.

The service of the altar, privileged exercise of this mediation,[250]

---

[248] This is what Ambrosiaster will express in a rather balanced way: "Compared to the stars, the light of a lamp is but fog; while compared to the sun, the stars are obscure; and compared to the radiance of God, the sun is but night. Thus are the things which, in relationship to us, are licit and pure, and are as if illicit and impure with respect to the dignity of God; indeed, no matter how good they are, they are not appropriate to the person of God" (*Quaestiones Veteris et Novi Testamenti*, 127. CSEL 50, 415. See above, pp. 224–25).

[249] Joannou, II, pp. 63–71.

[250] Purposely we do not use the phrase "ritual continence", which is loaded with pagan or philosophical (especially stoic) echoes that are not always in tune with the spirit of

demands the same obligations from all, starting from the moment that one is consecrated to it. With a constant agreement the documents associate in this way the three higher ranks of the clergy—deacons, priests, and bishops—under the same regulation. Indissociable in their functions, so too are they, as a consequence, regarding the type of chastity required for the liturgical universe. The exception provided for at the Council of Ancyra for a certain category of deacons, if there was such a thing, is only stressing by its unusual feature the universality of the rule. The principle used to justify continence led logically to an extension of the discipline to all the clerics attached in one way or the other to the service of the sacred mysteries (salvific intercession for the people of God, exercised *in persona Christi*). Being less and less seen as a servant of the temporal needs of the community, as were the Seven appointed by the apostles, but very soon entrusted, as a second, with the responsibility of priestly mediation, the deacon was inevitably entering a sphere in which the exercise of sexuality took on a negative value. The same phenomenon would later attract the subdiaconate into the orbit of continence, as we will see below.

We must also note about that period the admission of multiple infractions. It was not without reason that the councils intervened and promulgated severe sanctions. Epiphanius, Ambrose, and Siricius openly admit that many clerics, including bishops, continued to have relations with their wives and to sire children. That situation saddened them but did not impress them too much. Heresy or human weakness, the causes of such disorders were for them stimulants to reaction, and react they did with the awareness that it was not up to the Church to modify the status quo. The latter is a heritage of sorts, transmitted since the apostles; what is new is not the discipline, but the change that some would like to bring to it.

Summarizing in a formula laden with tradition the feelings of their predecessors, the Africans of 390 expressed what was for them the truth

---

Christianity. We prefer to speak, with the Fathers themselves, of "the service of the altar", and of "the priestly ministry", when we are referring to the central motivation invoked for the obligation of celibacy-continence. It is the liturgy, and the Eucharistic liturgy in particular, that, making the Paschal mystery become a reality, leads the Christian people and, in a special and permanent role, "the servant of the altar" to an identification with Christ praying and offering himself to the Father for the salvation of the world. Christ himself is present, God-Man, associating his ministers with his person and his sacrifice, and not an impersonal or abstract divinity generating irrational taboos. There is as much difference between "ritual continence" and the celibacy-continence of the priests of Jesus Christ as there is between the pagan rituals, no matter how respectable they are, and the sacrifice of the Cross.

of history: "What the apostles taught and antiquity itself observed, we too must keep" (Ut quod apostoli docuerunt, et ipsa servavit antiquitas, nos quoque custodiamus). The inquiry we conducted in the various regions of the Christian world, trying to unravel the complex intricacies of the problems, brings us back to that sentence. It seems to us that the affirmation of the Fathers of Carthage is not contradicted but rather confirmed by the documents of the early centuries and can be a useful conducting wire to go back to the origins of the law.

The second part of our records, extending to the Quinisext Council of 691, will open on the morrow of the Synod of Genethlius. It will provide us with the complementary information that is needed to judge the problem better.

From the Year 390 to
the End of the 7th Century

From 390 to the End of the 5th Century

1. THE ROMAN PONTIFFS

Innocent I (401/2–417)

Born in Albano, Innocent succeeded Anastasius I in the month of December 401 (or 402) and died on March 12, 417, at the end of a pontificate that remains, like that of St. Leo, one of the greatest in the history of the early centuries. In one of his letters St. Jerome affirms that Innocent was "the successor and the son of Anastasius". There would be nothing incredible in that. We also know the case of Pope Hormisdas (514–23), father of Pope Silverius (536–38), and that of Pope Felix II (483–92), who was the great-grandfather of St. Gregory the Great (590–604).

During his agitated reign (the barbarians were invading the West), Innocent I had to respond to various consultations from bishops having recourse to the Apostolic See on matters of discipline. The continence of clerics remained a concern. Three letters from the successor of Siricius, addressed to Victricius of Rouen, Exupery of Toulouse, and two bishops of Calabria (Maximus and Severus), indicate the proper behavior and the motives justifying in his eyes the maintenance of the former regulations. Directly inspired by the *Directa* decretal to Himerius of Tarragona and the *Cum in unum* decretal to the African bishops—they duplicate them literally at times—these answers of the Pope confirm the continuity of views animating the Roman pontiffs.

Here are the passages of this correspondence related to priestly chastity:

Letter to Victricius of Rouen (February 15, 404)

Moreover, the Church must absolutely maintain what is worthy, pure, and honest, to wit: the priest and the deacon must have no relations with their wives, because they are very busy every day with the necessities of the ministry; in fact it is written: "Be holy, for I am Yahweh your God." Indeed, if, in the past, the priests of God did not leave the temple during the year of their tours of duty, as we read about Zechariah, and had no contact with their households—these to whom the use of marriage had been permitted so as to ensure their continuance, no one [then] having the right to belong to the priesthood if he were not of the tribe and the race of Aaron—how much more reason do they have—from the day of their ordinations—to observe chastity, these priests and deacons whose priesthood or ministry is not hereditary and for whom there could not be a day without their [celebrating] the divine sacrifice and administering baptism? Indeed, if Paul writes to the Corinthians, "Abstain [from each other] for a while so as to free yourselves for prayer" and recommends this to lay people, how much more then must priests, whose function is to pray and to offer ceaseless sacrifice, always abstain from a [relation] of that nature. If anyone has been soiled by carnal concupiscence, with what audacity would he dare to offer the sacrifice? Or with what conscience does he believe [his prayers] would be granted when it is said: "All is pure to the pure, but to those who are defiled and have no faith, nothing is pure"? But [this one] believes, perhaps, that this thing is permitted because it is written: "the husband of an only wife". [The Apostle] did not talk about a man persisting in his desire to beget, but with regard to the continence [to be observed] in the future. In effect, he did not admit those who lacked perfect bodily integrity, he who said: "I should like everybody to be like me"; and he speaks even more openly: "But those who are unspiritual cannot please God; as to you, you are not any more unspiritual, but spiritual."[1]

Letter to Exupery of Toulouse (February 20, 405)

You have asked what behavior one must have with regard to the men who exercise the functions of deacon or priest and do not keep or have not kept continence, begetting children. The teaching of the divine laws with regard to them is very clear, and Bishop Siricius, of blessed memory, has set forth obvious instructions: those who do not observe continence, while they are established in such functions, must be deprived of all ecclesiastical dignity and must not be admitted to the ministry; the exercise of this ministry is, indeed, reserved only to the continent. There is indeed an old and holy law that has absolute authority and thereby was kept since the beginning:

---

[1] *Epist. ad Victricium episcopum Rothomagensem*, IX, 12. PL 20, 475c–77a (JW 286).

during the year of their tours of duty, the priests were ordered to live in
the Temple in order to keep themselves pure and purified of all defilement
by being at the service of the holy sacrifices and in order to obtain divine
favors; one did not have the right to admit [to the celebration of the]
sacrifices those who had carnal intercourse, even with their wives, for it
is written: "Be holy, because I am holy, I Yahweh your God." If conjugal
relations were permitted to these men [of the old law], it was so that they
could ensure their continuation, for no one was accepted for the priesthood
if he belonged to another tribe. How much more so must they, starting
from the day of their ordinations, observe chastity, these priests and deacons
whose priesthood or ministry is not hereditary, and for whom there is not
one day without their having to offer the divine sacrifice or administer
baptism. Indeed, if Paul writes to the Corinthians: "Abstain [from each
other] for a while, to free yourselves for prayer", and recommends this to
lay people, how much more so should the priests, whose function it is to
pray and ceaselessly offer the sacrifice, abstain continually from a relation
of that kind. If anyone is defiled by carnal concupiscence, with what
audacity would he dare offer the sacrifice? Or with what conscience, what
merit, does he believe his prayer would be granted, when it is said: "All
is pure to the pure, but to those who are defiled and have no faith, nothing
is pure"? But does [this one] believe, perhaps, that this thing is permitted
because it is written: "the husband of an only wife"? [The Apostle] did
not talk about a man who would persist in his desire to beget, but with
regard to continence [to be observed] in the future. Indeed, he did not
admit those who did not have a perfect bodily integrity, he who said: "I
would like everybody to be like me"; and he speaks even more openly
when he says: "[a man] who has children", not "[a man] who begets
[children]"; these are two separate things and quite distinct. Well, if it is
proven that this rule of ecclesiastical life, as well as the discipline that
spread in the [various] provinces since Bishop Siricius, has not reached the
awareness of some, their ignorance will be taken into account, and they
will be forgiven, on the condition that they undertake from now on to
abstain from [conjugal relations]; let them thus keep the ecclesiastical ranks
in which they would have been found, but they will not be permitted to go
higher; they have to consider it a favor that they are not losing the place they
occupy. But if it is discovered that they were aware of the rule of life sent
by Siricius and did not immediately reject the desire of passion, they must
by all means be rejected [from the ministry]; after having been apprised
of the warning [sent by Siricius], they decided that they preferred pleasure.[2]

Letter to Maximus and Severus, bishops in Calabria (401–7)

No priest should be unaware of the rule of ecclesiastical canons; it is quite
a dishonor when a pontiff does not know it, especially when religious lay

[2] *Epist. ad Exuperium episcopum Tolosanum*, I, 2. PL 20, 496b–98a (JW 293).

people know it and think that it should be observed. Our son Maximilian, involved in all kinds of matters, has filed a complaint, as you can see from the enclosed document. Guided by the zeal of faith and of discipline, he cannot stand by and let the Church be defiled by unworthy priests who, while exercising their priesthood—as he affirms—have begotten children. I would not allow myself to talk about this if I did not know that Your Prudence has a perfect knowledge of the law. And this is why, my very dear brothers, after having examined the text of the enclosed document, you will order that all those who are known to have committed such actions be exposed: you will discuss the accusations made against these priests; if it is possible to convict them [of fault], let them be excluded from the priestly function, for those who are not holy cannot touch holy things; and let them become strangers to the ministry that they defiled through an illicit life.[3]

These texts do not call for long commentaries. In essence they are, as their author himself wants it, a reprise of the instructions already formulated by Siricius and include the same theologico-scriptural considerations. St. Paul and Leviticus remain the cornerstones of such a *fortiori* argumentation. The discipline of clerical continence is founded, as Innocent and his predecessor saw it, on the divine law's authority ("De his divinarum legum manifesta est disciplina"). The Roman Pontiff is not its master but its interpreter. Hence the firmness of his interventions in response to numerous and complex human situations that would probably have led to compromise had this been a matter of pure ecclesial discipline. The only thing that is tempered is the severity of the sanctions, because of the good faith of many of the clerics found to be guilty. While Siricius demanded that they resign, Innocent takes extenuating circumstances into account for some of them: those who had no knowledge of Siricius' decrees will not be excluded from the clergy, but could be kept in their functions on condition that they amend their lives. This measure of exception conceded to the clergy of Toulouse, however, is not to be found in the letter to the bishops of Calabria. Writing to bishops Maximus and Severus, the Roman Pontiff posits as a principle that no priest should be unaware of the ecclesiastical canons. The indulgence granted to regions that are far from Rome was probably not meant for the provinces of the Italian peninsula. In conclusion, let us keep in mind the close kinship of thought between Innocent I and his predecessor in the Apostolic See.

This concern for continuity does explicitly proceed in Pope Innocent from his conviction to act with the full authority of the apostles' successor. In many circumstances he encouraged and congratulated the bishops of

---

[3] *Epist. ad Maximum et Severum episcopos per Brittios.* PL 20, 605b–c (JW 315).

Christendom who turned to him in order to solve important difficulties "as to the head and summit of the episcopate" (*quasi ad caput atque ad aciem episcopatus*).[4] We know that he exercised that right of intervention of which he was aware even in the affairs of the East; for instance, he gave his support to St. John Chrysostom when the latter was deposed by the Synod at the Oak. Truth to tell, one does not find under his pen any reference to clerical continence as such when he dealt with the Churches of those regions. But the emphasis with which he claimed for the Roman See a universal right of control and the theologico-scriptural foundation—thus independent from local contingencies—on which he deemed the obligation of continence imposed on the ministers of the Church to be established, cannot fail to generate a question. Would he not have written to the bishops of the East in the same terms as to a Victricius of Rouen or an Exupery of Toulouse if the situation of the clergy in those regions had been perceived by him as it was in Gaul, i.e., contrary to the ancient traditions? Must we think that he recognized in those Churches customs other than those he demanded the Western ones to keep unconditionally, with reference to Scripture and the apostolic tradition? This point seems worthy of attention.

St. Leo the Great († 461)

Born in Tuscany, Leo was the archdeacon of the Church of Rome when he was elected to succeed Sixtus (432–40) on Peter's Chair. He was then between forty and fifty years old. The twenty-one years of his pontificate, known to us mostly thanks to his speeches and correspondence, are among the most important in the history of the Church. St. Leo and St. Gregory were the only popes to whom posterity has given the adjective "great". In 1754, Benedict XIV proclaimed him a doctor of the Church. He died on November 10, 461.

It is commonplace to recall the sovereign pride with which St. Leo exalted the greatness of the priesthood. Amid the countless crises that he had to face, he never lost sight of this primary concern in his universal responsibility: the honor and dignity of the clergy. Many letters bear witness to this; sent to all the corners of the empire, here to enliven faith, there to specify a point of discipline, relentlessly they exhort the elite of the Christian people.

The issue of clerical continence provided him with the opportunity for two interventions, one in Illyria and the other in Gaul, in which he

---

[4] *Epist. ad Felicem episcopum Nucerinum.* PL 20, 603a (JW 314).

confirmed the traditional discipline by stipulating its scope and bringing to light the spirit that was to guide, in his eyes, the observance of the law.

Letter to Anastasius of Thessalonika (446?)

From the bishop of Thessalonika, whom he had appointed his vicar in Illyria, the Roman Pontiff asks an extension to subdeacons of the rule of continence:

> Indeed, if those who do not belong to the Order of clerics are free to enjoy conjugal relations and to beget children, we must, in order to manifest [what is] the purity of a perfect continence, not permit carnal relations even to subdeacons: "so that those who have [a wife] be as if they did not have one" and those who do not have one remain single. If it befits this Order—the fourth starting from the top—to observe [continence], how much more so the first, the second, and the third must observe it; let no one be deemed apt for the Levitical or priestly dignity or for the supreme dignity of the episcopate if it is found that he has not yet put an end to conjugal pleasure.[5]

Here, then, the Roman Pontiff endorses the law of continence, as recently formulated by Church councils in Africa, applied to subdeacons.[6] The reason he gives is that the subdiaconate represents the "fourth Order" within the Church's hierarchy. This definition suggests that the subdiaconate had some functions in common with the three higher degrees of Holy Orders; very likely St. Leo himself is, in this instance, of the opinion that the level of liturgical function immediately preceding the reception of deacons' Orders associates a cleric with the ministry of the altar. Those whose hands "touch the holy Mysteries" are for that reason obligated to the duty that belongs to that ministry's character of holiness.

It should be noted that when the Pope places upon the subdeacons of Illyria the obligation to observe continence, it is not his intention to inaugurate a new discipline above and beyond what was already being required of them. The way Pope St. Leo expresses himself simply shows that the rule was valid also for the Church of Thessalonika. There is every reason to suppose that this practice was already current in the Roman world. Because the discipline was relatively new as far as the canonical jurisprudence of the period was concerned, it may well be that there had been a change in the status of subdeacons. It is reasonable to think that until the early years of the 5th century, the subdiaconate constituted a

---

[5] *Epist. ad Anastasium Thessalonicensem episcopum*, IV. PL 54, 672b–73a (JW 411).
[6] This deals with the Councils of Carthage of 401 and 419. See below, pp. 266ff.

kind of senior grade embracing all levels of liturgical service below the major Order of the diaconate, or else that, while still above lectors, porters, or cantors, subdeacons might not quite have attained the status accorded to the sacred ministers.[7] That subdeacons are now being called to the duty of continence, a duty that thus far has been reserved to the sacred ministers, suggests that it is precisely at this time that the functions of subdeacons began to be raised to the dignity of what we today would call major Orders. As some fifth-century Churches were still exempting subdeacons from the obligation to perfect chastity, it would be understandable that this promotion did not occur equally in all parts of the Christian world.[8]

To extend the law of continence to the "fourth Order" is to maintain it all the more, as the Roman Pontiff stresses, for the first, the second, and the third. The law is to be interpreted in various ways depending on the family situation of the individual: single before his ordination to the subdiaconate, the cleric will have to remain so from then on; married, let him live according to the recommendation of the Apostle: "Ut et qui habent, sint tanquam non habentes" (1 Cor 7:29). One could argue about the relevance of this verse of the first epistle to the Corinthians to the total continence demanded from clerics, because St. Paul, addressing himself to lay Christians, never thought of advising them against conjugal life; but when transposing the phrase for the ministers of the altar, Leo the Great is not so much trying to give new foundations to the discipline (they remain implied) but rather defining with the help of Scripture the spirit of detachment required from married men promoted to the priesthood. Adapting spiritual advice offers him the advantage of accepting with flexibility various ways of achieving this detachment and of excluding extreme solutions. Under the concision of the style one perceives the pastoral approach of the great Pontiff and his sense of human realities.

Letter to Rusticus of Narbonne (458–459)

His judgment would be put even more clearly in the response addressed in 458 (or 459) to a letter sent by the bishop of Narbonne asking for

---

[7] The *Apostolic Tradition* of Hippolytus (c. XIV) mentions them explicitly in the list of lower ranks of the ecclesiastical hierarchy (*La Tradition apostolique*, trans. B. Botte, SC ii [1946], p. 43). The *Apostolic Constitutions* attest that their functions varied according to need: they watched over the doors on the women's side (VIII, XXI, 3), were responsible for the sacred vessels (VIII, XXI, 4), poured water on the priests' hands (VIII, XI, 2), and so forth. It was only with the *Ordines Romani* that their role of assistance to deacons was clearly defined in the celebration of the Eucharist. But it is known that the Roman ceremonies did not predate the 8th century.

[8] It seems this was particularly the case in the churches of Gaul. See below, pp. 414f.

advice, and we can see there, without any equivocation, exactly what he meant when he required married clerics to abstain from sexual relations.

> *Inquis. III*: About those who serve at the altar and are married: is it permitted for them to have conjugal relations?

> *Ans.*: The law of continence is the same for the ministers of the altar, for the bishops and for the priests; when they were [still] lay people or lectors, they could freely take a wife and sire children. But once they have reached the ranks mentioned above, what had been permitted is no longer so. This is why, in order for [their] union to change from carnal to spiritual, they must, without sending away their wives, live with them as if they did not have them, so that conjugal love be safeguarded and nuptial activity be ended.[9]

Thanks to his gift for lapidary formulas, St. Leo manages in one sentence to reconcile attitudes that were seemingly incompatible. A cleric must not send his wife away, but live with her as if he did not have one; so that the love of the couple be safeguarded and their embraces brought to an end: "Quo et salva sit charitas connubiorum, et cesset opera nuptiarum." This text, written by one of the greatest popes, attests in a felicitous manner to the trust of the Church in the power of human love, while she is asking of it the most severe renunciation.

In that middle of the 5th century such perspectives are not new. St. Leo is endorsing in a way, with his authority, the views that had already been expressed by the anonymous author of the booklet *De septem ordinibus Ecclesiae* as well as by the contemporary decisions of the 2d Council of Arles.[10] Under his patronage they now become the official norm of behavior. We are, however, entitled to wonder whether their formulation was not the result of certain influences that Pope St. Leo could hardly have ignored. At the beginning of his century there was already in circulation a pseudoapostolic collection introducing, in the form of canons, a broad gamut of disciplinary traditions. Known under the venerable title of *Apostolic Canons*, this compendium enjoyed the prestige attached to its name and was widely circulated without being suspected. Even before being claimed by the Council in Trullo in the 7th century, it was respected by the leaders of the Church as soon as it was published. Now, canon 6 of the famous collection specifically deals with the situation of the wife of a priest or a bishop and formally enjoins against sending her away:

---

[9] *Epist. ad Rusticum Narbonensem episcopum, Inquis. III, Resp.* PL 54, 1204a (JW 544).
[10] See below, pp. 273 and 313–15.

Let no bishop, priest, or deacon send away his wife with the excuse of piety; if he sends her away, let him be excommunicated, and if he persists, let him be deposed.[11]

We will return to the problems caused by the interpretation of this canon.[12] Whatever the meaning that the author himself had in mind, one thing seems almost certain: St. Leo was, with this text, in the presence of a directive claiming to have come from the apostles and thereby to be incontestable. Even if he must denounce other customs, he had to compromise with the "apostolic" interdict. Let no bishop or priest send away his wife with the excuse of piety, said the ancient regulation; a man must not chase away his wife, the successor of Peter would repeat, when he has reached service at the altar. But out of fidelity for what will always be for him a no less inviolable given, he will now live—as the Apostle requests—in perfect chastity: "*ut de carnali fiat spirituale conjugium*". One can certainly imagine other motivations that led St. Leo to harmonize in a difficult balance the double obligation formulated in the letter to Rusticus of Narbonne, but does not its pastoral sense find in the complex heritage of the apostolic laws the opportunity of an enrichment? We are inclined to think so and to consider with all the greater interest his concern for fidelity that the Eastern tradition itself would eventually give up. Claiming for priests and deacons the right to make use of marriage, the Fathers of the Council in Trullo will keep the discipline of conjugal continence for the bishop;[13] now, notwithstanding their solemn profession of attachment to the eighty-five apostolic canons,[14] the legislators of Constantinople will deem it more prudent to forbid "the shepherds beloved of God" to cohabit with their wives. In spite of their protests,[15] they preferred to ignore apostolic canon 6, which was in their opinion a source of too many difficulties. The position of St. Leo, in contrast to theirs, shows a desire of fidelity that is closer to

---

[11] Joannou, I, 2, p. 10.

[12] See below, pp. 311–12.

[13] See below, pp. 399–401.

[14] "This holy council has also made the very fine and important decision that henceforth the eighty-five canons received and confirmed by the holy and blessed Fathers who preceded us and transmitted to us as well, in the name of the holy and glorious apostles, would be kept whole and entire for the salvation of souls and the healing of the passions" (Quinisext Council, can. 2. Joannou, I, 1, pp. 120–21).

[15] "We are not saying this to break or invalidate the apostolic ordinances, but to see to the salvation of the peoples and their progress in virtue, in order not to offer any occasion of blame against the ecclesiastical discipline" (Quinisext Council, can. 12. Joannou, I, 1, p. 139).

the tradition and a daring that finds in this very tradition its reason for facing risks.

2. COUNCILS AND SYNODS

Council of Chalcedon (451)
4th Ecumenical Council

The fourth ecumenical council, called by Emperor Marcian, gathered in Chalcedon in October 451. From five to six hundred bishops participated, effectively presided over by Pope Leo's legates. The Pope ratified the doctrinal decrees and the disciplinary decisions of the Council, with the exception of canon 28, which he rejected as "being in opposition to the canons of Nicaea" and "against the rights of the particular churches". That canon, in addition to an honorific primacy acknowledged to the bishop of Constantinople by the Council of Constantinople of 381, gave to "the new Rome" a patriarchal authority over the metropolitans of the dioceses of Pontus, Asia (Proconsular), and Thracia, and was not approved by Rome until the 13th century.

Canon 14 of the Council of Chalcedon deals in part with the issue of clerical continence and thus finds its place in our records.[16]

Canon 14

Inasmuch as in certain provinces lectors and cantors have been permitted to marry, the holy council has decreed that none of them may marry a heretic woman; those who have had children after having contracted such marriages, if they already have had the children baptized among the heretics, must bring them for communion in the Catholic Church; should the children not yet be baptized, they must not have them baptized among the heretics or give them in marriage to a heretic, Jew, or pagan, unless the person who is to marry the orthodox party promises to embrace the orthodox faith. If anyone goes against this ordinance of the holy council, he will be struck with the canonical penalties.[17]

---

[16] About the question of which session promulgated the disciplinary canons of the fourth ecumenical council, see Joannou, I, 1, p. 68, and also Hefele-Leclercq, II, 1, pp. 649ff. Canon 14 was certainly part of the official collection of the council's acts and as such was ratified by St. Leo.

[17] Can. 14. Joannou, I, 1, p. 80.

It was incidentally that the Fathers of Chalcedon advised us of the permission granted in certain provinces: lectors and cantors may get married—their intention being to recall the decisions of the previous councils regarding marriage with heretics and stipulating the conditions. This information calls for some comments:

It is indirectly confirmed that the other categories of clerics, especially bishops, priests, and deacons, could not enter into marriage after ordination. Because there is no mention of subdeacons, the same law seems to apply to them. As to the problem of conjugal continence, it is beyond the perspectives studied by this decree. While the lectors and cantors who are authorized to marry can of course have children, nothing is said about the matrimonial situation of the other clergy members. We cannot draw any conclusions from this; we can only wonder why there was not at least a mention of the children that the latter could have had before they became deacons. Is this an indication that the candidates directly elected to the higher ranks of the clergy, without having to go through the other stages, were becoming fewer in number?

Concerning the permission to marry granted in certain provinces to lectors and cantors, it seems that the Fathers of Chalcedon are mentioning a relatively new custom. This is rather surprising because up to then we have not seen any document imposing the obligation of celibacy on lower clerics.[18] Still, we must put forward the hypothesis that until a period close to the fourth ecumenical council, it might have become a custom in the Churches, especially in the East, to forbid marriage as soon as one had crossed the threshold of holy Orders.[19] Historical evolution having led certain communities to adopt a more liberal attitude toward lectors and cantors, the special problems created by that situation would then have been discussed at Chalcedon and solved as stipulated in canon 14.

It is also interesting to note that the freedom granted to lectors and cantors seems to have been limited, by the Fathers of Chalcedon, to certain provinces. Now, canon 27 of the *Apostolic Canons*, whose authority was not questioned, makes provision on its part for a similar authorization, but one valid—as a tradition going back to the apostles—for the whole Christian world:

---

[18] The African councils will ask the lectors to marry unless they make a profession of continence. See below, pp. 266–70 and 411.

[19] With the exception of the three Roman legates and two African bishops, all the five or six hundred bishops who came to Chalcedon were from the Eastern provinces. It is therefore likely that their decisions concerned, by priority, the context of those provinces.

For those who have joined the clergy without having been married, we will permit marriage only to the lectors and cantors who desire it.[20]

The Council in Trullo of 692 would confirm explicitly this "apostolic" law.[21] How could it happen that the Greeks and Easterners of Chalcedon, who had more respect than the others for the documents reflecting the tradition of their Churches, submitted only partially to canon 27 of the apostles? It is not very satisfactory to say that they purposely ignored it or minimized it and even less that they simply decided to ignore it totally, if the famous apocryphal compilation was already widely known in the early years of the 5th century, as people seem to think at times.[22] It remains to be seen whether the best explanation for their attitude would not be simply that, when the fourth ecumenical council started, the Syriac collection had not yet been published or was still restricted to some limited circles. Unknown then by the members of the council, it would have remained outside of their deliberations. This could also explain the fact that only some provinces of the Christian world had, in the middle of the 5th century, dared to permit lectors and cantors to marry. Apostolic canon 27 would therefore represent a generalization of the local practices accepted in Chalcedon, a process that would be more normal than the opposite one and rather incomprehensible on the part of the leaders of the Eastern Churches. We may have here an indication helping us find a more precise date for the publication of the *Apostolic Canons.*[23]

AFRICA

17th Council of Carthage

Two hundred seventeen African bishops met in a general council in Carthage on May 25, 419, with Bishop Faustinus, legate of Pope Boniface, presiding. Aurelius, archbishop of Carthage and his colleagues, among them St. Augustine, decided particularly about the attitude to be taken

---

[20]Joannou, I, 2, p. 19.

[21]Can. 6. Joannou, I, 1, pp. 131–32.

[22]The question of the date of the *Canones apostolorum* aroused a long controversy. From the 2d to the 6th century all the hypotheses were studied. After F. X. Funk, *Die apostolischen Konstitutionen* (Rottenburg, 1891), p. 191, the general agreement today is that they date from the first half or the start of the 5th century. See a development on the issue in Hefele-Leclercq, I, 2, pp. 1206ff., and Joannou, I, 2, p. 1.

[23]If one takes into account the date of St. Leo's letter to Rusticus of Narbonne (458 or 459), a letter that seems to be inspired on a precise point by the 6th apostolic canon, it seems possible to locate the time when the pseudoapostolic collection might have been published sometime between the Council of Chalcedon and the year 459. But here again, considering the letter of St. Leo and the 6th apocryphal canon, which depends on which?

in the matter of Apiarius of Sicca. That priest of the Preconsular province had been deposed and excommunicated by his bishop, Urbanus, and then was rehabilitated by the Pope, to whom he had appealed. Pope Zozimus and his successor, Boniface I, had found in his favor on the basis of a Nicaean canon regarding the right of appeal to Rome. Not finding that canon in the copy of the acts of Nicaea kept in Carthage, the African bishops asked for an inquiry with the bishops of Constantinople, to obtain from them true copies of the decisions made by the First Ecumenical Council. All this pertaining to a point of ecclesiastical discipline shows the concern that prevailed in Africa, as in Rome, to conform faithfully to the decrees of Nicaea.

During the same council, the Fathers of Carthage renewed a whole series of ordinances enacted by previous African councils. The collection of canons, numbering 133, is known under the name of *Codex canonum Ecclesiae africanae*. Regarding the continence of clerics, one can read in it five canons, all of which had been promulgated by previous synods: the Council of Carthage in 390, the Council of Hippo in 393, and the Council of Carthage in 401.[24] Here is part of the text:

Codex canonum Ecclesiae africanae

Can. 3: Bishop Aurelius said: In a previous council, when the issue was normalization of the rules of continence and chastity, [the council dealt with] the three Orders that, by virtue of their consecration, are associated by a kind of bond of chastity; I mean the bishops, the priests, and the deacons. The opinion was, as is befitting [their state], that the very holy pontiffs, the priests of God, and also the Levites, i.e., those who are at the service of the divine sacraments, had to observe perfect continence so as to obtain in all simplicity what they asked from God: what the apostles taught, and what antiquity itself observed, we also have to keep.[25]

Can. 4: Faustinus, bishop of the church of Potenza, said: It pleases us that the bishops, priests, and deacons, in other words those who touch the sacred mysteries, guardians of chastity, abstain [from conjugal relations] with their wives. All the bishops declared: We agree that all those who are serving at the altar should keep perfect chastity.[26]

---

[24] For the sake of convenience, we discuss these five canons in the framework of the *Codex canonum Ecclesiae africanae* rather than in a chronological presentation of the councils where they were promulgated. Here is the concordance between the documents of 419 and the original texts from which they were borrowed: *Can. 3*: Council of Carthage under Genethlius (390), can. 2 (1st part). *Can. 4*: Council of Carthage under Genethlius (390), can. 2 (2d part). *Can. 16*: Council of Hippo (393), can. 18. *Can. 25*: Council of Carthage (401), can. 4. *Can. 70*: Council of Carthage (401), can. 4.

[25] Joannou, I, 2, pp. 216–17.

[26] Ibid., pp. 217–18.

Can. 16, 2d part: It was also decided that the lectors who had reached the age of puberty must either marry or make a vow of chastity.[27]

Can. 25: Bishop Aurelius said: As we have dealt with certain clerics, especially lectors, as regards continence with their wives, I would add, very dear brothers, what was confirmed in many synods, that the subdeacons who touch the sacred mysteries, and also the deacons, priests, and bishops, in conformity with the ordinances concerning them, will abstain from their wives "as if they did not have one"; if they do not do so, they will be rejected from any ecclesiastical function. As to the other clerics, they will be compelled to do so only at an advanced age. The whole synod said: What your holiness has regulated in justice, we confirm because it is worthy of the priesthood and pleasing to God.[28]

Can. 70: Moreover, as it was mentioned about the continence of certain clerics with respect to their own wives, it was decided that the bishops, priests, and deacons, in conformity with the decisions concerning them, will also observe continence with their wives; if they do not do so, they will be demoted from their rank. As to the other clerics, they will not be forced to do this, but the practice of each church will be observed.[29]

Canons 3 and 4 being a literal duplication of canon 2 of the Council of Carthage held under Genethlius (390), with which our study started, we will simply ask the reader to go back to the commentary on that canon in Chapter 1.[30]

The three other canons stipulate the discipline in the following manner: Having reached the age of puberty, the lectors are either to marry or to make a profession of continence. The intention of the legislators seems to have been to avoid a situation wherein clergy members would live in a way that could promote misbehavior or would remain undecided for too long a time as to their choice of a state of life. Because no one could be ordained a deacon before age twenty-five (can. 16), there were many years before a young lector would be admitted to the higher ranks of the clergy. In the meantime, he was asked to prove himself: married or continent, he had to bear witness to his aptitudes for the higher functions to which he aspired. It is known that fidelity in monogamous marriage was one of the conditions required among those who, after ordination, would have to commit themselves to total continence. The lector who chose to marry knew what would be asked of him at the time of the diaconate and could reflect at length during his conjugal experience about

[27] Ibid., p. 230.
[28] Ibid., pp. 240–41.
[29] Ibid., pp. 312–13.
[30] See above, pp. 3–8.

the choice that, while still young, he had made in opting for clerical life. As to the others, the profession of continence served as what we call today a formation: during several years he would himself judge, and others would judge for him, his capacities to observe celibacy. The African law seems therefore to have been essentially motivated by pedagogical reasons.

The two canons 25 and 70, voted earlier at a synod held in Carthage in 401, react against a relaxation of the discipline. In the background we discover troubles among the African clergy caused by the Donatist[31] schism. Certain bishops seemed to complain about the "incontinence" of the lectors, a reproach that the council did not, of course, take into account. Nothing prevented married lectors from living with their wives. It was stipulated, however, that the obligation of continence was extended to subdeacons. It is because they "touch the sacred mysteries" that sub-deacons are to be held by the same obligations. It can most likely be thought that until that date, the subdeacons did not form a part of the direct service at the altar, unlike the three higher ranks of the hierarchy, or that the category of subdeacon described all the lower clerics in a general way, without any precise definition.

Violations of the discipline are now accompanied by sanctions, which did not appear to have been provided for at the council of 390. Probably aligning themselves on the regulations of the Church of Rome, the Africans decided that clerics who would be found guilty should be forbidden to exercise their ministry (*ab ecclesiastico removeantur officio*).

The other clerics (i.e., under the Order of the subdiaconate) would not be held to the obligation of continence *nisi maturiore aetate*. This incidental phrase is somewhat enigmatic. Should we understand that, when reaching a mature age, even lower clerics had to live in perfect chastity? Though this seems surprising, it is difficult to interpret it otherwise. The council probably wanted to respond to the requests of some of its members who even complained about the "incontinence" of lectors. We would have here the first law—one that is in fact unique in the annals of the early canonical literature—prohibiting conjugal intercourse to the entire clergy. The only ones to be exempted were the clerics still too young (probably those under the age of twenty-five, the average age for admission to the diaconate) to have such a burden—generally carried by adults—imposed on them. It might be that men in their late twenties or early thirties were then relatively rare in the lower ranks of the clergy, and that measure was meant to encourage them to move up in the Orders

---

[31] Cf. R. Crespin, "Scandales et schismes dans le clergé africain, un grand souci pastoral de saint Augustin" (Doctoral thesis, mimeographed, Lyon, 1960).

by imposing on them all in any case the continence that made them hesitate. It must be noted, however, that this severe regulation did not please everyone, because canon 70 finally left to each Church the freedom to follow its own custom on this point.

SPAIN

1st Council of Toledo (400)

On September 7, 400, a council was held in Toledo, gathering eighteen Spanish bishops with Archbishop Patruinus of Merida presiding. It condemned the Priscillianist errors and adopted two documents regarding the reintegration of the bishops in Priscillian's party. The council also legislated by voting on twenty disciplinary canons.

The first of these canons deals with the problem of clerical continence:

Canon 1

> It seems good that the deacons be men who have kept their integrity by leading chaste and continent lives; even if they have wives, [let such men] be established in the ministry; however, if there are some who, even before the Lusitanian bishops had pronounced the interdict, did not observe continence with their wives, let them not be granted the honor of the priesthood; if a priest, before the said interdict, had children, let him not be admitted to the episcopate.[32]

First the deacons are asked to observe integral chastity; those who, while they have wives, lead a life of continence can be established in the service of the Church.

Measures are then enacted with respect to the deacons and priests who have lived maritally with their wives. If deacons behaved in such a way, even before the sentence pronounced by the bishops of Lusitania, they will not "be granted the honor of the priesthood"; and if priests, before said sentence, have had children, they will not be admitted to the episcopate.

We have no other knowledge about the Synod of Lusitania that is mentioned here.[33] As to the Fathers of Toledo, they meant to refer to dispositions that existed before the sentence pronounced by that synod, for they do not hesitate to pass sentence on infractions against continence

---

[32] Bruns, I, 203.

[33] According to Mansi 3, 998, note to can. 1, this would have been a council held a short time earlier to deal with the Priscillianist errors.

that could have been committed by clerics even before the Lusitanian decrees. A certain indulgence tempered their judgment, probably because there had not been for a long time a Spanish council urging the obligation to continence, and the violators thus had the benefit of extenuating circumstances.[34] Clerics recognized as guilty would not be deposed from their functions: it was simply forbidden to promote them to the next rank.

This canon on clerical continence, the first in the series of twenty canons promulgated in Toledo, follows directly a preface in which the president of the Council and his colleagues declare in which frame of mind they wish to make their decisions. It is rather interesting to find out about it:

> Bishop Patruinus said: Because we have started, all of us, to act in various ways in our respective churches, and this leads to so many scandals breeding schisms, let us decide, if all agree, what should guide bishops in the ordination of [their] clerics; I, for one, deem that we must above all continue to observe the canons of the Council of Nicaea and not to stray from them. The bishops said: We all agree; so that if someone, after having been made aware of the acts of the Council of Nicaea, has the audacity to act against what was decided [by that council], and deems that he is under no obligation to obey them, let [him] be held as excommunicated, unless a fraternal correction leads him to amend his life.[35]

The bishops of Toledo therefore explicitly propose to put an end to "scandalous" variations that have arisen in the method of ordaining clerics; to do so, Patruinus demands fidelity to the regulations of the first ecumenical council ("mihi autem placet et constituta primitus concilii Nicaeni perpetuo esse servanda nec ab his esse recedendum"), and he obtains the unanimous approval of his assistants. Notwithstanding this declaration, it is easy to recognize that the twenty canons of Toledo deal with points that, from what we know, had not been discussed at the Council of Nicaea. The notion of the Spaniards' direct dependence on the ecumenical assembly of 325 is therefore to be excluded. Must one then think that their intention to remain faithful to it was purely perfunctory? But how could they have hoped for an adhesion on the part of

---

[34] It is known that the first recorded Spanish council that had enacted laws on priestly continence had been, a hundred years earlier, the Synod of Elvira. That the law fell into abeyance or oblivion during that long period of time is not surprising. The *Directa* decretal of Siricius to Himerius of Tarragona, more recent, was certainly not yet known to all. Under such conditions one might think that the Fathers of Toledo desired to take into account the fact that in living with their wives several clerics had acted out of ignorance. Almost at the same date Pope Innocent I manifested a similar indulgence (*Epist. ad Victricium episcopum Rothomagensem.* PL 20, 502b. CC 148, 199).

[35] Bruns, I, 203.

the clergy if the very authority they claimed to have did not in some way justify their legislation? We are rather inclined to think that they were conscious of being faithful, if not to the letter, at least to the spirit of the First Ecumenical Council, and that their reasons to think so were sufficiently grounded as not to lead to criticism. If we are not mistaken, it would be fitting, as they themselves wished to do, to credit their decisions with more value than that granted by a provincial assembly in Toledo, and to place them in the Council of Nicaea's sphere of influence. This viewpoint would have quite important consequences, as can be understood, with regard to the discipline of clerical continence. We can only suggest it. In any case, it would seem rather difficult to imagine that the bishops of Toledo, at the very moment they affirmed their desire to conform with the decisions of Nicaea, could have been able to vote a decree on priestly chastity in a spirit opposed to the intentions of the First Ecumenical Council. Now, such would precisely be the case if the anecdote of Paphnutius' intervention related by Socrates were genuine. Our reservations with regard to that episode find here an additional confirmation.

GAUL

During the 5th century, three Gallic councils made or renewed decisions regarding clerical continence and thus are of interest to our study. The Council of Orange, which met on November 8, 441, in the *Justinianensis* (or *Justianensis*) Church of the diocese of Orange, was presided over by the metropolitan Hilary of Arles. Sixteen bishops, among whom was Eucherus of Lyon (father of Salonius, future bishop of Geneva, and of Veranus, future bishop of Vence), took part in the discussions of this synod leading to the promulgation of thirty canons. A Council whose date cannot be given with precision (between 442 and 506) met in Arles, Hilary presiding, and adopted a series of fifty-six canons, some of which were only the repetitions of previous ordinances. It was the second council legally held in the capital of Narbonnaise II, the first having been the Council of Arles of 314. At the occasion of the feast of St. Martin, in November 461, nine bishops gathered in Tours, around Perpetuus, bishop of that town, and reaffirmed thirteen old prescriptions. The presence of several metropolitans gave particular importance to that Council of Tours.

Council of Orange (441)

Can. 21: It pleases [us] that married men are not ordained anymore to the diaconate unless, with the firm intention of changing their lives, they have first made a profession of chastity.[36]

Can. 22: But if someone is found who, after having received the Levitical blessing, does not observe continence with his wife, let him be forbidden to exercise his ministry.[37]

2d Council of Arles (442–506)

Can. 2: One cannot elevate to the priesthood a man bound by marriage unless he has first converted [to continence].[38]

Can. 3: If a cleric, starting from the Order of the diaconate, dares to take with him a woman to "console himself", let him be rejected from communion. An exception is to be made for his grandmother [mother], sister, niece, or a wife who has converted [to continence]. If she refuses to separate [from the cleric], the woman will also be punished in the same way.[39]

Can. 43: It has seemed good, moreover, according to the decisions of this synod, not to order to the diaconate married men unless, in the firm intention of changing their lives, they first make a profession of chastity.[40]

Can. 44: But if someone is discovered, after having received the Levitical blessing, not to observe continence with his wife, let him be forbidden to exercise his ministry.[41]

1st Council of Tours (461)

Can. 1: In the first place, let the priests and ministers of the Church, of whom it is said "You are the light of the world", therefore lead a very holy life, inspired by the fear of God; let them direct their actions so as to be pleasing to divine clemency and to offer a good example to the faithful.

[36] CC 148, 84.
[37] Ibid.
[38] CC 148, 114.
[39] Ibid.
[40] CC 148, 122.
[41] CC 148, 123.

Just as it [is written]: "Woe to you, because of whom the name of God is blasphemed", they will obtain the glory of immortality, those whose actions benefit the name of God. If the faithful are advised to observe chastity, according to the doctrine of the Apostle, "so that those who have a wife be as if they did not have one", how much more the priests of God and deacons, attached to the service of the divine altar, must practice it; thus they will deserve, thanks to purity of heart as well as of body, that their prayers reach God's ears when they devote themselves to supplicate on behalf of the people; indeed, according to the authorized teaching of the Apostle, "those who are in unspiritual things cannot please God; as to you, you are not of unspiritual but of spiritual things", and again, "all is pure to the pure, but for those who are defiled and have no faith, nothing is pure; even their spirits and their consciences are defiled". Consequently, if a layman is admonished to practice [conjugal] abstinence so as to be answered when he frees himself for prayer and presents his supplications to God, how much more priests and deacons [are obliged]; they must be ready at any moment [to present themselves before God] with assurance, in all purity and cleanliness, in case they would have to offer the sacrifice or baptize should the circumstances call for it. If they defiled themselves through carnal concupiscence, what excuse would they find [for not fulfilling the requested ministry]; with what audacity would they dare [to fulfill it]; with what conscience, what merit, do they believe that they will be answered? [42]

Can. 2: Though it had been decided by the authority of our Fathers that the priest or deacon convicted of having accomplished the act of procreation be rejected from the Eucharistic communion, we have nevertheless decided, for our part, to temper the rigor of that law and to mitigate a decision [that is otherwise] legitimate; let the priest and deacon who remain attached with concupiscence to conjugal life and continue to devote themselves to procreation not be promoted to a higher rank and not have the presumption of offering to God the sacrifice, not take upon themselves the ministry on behalf of the people. Let it be enough for them not to be rejected from communion. [43]

Can. 3: And because it is necessary not to give in to the devil, we decree that the following point should be particularly observed: that clerics should have no familiarity with "outsider" women, so as not to give an excuse for calumnies and suspicions. Because of such circumstances contrary to decency, it frequently happens that the devil, watching like a lion in his den, works at the destruction of God's servants. If a cleric, after the interdiction made by his bishop, persists in being familiar with "outsider" women, let him be rejected from communion. [44]

---

[42] CC 148, 143–44.
[43] CC 148, 144.
[44] CC 148, 145.

The identity of canons 21 and 22 of the Council of Orange on the one hand and on the other of canons 43 and 44 of the 2d Council of Arles has certainly been observed. They all reflect the same law and are accompanied by the same sanction. Married clerics should not be admitted to ordination to the diaconate until after making a profession of continence. This step is described as *conversio* to stress the change of life requested from future deacons. Thus one can probably conclude that subdeacons were not bound, in those areas of Gaul, to the same obligations as deacons, contrary to what occurred in Africa. The required commitment seems to have been an explicit declaration pronounced in the presence of witnesses. It was no longer sufficient to make a tacit profession as was, for instance, still the case at the Synod of Ancyra.[45] It must be noted that these documents are the first in our records to refer to a promise of continence made for its own sake, perfect chastity having been habitually linked ipso facto to receiving Orders. It seems that when they inaugurated this rule, the Fathers of the Councils of Arles and Orange wanted to prevent on the part of some clerics a questioning of the implicitly contracted obligation. Accepted with open eyes before the imposition of hands, the profession could not provide any excuse for possible contestations. No one could argue thereafter that he was ignorant of the law, and that probably justified the gravity of sanctions provided for with regard to deacons returning to marital life with their wives: they would be sent away from their office.

The 2d Council of Arles reiterates the same ordinance with regard to priests: no married man could be elevated to the priesthood without a prior "conversion". Though the decree does not explicitly mention continence, the context leaves no doubt in this respect. Since deacons are the object of a similar decree, it remains obvious that this canon 2 of the Synod of Arles had no intention of indirectly conceding the freedom of conjugal intercourse to higher clerics who are not priests. If priests are specifically mentioned, it is likely because of the numbers of lay people who could have access to the priesthood without having to go first through the diaconate. There was also probably a desire to regulate the situation of married deacons who, before the Council, had not made a formal profession of continence.

The 3d canon of the Council of Arles offers an interesting variation in the rich canonical "literature" devoted to the συνείσακτοι (women admitted to the company of clerics). We recall that the hierarchy was concerned with the issue from the beginning, in order to guard clerics from dangerous or, at the very least, questionable companionships. A

---

[45] See above, pp. 169ff.

decree of the first ecumenical Council of Nicaea (325) had extended to the entire Church a discipline practiced until then in various ways in the Christian world, and led to the long series of similar decisions that we studied above.[46] In this legislative family concerning the συνείσακτοι, a quasi-stereotyped list (mother, sister, aunt, niece, and so on) was regularly used to indicate persons of the female sex authorized to live under the same roof with clerics. Now, while close female relatives are listed very precisely, the texts are silent about the one most closely united with a married man who has joined the clergy: was the wife naturally included in the list, or should we understand that the conjugal continence imposed on the husband and wife from then on made her presence inopportune under the roof of her husband? The synods promulgating or recalling in the clearest terms the obligation of perfect chastity have nothing to say on this point, even though they deal with the συνείσακτοι, and we have explained how this silence brought up the important question of knowing what disciplinary background could have motivated the famous canon 3 of the Council of Nicaea.[47] Here we have, for the first time, a council expressing itself clearly and shedding a noteworthy light on the situation of the wife of a deacon, priest, or bishop: for his "consolation" (in solacio sua), the church minister is free to keep at home his conversam uxorem, just like his close female relatives. The Gallic bishops of the 5th century were favorable to the presence at home of the woman united by the sacred bonds of marriage to a man promoted to the priesthood and were thus showing a less severe attitude than that of the laws prevailing in other regions of the empire.[48]

The condition required for this cohabitation is the "conversion" of the wife, meaning her commitment to continence.[49] United by new bonds—a chastity lived in common—husband and wife found themselves in some way committed to the priestly adventure, the daily presence gaining in quality of love what it had lost on the level of carnal relations. We find ourselves in the perspective evoked by the De septem ordinibus Ecclesiae of pseudo-Jerome,[50] the very same that Pope St. Leo defined: "Et salva sit caritas connubiorum, et cesset opera nuptiarum."

---

[46] See above, pp. 185–95.

[47] See above, pp. 185–95.

[48] St. John Chrysostom, for instance, considered the presence of the bishop's wife in the episcopal residence as a concession to the customs of apostolic times. The discipline of his time, in Antioch and Constantinople, on the contrary, required non-cohabitation. See below, pp. 291–94.

[49] Cf. Hefele-Leclercq, II, 2, p. 462, n. 2: "One called 'conversion' of the husband and wife continence in marriage."

[50] See below, pp. 313–15.

The long decrees of the Council of Tours reiterate the essentials of the theologico-scriptural arguments dear to Siricius and Innocent I, which exempt us from commentaries. Again it is a reminder of the same discipline. Canon 2, though, intends to temper the rigorous sanctions previously decreed against the guilty parties: they will not be admitted to the higher rank and any ministry will be forbidden to them, but they will not be excommunicated. Let us only observe the style of the preface:

> Gathered together in the city of Tours . . . the very holy bishops whose signature is appended herein below have deemed it necessary to confirm by the present text a decision made in agreement with the authority of the Fathers; on certain points of ecclesiastical discipline, a laxity of long duration had indeed favored a modification of the law; [the bishops decided on this] not with the intention of returning to what had previously and illegally been tolerated, but to foresee what could be beneficial to all; [their goal] is to observe the decrees of the Fathers in conformity with evangelical precepts and apostolic doctrine so that the Church of the Lord remain pure and immaculate.[51]

In Gaul, as in Africa and Spain, "a laxity of long duration" had modified the rule of ecclesiastical discipline. The Fathers of Tours decided to restore the discipline without returning to situations that were against the law and that had been previously tolerated, but in the perspective of the future and to everybody's benefit. Their purpose was to keep for the Church of Christ its "immaculate purity" by applying the decrees of the Fathers, which are in conformity with evangelical precepts and apostolic doctrine (*ut secundum evangelica precepta et apostolicam doctrinam patrum statuta servantes, ecclesias Domini pura et immaculata permaneat*). In the manner of the Council of Carthage gathered in 390 and of their many predecessors, the bishops gathered in Tours therefore wanted to link ecclesiastical discipline, especially priestly continence, to scriptural and apostolic origins. Their conviction of being the spokesmen of an ancient tradition is to be taken into account in our study.

ITALY

Council of Turin (398 or 401)

With a real concern to "keep the good of peace as well as traditional discipline and to bring a useful help", Bishop Simplician, who had succeeded St. Ambrose to the See of Milan, gathered a council in Turin "at the request of the Gallic bishops". The date that is generally accepted

[51] CC 148, 143.

today is September 22, 398, but it could be necessary to push it forward to the year 401. This interprovincial Council, one of the most important of its time, had to settle the issue of the Felician schism then dividing the Gallic episcopate and to deal with several matters of ecclesiastical jurisdiction created by the civil reorganization of Gaul at the end of the 4th century. Several points of discipline were also discussed.

Out of the eight canons that have come down to us from that Council is the following one:

> Can. 8: As to those who have been ordained in spite of [this] prohibition, or who, during their ministry, have sired children, the synod decreed with authority that they should not be permitted to reach the higher ranks of the Orders.[52]

The text is meant for clerics who were illegally ordained and "those who sired children while being in the service of the Church". The situation is similar to that of Siricius' time: a discipline demanding clerical continence is in force. Some clerics have violated the discipline by living as husbands with their wives and continuing to beget children. The synod enacts sanctions.

A few remarks are in order:

The canon does not stipulate that this is meant for all clerics without exception or for only the higher ranks of the clergy. However, the use of the word *ministerium*, generally reserved for the ministry of the altar, seems rather to imply that the decree concerns bishops, priests, and deacons. Only a few years after the decretals of Siricius, it would seem difficult for an Italian council to deem that lower clerics should be bound by the duty of continence. The sanctions for the guilty parties are not as severe as the penalties enacted by Siricius. The clerics are not forbidden to exercise their ministry, but only declared as unsuited for higher Orders. It goes without saying that the offense is not legalized by these means; kept in the clergy, the clerics remain from then on subject to the obligations of their state, including continence.

The synodal letter containing the eight canons of the Council of Turin is addressed to the bishops of Gaul.[53] Gathered in a provincial assembly, the Piedmont Fathers legislated for the benefit of Churches over which they normally had no jurisdiction. They did this most likely at the request of the interested parties, but the recourse to their competence seems to indicate that they represented a wider authority than simply a local one.

---

[52] CC 148, 58.
[53] Cf. Hefele-Leclercq, II, 1, pp. 129–33.

As to the issue of clerical continence, their intervention can be well understood only if we look at the background of a discipline that was common to all the Churches (at least in the West). It would be rather difficult to imagine that sanctions could have been enacted against the clergy of Provence in the name of customs specific to the Church of Piedmont.

With the exception of the Council of Chalcedon (451), which, as an ecumenical council, concerns all the Churches of the East and of the West, the only Eastern councils of the 5th century, as far as we know, having made decisions regarding clerical continence are those of the Armenian Church and those of the Persian Church.

ARMENIA

The So-called Canons of Gregory the Illuminator

An Armenian legend has it that the youngest son of Gregory, Aristakes, took part in the Council of Nicaea in 325 and returned to his country with a copy of the twenty canons promulgated by the First Ecumenical Council. Gregory would have them adopted by his clergy and his people after appending to them a series of special canons that he had composed himself. The latter, known as the canons of Gregory the Illuminator, are quite likely apocryphal. Most Armenian critics believe that they may have been written in Armenia around 365, at the time of Katholikos Sahak from the Aghbianos family.

Here is the text of the second of these canons, regarding the prohibition against priests' marrying after ordination:

> The priest who has taken a wife will have to do penance for seven years outside and then for two years inside the Church. He will not have the right to receive communion for another additional two years, and only then will he be admitted to communion.[54]

---

[54] *Canones sancti Gregorii Armeniorum apostoli*, can. 2. A. Mai, *Scriptorum veterum nova collectio*, X, 2, p. 269 (the Latin translation published by Mai was by Arsène Angiarakian [Rome, 1838]).

Council of Chahabivan (444)

It was in order to oppose the worrisome surge of Messialism that the Council of Chahabivan was gathered in 444 (or in 446–48), with Katholikos Joseph, a disciple of Mesrob, presiding. The Messialian heresy, derived from Gnosis, spread a contemptuous mysticism that disregarded dogmas and sacraments and was free from all morality. It had spread in many countries of the East, and under favorable political circumstances it reached all the classes of the population in Armenia. The clergy themselves had many disciples of that sect. The Council of Chahabivan reacted with extreme severity.

Among the twenty canons promulgated by the Armenian synod of 444, four penalize the offenses of fornication and adultery committed by clergy members (1, 2, 14, 19). We note here two texts of direct interest to our study:

> *Can. 2*: If the wife of a priest or a deacon is caught in the act of adultery, her husband will have to decide whether to choose either the Church and the priesthood on the one hand or his wife on the other. Should he choose the priesthood, let him send away his wife from the conjugal home and inflict a heavy penance on her. If the daughter of a priest is caught in the act of adultery, she will not receive her share of the Church's goods, will be sent away from the rectory, and will be subjected to a harsh penance: the same will be applicable to the priests' sons.[55]

> *Can. 14*: If a bishop, priest, or deacon, or anyone belonging to the Order of the ministers of the Church, has in his home an "introduced" woman who is the house mistress, as is the practice among those who have a concubine, let him be forbidden to exercise his ministry and held as a pervert and a publican: for the Holy Church and the sacred mysteries of the Lord call for holy and immaculate men: so that those who are defiled by their faults obtain salvation thanks to spotless ministers.[56]

The clause of rejection stipulated by canon 2 for the wife of a priest or deacon who would have committed adultery seems to have been inspired by canon 8 of the Council of Neocaesarea in Cappadocia (314–25) and calls for the same commentaries.[57] If the faithful wife of a cleric was authorized to live under his roof, it did not necessarily mean that they were free to have conjugal intercourse. During that first half of the 5th century, the Churches of the West were observing the rule laid down

---

[55] *Canones synodi Armeniorum*, can. 2. A. Mai, *Scriptorum veterum nova collectio*, p. 292.
[56] Ibid., p. 295.
[57] See above, p. 178, n. 94.

by St. Leo in his letter to Rusticus of Narbonne:[58] married deacons, priests, and bishops kept their wives with them, treating them like sisters. It is quite probable that such a *modus vivendi* had been adopted in Armenia, where the Church, until 491, remained in close communion with Rome.[59]

PERSIA

Council of Seleucia-Ctesiphon (410)

While the Churches of the Roman World were enjoying the Constantinian peace, the Persian Christian communities of the 4th century were being subjected to a long and violent persecution. Ordered by the King of Kings Sapor II in the year 339–40, it lasted until the death of the Sassanid monarch (August 19, 379). The precarious peace that followed allowed some kind of Church reorganization. But it was only in 410, after felicitous negotiations with Iazgerd I (399–420), that the Church was officially recognized by a royal ordinance that was considered to be the decree of Milan of the Persian Church. Mar Maruta, bishop of Maipherqat (in Mesopotamia), had been the "mediator of peace and concord between the East and the West". His first concern, as well as that of the newly elected Katholikos of the Royal Cities, Mar Isaac, was to call a general council that was to be for Persia what the Council of Nicaea had been for the Roman world. The Synod opened on February 1, 410, at Seleucia-Ctesiphon, with the participation of about forty bishops and apparently was of brief duration. Mar Maruta read "all the regulating canons enacted at the great synod held in the town of Nicaea", which the Fathers approved unanimously. The faith of Nicaea was becoming the only creed of the Syrian churches.

Among the twenty-one canons established by the Council of 410 is a decree relative to the *subintroductae*; the text of this decree follows:

> *Can. 3*: On the fact that the *subintroductae* must not live anymore with clerics, as was the prior custom.—With respect to the *subintroductae* we will do all that is stipulated in the synod;[60] now any bishop, deacon, subdeacon,

[58] See above, pp. 261ff.

[59] We think that the imperial law of 420 (adopted by the Theodosian Code of 438) authorizing cohabitation for a married cleric with his wife is to be interpreted in the sense of St. Leo's letter to Rusticus of Narbonne. See below, pp. 318–19.

[60] This is the 3d canon of the Council of Nicaea, whose text we give here as a reminder: "The great council has absolutely forbidden bishops, priests, and deacons—in a word, all clergy members—to have with them a sister-companion, unless she be a mother, a sister, an aunt, or one of the only persons who are above any suspicion" (Joannou, I, 1, pp. 25–26).

or cleric[61] living among women, and not alone, chastely, and in a holy way, as befits the ministry of the Church, men and women being separated, will not be admitted to the ministry of the Church.[62]

It will be noticed that, while affirming their desire to do "all that is stipulated in the Synod [of Nicaea]", the Fathers of Seleucia-Ctesiphon are more severe than the First Ecumenical Council and forbid clerics any cohabitation with a woman, without even providing for exceptions for "a mother, sister, aunt, or all the persons who are beyond any suspicion", as had been decided at Nicaea. The question is whether the Persian bishops did have a genuine copy of the Council of Nicaea's canons. If such was the case, as we have reason to think,[63] Mar Maruta and his colleagues could take responsibility to modify canon 3 of Nicaea relative to the *subintroductae* in a restrictive sense only because the discipline prevailing at that time in the Church of Persia was favorable to it. That would be a confirmation of what we read in the *Doctrina Aeddei* with respect to the clergy of Edessa: "All those who were devoted to the ecclesiastical service, men and women, were chaste, prudent, holy, and pure, since they lived separately [one from another] and [lived] a chaste and spotless life." [64]

Council of Beth Lafath (484)

Chased away from Edessa because of his Nestorian convictions, Barsumas became bishop of Nisibe thanks to the protection of King Peroz

---

[61] Literally, "sons of the Covenant" (*Bnay Qyāmâ*). This phrase, as well as its female opposite number "daughters of the Covenant" (*Bnât Qyāmâ*), is used several times in the Nestorian synods. At times it describes clerics, at times the virgins consecrated to God or the women in service of the Church. Only the context enables us to determine the category of persons appearing in a document. When they are clerics, as seems to be the case here, they are of the lower ranks, such as cantors, lectors, or subdeacons. Cf. T. J. Lamy, *Concilium Seleuciae et Ctesiphonti habitum anno 410* (Lovanii, 1868), c. 113–20; J. B. Chabot, *Synodicon orientale ou Recueil de synodes nestoriens* (*Notices et extraits des manuscrits de la Bibliothèque nationale et autres bibliothèques*, t. 37) (Paris, 1902), p. 254, n. 3. See also R. Murray, *Symbols of Church and Kingdom: A Study in Early Syriac Tradition* (Cambridge University Press, 1975), pp. 14–17.

[62] J. B. Chabot, *Synodicon orientale*, p. 264.

[63] Cf. J. B. Chabot, ibid., p. 259, n. 3: "What were these canons? Were they a translation of the twenty genuine canons or a version of the *Canones arabici*? I am inclined to believe that they were authentic canons, actually mentioned in canons 2, 3, 4, and 6 of this synod. It would thus have been an authentic version of the Council of Nicaea that Maruta had communicated to Isaac and to the Eastern bishops."

[64] See below, pp. 312–13.

and founded there a school, which gained fame quickly and contributed actively to the propagation of Nestorianism in Persia. The bishop of Nisibe was struggling against the primate of Seleucia-Ctesiphon. In April 484, he succeeded in gathering several bishops of his party and held a synod with them at Beth Lafath. Though it was disavowed the following year by Barsumas himself during the Council of Beth Edrai, and thus rejected from the official collections of the Nestorian synods, that Council of Beth Lafath had a great influence in the Persian Church from both dogmatic and canonical viewpoints.

The canon relative to the marriage of clerics that Barsumas defined in 484 in order to justify his own marriage with the nun Mamoe was ratified by the Council of Mar Acacius in 486 (can. 3) and by the Council of Mar Babai in 497. We do not know the original text because the acts of the Council of Beth Lafath were annulled, but we can certainly trust the testimony of the Nestorian Mare ibn Sulaiman, according to whom Barsumas had written a synodal letter authorizing priests and monks "who could not restrain themselves" to get married.[65] The Council of Mar Babai (497), when legislating on clerical marriage, would declare admissible—only on this point, however—the assembly of Beth Lafath. It is thus likely that the content of Barsumas' law was substantially identical to what we read in the acts of the Council of Mar Babai: "We have permitted that: from the patriarch down to the least in the hierarchy, everyone may openly contract a chaste marriage, with only one wife, to beget children, and make use [of marital rights]."[66]

Starting from 484, the Nestorian Church of Persia thus granted herself a legislation authorizing the marriage of clerics at all ranks of the hierarchy. The use of marriage was also explicitly acknowledged for these ministers, and there was never a question about perpetual or temporary continence.

Council of Mar Acacius (486)

The Persian Church, which, in 410, had solemnly ratified the decisions of the Council of Nicaea, was led into another direction after the Council of Chalcedon (451), when it adopted an attitude of denial with regard to the faith defined at the Fourth Ecumenical Council. Nestorianism became the official religion of the Christian communities in the Sassanid Empire. It is difficult to know exactly when and how this secession took

---

[65] Cf. J. S. Assemani, *Bibliotheca Orientalis Clementino-Vaticana*, III (Rome, 1728), p. 93.
[66] See below, pp. 287–88.

place because we have no historical source for that decisive period. If we are to believe the *Chronicle* of Michael the Syrian, it was Bishop Barsumas of Nisibe who convinced King Peroz to impose the Nestorian faith forcibly on his subjects: "If we do not proclaim in the East a dogma that is different from that of the Roman emperor, your Christian subjects will never be sincerely attached to you. But give me troops and I will make all Christians in your empire Nestorians. Thus they will hate the Romans, and the Romans will detest them." It is quite likely that things happened in a different way. The influence of the flourishing school of Nisibe, founded by Barsumas, probably had the primary role in the diffusion and success of the Nestorian doctrines in Persia. When Katholikos Mar Acacius called in February 486 the council of Seleucia that was to bear his name, the Persian Church was already cut off from Byzantium and Rome. The twelve bishops of the synod, around their president, labored to define the faith that now was its own (can. 1) and to give it a particular organization and discipline. Their decisions would mark the triumph of the ideas of Barsumas, he who had been the main architect of the new orientation adopted in Persia.

The last of the three canons promulgated by the Council of Mar Acacius is a long decree-treatise on clerical marriage and celibacy. To make its reading easier, we have introduced a few subtitles.

Canon 3

Celibacy cannot be imposed upon clerics
and the "Sons of the Covenant"

As to the way of life befitting the truth and worthy of the faith in Christ, this is our definition: now and forever let no bishop place any obstacles or difficulties to prevent marriage in the country he is ruling and in the Church where he exercises his functions. Sufficient are the evils that have struck our dioceses through fornication and adultery, the iniquity of which spread and came to the ears of foreigners, so that contempt and derision toward us have been aroused against us in the conscience of all the peoples. Let no one among us forcibly impose this commitment on his clergy, either among the village priests or the clerics under his authority; but let his teaching on this point be in conformity with the teaching of the holy books, and that through his own weakness he recognize other peoples' weaknesses. Christ our Lord did indeed tell the apostles who asked him whether it was useful for them to stay away from marriage: "Not all men are capable of these things"; and shortly thereafter he entrusted the matter to the will of the apostles, saying: "Let the one who can do it, do it." In accordance with the doctrine of our Savior, the blessed Apostle instructed the Corinthians, who had written to him asking whether they should stay away from marriage, by saying, "About the things you wrote to me, it is good for a man not to have a wife; but because of fornication it is better for each one to have his wife and for each woman to have her husband." Elsewhere the Apostle, considering human weakness and the difficulty of the matter, instructed those who voluntarily bound themselves through this promise, and said: "And I say to those who are not married and to the widows that it is good for them to remain like me; but if they suffer, let them marry; for it is better to take a wife than to burn with concupiscence." And we too—now that we all know the damage we as well as our flock suffered because of the laxity of the incontinent who scandalized the consciences of many people—we reveal our sufferings; we unveil our faults and are not ashamed of the remedy openly offered to the sick among us, as to our behavior, and of the penance that we rightly impose on ourselves and on our people. And in fact we testify to these words of the great Doctor: "It is better to take a wife than to burn with concupiscence."

Let each one choose: either perfect continence or a regular marriage

Each one of us will choose one of these two things, perfect continence or a regular marriage, according to the teaching of Blessed Paul who, about the things that befit the episcopate, gives his instructions to Timothy in his letter, as follows: "If anyone wants to be a bishop, it is a good thing. The bishop must be beyond reproach and married to an only wife." The consequence of this doctrine is therefore that everybody who is married to an only wife fulfills through his marriage the law of the Apostle.

The marriage of deacons

It is also permitted to each of the deacons who have already received the ordination of the diaconate to be united to one woman by a regular and legitimate marriage, and to be freed from the ancient custom that, because of the laxity of the profligates, is blamed and derided by outsiders. As to those who come for the first time for the imposition of hands of the diaconate, they will be questioned about their other works, including their legal union, and if they are legitimately married, they will be ordained deacons so that they will be able to fulfill the apostolic doctrine that teaches "Let deacons be the husbands of only one wife, taking good care of their sons and their daughters." Moreover, so as to heal completely, even against their will, those among us who are sick—i.e., those who, in the words of the apostles, have cut themselves off from any hope and have surrendered avidly to indecency and the practice of all kinds of defilements; those who take pleasure in fornication and adultery; those who, not being regularly united, do not beget and raise [their children] legitimately according to God's will—we will add this to the canon: "Now and forever let no bishop confer the ordination of the diaconate to a man of his town or the villages under his jurisdiction without having found out beforehand if his behavior is good and worthy of the ordination for which he presents himself, and also if he has a legitimate union and children; so as to erase carefully from the Church of Christ all the arrogance and ostentation of the false doctors who call marriage and procreation evil and appease their desires in adultery, fornication, and bad artifices.

Those who freely choose not to marry must live in a monastery

All of us, with a vigorous spirit, despising vain glory, have decided unanimously to remove from our flocks old and nefarious traditions, and to establish just and correct rules for those who are married and for the single men in the dioceses entrusted to us by divine grace.—We teach that the one who voluntarily chooses to stay away from marriage must live alone and without dissolute ways in a monastery, in purity and continence.

Canonical sanctions

And if the one who had preferred to serve and honor Christ in chastity and the renunciation of all earthly things is convicted of adultery or fornication, after this open permission to contract a legitimate marriage and to beget children, he will have to be subjected to the penalty stipulated by the canons; if he has the title of priest, let him become an outsider of the priestly ministry until he has done the penance fitting his transgression and seems worthy of absolution. On his part, he who having contracted a legitimate marriage dares to use other women besides his wife, and the one who, being regularly married, prevents the fruit of marriage [from ripening], outside of the natural sickness of sterility, must also be deprived from the communion of the Church and from the priestly Order.

Priests can marry or remarry after the deaths of their wives

If a priest is not married yet and wishes to marry and beget children legitimately, or if the one whose first wife died wishes to take another wife and observe the legality of his union with his second wife as was the case with the first one, his bishop has no right to oppose his desire: for legitimate marriage and procreation of children, either before or after the priesthood, is a good thing and one acceptable to God. A brother must be regarded as having been united to only one wife even though the latter changed through death or necessities happening in this world, even though he took two wives, one after the other. We prescribe and teach that this must be so, so that the choice of perfection, preferably to marriage, to legitimate union and procreation of children, be free of any constraint and obstacle.

Anathema against whoever teaches the contrary

> If anyone rebels against this true doctrine or thinks in his pride that it is contemptible, or prefers to do and teach things that are in keeping with that hypocrisy which, with the help of Christ, we have unmasked and want to keep away from us; if anyone cannot be brought to hold to the truth of our faith recorded in this book and to observe faithfully one of the following two things: either perfect sanctity or a legitimate union crowned by the chaste procreation of children; if he does not adhere to the sentence we have recorded above against the seductors calling themselves ascetics, though they are quite far from the reality [of asceticism]; if he does not affirm his adhesion to all these things with goodwill and a spirit free from all artifice, with his seal and signature; if he is a bishop, priest, or monk who teaches the opposite of these things and does not adhere to all that is recorded above and defined in this work: he will not have any communion with us, we will abstain from participating with him, and we will forbid him to exercise his priesthood as well as prevent him from serving in any other Order of the Church; and if he is a lay person, let him be censored and anathematized.[67]

Council of Mar Babai (497)

Shortly after his election, Katholikos Mar Babai, son of Hormizd, received an edict from Zâmâsp, King of Kings, asking him that "the bishops under his authority be gathered by him and that they establish a reform with regard to legitimate marriage and procreation of children for all clerics in all countries". The Council that met at Seleucia-Ctesiphon in November 497 gathered from thirty-three to thirty-nine bishops (depending on the lists). In addition to the measures relative to the marriage of clerics—the purpose of the synod—the Council reaffirmed the absolute primacy of the patriarch of the Church of Persia. It was also decided that general councils would henceforth be gathered every four years. Finally, certain episcopal elections were validated, and severe measures were taken against Monophysite propagandists.

Here is how the Persian bishops conformed to the edict of Zâmâsp:

> All of us bishops, whose names are recorded above, conforming in the same spirit to the perfection of Christ's laws, have made reforms that are

---

[67] J. B. Chabot, *Synodicon orientale*, pp. 303–6.

good for our people and our flocks with respect to marriage and the procreation of children, and we have permitted that from the patriarch to the
least in the hierarchy[68] all can openly contract a chaste marriage, with an
only wife, to procreate children and use the marital rights.

We also accept, but only on this point, the assembly that took place in
the country of Beth Huzayeh, in the city of Beth Lafath, in the year 27
of Peroz, King of Kings; as well as the text started at Beth Edrai during
the second year of Balas, in the time of Mar Acacius, and completed in
the country of Beth Aramayeh; and the true faith established by the authority and doctrines of the Holy Books.[69]

This text of the Council of Mar Babai enables us to know indirectly the
text of the decisions relative to the marriage of clerics that had been
made thirteen years earlier by Barsumas of Nisibe at the Synod of Beth
Lafath.[70] The reference to "reforms that are good for our people" cannot
be interpreted, coming from the mouth of the bishops of 497 as an
announcement of a change in discipline now authorizing clerics to do
what had previously been forbidden to them, inasmuch as marriage had
already been permitted at all ranks of the hierarchy of Barsumas (484)
and by the Council of Mar Acacius (486). If there was a concern for
reform, it was because the state of mores had seriously declined in the
Persian empire, especially under the influence of one Mazdak, who
preached the community of goods and women. It is likely that the
customs of the Persian clergy had been somewhat influenced by this.
The Council of Mar Babai contributed to the necessary reform by recalling the previous decisions. That legislation authorizing marriage and its
use by all clerics "from the patriarch to the least in the hierarchy" will
remain in force until Mar Aba I, elected Katholikos in 540, who would
forbid ordaining as bishop or patriarch a married man.[71]

3. PATRISTIC WRITERS

St. Augustine (354–430)

Born at Tagaste (Suk-Ahras) on November 13, 354, Augustine was the
son of a pagan father—baptized on his deathbed—and of a Christian
mother, the future St. Monica, who had a decisive influence on him.

[68] Literally, "Until the lowest who is in the Covenant (Qyāmâ)".
[69] J. B. Chabot, *Synodicon orientale*, p. 312.
[70] See above, pp. 282–83.
[71] See below, pp. 348–49.

After studying in Carthage, he devoted himself to teaching, first in Tagaste, then in Carthage (375–83), and last in Milan. In that city, whose bishop was then St. Ambrose, he converted to the Christian faith—which had been the faith of his childhood—after harrowing inner struggles. He gave up Manichaeism, to which he had adhered for nine years. Baptized by St. Ambrose himself on Easter 387, the author of the *Confessions* started a new life in the Church, and from monastic solitude moved rapidly to the priesthood and the episcopate. From 396 until his death, on August 28, 430, he was the head of the Church of Hippo, a bishop of untiring charity, of sure and luminous doctrine, and of eminent sanctity. He took part in most of the councils that were held in Africa in his time—from the plenary Council of Hippo (where as a young priest he gave a speech that is still famous) until the Council of Carthage in 419, where he, with his friend Aurelius of Carthage, provided inspiration and was instrumental in the actual composition of the *Codex canonum Ecclesiae africanae*.

The active participation of the bishop of Hippo in the African synods probably explains why he did not feel the need to formulate for his clergy a disciplinary regulation regarding continence that was already promulgated by the official canons. Moreover, the monastic style that he was able to impart to his presbyterium made the observance easier.

Adulterous unions (end 419)

The only reference to this issue found in the Augustinian works is at the end of a treatise dedicated to one Pollentius regarding adulterous unions. Evoking the situation of married men who are separated from their wives, who believe that remaining chaste is impossible, and who even deem it at times a male virtue to have sinful affairs, St. Augustine says that he likes to propose as an example the great number of clerics called also, by dint of circumstances, to a life of continence:

> This is why when we inspire these men, for whom the superiority of their sex means the freedom to sin, with the fear of eternal death if they contract adulterous marriages, we are accustomed to give them as an example the continence of these clerics who were frequently forced against their wills to carry such a burden. Nevertheless, as soon as they have accepted it, they carry it, faithful to their duty, until death. Thus we tell these men: If the violence of a pious people were to compel you to observe it, what would you do? Would you not chastely fulfill the duty imposed upon you? Would you not turn immediately to God to obtain from him a strength you never thought of asking him until that day? But, they say, honor is a handsome consolation for clerics! And you, we would retort, do you not have the even more powerful motivation of fear to moderate your

concupiscence? If a great number of the Lord's ministers accepted all of a sudden and without warning the yoke imposed on them, in the hope of receiving a more glorious place in Christ's inheritance, how much more should you avoid adultery and embrace continence, for fear, not of shining less in the Kingdom of God, but of burning in the Gehenna of fire.[72]

A comparison is made here between men separated from their wives through circumstances and clerics who were involuntarily (*inviti*) placed under the yoke of continence. In either case the men are bound by a situation they did not choose, though they are not thereby exempted from being faithful to it. Making a virtue out of necessity, as it were, the clerics accept their harsh obligations and with God's grace observe them fully. Let the men deprived of their wives meditate on their example. Constrained also to conjugal abstinence, though for other reasons, they are asked to have the same attitude and the same divine grace is offered to them. Let them not say: the clerics find a compensation in the honors of their duty. The fear of punishment is more powerful than honor when it comes to curbing adulterous desires. Let them rather consider their duty and God's judgment, and carry faithfully the burden of their continence.[73]

We know that it was not rare in the early Church to see men suddenly taken away from their usual occupations in order—like it or not—to be ordained priests. Ambrose's friend remembered the governor of Milan, chosen by a plebiscite against his will and switching from a secular life one day to an ecclesiastical life the next; as to Augustine himself, had he not been in a way "volunteered" by old Valerius and the people of Hippo, and forced to accept the imposition of hands? When the Church needed a shepherd, it happened frequently enough that the man himself was not consulted.[74] Obviously, Augustine was thinking about such situations in the passage we just read. Most of the time (*plerumque*), the clerics were compelled to carry the burden of continence. To understand the sentence as if only some of the clergy were bound to continence, while others would have been free to have a conjugal life, would be nonsensical

---

[72] *De conjugiis adulterinis*, II, 22. CSEL 41, 409; trans., G. Combes, *Oeuvres de saint Augustin*, 1st ser., II (Paris, 1937), pp. 225–27.

[73] The Council of Toledo, in 653, would draw a parallel between the situation of the one baptized against his will and that of the cleric ordained against his will: just as the former is bound to obey the universal law, though he was baptized without his consent, the latter must also observe priestly continence (Can. 7. Mansi 10, 1217–18).

[74] It was the case, for instance, for Severus of Ravenna, Germanus of Auxerre, Lupus of Troyes, Synesius of Ptolemais, Gregory of Langres, and others (see above, chap. 5, nos. 42, 84, 89, 98, 143).

given the contemporary discipline of the African Church as described by the councils; it would also undo the strength of the comparison. Augustine does place the stress on the unforeseen nature of the two situations he compares as parallel: on the one hand, husbands who are separated from their wives, and on the other, men elevated to the clergy, all being bound against their wills to a style of life calling for continence. If only part of the clergy, even the majority, had been bound to total chastity, it would not have been very efficacious to give them as an example, and such a discrimination would be inconceivable in any event. On the other hand, the argument gains its full value when we deal with men enrolled forcibly in the ranks of the clergy, as unwilling as husbands could have been when separated from their wives, and thereby committed to the obligations inherent in the priestly functions. Mobilized for a service demanding continence, they were an example that laymen who became bachelors against their wills could use as an inspiration for their own behavior. It seems, from the logic of his argumentation, that such was indeed Augustine's thought. Moreover, it only confirms what we already knew: the existence of an African discipline, in those early years of the 5th century, demanding that married clerics abstain from conjugal relations.[75]

St. John Chrysostom (344/54–407)

John, called "Golden Mouth" (Chrysostom) by posterity, was born in Antioch between the years 344 and 354. Shortly after his baptism, received as an adult, he was ordained lector and led an ascetic life. It does seem, however, that he did not take up a life of solitude outside Antioch until the death of his widowed mother. Six years later he returned to his native town for reasons of health, and he was promptly chosen for the diaconate (381). In 386, his bishop Flavian called him to the priesthood and appointed him preacher, a task that he fulfilled for twelve years with unique talent and influence, thereby earning an immortal fame. In 397, he was abducted by surprise and consecrated bishop of Constantinople. In his See in the imperial capital he remained the ascetic preacher he had been, while facing the new duties of his functions with a fully evangelical freedom of speech that did not spare the wealthy and powerful. He did not acquire only friends! Theophilus of Alexandria's intrigues and

---

[75] Quite likely this passage deals only with the higher ranks of the clerical hierarchy. It appears that no one was forcibly enrolled for the office of lector or porter but only for the priesthood or the episcopate.

Empress Eudoxia's rancor led to his being deposed and banished from Byzantium. A first rehabilitation did not last long. He had to take the road to exile once again and died of exhaustion on the way in Comanes, Pontus, on September 14, 407. His many works and sanctity earned him his place among the greatest doctors of the Church.

Commentary on the first epistle to Timothy (392–397)

In one of his homilies on the Pauline epistles, St. John Chrysostom tackles an objection raised by the admission of married men to the episcopate:

> If, then, the married man has worldly concerns, and if, on the other hand, a bishop should not have them, how can the Apostle say, "the husband of an only wife"? Some say that we are dealing here with the case of a man who has been freed [from his ties with] his wife; if such is not the case, it is permissible that he be a man having a wife [on condition that he live] as if he did not have one. At that time this was indeed rightly permitted because of the prevailing situation. For it was possible to lead such a life honorably if one wished to do so. Indeed, though it is difficult for a rich man to enter the Kingdom of Heaven, there have frequently been rich people who did so; the same is true for marriage.[76]

The objection raised by the *unius uxoris virum* of St. Paul does not aim, as is the case with Jovinian, to question the discipline of clerical continence: the listeners of the Antioch preacher are rather surprised by an apparent contradiction in the teachings of the Apostle: if the married man has worldly concerns, how can one still elect to the episcopate men who are bound by marriage? The question is posed because of the obligations known to be those of the head of the community: detached, out of duty, from "worldly" preoccupations, how could a married bishop be in conformity with such an ideal? The orator then wishes to show that, married or not, the candidate to the episcopal See is called to that conformity. The *unius uxoris virum* can be understood in two ways: some deem that being monogamous, the future bishop must be freed from his marital bonds when he is elected. In other words, only widowers could aspire to priestly functions. Chrysostom does not directly endorse that opinion but mentions it without criticism. One thing is certain, however: if the bishop is still permitted to have a wife, it is on condition that he live as if he did not have one.

Meant to reassure the faithful about the inner freedom of their shepherds, this discourse is obviously not the canonical expression of a

---

[76] *In epist. I ad Timotheum*, cap. III, homilia X, 1–2. PG 62, 549a.

discipline; it only supposes it and thereby indirectly bears witness to its existence. If the first way of understanding the *unius uxoris virum* of St. Paul is only an optional interpretation, the second is presented as a required minimum, a condition for accession to the episcopate within which it seems there was no room for exceptions. Facing an audience that was as knowledgeable of the Church's customs as he was, Chrysostom could not have allowed himself to invent a discipline that did not exist. If he explains it, it is in order to show that it answers exactly the legitimate preoccupations of the faithful: bound to continence, the married bishop is detached from "the things of this world" as St. Paul wanted it, just as a single man is.

Finally, let us note that the above commentary deals only with bishops. The orator comments on the verse of the first epistle to Timothy concerning episcopal functions (1 Tim 3:2) and does not refer to the situation of priests and deacons.

Dialogue on the Life of Saint John Chrysostom (408)

Having become the bishop of Constantinople, the former preacher of Antioch had to make people respect that discipline on whose validity he commented. An episode reported by Palladius in his *Dialogue on the Life of Saint John Chrysostom* does indeed mention a synod presided over by John in the year 400 during which sanctions were taken against one Antoninus, bishop of Ephesus. Among the seven counts leveled at the guilty man was the following: "Sixth, after having been separated from his wife, he went back to common life with her and had children." [77]

Some authors opined that the bishop of Ephesus was sentenced for having failed in an attempt at continence that had not been imposed upon him, but that he had voluntarily undertaken. [78] We think that this would minimize the gravity of the accusation leveled at him. The behavior of Antoninus was severely punished (he was deposed) and described in the most reprehensible terms: "Every point of these different chapters is the epitome of impiety and forbidden in any case by the holy laws." [79]

Had married bishops been free to live with their wives and to sire children, no one would have judged so severely a man who had simply changed a personal decision, no matter how much inconstancy might be blameworthy in a bishop. Moreover, we have nothing in patristic literature

---

[77] PG 47, 48a.

[78] Cf. E. Vacandard, *Les origines du célibat*, p. 85; F. X. Funk, "Cölibat und Priesterehe in christlichen Altertum", in *Kirchengeschichtliche Abhandlungen und Untersuchungen*, I (Paderborn, 1897), pp. 134–35.

[79] PG 47, 49a.

about laws sanctioning possible infractions to what we would call today a free vow of continence. Now Antoninus was reproached for having committed an act "forbidden by the holy laws". We could think that in this case it was indeed a free commitment but one that the Church had officially recognized, which made it a juridical obligation. But the text has nothing to say about this, and the emphasis is placed on the offense itself rather than on the nature of the violated decision. The decision does indeed seem to be linked to the episcopal function, independently from a freely accepted option, and the incidental clause "after having separated from his wife" simply bears witness, we think, that the guilty bishop had at first conformed to a general discipline.

If one compares the synod presided over by John with the homily he had preached several years earlier in Antioch, it will be easier to see in this synod the application to a specific case of a regulation on clerical continence that had already been attested by the young preacher.

St. Jerome (ca. 347–419/20)

Adversus Jovinianum (393)

The ideas developed by St. Jerome in his commentary on the epistle to Titus[80] are found again, as could be expected, in the occasional writings inspired by his controversy with Jovinian, an opponent of celibacy and virginity. As soon as he had received the *Commentarioli* of Jovinian, the monk of Bethlehem hastened to refute his theses. Attacking his adversary, he plied him with questions and opposed him with the traditional doctrine of which he made himself the spokesman. Thus, an objection that Jovinian had drawn from St. Paul brought Jerome to explain the discipline regarding clerical continence: "It is futile for you [said Jovinian] to make this discourse, since bishops, priests, and deacons must be men married only once [to an only wife] and have children, according to what the Apostle had established."

The Pauline instruction of *unius uxoris virum* having been taken as the basic scriptural argument, Jerome takes the same stance:

> [The Apostle] did not say: Let us choose as a bishop a man married to one wife and siring children but: a man who has had only one wife and keeps his children in perfect submission. You surely admit that he who goes on siring children during his episcopate cannot be a bishop. For if people find out about it, he will not be considered a husband but condemned as being

[80] See above, pp. 238–39.

adulterous. [One thing has to be decided]: either you allow priests to exercise their nuptial activity so that there is no difference between virgins and married people; or, if priests are not allowed to touch their wives, [you have to admit that] they are holy, precisely because they imitate virginal purity. But let us go further. If a lay person, any member of the faithful, cannot devote himself to prayer without setting conjugal intercourse aside, the priest who must offer the sacrifice at all times has to pray unceasingly. If he must pray unceasingly, he must continually be free from marriage. Even under the old law, those who offered victims for the people not only did not reside in their own homes, but also purified themselves by abstaining temporarily from living with their wives; neither did they drink wine or fermented beverages, which generally excite the libido. I will not deny that married men are chosen for the priesthood; the reason is that there are not as many virgins as are needed for the priesthood. If, in an army, the strongest are recruited, does one not also take those who are weaker since not all can be strong?[81]

Let us follow his reasoning:

Jovinian is wrong about the meaning of *unius uxoris virum*. St. Paul did not ask to choose as bishops men who, at the time of their episcopate, unite themselves with an only wife and beget children, as if the unstated verb were at the present time, but candidates who, in the past, before their election, had only one wife and had kept their children in perfect discipline. Jerome is almost disputing a point of grammar. One has the impression that he is less concerned with the interpretation of the Pauline instruction, as Ambrose and Siricius had been, than with its correct translation. Could he have a more explicit version than we do? Or did he imagine, for the sake of expediency, a verb in the past tense? It is difficult to answer. The fact is that the real meaning of the Apostle's recommendation seems incontestable to him. Jovinian and his followers are basing their argumentation on a misunderstanding.

Not only Scripture but also Church practice are on Jerome's side. There cannot be a bishop who, while exercising his functions, goes on begetting children; if he does so and the matter becomes known, he will be condemned as being adulterous; he will not be judged as a husband. Jovinian is taken to witness here: "You will surely admit that there cannot be a bishop. . . . " Invoking a point of law, the apologist means to lean on a solid argument. No one, he opines, could refute him, not even his adversary. The risk would indeed have been serious for Jerome if he had exposed himself to a refutation on such a ground; if the disciplinary practice of the time had been different, Jovinian would not have failed to stress it in response, and Jerome would have been discredited.

---

[81] *Adversus Jovinianum*, I, 34. PL 23, 257a–c.

Everything leads us to believe that whereas the instances of noncontinent bishops were not rare, the legislation attested in the *Adversus Jovinianum* did correspond to reality.

These premises being established, we have to deal with the argument itself. For if Jovinian does contest the exegesis of St. Paul and current discipline, it is because he places marriage and virginity on the same plane. The hermit of Bethlehem has grasped the core of the debate and expressed it as an alternative: either one permits priests to have conjugal relations and thus suppresses all difference between virgins and married people, or one does not permit them to live with their wives and then they are saints, exactly according to the model of virginal purity. For Jerome, as it was for Siricius, priestly continence is above all a matter of "sanctity". To fight it is to deny that the priest must be distinguished from the mass of the faithful. And Jerome the churchman firmly holds onto that distinction, which to him seems to be an inherent feature of the Christian people. There is a hierarchy of "sanctity" based on a hierarchy of functions. Then he brings up the two scriptural motivations already made familiar to us by his contemporaries: if a layman must temporarily give up sexual relations in order to free himself for prayer, according to the advice of St. Paul, how much more should the priest do so, since he is, owing to his function, held to perpetual prayer: "Si semper orandum est, ergo semper carendum matrimonio." And in the Old Law, did not the Levites in charge of the sacrifices separate from their wives when their functions demanded it? The strength of these arguments is such, in Jerome's eyes, that he deems the case settled.

Should one still object, wondering why the Church also chooses her ministers among married people, Jerome has a ready answer: there are not enough virgins ("Quia non sunt tanti virgines, quanti necessarii sunt sacerdotes"). A reason of sheer expediency and, he adds, of practical realism: it is not because an army recruits the strongest, that it must, by the same token, deprive itself of the weak. One should not expect Jerome, who easily emphasized the inconveniences of conjugal life, to see in the choice of monogamists an honor rendered to the dignity of marriage; one is all the more grateful to Epiphanius and others who did so.

The *Adversus Jovinianum* contained more than derogatory implications regarding married people. Scandal and protests followed. Jerome had to defend himself and did so in his famous *Letter to Pammachius*. It is of interest to us because of a new reference to priestly continence:

> Here then is what we have clearly said: marriage is permitted in the Gospel, but women, if they persist in accomplishing the duty that is theirs, cannot receive the reward promised to chastity. Let the husbands, if they grow

indignant at this opinion, be irritated not with me but with Holy Scripture, better yet with the bishops, the priests, the deacons, the entire priestly, even Levitical choir who know that they cannot offer sacrifices if they accomplish the conjugal act! . . . Therefore, as we had started to say, the virgin Christ and the virgin Mary have consecrated for each sex the beginnings of virginity: the apostles were either virgins or continent after having been married. Bishops, priests, and deacons are chosen among virgins and widowers; in any case, once they are ordained, they live in perfect chastity. Why delude ourselves or get upset if, when we are constantly seeking the conjugal act, we are refused the recompenses promised to purity? [82]

Leaving aside the properly apologetic aspects, let us retain what pertains to our subject matter: to justify himself in the face of the criticisms he received, Jerome takes refuge in the authority of Scripture and the official witness of priestly chastity. The latter is not given as an ideal to be pursued but as a fact admitted by all: bishops, priests, deacons, and "the universal choir" of priests and Levites know that they cannot offer the sacrifice if they have conjugal intercourse. By using such examples the author of the letter also attests to the existence of a discipline imposing sexual abstinence on the clerics of the hierarchy. No more than in the *Adversus Jovinianum* could Jerome have used such an argument if reality had denied it. The information is therefore important and confirms again what we learned from other sources.

Priestly chastity is also the rule for recruiting; bishops, priests, and deacons are all chosen from one of the following categories: virgins (today we would say "single men"), widowers, or married men who, after ordination, will observe perfect continence. Here too Jerome does not use the optative; he posits a fact. Given the prudence that polemics necessarily imposed on him insofar as word choice was concerned, it is rather unlikely that he would venture to affirm such an important thing without being sure it was indisputable. We can believe him when he sums up, in his concise style, the criteria used in his time for priestly recruiting. It is also interesting to note that, on this point as on the previous one, the Holy Land writer does not give the impression of knowing any difference between the various Churches. Would he have used the same terms if it had been public knowledge that several provinces, especially in the East, applied other disciplinary rules?

In justifying these criteria by the example of the apostles, Jerome echoes a tradition that, as we have seen, is unanimous in affirming that those of the apostles who might have been married before being called

---

[82] *Apologeticum ad Pammachium. Ep.* 49, 10 and 21. CSEL 54, 365 and 386–87. J. Labourt, trans., Coll. "Budé", II, pp. 130–31 and 149–50.

by the Lord to follow him had practiced continence from then on. In this respect Jerome's formula expresses the general consensus of the Fathers: "Apostoli, vel virgines vel post nuptias continentes".[83] Let us also note the principle that, according to him, is the source of all chastity: "Christus virgo, virgo Maria utrique sexui virginitatis dedicavere principia". It is the living law of virginity lived by Christ and his mother that is the origin of the virginity lived in the Church by the faithful of both sexes. Now freely accepted by some, it is for priests the principle of "sanctity" called for by their ministry, and at their level it is translated into the special demands of continence. Though he does not explicitly say so here, his thought remains animated by the sentence quoted above: "Si sacerdotibus non licet uxores tangere, in eo sancti sunt, quia imitantur pudicitiam virginalem"; the imitation of virginal purity, inaugurated by Christ and his mother, is from now on the rule of the new priesthood; it explains what criteria are used in the Church for recruiting clerics. Going beyond the arguments drawn from Leviticus, Jerome highlights the fundamental principle that appears to him to govern, from its beginnings, the ordering of ecclesiastical discipline.

Adversus Vigilantium (406)

On returning to Languedoc, the priest Vigilantius, who harbored a grudge against Jerome for having suspected him of Origenist sympathies, launched a campaign to disparage a whole series of Christian customs that had up to then been highly respected: the cult of the martyrs, the veneration of relics, the invocation of saints, renunciation of one's worldly goods for the sake of the poor—all these things met with his scorn; even clerical continence was a target for this follower of Jovinian. Vigilantius saw continence as nothing but heresy and an occasion of sin. This kind of talk was all it took to make Jerome break his silence. As soon as Jerome had been alerted to all this by a courier from Gaul, he worked feverishly all night long dictating his rebuttal; Jerome's refutation, as far as one can tell, silenced the troublemaker from Languedoc once and for all.

What exactly had Vigilantius said? His writings have been lost, and our information is limited to what the monk of Bethlehem was willing to retain. In any case, we are not interested here in the theories of priestly continence's enemy, but in the reflection that sprang out from Jerome's pen with regard to the discipline attacked by his adversary:

Alas! It is said that [Vigilantius] has bishops on his criminal side; if we [still] have to call them bishops, these people who ordain no one to the

[83] See above, pp. 79–83.

diaconate unless [the candidates] are already married, and who do not trust the chastity of a single man; they go so far as to show what "holy" life they lead, they who suspect evil in everybody else, and who, if they do not see the wives of clerics pregnant or infants crying in their mothers' laps, do not grant the sacraments of Christ. What would the Eastern Churches do? What would [those of] Egypt and the Apostolic See do, they who never accept clerics unless they are virgins or continent men, or if [they are clerics who] had had a wife, [accept them only] if they give up matrimonial life? . . . [84]

Thus, if we believe the polemic, the bishops of Vigilantius' party lived freely with their wives, refused to ordain unmarried men as deacons, and did not at all trust the chastity of single men. To this unedifying picture Jerome opposes the practice that he knows to be traditional: With such men, what would happen to the Churches of the East? What would happen to the Churches of Egypt and those of the Apostolic See, which accepted only clerics who were virgins or continent men, or, in the case of clerics who had already been married, [asked them] to give up relations with their wives? In the face of the disorders prevalent in the Narbonne province of Gaul, the author of the *Adversus Vigilantium* calls the major part of Christendom as witness. Though he was quite carried away by the fire of polemic, we have no reason not to believe him when he gives as an example the discipline of continence practiced in large areas of the empire. Should we go further and discern in Jerome's allusion not only the indication of a widely spread custom but a witnessing to a formal law regulating, as he describes it, priestly recruiting? In itself the text does not permit any extrapolation and the fact has rightly been stressed.[85] But if we place this passage of the *Adversus Vigilantium* in the general context of Jerome's writings regarding the same problem, we will have no difficulty in admitting that the commentator of the epistle to Titus who defined the meaning of the Pauline *unius uxoris virum* in the same way as Siricius or Ambrose—and the writer who had launched against Jovinian an offensive based on contemporary legislation—had in mind more than a custom when he hurled the lines we have just read.

Isidore of Pelusium († ca. 431)

Born probably in Alexandria around the years 360–70, Isidore led a monastic life in a monastery located not far from Pelusium, east of the

---

[84] *Adversus Vigilantium*, 2. PL 23, 340b–41a.
[85] Cf. Hefele-Leclercq, II, 1, p. 1332; Funk, *Die apostolischen Konstitutionen*, p. 135.

Nile delta. Priest, ascetic, and exegete of high caliber, he had a deep influence on his time. Cyril of Alexandria called him his "father". His prophetic freedom of speech, together with an elegant style, made him a remarkable letter-writer. We still have over two thousand letters out of the three thousand he is said to have written. Through this correspondence we perceive a cultured mind and a spiritual master who did not hesitate to remind his contemporaries of their duties: "Priests, bishops, monks, provincial functionaries, great men of the court, he reprimanded them all with the greatest freedom; even the emperor, pious Theodosius II, did not escape the dressing down of the holy Egyptian. But it was especially the clergy of Pelusium, and even more their head, Bishop Eusebius, who received the brunt of his invectives" (L. Duchesne).[86]

Is there in Isidore of Pelusium's writings any explicit allusion to a discipline of continence for married clerics? The lofty idea he held about priests, imitating St. John Chrysostom, whom he deeply admired, allows us to suppose with enough certainty that he, for one, was favorable to it: "Those who exercise the priesthood", he wrote to Bishop Palladius, for instance, "must be holier and purer than those who settled in the mountains [i.e., the monks]."[87] But is it also possible to affirm even more and to say that the monk of Pelusium is a witness for Egypt, at least an indirect one, to the existence of a legislation similar to that of the Western councils of the 5th century? Bickell thought that he could do so in connection with a letter from Isidore that thus became a controversial document in the records of ecclesiastical continence. We refer to the reply that the Egyptian exegete sent to one Bishop Theodosius, who had questioned him about the exact meaning to be given to the phrase of St. Paul: "Offer your bodies as a living sacrifice, pleasing to God . . . ."[88] Here is the text:

To Theodosius, bishop

Those declared priests by the divine Paul, O excellent friend, are those who accomplish [the work of] piety not through animal sacrifices but by the very offering of their being, in all its nakedness, only those who, of their own volition, make their bodies into a pure libation. For the best of

---

[86] On this problem of authenticity of the letters and even the person of Isidore of Pelusium, see P. Évieux, "Isidore de Péluse, État des recherches", *Recherches de Sciences Religieuses* 64 (1976), pp. 321–40.

[87] II, 284. PG 78, 713b. One may also recall that in another of his letters, Isidore of Pelusium had opined against an interpretation of 1 Cor 9:5 that could have led us to think that the apostles continued their conjugal lives after they had been called by Christ (see above, p. 81).

[88] Rom 12:1.

all sacrifices is to have a soul exempt from stain and a chaste flesh. This is why he also said these words, about which you asked for an explanation: "Offer your bodies as a living sacrifice, pleasing to God; this is the reasonable worship you have to give." And, in truth, when he made this regulation he was not addressing only priests, as you think, but the entire Church. He asked everyone, in this sphere, to be a priest. But if chastity makes priests of those who are in an inferior position, sexual misbehavior, for its part, obviously deprives priests of their dignity. The laws prescribe it, even though it does not always happen that way. It is not for me to state the reasons. As to those who have received the crown of the divine priesthood and who have truly deserved the presidency, if they still keep bodily chastity, they are the holiest of all. For as was the case in the Old Covenant, only the priests offered sacrifices, whereas at the time of Passover all were somehow honored [because each one immolated a lamb]; such is also the case in the New and perpetual [Covenant], when all who are permitted to offer it exercise in a special way the liturgy of the unbloody sacrifice. Each one is ordered priest of his own body, not in order to claim power over others, if he has not received the imposition of hands, but to transform his whole body—by mastering his passions—into a sanctuary or temple of chastity.[89]

Bickell opines that the "misbehavior" (λαγνεία) depriving priests of their dignity that is mentioned in this letter is to be understood above all as a continuation of conjugal life by those of the men who were ordained after they had already been married. To support his interpretation, the German professor stresses the remark that follows immediately afterward: "The laws prescribe it even though it does not always happen that way." Had Isidore made only an oblique reference to sins of impurity in general, Bickell points out, the latter remark would have been superfluous and the former inaccurate. The reason is therefore that he also holds, in a very explicit way, the priests' obligation to continence to have been an ecclesiastical law.[90] What can we think about this interpretation of the letter from Isidore? As far as vocabulary is concerned, the word λαγνεία generally described sexual relations[91] and could indeed be used in connection with conjugal intimacy. However, Isidore generally uses in his correspondence the term λαγνεία and words derived from the same root to denote license and impurity.[92] To restrict the meaning in

---

[89] III, 75. PG 78, 781a–84a.

[90] G. Bickell, "Der Cölibat eine apostolische Anordnung", in ZkTh (1878), pp. 52–53.

[91] Cf. H. G. Liddell and R. Scott, A Greek-English Lexicon, 6th ed. (Oxford, 1932), p. 1022: λαγνεία, the act of coitus, sexual intercourse. P. Chantraine, Dictionnaire étymologique de la langue grecque. Histoire des mots, III (Paris, 1974), p. 611: λαγνεία, sexual relations, salacity.

[92] Cf. I, 135 (PG 78, 272b); IV, 129 (PG 78, 1208b, 1209b).

the above letter to conjugal relations would be legitimate only if the context permitted it. Now, contrary to what Bickell thinks, it is not inaccurate that the offenses of fornication and adultery would have been forbidden to clerics by ecclesiastical law. We have more than one canon of the early centuries enacting severe sanctions for such offenses, especially the penalty of deposition.[93] Notwithstanding the comment of the monk of Pelusium admitting that "such things do not always happen", many abuses, according to Isidore himself, were widespread in the ranks of the Egyptian clergy[94] and especially in the Church of Pelusium, where the unworthy Eusebius' accession to the episcopal See had encouraged the ordination of men who were not meant for the priesthood. Thus the remark is not as "superfluous" as Bickell wishes it to be judged.

Funk is therefore right, we believe, in criticizing Bickell's position on this point, by noting that "it is daring enough to see in the impudicity of the priests the mere continuation of a matrimonial life started before ordination".[95] But the reasons invoked by the Tübingen professor are not convincing in themselves: "To judge on the basis of the remark that follows immediately", he says, "this interpretation [of Bickell's] seems frankly incorrect." We read: "If the heads of the Church keep also bodily purity, they are holier than the priests."[96] The original Greek of that sentence is as follows: εἰ καὶ τὴν τοῦ σώματος ἁγνείαν φυλάξοιεν ὄντως ἱερῶς εἰσιν ἱερώτεροι. By translating the words ὄντως ἱερῶν κτλ. as "they are holier than the priests", Funk has a correct meaning from the viewpoint of syntax. Such a translation would, however, give a rather obscure general meaning to the sentence, putting in Isidore's mouth such words as "As to those who are crowned with the divine priesthood . . . if they still keep bodily chastity, they are holier than the priests", meaning holier than themselves. Which is why we prefer the translation: "They are the holiest of all", manifesting the eminent sanctity achieved by the heads of the Church when they also keep chastity.[97] Isidore does not

---

[93] See, for instance, *Council of Neocaesarea* (314–19), can. 1 (Joannou, I, 2, p. 75); Basil of Caesarea, *Canons to Amphilochius* (ca. 370), can. 3 and 70 (Joannou, II, pp. 100–101 and 149–50); *Codex canonum Ecclesiae africanae* (419), can. 27 (Joannou, I, 2, p. 243); *Canones apostolorum* (5th century), can. 25 (Joannou, I, 2, p. 19); etc.

[94] See, in particular, the letter to Cyril of Alexandria, in which Isidore blames the behavior of Bishop Eusebius of Pelusium: II, 127 (PG 78, 565a–72c). A description of the disorders that had crept into certain Churches is also given in the letter to Bishop Leontius, published by R. Aigrain, in *49 lettres de saint Isidore de Péluse* (Paris, 1911), pp. 44–46.

[95] F. X. Funk, "Cölibat und Priesterehe", p. 135.

[96] Ibid.

[97] This is also the translation adopted by J. Billy in PG 78, 782d–83a ("At vero qui divino sacerdotio redimiti, ac praefecturam digne consecuti sunt, si corporis quoque castitatem custodiant, vere plusquam sacrosancti sunt"), and by R. Gryson, *Les origines du célibat*, p. 51.

imply by this that conjugal continence was optional for the members of the higher clergy. He simply highlights the effects of the virtue of chastity on the priests who practice it, be they married or not. The question whether properly defined continence, for married or single clerics, was compulsory or not does not belong to his subject matter here.

To summarize, the letter of Isidore of Pelusium to Bishop Theodosius is not, in our view, a specific part of the records on clerical continence during the early centuries of the Church. We cannot follow Bickell when he sees in the reference to the "misbehavior" of the priests an allusion to a continuation of conjugal life after ordination; but, inversely, we cannot follow Funk's reasoning all the way and affirm that the letter bore witness to a freedom to practice or not to practice conjugal continence that had been given to the sacred ministers. In fact, the monk of Pelusium who saw many disorders in the ranks of the clergy of his country is thinking about fornication and adultery and not the continence (or "incontinence") of married clerics.

Synesius of Ptolemais (370/75–413/14)

Eclipsed by the prestige of the great Churches of Alexandria and Carthage, the modest province of Cyrenaica, located between those two lighthouses of the Christian world, seems to have had a rather dull existence. However, one name, at the threshold of the 5th century, illustrates the annals of the Libyan Church. Around the year 410, the "Mitered Platonist"—a nickname that is almost a biography—Synesius of Cyrene was selected through plebiscite to the episcopate by the faithful of his country who owed their lives to him. He would gladly have done without such an honor. Born into a rich family, brought up with a love of literature and philosophy, he had a passion for hunting, was not adverse to pleasure, loved his privacy, and was not too keen on preaching a doctrine in which his personal convictions were not always represented. Describing himself as such in a fascinating correspondence, he gave us an open book on his inner struggles. It was no small battle for that man of war, a great lord of the spirit also, to overcome his own resistance in order to accept the responsibilities that were to tie him down.

Letter 105 (ca. 410)

Synesius admits candidly that there was one obstacle holding him back more than anything else. It had not been long since "God and the law, by the consecrated hand of Theophilus" had given him in marriage a wife whom he dearly loved, and they had already been blessed with three sons. As a husband truly happy in his family life, he was not looking forward to a state of life that would require him to give up these lawful sources of happiness. He was not sure how to reconcile the duties of a bishop with the conjugal love of married life, for a bishop's life had to be "godly" in every way, and upon a bishop, as he knew very well, physical pleasure could have no claim. Would he resign himself to being separated from his wife? How could he, who had always lived in peace with God, with a clear conscience, bear to go on living with her when their life together had become unlawful, when he would be called an adulterer if he tried to wear a miter and be a husband at the same time? So, he took up his pen, and Theophilus of Alexandria received a letter from him. It will be worthwhile to examine a few passages from that letter:

But a bishop must be a godly man; like God himself, a bishop truly must not allow himself to be attracted to life's pleasures, for he is kept faithful to his charge by the watchful eyes of thousands; however, this scrutiny is no protection to him and does him no good at all if he is a man who is easily led astray and does not know how to conduct himself with tremendous reserve. . . . And every time anyone asks me, I do not hesitate to tell him frankly that a bishop must be above ordinary men in every respect. His reputation must be spotless, and thus he must be far removed from everyone else, seeing that he is the one whose job it is to cleanse the stains from everyone else. . . . Now then, God, and the law, and the anointed hand of Theophilus, have given me a wife. Well, I confess before all men and I freely admit: I do not want to be separated from her for ever, or to live with her in secret, like an adulterer. For the first attitude would be contrary to love, and the second unlawful. But I would hope and pray [without ceasing] to have lots of fine children. I want to be absolutely sure that the bishop responsible for the ordination knows exactly how I feel on this point. . . . If, knowing the thoughts I have confessed openly—and I certainly would never try to hide them—the man whom God has given the power to elevate me to the episcopate decides to go ahead with making me a bishop, I will obey because it is necessary, and I will accept it as a word that comes from God. If the king, or some evil genius of an imperial bureaucrat, were to give me an order, and if I had to disobey that order, I would deserve to be severely punished. But one must obey God freely and not out of fear of being punished. And if God does not wish to have me as a minister of the liturgy, then, I think, first of all it is necessary to love God's most holy Will and God's truth, and one must not insinuate oneself into God's service while one's mental attitude is diametrically opposed to the mind of God, as it would be if he lied, for example. Please make certain that the properly qualified persons know all about what I have just said and are made fully aware of what I think.[98]

From its very outset this plea shows the lofty conception Synesius held of the office of bishop. However human he is, a bishop is nothing less than "divine", θεοπέσιον, and must remain as detached as God himself from the attraction to pleasure. The watchful scrutiny of myriads of eyes, furthermore, will not do him much good if he is not already naturally inclined toward an austerity of life that will qualify him to purify the lives of others. As a Christian thinker, he says that to anyone who is willing to listen: as one who loves his life just as it is, he is not unaware that the work of a pastor and the pursuit of pleasure are mutually exclusive. These exemplary statements are truly in line with their times; they express, along with other pages from the writings of the future bishop of Cyrene, "the high ideal educated men upheld, at the beginning of the 5th century, of the Christian priest and his work; that ideal is worthy of a place beside the De Sacerdotio by St. John Chrysostom and several other writings of the same kind." [99]

Having said that, the husband comes to what is closest to his heart. He has a wife, to whom he has every legitimate right, since God himself and the law and the consecrated hand of Theophilus have given her to him. He does not want to be separated from her, or to live with her secretly like an adulterer. The first solution would be contrary to love, the second against the law (ἥκιστα νόμιμον). Further, he expects to have many more fine children. . . .

The commentators differ on the meaning of these sentences. Some think that by discussing his problem of conscience, Synesius would have been placing a *sine qua non* condition on his acceptance of the episcopal office, and, since the episcopacy was actually conferred on him, they come to the conclusion that he had been authorized to go on living openly with his wife.[100] Such a hypothesis does not seem to take sufficient account of the vocabulary Synesius uses. When he thinks about what would happen if he continued to live with his wife after his consecration, what he has in mind is not a conduct that would have been condemned by a mere custom, and therefore could have been legitimately tolerated from him. He was thinking about a literal violation of laws governing ecclesiastical discipline. The word νόμιμος, as it is used here, is the same

---

[98] *Epist.* 105. PG 66, 1484a–88d. R. Hercher, ed., *Epistolographi graeci* (Paris, 1873), pp. 704–6.

[99] G. Bardy, "Synésius", in DTC 14, 3001.

[100] Cf. Hefele-Leclercq, II, 2, p. 1332, and J. Quasten, *Patrology*, III (Westminster, Md.: Newman Press, 1960), p. 107.

word Synesius has just used a moment ago to defend the value he places on his own marriage. While the marriage he had so recently contracted was legal in every respect, when he became a bishop his presently legal marital relationship would become illegal. The Libyan gentleman, therefore, is clearly affirming the existence of legislation binding the bishops of his province to perfect continence.[101] It is the knowledge of this law that holds him back from undertaking to enter into a state of life that would cause his marital relationship, now legal, to become illegal. When he says that living openly with his wife after becoming a bishop would cause him to be called an adulterer, it is not because he is determined, come what may, to go on living with his wife and having more children by her, but because he would prefer not to be made a bishop, so attached is he to the home he would not leave voluntarily.

The end of the letter makes his thought clear. Being as loyal toward God as he is toward his prince, Synesius adds that he will obey if he who holds divine authority gives him the order. It will be for him a divine command (θεῖον σύνθημα). Because he obeys the emperor, all the more so and spontaneously will he give in to God himself. Love of truth will forbid him from slipping into the ministry with hypocritical intentions. Let the judges decide. We know what they decided! The philosopher was elevated to the episcopate, and we have no reason to believe that having become, in his turn, a "divine man", he lived against his conscience as well as against the law, in adultery.

We think that this interpretation respects the internal structure of the letter and can still be confirmed by documents relative to the Eastern discipline that we have already seen,[102] and to which we must add here a letter written by Cyril of Alexandria to the bishops of Libya and Pentapolis (ca. 443), asking that before they admit a cleric to the imposition of hands they should examine his life: "If he has taken a wife or not; how and when he contracted a marriage and if he abstained from doing so".[103] Coming later than Synesius of Cyrene's elevation to the

---

[101] Misunderstanding the phrase ἥκιστα νόμιμον, H. Leclercq translated this passage: "Separation would be impious; clandestine relations would be contrary to the rule of marriage" ("La législation conciliaire relative au célibat ecclésiastique", *Histoire des Conciles* Appendix VI, II, 2 [Paris, 1908], p. 1332). The rule that Synesius is talking about is not that of marriage, which would make the hypothesis of clandestine relations an absurdity, but truly the ecclesiastical law of continence.

[102] See above, pp. 245–47, 298–99.

[103] Here is the Greek text of this document:

(γ) Περὶ τοῦ πῶς καὶ πότε δεῖ χειροτονεῖν καὶ τίνα δεῖ ἐξετάζειν.

Ἐπειδὴ τοίνυν πρὸς οἰκοδομήν, ὡς ἔφην, τῶν λαῶν πάντα χρὴ πράττεσθαι παρ᾽ ἡμῶν,

episcopate, that letter is a reminder of an already ancient obligation, in agreement with the testimony of Synesius himself, who indirectly bore witness to its existence.

For all these reasons we think that the episode of the Libyan bishop's election is to be placed with the texts attesting to a formal law imposing the duty of conjugal abstinence on the higher clergy, especially on the heads of communities.[104]

4. ANONYMOUS AND APOCRYPHAL TEXTS

The Apostolic Constitutions
(late 4th century–early 5th century)

The pseudoapostolic compilation entitled Διαταγαὶ τῶν ἁγίων ἀποσ-τόλων διὰ Κλήμεντος τοῦ Ῥωμαίων ἐπισκόπου τε καὶ πολίτου, ἢ καθολικὴ διδασκαλία must have appeared in Syria (Antioch) or in Palestine toward the end of the 4th century or the beginning of the 5th. Wrongly credited to St. Clement of Rome (92–101), it was the work of a semi-Arian who used prior sources. The text was published for the first time in Venice in 1563 by the Jesuit Fr. Turrianus, or Torres, who also presented a Latin version a few years later (1578). While unknown

---

ἐπιτηρείτω ταῦτα ἡ θεοσέβεια ὑμῶν; καὶ εἰ μέλλοι τις χειροτονεῖσθαι κληρικός, περιεργαζέσθω τὸν βίον αὐτοῦ, καὶ πότερόν ποτε γαμετὴν ἔχει ἢ οὔ, καὶ πῶς ἢ πότε ἠγάγετο, καὶ εἰ ἀπέσχετο; καὶ εἰ μή τίς ἐστι τῶν ἐκβεβλημένων ἢ παρ᾽ ἑτέρου θεοσεβεστάτου ἐπισκόπου ἢ ἐκ μοναστηρίων. καὶ τότε χειροτονείτω, ἀδιάβλητον εὑρεθέντα. Τηρήσομεν γὰρ οὕτω καθαρὸν καὶ τὸ ἑαυτῶν συνειδὸς καὶ ἀδιάβλητον τὴν ἱερὰν καὶ σεπτὴν λειτουργίαν (Joannou, II, p. 283). R. Gryson, who quotes this text of Cyril, omits the phrase καὶ εἰ ἀπέσχετο ("and he abstained from it"), which is, however, essential for the interpretation of this passage (*Les origines du célibat ecclésiastique*, p. 50).

[104] Cf. H. Druon, *Les oeuvres de Synésius, évêque de Ptolémaïs dans la Cyrénaïque au commencement du 5ᵉ siècle, traduites pour la première fois en français et précédées d'une étude biographique et littéraire* (Paris, 1878). See the introduction. Druon deems that Synesius actually ceased to live with his wife after his elevation to the episcopate. This is also the opinion of C. Knetes in *Ordination and Matrimony in the Eastern Church*, JTS (1910), p. 486: "This view is, to a certain extent, confirmed by the sense of desolation expressed in some letters of Synesius, written after his elevation to the episcopate (*Ep.* 8, 79, 57, 93, 89, 126, 70, 10, 16), and by the fact that no child was born to him after his consecration, for all his three sons were born during the five years before he became a bishop." More recently, C. Lacombrade concludes in the same vein: "It is more than likely that he renounced his conjugal life" (*Synesios de Cyrène. Hymnes.* Coll. "Budé" [1978], p. xxxviii).

in the West before that time, it seems the *Apostolic Constitutions* had a very great authority in the East until the Council in Trullo (691), when they were condemned as tainted with heresy, except for eighty-five canons called "of the apostles" appearing at the end of the work. The *Apostolic Constitutions* comprise eight books: the first six are an amplification and adaptation of the apostles' *Didascalia*; the seventh is related to the *Didache*, or *Doctrine of the Twelve Apostles*; the eighth and last book is likely derived from Hippolytus' *Apostolic Tradition*.

In chapter 17 of book 6, a passage of the *Apostolic Constitutions* deals with the issue of clerical marriage, taking its scriptural basis in the Pauline instruction of the *unius uxoris virum*:

> Ἐπίσκοπον καὶ πρεσβύτερον καὶ διάκονον εἴπομεν μονογάμους καθίστασθαι, κἂν ζῶσιν αὐτῶν αἱ γαμεταὶ κἂν τεθνᾶσι; μὴ ἐξεῖναι δὲ αὐτοῖς μετὰ χειροτονίαν ἀγάμοις οὖσιν, ἔτι ἐπὶ γάμον ἔρχεσθαι, ἢ γεγαμηκόσιν, ἑτέραις συμπλέκεσθαι, ἀλλ' ἀρκεῖσθαι, ἧ ἔχοντες ἦλθον ἐπὶ τὴν χειροτονίαν.

As bishops, priests, and deacons, it is necessary to install, as we have said, monogamists, whether their wives be still alive or already dead; should these men have been single, it is not permitted to them, after the imposition of hands, to contract a marriage or, if they were married, to unite themselves with other wives [or: to marry a second time]; let them be content with the wives they had when they were admitted to the imposition of hands [or: let it be enough for them to have reached the imposition of hands while having wives].[105]

This text brings up a specific problem because, after having evoked the rule of monogamy for the choice of candidates to the major Orders, the pseudo-Clement adds a sentence that can be interpreted in two different ways: ἢ γεγαμηκόσιν ἑτέραις συμπλέκεσαι, we read, 'αλλ' ἀρκεῖσαι ἧ ἔχοντες ἦλθον επὶ τὴν χειροτονίαν. In his 1563 edition—the first after the invention of the printing press—Fr. Torres (Turrianus) translates the Greek text as follows: "Si uxores non habent, praecipimus ut non liceat amplius ducere, aut si antea duxerant, non alias in matrimonium accipere, sed potius, quod cum haberent ad ordinationem venerunt, contentos esse."[106] Men married before the diaconate (or the priesthood)

---

[105] PG 1, 956a–57a. F. X. Funk, *Didascalia et Constitutiones Apostolorum*, I (Paderborn, 1905), pp. 339–41.

[106] Mansi 1, 462–63. See the commentary on this translation by the author himself in Fr. Turrianus (Fr. Torres), *Apostolicarum Constitutionum et Catholicae doctrinae Clementis Romani libri VIII* (Antwerpen, 1578), pp. 234–37.

are not authorized to contract a new marriage, but should rather feel privileged to have been able to reach ordination while having a wife. Whether that measure—presented as a provision for preferential treatment—also included the freedom to use marriage once the cleric had passed the threshold of the clergy's higher ranks is not what the author is asking himself, but such as it is the translation easily supports a commentary legitimizing the regulation prevailing in the Roman world, in the way Siricius, for instance, understood the exegesis of the Pauline *unius uxoris virum*: let the monogamists be happy to have been chosen since they have the same privilege as single men, though it remains understood that being elevated to the priestly ministry demands from them, as it does from all, observation of perfect chastity. We do not say that this meaning is directly implied in the sentence of the *Constitutions*, but that it can be claimed quite rightly by the Latin tradition, and this explains why the Western commentators did not generally place the chapter of the pseudo-Clement among the texts creating difficulties.

A second Latin translation, published in 1672 by Cotelier, on the other hand, could have implied an approval of continuing conjugal relations: "Si uxores non habeant", as the author understands it, "[non licere] matrimonium contrahere, aut si uxores habeant, cum aliis copulari: sed contentos esse ea, quam habentes, ad ordinationem venerunt." [107] Married ministers must content themselves with the women they had before ordination and not seek others; in this way, it would seem legitimate to understand that their right to unite with their wives is recognized. Though it gives an explanation, in itself, for the practice that will become legalized in 691 by the Quinisext Council, such an interpretation still shifts the emphasis of the Greek sentence and thus does not respect, in our view, the original meaning: it is not said the married candidates will have to be content with only one wife (as if one wished to protect them against the temptation of adultery), but that they must feel content that, having a wife, they are (nevertheless) elevated to ordination, the word ἢ being the equivalent of the conjunction εἰ, and the participle ἔχοντες having the grammatical role of an incidental clause clarifying the reason that should give to the parties an appreciation of the favor done to them. All in all, it is Fr. Torres' Latin that seems to give the precise meaning of ἀλλ᾽ ἀρκεῖσθαι ᾗ ἔχοντες ἦλθον ἐπὶ τὴν χειροτονίαν, and we can limit ourselves to the remarks that he suggests. In itself the passage in the sixth book of the *Apostolic Constitutions* is not a determining factor in deciding what could have been the discipline relative to clerical continence underlying the thought of the fifth-century Syrian writer; it equally lends

---

[107] PG 1, 958a.

itself to an interpretation conforming to the Trullan discipline and to a meaning in line with Siricius' decretals or the Western councils, and both traditions can recognize themselves in it.[108]

If we also take into account the fact that the Fathers of the Quinisext Council rejected the *Apostolic Constitutions* as distorted by heretical interpretations[109] and that the text of the pseudo-Clement remained unknown in the West until the 16th century, we can reasonably conclude that, at all events, the passage in question does not represent an essential witness to the early centuries' history.[110]

The Apostolic Canons
(late 4th–early 5th century)

The eighty-five canons known as *Apostolic Canons* are found at the end of book 8 of the *Apostolic Constitutions* and are perhaps the work of the same author. They are written as conciliar canons and reflect, for the most part, the decisions of the Council of Antioch (341) and the Council of Laodicea (late 4th century). The first fifty were translated into Latin by Denys the Minor (6th century) and thus became widespread in the West. In the East, the eighty-five canons were all adopted by the Quinisext Council of 691 (can. 2).

---

[108] For informational purposes, here is the conclusion of Fr. Torres about this passage: "Qui vero hic accipiendum putant, contentos esse ea quam habebant, aut sic contentos esse habere nunc, sicut prius, hi traditioni Apostolorum atque ipsis Patribus repugnant, ipsa etiam natura, et constructione verborum contradicente" (*Apostolicarum Constitutionum*, p. 327). Cotelier himself deems that it would be an unwarranted extrapolation of the text's meaning to see in it an implicit authorization for clerics to use their marital rights after ordination: "Nihil a nostro de licentia maritali dicitur" (PG 1, 957, n. 97).

[109] Quinisext Council, can. 2: "But because in these [apostolic] canons we are ordered also to receive the Constitutions of the very holy apostles as drawn up by Clement, to which formerly the heretics, to harm the Church, added things that are false and alien to the true faith, that tarnished the noble beauty of the divine truths, we have decided to reject, as it was right to do, these very Constitutions, for the edification and security of the most Christian people, by disapproving absolutely the madness of the heretical lies, basing ourselves on the pure and complete teaching of the apostles" (Joannou, I, 1, pp. 121–22).

[110] For a critical study of the *Apostolic Constitutions*, see H. Leclercq, *Constitutions apostoliques*, DACL 3, 2732–48, and F. X. Funk, *Didascalia et Constitutiones Apostolorum*, I (Paderborn, 1905).

Canon 6 (5)

The sixth (or fifth) of these canons placed under the patronage of the apostles had an important role in the history of the clerical discipline of celibacy-continence. Here is the text:

> Let no bishop, priest, or deacon send away his wife with the excuse of piety; if he sends her away, let him be excommunicated, and if he persists, let him be deposed.[111]

Two different interpretations were given. A first line of interpretation seems to have been started by Pope St. Leo in his letter to Rusticus of Narbonne.[112] While accepting the "apostolic" request not to send away the wife from the home of the married cleric under the excuse of piety, the Roman Pontiff nevertheless asks the couple to observe perfect chastity. Husband and wife, the cleric and his companion must live after ordination as though they were brother and sister, living their love at a level excluding carnal relations so as to achieve a higher union: "Ut de carnali fiat spirituale conjugium, oportet eos nec dimittere uxores, et quasi non habeant sic habere, quo et salva sit charitas connubiorum, et cesset opera nuptiarum [So that (their) carnal union become a spiritual one, they must, without sending away their wife, live with her so that they safeguard conjugal love and cease nuptial activity]." Such a difficult balance was to become the rule, not only in Rome but in the provinces of Gaul, Spain, and Africa, where the councils from the 5th to the 7th century would echo for a long time the Leonian directives.[113]

A second line of interpretation will be adopted, as we will see, by the Eastern Fathers of the Quinisext Council of 691 in Trullo, who based

---

[111] Ἐπίσκοπος ἢ πρεσβύτερος ἢ διάκονος τὴν ἑαυτοῦ γυναῖκα μὴ ἐκβαλλέτω προφάσει εὐλαβείας; ἐὰν δὲ ἐκβάλλῃ, ἀφοριζέσθω, ἐπιμένων δέ, καθαιρείσθω (Joannou, I, 2, p. 10).

[112] See above, pp. 261–64.

[113] If the evolution of ecclesiastical institutions was to bring certain provinces to stray from it little by little, to give way to a monastic lifestyle, it seems that Africa, in particular, always remained faithful to this principle, respecting both the rights of love and of chastity, as is attested in the *Breviatio Ferrandi* and especially the *Concordia Cresconii* (see pp. 324ff. and 383ff.). In the early 6th century, apostolic canon 6 was still ruling, in the Leonian sense, Western law, if we can judge by the title used by the Roman compiler Denys the Minor at the head of his translation of the Eastern councils: "Ut episcopus aut presbyter uxorem suam, quam debet caste regere, non relinquat" (Joannou, I, 2, p. 10). Not to abandon one's wife but to guide her in chastity was the traditional interpretation of the famous decree in the Church of the Latin world, which did not have a double standard—for bishops on the one hand and priests and deacons on the other—but which recognized for all of them the right to keep at home the companions of their lives.

themselves on this sixth canon "of the apostles" to justify the right of priests and deacons to use their marital rights.[114] It is noteworthy that the Trullan legislators were the first, in the East, to give such an interpretation.[115] On the other hand, while invoking the authority of the pseudoapostolic law, the Byzantine assembly of 691 will limit its scope to the above-mentioned ranks, keeping the obligation of marital separation for bishops (can. 48).

These two types of interpretation show the complexity of the problem and invite the modern historian not to prejudge in abstracto the meaning of the sixth apostolic canon. The latter depends essentially on the disciplinary context in which it is received: today we have to read it in light of that context, which was different in the East at the end of the 7th century from what it had been since the time of St. Leo for a great part of the Christian communities of the Roman world.

The Doctrina Aeddei (ca. 400)

In the first book of his *Historia Ecclesiastica*, Eusebius of Caesarea relates a legend according to which the Lord sent Thaddeus, one of the seventy-two disciples, to King Abgar of Edessa (I:13). Around the year 400, an unknown author composed an edifying narrative around that Mesopotamian tradition, and it has come down to us in the manuscripts of the 5th and 6th centuries. Known under the title *Doctrina Aeddei*, it offers a long recension of a third-century Syriac work: *The Acts of Thaddeus.*[116]

Before he died, the apostle Addai (*alias* Thaddeus) allegedly left to his clergy some recommendations to which the apocryphal narrative purports to link the discipline of the Edessa Church. That spiritual testament contains in particular the following logion: "He [Addai] has carefully prescribed [to his clerics] to keep their bodies in purity and sanctity, as befits men standing in the presence of God's altar."

That recommendation was perfectly observed, as we read further: "All those who were devoted to the ecclesiastical service, men and women,

---

[114] See below, pp. 405ff. Quinisext Council, can. 13. Joannou, I, 1, p. 143.

[115] Emperor Justinian, who, in the 6th century, will also place the *Apostolic Canons* among the canons of the Church, will nevertheless demand that deacons, priests, and above all bishops abandon all relations with their wives. Our 6th canon did not seem to be, for him, an equally explicit motive in favor of conjugal freedom for clerics, no more than it would be for the conciliar assembly of 691.

[116] Cf. I. Ortiz de Urbina, *Patrologia syriaca* (Rome, 1958), pp. 41–42. J. Tixeront, *Les origines de l'Église d'Édesse et la légende d'Abgar* (Paris, 1888).

were chaste, prudent, holy, and pure, because they lived separately [from one another] and [lived] chastely and without stain." [117]

As is the case with the *Ecclesiastical Canons of the Holy Apostles*, published in the 4th century among the Egyptian Christian communities,[118] we are dealing here with an original literary genre. It is a question of putting under the authority of an apostle a discipline whose validity one is trying to justify, or to promote its application. This entails many precautions. Given the favor enjoyed in those days by such narratives, it must, however, be deemed that the *Doctrina Aeddei* is not to be eliminated *a priori* from our records, and that we should take into account the indications that it gives us about the state of mind in certain Edessian circles.[119] An apostolic tradition had it that clerics employed at the service of the altar (*qui coram altaribus Dei starent*) kept perfect bodily purity. That was not a mere matter of external purification rites but of chastity; the description evoking the morals of men and women "devoted to ecclesiastical service" is quite clear on this point. They were all *casti, cauti, sancti et puri*, men and women living separately and keeping themselves from any fault.

The discipline of the Church of Edessa, such as the apocryphal author wished it to be or actually described it, would correspond to what we know about other Churches through contemporary documents. Continence was demanded from clerics at the service of the altar, whom we must understand as being, in all likelihood, bishops, priests, and deacons. As to the women, the reference is probably to deaconesses, bound for the same "liturgical" reasons to perfect chastity. The same discipline is attested in Persia by the third canon of the Council of Seleucia-Ctesiphon in 410.[120]

The De Septem Ordinibus Ecclesiae (ca. 417) (Pseudo-Jerome)

As indicated by its title, this booklet is a short treatise on the various ranks of the ecclesiastical hierarchy. In this book the author, who was likely a priest (or even a bishop) from the area of Arles-Marseilles, living

---

[117] Translation based on the Latin text of H. Hurter, *Theologiae dogmaticae compendium*, III, 9th ed. (Oeniponte), p. 522.

[118] See above, pp. 203ff.

[119] They can even testify to a rather ancient period, if one accepts with Tixeront that "the legend of Abgar started . . . to take shape around the middle of the 3d century" before becoming, more than a hundred years later, the *Doctrina Aeddei* (*Les origines*, p. 158).

[120] See above, pp. 281–82.

at about the same time as Jerome, addresses a layman who has been suddenly elevated to the episcopate, exhorting him to fulfill worthily the duties of his functions.[121]

A passage from the *De septem ordinibus* is of special interest in view of our subject:

> Because of the ancient custom and the damage to the priesthood [that can result from it], do not give to your wife power over your soul. . . . Of course, you must love your wife, but as you love the Church or the temple of God; pray with her, read [with her], abstain [from conjugal relationships], commune at the altar and not in the act [of the flesh]. As to her, she also must venerate you, because of the law that unites you, not desire you because of the customary ending [of the common life]: you know indeed quite well that the use of marriage is forbidden to you as soon as you learn that you will become a bishop.[122]

The addressee is thus reminded of the principles reconciling, in a bishop, love of his wife and conjugal continence. As far as we know this is the first document—chronologically—where we can see a viewpoint taking into account the demands of the affection uniting husband and wife, even beyond the change of lifestyle begun at ordination, and it is noteworthy. The "bodily separation" requested from the couple is not a denial of love, contrary to what the dryness of the laws might let us feel at times, but its "sublimation", if we wish to use a modern word, in a kind of relationship lived on a higher level. In other words, this is transcending conjugal love that from a carnal stage passes to a consummation in spiritual union: "Amanda quidem uxor est, sed sicut Ecclesia aut Templum Dei, orandum cum ea, legendum, abstinendum, communicandum in altario, non in opere; spiritu, non carne vivendum." Here we have the first formulation of the rule that will be enunciated by Pope St. Leo in 458–59: "Et salva sit caritas connubiorum, et cesset opera nuptiarum."[123]

As lofty as it is, the ideal just described is not simply proposed as a remote goal, an effort of spiritualization more or less compatible with forgivable human fumblings; by accepting the episcopate, the newly elected bishop knows what his commitment is: "Quia aperte tibi usum conjugii interdictum esse perpendis, cum te episcopum esse cognoscis." The new way of life, in accordance with the law, begins with it. Through the exhortations of pseudo-Jerome we recognize the substance of the

---

[121] See above, pp. 100–101.

[122] PL 30, 159c–d.

[123] *Epist. ad Rusticum Narbonensem episcopum, Inquis. III, Resp.* PL 54, 1204a.

decrees in force in those regions of the Christian world where our historical inquiry has already led us.

In asking the married bishop to transpose his conjugal existence to a new level, the writer of the *opusculum* is careful enough not to offer him what we would call a bachelor's spirituality. Husband he is and husband he remains, and this essential dimension of his life finds its true blossoming in the covenant uniting him with the people entrusted to him, his paternity extending to the multitude of God's children: "What better wife than the Church of God, I ask you, [can] a bishop look for? What better children than the people of God? . . . " [124]

Here are new reasons dictating his behavior and that of the men he will have to choose for the priesthood. To return to a "carnal" love of his wife would deserve the reproach of adultery, because he is not so much being faithful to the old conjugal tie as he is perjuring the commitment to chastity: "For the man is guilty of adultery if after repudiating [his] God, he becomes a prisoner to the love of his wife; he uses less the old law of marriage than he shows himself ready to violate the new one, the one that compels him to remain pure." [125]

In the framework of a familiar exhortation, the *opusculum de septem ordinibus Ecclesiae* is therefore an interesting witness to the discipline of priestly continence in the south of Gaul, and at the same time it is an essay on priestly conjugal spirituality elaborating the theme of human love's transcendence in couples called by the priesthood of the husband to a more perfect life.

The Testamentum Domini Nostri Jesu Christi
(late 5th century)

This apocryphal collection was probably written in Syria by the end of the 5th century. The work of an unknown author (perhaps a Monophysite), it was written in Greek, but today we have only its Syriac, Coptic, and Ethiopian versions. It was published for the first time in Syriac, together with a Latin translation by H. E. Ignatius Ephrem II Rahmani, Syrian Patriarch of Antioch, in 1899. The complete title is: *Testament or Words That Our Lord Jesus Christ Told to His Holy Apostles and That Were Written by Clement of Rome, Disciple of Peter.* It is divided into two books: in the first, Jesus gives his instructions to his disciples before his Ascension; in

---

[124] G. Morin, "Pages inédites de deux pseudo-Jérômes, des environs de l'an 400", *Revue Bénédictine* 40 (1928), p. 312.

[125] Ibid., p. 314.

the second, which is the canonical part of the book, there are rules about the sacraments and Christian life. The collection depends on Hippolytus' *Apostolic Tradition*.[126]

Two passages of the *Testamentum* regarding priestly continence are to be entered into our records. One concerns bishops, and the other, deacons:

I. *Institution of a bishop*

XX: After having built the house [of the church] as is also necessary, let the bishop be ordained; he must be elected by all the people according to the desire of the Holy Spirit; this surely ought to be an irreproachable man, chaste, meek, humble. . . .

It is best for the man [elevated to the episcopate] not to have a wife; at least let him be a man who has had only one wife, so that he be able to share the distress of widows.[127]

II. *Institution of a deacon*

XXXII: *Of the deacons.*
The candidate chosen in conformity with the previously listed [conditions] will be ordained a deacon: let him be of good behavior, pure, and chosen because of his purity and [voluntary] inexperience of the senses' charms. At least let him be a man who was married to only one wife.[128]

It is asked that the bishop preferably be a single man; at the least, that he had had only one wife, so as to be able to share the distress of widows. The Pauline instruction of the *unius uxoris virum* is given here in the past tense of the verb *fuit*; one can wonder whether the author knew a biblical text that truly expressed such a grammatical shade of meaning, or whether he did not take upon himself to introduce it in the Pauline verse so as to adapt it to the discipline he recommended. I. E. Rahmani affirms that the *Testamentum* uses the Syriac version of the New Testament, known by the name of *Peschitta*, in which the passage of the epistles to Timothy and Titus regarding the choice of monogamists has a past-tense verbal form: *Wa-hwā ba'lā da-ḥ dā'anttā (qui* fuit *unius uxoris virum).*[129] Now, the Syriac translation of the New Testament, whose presumed author,

---

[126] Cf. F. X. Funk, *Das Testament unseres Herrn und die verwandten Schriften* (Mainz, 1901); O. Bardenhewer, *Altkirchliche Literatur*, IV (1924), pp. 262–75; E. Amann, *Testament de Notre Seigneur Jésus-Christ*, DTC 15, 194–200; I. E. Rahmani, *Testamentum Domini Nostri Jesu Christi, texte syriaque et traduction latine* (Mainz, 1899) (I. E. Rahmani thought that he could date the collection from the 2d century).

[127] I. E. Rahmani, ibid., p. 27; our emphasis.

[128] Ibid., pp. 79–81.

[129] Ibid., p. 157.

Rabbula, was bishop of Edessa at the time of the Council of Ephesus (431), shows, in comparison to the "Western" lessons, original features that seem to have come from a rather ancient source.[130] It would not be impossible, therefore, that the incidental clause *qui fuit unius uxoris virum* comes from a biblical source more genuine because of its antiquity than we are tempted to suspect at first glance.[131]

The instructions of the *Testamentum* regarding the institution of deacons express in partially different terms the principles already enunciated for the choice of bishops. The circumlocution "let him be . . . pure and chosen because of his purity and [voluntary] inexperience of the senses' charms" (si purus, si propter suam puritatem et exemptionem ab illecebris fuerit electus) obviously describes the state of a single man. It is in fact immediately followed by the conjunction *sin minus*, indicating an alternative. In case there are no men who have the described qualities, one should at least choose a former monogamist ("qui conjunctus fuit matrimonio cum una uxore"). Such qualities cannot therefore logically be applied except to men who were never married. If the instruction uses "purity and inexperience of the senses' charms [puritatem et exemptionem ab illecebris]", instead of simply saying "sine uxore sit", it is undoubtedly to stress the morals of the candidate rather than the situation, in itself morally indifferent, of the single state.

It goes without saying that these conditions required at the diaconate level are also valid for priests, though the *Testamentum* does not prescribe anything concerning them.

Finally, let us note that the formula *qui conjunctus fuit matrimonio cum una uxore* does not impose the understanding, as clearly as for the bishop, that this means monogamists who became widowers. Though the use of the past tense suggests a preference for such an interpretation, one is left free to think that if the layman were married before his ordination, he still could receive the diaconate while his wife was alive. The general context of the instruction seems, however, to indicate clearly that from then on he was bound to observe perfect continence.[132]

---

[130] Cf. E. Amann, *Versions de la Bible*, DTC 15, 2726.

[131] With respect to the Coptic translations of the Bible, R. Kasser pointed out something that is, we think, equally true for the Syriac *Peschitta*: "It would not surprise us to find out, one day, by some new testimony, that the first biblical translations in Coptic language had already been done in the second half of the 2d century or at least at the end of the 2d century. Through these translations one could then perceive original texts that were as ancient as, or even more ancient than, most of the oldest witnesses of the Greek Bible. This is a possibility that we must take into account each time we use the archaic Coptic versions in a study of textual criticism" (R. Kasser, "Les origines du christianisme égyptien", *Revue de Théologie et de Philosophie* I [1962], p. 28).

[132] The text adds: "Si vero habuit jam uxorem vel si ei liberi sunt, discant ipsius filii

5. IMPERIAL LAWS

Theodosian Code (438)

This name applies to the genuine collection of the imperial constitutions enacted from Constantine the Great (306–37) to Theodosius II (408–50). Prepared by order of the latter, it was published in the East on February 5, 438, and came into effect on January 1, 439. This *Codex Theodosius* was sent in late 438 to the Senate of Rome, which adopted it officially. Thus was achieved, at least temporarily, the legislative unification of the Roman world. In 529, the Theodosian Code would be replaced by the Justinian Code.

An entire book of the code—which comprises sixteen books—is devoted to religious matters. It is book 16 in which we find a copy of an ordinance sent jointly by Western Emperor Honorius (395–423) and Eastern Emperor Theodosius II (408–50) to Palladius, prefect of the praetorium. Dated May 8, 420, it reiterates in particular the prohibition against clerics living with "outsider" women:

Honorius and Theodosius, August Emperors,
to Palladius, prefect of the praetorium

> It is not fitting that he who practices an estimable rule [in the eyes] of the world be ill considered by [the company of women] called by the name of "sisters". Therefore, those who, at whatever degree, are covered by the splendor of the priesthood or those who are affiliated with the dignity of the clergy must know that a community of life with "outsider" women is forbidden to them; they may only be granted the option of keeping in their house their mother, their daughters, and their sisters; the natural ties, indeed, do not permit casting any evil suspicion over the latter. A chaste love also invites one not to send away those who, before the priesthood of their husbands, had been worthy [of union with them] through a legitimate marriage: indeed, it is not without reason that they are associated with clerics, those who, through their behavior, made their husbands worthy of the priesthood.[133]

The recommendation inviting clerics not to abandon their wives is to be compared to the sixth (fifth) apostolic canon. What is directly

---

pietatem colere, et puros se exhibere." The turn of phrase seems to indicate that those are children he might have had before his ordination.

[133] T. Mommsen and P. Meyer, *Codex Theodosianus*, I, 2 (Berlin, 1903), p. 851.

concerned is not the issue of conjugal relations but the duty binding a man—even though he is a priest—to his wife and preventing him, under whatever excuse, from sending her away. In itself the Theodosian document does not allow one to clarify whether the presence of the wife in the home of a cleric—which is permitted here, or, to be more exact, strongly encouraged—is tantamount to an implicit freedom of the use of marriage. Such a distinction was common, as we know, during the 5th and 6th centuries. The phrase *castitatis adfectio* (a chaste love) would rather insinuate that chastity, in the exact meaning that we have seen it acquiring in the documents of that time, perfect continence, was for imperial legislators the condition legitimizing their ordinance. The justifying considerations through which they feel they must prove its validity ("Indeed, it is not without reason that they are associated with clerics . . . ") also give the same impression. And this all the more so that, after having authorized "all those who are counted in the honor of the clergy" to live together with their close relatives, Honorius and Theodosius now limit their field of observation to the sole ministers of the higher hierarchy. It is not for the mass of clerics that they raise the issue of the wife, but only for those who reach the priestly Order itself. The wives of whom they speak are those who "before the priesthood of their husbands" deserved to be united to them; and it was quite proper, they comment, to give them in marriage to (lower) clerics, they who by their behavior have made their husbands worthy of the priesthood.

This body of remarks strongly inclines us to believe that the decree of the *Codex Theodosius* is exactly in line with the letter of St. Leo to Rusticus of Narbonne[134] defining the *modus vivendi* particular to bishops and priests: they must not send away their wives but simultaneously cease their conjugal relations. In the absence of other Theodosian documents that would enable us better to measure its scope, however, we have to leave this text in a state of indetermination and recognize that it can be understood differently depending on the disciplinary context in which it is integrated. Just as for the sixth (fifth) apostolic canon, we can do no better than conclude with such an observation.[135]

[134] See above, pp. 261–64.
[135] See above, pp. 311–12.

6. HISTORIANS

Socrates

Historia Ecclesiastica, V, 22 (ca. 440)

The Byzantine historian Socrates, to whom we already owe the narrative of the episode of Paphnutius' intervention at the Council of Nicaea, relates in another chapter of his *Historia Ecclesiastica* a custom that he says he observed during his travels. In Thessalonika, the clerics who go on having conjugal relations with their wives after having been admitted to the clergy are excommunicated. And Socrates is surprised because, as he avers, this particular point is not the object of any legal prohibition in the entire East; everyone is free to practice continence as he wishes:

> I was told about another custom while I was in Thessalonika. There, if a cleric, after having joined the ranks of the clergy, has relations with the wife he had legitimately married before becoming a cleric, he is excommunicated. In the East [on the other hand], all practice continence as they wish and even the bishops do it only if they want to, without being under the constraint of a law. Among them, indeed, many have had children from their legitimate wives while they were bishops.[136]

The Thessalonian custom whose existence is affirmed by the Greek author agrees in the main with the information given in the letter of St. Leo to Anastasius of Thessalonika.[137] On one point, though, an inaccuracy can be discerned: it was not from their entrance into the clergy—as Socrates relates it—that clerics were requested to practice continence, but only when they were admitted to the Major Orders. Until 444, date of the request addressed by the Roman Pontiff to his colleague of Illyria, the subdeacons themselves seem not to have been compelled to it. The stay of the Byzantine traveler in Thessalonika having taken place several years before that document,[138] the state of discipline in that province was then like the one we saw in several Churches of the 5th century: lectors, cantors, and, generally speaking, all "the lower clerics" were authorized to take a wife and live with her; only ordination to the diaconate

---

[136] PG 67, 637a.

[137] See above, pp. 260–61.

[138] Because the *Historia Ecclesiastica* was written around 440, the stay of Socrates in Thessalonika occurred before this date, and thus before St. Leo's letter to Anastasius of Thessalonika.

became the threshold of a compulsory continence. No matter how secondary it is, the error of the historian of Constantinople shows that his information was not quite trustworthy.

As to the Churches of the East, the testimony of Socrates has against him several documents of the 4th and 5th centuries bearing witness to the existence of laws requesting or implying conjugal abstinence for the higher ministers of the ecclesiastical hierarchy, and most particularly the bishops. We can limit ourselves to listing them, since we already have had the opportunity of studying them at length:

1. ca. 300–350: *Ecclesiastical Canons of the Holy Apostles.*[139]
2. 374–77: Epiphanius, *Panarion (Adversus Haereses)*, Haer. 59 and 69; *Expositio fidei.*[140]
3. 386–407: St. John Chrysostom, *Commentary on the First Epistle to Timothy*; Palladius, *Dialogue on the Life of St. John Chrysostom.*[141]
4. ca. 400: *Doctrina Aeddei.*[142]
5. 406: St. Jerome, *Adversus Vigilantium*, I:1.[143]
6. ca. 410: Council of Seleucia-Ctesiphon, can. 3.[144]
7. ca. 410: Synesius of Ptolemais, *Ep.* 105.[145]
8. late 5th century: *Testamentum Domini Nostri Jesu Christi.*[146]

All these Eastern texts, or texts relative to Eastern communities, are so many denials opposed to the assertions of the Byzantine writer. Nothing could be more likely than some bishops, here and there, having relations with their wives and siring children, and this has been confirmed directly or indirectly by the above-listed witnesses. But Socrates is practically the only one to affirm that such facts were in conformity with ecclesiastical regulations. No echo to this could be found except in the sixth apostolic canon, but in addition to the fact that the apocryphal collection to which it belongs could be posterior to the date of writing of the *Historia Ecclesiastica*, the meaning of this decree has lent itself, as we have seen, to conflicting interpretations[147] and moreover was never used, in any case, to justify the use of matrimonial rights for bishops. In this respect, the *Corpus juris civilis* of Justinian and the anti-Roman

[139] See above, pp. 203ff.
[140] See above, pp. 226ff.
[141] See above, pp. 291ff.
[142] See above, pp. 312ff.
[143] See above, pp. 298ff.
[144] See above, pp. 281ff.
[145] See above, pp. 303ff.
[146] See above, pp. 315ff.
[147] See above, pp. 311f.

decisions of the Quinisext Council themselves would maintain in the East—for the leaders of the Church—the principle of perfect continence.

One could therefore accept only with great reservation the testimony of Socrates; taking a custom as a right, the narrator of Paphnutius' episode might have believed that he could draw an argument from particular cases so as to generalize a situation whose legality seemed guaranteed to him by the First Ecumenical Council. The conclusion of Valois, in his Migne edition, seems justified to us: "It is certain", he writes, "that Socrates has gone here beyond the limits of the truth." [148]

[148] PG 67, 638, n. 81.

6th Century

I. COUNCILS AND SYNODS

AFRICA

Oppressed under the yoke of the Vandal invaders, the Church of Africa endured almost a century of the harsh rule of merciless persecution. The death of Augustine in the besieged Hippo (430) sounded, as it were, the knell for a Christianity that had until then blossomed in an extraordinary way. Hunted, pursued, exterminated, the heads of many African communities, with few exceptions, were kept from exercising an essential part of their office: that of holding conciliar meetings. While the Gaul of Caesarius of Arles started a broad movement of reform, on this side of the Mediterranean the bishops were crushed by the boot of Genseric and his successors and reduced to silence, while Christian life was paralyzed. One had to wait for a lull.

This was provided to martyred Africa by Hilderic the Catholicizer, beginning the day after he arrived (523); and the churches, which had recovered their freedom, held their first council on February 5, 525, presided over by Boniface, a worthy disciple of Aurelius, the new metropolitan of Carthage whom the Vandal agreed to give to his people. The sixty bishops who gathered in the *secretarium* of the Agileus basilica devoted themselves vigorously to this urgent program: reorganization of the neglected Christian communities and restoration of the old discipline. According to a method dear to the Africans, the canonical archives of Carthage were read, thus renewing the previous regulations in their entirety.[149] If the old decrees on clerical continence did not receive an explicit mention, nonetheless it remains certain that they were in fact renewed together with the others. Reborn Christian Africa was keeping its traditions.

The same observation quite likely applies to the plenary Council of the African Church gathered in 536 by Reparatus, successor to Boniface, and celebrated in the enthusiasm of the Byzantine liberation. Freed from Arianism by the victory of Belisarius' soldiers, the Africans proclaimed

---

[149] That measure was taken at the suggestion of an assembly member who asked Boniface to restore the institutions of his predecessor Aurelius "of pious memory" (Mansi 8, 651).

their faith and their fidelity to the old discipline.[150] The only fragment that we have of the minutes of that Council deals solely with the relationships between the monasteries and the bishops, but we can hardly be wrong in supposing that the whole *Codex canonum Ecclesiae africanae* was put back into effect by Reparatus and his colleagues.

The Breviatio Ferrandi (before 546)

An explicit confirmation of these disciplinary decisions taken by the African episcopate during the period is effectively provided by the *Breviatio Ferrandi*, a sort of digest of the legislation of the Church under the jurisdiction of Carthage in the mid 6th century; it was the work of deacon Ferrandus, who wrote it, he said, by order of Boniface himself in order to restore the old regulations.[151] A selection of 232 canons, both Eastern and Western, constitutes this original compilation, which belongs to the literary genre of the "breviaries". The text is abbreviated and followed by references to the authentic acts. In this long list several decrees related to priestly continence are to be retained:

16. Let the bishops, priests, and deacons abstain from [relations with] their wives (Council of Carthage, can. 1, Council Zelleus).

89. Let no one have the audacity not to receive communion from the oblation [celebrated] by a married priest (Council of Gangres, can. 4).

98. If a priest gets married, let him be deposed; if he has committed [the sin of] fornication, let him also be constrained to do penance (Council of Neocaesarea, can. 1).

122. Let not clerics live with "outsider" women (Council of Nicaea, can. 3; Council of Carthage, under Gratus, can. 3; general Council of Carthage).

129. When they reach the age of puberty, let the lectors be compelled either to marry or to make a profession of continence (Council of Carthage, can. 27).[152]

---

[150] In their synodal letter to Pope John II, the 217 bishops gathered at Carthage said in particular: "Africana ecclesia in pristinam libertatem vindicata, ad restituendam collapsam ob longam servitutem ecclesiasticam disciplinam convenerunt episcopi, scriptaque ad Joannem pontificem epistola synodica, ad eumdem legationem miserunt" (Mansi 8, 839).

[151] Cf. P. Fournier and G. Lebras, *Histoire des collections canoniques en Occident*, I (Paris, 1931), p. 35.

[152] PL 67, 950b–c, 954c, 954d–55a, 956a–b, 956c.

The particular interest of the *Breviatio Ferrandi* is its universality of selection. It groups documents published at various times, in Africa as well as in the rest of the Christian world—East included—without seeing any contradiction in them, attesting, on the whole, to a profound harmony between these canons of various origins and making them concur with the foundation of one single discipline. It is, however, only too clear that such a harmonizing reading on the part of Deacon Ferrandus, occurring a long time after the promulgation of the decrees, does not allow us to prejudge with an assurance equal to his the meaning that some of those texts could have had at their origin. But Africa being then in the sphere of Byzantium, the interpretation of the Eastern canons by the compiler of Carthage is an indication to take into account. Since the Africans were looking toward Constantinople, it would have been difficult for them to distort intentionally the significance of disciplinary acts coming to them from Eastern Churches. We also know already that the Code of Justinian, contemporary to the *Breviatio*, expressed in essence identical views in matters of canon law. By this very fact, the summaries on the issue of priestly continence that we have just read provide, through their comparison, useful information.

Thus we see, placed together with the canon of Carthage from 390 forbidding bishops, priests, and deacons to use their marital rights, the fourth decree of the Synod of Gangres on the subject of the celebration of the Eucharist by married priests. In the mind of Deacon Ferrandus, there is no doubt that the priests referred to by the Eastern canon are clerics who had contracted a marriage before their ordinations and are now living in the required chastity. To refuse communion from their hands is an offense to the dignity of the sacrament of marriage and a contempt for ecclesiastical laws recognizing the rights of monogamists to enter the priesthood. It is such an attitude, of Encratist inspiration, that the author of the *Breviatio* intends to reject in the wake of the Council of Gangres. The idea of interpreting the old law of 340 in the meaning of an implicit authorization that would have been granted to those married priests to practice conjugal relations freely was obviously outside of his perspective. Placing the particular decrees in the general context of discipline, Deacon Ferrandus thus seems to warn us unknowingly not to give way to the temptation of mistaking a part for the whole, and of accidentally or anachronistically distorting the original intention of the legislators. It is necessary to make an honest note of this indication; it confirms the hypothesis that we had already voiced in response to the problem raised by the canon of the Council of Gangres.[153]

---

[153] See above, pp. 201–2.

A similar observation is suggested by the insertion of the third canon of the Council of Nicaea in the *Breviatio Ferrandi*. Considered in light of the entire law on continence, the prohibition against clerics living with women not of their kin appears here obviously as a corollary law, meant to safeguard the reputation of the ministers of the Church and to help them observe chastity.[154]

SPAIN

The conciliar activity of the Church of Spain, slowed during the 5th century by invasions, began again thanks to a temporary peace in the early 6th century. First there was the Council of Tarragona (516), then a series of episcopal assemblies that all endeavored to reorganize the clergy and the liturgy. Several laws relative to the discipline of celibacy-continence were voted or reinstated in the various towns of the peninsula. They are described here in chronological order.

Council of Girona (June 8, 517)

The Council gathered on June 8, 517, at Girona, a suffragan town of Tarragona, promulgated ten canons, among which we can read the following decree:

Can. 6: *Let the married [clerics], from bishop to subdeacon, not live without a witness.*

Here is how [the clerics] should behave, from bishop to subdeacon, after having received their honorific functions: should some of them have been married before their ordinations, they should not live with their wives—the latter now being sisters to them—if they have no access to brothers to serve as their witness. If they wish to live [with their wives], they must ask for the services of a brother, whose presence as a witness will compel them to live in all openness.[155]

The subject of the law is the problem of a possible cohabitation of high clerics (starting with subdeacons) with their wives. It is stipulated that the former conjugal relations must give way to brotherly affection: the minister of the Church will see his wife as a sister, a term we meet

---

[154] Canons 98 and 129 of the *Breviatio Ferrandi* do not call for any particular comment here. They are a duplication of the 1st canon of the Council of Neocaesarea and of the 16th canon of the *Codex canonum Ecclesiae africanae*. See above, pp. 177 and 267.

[155] Bruns, 2, 19.

for the first time in this era's legislation, defining in its way the new type of relationships, both human and spiritual, that should unite husband and wife in the priestly state.[156] In so doing, the bishops of Girona belong to the tradition started by Pope St. Leo.[157] A practical measure is added to the previous regulations: if one of the clerics bound to continence wishes to continue living with his wife, let him take "a brother" (which quite likely means another cleric) into his home to help him and bear witness to his behavior.

2d Council of Toledo (531)

The issue of marriage and matrimonial life of clerics was the object of yet another canonical notice, for once a long and detailed one, at the 2d Council gathered in 531 in Toledo, the metropolitan Montan presiding.[158]

> *Can. 1*: With regard to those who, since early childhood, were consecrated to the service of the clergy, we have decided to observe what follows: as soon as they have received the tonsure and have been set apart for the service of the "elected" [for baptism], they will have to reside in the house of the bishop, live with him, and be taught by [a responsible person] appointed over them. Having reached the age of eighteen, they will be questioned by the bishop in the presence of the people and of all the clergy, to ascertain whether or not they want to marry. If God inspires them to desire the grace of chastity, and if they promise to remain faithful to their promise of continence without having [later] need to get married, let them be subject to the very sweet yoke of the Lord as candidates to a very difficult life. After a time of testing their profession, they will first receive, at the age of twenty, the function of subdeacon. If they reach the age of twenty-five without having committed a fault or having been the object of reproaches, they will be promoted to the function of deacon, if the bishop has proof that they are capable of discharging it competently. One must watch, however, to be sure that they do not forget their promise or slide back, either by marrying or by practicing a clandestine affair. Should they do so, let them be condemned as guilty of sacrilege and held as strangers to the Church. As to those whose free will, at the time of questioning, inspired them to marry, we cannot deny them the concession granted by the apostles; married and having reached a [later] age, they will

---

[156] The Gallic councils would adopt the same formula. See below, pp. 339ff.

[157] See above, pp. 261–64.

[158] Hefele and Leclercq deem that the Synod took place on May 17, 527 (II, 2, p. 1081).

PATRISTIC RECORDS ON PRIESTLY CELIBACY-CONTINENCE

be able to aspire to Holy Orders, if they promise in common agreement [with their wives] to give up the works of the flesh.[159]

This decree can be divided into two parts. The longer one studies the case of the young clerics who agree, in the presence of witnesses, to make a perpetual profession of continence. At the age of eighteen, these adolescents, who have already been tonsured, will have to make an official decision in the presence of the bishop, the clergy, and the Christian people. If they do it, knowingly, they will be able to receive the subdiaconate two years later. The time spent in that office will serve as a probation; the bishop will judge their merits and will eventually raise them to the diaconate at the age of twenty-five. If later they fail in their commitment, they will be condemned as "sacrilegious"; they will be excluded from the Church.

The second part of the ordinance considers the case of young clerics of eighteen who, in contrast, declare their intention of marrying. It is their right, the Council declares, and one cannot deny them a concession granted by the apostles ("Concessam ab apostolis sententiam auferre non possumus"). It is likely that such a concession, described as "apostolic", is none other than canon 27 of the apocryphal collection placed under the aegis of the apostles, whose authority had long since been admitted in the Christian world.[160] But the married lectors or cantors, once they reach adulthood (*provectae aetatis*), in their turn will have to promise to give up conjugal life if they aspire to the higher ranks of the clergy. This profession of continence would have to be made in common agreement with their wives (*pari consensu*). Thus understood, the Spanish decree confirms the law of continence for the Major Orders, including the subdiaconate, in harmony with canon 16 of the *Codex canonum Ecclesiae africanae*, of which it offers a commentary of sorts.[161]

2d Council of Braga (572)

Out of the long series of canons published at the 2d Council of Braga (572), we retain two documents related to our inquiry, presenting them in inverse numerical order so that one can clarify the other. Martin of Braga, president of the synod, indicates that this canonical collection is an anthology composed on the basis of ancient Eastern councils and

[159] Bruns, I, 207–8.
[160] See above, p. 310.
[161] See above, p. 267.

translated by him into Latin.[162] We already had the opportunity to use this translation of Martin of Braga with regard to canon 10 of the Council of Ancyra.[163] We now return to it as a testimony to the Spanish discipline. Here are the texts of the two canons concerning our study:

> Can. 39: On those who are elected to the diaconate.
> If someone elected to the ministry of the diaconate declares [his desire] to contract a marriage and is not able to persevere in chastity, let him not be ordained. But if during the ordination he keeps silence, is ordained, and later on attempts to marry, let him be excluded from the ministry and eliminated from the clergy (Ancyra, 10).[164]

> Can. 28: On those whose wives commit adultery.
> If someone has a wife caught in the act of adultery, he will not in any way be led to the ecclesiastical ministry. But if a cleric, after ordination, [finds out] that his wife committed adultery, let him send her away; if he refuses and remains with her, let him be excluded from the ministry (Neocaesarea, 8).[165]

This canon 39, which is said to be a translation of canon 10 of the Council of Ancyra (314), expresses a discipline similar to that designed by the Fathers of Toledo.[166] No one will be ordained unless he has made a profession of continence. There are two differences with respect to the first canon of Toledo that are ascribable to the decree of Ancyra itself: the commitment of chastity is required at the level of the diaconate and not at that of the subdiaconate; it is tacit: the mere fact of accepting ordination amounts to a promise. Let us note that these differences do not imply that the bishops of Braga want to cancel the decisions made in Toledo; they simply copy an old Eastern text (all question of exactitude being set aside) to prop up the current discipline. One can suppose that they had no special reason to annul the modalities stipulated by their Spanish colleagues (explicit profession of continence as early as the sub-diaconate) in order to return to a law developed at a time and in a historical context that were different from theirs. The literary genre adopted by the collection of Martin of Braga—that of anthology—aims rather at showing the continuity of the practice of the Churches of Spain with the tradition of the previous councils.

---

[162] About the personality and work of Martin of Braga, see above, pp. 171–72, n. 76.
[163] See above, p. 171.
[164] Bruns, 2, 52.
[165] Ibid., 50.
[166] See above, pp. 327–28.

This continuity, in its turn, explains the meaning that the Fathers of Braga could give to canon 8 of the Council of Neocaesarea (314–19), whose interpretation poses, as we have seen, a problem.[167] The Fathers of Cappadocia had ordered married clerics to send away their wives if the latter were guilty of adultery. Canon 28 of the 2d Council of Braga adopts the decision. Outside of any context, one could infer from this that a cleric whose wife was faithful, having no reason to send her away, could openly lead a normal conjugal life. But we already know, through the contemporary legislation of the Councils of Girona and Toledo, what original type of relationships the Spanish bishops meant to establish between a cleric and his wife. There is no doubt, then, that in incorporating the Eastern decree in his canonical collection, Martin of Braga had no other thought. Was he faithful, in this way, to the intention of the Cappadocian legislators? Can we suppose that the early background of the canon of Neocaesarea, just as in the day of its rereading by the Spanish bishops, was already that of a continence lived in common by the man consecrated to the service of the Church through the imposition of hands and by his wife? It seems to us that the Spanish canons of that time, like the canons of the Council of Elvira, can effectively supply an indication to help us discern the exact meaning of canon 8 of the Council of Neocaesarea.

3d Council of Toledo (589)

After the conversion of King Recaredos, Catholic Spain, paralyzed for a long time by Arianism, enjoyed a genuine resurrection. The third Council of Toledo opened with triumphal celebrations during the month of May 589, and the seventy-four Fathers who applauded the converted Visigoth hastened to renew, with their profession of faith, the old disciplinary canons. In a word, the decisions of the previous councils and the Roman decretals were put back into effect.[168] This global approval of tradition was stressed by the national Council through the promulgation of twenty-three new disciplinary canons. Among them the continence of clerics is the object of a special decree:

Can. 5: It has come to the knowledge of the Holy Council that bishops, priests, and deacons, who were once heretics but returned [to Catholicism],

[167] See above, pp. 178, n. 94.
[168] Can. 1: "Omne quod priscorum canonum auctoritas prohibet sit resurgente disciplina inhibitum, et agatur omne quod praecepti fieri; maneant in suo vigore conciliorum omnium constituta, simul et synodicae sanctorum praesulum Romanorum epistolae" (Bruns, 1, 212–13).

still [gave in] to carnal desire and united with their wives; so that it does not happen again in the future, we have ordered as follows, which had already been decreed by previous canons: that it not be permitted [to these clerics and their wives] to lead a common life favoring incontinence, but that, while keeping conjugal fidelity toward each other, they watch to what is mutually beneficial to them both and not share the same room. With the help of virtue, it would be even better that [the cleric] find for his wife a new home, so that their chastity enjoy a good witnessing before both God and men. But if, after this warning, someone prefers to live in incontinence with his wife, let him be considered a lector; as to those who are still subject to the ecclesiastical canon, if they live in their cells, contrary to the elders' orders, in the company of women apt to raise suspicions harmful to their reputation, let those be struck with severe canonical penalties; for their part, the women in question will be sold by [the intermediary of] the bishop, and the money [resulting from the sale] will be distributed to the poor.[169]

The Fathers of Toledo wished to remedy the abuses that had penetrated the discipline of the clergy from the Arian heresy. Bishops, priests, and deacons who had returned to the Catholic faith after having abandoned it no longer considered chastity an obligation of the priestly state. Matrimonial life had reasserted its rights, a finding that sheds useful light on the ups and downs in the practice of continence when we remember the inroads of Arianism, long after its official defeat at the Council of Constantinople (381), in many countries of the Mediterranean world. One must certainly take it into account, besides other independent causes, to explain the resistance met by the legislators of the 5th and 6th centuries in obtaining fidelity to the discipline.

Canon 5 of that Council of Toledo renewed in general terms the old prescriptions. For the Spanish bishops as for Caesarius of Arles, or earlier for Siricius, the Tradition is one. It is the same from the beginning wherever heresy and man's negligence have not defeated it. Commenting in their turn on the common theme, they remind the interested parties that they are no longer allowed to have a *vita libidinosa*, a term that, all things considered, was no more derogatory than the term *incontinence* used by the previous councils. It is a technical expression of sorts, in the same way as its antonym *castitas*, also used without a shade of meaning to qualify the state of perfect continence. To take offense would be to credit men of the 6th century, anachronistically, with a linguistic sensitivity that did not exist in their time. The principle being set, the Fathers of Toledo invite husbands who have received the priesthood to take

---

[169] Bruns, I, 214.

measures so that their "chastity" appears as what it is before God and men: a good witness. Let them keep conjugal fidelity toward their wives, so that they can continue leaning on each other. But let them avoid sharing the same room, and if the voice of virtue is not strong enough, let them go as far as separating their respective homes. This regulation still takes into account the heart's affection, notwithstanding the severity of the principle, in line with and in respect of a tradition that honors the Church. St. Leo was able to define a balance of love and chastity that was to leave its mark for centuries on the face of the Christian priesthood.

As usual the law has its sanctions. The ministers guilty of having resumed conjugal relations will be demoted to the rank of lectors, a relatively mild measure because excommunication is not even thought of: such a semi-indulgence probably takes into account the special circumstances created by the return of many Arians to the Catholic faith. On the other hand, the customs of the time were not kind to women! Those who will persist in sharing the cells of clerics will be sold by the bishop, and the proceeds of the sale will be spent on the poor! The bishops of King Recaredos were no less Visigoths than their princes.

Two other Spanish councils, in that late 6th century, will again call bishops', priests', and deacons' attention to the chastity of their state. Since those canons were written to be rather general, we do not think it necessary to include them here, except to note that chastity is still to be understood as an obligation to perfect continence.[170]

GAUL

Councils Held under St. Caesarius of Arles

Born in 470 (or 471) at Châlon-sur-Saône, Caesarius entered the monastery of Lérins when he was about forty, after having spent two years as a cleric in his native town. Reasons of health, among others, seem to have made him leave the cloister and come to settle in Arles, where Bishop Eone, a fellow countryman, called him to the priesthood (498–99) and placed him in charge of a monastery. When Eone died, Caesarius was chosen to succeed him (503). Here was a tireless preacher, a doctor to whom councils listened, and the monastic legislator of Gaul; he presided over the Church of Arles for forty years and died on April 27, 543

---

[170] Those are the 1st canon of the 2d Council of Saragossa (592) and the 1st canon of another council held in Toledo (597) (Bruns, 2, 64; 1, 219).

(or 542). "When he died he left behind him a tremendous body of work for which he can be considered one of the founders of the Church of France" (Lejay).

The legislative work of the Gallic councils during the first half of the 6th century is linked to the influence of St. Caesarius. To learn about it is to discover at the same time the character and problems of the clergy in the provinces of Aquitaine, Auvergne, Orléanais, and Provence, as well as the reforming ideas of the great bishop of Arles. The continence of the ministers of the Church holds an important place in them, as the Gallic temperament and the laxity of morals at that time of invasions were combined in a tenacious resistance to the discipline.[171]

Council of Agde (506)

Thirty-four bishops who came from all parts of the kingdom responded to the call of Caesarius of Arles and held the Council of Agde in the Languedoc during the month of September 506. Out of the collection of seventy-one canons developed by the synod in order to reform and consolidate the clerical institutions,[172] two have a place in our data. These are canons 9 and 16:

> Can. 9: It also seemed good, if married deacons or priests have deliberately returned to the bed of their wives, to observe [with respect to these men] the ordinance of Pope Innocent or the decree of Siricius inserted in the present canons [here follows the passage of Innocent I's letter to Exupery of Toulouse that was inspired by Siricius' decretal].[173]

> Can. 16: Let the bishop absolutely not confer the blessing of the diaconate on [men] less than twenty-five years of age. If married men who are still young accept ordination, one will still have to obtain the consent of their wives; [these young men] will be ordained after they have renounced conjugal life and made a profession of holy life, and after they and their wives have been converted [to continence].[174]

In renewing the pontifical ordinances reminding higher clerics of their duty of continence, the bishops of Agde are dealing with a situation

---

[171] It is always useful to refer to A. Malnory, *Saint Césaire évêque d'Arles* (Paris, 1894), which remains, on many points, one of the best studies.

[172] In fact, only forty-seven of these canons are deemed to be authentic; the others belong to different councils. Cf. Hefele-Leclercq, II, 2, 980.

[173] CC 148, 196.

[174] CC 148, 201.

similar to what had already caused Pope Innocent's intervention in Aquitaine a century earlier. It seems that the latter had become a thing of the past for many, the voice of the Roman Pontiff having been rapidly muted by the Visigoth invasion (419). Same ills, same cures. We find in the canon of 506 the substance of the decretals that are already familiar to us. It is therefore not necessary to spend too much time on it. What is noteworthy, though, is the attitude of Caesarius, eager to put the Churches of Gaul in harmony with the universal discipline. A. Malnory has some useful observations in this regard:

> The particular care in the composition of the canon concerning the continence of the sacred Orders (can. 9) shows how much the author was involved with what he did. He does not hesitate to depart from the customary brevity of the canons so as to bring to everybody's knowledge, through the very text of the Council, the authorities that determined the law, according to him, in the issues under study. Those authorities were three decretals of Roman pontiffs, which at that time were kept in the archives of all the well-organized churches. . . . All those documents, though they were addressed to particular churches, had a character of universality that the popes themselves had been careful to stress by recommending that their addressees give them the greatest possible publicity. Their insertion in the text of the Council is tantamount, on the part of the Fathers, to recognition of their authority, which is not the least remarkable feature we find in the history of that Council.[175]

Insofar as there was a Caesarius to give them "the greatest publicity", the Roman pontiffs' decretals did obtain the expected results. The discipline of the Western Churches bears witness to this.

Canon 16 determines the minimum age required for admission to the diaconate: twenty-five, in conformity with the customs prevailing in other Churches, particularly in Africa.[176] It is deemed prudent not to entrust men who are still young with an honor to which serious obligations are bound. The obligation of continence in particular required a candidate who had given proof of an exemplary life. To these conditions of maturity were added the measures recently inaugurated by the Council of Orange (441): the "blessing" of the deacon is subordinate to an explicit profession of continence.[177] But it is now stipulated that the wife of the future deacon, just like her husband, must also make in full knowledge and respect of conscience (*etiam unorum voluntas ita requirenda est*) this promise of chastity. This is an improvement in discipline indicating a

---

[175] A. Malnory, *Saint Césaire*, pp. 77–78.
[176] See above, p. 268.
[177] See above, p. 273.

greater recognition of the rights of women. Husband and wife must both be "converted", through a free decision, so that the man can commit himself to the clergy.[178] The experience of the legislators seemed to be enriched by taking into account the problems that the difficult practice of priestly continence unceasingly raised.

4th Council of Arles (524)

Old habits are not uprooted in one day. The slowness with which the clergy followed the bishop of Arles was equaled only by the latter's perseverance in multiplying his warnings. In his metropolis, now ruled by Theodoric, the former monk of Lérins continued his policy of reforms. The 4th Council of Arles, solemnized on June 6, 524, with the gathering of thirteen bishops and four episcopal delegates, insisted again on the conditions of regularity required for promotion to the Major Orders: prior "conversion" and periods of probation. Refusing to give in to the "importunate and disorderly" protests of the malcontents and faced with a growing ecclesiastical population, the Synod of Arles reaffirmed its will to keep the old regulations: no one under the age of twenty-five will be ordained a deacon, and no one will receive the honor of the priesthood or of the episcopate until he is thirty. The *praemissa conversio* will have to be made one year before ordination if the candidate is still a layman; this is a legislative innovation, obviously aimed at trying the worth of future ministers. In sum, the Council of 524 is only repeating the measures taken, eighteen years earlier, in the Languedoc city. We now have to read the texts:

It is known that the former regulations of the Fathers concerning ordination of clerics are not totally observed as they should be; this is why, in order to prevent bishops of the Lord from giving in out of exhaustion to the importunate and disorderly requests of some and from being compelled to transgress precepts so frequently [promulgated], [the Fathers of the Council] declare unanimously that the following must be observed: let no bishop take it upon himself to ordain a deacon if the latter has not reached the age of twenty-five; as to the episcopal or priestly dignity, let no layman receive it unless he has previously converted "to continence" and is thirty or over. With regard to laymen, the Fathers of old established on many occasions the rules that must be observed; however, because of the increase

---

[178] For the meaning of the word *conversio*, see above, p. 275. Cf. also Hefele-Leclercq, II, 2, 988, n. 1; E. Griffe, *La Gaule chrétienne à l'époque romanine*. III. *La cité chrétienne* (Paris, 1965), pp. 129–32.

in the number of Churches, we have to ordain many clerics, and this cannot be done, in truth, with some and others without an obvious prejudice to the old canons: this is why [we decide as follows]: let no metropolitan bishop grant the episcopal dignity, and let not the other bishops permit themselves to confer the honor of the priesthood or of the diaconate on any layman, unless the latter, a full year prior to this, has converted [to continence].[179]

The episode of Contumeliosus, bishop of Riez, gives us a concrete illustration of the principles of general discipline enunciated by St. Caesarius and the Gallic councils. Accused of sins against morality—he is described as adulterous—the suffragan of the bishop of Arles was arraigned before a council gathered in Marseilles during the month of May 533 and sentenced to do penance in a monastery. Less than a year had elapsed before the repentant man, by his own initiative, was settled again in his episcopal residence. The affair was brought to the attention of the Holy See.

Caesarius is determined that the canons be observed, and they call for the deposition of the guilty party. Of the three letters by Pope John II that he received as a response, the one addressed personally to him[180] contained a brief anthology of the decrees, the purpose being to restate the law. Caesarius completed it in his own way and sent the package to his colleagues. This decretal, of a new kind, condemned the behavior of the bishop of Riez by invoking a series of authorities, among which we note the following citations:

—Letter of Siricius to Himerius of Tarragona, 7.
—A canon from the Council of Nicaea reading thus: "If it should happen that people were promoted to the priesthood without an inquiry and then reveal themselves as having committed a serious fault, either spontaneously or after having been convinced by others, let them be deposed."[181]
—Canon 22 of the Council held in Orange in *Ecclesia Justinianensis* (441) reading thus: "If it should happen that after having received the

---

[179] Fourth Council of Arles, 1 and 2. CC 148 A, 43–44.

[180] The other two are addressed to the bishops of Gaul and to the priests and deacons of Riez, respectively.

[181] G. Morin, *S. Caesarii Arelatensis episcopi opera*, II (Maredsous, 1940), p. 23. This text is, in substance, the 9th canon of the Council of Nicaea. Denys the Minor's version is slightly different: "Si qui presbyteri sine examinatione sunt promoti vel cum discuterentur, sua peccata confessi sunt et homines moti contra canones confessis manus imponere temptaverunt, tales regula non admittit, quia quod inreprehensibile est, catholica defendit ecclesia" (Joannou, I, 1, pp. 31–32).

Levitical blessing a deacon or a priest does not keep continence with his wife, let him be deposed of his functions." [182]

The choice of documents suggests the following reflections:

Though the accusation leveled at Contumeliosus is formulated in very general terms, [183] the main charge seems to be a return to conjugal life, if we base ourselves on the reminder of Siricius' decretal and of canon 22 of the Council of Orange. The fact that he is described as "adulterous" can be explained by the context of the time; we recall the observation of St. Jerome in the *Adversus Jovinianum*: "You surely admit that he who goes on siring children during his episcopate cannot be a bishop. For if people find out about it, he will not be considered a husband but condemned as being adulterous." [184] If such is the case, the use of canon 9 of the Council of Nicaea indicates in what spirit St. Caesarius interprets the discipline of the First Ecumenical Council. For him the "crimes" that, according to the legislation of 325, make a cleric irregular include offenses against conjugal continence. If such an interpretation goes beyond the letter of canon 9, it still has the advantage of letting us know the position of the bishops of Gaul with respect to the Council of Nicaea. The idea that, by condemning clerics who had used their matrimonial rights, they could violate the intentions of the First Ecumenical Council was far from their minds.

The anthological method adopted by John II and Caesarius in settling the matter of Contumeliosus manifests once again the desire to remain in line with authentic tradition. Both want to follow the Fathers, and to legislate is, for them, only acting in a spirit of adherence to the will of the 318 bishops of Nicaea *"qui per omnes ecclesias concilia fieri praeceperunt"*. As for the councils that he convenes so carefully and the regulations he enacts according to the practice of the Africans and the other Churches "of the whole world" for the purpose of promoting ecclesiastical discipline, Caesarius warns anyone who holds these things in contempt that such behavior reflects on the Fathers of the ecumenical council themselves and on the universal Church:

> Weigh the matter carefully and see whether it is possible and legitimate on our part, in defiance of the canons of such great and numerous bishops, mentioned hereinabove, to take the risk of observing something else and acting otherwise than as those bishops decided; all the more so because if

---

[182] See above, p. 273. The words *deacon and priest* are not to be found in the present edition of the Council of Orange's acts.

[183] "Multa turpia et supradictus Contumiliosus convictus ore proprio se confessus est perpetrasse" (G. Morin, *S. Caesarii Arelatensis*, II, p. 21).

[184] See above, pp. 294–95.

we neglected the holy decrees of those 318 bishops, ordering that councils be held in all the Churches, we would despise not only them but, as it has already been said, the African pontiffs and all the others who, by order [of the Fathers of Nicaea], established in the whole world regulations related to ecclesiastical discipline.[185]

That discipline of priestly continence was inherited from the previous centuries, like all the rest, and the bishop of Arles stresses: "One must also watch carefully so that the clerics who eventually return [to conjugal relations] with their wives are completely suspended from their functions, in conformity to what was said above."[186]

From the Council of Marseilles until his death (543) St. Caesarius no longer had the opportunity or the possibility of taking an active part in the synodal assemblies of the Frankish kingdom. The four episcopal meetings that took place in Auvergne and the Orléanais during that period were marked by his influence, however; they are deeply inspired by the dynamics started at the Council of Agde. One can follow the march of the reforms launched by the bishop of Arles in the new canons on the continence of clerics promulgated in his absence.

Council of Orléans (533)

First there was a decree of the 2d Council of Orléans (June 23, 533) concerning deacons:

> Can. 8: If a deacon married while a captive, let him be, upon his return, completely excluded from the ministry pertaining to his function. It will be enough for him, given the instability of his behavior, to fulfill his penance, and as a satisfaction [for his penalty], [to take part] in communion.[187]

The thirty-one members of that synod—"a kind of national council of the Frankish nation"[188]—do not mitigate their severity, as we can see, even against deacons who had been taken into slavery. Victims of circumstances, the clerics are not thereby exempted from their duties. If some of them, willingly or unwillingly,[189] took wives while they were captive, upon their return they must be deposed from all ecclesiastical functions. Their behavior is seen as a weakness: they will have to consider themselves fortunate to be still admitted to communion once they have done penance.

---

[185] G. Morin, S. Caesarii Arelatensis, II, pp. 24–25.
[186] Ibid., p. 25.
[187] CC 148 A, 100.
[188] Cf. Hefele-Leclercq, II, 2, 1132.
[189] The formula uxori fuerit copulatus can be understood in both meanings.

Council of Clermont (535)

Two years later, a council held at Clermont (November 8, 535) again recalls the law of continence, taking its inspiration from the new principles formulated by Pope St. Leo. The conjugal relationship must rise from a "carnal" one to the level of a "spiritual" affection:

> Can. 13: When men are called to the sublime dignity of the priesthood and of the diaconate, let them totally repudiate the works of the world; chosen for the sacred mysteries, let them renounce carnal relations and change into fraternal affection the sexual intimacy they had had until then [with their wives]. And let every priest or deacon, after having, by God's grace, received the [Levitical] blessing, immediately become the brother of his former wife. We have learned that some, aflame with the ardor of their passion, rejected the cincture of the [priestly] militia and returned to their vomit; they resumed conjugal life that was forbidden to them, and through an incest of sorts, brought prejudice against the splendor of priestly dignity, to such an extent that they even sired children. If someone has publicly committed this kind [of offense], let him be deprived forever from his dignity; he had [in any case] lost it when he agreed [to commit] his offense.[190]

The words *brother and sister* to describe the type of affection uniting husband and wife from then on seem to have been taken from the Council of Girona (516).[191] It explains, in an unmistakable formula, the kind of life legitimized for more than a century by St. Leo, a reconciliation of love and chastity. The recognition of the "brotherly" ties between the priest (or deacon) and his wife lets one suppose that they were normally permitted to live in the same house. But at the same time the possible return to sexual relations takes on a specially serious nature: it is a kind of incest (*incesti quodammodo crimine*), also a new term in the vocabulary of our records. No excuse could be accepted now; the guilty party will be deprived forever of his dignity.

Council of Orléans (538)

The old canons are renewed again during the supraprovincial council held at Orléans on May 7, 538. From the subdiaconate upward, whoever persists in having conjugal relations with his wife will have to be deposed.

---

[190] CC 148 A, 108.
[191] See above, pp. 326–27.

The bishop is now held responsible; should he close his eyes to such situations, he will be suspended for three months and subject to penance. On the other hand, a man who of his own will enters the clergy must know that marriage is forbidden to him under penalty of excommunication. If he has been forcibly recruited, he will then be admitted as a lay communicant, while being deprived of his functions. The ordaining bishop will then have to pay for the offense: for a full year, he will not be permitted to say Mass. Here are the texts of these two canons:

> Can. 2: No cleric, from the subdiaconate upward, is entitled to take a wife into the new life he has chosen. If it happens that he already has one, he will not have relations with her anymore. Should he do so, he would be deposed of his functions, in conformity with the regulations of the old canons, and would have to be content with lay communion. If his bishop, knowing that he practices such sexual relations unworthy [of the ministry], nevertheless continues to admit him to [ecclesiastical functions], he will be excluded also from his [episcopal] function for a period of three months in order to do penance.[192]

> Can. 7: As to the single clerics who, after receiving the [Levitical] blessing, thought it good to choose a wife [here is what we have decided]: should they be clerics who were ordained at the requested age, voluntarily and without any excuse of protest on their part, let them and the wives they took be struck with excommunication; should they be men who were ordained against their will and in spite of their protests, let them be deposed of their functions but not excluded from communion. As to the bishop who took it upon himself to ordain anyone against his will and in spite of his protests, let him not have the presumption to say Mass for a year, and let him be subject [during the same time] to penance.[193]

Council of Orléans (541)

Strongly represented at the great Frankish national council that gathered at Orléans in 541, the province of Arles expressed in all likelihood the views of St. Caesarius: "It is in such a way, it was rightly observed, that the council is linked to his work and can be considered as the crowning achievement of those he personally convened."[194]

The seventeenth of the thirty-eight canons promulgated by the synod endorses the previous regulations on priestly continence and realistically

---

[192]CC 148 A, 114-15.
[193]CC 148 A, 117.
[194]A. Malnory, Saint Césaire, p. 165.

stipulates certain details on which silence had been kept up to that point: priests or deacons must not share the beds of their wives nor their rooms. We must then believe that some of them, even living as "brother and sister", did not deem it necessary to change their domestic habits. The Fathers of Orléans decided to put an end to any risk of suspicion, and those who are exposing themselves to it are deprived of their office:

> Can. 17: Let the priests and deacons not share the same bed or same room with their wives, lest they be suspected of [still having] carnal relations and their [reputation] in religious life be thereby stained. Should some do so, let them be demoted from their function in conformity with the old canons.[195]

At the end of that period, deeply marked by St. Caesarius' stamp, the Churches of Gaul thus began a movement of reform that extended to the provinces of the Frankish kingdom the discipline of priestly continence recommended by Siricius and the Roman pontiffs. With shades of meaning attesting to the resistance that concrete situations brought against the rigor of the laws, as well as to the legislators' growing attention to human problems, the Gallic councils led their clergy in what was, in their eyes, the line of authentic tradition. Their work, under the leadership of Caesarius of Arles, was a milestone in France's history.

The Councils of the Second Half of the 6th Century

After Caesarius' death, the Churches of the Frankish kingdom continued the conciliar work that, as we have seen, the bishop of Arles had set in motion. Five of these Gallic councils, during the second half of the 6th century, dealt again with the discipline of clerical continence because it continued to meet some opposition.

Council of Orléans (549)

The Council of Orléans (October 28, 549) was called by Childebert I to stop the advance of Arian heresy.[196] The seventy-one Fathers of the synod, among whom were forty-three bishops and seven archbishops, promulgated disciplinary canons at the same time. The fourth on the list reads as follows:

---

[195] CC 148 A, 136.
[196] Hefele and Leclercq deem that this was, rather, Monophysism and Nestorianism (III, 1, 159).

Can. 4: If a cleric who has received the [Levitical] blessing—in whatever area and at whatever rank—dares return to the conjugal bed that is now forbidden to him, he will be deposed from his function and from the honor [attached] to the Order he received until the end of his life, as stipulated by the canons of the ancient Fathers; he will simply be conceded [lay] communion.[197]

The decree seems to apply to all the Churches of Gaul; indeed, it comes from an assembly in which the vast majority of these Churches were represented, and stipulates that the clerics concerned are subject to the decree without any distinction of place (*cuiuslibet loci*). Though this means all clergy, without distinction as to hierarchical rank, one has grounds to think that the Major Orders are primarily involved. The formula "a cleric who has received the blessing (*qui clericus post acceptam benedictionem*)" recalls similar phrases during previous Frankish councils, when the word *benedictio* meant ordination to the diaconate.[198]

The object of the prohibition is the return to conjugal life. It is recalled that it is illicit and struck with sanctions by "the canons of the ancient Fathers". The same penalties are reenacted: deprivation of the dignity attached to the received Order and deposition from the function. The guilty parties are only authorized to receive [lay] communion.

Council of Tours (567)

On November 18, 567, an episcopal meeting presided over by Euphronius, archbishop of Tours, and counting among its members the archbishops of Paris and Rouen, met in the ancient capital of Touraine. Two of the twenty-seven ordinances promulgated by the Council tackle, one verbosely, the problem we are studying. Here are the texts:

Can. 13 (12): Let the bishop treat his wife as a sister, and let him rule all his house, the church as well as his home, in such a holy way that no motive of suspicion could arise. And even though by the favor of God and thanks to the witness of his clerics he leads a chaste life, it must be taken into account that the relatives who share his quarters follow him wherever he goes and that priests and deacons and even a crowd of young clerics, with God's help live [with him]: this is why, given the jealousy of our God, he should put a distance between himself and his relatives and live in a different house, so that even those who depend on the bishop's

---

[197] CC 148 A, 149.
[198] See above, p. 273.

generosity and are given food by the servants of clerics, may not be contaminated by the proximity of female servants.[199]

Can. 20 (19): Many archpriests, deacons, and subdeacons of the countryside—though not all, to be sure—are held in suspicion by the people because
they have a common life with their wives. This is why it has seemed good
[to us] to observe [the following]: Each time an archpriest will reside in a
village or will go to a country home, one of his appointed lectors, or at
least another clergy member, will go with him and serve as his witness
by sleeping in the same cell where he rests. Let him be granted, however,
seven [chosen assistants] among the subdeacons, lectors, and laymen; taking
turns during the week, they will take care to help him in everything [that
has to be done]; let him who refuses be beaten. And if it be found out that
a priest was negligent on this point and did not do as he was told, he will
be deprived of communion for thirty days, for which period he will do
penance and return to grace. Let the other priests, deacons, and subdeacons
of the countryside see to it that their servants reside with their respective
wives; as to them, let them live separately, alone in their cells, to pray and
sleep there. Those who have no wives also should have separate cells, far
from their servants, where they can pray and sleep alone. If a priest is
discovered in the company of his priestess, a deacon with his deaconess,
or a subdeacon with his subdeaconess, let him be excommunicated for a
whole year and demoted from all clerical functions; let him know that he
has to stand apart from the lay people, with the exception of his taking
his place among the lectors during the choral chanting of the psalms. As
to the archpriests who neglect to manifest such prudence with regard to
their subordinates and do not guide them while themselves being careful
to live separately, let them be urgently recalled to town by their bishop
and remain [locked up] in their cells for a full month, on bread and water;
[thus] they will do penance for the clergy entrusted to them, because no
cleric is permitted, in conformity with the canons' decisions, to live in
common with his wife, and because it was the instability of Nicolas that
brought about the heresy of the Nicolaitans, as it is written: "This heresy
of priests was first brought about by the fault of a certain priest"; no one
could have imagined that a man consecrating the Body of the Lord would
dare perpetrate such actions if, because of our sins, these [heresies] had not
recently arisen [again]. If those deacons were condemned by a general
decision of the bishops and reputed heretics, just as they would have been
for the same reason by the decrees of the Fathers, and were thus vowed
to the curse, what do these unfortunate priests, guilty of such a great sin
[not incur]? Are they not leading to their perdition, along with themselves,
those who see them living in such a manner? They who should be a model
of precept are showing themselves first as a model of sin. If the head is
sick and incurable, it is better to cut it off rather than let the flock be infected

[199]CC 148 A, 180–81.

by its fault. Such priests and shepherds who refuse to amend their lives are a manifest example of vice and not of discipline, and must not be venerated but denied by the people.[200]

Let the bishop treat his wife as a sister! Canon 13, which we have just read, remains in line with the previous councils. Relationships of chaste fraternal love must unite the bishop and the companion of his life. The honesty of their behavior is guaranteed by the constant witnessing of the people living with the shepherd: priests, deacons, and whole cohorts of young clerics do not, as it were, let him take a step by himself. But these companions of the bishop are a source of concern to the Fathers of the Synod of Tours: What if the female servants of the episcopal residence were to be an occasion of fault? There is only one solution: to separate the quarters. Let the bishop and "his sister" put a good distance between themselves. With time the regulations will become more precise, more severe. It will be noted that the case of married priests and deacons is not even studied. They could probably continue to lead a common life of sorts with their wives under the vigilant eyes of another cleric. Things are different for the bishop. He is not alone, the episcopal "house" already having the characteristics of a genuine monastery, and he must watch over the general atmosphere. In passing, let us note, in the background, what seemed to have become commonplace in sixth-century Gaul: a numerous community of single clerics—or clerics living apart from their wives—shared the daily existence of the heads of the hierarchy.

The situation remained quite different in the countryside. Less organized, the clergy was more at the mercy of lax tendencies. Canon 20 of our synod laments the fact that many archpriests, deacons, and subdeacons, by living with their wives, cause people to talk, hence a series of meticulous prescriptions to suppress such causes of scandal. It is not very interesting to study in detail these police-like methods, all of which are summarized by the formal obligation of having separate bedrooms. Let everyone stay quietly in his cell and pray there, the cleric on his side, and the wife on hers. There are sanctions, of course: temporary excommunication, penance, deprivation of office, when they do not include the whip and dry bread. More remarkable—and surprising—is the reference to the heresy of the Nicolaitans, which seems to have revived in Touraine and other provinces of Gaul at a relatively recent time ("No one could have imagined that a man who consecrates the Body of the Lord would dare perpetrate such actions if, because of our sins, these [heresies] had not recently arisen again"). Did the old sect, condemned

---

[200] CC 148 A, 183–84.

by Revelation in the letters to the Churches of Thyatira and Pergamum (Rev 2:6, 14–15, 20) and denounced by Peter and Jude as "the way of Balaam", find disciples even in the French countryside, after several centuries of such a mysterious existence that historians generally give up following its traces?[201] Or must one understand that the bishops of Tours used the expression "Nicolaitans"—i.e., apostles of fornication—as a general derogatory term for the clerics who persisted obstinately in living a conjugal life the better to stigmatize their behavior? It is difficult to answer. In any case, the bond, real or fictive, established between the reprehensible behavior of certain members of the clergy and an ancient heresy of apostolic times attests, in the eyes of the bishops of Tours, to the long-established discipline of priestly continence. By going back to Nicolas they intend to refer to the first priest who dared "perpetrate" actions similar to those of the accused clerics "because no cleric is permitted, in conformity with the canons' decisions, to live in common with his wife, and because it was the instability of Nicolas that brought about the heresy of the Nicolaitans, as it is written: 'This heresy of priests was first brought about by the fault of a certain priest.'" What was at times directly affirmed by their predecessors is said differently by the Gallic bishops: for them the perfect chastity of the clergy is of apostolic origin.

Council of Mâcon (581 or 583)

Mâcon, November 1, 581 (or 583). Twenty-one bishops, from all parts of France, decree new canonical regulations. In the list, which starts with a reminder of canon 3 from the Council of Nicaea, we find the following notice:

> Can. 11: When men are elevated to the sublime dignity of the episcopate, the priesthood, or any degree of the honorary clergy, let them totally repudiate the works of the world; chosen for the sacred mysteries, let them renounce carnal intercourse and transform into fraternal affection the sexual intimacy they had had until then [with their wives]. And let any man, after having, by God's grace, received the [Levitical] blessing, become immediately the brother of his former wife. We have learned that some, aflame with the ardor of their passion, rejected the cincture of the religious life and returned to their first vomit; they resumed the conjugal life that was forbidden to them, and through an incest of sorts, brought prejudice to the splendor of the priestly dignity, to such an extent that they even

---

[201] For the history of Nicolaism, see J. Danielou and H. Marrou, *Nouvelle Histoire de l'Église* (Paris, 1963), pp. 90–91. See also above, pp. 87–88, n. 4.

sired children. If someone has publicly committed this kind [of offense], he will be deprived forever of his dignity; he [already] lost it from the moment he agreed [to commit] his offense.[202]

Nothing new here with regard to the previous Gallic councils. Bishops, priests, and all clerics having a superior dignity (deacons and probably subdeacons) must completely give up the works of the world. Any resumption of conjugal intercourse is for them a kind of incest and is stigmatized as such. Infractions will be punished by permanent deposition.

Council of Lyon (583)

In May 583, a council held in Lyon reiterates the same discipline:[203]

Can. 1: The venerable Fathers of past times made several decisions with authority; now that divine favor has permitted a progress of the faith, it is necessary that the salutary prudence of the bishops renew these decisions with improvements, in the interest of the clergy and of the entire Catholic people. This is why, remembering the decrees of the very blessed Fathers, we have decided to enact the following canon: Let no cleric from the Holy Order of the episcopate down to the rank of subdiaconate have the right to keep in his home any woman, with the exception of his mother, aunt, or sister. It has also seemed good to us that if men bound to wives in some way attain the Order of the diaconate or the priesthood, they should not only stay away from the beds of their wives, but abstain from seeing [their wives] every day. If, God forbid, after having received the [Levitical] blessing, they were to have children on account of familiar cohabitation with [their wives], let them be deprived of the rank [corresponding to] their function.[204]

The reminder of the ancient laws is justified by the progress of the faith and the need for a better renewal. After an almost literal quotation of canon 3 of Nicaea, there is an immediate instruction to abandon the conjugal bed. More rigorous than their Spanish colleagues[205] of the same period, the Lyonnais make an authoritative separation between the higher clerics and their wives: they must abstain from seeing each other daily. Where the Fathers of Toledo still left to each one's virtue the freedom of deciding, our Gallic synod prescribes an obligation. Cohabitation as

---

[202] CC 148 A, 225.

[203] Hefele and Leclercq place this synod in 581 (III, 1, 206). We will follow here the date suggested by C. Munier in CC 148 A, 232.

[204] CC 128 A, 232.

[205] See above, pp. 326ff.

such is not punished by canonical penalties, however. Only the possible risks of a common life's familiarity are the object of similar measures: if there is, "God forbid", a child born, the trespasser will be deprived of his ministerial rank.

Council of Auxerre (between 561 and 605)

Toward the end of the 6th century a diocesan synod in Auxerre, presided over by Bishop Aunacharius, who had taken part in the Council of Mâcon (583), promulgated new ordinances regarding the chastity of clerics.[206] Two final Gallic canons are thus added to our chapter:

> *Can. 20*: If a priest, as we are ashamed to say, a deacon, or a subdeacon has begotten children after having received the [Levitical] blessing or committed adultery, without the archpriest informing the bishop or the archdeacon, he will not take part in communion for a full year.

> *Can. 21*: It is not permitted for a priest, after having received the [Levitical] blessing, to sleep in the same bed as his wife [*presbytera*], so as to get involved in sins of the flesh. The same is true for the deacon and the subdeacon.[207]

These two decrees form a whole, as it were. Priests, deacons, and subdeacons must not share the beds of their wives.[208] The archpriest who neglects to point out to the bishop or the archdeacon those who go on having children will be excluded from communion for a full year. There is the same sanction for those who close their eyes to possible offenses of adultery committed by clerics who have received the (Levitical) blessing. No penalty is indicated for the culprits themselves, but it goes without saying that they will be covered by the previous regulations.

---

[206] The exact date of this synod remains vague. The similarity of its canons with those of the councils of Mâcon leads one to suppose that it took place after 503: Cf. Hefele-Leclercq, III, 1, 214. C. Munier avoids giving a date and places it vaguely between 561 and 605: CC 148 A, 265.

[207] CC 148 A, 267–68.

[208] Notice the use of the word *presbytera* for the priest's wife. The 20th canon of the Council of Tours (567) had already mentioned, in the same meaning, the *presbytera*, *diaconissa*, and *subdiaconissa*. See above, pp. 343f.

PERSIA

Mar Aba I (540–552)

The Nestorian Church of Persia honors as a saint Katholikos Mar Aba I. Born into a Mazdeist family, he practiced the religion of Zoroaster until the day when the witnessing of a Christian student of Nisibe made him convert and ask for baptism. He then pursued brilliant studies at the School of Nisibe, founded by Barsumas, and started a long voyage that took him from Edessa to Constantinople, through Palestine and the Egyptian monasteries. Compelled to flee Constantinople, where his refusal to condemn Theodore of Mopsuestia and the Nestorian doctrines almost cost him his life, he returned to Nisibe, where he spent five to six years teaching. When the old Katholikos Paul died, he was unanimously elected patriarch of the Persian Church and, against his will, was elevated to the primate's See of Seleucia-Ctesiphon (February 540). His first care was to bring an end to the schism that had occurred from the competition between Mar Elisea and Mar Narses and to promote orthodoxy of the (Nestorian) faith as well as moral reform. Being the target of the magi's hostility, he had to suffer in prison and exile. He died at Seleucia on February 29, 552, leaving behind himself a trail of light.

Synod of Mar Aba (544)

This is the name given to a meeting of bishops held in December–January 543–44, during which the Katholikos and his colleagues gathered a collection of the main constitutions that had been prepared "under the inspiration" of Mar Aba.[209] It was probably during that synod that the decision was made (or promulgated) to forbid from then on the choice of married men as bishops or patriarchs if, however, such a measure was truly adopted by the Persian reformer. We have no other assurance than

---

[209] Here is the list of these constitutions, such as we can read it in the acts of the Synod of Mar Aba: "Among these writings are: (1) the orthodox synod of the provincial reforms; (2) those concerning the orthodoxy of faith and proving its integrity; (3) those concerning the rectitude of good morals; (4) those informing us about the deposition of the two persons who introduced duality, as well as the concessions and sanctions relative to those who had been installed by those persons; (5) those concerning the definitions and the canons relative to the differences of the ecclesiastical government; (6) the *Practica*, which includes the major part of these matters and adds the explanation of each one of them, and so forth" (J. B. Chabot, *Synodicon orientale* [Paris, 1902], p. 319).

the testimony of Mare ibn Sulaiman, during the 12th century, and facts seem to go against such an assertion, inasmuch as in 570 we see the son-in-law of Katholikos Paul receiving the episcopal See of Seleucia.[210] Nevertheless, we find that references to married clerics in the Nestorian councils held during the sixth century, after Mar Aba, mention deacons and priests but never bishops.[211]

Mar Joseph (552–564/67)

The man appointed by King Chosrau to replace the Katholikos Mar Aba I in May 552 was as obnoxious as his predecessor had been esteemed. The twelve (or fifteen) years that he spent on the seat of Seleucia were an opportunity for him to exert his despotism on the bishops and to commit many misdeeds. A synod deposed him. Some consider that Katholikos Joseph was illegitimate and his name was erased from the diptychs of the Nestorian Church.

---

[210] See above, p. 122.

[211] See below, the section on the Synod of Joseph, as well as the section on the synod and canons to Mar James by Katholikos Mar Jesuyahb I.

The *Chronicon Ecclesiasticum* by Bar Hebraeus (1286) relates a discussion between King Chosrau, described as "*rex sapiens*", and patriarch Mar Aba, during which the Persian monarch expresses his surprise about the fact that the Nestorian bishops and Katholikos kept their wives with them while, as he points out, this is not done elsewhere: "Where does one hear that the Katholikos or the bishop has a wife living by his side as you do? Or yet, where [does one hear] that a cleric takes another wife after the death of his first one, and yet a third one after the second, as your clerics are doing? The Katholikos replied: 'As far as wives are concerned, I personally do not have one, and never had any; as to my predecessors, it was the divine Apostle who gave them permission when he said: "Let the priest be the husband of only one wife", meaning that he should not have two at the same time, though he did not forbid successive bigamy.' King Chosrau replied: 'All these allegations do not hold. . . . As to the "It is better to marry", the Apostle said that for the people of the world who are in the grip of carnal libido; now he who is established in an apostolic rank must burn with love of God, not with the desire for a wife. Lastly, when it comes to the instruction "Let the priest be the husband of an only wife", if it were permitted to a layman to have two wives at the same time, perhaps we could think that it was that and only that which had been forbidden to priests. This is why, O Katholikos Aba, I advise you to abandon such beliefs and to adhere to [the beliefs] of the other Christian people. It will be for you an honor in our eyes and in theirs'" (Bar Hebraeus, *Chronicon Ecclesiasticum* [J. B. Abbeloos and J. J. Lamy, eds., IIIc, 92–96]). This anecdote, quite probably invented by Bar Hebraeus on the basis of conversations of Barsauma and his disciples, remains interesting because of the development and discussion of the Pauline arguments invoked to justify marriage for clergy members in the Nestorian Church.

Synod of Mar Joseph (554)

After putting off for a long time and for various reasons the meeting of the general synod of the Persian Church, which was usually gathered as soon as a Katholikos had been appointed, Joseph called the episcopal assembly in Seleucia in January 554. In addition to a solemn profession of the Nestorian faith, the conciliar Fathers composed twenty-three ecclesiastical canons. Canon 10 stipulates penalties for clerics marrying pagan women, and thus attests indirectly that the authorization to marry granted to members of the priestly hierarchy by the Councils of Mar Acacius and Mar Babai were still in effect. Nothing is said about bishops, however.

> *Can. 10*: It has been said that priests, deacons, clerics go and take pagan wives, some of whom convert, and that they beget children from them. After a while, when the magis find out about this, they seize these women, chain them, and they give up their Christianity; and certain priests and deacons are dishonored by apostate children. This is why we have decided canonically that: Those who act in such a manner will not be admitted to the exercise of the priesthood.[212]

Mar Jesuyahb I (582–594/95)

Elected through the favor of King Horzmid IV to succeed the patriarch Ezechiel (570–82), Katholikos Jesuyahb I, a former student of the School of Edessa, was a man knowledgeable in canon law and liturgy. Under his pontificate the Nestorian Church of Persia underwent a great development on the doctrinal plane as well as in the field of monastic life. Compelled to flee when King Chosrau II came to the throne, he died in 594–95 in the area of Hira near Babylon, where the Arab prince had asked for baptism.

Synod of Mar Jesuyahb I (585)

During the fourth year of his pontificate, Mar Jesuyahb I held a council in Seleucia with the participation of two metropolitans and twenty bishops. Among the thirty-one canons that were adopted, two contain measures related to the marriage of clerics:

---

[212]J. B. Chabot, *Synodicon orientale*, pp. 359–60.

Can. 5: Let the behavior of the priests, deacons, and ministers of the altar of the New Covenant respond to the sublimity of their ministry. . . . We have learned that many priests and deacons have left the right path and gone to the left, taking care of their bodies and neglecting their souls; starting, ending, and directing their deeds and designs; binding and loosing, with iniquity and not with justice, fraudulently and not correctly. Others have strayed from the road of pure and noble behavior befitting the ministry entrusted to them; they married shamefully and illegitimately, and because of them the priesthood is despised, authority outraged, and Christianity insulted. And the people became like the priests, because the doctrines have been despised through the laxity of the doctors' morality.

We therefore exhort and prescribe, by the word of our Lord, to all those in the ranks of the clergy, to conform their way of life totally to the precious models befitting ministers and workers of Christ.[213]

Can. 23: That it is not fitting for clerics to become prosecutors, stewards, or lawyers in a trial that is not of their concern; not to take abandoned [women]. . . . It has been said before the synod of the Fathers that some clerics do not apply themselves to the rules of their functions and do not wish to behave in conformity with the purity of the rank of those who are ministers of the Spirit. . . . [Some] dared to take abandoned women who had been defiled in shameful acts, and through their imprudence, caused by carnal desire, they have become an object of scandal and reproach for many people.—We therefore prescribe and order that now and from this point on, priests, deacons, and clerics will not be permitted to take interest or be hired as lawyers in trials that are not of their concern. . . . Let them not take either now or from this point on abandoned women who have dishonored themselves; for if a man who took a legitimate wife has to send her away and turn from relations with her when she has been dishonored by adultery, all the more so must the members of the clergy stay away from all those who are despicable and unworthy of the rank of their ministry. . . . Now and from this point on, let all those who are counted in the ranks of the clergy not even be in concert with abandoned women who did not dishonor themselves, in order to avoid contempt and evil suspicions. And if anyone, of any rank whatsoever in the clergy, took in his folly an abandoned woman who dishonored herself by adultery, let him not keep her. It is not permitted to do so by the word of God.[214]

Canon addressed to Mar James

The Eastern *Synodicon* has also kept for us a letter from Katholikos Mar Jesuyahb I, addressed to Mar James, bishop of the isle of Darai in the Persian Gulf, in answer to a series of questions concerning "priestly rules

[213] J. B. Chabot, *Synodicon orientale*, pp. 403–4.
[214] Ibid., pp. 416–17.

and ecclesiastical canons of the ministry of spiritual work".[215] Canon 11
of that letter states the case of a married priest who commits adultery
or fornication and orders appropriate sanctions.[216] This is, once more,
a direct testimony to the upkeep of the Nestorian discipline authorizing
priests and sacred ministers to marry.

2. IMPERIAL LAWS

The Imperial Legislation of Justinian (527–565)

In parallel with the legislative action of the Western councils, the Byzantine East during the 6th century was erecting a monument of civil and
ecclesiastical law to which history would give the name *Corpus juris civilis*.
Through a constitution dated February 13, 528, Emperor Justinian undertook a restructuring of the law by integrating in one sole work the ancient
Gregorian (291), Hermogenian (3d–4th centuries), and Theodosian (438)
codes in particular. Published on April 7, 529, the Code of Justinian gave
way five years later to a second edition, enlarged with new imperial laws
that had been promulgated in the meantime. It is that edition of 534 that
the manuscripts have kept for us. Later on the code itself was regrouped
with "Digests", "Institutes", and "Novellae" that had been promulgated
by Justinian at various dates. French jurist Denys Godefroy gave to that
legislative body of work the name of *Corpus juris civilis*, in 1589.[217]

Justinian's Caesaropapism did not leave aside any issue connected with
ecclesiastical discipline. While the Eastern councils following from Byzantium were preoccupied above all with particular problems or doctrinal
issues and did not seem to wish to have anything to do with canonical
legislation,[218] the emperor collected the rules meant for bishops, clerics,
and monks.

The set of laws and novellae specifically related to priestly continence
constitutes in itself a rather thick compendium. In spite of the length
and number of these texts, we think it useful to quote them here as
documentary information:

---

[215]J. B. Chabot, *Synodicon orientale*, p. 426.

[216]Ibid., pp. 438–39.

[217]Concerning the formation of the *Corpus juris civilis* and the presentation of manuscripts,
see the article of C. de Clercq, "Corpus juris civilis", in DDC 4, 644–68.

[218]Or not to be able to. It is likely that the emperor's pretensions in legislative matters
took away any possibility of initiative from the bishops.

To Atarbius, prefect of the praetorium (March 1, 528)

Always responsible for all the concerns of the very holy Churches, for the honor and glory of the holy, immaculate, and consubstantial Trinity, through whom we believe we will be saved, we and the community of our subjects, and also following the teaching of the holy apostles concerning the ordination of priests, who must be irreproachable, having received above all the mission to gain in the interest of public affairs the favor of God who loves men, we ordain by the present law [the following]: Anytime there will be a vacant apostolic See in a town, a decree will be put forth by the inhabitants of that town with regard to three [candidates] whose rectitude of faith, honesty in life, and other [required] qualities will have been attested so that the most suitable among them will be proposed for the episcopate. . . .

This is why it is fitting to elect and ordain as bishops men who have neither children nor grandchildren, considering that it is not possible for a man subjected to concerns of daily life, especially those that children bring to their parents, to apply all his zeal and spirit to divine liturgy and ecclesiastical matters. Because some people, through the effect of their hope in God and for the salvation of their souls, rush to the very holy Churches, bringing their goods and giving them up to be spent for the unfortunate and poor and for other pious uses, it is quite unfitting for bishops to take [these goods] for their personal profit or spend it for their own children and families. Because the bishop must not be hindered by natural inclination toward the children of his own flesh and must be the spiritual father of all the faithful, we now forbid ordaining as bishop anyone who has children or grandchildren.[219]

The preamble of the imperial ordinance first expresses the concern about the "very holy Churches" for which Justinian feels responsible. This sacred mission motivates the interventions of the emperor-pontiff in the choice of bishops. In the exercise of his functions we see him professing his fidelity to "the doctrine of the holy apostles": to follow the path they opened and confer episcopal ordination only on men who have been purified of any vice, able to obtain for the common good the divine favor and goodwill thanks to their prayers—such is the motive of the present law.

Its object is multiple: examination of a candidate by a jury of three persons who are particularly well chosen; detachment from wealth; absence of direct heirs. It is this last point that holds our attention. More demanding than many Western councils, the emperor of Byzantium forbids elevating family men to the episcopate: "It is fitting to elect and

---

[219] *Codex Justinianus*, I, 3, 41. CJC (J) 2, 25–26.

ordain as bishops men who have neither children nor grandchildren." [220]
In other words, there are only three categories of people who fulfill such
conditions: single men, widowers or married men without children,
widowers and married men whose children and possibly grandchildren
are no longer alive. The decree does not specify whether a still-married
bishop can keep his wife by his side,[221] but the prohibition against having
sons implies, of course, conjugal continence.

The particular reason invoked for this measure is of a pastoral order.
It is not right for a bishop to put the interests of his own relatives before
the good of his Church. It is to her that he must give all his care and all
his wealth. The latter has to be used by the "spiritual father of all the
faithful" whose mission it is, for the good of the poor, the hospices, the
various works of mercy. To alienate it for the benefit of his children or
grandchildren would be unworthy of him. To prevent such a temptation,
the emperor prefers to suppress its causes. This is an example of adaptation of Roman law to the concrete conditions of the Byzantine world.
Justinian does not lose sight of the spiritual principles: he did not fail to
cover himself with the authority of the apostles, to speak first about the
conditions of sanctity required for prayer—and we do grasp here, effectively, an echo of the theological foundation common to a whole tradition—but the chief of State is perhaps even more alert to the social and
economic aspects of pastoral responsibilities. The distinction between
the temporal and the spiritual is unknown in Byzantium. The features
of the Eastern episcopate in the 6th century become better defined than
in the West, the absence of family responsibilities also appreciably
simplifying the problems posed by the state of continence.

To Julian, prefect of the praetorium (October 18, 530)

Though the holy canons do not allow priests who are much loved by God
or the very religious deacons or subdeacons to marry after such an imposition of hands and grant such a right only to the very religious cantors and
lectors, we see that some of them despise the holy canons and beget children
from the wives with whom, according to the priestly rule, they are not
permitted to have relations. The only punishment for such an offense has
always been dismissal from the priesthood, but our own imperial laws are
made for the express purpose of enforcing the holy canons just as strictly
as the imperial laws themselves. We therefore order that whatever is decided
by the holy canons has the force of law as far as the interested parties are
concerned, just as if those decisions had been written into the civil law

---

[220] We translate ἔγγονος as "grandson" rather than "nephew"; the second meaning would
give to the law an extension that seems excessive.

[221] This question comes under other ordinances. See below, p. 357.

itself; let such men be deposed from the priesthood and from the sacred ministry, and likewise let them be deprived of the dignity that they have enjoyed heretofore. Clearly, if such actions are forbidden by the holy canons, in the same way the crime must be stamped out according to our civil laws; besides the aforementioned penalty of deposition, we order that not even children previously considered legitimate be accounted as legitimate any longer, for children who are born into, or whose birth contributes to, the willful corruption of both spouses partake of the shame of those who have brought them into this world. . . .[222]

Like the previous one, this imperial ordinance is addressed to a prefect of the praetorium. It therefore examines the ecclesiastical discipline from a particular angle: the consequences of canon law on civil law. It is only occasionally, as it were, that the content of the previous laws is recalled—Justinian seems to refer especially to canon 14 of the Council of Chalcedon,[223] forbidding marriage to subdeacons and other major clerics. We record this reminder as a confirmation by the Byzantine code of an already-known regulation.

Prefect Julian is informed that the penalties set by Church legislations must from now on be applied exactly as if they were civil laws: the parties concerned who continue to have children from those illegitimate marriages will be deprived of their functions and deprived of the dignity itself. We could say that secular power is lending its arm to ecclesiastical justice.

Other civil effects: the children born of the guilty unions will bear the fault of their parents and will not be able to be legitimized.

Finally, let us note that lectors and cantors are permitted to marry, and that the imperial decree does not approach the issue of whether conjugal continence was or was not required from men who could have been married before the imposition of hands.

To John, prefect of the praetorium (July 29, 531)

We order that no one be proposed for the episcopate unless he is, among other things, virtuous and good; that he not be living with a wife and not be a family man, but that instead of a wife he be attached faithfully to the most holy Church, and that instead of children, he possess all the Christian and Orthodox people. Let him know from the start that such has been our design regarding the succession of the bishops much beloved of God; and it is in this line of thought that we have promulgated the law (let it be also known), they who act or have acted against these regulations are

---

[222] *Codex Justinianus*, I, 3, 44. CJC (J) 2, 30–31.
[223] See above, p. 264.

absolutely unworthy of the episcopate. Therefore, those who, after this disposition that we have taken, will have the audacity to confer the episcopate upon anyone or become bishops will not be [counted] in the episcopate and will not remain among the bishops; but chased away from their places, they will leave them to others for an ordination in conformity with the norm and pleasing to God in every aspect.[224]

The present law does not refer, for obvious reasons, to the "most sacred canons" of the Fathers. Justinian is innovating, as he had already done three years earlier in his letter to Prefect Atarbius:[225] the bishop, who must be at all events "good and apt", must be chosen from among those who do not live with a wife and have no children. The wife he will embrace will be the most holy Church, and the orthodox and Christian population will become his progeny. Such mystical-sounding considerations might remind us of the sermons of St. Augustine or of the spiritual exhortations of the *De septem ordinibus Ecclesiae*.[226] But the real preoccupation of the pontiff-sovereign [the emperor] is of another order, though this does not exclude the sincerity of the premises. He intends to keep away from the bishop's will any direct heirs, and to him the very nonexistence of such heirs seems to be the most efficacious method. The goods acquired by the bishop since his elevation to the episcopal See belong by right to his Church; any alienation of property to the benefit of individuals, and in particular to possible members of the bishop's family, is illegal, in any form or manner, as the Code of Justinian had decreed it for several years.[227] John, prefect of the praetorium, is advised that those dispositions are still in effect and that he has to make them respected: the bishops who dare violate them are unworthy of their function.

Inasmuch as the responsibility for wrongful and illegal instances of ordination rested squarely on the shoulders of the bishops performing the illegal consecrations, the Constitution of the empire provided equally for the deposition of ordaining bishops who, contrary to the law, chose to consecrate family men or men who were bound to wives. By means of a series of laws against progressively worse infractions, the Byzantine lawgiver intended to build an effective wall of security around the goods that belonged to the Church—we might say, he was nationalizing the Church's property. Reasons of State fit in only too well with a spiritual discipline of continence that made its own automatic contribution to the empire's best interests.

---

[224] *Codex Justinianus*, I, 3, 47. CJC (J) 2, 34.
[225] See above, p. 353.
[226] See above, pp. 313–14.
[227] *Codex Justinianus*, I, 3, 41. CJC (J) 2, 26.

Novella 5:
To Epiphanius, archbishop of Constantinople (March 20, 535)

Chap. 8: If anyone of those who profess monastic life deserves priestly ordination, let him persevere in fidelity to a pure life. Should he, once ordained a cleric, abuse the trust [given to him] and have the audacity to get married—[we are speaking,] of course, of a man who is not included in the clergy at a rank allowing him to take a wife: i.e., at the level of lectors or cantors; at all other levels, we absolutely forbid marriage, in conformity with the holy rules, or life with concubines, or a life of license— let him be, by all means, excluded from the clergy, as having covered with shame his previous way of life and solitary life itself.[228]

This novella, meant for all the patriarchs so as to bring them to the attention of the metropolitans, bishops, and monasteries under their orders,[229] deals with monastic life. The chapter we have just read is of interest to us because it recalls, in passing, an ancient law already endorsed by the Council of Chalcedon. It brings up the issue of monks who deserved priestly ordination. Those who would wish to use their admission to the clergy in order to contract a marriage will be excluded from the clergy by all means, as they have dishonored their previous existence as solitaries. By way of an incidental clause, the emperor explains that he does not foresee such a possibility except at the very first levels of the ecclesiastical hierarchy—lectors and cantors—it being well understood that at the higher ranks, any possibility of marriage is forbidden by the "divine canons". It is this incidental clause that we will note here as confirming the validity of canon 14 of the Council of Chalcedon—and the ancient discipline that it bore witness to—in the territories of the Byzantine empire during the first half of the 6th century.

Novella 6:
To Epiphanius, archbishop of Constantinople (March 16, 535)

We believe that this [i.e., the prosperity of public affairs] will be possible if people continue to observe the holy rules that the apostles, rightly praised and venerated as commentators and ministers of the Word of God, passed on [to us], and that the holy Fathers kept and explained.

Chap. 1: Here is, therefore, what we order, in full conformity with the holy rules: when in the future someone will be led to episcopal ordination,

[228] CJC (J) 3, 33–34.

[229] "Haec igitur omnia sanctissimi patriarchae sub se constitutis deo amabilibus metropolitis manifesta faciant, at illi subiectis sibi deo amabilibus episcopis declarent, et illi monasteriis sub ordinatione constitutis cognita faciant" (*Nov. 5, Epilogus*, CJC [J] 3, 34–35).

the first step will be to examine [the nature of] his life according to [the recommendations of] the holy apostles: [to see] if it is honest and free of fault and irreproachable on all points; it is also [necessary] that people of good reputation witness on his behalf and that his life be worthy of a bishop. . . . (3) [The candidate] must not be bound either to a wife, but must have always lived as a virgin; or, if he does have a wife, [it is necessary] that the latter, when she came to him, was a virgin, not a widow, a woman separated from her husband, or a concubine. (4) He must not have children or grandchildren, whether or not they are recognized by the law; otherwise, if anyone acts against these dispositions, he will be personally demoted from the priesthood; as to the one who ordained him, he will be rejected from the episcopate as having trespassed against said law. . . . (6) No one can have access to the episcopate if he does not know the holy decrees. (7) But he must have previously professed monastic law or have been included in the ranks of the clergy for at least six months, without, however, being bound to a wife or having children or grandchildren. We do seek this above all among the bishops much beloved of God, as it had already been decided by the two holy constitutions that we have promulgated; in those we requested an inquiry [to know whether the candidates] were not bound to wives, neglecting all the rest and not permitting anyone in the future and in virtue of the law to impose hands on a man bound to a wife. Today we renew this law again; if by chance anything were done against these dispositions, [the concerned party] would be dismissed from the priesthood and would, at the same time, cause the exclusion of the ordaining [bishop]. Let the one to be ordained therefore be chosen among the monks or clerics; and in this kind of life let him, in addition, have good testimonies, be honest, have a good reputation, and bring to the episcopate this foundation of life.[230]

The main addressee of the novella is Epiphanius, archbishop of Constantinople. Copies were simultaneously sent to the metropolitans of Alexandria, Theopolis (Antioch), and Jerusalem, as well as to the prefect of the praetorium of Illyria.[231] The scope was thus extended, from the start, to the entire Byzantine world.

The preamble mentions the observation of the "sacred rules" transmitted by the apostles, kept and explained by the holy Fathers. Addressing himself to patriarchs, Justinian manifests his intention to remain faithful to the ancient tradition of the Churches. *Captatio benevolentiae*, of course, but agreeing, at least on certain points, with the views expressed at various times by the Roman pontiffs and many patristic authors. In the matter of ecclesiastical discipline, the emperor who desired to place his

[230] CJC (J) 3, 36–37.
[231] CJC (J) 3, 47.

code under the sign of the "Supreme Trinity and the Catholic faith"[232] knows that he can claim a fairly general consensus on the part of the Christian people when he declares himself as heir to the patrimony bequeathed by Peter.[233] The fact is that this does not prevent him in the least from inaugurating new regulations for the purposes of his policy, as we have already seen in several instances, but he is careful not to do so in a direction that might, in his eyes, relax the principles that he appointed himself to defend.

The object of the law concerns the conditions required for admission to the episcopate. Remote conditions, one might say, and immediate conditions. In the past of the candidates, which must be, according to the word of the Apostle, irreproachable, one will examine in particular his matrimonial situation: his wife, if he has had one, must have been a virgin at marriage; married to a widow or a woman separated from her first husband, or bound to a concubine, the candidate will be rejected from the priesthood.[234] Same obstacle if he happens to have children or grandchildren, whether or not they are recognized by civil law. In case of infraction, the candidate and the consecrating bishop will be deprived of their dignity.

For definitive admission the future bishop must also make a profession of monastic life or already be a member of the clergy for at least six months. According to the already-established prescriptions, he will have ceased to live with his wife and will not be supporting any children or grandchildren.[235]

Through this letter addressed to Eastern patriarchs and to the prefecture of Illyria the bishops under the jurisdiction of Byzantium were thus reminded of the duty of conjugal continence:

> *Chap 5*: One must not ordain deacon or priest a man who is now or has been previously remarried; [nor will one ordain a man] bound to a wife who had separated from her husband and abandoned him, or a man who

---

[232] CJC (J) 2, 5.

[233] See, for instance, the first words of the code: "Cunctos populos, quos clementiae nostrae regit temperamentum, in tali volumus religione versari, quam divinum Petrum apostolum tradidisse Romanis religio usque ad nunc ab ipso insinuata declarat" (CJC [J] 2, 5).

[234] These conditions for admission to Orders, directly inspired by Leviticus, were always observed in the early Church. We have not mentioned all the many documents testifying to it, this aspect of chastity being a marginal one as far as our study is concerned. There is a good exposition in J. Lafontaine, *Les conditions positives de l'accession aux ordres dans la première législation ecclésiastique* (Ottawa, 1963).

[235] This is, in substance, a repetition of the ordinance of 528 to the prefect Atarbius. See above, pp. 353-54.

has a concubine; but [one will ordain] him only if his wife lives in chastity and was a virgin [at her marriage]. Indeed, nothing is more [sought] in the holy ordinations than men living in chastity or not living with wives, or whose wives, if they have been or still are married—and monogamous— chose chastity, made by the divine canons the first principle, the foundation and cornerstone of all the other virtues. Should it happen later that a priest, deacon, or subdeacon take a wife or a concubine, either overtly or covertly, let him be immediately demoted from his holy rank and held from then on as a mere faithful. If against these dispositions a lector marries for the second time, and this possibly because of an unavoidable necessity, let him not be admitted to any higher rank and thus enjoy a superior level in the hierarchy. Let him not contract a third marriage; it is indeed enough for him to have married twice. If he actually remarried and promptly sought a higher rank, by this fact he will be considered a mere layman and demoted from all sacred ministry. For us the life of chastity is in fact a matter of concern above all others. For if they are thus established [in chastity]—those who, oriented toward the clergy, received the imposition of hands—they will have an easy promotion to the episcopate; in a crowd of good men it will not be difficult to find [subjects] who are worthy of promotion to the priesthood.[236]

This chapter is part of the sixth novella concerning deacons, priests, and lectors. For the first two categories of clerics, first their matrimonial situation is stressed: one should not elevate to the diaconate or the priesthood a man who married a woman separated from her husband, or one living with a concubine; remarried widowers are also excluded. The conditions to be fulfilled are the following: either living in chastity or not living with one's wife, either having been or still being the husband of an only wife, who also must live in chastity and have been a virgin at marriage. We follow up here the Greek text:

[IB] μήτε δὲ τὸν δευτέρους ἔχοντα γάμους ἢ σχόντα χειροτονεῖθαι διάκονον ἢ πρεσβύτερον, μήτε εἰ γυναικὶ συνοικοίη διεζευγμένῃ καὶ τὸν οἰκεῖον ἄνδρα καταλιπούσῃ, μήτε εἰ παλλακὴν ἔχοι; ἀλλὰ καὶ αὐτοὺς ἢ μετὰ σοφροσύνης ζῶντας ἢ γαμεταῖς οὐ συνοικοῦντας, ἢ μιᾶς γαμετῆς ἄνδρα γενόμενον ἢ ὄντα, καὶ αὐτῆς σώφρονος καὶ ἐκ παρθενίας.[237]

---

[236] CJC (J) 3, 42–43.

[237] The "renewed" Latin version by P. Krueger and G. Kroll effectively corrects, according to the Greek, the so-called authentic version, and suggests the following rendition of this passage: "sed et ipsos cum castitate viventes aut uxoribus non cohabitantes, aut unius uxoris virum qui vel fuerit vel sit, et ipsam uxorem si cum castitate et ex virginitate sit" (CJC [J] 3, 4–43, note).

The word σώφρων is used for both the man and the woman. The single men chosen for the diaconate or the priesthood must be μετὰ σωφροσύνης ζῶντας; for her part, the virgin who married the future cleric must also become σώφρων. The chaste life of the deacon's or priest's wife must thus be understood as one of perfect continence, of the same kind that is required from an unmarried future minister.[238] The reason for these demands is explained at the end of the chapter: such men, if chosen for the clergy, will easily be elevated to the episcopate, and one would have, so to speak, plenty of choice: "If they are well established [in chastity], those who, oriented to the clergy, received the imposition of hands will have an easy promotion to the episcopate; it will be easy to find in a crowd of good men [subjects] who are worthy of promotion to the priesthood." If we recall that one of the conditions required of the bishop by the Code of Justinian is that the candidate must not have children, we will understand that he extended the obligation of continence to the deacons and priests whose wives were still alive.

As to the lectors, the novella forbids them to remarry if they want to be promoted to a higher rank of the clergy. We already knew that they were allowed to be married and can make a quick note of this confirmation.

Novella 22:
To John, prefect of the praetorium (March 18, 536)

Chap. 42: If a man included with the very venerable clerics has contracted a marriage [we are not talking about lectors and cantors], we decide and wish him to be, in virtue of our constitution, demoted from the priesthood. If a married lector, for his part, later comes to a second marriage on account of an unavoidable necessity, let him not be raised in any way to the higher clergy, but let him remain with his wife because he chose her love above a better promotion. If he is a layman who desired to reach ordination of the subdiaconate, the diaconate, or the priesthood, and later on it is discovered that he had married either a woman who was not a virgin [at the time of the marriage] or a woman separated from her husband, or if [it is discovered that that woman] was never legitimately united to him from the start, or if he contracted a second marriage, he will not obtain the priesthood, and in case he manages to do so by hiding [the truth], he will resolutely be demoted.[239]

---

[238] The meaning of the word σώφρων is confirmed again by its use in chapter 12 of the 123d novella, where the clerics are reminded that they should be either husbands of an only legitimate wife or perfectly chaste men: "Clericos autem non aliter ordinari permittimus, nisi . . . caste (σώφρων) viventes aut uxorem legitimam et ipsam unam et primam habentes" (CJC [J] 3, 604).

[239] CJC (J) 3, 176.

Marriage is forbidden to subdeacons and major clerics; remarried widowers or those who, married, did not take a virgin are excluded. This novella is in line with the previous ones.

Novella 123:
To Peter, prefect of the praetorium (May 1, 546)

Chap. 1: We therefore decide that each time it will be necessary to elect a bishop, the clerics and the main notabilities of the town where the ordination is to take place should quickly write decrees relative to three persons; [let them do it] in the presence of the most holy Gospels and at the risk of their souls, declaring in said decrees that it is not because of a donation or because of any promise, or out of friendship, or for any other reason, that they chose those men, but because they know them as having an orthodox and Catholic faith, leading honest lives and being knowledgeable in [Holy] Writ; [they also have to declare] that to their knowledge none of them has either wife or children, that he has not had and still has no concubine or children out of wedlock; if one of them at one time had a wife [he must also declare] that she was truly the only and the first, that she was not a widow, nor an already-married woman, nor a person guilty under the laws or sacred canons.[240]

The 123d novella, addressed to "the most glorious Peter", prefect of the praetorium, to make certain that it is observed everywhere,[241] is among the more important ones in the legislative work of Justinian. Approaching a group of problems concerning bishops, clerics, and monks, it renews and amends on certain points the previous constitutions.

The first chapter, above, goes back to the essential points of the letters to prefects Atarbius and John and of the constitution of 535 sent to the Eastern patriarchs about the ordination of bishops.[242] The elected will have to be the object of a meticulous inquiry, no consideration inspired by favoritism or interest entering into such a serious matter. The rectitude of his faith and the honesty of his morals are the first and fundamental criteria. Then come the usual questions regarding sexual and conjugal life. The future bishop must have had no wife or children; there will also be an inquiry to discover whether he might have had a concubine and sired illegitimate children. In the case of his having been married, did his wife belong to the category of women who constitute, in virtue of "the laws or the sacred canons", an obstacle to the priesthood? All these

---

[240] CJC (J) 3, 594.

[241] "Tua igitur gloria quae per praesentem legem in perpetuum valituram nostra sanxit tranquillitas per omnia custodiri provideat" (Nov. 123, Epilogus. CJC [J] 3, 625).

[242] See above, pp. 353, 355–56, 357–58.

conditions, as we can see, prepare the ground for the kind of life required from a bishop. Married or not at the time of his lay life, he will have to remain childless and observe perfect continence.

> *Chap 12*: We will not permit the ordination of clerics unless it is with the condition that they are knowledgeable in [Holy] Writ, have an upright faith and life, did not have and still do not have a concubine or children born out of wedlock, but live chastely; or, if they have a legitimate wife, that she is the only and the first, and that she is not a widow or a woman separated from her husband, nor a woman subject to the interdicts of the laws or the holy canons.[243]

The preliminary inquiry for ordination in the various categories of clerics, including lectors and cantors, concerns the same points as the examination of the bishop's aptitude: rectitude of faith and morals, matrimonial situation. To be received in the clergy, one must, in particular, bear witness to a behavior in conformity with the "laws and holy canons", i.e., have lived in perfect chastity or have married only once and to a virgin. This chapter does not deal with the continence that will or will not be required from new ministers in the future. Concerning the first ranks of the clergy as well as the Major Orders, it leaves aside an issue of special interest to bishops, priests, and deacons.[244]

> *Chap. 14*: But if a deacon about to receive the imposition of hands has no wife united to him [in marriage] as was stated above, let no one impose hands on him before the bishop questions him and he has promised to live worthily and without a legitimate wife after the imposition of hands; the ordaining [bishop] has no power, at the time of imposition of hands, to permit the deacon to take a wife after the imposition of hands; should such a thing happen, the bishop who gave the permission would be excluded from the episcopate; if, after the imposition of hands, a priest, deacon, or subdeacon contracts a marriage, let him be rejected from the clergy and delivered, body and goods, to the council of the town where he was a cleric.
>
> If a lector, on his part, contracts a second marriage, or if his first wife was a widow or a woman separated from her husband or a person under the interdicts of the laws or the holy canons, let him not be promoted to

---

[243] CJC (J) 3, 604.

[244] We may take this opportunity to note the age limitations set in the following chapter for admission to the different Orders: thirty-five for the priesthood, twenty-five for the diaconate or the subdiaconate, ten or eight years old as a minimum for the lectorate. It is understandable that when they reached marriageable age the lectors were authorized to marry, while they waited to make up their minds—and to be judged worthy—for their admission to the subdiaconate some years later. Cf. CJC (J) 3, 604.

another ecclesiastical rank; and if he was elevated in any manner to a higher rank, let him be sent away and demoted to his previous rank.[245]

The first part of this chapter is not without reminding us, as we have seen, of the 10th canon of the Council of Ancyra.[246] It is composed according to the same framework, and it is the same question, raised during the ceremony of ordination itself, by the possible desire of a future marriage. While the interpretation of the rule as enunciated here was afterward extended to include subdeacons, the addendum to the code [Novella] starts, however, with the mention of deacons by themselves, confirming the impression that the main idea of the decree was borrowed from the older pattern set by the Council of Ancyra. It may very well be, let us note further, that the Byzantine emperor had the deliberate intention of modifying the ancient Eastern discipline in a restrictive way, in order, for example, to cut through the red tape of ambiguous situations: after all, any deacon could always protest that even though he was silent at the moment of the laying-on-of-hands, he had never made up his mind formally to make a vow of perpetual chastity. Further, Justinian's reforms as far as ecclesiastical discipline was concerned make this hypothesis even more plausible. But it is just as possible to wonder whether we do not have in this addendum to the Code an interpretation and a clarification that are faithful to the canon law voted at Ancyra, the Greek text we possess of that law not being nearly as clear as one might wish.

In any case, the legislation of 546 stipulates that candidates to the diaconate will be ordained only after a formal questioning on the part of the consecrating bishop and an explicit promise to remain single. Could those who had been married before continue their conjugal existence? This point, which is the subject of a special chapter in the sixth novella,[247] is not studied here. It is simply specified that the same question will be asked of subdeacons.

In keeping with his habits, the emperor promulgated sanctions against possible culprits. The first to be held responsible is the ordaining bishop. Should he authorize a subdeacon or a deacon to marry, he himself would be deprived of his episcopal function. As to the concerned parties, they would return to the lay state; the city where they exercised their function would decide their fates.

In the second part the decree reiterates the conditions required for entry to the lectorate; if a lector decides to remarry, or if it happens that his

[245] CJC (J) 3, 605.
[246] See above, pp. 172–73.
[247] See above, pp. 357–61.

wife does not fulfill the conditions mentioned by "the laws or the holy canons", he will not be able to rise to the higher dignity. Should he manage to bypass this condition, he would be demoted to the echelon he should never have left.

> *Chap. 29*: As to the priests, the deacons, and the subdeacons, and all those who, not having wives, were enrolled into the clergy in conformity with the divine canons, we also forbid them, on the authority of the holy canons, to bring into their own homes any woman whatever, with the exception, however, of a mother, a daughter, a sister, or other female persons above all suspicion. Should anyone stray from this regulation and keep in his house a woman able to bring suspicion upon him, and after a first and a second warning from his bishop or clerics requesting him not to live with such a woman, should he refuse to send her away or if somebody comes to accuse him and provides a proof that he lives in a dishonest way with that woman, his bishop will then have to demote him from the clergy, according to ecclesiastical canons, and surrender him to the council of the town where he was a cleric. As to the bishop, in no way do we permit him to have a wife or live with her. If it is proven that he does not observe this regulation, let him be rejected from the episcopate; he himself shows that he is unworthy of the priesthood.[248]

This law is inspired by canon 3 of the Council of Nicaea (325), although it is not mentioned by name, and its application to bishops is reinforced. All clergy members who are widowers or bachelors—including the lower clerics—must be forbidden to live with women who are not their kin. The reason that is invoked, as usual, is the risk of suspicion that the presence of such women under their roofs could bring upon the clerics. The insertion of this regulation, which was more than two centuries old, into the *Corpus juris civilis* proves that the custom of the συνείσακτοι had, among the Eastern clergy members, a life that was as tenacious as it had in the West.

On the list of close female relatives "above any suspicion", the wife of the cleric who might have been married before ordination is not mentioned. Therefore, nothing can be concluded here, with the exception of the bishop's case, unless her presence, if it were admitted, was not considered more damaging to the reputation of the Church minister than that of a mother, sister, or daughter. In light of the sixth novella, one can think that the chastity required from the wife normalized, in the eyes of public opinion, her living at the conjugal home.[249]

[248] CJC (J) 3, 615–16.
[249] See above, pp. 360–61.

Keeping his distance as regards the tradition of Nicaea, the emperor decided, on his own authority, measures that were stricter concerning bishops. No woman, not even a close relative, could find room in the episcopal house. The transgressor risked serious sanctions, nothing less than the loss of his See. One might be ready to believe Justinian when he declares "unworthy" of the priesthood bishops who keep at home a mother or a sister, but more practical considerations were undoubtedly at the basis of a severity that is difficult to justify with motives of priestly spirituality; the problems of succession are certainly playing a greater role here. To eliminate the risk of alienating Church goods for the benefit of the bishop's kin was, as we saw, one of the major concerns of Justinian's policy. But inasmuch as we are talking here about women, the unconditional decree shutting the door of the bishops' house in their faces seems to reveal even more the design shaping the episcopal lifestyle according to the model of the monasteries. The monasteries were influential in an empire that counted hundreds of them at that time, and Justinian did not cease to shower on them financial favors and marks of admiration.[250] This is true. The real reason for such an assimilation, favored but never imposed in the West, escapes us, however. Or was the husband of Theodora so suspicious of female influences that he wished at all costs to guard his mitered functionaries against them?

Novella 137:
To Peter, master of the sacred palace (March 26, 565)

Chap. 1: Because we take God's judgment very seriously, we deem it proper to proceed immediately to the examination and the canonical reform of various subjects presented to us. Indeed, if the civil laws do not permit the offenses committed by lay people to be treated carelessly, without inquiry or punishment, how could we allow the canonical regulations, enacted by the holy apostles and the holy Fathers for the salvation of all men, to be disregarded? Now, we are convinced that if many fell into sin, the main reason is that the consecrated bishops did not hold a synod as the holy apostles and the holy Fathers directed them to do. If indeed such a point had been observed, everyone would fear condemnation by the synod and would make a serious effort to devote himself [wholly] to the divine liturgies and to live honestly in order not to fall under the sanction

---

[250] He did not hesitate to entrust the temporal prosperity of the State to the prayer of the monks: "Si enim illi puris manibus et nudis animabus pro re publica supplicent (deo, manifestum quia et exercitus) habebit bene et civitates bene disponentur . . . terraque nobis offeret fructus et mare quae sua sunt dabit, illorum oratione propitiationem dei ad omnem rempublicam deducente" (Nov. 137, cap. 5. CJC [J] 3, 674).

of the holy canons. And several people have found an excuse to sin that was not a minor one because bishops, priests, deacons, or other clerics at various degrees had been ordained [among the recruited candidates] without a preliminary inquiry and without [questioning] witnesses about the rectitude of their faith and the seriousness of their morals. Now, if those who received the responsibility of praying for the people are found to be unworthy of the ministry of God, how could they appease God for the sins of the people? That the appointment of the priests must be undertaken with great care, this is what we are also taught by Gregory the Theologian, held in honor of sanctity, following [in this] the holy apostles and the holy canons [here are some quotations from Gregory Nazianzen]. . . . Basil, also held in honor of sanctity, teaches us that the holy canons forbid access to the clergy to all those who remarried: those who contracted a second marriage, he says, are excluded formally, by the canon, from the ministry. Such is the opinion of Basil, held in honor of sanctity. The holy Fathers bore witness to such a great concern for the priesthood that the [bishops] gathered at Nicaea enacted a canon as follows: the great council absolutely forbids bishops, priests, and deacons, and, in a word, all the members of the clergy, to have a sister-companion with them unless she is a mother or an aunt or the only persons above suspicion.

Chap. 2: Conforming ourselves therefore to the regulations specified by the holy canons, we enact the present law, through which we order [the following]: each time it will be necessary to appoint a bishop, the clerics and the main notabilities of the town where the bishop is to be appointed will have to gather, and before the holy Gospels write decrees about three persons: each one of them will have to take an oath on Holy Scripture and attest in writing [in these decrees] that he did not choose these [candidates] on account of gifts [that had been made to them], or in virtue of a promise, or out of friendship, or for any interested motive, but because he knows that they have an orthodox and Catholic faith and lead honest lives; [he must also attest] that to the best of his knowledge none of them has a wife or children, and that he has not had and still does not have a concubine and children born out of wedlock; if one of them once had a wife [he must also attest] that the latter was truly the only one and that she was not a widow, or a woman separated from her husband, or a person under the interdicts of the holy canons (and the laws).[251]

This lengthy novella, proudly bedecked with all the titles that the emperor had acquired at the price of exhausting campaigns, is dated from the second year of the reign of Justinian. His main addressee, Peter, the master of the sacred palace, is in charge of disseminating it throughout the world and transmitting it to the governments of the provinces.

[251] CJC (J) 3, 695–97.

In substance it does not teach us anything new: the regulation concerning the consecration of bishops is a literal copy of the constitution of 546, addressed to the same functionary, which also renewed anterior ordinances.[252]

Two references that are more precise intend to link the spirit of the law and the traditional doctrine: the authority of Gregory of Nazianzen and of Basil of Caesarea on the one hand, both with the prestigious halo of the saints, and on the other hand, canon 3 of the Council of Nicaea, related to the female guests of clerics. This is an anthological procedure that Justinian had not yet shown to us; did the old monarch feel a need to base his decisions on those whose authority was less contested than his own?

We must note also the passing complaint that escapes from his pen: Justinian laments the shirking of the bishops who neglected to hold councils, contrary to the prescriptions of "the holy apostles and the holy Fathers", and who are responsible for a general laxity of the discipline ("If many fell into sin, the main reason is that the consecrated bishops held no synod, as they had been directed to do by the holy apostles and the holy Fathers"). Such a reproach may be perplexing when one knows the care with which the emperor had guarded, all his life, the monopoly on ecclesiastical matters. One would rather think that his meddling in all matters was not the least responsible for this slowing down of conciliar activity in the Eastern patriarchates. As he was declining in power, did the authoritarian legislator become aware of the weak points in his Caesaropapism? It remains a fact that he was conscious of a real evil where we might perhaps find one of the profound reasons explaining the ups and downs in the discipline of priestly continence in the Eastern world. When we compare on this point and for the same period the influence of the councils of Gaul or Spain, on the one hand, with the action exerted by only one man (even if he was the great Justinian and such an action was a monumental legislative enterprise), on the other hand, we cannot help but think that it would certainly have been more efficacious to put into the hands of the bishops the responsibility of disciplinary decisions, even if they had to be forcibly pushed to meet frequently in councils (if it is true—but we are allowed to doubt it—that they had no such desire).[253]

---

[252] See above, pp. 362–63.

[253] This is precisely what the emperor made up his mind to do in that last year of his reign, when he admitted his own negligence (Nov. 137, cap. 4. CJC [J] 3, 698).

Emperors Honorius and Theodosius
to Palladius, prefect of the praetorium (May 8, 420)

It is not fitting that the one who practices an estimable rule [in the eyes of the world] be discredited by [the company of women] to whom is given the name of "sisters". As a consequence, all those who, at any level whatever, are covered with the splendor of the priesthood or who are affiliated to the dignity of the clergy, must know that common life with women who are "outsiders" of their houses is forbidden to them; we concede only the option of giving refuge in their houses to their mothers, their daughters, and their sisters; the ties of nature do not permit any evil suspicion about them. A chaste love still calls for not abandoning those who, before the priesthood of their husbands, had been worthy [of union with them] through a legitimate marriage: it is indeed not without reason that they are associated with clerics, those whose behavior made their husbands worthy of the priesthood.[254]

We have intentionally kept for the end this document, which, because of its date, should have been placed at the head of the series of Justinian's laws. This is, as can be seen, the constitution promulgated in 420 by the emperors Honorius and Theodosius as it applies to the problem of clerics' cohabitation with so-called outsider women. Its interpretation at the level of the Theodosian Code brings up a problem that we have already had the opportunity to study.[255] It is the document's place in the Code of Justinian published in 534 that demands our attention now, and the scope given to it by the general context of the *Corpus juris civilis* in which it is inserted.

Faithful to his project of collecting the main ordinances of his predecessors, the emperor of Byzantium reedited the text without changing the letter. The law we just read reproduces faithfully the content of the Theodosian document such as the manuscripts have kept it for us.[256] Does this fidelity mean that its content is ipso facto endorsed, without any shading of meaning, by the new legislation? The answer is easy when one has a proper knowledge of the Justinian decrees and novellae of the *Corpus juris civilis*. As to the presence of women in the houses of clerics, the decrees are summarized, as we will recall, in the following givens:

No woman, not even a close relative, is authorized to live in the episcopal residence. The possible wife of the bishop is no exception.[257]

---

[254] *Codex Justinianus*, I, 3, 19. CJC (J) 2, 20.

[255] See above, pp. 318–19.

[256] *Codex Theodosianus*, 16, 2, 44. T. Mommsen, ed., *Theodosiani libri XVI cum constitutionibus Sirmondianis*, I, 2 (Berlin, 1904, 1954), p. 851.

[257] See above, pp. 357ff.

Subdeacons, deacons, and priests may keep by their sides their mothers, sisters, and daughters, or any other female person whose company does not provoke suspicion. Though wives are not mentioned, the chastity required from them seems to imply that they belonged to the latter category.[258] In this form, the Code of Justinian is close to the Western legislation of St. Leo or the Gallic councils in its attempt to find a harmonious solution to the rights of conjugal affection and the demands of chastity.[259]

As to the lower clerics, lectors and cantors, because they were free to marry, it goes without saying that they could have a conjugal life.[260]

Thus, one can readily judge the meaning that the Theodosian decree could have in the mind of Theodosius' successor on the throne of Byzantium. First, it is clear enough that the case of lectors and cantors, who could marry, is outside his perspective, the problem at hand being that of wives who "before the priesthood of their husbands deserved to be legitimately united with them [*quae ante sacerdotium maritorum legitimum meruere coniugium*]". The situation concerns men who were already married and are advancing toward the higher Orders. Restricting the clauses of the law of 420, Justinian excludes for bishops the possibility of cohabitation with those "deserving" wives. The affection—bond—of chastity that justified in Theodosius' eyes his advice "not to abandon those who, through their behavior, made their husbands worthy of the priesthood", is no longer taken into account. On the other hand, it is not seen that the Byzantine legislator of the 6th century denied its value for subdeacons, deacons, and priests. We do not risk being wrong in thinking that he recognized for them the right to live with their wives, according to a *modus vivendi* regulated by continence, for the very reasons expressed in the decree he wanted to preserve from oblivion: "A chaste love still calls for not abandoning those who, before the priesthood of their husbands, had been worthy [of union with them] through a legitimate marriage: it is indeed not unreasonable that associated with clerics are those whose behavior made their husbands worthy of the priesthood." Incorporated into the new code, the Theodosian law was thus modified, as happened frequently in the *Corpus juris civilis*. To be more precise, it became relativized through the promulgation of new ordinances defining the discipline of the time, which is why we placed the commentary at the end of this section.

---

[258] See above, pp. 359ff.
[259] See above, pp. 261ff., 272ff.
[260] See above, pp. 361, 363.

3. THE ROMAN PONTIFFS

Gregory the Great (590–604)

It was St. Gregory who, for the first time in history, took the title of *Servus servorum Dei*, which has become the distinctive appellation of the sovereign pontiffs. Born in Rome around the year 540, from a family of noble origins that had already given a pope to the Church (Felix III, great-grandfather of Gregory), he gave up a brilliant political career to answer the call to monastic life. Selling his goods enabled him to found six monasteries in Sicily and a seventh in Rome, where he withdrew from the world. But Pope Pelagius soon pulled him out of seclusion to make him his apocrisiarius (nuncio) in Constantinople; he stayed in the imperial capital from 578 to about 585, devoting the leisure of his official functions to the composition of an ascetic treatise, the *Moralities on Job*, which remains one of the masterpieces of spiritual literature. Back in Rome, he directed the monastery that he had founded, but the cloister was not able to keep him for long. At the death of Pelagius II, Abbot Gregory was obliged to sit on Peter's throne (590). The fourteen years of his pontificate would have been enough to give him the title "Great" that posterity attached to his name. Moralist, director of souls, contemplative of a prodigious activity, master preacher, this "Benedictine" who became Pope was a man of government who combined a keen sense of his universal authority in the Church with a peaceful humility "that knows how to make itself loved without trying too hard to please". He died on March 12, 604.

We still have today 848 letters of St. Gregory the Great collected in fourteen books. If they are only a small part of the huge correspondence of the Roman Pontiff (the original collection gathered while Gregory was still alive has been lost), they nevertheless provide us with important testimonies on the many issues that called for his intervention and on the nature of his pastoral methods. On the specific problem of priestly continence, the *Register Epistolarum* preserved for us several letters in which we see the successor of Peter affirm the traditional discipline while adapting his decisions to concrete situations.

To Peter, subdeacon of Sicily (May 591)

Writing to a certain Peter, subdeacon and administrator of the pontifical patrimony in Sicily, Gregory instructs him to obtain from the bishops that they show moderation when they extend to subdeacons the obligation of continence:

> Three years ago it was absolutely forbidden to subdeacons of the Churches of Sicily, according to the customs of the Roman Church, to have relations with their wives. It seems to me harsh and inopportune to compel a man to separate from his wife when he has not discovered the advantages of continence and did not himself previously propose to [observe] chastity; this makes him fall, God preserve us, into a worse [situation]. This is why it seems good to me to request that all the bishops from now on should not allow themselves to ordain as subdeacon someone who would not have [first] promised to live in chastity . . . in order not to demand by force what was not first desired with a well-considered intention and carefully to avoid future [disasters]. As to those who, after said interdiction enacted three years ago, kept continence with their wives, they must be praised and rewarded and exhorted to persevere in their good [resolution]. As to those who, on their part, [still] refused to abstain from [relations] with their wives after interdiction, we oppose their admission to the sacred Order, since no one can have access to the altar if his chastity has not been tested and recognized before receiving the ministry.[261]

Three years earlier, the bishops of Sicily had decided to conform to the customs of the Church of Rome and had forbidden subdeacons to have conjugal relations. This preliminary observation informs us indirectly that deacons, priests, and bishops of Sicily, for their part, had been bound for a long time to continence. The extension of the obligation to the fourth Order was the result of an evolution similar to that of other ecclesiastical provinces, probably taking into account that subdeacons participated in a closer way in the higher functions of the clergy.[262]

The decision made by the episcopate of the island concerned future candidates as well as the men already ordained subdeacons. Between one day and the next, as it were, unprepared people had thus been asked to cease their common life with their wives—an excess of zeal that Gregory, being an experienced shepherd, did not hesitate to denounce. It seems to him harsh and inopportune (*durum atque incompetens*) to force anyone to such a separation if he has not first discovered the advantages of continence and did not himself freely propose to be bound by it. A worse fall would be in store for him. Gregory certainly does not intend to grant to the subdeacons of Sicily a freedom that he deems, as does his correspondent,

---

[261] *Ep.* I, 42. MGH, *Gregorii I Papae registrum epistolarum*, I (Berlin, 1891), p. 67.

[262] Such was the case, as we have seen, at the same time in the Churches of Gaul, Spain, Africa, and, of course, Rome.

incompatible with their functions. But he insists that no violence be done to some by requiring from them a sudden discipline, and that in the future one act with prudence to the others. This double preoccupation dictates the action to be taken: from now on, let the bishops not take the risk of elevating to the subdiaconate someone who has not first promised to lead a chaste life. As to the subdeacons already in position, if there are among them some who have actually observed conjugal continence since the recent interdiction, one must praise them, reward them, and encourage them to persevere on the right path. As to the others, rebelling against a law that took them by surprise, the Pontiff calls for a compromise: they will have no access to the sacred altar because no one must approach the ministry of the altar without having first been approved as chaste; but without saying so openly, Gregory nevertheless recognizes their right to retain this function. These transitional measures did in fact create two categories of subdeacons, only the continent being organically linked to the higher ranks of the hierarchy and able to be promoted eventually. With the disappearance by attrition of the others, in a few years the Church of Sicily would smoothly catch up with the statute of the communities of the Roman world.

To Symmacus, defender[263] (June 591)

After having given to his representative in Corsica his instructions on the choice of a site for the erection of a monastery, and having invited him to take good care in reforming the monks on the nearby island of Gorgona, the Pope adds: "Moreover, we desire that the priests residing in Corsica be forbidden to live with women, with the exception of a mother, a sister, or a wife, the last being guided with chastity."[264]

This reminder of canon 3 of Nicaea on the cohabitation of clerics with *subintroductae* is accompanied with particulars concerning the wife. She, in conformity with the practice officially approved by St. Leo in his letter to Rusticus of Narbonne,[265] is authorized to live with her husband after he has been ordained. She is to be counted among the women whose presence at the cleric's home would not constitute a cause for scandal, on condition that she be "guided with chastity (*quae caste regenda est*)". This

---

[263] The "defenders" were, at the time of St. Gregory, pontifical functionaries who were entrusted with the administration of Peter's patrimony. In Corsica, where the Holy See owned important domains, the defender had a great authority, both over the leasing farmers (*conductores*) and over the bishops themselves.

[264] *Ep.* I, 50. MGH, *Gregorii I*, I, p. 76.

[265] See above, pp. 261–64.

way of interpreting the canon of the Council of Nicaea is in line with the previous councils and pontifical declarations.

To Boniface, bishop of Reggio (Calabria)(September 593)

In this letter, meant to revive in a bishop the sense of his responsibility with respect to his clergy, we read the following passage: "As to your subdeacons, our will is that they observe what we stipulated with regard to the Sicilians. Do not let it happen that obstinacy or temerity on anybody's part reduce to nothing what we have thus determined." [266]

Though located in Calabria, the town of Reggio, on the strait of Messina, was in practice linked to the episcopal Sees of Sicily. [267] This explains why in 588 the subdeacons there had been subjected to the same measures as those Gregory referred to in his letter to the subdeacon Peter. The same moderation in the method to be followed for progressively extending to the members of the clergy's "fourth Order" the obligation of continence is thus to be used: namely, to encourage those subdeacons who already practice continence; not downgrading the others but not promoting them to a higher rank either.

To John, bishop of Cagliari (Sardinia) (May 594)

The bishop of Cagliari was letting his inclination to simplicity prevail over the necessary firmness. Gregory reminds him of his duty:

A report from our brother and fellow Bishop Felix and of Abbot Cyriacus informs us that on the island of Sardinia the priests are oppressed by lay judges, and the agents of the civil power despise your fraternity. And although you are only seeking simplicity, insofar as we can understand it, discipline finds itself neglected. I am therefore exhorting you to rule, by divine authority, the Church entrusted to you, without giving any excuse, and to see to the discipline proper to the clergy without fearing anyone's words. According to what I have been told, you have forbidden your archdeacon to live with women, and until this day he has paid no attention to your prohibition. Unless he has already obeyed your injunction, we want this man to be deprived of the sacred Order. . . .

We have also heard that some people, after having strayed from sacred Orders, were reinstated in their ministerial function, either after having done penance or before, which we absolutely forbid. In so doing they also violate the holy canons. From now on, anyone who, after his ordination, falls into the sin of the flesh will have to be deprived of the sacred Order and not be admitted in the future to the ministry of the altar. But to prevent

---

[266] Ep. IV, 5. MGH, Gregorii I, I, p. 237.
[267] Cf. also Ep. VII, 19. Ibid., I, p. 462.

that those who have been ordained perish, one must take thought and check those who are candidates to Orders; first let it be examined whether they have led a continent life for many years, whether they have demonstrated a taste for the study [of Holy Scripture], whether they liked giving alms. One must also find out if they were not, by chance, bigamists.[268]

This letter is of interest to us because it contains a reminder of canon 3 from Nicaea. We also see the Roman Pontiff manifest an equal severity with respect to the offenses of fornication committed by clerics. The penalty of deposition is to be strictly applied, without leaving to the culprits the possibility of resuming their ministries, even after a period of penance. Gregory is firm on discipline, his concern being obviously to associate continence with the ministry of the altar in an exclusive manner.[269] It is forethought in the choice of candidates that will make it possible to avoid the entrance of men who are not particularly inclined to continence into the clergy. A man will be accepted for ordination only if he has already practiced that discipline for several years. Given that the subdiaconate was generally considered a sacred Order by that time, should one understand that St. Gregory demanded of lectors, cantors, and the other clerics of lower ranks, as well as of lay people directly elevated to one of the higher ranks of the hierarchy, that they practice continence for a rather long time before being admitted to the subdiaconate? It does seem that this is the spirit of the letter to John of Cagliari.[270]

To Leo, bishop of Catania (Sicily) (July 594)

Three years after his letter to Peter, subdeacon of Sicily, St. Gregory returns to the issue of the subdeacons' continence in an epistle to one of the bishops of the island:

---

[268] *Ep.* IV, 26. Ibid., I, pp. 260–61.

[269] The correspondence of St. Gregory includes other instances of clerics guilty (or suspected) of offenses of fornication. See, in particular, *Ep.* III, 44 and 45 (ibid., I, pp. 200–201); *Ep.* V, 17 (ibid., I, pp. 298–99); *Ep.* V, 18 (ibid., I, pp. 299–301); *Ep.* VIII, 24 (ibid., II [Berlin, 1899], p. 26); *Ep.* X, 2 (ibid., II, pp. 237–38); *Ep.* XI, 46 (ibid., II, pp. 318–19). The Roman Pontiff always intervened with the same severity in conformity with the legislation then in effect.

[270] On this point, see also the letter of St. Gregory to the clergy and nobility of Naples, in which he disagrees with the election to the episcopate of a deacon who was the father of a little girl. The context shows that it was a daughter the deacon had had before he was ordained (otherwise, Gregory would simply have asked for his deposition), but the age of the child attested that the candidate to the episcopate of Naples had not started to observe continence until a relatively recent date. Hence the objection of St. Gregory: "Nam qua praesumptione ad episcopatum audet accedere, qui adhuc longam corporis sui continentiam filiola teste convincitur non habere?" (*Ep.* X, 19. Ibid., II, p. 254).

Many reports have informed us that there was a custom in the past, among you, permitting subdeacons to have relations with their wives. So that no one will again have the audacity to act in such a way, an interdiction was brought by Servus-Dei, deacon of our [Apostolic] See, on the authority of our predecessor: those who were already united to wives had to choose between two things; either to abstain from conjugal relations or not to have the presumption to exercise their ministries under any pretext. According to what I have been told, Speciosus, who was then a subdeacon, resigned from his function for that reason and until his death was a notary, ceasing to exercise the ministry that he would have had as a subdeacon. After his death, his widow, Honorata, contracted a second marriage, for which reason it is said that your fraternity consigned her to a monastery. Therefore, if it is true that her [first] husband did resign his functions, one must not hold it against that woman if she remarried, especially since she had not married that subdeacon with the intention of abstaining from the pleasures of the flesh. If you are certain that the truth is such as we have been informed, then you must permit that woman to leave the monastery so that she will be able to return without fear to her husband.

But let your fraternity be quite watchful now. Let it watch with the greatest care so that the men promoted to this function [of the subdiaconate] do not enjoy the freedom of relations with their wives, should they have one. But following the example of the Apostolic See and with no less severity, let your fraternity take dispositions so that they observe [all that is prescribed].[271]

This letter brings particulars with regard to the way the measure had been taken when it extended the obligation to continence to the subdeacons of Sicily. One Servus-Dei, deacon of Rome, had been entrusted by Pelagius II in 588 to put an end to a custom that had been kept on the island for a long time. The concerned parties had been called to choose: either practice continence and remain in their functions, or continue conjugal life, and in that case, be demoted to a lower rank. We saw above how such a method had been deemed "harsh and inopportune" by St. Gregory, concerned as he was to have a necessary transition. His pastoral prudence is again visible here in the settlement of a litigious situation: the widow of a subdeacon who had voluntarily resigned from his functions after the interdict of Pelagius II is declared perfectly free to remarry by St. Gregory. The bishop was wrong to lock her up in a monastery, because her first husband had resigned his subdeacon's functions, and she herself never had the intention of living with him in continence. Indirectly we learn that the widow of a subdeacon or of another major cleric did not then have the option to remarry. Her profession of continence was as definitive as her husband's, such a quality of commitment being likely, as we can easily understand,

---

[271] *Ep.* IV, 34. Ibid., I, pp. 269–70.

an indispensable condition for conjugal fidelity between husband and wife.[272]

To Romanus and Fantinus, defenders; to Savinus, subdeacon; to Hadrian and Eugenius, notaries; to Felix, subdeacon; to Sergius and Boniface, defenders; and to six lawyers (February 599)

This letter, entirely devoted to the problems of priestly cohabitation with female persons, is addressed to functionaries of Sicily (Romanus, Fantinus, and Hadrian), Calabria (Savinus), Latium and the Roman Campana (Felix), and Apulia (Sergius).[273]

> Just as a thoughtful prudence is a hindrance to faults and can remove sources of trouble, negligence opens the path to excesses and ordinarily brings about what is to be feared. Under such conditions we have to employ the greatest zeal and watch over the reputation of our brothers and priests, as well as over their safe-conduct. Now it has come to us that, with the excuse of finding consolation, certain bishops live under the same roof with women. In order not to give to the scorners a just opportunity for disparagement or provide the ancient enemy of the human race with favorable ground for his tricks, we exhort you seriously in this present letter to be diligent and zealous: if one of the bishops living within the boundaries of the patrimony entrusted to you is living with women, you must absolutely put an end to this; and from now on, do not tolerate in any way the residence of women [with bishops] save those who are authorized by the holy canons, i.e., a mother, an aunt, a sister, and other women who—in the same way—cannot cause evil suspicions. It would be best even to abstain from living with such women, however. We read, in fact, that Blessed Augustine could not consent to live with his sister: "The friends of my sister", he would say, "are not my sisters." The prudence of a wise man must therefore be a great lesson for us. . . . Moreover, be careful to exhort these very same bishops, our brothers, to warn those of their subjects who are settled in holy Orders to follow their example and to observe perfectly what they themselves observe, adding simply, as required by canonical authority, that those who have a wife do not abandon her. They have to guide her with chastity.[274]

Here again we have a reminder of canon 3 from the Council of Nicaea, accompanied by the customary clause authorizing the wife of a subdeacon, deacon, or priest to share the home of her husband, on condition that she live in continence with him. It is noteworthy that St. Gregory made no explicit mention of the wife when it came to bishops but limited

---

[272] Cf. also *Ep.* XIV, 5. Ibid., II, 423–24.

[273] It is not known from which areas came the notary Eugenius, the defender Boniface, and the six lawyers (*patroni*).

[274] *Ep.* IX, 110. MGH, *Gregorii I*, II, pp. 115–16.

himself to speaking, in a general way, about women "who cannot cause evil suspicions". We can think with sufficient certainty that he also included in the latter category the wives of men elected to the episcopate, for we know that in his days there were still a certain number of married bishops.[275] Nevertheless, the reserve of St. Leo's successor with respect to bishops can also be explained by a concern to conform with Justinian's legislation, because the Emperor had forbidden bishops to live with wives.[276] It is also likely that, more than half a century after the imperial laws stipulating that no man still bound by marriage could be ordained a bishop,[277] the number of married men chosen for the episcopate had diminished, even in the West. The letter we have just read seems to indicate that Pope Gregory personally favored such a trend.

To Syagrus, Aetherius, Virgil, and Desiderius, bishops (a paribus) of Gaul (July 599)

The four addressees of the letter are Gallic bishops: Syagrus of Autun († 599–600) was a famous bishop, frequently mentioned by Gregory of Tours, Venantius Fortunatus, and Gregory the Great, his contemporaries. Aetherius of Lyon († 602) was the successor of St. Nicetus; he had the honor of celebrating the episcopal ordination of St. Augustine, first archbishop of Canterbury, who had been sent with forty monks by Pope Gregory to convert England. Virgil, a former abbot of Autun, had been elected in 588 to the See of Arles, metropolis of Gaul, on the recommendation of Syagrus. Finally, the one who was to become St. Desiderius was elevated to the See of Vienne after refusing several bishoprics out of humility. After some plots, he would be deposed by a council in 602 (603) and exiled to an island. He was assassinated, a victim of Brunhilde and King Thierry II, whom he had admonished for having concubines. The long epistle addressed by St. Gregory to these four men in July 599 touches upon several questions of ecclesiastical discipline: prohibition against practicing simony and raising laymen to the episcopate without preparation, yearly gatherings of diocesan synods, cohabitation of clerics with "outsider" women. Here are the passages of the letter concerning this last point, which continued to be a problem in Gaul at the dawn of the 7th century:

---

[275] See above, pp. 109–12, regarding several instances of married bishops in the 6th century. Some of them are even known to us through the correspondence of St. Gregory (Blandus of Ortona [133], Eusanius of Agrigentia [138], Lucillus of Malta [147], Passivus of Fermo [152]).

[276] See above, pp. 357ff.

[277] See above, pp. 362ff.

We cannot remain silent, through negligence, on what has also to be improved. Indeed, what is the purpose of having erected fortifications everywhere if one leaves a passage through which the enemy can enter? This is why it is forbidden to those who are members of the sacred Order to reside with women. We must avoid making the ancient enemy of the human race happy, and because of this we decree unanimously that they are forbidden to have a woman with them, exception being made for those listed in the holy canons. It might seem for a while that such interdiction is bitter to some, but there is no doubt that it will later become sweet thanks to the advantages that it provides the soul, if the enemy is vanquished where he could have triumphed. . . .[278]

This is why we desire that your fraternity, in virtue of divine authority, gather a synod and that through the intermediary of our very reverend brother, Bishop Aregius, and our very dear son Cyriacus, all that we have already stated as contrary to the holy canons be strictly condemned under penalty of anathema: let no one dare give gifts to obtain ecclesiastical Orders or receive them for having conferred Orders; let no one have the audacity to switch abruptly from lay life to a position in the sacred hierarchy, and let the priests live with no other women than those authorized by the holy canons, as stated above.[279]

To Augustine, bishop (July 601)

Consecrated archbishop of Canterbury on November 16, 597, by Virgil of Arles, the monk Augustine maintained a close relationship with Pope Gregory, whom he consulted on numerous problems encountered in the organization of the young Church in England. The answers that the Roman Pontiff sent him, Augustin Thierry wrote, "are admirable in their practical wisdom, their high prudence, and their moderation".[280]

In the long letter that left Rome for Canterbury during the month of July 601, Gregory the Great encourages his English colleague to live in community with clerics, most of whom were monks. Then he adds: "But if there are clerics outside of the holy Orders who cannot contain themselves, they must choose a wife and receive their stipend outside [of the presbyterial community]." [281]

We can see from this brief instruction that Gregory the Great extended to the Church in England, as soon as it was founded, the law in effect in the universal Church, according to which only clerics of the lower Orders (porters, cantors, lectors) were permitted to marry. The letter does not mention the continence to be observed by those subdeacons

---

[278] Ep. IX, 218. MGH, Gregorii I, II, p. 209.

[279] Ibid., p. 210.

[280] Quoted by F. Cabrol, L'Angleterre chrétienne avant les Normands (Paris, 1908), p. 66.

[281] Ep. XI, 56a. MGH, Gregorii I, II, p. 333.

and other clerics "established in the holy Orders" who could have been married before their ordinations. This is probably because Augustine of Canterbury had not felt the need to question the Roman Pontiff on this particular point: most of the English clerics were monks; on the other hand, the direction to follow in this field does not seem to have been the object of any hesitation on the part of the first legislators of "the British Isles", if one can judge this by the firmness with which the penitential books, principal expression of the ecclesiastical discipline in those communities, demand that deacons and other major clerics observe continence.[282]

To Gattulus, Romanus, and Wintarit (June 603)

We do not know these three men of high rank to whom Gregory the Great wrote, in June 603, asking them to help Optat, the defender, to put an end to clerics' cohabitation with "outsider" women in the territory of Nursia. Here is the letter they received:

> We have been informed that, in the territory of Nursia, those who are established in the holy Order live with "outsider" women, This being totally against decency, we have ordered the defender Optat that, if such is the true situation, he should exhort and discourage [these clerics] from living with "outsider" women. In case they were to neglect his warnings, we also enjoined him to inform our brother and fellow Bishop Chrysanthes so that he himself may remedy the situation or that, with the help of his authority, the defender [Optat] may endeavor to correct it himself. Let your Eminence lend support in this matter as befits you, and consider the defender as completely trustworthy. Thanks to your support, may he accomplish his mission in good conditions, and for the rest, may he not be able to act in an unreasonable manner.[283]

---

[282] Canon 27 of the *Pénitentiel de Vinniaus* (late 6th century) already makes provision for a severe penance for the cleric (*diaconus aut alicujus gradus*) who, married before ordination, has resumed conjugal relations with his wife and begotten other children, because—as it is stressed—his sin is no less than that of a cleric who, belonging to the clergy since his youth, erred with a young girl. (F. W. H. Wesserschleben, *Die Bussordnungen der abendländischen Kirche* [Halle, 1851; Graz, 1958], p. 114). Canon 28 of the *Pénitentiel de saint Colomban* (ca. 600) reiterates the same dispositions in a clearer style: "If a deacon or a cleric of any rank, who was a family man during his life as a layman, resumes relations with his companion (*clientela*) and begets new children, let him know that he has committed adultery and has sinned no less than if he were a cleric since childhood and then erred with a young girl; for it was after his vow that he sinned, after he had consecrated himself to the Lord, and his vow has been negated by him; therefore he will do penance for seven years on bread and water" (ibid., p. 356). For a good introduction to the "insular" (Ireland and Britain) Penitential books, see A. M. Stickler, *Historia Juris canonici latini*, I, *Historia fontium* (Pas-Verlag, 1950, 1974), pp. 84–95.

[283] *Ep.* XIII, 38. MGH, *Gregorii I*, II, pp. 401–2.

To Chrysanthes, bishop of Spoleto (June 603)

By the same mail, the bishop of Spoleto, who has been mentioned above, also received a letter from Gregory the Great urgently asking him to intervene:

> We have learned from several sources that priests from the territory of Nursia live with "outsider" women. Let your fraternity know that we are very sad about this affair, for you have tolerated that nothing be done to stop such [behavior], assuming that you had full knowledge of the facts. We have ordered defender Optat to remedy the situation by all means: if one of these [priests] were to prove obstinate, he must bring him to judgment before your fraternity. This is why we deemed it necessary to write to your holiness, so that if you find out that certain priests belonging to your diocese live with "outsider" women or if you acquired such certainty through the reports of defender Optat, you will hasten to remedy the situation because we absolutely cannot bear such news. Start with a priestly admonition, and if the matter demands it, go so far as to apply canonical discipline.[284]

These various letters of Gregory the Great attest, on the occasion of concrete situations, to the concern that the successor to Siricius, Innocent I, and St. Leo had in maintaining and applying the discipline set by the papal councils and decretals. No search for innovation characterizes the action of the Bishop of Rome when he asks his correspondents to see to it that the canon of Nicaea regarding "outsider" women be observed or when he reminds the higher ministers of the clergy that they must live in perfect continence with their possible wives. If he intervened in Sicily with regard to subdeacons, it was not in order to extend to them the law of continence, but because the methods that had recently been used on the island to attain such a result seemed "harsh and inopportune" to him.

Nowhere in this correspondence does Gregory the Great seem to feel the need to explain the motivations justifying in his eyes the discipline of chastity and continence of priests. All is understood as an accepted fact, considering that the addressees of his letters also knew what the issues were. If we, on our part, want to ask Gregory to show us the core of his thought, nothing seems better than to open the *Regula pastoralis*, that book he wrote when he was still a young Pope to elaborate on his conception of the priestly ideal. One page, among many others, shows how much the function of intercessor with God, which is that of

---

[284] *Ep.* XIII, 39. Ibid., II, p. 402.

the priest, was in the theology of St. Gregory a specific demand for a more perfect life:

> A shepherd must, by obligation, give a good example in all things; he must, dying to all the passions of the flesh, already live here below in a spiritual life; and having said goodbye to the advantages of this world, he must not be afraid of any adversity and desire only interior goods. He must . . . have learned, by habit and the experience of prayer, that it is possible to obtain from God what he will ask: for it is to him that, practically and specifically, this word of the Lord is addressed: "Before your prayer is over Yahweh will say, 'Here I am'" (Is 58:9).
>
> If, indeed, someone came to ask us, by chance, to intercede in his favor with a high-placed person who is angry at him, and who, in addition, is unknown to us, we would immediately answer as follows: "It is impossible to do this, for we have no relation of friendship with that man!"
>
> If a man dares not become an intercessor with another man of whom he can expect nothing, how dare he arrogate to himself the role of intercessor of the people before God if he has not become, through the merit of his life, accustomed to celestial favor? Again: how will he ask grace for others, if he does not even know whether God is favorable to him? [285]

One would think that this is a commentary on the phrase in which the Fathers of Carthage, in 390, expressed an essential finality for priestly continence: "*quo possint simpliciter quod a Deo postulant impetrare* [so that they can in all simplicity obtain from God what they are asking]".

7th Century

COUNCILS AND SYNODS

AFRICA

For the land of Africa the 7th century was the century of the Moslem invasion. One can never approach without emotion the history of this tragic watershed in which the flourishing Church, fecundated by the blood of Cyprian and illustrated by the most prestigious names of the Christian origins, was to be engulfed for more than a thousand years.

---

[285] *Regula pastoralis*, I, 10. J. Boutet, trans., *Le Pastoral de saint Grégoire le Grand* (Paris, 1928), pp. 27–29.

In 647, when the Egyptian Abdallah ibn Saad obtained from Khalif Othman, successor of Omar, license to venture into the "remote and perfidious Maghreb", the fate of Byzantine Africa was sealed. Fifty years of inexpiable struggles would deliver it to Islam, leaving only the immortal memory of a glorious past.

During the first half of that tragic century, the ecclesiastical provinces under the jurisdiction of Carthage still devoted themselves to tasks of organization. In spite of its mediocrity, the African episcopate, pushed by Gregory the Great, found the strength to stop a renewal of Donatism; under pressure from the exarchs, many churches were built and the danger of Monotheistic heresy caused a renewal of conciliar activity, last signs of life, if we may dare to say, of a long-dynamic Church. In the area of discipline the Church of Africa's "swan song" took the form of a canonical compilation whose exact date and author remain rather uncertain, but which can rightly pass as the last legislative code of Carthage.

The Concordia Cresconii

Was this book the work of a bishop, as asserted in a tenth-century manuscript, or must it be credited to that Cresconius who celebrated in verse, at the end of the 7th century, the victories of the patrician Johannes over the Saracens? We do not know. Certainly anterior to the 8th century, that rich systematic collection may have been written around the year 600 or 700; it appears as a rewrite of the *Breviatio* of the deacon Ferrandus.[286] Grouped under three titles, the 300 (or 301) canons it includes offer a range of documents concerning ecclesiastical institutions and certain doctrinal points. Its literary genre is a duplicate of that of the *Breviatio Ferrandi*, the anthology: a great selection of quotations from councils and pontifical documents, copied in extenso in their Latin version or translation, altogether no fewer than 113 columns of the present Migne edition.[287] As we could have expected, a relatively important number of

---

[286] PL 88, 830c–d. For questions related to the date and author of the *Concordia*, cf. Maassen, 806–13, and P. Fournier and G. Lebras, *Histoire des collections canoniques en Occident*, I (Paris, 1931), p. 35.

[287] Here is the title, developed as a table of contents: *Crisconii episcopi africani Breviarium canonicum, hic habetur concordia canonum conciliorum infra scriptorum, et praesulum romanorum, id est canonum, apostolorum, niceanorum, ancyranorum, novaecaesariensium, gangrensium, antiochensium, laodicensium, chalcedonensium, sardicensium, carthaginensium; item praesulum Siricii, Innocentii, Zosimi, Caelestini, Leonis et Gelasii* (PL 88, 829–30).

these documents are related to priestly continence. It is not necessary to retranscribe them, their content being already known to us, but the rapid inventory that we give below offers useful information on the last state of the issue in Byzantine Africa. Here are the titles or references listed in the same order as in the *Concordia Cresconii*:

1. Siricius, *Letter to Himerius of Tarragona*, chap. IX[288]
2. *Canones apostolorum*, can. 6[289]
3. Siricius, *Letter to Himerius of Tarragona*, chap. VII[290]
4. Innocent I, *Letter to Victricius of Rouen*, chap. XXI[291]
5. *Canones apostolorum*, can. 27[292]
6. *Codex canonum Ecclesiae africanae*, can. 16 (= Council of Hippo of 393, can. 18)[293]
7. *Council of Chalcedon*, can. 14[294]
8. *Council of Ancyra*, can. 10[295]
9. *Council of Neocaesarea*, can. 1[296]
10. Innocent I, *Letter to Victricius of Rouen*, chap. 16[297]
11. St. Leo the Great, *Letter to Rusticus of Narbonne*[298]
12. *Codex canonum Ecclesiae africanae*, can. 25 (= Council of Carthage of 401, can. 4)[299]
13. *Council of Nicaea*, can. 3[300]
14. Siricius, *Letter to Himerius of Tarragona*, chap. 12[301]
15. *Council of Gangres*, can. 4[302]
16. *Council of Neocaesarea*, can. 8[303]
17. St. Leo the Great, *Letter to Anastasius of Thessalonika*, chap. 4[304]

The eclecticism of these documents calls for remarks similar to those already suggested by the *Breviatio Ferrandi*. We are in the presence of an

---

[288] PL 88, 835a–b.
[289] Ibid, 840b.
[290] Ibid., 849c–50c.
[291] Ibid., 850c–51c. In fact, this is the letter to Exupery of Toulouse, chapter 1.
[292] Ibid., 852c.
[293] Ibid., 852c–d.
[294] Ibid., 862b–c.
[295] Ibid., 877a–b.
[296] Ibid., 882b.
[297] Ibid., 882c–d. In fact, this is chapter 10 of the same letter.
[298] Ibid., 883a.
[299] Ibid., 883a–b.
[300] Ibid., 883b.
[301] Ibid., 883b–c.
[302] Ibid., 883c.
[303] Ibid., 884b.
[304] Ibid., 922b–c.

attempt at harmonizing, in one sole legislative collection, ordinances of various origins, as diverse in time as they had been in space. The editor does not hesitate to associate the decretals of Siricius and Innocent I, not only the apocryphal *canones apostolorum*, but even those Eastern councils that seemed at times to attest to a discipline different from the one expressed by the voice of the Roman pontiffs (Gangres, Ancyra, Neocaesarea). It is obvious that, in the mind of Cresconius, such a collection is not heterogeneous; his explicit intention is, on the contrary, to compile in an easy-to-consult manual a choice of texts that are representative of the Tradition of the Church since her origins.[305] For him, as it was for Deacon Ferrandus, there is only one disciplinary tradition that he applies himself to collect in the archives of the West and of the East, and we would be attributing to him a mind set very alien to his own if we saw in the selection of such canon or other the recognition of customs opposed to those practiced in the Church of Rome or of Africa. His reading of canon 4 of Gangres, of canon 10 of Ancyra, or of the sixth apostolic canon is that of a man for whom the general rule serves as a key to interpretation and who records such diverse documents as being the application of concrete historical situations in the common law. It may be that such a way of understanding texts that were several centuries old resulted from a deliberate intention, and we have the right to wonder about it. But when a seventh-century African does not mention, in a compilation of encyclical type, any concern about setting aside certain Eastern documents, but on the contrary retains them to support a canonical building that he intends to be homogeneous, the fact cannot help but be food for thought. It is yet another indication, and not without value, calling for a careful reconsideration of the meaning that several modern historians thought they could give to those Eastern canons. The unknown author who, on the eve of the Moslem invasion, was erecting in his retreat in Africa this small monument of ecclesiastical law will have rendered an appreciable service to us by bearing witness to the unity of discipline in the entire Christian world, warning us that we should not hasten to question it on the basis of documents whose true significance, with the passage of time and ignorance of the general context, we easily run the risk of mistaking.

---

[305] It is written in his letter of advice to the Pontiff Liberinus: "Praecipis ut cuncta canonica constituta quae ab ipsis exordiis militiae Christianae tam SS. apostoli, quam apostolici viri per successiones temporum protulere vobis colligamus in unum, eorumque concordiam facientes, ac titulorum praenotationem interponentes, ea lucidius declaremus" (PL 88, 829d–30c).

SPAIN

Isidore of Seville and the 4th Council of Toledo (633)

Born in Seville, quite likely, around the year 554, Isidore belonged to a family who had emigrated to that town during the invasion of the Arian Goths. His sister Florentina became a nun. His two brothers were promoted to the episcopate—Fulgentius to the See of Carthage; and Leander, the elder, to the See of Seville, where, around the year 600, Isidore was to be his successor. Archbishop of Seville for thirty-six years, he exerted a primary influence in the affairs of the Church of his time, especially in continuing the reforms of the old Spanish councils. Though he did not have the genius of Augustine, Isidore, who remained for history "the last Father of the Western Church", put at the service of the Church the resources of a vast scholarship and was the soul of Catholicism on the peninsula. Bishop Braulio of Saragossa, his friend and first panegyrist, already spoke about him as "the man providentially sent by God to save the documents of antiquity, renew Spain, and prevent it from falling into rusticity". He died in April 636. Innocent XIII declared him a doctor of the Church.

The De Ecclesiasticis Officiis (before 620)

The metropolitan of Betica manifested his attachment to tradition in all fields, but more particularly so in the issues concerning the ecclesiastical ministry. His treatise *De ecclesiasticis officiis* is totally devoted to them; rich in information about the organization of the seventh-century Gothic Church, it sets out to develop the scriptural principles and customs of antiquity that constitute its foundation. The intention of the author is less to describe than to justify, by showing the link connecting present institutions to an ancient past. Thus, when talking about priestly continence, he reviews the argumentation drawn from Leviticus and from the Pauline epistles. The three following texts, concerning bishops, priests, deacons, and subdeacons, are of direct interest to us:

> *About the bishop*: Let those who are elected to the Order of the episcopate be [the husbands] of an only wife, virgin [at marriage]; thus it was ordered by the ancient law and instructed even more fully for us by the Apostle in these words: "the husband of an only wife". Indeed, the Church desires

for bishop either an ex-monogamist ordained [priest] or a man chosen from among the virgins and consecrated [to God]; as to the remarried man, it is precluded that he [could] exercise the priesthood.[306]

About the deacons: It is fitting indeed that the Lord have for ministers men who are not marred by any carnal defilement, but rather radiate with the [splendor] of an eminent chastity. The Apostle Paul specified in his letter to Timothy who these men are that must be ordained as deacons. After having spoken about the selection of bishops, he continues: the deacons, also, [must be] irreproachable, that is, without stain, like the bishops; pure, of course, that is, keeping continence.[307]

About the subdeacons: Those, therefore, receive the offerings made by the people in the temple of the Lord and serve submissively the Levites, offering also to the deacons the [sacred] vessels of the Body and Blood of Christ so that [they can bring them] to the altar of the Lord. Because they touch the sacred mysteries, it has seemed good to the Fathers that these men be chaste and keep continence with their wives and be free of any carnal impurity, according to what had been commanded to them by the prophet: "Purify yourselves, you who carry the vessels of the Lord."[308]

These instructions of Isidore are interwoven with reminiscences borrowed from Scripture, the Fathers, and the previous councils. The note on the first rank of the priestly Order invokes the dual testimony of the Leviticus prescriptions and the *unius uxoris virum* in the epistle to Timothy. The bishop of Seville discerns an echo of what the Old Law called for, i.e., that the high priest take as wife a woman still a virgin,[309] in the Apostle's instruction setting the norms of episcopal recruiting. The New Law is also calling for monogamists because of the sanctity of the ministry. But the author is careful to stipulate that St. Paul expressed himself in a fuller way (*plenius*) than did the old code of the Levites. Such a remark would be rather surprising at first sight, because the verse of the letter to Timothy seems to ignore the Old Testament's criterion relative to the wife of the priest. If it is said that the priest must be the husband of an only wife, the representative of Paul at Ephesus did not seem to have to concern himself with knowing whether or not the wife of the future bishop had to be a virgin at marriage. But the fullness attested by the Apostle, in the view of Isidore of Seville, has another context: it is not so much the conditions preliminary to the episcopal functions that have to be examined but the quality of life required after ordination. Explaining his thought, the author of *De ecclesiasticis officiis* immediately

---

[306] *De ecclesiasticis officiis*, II, 5. PL 83, 783b.
[307] Ibid., II, 8. PL 83, 790a.
[308] Ibid., II, 10. PL 83, 790c–91a.
[309] Lev 21:13.

adds, after a sentence that seems to have come straight out of St. Jerome, "The Church indeed wants a bishop to be either an ordained ex-monogamist [priest] or a man chosen from among the virgins and consecrated [to God]."[310]

While the old tradition, concerned with ensuring a descendance to the tribe of Levi, made it a sacred duty for the priest to marry, the Christian Church calls to the priesthood not only husbands, but men who have lived in perfect chastity. And for the former as for the latter, the threshold of ordination inaugurates a new existence, marked by the definite choice of continence. Though he does not put it as clearly, the bishop of Seville lets it be understood by the very style of his phrases (de monogamia, de virginitate) that the men recruited from "the bosom" of monogamy or virginity are called to a purity excluding any return to conjugal life from that point on. If any doubts could linger in this respect, the following texts would be enough to dispel them.

This fullness of demands is, as always, emphasized by the epistle to Timothy in the recommendations made to deacons. The Apostle expressed himself plenissime, Isidore deems, when he demands from the latter that they be irreprehensibiles, exactly like the bishop, and pudici utique[311]—two words to which the author of the De ecclesiasticis officiis adds short commentaries—sine macula, a libidine continentes—for he sees here a formal invitation to perfect chastity. Such is the note, according to him, that distinguishes the New Covenant ministers, these men who must "be resplendent with the excellence of chastity".

Ministers also, because they offer the sacred vessels of the Body and Blood of Christ to the deacons who bring them to the altar, the subdeacons are called in turn to a chaste life and must abstain from their wives. Here the bishop of Seville knows that he cannot quote St. Paul, subdeacons being a recent institution in the Church. He has recourse to the judgment of the "Fathers", in a choice of quotations directly borrowed, it would seem, from canon 25 of the Codex canonum Ecclesiae africanae, derived from the Council of Carthage presided over by Aurelius in the year 401: "As they touch the sacred mysteries, it has seemed good

---

[310] In the Apologeticum ad Pammachium St. Jerome had affirmed: "episcopi, presbyteri, diaconi, aut virgines eliguntur aut vidui, aut certe post sacerdotium in aeternum pudici". See above, pp. 296–98.

[311] In fact, the epistle to Timothy does not use the word irreprehensibiles to define the qualities required from a deacon. Isidore is probably quoting from memory, hence the confusion, unless he had a version which was different from ours. If he did not rigorously follow the Pauline text, the Spanish bishop did, however, respect the general meaning of the Apostle's thought.

to the Fathers that these men be chaste and observe continence with their wives and be free of any carnal impurity." [312]

The theological justification invoked to support the law—*quia sacra mysteria contrectant*—seems to indicate, as it did with Gregory the Great, that continence is not merely a contingent duty for subdeacons starting from the moment when, from simply being entrusted with subaltern offices, they find themselves associated closely and in an institutional way with the ministry of the deacons. It is not the link between perfect chastity and service of the altar that would have been recently established in the Church, but the participation of a certain rank of clerics, in this case the fourth Order of the hierarchy, in this service that cannot be dissociated from continence. Indirectly the extension to the subdiaconate of the law of conjugal abstention shows the force that the scriptural principles represented in the eyes of Isidore of Seville, as in those of his predecessors. To the arguments used in favor of the diaconate, this even adds a new one, drawn from the book of Isaiah, for the more special case of the subdiaconal functions: "Mundamini, qui fertis vasa Domini." [313] A simple expediency, though it goes without saying the Spanish bishop wishes to see more in it (*jubetur*), but one that bears witness to the same concern to attach the discipline to God's will.

4th Council of Toledo (633)

The metropolitan of Betica had the opportunity to promote that discipline so dear to his heart in the whole peninsula through the 4th national Council of Toledo (633), which he presided over and animated. Gathered at the order of King Sisenandus, the assembly was to be a milestone in the history of the Church of Spain through the number and importance of its decisions. The seventy-two bishops, some of whom even came from Narbonnaise Gaul, specially endeavored to reform the institutions, according to the customary method of the early centuries, in conformity with the ancient canons. Out of seventy-five *capitula*, here are four connected with our study:

> *Can. 21*: All those who have a rank in God's priesthood must be irreproachable as attested by St. Paul: the bishop must be irreproachable. It is

---

[312] The text of the African canon read, as will be remembered, as follows: "Placuit quod et in diversis conciliis firmatum est, subdiacones qui sacra ministeria contrectant et diacones, presbiteri, sed et episcopi secundum propria statuta, ab uxoribus se contineant, ut 'tamquam non habentes videantur esse'." See above, pp. 267–68.

[313] Is 52:11.

therefore fitting that the priests of God be protected against the encroach-ments of [sin], without stain, without defilement by acts of fornication; but let them live chastely and present themselves with purity to the celebra-tion of the mysteries. Let us therefore abstain from every evil deed and remain free from carnal defilement so that, pure in body and purified in spirit, we can worthily reach the sacrifice of Christ and supplicate God for everyone's sins.[314]

Can. 22: Though the essential, for us, is to have a pure conscience in God's eyes, it is also fitting to keep an excellent reputation in the eyes of men, so that, in keeping with the apostolic precept, we can have the witness of a holy life not only before God but before men. Now, certain priests have caused a great scandal until now: they are accused of lewdness, and, because of their behavior, they do not enjoy a good reputation. As a consequence, from now on, in order not to provide the opportunity to men of the world to deprecate [us], the bishops must have in their lodgings people worthy of trust and serving as their witnesses; thus they will be more pleasing to God through the purity of their conscience and to the Church thanks to an excellent reputation.[315]

Can. 23: It has seemed good [to us] also, just as it has for the bishops, that the priests and deacons whom age and health no longer permit to stay in the residence of the bishop should also have in their cells witnesses to their life, and that they conform, in name as well as in merit, to the [kind of] life that is theirs.[316]

Can. 27: When priests or deacons are installed in country churches, the bishop must have them make a profession of pure and chaste life, for fear of God, so that, thanks to the bonds of such a profession, they be kept within the boundaries of a holy life.[317]

The measures taken here by the Council of Toledo do not concern the specific problem of conjugal continence, but more generally the virtue of chastity. Irreproachable, according to the word of St. Paul, the bishops and priests must live a thoroughly chaste life, free from all fornication, so as to present themselves worthily to the celebration of the holy mys-teries. With a remarkable constancy, the tradition expressed by the voice of Isidore and his Spanish colleagues continues to draw from the function of mediation the demands that are particular to clerics. It is as interces-sors of the people that the priests of God must keep themselves "pure of body and of spirit", free from all carnal defilement. The perspective that

---

[314] Bruns, I, 230.
[315] Ibid.
[316] Ibid., 230–31.
[317] Ibid., 231.

is enlarged to all forms of chastity, which explains in part the derogatory vocabulary of the Council (*fornicatio*, defilement), manifestly includes abstention from relations with the legitimate wife. In the context of a discipline that had been in effect for a long time in the Church of Spain, the use of matrimonial rights constituted on the part of ministers of the altar a crime that tended to be assimilated without many shades of meaning to other faults against continence. It is not surprising to find in the text inspired by Isidore of Seville an implicit identification between conjugal intercourse deemed to be illicit and impurity itself, when one is already familiar with the tone of the *De ecclesiasticis officiis*.[318]

This being noted, the first three decrees that we just read call for only a brief commentary: They aim to protect the very reputation of clerics belonging to the higher ranks of the hierarchy, as well as their virtue, by prescribing regulations similar to those of the Churches of Gaul. The bishops must have in their homes worthy people who can become witnesses to the honesty of their conduct; as to the deacons and priests who, for serious reasons [sickness or old age] do not live in community in the episcopal residence, cell companions will be, in the same way, witnesses to their chastity. In other words, the thorny problem of the clerics' cohabitation with women tends more and more to be solved through the adoption of a community lifestyle: one cohabitation chases the other away.

Sent to parishes, most frequently in the countryside, priests and deacons could nevertheless find themselves alone, under conditions that made it impossible to apply these prudent regulations. In order to palliate this, canon 27 has an expedient of sorts: let them promise to their bishop that they will live chastely (*caste et pure*). The fear of God will be their safeguard and will keep them in the discipline of a holy life. The promise is in addition to their profession of continence already tied to the reception of Orders, and aims at ensuring the fidelity of clerics called to live without witnesses in more difficult situations.

Through this series of measures, as we can see, the Spanish episcopate at the time of Isidore of Seville kept and reinforced the traditional organization of discipline pertaining to priestly continence.

---

[318] About the subdeacons the Spanish author had written: "Let these men be chaste and keep continence with their wives, and let them be free of any carnal impurity." See above, p. 387.

The Last Spanish Councils of the 7th Century (653–655)

Two councils held in Toledo around the mid 7th century still had to concern themselves with the same problems. The interest of their documents becomes weaker insofar as they repeat what we have heard many times, but they attest to the continuity of the discipline. We can rapidly make note of them, limiting ourselves mostly to reading the texts.

8th Council of Toledo (653)

Four canons on chastity of clerics are at the beginning of the acts of the 8th Council of Toledo gathered on December 16, 653, by Receswinthes, the new king of Spain. Here are the contents:

> *Can. 4*: This is why, along with other virtues, all the bishops must shine even more in their bodily purity; so that those who listen to them, seeing that their masters are not dishonored by impurity, would [themselves] come to desire purity. If therefore it is found out that bishops have defiled themselves in a loathsome and vicious way with women or have fallen [with them] into excessive familiarity, let [these bishops] know that they are under the irrevocable law of the Fathers, to wit: the deprivation of the dignity attached to their See and their rank.[319]

> *Can. 5*: During the fifth [conciliar] action, it has come to the knowledge of the holy council that priests and ministers, oblivious of the old rules established by the ancients, dishonored themselves through an impure common life with various women; in the obstinacy of their hardened hearts they go against Holy Scripture as well as against the rules of the Fathers; in their instability they neglect to keep in mind what Scripture said: "Be holy, for I am Yahweh your God" and that other apostolic word: "Mortify your earthly members, that is, fornication and impurity, evil desires and greed." The more obstinate their inclination to evil, the more austere must be the decrees with which we shall have to [oppose] them. Because of the shame attached to this vice, the holy council has most especially decided [the following]: all bishops must have the concern to seek carefully [to know whether] this [fault] is not to be found among their subjects; and if they happen to find it with certainty, let all consider themselves bound, in virtue of this prudent common resolution, to act in such a way that in the future no more abominable acts of the kind be committed. As to the women associated in the shame of [the incriminated clerics], whether they be slaves or free, by all means let them be separated [from their companions]

---

[319]Bruns, I, 279.

or at least sold, so that any access [to the clerics] conscious of their fault be now forbidden to them; as to clerics, if they cannot be compelled in any way [to separate from the women], let them be sent to a monastery until the end of their lives and remain under a penitential discipline.[320]

Can. 6: During the 6th [conciliar] discussion, dishonorable accusations were made against certain [clerics] ill advised [of their obligations]. Indeed, it has been reported to us that certain subdeacons, after their accession to this sacred Order, defiled themselves with carnal impurities—while it is written: "Purify yourselves, you who carry the vessels of the Lord"—and moreover, as we are ashamed to say, they contracted new marriages; they pretend that this is permitted to them because, insofar as they know, they did not receive a blessing from the bishop. This is why we [wish] to rip the veil [behind which all these clerics] try to justify themselves, and we order that [which follows] to be observed: When a bishop ordains subdeacons, let him confer upon them the blessing at the same time he gives them the [sacred] vessels of the ministry as [is required] by an ancient tradition in certain Churches; it is well known that this holy custom expresses for them [the obligation] to keep themselves from any defilement and any familiarity with women. In the future, if they are hurt by this wound, they will have to be sent to a monastery immediately to bear there the burden of penance until the end of their lives.[321]

Can. 7: Upon taking up point 7 of our agenda, our assembly was struck by a number [of problems]: it was as much a question of increasing defiance as it was of a kind of pride we had never before encountered [until now], an ignoble, detestable presumption. We have learned, actually, that certain men have accepted Church positions and ecclesiastical honors either under duress or in order to escape [various] dangerous situations. They insist that they were not free to make their own choices when these [offices] were imposed on them, and therefore they take the opportunity to renounce their ministries and to revert to their former married states; they unscrupulously dispense themselves from [their] sublime responsibilities and quickly demonstrate how captivated they are by the charm of earthly things. . . .

—In order to stamp out [their] futile plottings and subterfuges, let [these clerics] hear the objection we are justified in putting to them: the inestimable gift of baptism is often, and irrevocably, granted not only to people who do not ask for it, but what is more, it is even granted to people who have no idea what it means; still, no one is permitted to profane it. . . .

—Therefore, let them pay attention [to this objection], those shameless men who plead for such desires, and even though they have received in spite of themselves something they did not deserve to get, let them nevertheless keep in good faith the heavenly reward that goes with it; they

---

[320] Bruns, I, 279–80.
[321] Ibid., 280.

obtained it without desiring it, thanks to an earthly necessity; well, let them [take some time and] eventually learn to desire and to love the blessings that they can obviously see it is useless to resist. And let any man who, after this ordinance is promulgated, remains obdurate and refuses to apply himself sincerely to holy religion, and who rather, rejecting the grace he has received, attempts to return to his former married state and to the ways of this world—and does so publicly—let that man be immediately stripped of all dignity attached to whatever rank he holds in the Church, and in truth, let him be held henceforward to be an apostate, expelled from the threshold of holy Church and from the communion of the faithful; he shall be forcibly confined to a monastery, there to do penance to the end of his days.[322]

What we can retain from these long texts, in addition to the customary reminder of chastity and continence, are some more original details. The Council intends to react against seemingly numerous abuses on the part of clerics in Major Orders who have culpable relations, either with their wives or with concubines. Their behavior is stigmatized in the most severe terms, and no distinction is made between the use of marriage and scandalous unions. One feels that, with time, the attitude of the legislators hardens in response to the resistance still encountered by the ancient discipline. Far from giving in under the pressure of the number and kind of objections, authority attempts to stop the evil by stressing with greater emphasis the dishonorable nature of the transgressions and by weaving a tighter network of regulations. Not only will the culprits be deprived of their dignity, excluded from the communion of the faithful, or sentenced to do penance in a monastery, but the women themselves, whatever their condition, will pay the price of their complicity: separated willingly or unwillingly from their companions "of shame" they may even be sold as slaves, a measure that the harsh Spanish society of the 7th century seemed to have accepted without any scruples.

No consideration inspired by clemency is as yet foreseen with regard to those who believe they can argue that they were ignorant or suddenly compelled. The subdeacons will be deprived of any excuse to enter into illegal relationships with females by letting them clearly know their obligations at the moment of blessing accompanying the tradition of the sacred vessels. If they persist in desiring to contract a marriage, they will be penalized by perpetual reclusion in a cloister. There is the same absence of indulgence for the ministers who received Orders by force or under the duress of a strong fear; these are not extenuating circumstances that could excuse a resumption of conjugal life. No more than baptism is a

---

[322] Bruns, I, 280–81.

revocable gift, the Fathers of Toledo specify, when it is given to men who receive it against their will or without their knowledge, ordination, even if it is imposed by force, cannot put up with reversals. The clerics-in-spite-of-themselves must make the best of it, as it were, and learn to love what they could not contest anyway. Otherwise, serious canonical penalties are awaiting them, including penitential claustration.

9th Council of Toledo (655)

The laws became even more intransigent with the provincial council, the ninth in Toledo, gathered two years later in the Spanish metropolis. The situation was visibly deteriorating while the leaders of the Church countered it with an increasing rigor:

> *Can. 10*: Heretofore the Fathers have made numerous decisions concerning the incontinence of clerics; notwithstanding [those regulations], people have not yet managed to correct their morals to the extent that the offenses they committed compelled judges to give greater scope to their decisions: it is not only against the perpetrators of unlawful acts, but also against the descendants of the [clerics] who were punished, that sanctions will be taken. This is why [this present decision has been made with respect to] anyone, established in dignity, from the bishop to the subdeacon who would have had children from guilty relations with a slave or a free woman. Those for whom we have the proof that they are truly the fathers of these children will be under canonical censorship. As to the children born from such an impure [relation], not only will they never inherit the goods of their parents, but they will remain, in virtue of an irrevocable right, at the service of the Church to whom belonged the priest or minister through whose shameful fault they were born.[323]

This time not only are the guilty parents struck with sanctions that had already been foreseen, without exceptions, but the children themselves, born from the forbidden unions, will have to suffer for the fault of those who brought them into this world.

As we can see, there is a harsh struggle between the guardians of the discipline and the impenitent rebels who continue here and there to transgress it. Because of her councils, firmly faithful to the Tradition, Visigoth Spain did not fall into a disciplinary schism for which circumstances were only too favorable.[324] If those seventh-century prelates seem to

[323] Bruns, I, 295.

[324] One can appreciate the determining role played by the Spanish synods of the 7th century in the maintaining and restoring of discipline when one sees how fast faith and morals had a tendency to deteriorate in the Visigoth society of the time. It was for this

us excessively rigorous, one must recognize that they were dealing with difficult adversaries and that, given the mentality of their time, the inflexibility of the conciliar decisions was probably the indispensable weapon of virtue. Nor should one forget that the Spanish assemblies, which were generally called by the king and whose program was meticulously drawn up by him, were influenced by the iron hand of the monarch. Taking such a context into account, and with the advantage of hindsight, we find that one thing seems certain: the Councils of Toledo were the severe but efficient instrument through which the Church in Spain, in spite of a thousand obstacles, remained bound to the secular discipline of priestly continence. When the Arab invasion occurs, the work of Isidore of Seville and his successors will remain buried in the Christian memory, witness to an indefectible fidelity and a promise of rebirth.

Quinisext Council in Trullo (691)

While Christian Africa was agonizing under the blows of Islam, the Byzantine Empire was threatened on all sides by invaders. From 635 to 642, Syria, Palestine, Mesopotamia, and Egypt had fallen with terrifying speed, one after the other, into the hands of the Moslem chiefs. Out of four Eastern patriarchates, only one—the See of Constantinople—was still standing, bearing from then on in that part of the world the whole responsibility for the future of the Church. On the northern borders the danger was no less significant. Slavic and Bulgarian invasions succeeded one another, creating a completely new situation in the areas located south of the Danube. After Illyria fell, Mesia, Macedonia, Greece, and the islands of the archipelago were forced to accept foreign invasion. The emperors of Byzantium had to compromise with the danger and tolerate in those territories the settlement of many "sclavinias", outposts that were to leave a deep stamp on Hellenic civilization.[325]

---

reason that the 11th Council of Toledo, gathered on November 7, 675, deplored the "Babylonian" confusion that had crept into society and the Church and particularly blamed the long intervals between meetings of synods (more than twenty years had elapsed since the last episcopal assembly of Toledo) (Bruns, I, 306). Therefore, it is not surprising to see the Fathers of the Council go so far as to study the case in which a bishop would commit adultery with the wife, daughter, or niece of a high-ranking person and edict sanctions of a harsh severity (can. 5, Bruns, I, 311).

[325] For this period of the Byzantine history, see C. Diehl and G. Marcais, *Histoire du Moyen-Age*, III, *Le monde oriental de 395 à 1081* (Paris, 1936), pp. 211–49, and A. A. Vasiliev, *Histoire de l'empire byzantin*, I, (Paris, 1932), pp. 255ff.

A deep transformation, felt in all domains, was brought about: not only did the ethnic features of the empire change completely, but the consequences affecting administration and the religious and social evolution were overwhelming. That century of upheavals, which almost spelled the ruin of Byzantium, dragged the East into a decline that the spiritual energy of its leaders did not manage to overcome for a long time. The political shake-up had its effects on intellectual and moral life, bringing Byzantine society into an anarchy that can be compared to the disorders of the 5th century, after the fall of the Roman Empire. That period of iron

> shows a deep intellectual decadence. People did not write anymore; the Byzantine literature of the 7th century was represented only by some theological works or lives of the saints. People did not build anymore: after the great strides that art had known during the reign of Justinian, barely two or three churches were built in the city. Morals became more uncivilized, superstition increased at the expense of faith; it seemed that the Christian world was about to collapse, carried away by the formidable storm of Islam (C. Diehl and G. Marçais).

Prey to such internal dislocations, Byzantium also knew increasing difficulties with Rome. Since the serious matter of canon 28 of the Council of Chalcedon, a misunderstanding had been brewing between the two parts of the Christian world, and the cracks in unity were patched over only thanks to mutual concessions and subtle diplomacy. The adroit religious policy of Justinian, who had managed to reconcile his Caesaropapism with fidelity to the Apostolic See, extended the status quo without suppressing the causes of a movement almost fatally leading to a break. This became obvious when his successor, Heraclius, undertook to put an end to the Monophysite dissidence of the great patriarchal sees by rallying the people's spirits around a new formula of concord. His "Monothelism", imagined out of expediency, succeeded only, after many ups and downs, in aggravating the tension with Rome, where Pope John IV wound up condemning the famous doctrine that was, however, approved by a Council of Constantinople. Forty years were to pass before the sixth ecumenical council, gathered in November 680 by Emperor Constantine IV, was able to reestablish peace by a solemn rejection of the Monothelitic doctrine. But it was an ephemeral peace, sapped from within by a veiled distrust on the part of the Latins who did not know Greek, and on the part of the Greeks who were contemptuous of anything but their own language; a peace that political chaos on the one hand and the clumsy ambition of young Justinian II on the other were soon to jeopardize irreparably.

The Quinisext Council, better known as the Council in Trullo, thus opened at the end of the year 691 in a climate of open hostility toward Rome.[326] Meant to complete the work of the fifth and sixth ecumenical councils—hence its name *Quinisext, πενθέκτη*—it practically left dogma aside to devote itself to problems of discipline that the two previous synods had neglected to treat. One hundred and two disciplinary canons were signed by approximately 215 Fathers, all Greeks, Eastern churchmen or Armenians, who worked at that task. A genuine code of law, the text published by the Council held "under the dome" was to determine Byzantine legislation for centuries, and until today, and it has been rightly written that the seventh-century document is "the last word on ecclesiastical discipline for the Greek Church".[327]

The brief historical landmarks that it was necessary to recall help us better understand the schismatic climate that prevailed at the deliberations of 691. Although the intention was to reform the abuses and errors of its time, the Council of Constantinople meant to do so in its own way, distancing itself from Rome and flaunting its disagreement with the Latin traditions. "There is no doubt as to the clearly separatist spirit of the Trullan legislation, as has been rightly pointed out; the Council's rulings are intended to pose as Byzantine, which is why those canons are so forcefully directed against both the Latins and the Armenians, not on issues of principle, to be sure, but, aside from orthodox principles of faith, on issues of clerical and liturgical discipline."[328] And on the part of Rome, for the first time in history, there was a formal disavowal of the Eastern discipline, Pope Sergius (687–701), though he was of Syrian descent, declaring that he would rather die than approve of certain canons that were "against the order of the Church".[329]

Out of all the conciliar acts of the Eastern assembly, seven canons are specifically of interest to our subject. Several of them include positive obligations demanding continence from the ministers of the altar. Notwithstanding the division with Rome, it is known indeed that on more than one point the East has kept customs that are rather close to those of the Latin Church. Those are the documents that we will study first,

---

[326] Joannou deems that "the date of the council is definitely resolved by the manuscript tradition of canon 3, which gives, against the 6109 of the Vulgata 'the year 6199, after January 15 of the 4th elapsed indiction', i.e., after September 691 and, more precisely, before January 692; 'elapsed' January 1, belonging to the 4th indiction (690–91) and the latter having also 'elapsed': therefore, between September 1 and December 31, probably in October 691" (I, 1, p. 98).

[327] E. Vacandard, *Les origines du célibat ecclésiastique* (Paris, 1913), p. 101.

[328] Joannou, I, 1, p. 98.

[329] For a detailed history of the Quinisext Council, cf. Hefele-Leclercq, III, 1, pp. 560ff.

and we will come later to the other texts authorizing certain clerics, under certain conditions, to use their marital rights.

The bishops

First we note two canons concerning bishops:

> *Can. 12: Let no bishop live with his ex-wife.*
> It has come to our knowledge that in Africa and in Libya and other places, the shepherds beloved by God of these territories did not cease to live with their wives, even after having received the episcopate, thus becoming an obstacle and a scandal for the people. Having therefore a great concern that all be done for the edification of the peoples that we have to govern, we decided that such a behavior should no longer occur. We are not saying this to violate or overturn the apostolic ordinances, but to provide salvation for the peoples and progress in their virtues and to offer no opportunity for blame against the ecclesiastical discipline; indeed, the divine Apostle said: "Do everything for the glory of God, give no scandal to the Jews nor to Greeks, nor to the Church of God; it is thus that I myself endeavor to please everyone in all things, seeking not my own advantage but that of the greatest number, so that many men be saved; be my imitators as I am myself [an imitator] of Christ." Should anyone be caught doing that [i.e., giving scandal], let him be deposed.[330]

> *Can. 48: Let the wife of the bishop, after having separated from him, in common agreement, enter into a monastery after the elevation.*
> The wife of him who is promoted to the episcopate, having separated from her husband in common agreement, after his elevation will enter a monastery located not far from the episcopal residence and enjoy the material support of the bishop; if she be worthy of it, let her be promoted to the dignity of deaconess.[331]

The occasion for the first of those decrees was given to the Eastern legislators by the lifestyle of certain bishops in the areas located far from Byzantium, especially in Africa and in Libya. They heard that such shepherd or other did not hesitate to live with his wife, without any thought of the scandal that his behavior could create in public opinion. They wish to put an end to the scandal, out of concern for the faithful's edification. We must note from the outset that they do not reproach these churchmen for continuing to have conjugal relations with their wives, but only for sharing the same house with their companions. The two things are, indeed, distinct, and we know that Latin tradition, in particular since St. Leo, authorized for a long time the clerics of the hierarchy to

---

[330] Joannou, I, 1, pp. 138–39.
[331] Ibid., p. 186.

keep their wives with them while observing strict continence. If, during the course of the 6th and 7th centuries, the organization of the episcopal house had taken here and there, in Gaul and also in Spain, the appearance of a monastery from which all women were excluded, such was not the case in Africa, it seems, where the ancient customs were still kept. Neither the *Breviatio Ferrandi* nor the *Concordia Cresconii* mention any prescription forbidding bishops to live in the company of their wives; they continue, on the contrary, to consider as valid the 6th apostolic canon ordering priests not to send away their wives with the excuse of piety. It is therefore quite plausible that several African bishops did not have any problems of conscience—they might even have thought it a duty—when settling in their homes the women united to them by marital bonds. That the risks inherent in such a situation were at times accompanied by a true resumption of genuine matrimonial life seems to be quite likely, especially in the Maghreb overwhelmed by Moslem invasion. But in the eyes of the Fathers of Byzantium the crux of the matter is, we have to stress again, cohabitation itself, and not the question of a possible resumption of conjugal intercourse. This συνοίκησις had been formally prohibited more than a century earlier by the 123d novella of Justinian,[332] and the imperial decree had been very likely kept in effect, later on, in the Eastern patriarchates. The authority of that already long tradition is justified, in the eyes of the members of the Council in Trullo, by pastoral motives. A bishop living with his wife is a stumbling block for the Christian community, they think, and one must not give any grounds for scandal to anybody. Quoted here is St. Paul, who had declared to the Corinthians that he was seeking above all the advantage of the greater number rather than his personal advantage. This apostolic argument wins over other ordinances enacted by the apostles, as the Fathers of Constantinople note, and we do sense a certain uneasiness in them as they try to solve the difficulty represented by the 6th *canon apostolorum*. Though they do not explicitly refer to it, it is obvious that the document, whose apocryphal nature they and their contemporaries did not even suspect, is embarrassing to them.[333] All the more that, at the start of their collection, the participants in the Council solemnly affirmed their fidelity to "the eighty-five canons received and confirmed by the blessed Fathers who came before us and transmitted them to us also under the names of the saints and glorious apostles".[334] The legislation inherited from

---

[332] See above, pp. 362ff.

[333] The Byzantine commentators of the 12th century—Balsamon, Zonaras, and Aristenes—agree on this point (PG 137, 556a–60a).

[334] Can. 2. Joannou, I, 1, pp. 120–21. It is known that, contrary to the Easterners, Rome accepted only the first fifty apostolic canons.

Justinian had to be quite vivid to give these seventh-century bishops, respect-ful as they were of the Apostolic Tradition, the audacity to come to terms with such a well-known authority. To a perfectly valid decree they oppose a passage from Corinthians, about which the least that can be said is that it does not have the value of a precept, to confirm the customs of Byzantium and extend them to the provinces of Africa and Libya. St. Leo, who seemed to have known the 6th apostolic canon, did not, for his part, think that he could afford to discount it.[335] But under the pressure of circumstances and to guard the chastity of clerics by more favorable conditions, many ecclesias-tic provinces in the Latin world had, little by little, asked for a separation from the wife. Thus, in different ways East and West had reached the same practical conclusions, and it is rather interesting to note this convergence. For the bishop, the law of conjugal continence is the same in Rome as in Byzantium, and if the latter, at the end of the 7th century, shows some originality, it is in rejecting in practice the 6th canon of the apostles, which still had kept its normative value in several Western Churches.

Canon 48 of the Quinisext Council deals with the wife of the bishop and is only of indirect interest to us insofar as it implies the obligation of perfect continence recalled by the previous text. It is in common agreement with her husband that the wife of the candidate to the episcopate must accept the separation; otherwise, we are to understand, the latter will not be ordained. As a consequence, this agreement leads to a commitment to a life of chastity, the wife who is alone from then on not being free to remarry, of course, but on the contrary placed under the obligation of entering monastic life. She will remain under the "providential" care of the bishop and, if she is judged worthy of it, will become a deaconess.

Priests, deacons, and subdeacons

While strictly faithful to the Code of Justinian with regard to the leaders of the hierarchy, the Trullan legislation authorizes priests and deacons to use their marital rights. We will came back to this point. For the moment we add to our records two other canons stipulating, for the major clerics, various obligations of chastity:

> Can. 3: About the place in the sanctuary for priests who have contracted second marriages or married after ordination, and for those who married widows or rejected wives.
>
> As our pious emperor beloved of Christ asked in his discourse to this holy and ecumenical council to make all those who belong to the ranks of the clergy, and through whom men receive the graces of the sacraments,

[335] See above, pp. 262f.

pure and irreproachable ministers, worthy of the spiritual sacrifice of the great God, victim and pontiff at the same time, and to purify them from the defilement of their illicit marriages; as, on the other hand, those of the most holy Roman Church wish to follow the very severe discipline, and those of this imperial city guarded by God the rule of humanity and condescension, we have combined the two tendencies into one so that meekness not fall into laxity nor austerity into bitterness, keeping in mind, above all, faults of ignorance that concerned a quite numerous crowd of men; we decide that the clerics who let themselves fall into a second marriage and, being slaves to sin, did nothing to amend themselves until the fifteenth day of January last in the fourth indiction started in the year six thousand one hundred and nine, be condemned to canonical deposition.

While those who fell into that defilement of a second marriage but recognized their spiritual interest before our meeting and put the evil away from themselves by breaking this strange and illegitimate union, or those whose second wives already died, or those who themselves took care of their return to God, resuming the practice of chastity and making haste not to think about their past iniquities; if such clerics are priests, deacons, or subdeacons, it was decided that they should be deprived of all priestly functions, or any activity, after having done penance; they will still take part in the honors of the See and the position occupied by those of their rank, contenting themselves with this precedence and imploring the Lord for his pardon of the iniquity committed out of ignorance; it would indeed be unreasonable to bless another man when one needs to bind his own wounds.

Those who had only one wife but one who was a widow, and also those priests, deacons, and subdeacons who, after ordination, contracted an illegitimate marriage, after a short time of suspension from their sacred functions and penance, will be given back their own rank, without having the right to a promotion, the illegal marriage being, of course, dissolved.

On our episcopal authority we have formulated these rules concerning those who were caught in only the above-mentioned faults until January 15, as we have said, of the fourth indiction, and we order today and renew the canon that states: "He who after baptism married twice or had a concubine cannot be a bishop, a priest, or a deacon, or even a member of the clergy"; in the same way, "he who has married a widow or a woman sent away by her husband, or a courtesan, or a slave, or an actress, cannot be a bishop, a priest, a deacon, or even a member of the clergy." [336]

Can. 6: It is not permitted for priests and deacons to contract a marriage after ordination.

As is said in the apostolic canons, "Among the single men promoted in the ranks of the clergy, only lectors and cantors can marry", we too,

---

[336] Joannou, I, 1, pp. 125–30.

observing this prescription, order that from now on, no subdeacon, deacon, or priest be permitted, once he has received ordination, to contract a marriage; if he dares do so, let him be deposed. If anyone among those who enroll in the clergy wishes to unite with a woman through the bonds of a legitimate marriage, let him do so before his ordination to the subdiaconate or the diaconate or the priesthood.[337]

These decisive texts of the Byzantine law can be summarized in a few points:

It is forbidden for any clerics, whatever their rank, to contract a second marriage. The council sets a date (until January 15 of the past fourth indiction, i.e., of the year 6109 = 692), after which those who are actually married for the second time must mend their ways. The rebels will be condemned to canonical deposition. The others will be forbidden to exercise their priestly functions if they are priests, deacons, or subdeacons but will keep the honors due to their seat and rank.

Subdeacons, deacons, and priests cannot marry. If they want to do so, let them take a wife before the subdiaconate. This decision is supported by canon 27 of the apostles, according to which only lectors and cantors, among the members of the clergy, enjoy such a freedom.[338] Those who, against the law, will dare henceforth to contract an illegitimate union will be struck by deposition. Canon 3 of 691 stipulates, however, that on condition of doing penance and dissolving their matrimonial bonds, the guilty parties will be permitted to regain their functions, though not to aspire to a higher rank. One must stress the adverb *deinceps* (henceforth), which seems to show that, before the Quinisext Council, there was a tolerance concerning many illicit situations. One has grounds to suppose that because of the upheavals in the Byzantine Empire characteristic of the 7th century, a rather large proportion of men belonging to the higher ranks of the clergy had entered into matrimony. A practical disregard of the Justinian legislation, to say nothing of more ancient laws, led to a notable change in the customs of the Eastern clergy and shed light on the historical background against which the decisions of the Trullan Council were made.

Only monogamists can be admitted to the clergy, and still further promoted to the subdiaconate, but on condition that their wives had been

---

[337]Joannou, I, 1, pp. 131–32.

[338]It will be noted that the Fathers of the Council in Trullo do not mention canon 14 of the Council of Chalcedon, probably because the fourth ecumenical council, while taking into account the same authorization, presented it only as a custom peculiar to certain provinces. In addition to this, the "apostolic" authority of canon 27, in the eyes of the Trullan bishops, superseded a conciliar decision.

virgins, free, and had not exercised professions deemed to be dishonorable. In other words, the Council excludes from the ecclesiastical ministry: men married twice; those who have a concubine; or those who married a widow, a woman sent away by her husband, a courtesan, a slave, or an actress. These measures are explicitly referring to the 17th and 18th apostolic canons.[339]

These prescriptions of the Quinisext Council, which even today define the particular law of the Eastern Churches, bear witness, as we have been able to see, to a deep concern of fidelity to the Apostolic Tradition. Except for the authorization given to clerics married before the subdiaconate to pursue their conjugal lives, they coincide exactly with the rules of the Latin Church. The only difference lies in the choice of historical precedents. While the communities of Gaul, Spain, and Africa refer in preference to the decretals of the Roman pontiffs or to a canonical tradition or an oral tradition going back to the apostles, the bishops of Byzantium chose to skip the intermediary stages in order to give priority to the *canones apostolorum*, that collection providing them with bases that they deemed incontestable in grounding their discipline on the most authoritative foundation. The conformity of those documents, which today we know to be of apocryphal origin, with the essence of the customs prescribed by Rome, had the felicitous result of safeguarding on many points organic unity of the Latin and Eastern traditions, in spite of the schism dividing the Christian world. We believe that the role of that so-called apostolic collection in the history of the legislation related to priestly continence cannot be emphasized enough. If it gave way to important divergences, as we will see, it contributed just as much and in a decisive way to the disciplinary rapprochement of the separated Churches. This is no small merit. Though they were deceived, unknowingly, by the undue authority of those ordinances placed under the aegis of the apostles, the Fathers of Constantinople also had the merit, from the viewpoint of history, to have reacted against the abuses of their time through a recourse to the most venerable traditions. Rome and Byzantium agree as far as the essentials are concerned: the demands of chastity of the ministers of the Church do and can have no other foundation than the will expressed since the origins of Christianity by its very founders.

---

[339] Joannou, I, 2, p. 16.

Canon 13

Out of all the legislation promulgated by the Quinisext Council, the decree limiting the obligation of chastity for married men ordained as deacons or priests to a simple temporary continence is the one that provoked the strongest reaction on the part of Rome. The text is as follows:

Can. 13: About priests and deacons, that they can keep their wives.

As we have learned that in the Church of Rome the rule was established that candidates, before receiving ordination as deacon or priest, make a public promise not to have relations anymore with their wives; we, conforming ourselves to the ancient rule of strict observation and apostolic discipline, want the legitimate marriages of consecrated men to remain in effect even in the future, without dissolving the bond uniting these men to their wives, nor depriving them of mutual relations at the appropriate times. In such a way, if someone is deemed worthy to be ordained subdeacon, deacon, or priest, let him not be prevented from growing in this dignity because he has a legitimate wife, and neither should it be demanded that he promise, at the time of his ordination, to abstain from legitimate relations with his own wife; for otherwise we would insult marriage, which was instituted by God and blessed by his presence, while the voice of the Gospel calls to us: "Let no man put asunder those whom God has united", and the Apostle teaches: "Let marriage be respected by all and the conjugal bed be without stain"; and again: "Are you tied to a wife by the bonds of marriage? Then do not seek to break them."

On the other hand, we know that the Fathers gathered at Carthage, as a precautionary measure because of the seriousness of the morals of the ministers of the altar, decided that "the subdeacons, who touch the sacred mysteries, the deacons and the priests too, should abstain from their wives during the periods that are specifically [assigned] to them, . . . thus we also will keep what was taught by the apostles and observed since antiquity, knowing that there is a time for everything, especially for fasting and prayer; it is indeed necessary that those who approach the altar, when they touch holy things, be continent in every respect so that they can obtain in all simplicity what they are asking from God." If, therefore, anyone, acting against the apostolic canons, dares deprive a cleric in sacred Orders—i.e, a priest, a deacon, or a subdeacon—from conjugal relations and the society of his wife, let him be deposed; in the same way, "if a priest or deacon sends away his wife with the excuse of piety, let him be excommunicated, and if he persists, deposed".[340]

---

[340] Joannou, I, 1, pp. 140–43. We have modified the translation given by Joannou of the incidental proposition κατὰ τοὺς ἰδίους ὅρους and have rendered it as "during the periods that are particularly [assigned to them]" in conformity with the commentaries of the Byzantine Balsamon, Zonaras, and Aristenes (PG 138, 33a–37a, and PG 137, 561a–64d).

Directed from the start against the rule in effect in the Church of
Rome, the Trullan canon protests against any attempt aiming to break
the matrimonial bonds of men called to the subdiaconate, the diaconate,
and the priesthood, and to forbid all conjugal relations with their legitimate wives. Placing one law in opposition to the other, it decrees that
no one should be prevented from a promotion to these different Orders
if he had already contracted a marriage before his ordination, nor compelled on the day of his ordination to make a profession of continence.
It is the latter condition, we must remark, that characterized the Roman
discipline and constitutes the point of dispute. Contrary to where the
preamble of the Fathers of Byzantium might lead the unknowing reader,
the Latin legislation did not see marriage as an obstacle to entrance into
the priestly ministry; being indissoluble, the bond could not be dissolved
after consecration and kept all its force, as we have seen when St. Leo
authorized husband and wife to live in the same home and took into
account the bonds of mutual love that still attach them to each other.
By prescribing total chastity to married clerics, Rome did not mean "to
put asunder what God has united" but to elevate their kind of life,
together with their wives, to a level she deemed compatible with what
service at the altar demands. Polemics or lack or information induced
the Quinisext Council to ignore such an essential aspect. On the precise
problem of continence, however, the Eastern Church is clearly of another
mind. Here is the true and—it must be stressed—the only subject of
contestation between the two Churches.

The bishops of Constantinople base their claim on "the ancient rule
of strict observation and the apostolic discipline". This profession of
fidelity formulated in general—one would be tempted to say "vague"—
terms will, however, be explained further by a recourse to two "traditional" authorities: the Councils of Carthage and the 6th apostolic canon.
We have already made all the remarks that we deem necessary about the
latter and about the selective exegesis given to it by the Byzantines who,
in its name, granted to deacons and priests what they refused to bishops,
thus overlooking the very same decree. As Hefele and Leclercq—not
otherwise suspected of a purposeful derogation of the Greek tradition's
value—observe rightly, "It is easy to see the inconsistency into which
the Greeks fell; they order that if a married man becomes a priest, he
must keep his wife; on the contrary, if he becomes a bishop, his wife
must retire to a convent." [341]

The reference to the Councils of Carthage is no less surprising. One
would have easily identified the origin of the quotations used in the

---

[341] Hefele-Leclercq, III, 1, p. 565, n. 1.

Eastern canon: they come from articles 25 and 33 of the *Codex canonum Ecclesiae africanae* (419), respectively enacted by the council held in Carthage in 401 (can. 4) and the synod presided over by Genethlius in 390 in the African metropolis (can. 2). Proceeding by way of anthology, the Fathers of 691 combine those two texts into one, not without having cut them somewhat and also having introduced a brief paraphrase.[342]

[342]Their intention will be better understood with a synoptic reading of the African canons and the passage of the Council in Trullo referring to them.

Council in Trullo

On the other hand, we know that the Fathers gathered in Carthage, with foresight in connection with the seriousness of the morals of the ministers of the alter, have decided *that the subdeacons who touch the holy mysteries, the deacons, and also the priests,* must abstain from their wives DURING THE PERIODS THAT ARE PARTICULARLY [ASSIGNED] TO THEM:

Codex canonum Ecclesiae africanae

Aurelius said: As it has been a question of certain clerics, especially lectors, with regard to continence toward their wives, I would add, very dear brothers, what was confirmed in many a synod, *that the subdeacons who touch the sacred mysteries and the deacons and the priests,* AND ALSO THE BISHOPS, IN CONFORMITY WITH THE ORDINANCES CONCERNING THEM, *will abstain from their wives* "AS IF THEY DID NOT HAVE ANY"; that if they do not do so, they will be removed from any ecclesiastical functions. As to the other clerics, they will be compelled to it only at an advanced age (can. 25). . . . Moreover, as mention was made of the continence of certain clerics with their own wives, it was decided that the BISHOPS, *priests, and deacons,* IN CONFORMITY WITH THE DECISIONS CONCERNING THEM, *will observe continence with their wives also;* if they do not, they will be demoted from their ranks. As to the other clerics, they will not be compelled to this, but the usage of each Church will be observed (can. 70).

Bishop Aurelius said: In a previous council, when one spoke of normalizing the rules on continence and chastity [one dealt with] the three Orders that, by virtue of their consecration, are associated by a kind of link of chastity. I am talking about: THE BISHOPS, *the priests, and also the deacons.* We agreed, as is fitting to [their state] that THE VERY HOLY PONTIFFS, *the priests of God, and also the deacons—i.e., those who are at the service of the divine sacraments—observe a* PERFECT *continence, so that they can obtain in all simplicity what they are asking from God; what the apostles taught and what antiquity itself*

Just like the African Fathers, the legislators of Byzantium claim a tradition of apostolic origin. The decrees of Carthage are used by them as a step to go back to that remote antiquity, proof of the importance that the decisions of Genethlius and his successors had in their eyes as testimonies of the early discipline. By adopting the declaration of the fourth-century bishops, they see it as what it meant to represent: a voice faithfully transmitting the discipline of the apostles. In so doing the Council in Trullo confirms the exceptional importance of the African canon of 390 for the history of the law on priestly continence.

Nevertheless, two essential points constitute the originality of the Byzantine decree with respect to its source: the mention of the bishops has disappeared for reasons that we know, and the continence demanded from clerics "who touch the holy mysteries" is only temporary, limited only to their periods of liturgical service. It is through the intermediary of a Greek translation playing on the two possible meanings of the phrase κατὰ τοὺς ἰδίους ὅρους that the Easterners of 691 based themselves on the African text to restrict in such a manner the scope of the law. The *secundum priora* (or *propria*) *statuta* of the Latin manuscripts having been translated by the Greek phrase κατὰ τοὺς ἰδίους ὅρους, a slippage in the text was facilitated, enabling the Council of Carthage to say what the Easterners deemed to be the authentic interpretation.[343]

Taking this difference into account, we find it noteworthy that the traditions of Byzantium and Rome are in basic agreement: the apostolic origin of the duty of (temporary or perpetual) continence imposed upon the ministers of the altar, on the one hand; the theologico-scriptural

---

thus we will keep also what was passed on to us by the apostles and observed from all antiquity. KNOWING THAT THERE IS A TIME FOR EVERYTHING, ESPECIALLY FOR FAST AND PRAYER, *it is necessary indeed that those who approach the altar,* AT THE TIME WHEN THEY TOUCH THE HOLY THINGS, *be continent in everything, so that they can obtain what they are asking in all simplicity from God.* (Joannou, I, 1, pp. 141–42)

observed we must also endeavor to keep (can. 3).

Faustinus, bishop of Potenza, said: It pleases us that THE BISHOPS, *the priests, the deacons, all those who, in other words, touch the sacred mysteries, the keepers of chastity, abstain [from conjugal intercourse] with their wives.* The bishops unanimously declared: we agree: let them keep a PERFECT chastity, all those who serve at the altar (can. 4). (Joannou, I, 2, pp. 216–17, 240–41, 312–13)

N.B.: Italics indicate passages where the same idea is expressed in both documents (at times word for word); the words or phrases in capitals are those where important differences appear.

[343] The Greek version of the *Codex canonum Ecclesiae africanae* is posterior to the *Dionysiana*. So far the author remains unknown.

foundation of that obligation on the other hand. It is as servants of the divine mysteries (τοὺς τῷ θυσιαστηρίῳ προσεδρεύοντας) and mediators of the people through prayer that the major clerics are bound to abstain from sexual relations. The reference, implicit in the Trullan document, is the very same that we saw many times developed by the patristic authors: prescriptions of Leviticus and Pauline instructions related to conjugal abstinence needed for prayer.

This identity of views on issues that are so fundamental is to be emphasized; it attests that, in spite of certain divergences, East and West never thought it possible to justify the difficult discipline of priestly chastity[344] in any other way than by a positive command of the apostles themselves. Any idea of progressive development in line with a trend favorable to virginity and continence that would have occasioned, rather late in the day, the placing of such demands on the clergy in particular, was clearly alien to their thinking. Rome and Byzantium also show by their agreement the strength of motivation that both recognize in the scriptural principles. Here too it is on no other foundation than the Word of God that they agree to ensure the bond between sexual purity and the liturgical ministry. This bond is not questioned by the Eastern legislation of 691, but in a certain way is more strongly emphasized by the periodical nature of the obligation of continence. It is because they approach—and when they approach—the sacred mysteries that the Levites of the New Covenant must abstain from relations with their wives. It can be supposed that if the use of daily celebration had become established in the Churches of the East, the a fortiori argument that played such a great role, as we saw, in the thought of Siricius, in explaining that the laws of the Old Testament that had been temporary now had to become permanent, the same argument would possibly have been used with similar effects in the seventh-century Byzantine world. Or, inversely, it would have been very difficult for the Latins to maintain the principle of daily continence if, in one way or the other, the prayers of the people's intercessors had not been conceived by them as an uninterrupted mission. This common basis of the two traditions, which too often one tends to imagine as being independent one from the other, is all the more remarkable in that it is nourished by the testimony of the same inheritance, the Council held in Carthage in 390, considered the essential link on the path connecting the living conscience of the Church with apostolic times.

The silence of the Eastern Church regarding any decision of the Council of Nicaea authorizing the ministers of the hierarchy to use their marital

---

[344] The temporary continence of the Easterners is also not without a real asceticism.

rights, as we also remarked, is no less significant because of the doubt it continues to bring to bear on the famous episode of Paphnutius' intervention. Was the *Historia Ecclesiastica* of Socrates unknown to the Fathers of the Council in Trullo? It is unlikely. The fact remains that they did not deem it good to use a document in which, for reasons partially similar to those of Rome, they did not recognize the genuine expression of Tradition. In spite of what a certain historical criticism attempted to accredit, that text of uncertain origin, unanimously set aside by the West and by the East, is nothing like a demarcation line between the two disciplinary trends of the Christian world. Far from separating them, it is, on the contrary—by its very rejection—an element of rapprochement between them.

All in all, the study of canon 13 of the Quinisext Council reveals a closer kinship than it seems to have at first sight between the legislators of Constantinople and the synodal assemblies that, from the 4th to the 7th centuries, developed in many provinces the ecclesiastical rules we know. On one side as on the other, what we would call today a same view of the problems governs the decisions on the chastity of clerics and brings about ordinances that are in agreement on more than one point. If divergences appear in the appreciation of the degree of continence compatible with the exercise of the priesthood, we believe that the cause is the particular circumstances that shook up the Byzantine Empire during most of the 7th century[345] and put the clergy into a de facto situation that proved stronger than the Justinian legislation. The schismatic climate prevailing then in Byzantium probably prevented the Eastern Church from remedying this situation in the direction that the African councils—which constituted for them the traditional line—would normally have demanded, and they endeavored to legalize it, probably in good faith, though without recognizing that this recourse to the Carthaginian authority manifested by the same token the divergence of their discipline from that of the early centuries. It remains true that, by this very reference, the Council in Trullo retains the very great merit of having sought to hold to the original Tradition and to retain for priestly continence the theologico-scriptural bases common to the entire patristic period.

[345] See above, pp. 397–98.

LEGISLATION ON MARRIAGE AND CONTINENCE FOR THE LOWER CLERICS

In order to avoid repetition, we have grouped here, in one chapter only, the data relative to marriage and continence for lectors, cantors, and subdeacons provided by the documents of the 5th, 6th, and 7th centuries.

LECTORS AND CANTORS

It was only at the end of the 4th century that the legislation of the Churches began to mention lectors explicitly, stipulating their statute with respect to the general discipline of clerical chastity.

The first of these documents is a canon of the *Breviarium Hipponense* of 393 asking that when they reach the age of puberty, the young men acting as lectors choose between marriage and a profession of continence. This law, meant to test the aptitude of future deacons to accept the obligations of perfect continence that would one day be theirs, would remain to the end the particular charter of this category of clerics in the African Church. We find it also without changes in the *Codex canonum Ecclesiae africanae* (can. 16), the *Breviatio Ferrandi* (can. 129), and the *Concordia Cresconii*.[346]

For Rome, the right of lectors to contract marriage is attested by a letter from St. Leo to Rusticus of Narbonne.[347] The Roman Pontiff makes only a brief reference to it, in passing, which leads us to think that the law was older. Because he addresses a Gallic bishop, it can also be considered that the situation of the lectors was regulated in that country by canonical practices identical to those of the Italian provinces.

No Gallic council during the period under study directly approached the problem of the lectors' marriage, but the entire legislation of the Frankish kingdom does not leave any doubt on the point. It is only from the diaconate up, and later from the subdiaconate, that clerics are forbidden to take wives or use their conjugal rights.

---

[346] See above, pp. 267, 324, 383–84.
[347] See above, pp. 261f.

Dispositions similar to those of the African Church are taken by the 2d Council of Toledo (531) and confirm that Spain acknowledged the same liberties for the young clerics, before their admission to the subdiaconate. As we pointed out about Gaul, all the Spanish laws on continence for the Major Orders imply indirectly the authorization of marriage for lectors and cantors.

In the East, the basic texts are provided by canon 14 of the Council of Chalcedon and the 27th apostolic canon, whose influence is also felt in the Latin Churches.[348] One will, however, take note of the fact that the Fathers of Chalcedon do not seem to consider that the custom of permitting marriage to lectors and cantors was then in effect in all the provinces of the Christian world. It is possible that in the mid 5th century a certain number of Churches did not yet make a distinction in this regard between the various members of the clergy.[349] In any event, the law became generalized, especially after the dissemination of the *canones apostolorum* (5th century). The Code and Novellae of Justinian record it and confirm it several times.[350] Finally, the 27th apostolic canon will be repeated in the letter by the Fathers of the Quinisext Council and definitively integrated into the Eastern Code.

SUBDEACONS

AFRICA

The first text of law concerning subdeacons is canon 4 of the Council held in 401 at Carthage, adopted later by the *Codex canonum Ecclesiae africanae*.[351] Put in the same category as the ministers working at the service of the altar, the clerics of the fourth Order partake of the same obligations of chastity. The reason that is invoked—*qui sacra ministeria contrectant*—is akin to the motive for which canon 3 of the Council of Carthage demanded conjugal abstention from bishops, priests, and deacons—"condecet sacros antistites ac dei sacerdotes, nec non levitas,

---

[348] See above, pp. 264–66.

[349] The letter of St. Leo to Rusticus of Narbonne being posterior by several years to the Council of Chalcedon, one could think that those Churches instead belonged to the Latin world. The Roman Pontiff probably wanted to take into account the decisions of the fourth ecumenical council by officially approving the law authorizing lectors to marry.

[350] See above, pp. 361, 363.

[351] *Codex canonum Ecclesiae africanae*, can. 25. See above, p. 267.

vel qui sacramentis divinis inserviunt, continentes esse in omnibus"—from which one can reasonably conclude that subdeacons began being held to continence from the moment their functions associated them more closely to the ministry of the deacons. Such an evolution probably took place in Africa between the end of the 4th century and the Council of 401, since no mention is made of them in the acts of the synod of 390, unless the phrase *vel qui sacramentis divinis inserviunt* covers them in a paraphrastic way. In any event, starting with the year 401 the extension to the subdiaconate of the law of continence is a fact in the African provinces. Its renewal at the general council of 419 and then its insertion in the *Concordia Cresconii* testify that it remained in effect until the Moslem invasion.[352]

ROME

In Rome the issue evolved in a similar way. The decretals of Innocent I to Victricius of Rouen (404) and to Exupery of Toulouse (405) record, without modifications, the instructions of Pope Siricius and do not seem to extend to subdeacons the demands proper to the Major Orders.[353] The question remains whether, as was the case in the African Church, that was the result of the fact that the subdiaconate was still a subaltern office, without any direct tie to the properly called service of the altar. Insofar as it was more and more considered "the fourth Order" in the hierarchy of the sacred ministries, it tended, of course, to be subjected to the law of continence already required of the three higher Orders. This was the reason given by St. Leo in his letter to Anastasius of Thessalonika (444).[354] By the time of St. Leo's pontificate, the process of raising the subdeacons to the honors and functions of the priestly ministry seems clearly complete. They are not only forbidden to marry but also forbidden to devote themselves to conjugal relations if they were married before receiving ordination. At the end of the 6th century, Gregory the Great would again bear witness to this discipline in his letters to Peter, subdeacon in Sicily; to the defender Symmacus, and to Boniface of Reggio;[355] and the rejection by Pope Sergius of the Quinisext Council's decisions (691) also manifests that if the Bishop of Rome agreed with the Eastern Church in refusing subdeacons the right to marry, he

---

[352] Even though that law was not mentioned in the *Breviatio Ferrandi*, there is no reason to suppose that it had been abandoned during the 6th century.

[353] See above, pp. 256–57.

[354] See above, p. 260–61.

[355] See above, pp. 371–73, 373–74, 374.

also asked them, unlike the Fathers of Byzantium, to abstain from marriage in case they had taken a wife beforehand.

GAUL

The Gallic Councils of the 5th century also ignored subdeacons in their decrees pertaining to priestly continence.[356] Canon 11 of the Council of Vannes (461–91) and canon 39 of the Council of Agde (506) mention them in the list of clergy members who must remain single, without stipulating whether those who had been married before now had to abstain from their wives.[357] The other canons of the Council of Agde, as well as the first synods held in Gaul during the 6th century, demand clerical continence starting only from the diaconate.[358] It was the Council of Orléans in 538, as far as we know, which on this matter inaugurated a series of laws including the subdiaconate in the hierarchy of ranks bound to keep perfect chastity. It seems surprising that the Churches of the Frankish kingdom had to wait almost a century to align themselves with the Roman practices, especially if we recall that the first assemblies of the 6th century were directed by Caesarius of Arles himself. Concerned as he was to promote universal discipline, it seems strange that he could have deliberately neglected the directive of St. Leo. Here, we may also wonder whether, until a period close to the Council of Orléans, the subdeacons of the French provinces did not remain exempt from the law of continence because they generally were not yet among the ministers in charge of the altar service. It is known that the minimum age required for the diaconate was twenty-five, and the period of probation demanded from the acolytes or subdeacons, since the time of Siricius, lasted five years.[359]

---

[356] Can. 21 and 22 of the Council of Orange (441); can. 3, 43, and 44 of the 2d Council of Arles (442–506); can. 1 and 2 of the 1st Council of Tours (461). See above, pp. 273–74.

[357] CC 148, 154, and 209.

[358] Can. 9 and 16 of the Council of Agde (506); 4th Council of Arles (524); can. 13 of the Council of Clermont (535). See above, pp. 333, 335ff., 339.

[359] Epist. ad Himerium Tarraconensem episcopum, I, 9–10. PL 56, 560a–c. Caesarius of Arles, for his part, seems to have postponed the admission age for the major Orders until thirty, if we are to believe his biographers: "ut nonquam in Ecclesia sua diaconum ordinaret ante tricesimum aetatis eius annum" is written in Sancti Caesarii Vita ab ejus familiaribus scripta, lib. I, n. 56 (G. Morin, S. Caesarii opera omnia, II, p. 320). He had to rally against his will to the decisions of the Council of Agde, setting the age at twenty-five, but not without openly regretting what he thought to be a detestable custom: cf. Sermo I, n. 14 (G. Morin, S. Caesarii, I, pp. 12–13). Concerning the entire question, see the critical study of P. H. Lafontaine, Les conditions positives de l'accession aux ordres dans la première législation ecclésiastique (300–492) (Ottawa, 1963), pp. 136ff.

As early as his twentieth year, a lector could thus be ordained subdeacon; this young age probably explains why there was delay in subjecting clerics of the "fourth Order" to obligations of chastity that were more compatible with maturity. Only the progressive participation of subdeacons in liturgical functions considered as "sacred" could have been the determining factor, we believe, in the discipline's evolution and also bring legislators to demand from subdeacons that they abstain from their wives. Once the principle of an indissoluble link between altar service and continence was posited, such an evolution was in the logic of things. Starting with the Council of Orléans of 538, if not earlier, the Gallic provinces would now associate the subdiaconate with the higher ranks of the clergy to impose upon it the duty of continence.[360]

SPAIN

In Spain the change did not occur, in all likelihood, before the end of that same period. The only conciliar text related to our study—canon 1 of the Council of Toledo of the year 400[361]—does not mention subdeacons. But as soon as the synodal assemblies started again, at the threshold of the 6th century, the Spanish bishops subjected subdeacons to the traditionally prevailing regulations for the ministers of the hierarchy, and from the Council of Girona (517) to the one held in Toledo in 655—the last of our series—there would be many and invariable ordinances reminding married men promoted to the subdiaconate of their duty of perfect chastity.[362]

BYZANTINE EAST

The first Eastern texts explicitly mentioning subdeacons, forbidding them marriage, are found in the *Corpus juris civilis* of Justinian (529–46).[363] Yet it does not seem that the emperor wished to extend to clerics of

---

[360] Can. 20 (19) of the Council of Tours (567); can. 11 of the Council of Mâcon (583); can. 1 of the Council of Lyon (583); can. 20 and 21 of the Council of Auxerre (late 6th century). See above, pp. 342–45, 345–46, 346–47, 347.

[361] See above, p. 270.

[362] Can. 6 of the Council of Girona (517); can. 1 of the 2d Council of Toledo (531); Isidore of Seville, *De ecclesiasticis officiis*, II; can. 6 of the 8th Council of Toledo (653); can. 10 of the 9th Council of Toledo (655). See above, pp. 326, 327–28, 386–87, 393, 395.

[363] *Codex Justinianus*, I, 3, 44; *novella* 5, 8; *novella* 6, 5; *novella* 22, 42; *novella* 123, 14 and 29. See above, pp. 353–54, 357, 359–60, 361–62, 363–65.

that category, when they had been married before ordination, the obligation of conjugal continence that he demanded from deacons, priests, and bishops.[364] The insertion of the Theodosian document on the cohabitation of clerics with female persons in the *Corpus juris civilis* might lead one to think that, in the mind of the imperial legislator, the subdiaconate was also obligated by the law, but in the absence of formal texts, we can only formulate a hypothesis.[365] It is quite likely that the Byzantine Eastern legislation in the first half of the 6th century still left to clerics of the fourth Order the freedom to live maritally with their wives while refusing to those who were still bachelors the right to marry.

Last came the Council in Trullo (691), which undertook to defend categorically "the honor of the conjugal bed" and opposed any attempt to require Church ministers, with the exception of bishops, to abstain from legitimate relations with their wives (can. 13). The decision concerns priests and deacons as well as subdeacons, as we have seen.[366] It is enough here to note that at the end of the 7th century, the code of the Eastern Churches under the jurisdiction of Constantinople officially authorized clerics promoted to the subdiaconate to use their marital rights, upholding, however, the prohibition against taking a wife for those who had not done so before. In general, the East does not show any clear trace of evolution comparable to that of the Western Christian communities with respect to the discipline of chastity required from subdeacons. Nevertheless, the latter were progressively assimilated into the higher ranks of the hierarchy, as is attested by laws forbidding marriage once a man passed the threshold of ordination and the temporary conjugal abstinence that was still demanded from men connected with the sacred service of the altar.[367]

CONCLUSION OF SECTION B

At the end of this long inquiry through three centuries of history a salient fact becomes evident following an overall look at the period: the intense conciliar activity of the Western Churches.

---

[364] See above, pp. 359–60.

[365] See above, pp. 369–70.

[366] See above, p. 405.

[367] We have seen that the Nestorian Church of Persia gave herself, starting with the Council of Beth Lafath in 484, a proper legislation authorizing clerics to marry and use marriage "from the patriarch down to the lowest in the hierarchy". See above, pp. 282–83.

Reduced to silence by invasions, shaken by the Priscillanist and Arian crises, Spanish Christendom regularly seized the opportunity of quieter periods provided by circumstances to hold synods and oppose the contrary tendencies threatening its institutions. From 400 to 655, i.e., from the 1st to the 9th councils of Toledo, including the assemblies of Girona and Braga, the results of this tenacious perseverance led to the fidelity of the Iberian peninsula to the discipline promulgated by the Council of Elvira (ca. 300), which was in perfect tune with the Roman legislation.

On their part, the dioceses of Gaul and of the Seven Provinces, deprived of genuine leaders for the whole of the 4th century, undertook at the Council of Orange, presided over by Hilary of Arles in 441, a work of reform that would progressively extend its influence over the entire Frankish kingdom, giving to the clergy the definitive stamp that we have seen. The leader of this long-term venture, which was tremendous in proportion to the obstacles that were overcome, remains for the observer that ancient monk of Lérins promoted to the metropolitan See of Southern Gaul, Caesarius of Arles, the soul of the episcopal conferences of his time. To him Christian France still greatly owes what it is today.

As for Augustine's Africa, it is enough to evoke the general council of 419—the sixteenth held in Carthage in less than a century—to have an idea of the energy with which his multitude of bishops vigorously endeavored to keep and restore the traditional ordinances. The voluminous *Codex canonum Ecclesiae africanae*, put together during those sessions, will remain the charter of the African Churches until the Moslem invasion. By turns glorious or bleeding to death, the communities of the Maghreb will gather from this legislation the letter and the spirit of perpetual renewals. The *Breviatio* of Deacon Ferrandus in the 6th century and later the *Concordia Cresconii* will show, each in its own way, the homogeneity of Carthage's archives with the apparently heteroclite collection of the ancient canons coming from all parts.

The living source and direct inspiration of the movement confirmed by the Latin world, Rome, is better expressed through the voice of the Roman pontiffs themselves. With the exception of the Council of Turin (398 or 401), the legislative calendar of Italy, from the 5th to the 7th century, is uniquely marked by their interventions: Innocent I, St. Leo, and Gregory the Great echo, one after the other, the teaching inherited from the past, holding the rudder through powerful storms, keeping their eyes trained on a line that came, as they believed, from the apostles, and thus determine the course to be followed by the Apostolic See. The discipline that became consolidated at that time in many of the Mediterranean lands is their work, just as much as that of Aurelius of Carthage, Caesarius of Arles, or Isidore of Seville. It is characterized, as was the case in the previous centuries, by the intention to link priestly continence with the very origins of the Church and to support its theologico-scriptural foundations by the exegesis of Leviticus' prescriptions and St. Paul's instructions. Through many ups and downs that intention did not change, and it patiently built, for future generations, the rule of life for the Western clergy.

The parallel history of the Eastern patriarchate offers, for its part, a diversity of testimonies in which it is more difficult to find one's bearings. Justinian's Code, apart from certain initiatives of secondary importance, is essentially in harmony with the trends and laws of the Roman Church. Jerome guarantees the conformity of the Eastern Churches with the rest of the empire, a certainty corroborated at the local level by the writings and sermons of St. John Chrysostom as well as by the plea of Synesius of Cyrene. The Egypt of Cyril welcomes and disseminates the *Doctrina Aeddei*, and the Syrian circles of the late 5th century welcomed and spread the apostolic pseudoritual known as the *Testamentum Domini Nostri Jesu Christi*. The latter two works contain ideas that could pass for Latin; other documents, however, introduce a different note into that unity.

We thought it better to leave aside, for serious reasons, the passage from Socrates' *Historia Ecclesiastica* affirming, flatly, that the Eastern clergy, bishops included, did not know any regulations related to conjugal abstinence. That categorical assumption which other and more trustworthy witnesses deny is to be understood, we believe, as a marginal disciplinary trend.

A rift that is easier to discern between the two traditions of the Christian world is found in the Theodosian law of 420 and, at about the same date, in canon 6 (5) of the apocryphal collection that anonymous Syrian or Byzantine editors placed under the aegis of the apostles (*canones apostolorum*). The study of those problematic writings and of their influence in the context of that time, brought to light, as we have seen, the latent ambiguity of the formulas. Assimilated without difficulties by St. Leo, incorporated into the conciliar legislation of Gaul and Spain, the instruction given to priests not to "send away" their legitimate wives was translated, however, by the Quinisext Council (691) into an official recognition of their right to make use of their marriages. In other words, the decrees of Theodosius' Code, and more particularly the 6th "apostolic" canon, by themselves, do not give us a clear definition of their meaning, for the latter depends above all on an interpretation. It is all but certain, in the last analysis, that the rift we referred to was effectively started as early as the 5th century. We are rather inclined to think that the contrary was true. If the *canones apostolorum* encountered, as soon as they were published, an institutional atmosphere different from the official positions presented by St. Leo and the Western councils, the decree forbidding "sending back the wife with the excuse of piety" would have been annexed by it as an indisputable authority in favor of the clerics' freedom to continue conjugal relations. Canonized under that form, it would have made practically impossible any later attempt to impose upon the Eastern Christian communities a law on perpetual continence, which would certainly have been branded as unfaithful to the apostolic tradition.[368] Now, not only do we see the *Testamentum Domini Nostri Jesu Christi* continue to recommend perfect chastity to the ministers of the altar, but also Justinian's legislative corpus, praising the apocryphal collection, retains for deacons, for priests, and even more strongly for bishops the obligations we know, and it even claims as a source of authority the teaching of the holy Fathers and the holy apostles. And the insertion of the Theodosian law in the Byzantine Code of the 6th century confirms that the emperor of Constantinople had read the text and had interpreted the formal instruction not to separate a cleric from his wife in the same way St. Leo had done in his letter to Rusticus of Narbonne.

If we closely study the entire period, it seems clear enough that the Fathers of the Quinisext Council (691) were the first and only ones to read officially in the 6th (5th) "apostolic" canon, as self-explanatory, the authorization of conjugal relations. The line of demarcation between the East and the West was effectively drawn through the intermediary influence of the apostles' pseudologion, but the separation came about more than two hundred years after the pseudologion was written, at a time when political upheaval and dissensions within Christendom itself favored, quite strongly, divergences in many areas.

Historical objectivity does not seem to us to justify with enough certainty the hypothesis according to which the Churches of the East had been ruled, before the 7th century, by a legislation on clerical continence that was essentially different from that of the Latin-speaking provinces. The reconstruction we can make on the basis of the documents of unequal importance that mark that period offers, rather, the evidence of a discipline such as the one Jerome in Bethlehem or Chrysostom in Antioch knew, judging by what they say.[369] Though one must accept such a view

---

[368] We have here, as it will have been observed, an example of applying the "principle of comprehensive interpretation", according to which one has to take into account all the givens converging on a point of history or a text so as to clarify its signification. See above, pp. 63–64.

[369] One should also take into account the indication provided by the Council of Seleucia-Ctesiphon in 410, during which the leaders of the Persian Church solemnly approved the canons of the First Ecumenical Council. The 3d canon of that synod, called "of Mar Isaac", promulgated anew the 3d canon of Nicaea on "subintroductae" women for the Persian

of things with the reservations imposed by the vagueness of certain testimonies and not assert more than one should, we still can draw attention to the direction in which, insofar as we are concerned, we see the history of the East organize itself in the most likely way.

On this general background various observations provided by documents published after the Carthaginian Council of 390 may be regrouped here.

No more than during the previous period did we encounter a law of celibacy in the strict sense of the term. A rather large number of ministers of the ecclesiastical hierarchy were chosen from men bound by marriage, both because of the scarcity of single candidates—as St. Jerome, who was not exactly favorable to women, lamented—and because of the respect due to the sacrament of marriage; and St. John Chrysostom was right to stress that point, reflecting a more objective attitude. In all the dioceses of the Roman or Byzantine Empire, priests and deacons were family men and had a personal experience of conjugal life. One must keep that situation in mind to appreciate the magnitude of the sacrifices that were undertaken, the original features of the priesthood in the early centuries, and the specific difficulties to which the legislators tried to adjust.

The Pauline principle of the *unius uxoris virum* governed, as it had formerly, the policy of clerical recruiting. Faithful to the exegesis of Siricius, Innocent I interpreted the directives of the first epistle to Timothy to demand perfect continence from the monogamists admitted to ordination, and he was followed by the Western episcopates, as is attested in particular by the Councils of Agde and Marseilles and, in Africa, by the canonical collection of Cresconius. In the same vein, St. John Chrysostom explained to his listeners in Antioch that the married bishop must live with his wife "as if he did not have one"; without adopting it, he reiterated the opinion of certain people, according to whom the future shepherd could be elected only on the condition that he be freed from his matrimonial bonds.

This last way of understanding the thought of St. Paul seems to have been favored in certain Eastern circles, if we go by the *Testamentum Domini Nostri Jesu Christi*, which speaks of the bishop as a widower. One interesting detail: this regulation of ordination translates μιᾶς γυναικὸς ἀνήρ by a grammatical device employing a past-tense verb

---

clergy; as we have seen, it seems to unveil in the background the existence of a discipline of clerical continence similar to (even stricter than, as far as cohabitation is concerned) that of the Western Churches. It was only after the conversion to Nestorianism that the Church of Persia would adopt a different discipline extending the use of marriage to clerics, whatever their rank in the hierarchy (Council of Beth Lafath, 484). See above, pp. 281–83.

(*qui* fuit *unius uxoris virum*) and thus seems to have known a version of the Pauline text that would have been different from our Greek manuscripts. For his part, Jerome argued against Jovinian on the basis of a formula of the same type: St. Paul did not say, he protested, "Eligatur episcopus, qui unam ducat uxorem sed qui unam habuerit uxorem. . . ." It all happened as if the true meaning of the scriptural verse was rooted, for these authors, not on an *a posteriori* exegesis, but in the very letter of the Apostle. The fact that St. Jerome was not the only one to represent that tradition deserved not to be ignored. It may not be impossible that the Syriac version kept a style closer to the Pauline original than the Greek language parchments had. In any case, its influence on Eastern customs was not negligible and helps us have a more exact idea of the tendencies that may have prevailed in certain of those communities.

With the *Corpus juris civilis* of Justinian, the rule prescribed by the epistle to Timothy was interpreted in a strongly rigorist way that has more to do with the reason of State than with hermeneutics. To avoid the alienation of ecclesiastical assets—the greatest wealth in Byzantium—for the benefit of the bishop's family, the emperor removed from their episcopal office men who had heirs in direct line, children or grandchildren. Such a measure was intended to make absolutely sure that men selected as bishops were for the most part widowers or bachelors, because married men without children or men who had always kept perfect chastity with their wives were likely to represent only a very small proportion of the total number. From the other higher ranks of the clergy he also demanded total continence, with the calculated intention of having easy access to priests qualified for the episcopate, the "divine rules" of the priesthood being happily favorable to the necessities of his politics. The narrow gate leading to the summit of the hierarchy was to remain in the canon law of the Eastern Church in the way Justinian wished it to be. As a consequence, the monasteries became, little by little, the only source providing subjects fulfilling the set conditions, while historical circumstances favored—for the secular clergy—the normalization of conjugal life.

If the rule of the *unius uxoris virum* still remained an underlying factor for the Quinisext Council—deacons and priests having been married only once and to a virgin—the practical interpretation tended toward a new exegesis of the Pauline principle. We say "practical" because the anti-Roman faction claimed, for its part, to be faithful to the original Tradition. It was not a perpetual continence but a chastity limited solely to the days of liturgical service, according to the pattern of the Old Testament laws, that the Fathers of 691 deemed to conform to the apostolic discipline. The sixth of the *canones apostolorum*, an apocryphal document ambiguous in interpretation, and above all canon 2 of the late fourth-century African synod, both invoked to support the Trullan legislation, show in fact that the latter moved away from the traditional exegesis of the epistle to Timothy. From the viewpoint of history, the recommendation of St. Paul has defined, since Siricius, the rule of priestly behavior according to a reading that no document prior to the Council in Trullo questioned with certainty. The rare texts seeming to do so (*Apostolic Constitutions*, Theodosian Code, and canon 6 of the *canones apostolorum*) were integrated easily in the general context of Western thought and therefore cannot be objectively seen as steps that would have foreshadowed the customs legalized in Byzantium in 691. This observation, which of course cannot enable us to prejudge the meaning that the *unius uxoris virum* could have had to St. Paul himself, warns us that we are confronted by two disciplinary traditions whose essential references to Scripture were developed over several centuries: on the one hand, the exegetic current represented by Siricius and the Council of Carthage in 390 that corresponded to his views, and on the other, the interpretation explicitly claimed here for the first time, at the end of the 7th century, at the Quinisext Council.

Whatever the divergences might have been between Rome and Constantinople, the same theological foundation continued to support solidly the discipline throughout the period: the indissociable bond between service at the altar and continence (perpetual or temporary) demanded from ministers. If the episcopal conferences did not always feel the need to mention it, it remained present in the minds of the legislators, as was attested by the documents incorporating the full texts of Siricius' decretals (letters of Innocent I, Councils of Agde and Marseilles, *Concordia Cresconii*) or arguing tirelessly on the basis of the "divine laws", i.e., the prescriptions of Leviticus and the abstinence-for-prayer requested by St. Paul from Christian couples (Innocent I, 1st Council of Tours, Isidore of Seville, Code of Justinian, Council in Trullo).

As usual, the emphasis was placed on the function of mediation. Responsible for the spiritual interests of God's people, the man in charge of the liturgy must be in a position that will permit him to obtain a divine audience and ensure the success of his prayer. From this viewpoint, abstaining from sex seems to be an essential condition, set from the very beginning of the institution of the priesthood, without its justification through philosophy or a study of anthropology of some sort being deemed necessary. The *Quo possint simpliciter quod a Deo postulant impetrare* of the Council of Carthage underlies the problems of the time and was mentioned in a textual quotation during the Quinisext Council. Just as was the case with the Tent of Sacrifice or the Holy of Holies, the altar of the New Covenant is the privileged locus of intercession. The latter is thus identified, as it were, with the liturgical service, and continence seems equally demanded by the "sacred" character of the mysteries taking place there. The formulas of the kind *qui divinis mysteriis inserviunt* (Council of Carthage in 390) and *qui sacra ministeria contrectant* (Council of Carthage in 401) are frequently added to the considerations centered on the original character of the priestly mediation and at times run the risk of sidetracking us by seeming to localize the ministerial activity. Being an intercessor personally committed to a dialogue with the living God, the minister of the altar can then appear as a mere leader of the chorus, moving about in a sacred environment and manipulating objects that possess an intrinsic constraining value. We cannot escape such an impression when we see Isidore of Seville, for instance, draw his inspiration from a passage of Isaiah in order to exhort subdeacons to continence, reminding them: "Mundamini, qui fertis vasa Domini." Such phrases will favor at certain periods in the history of the Church a process of sacralization tending to relativize the dominant note of patristic thought and to substitute for the first motivation reasons of a strictly ritual character. Until the end of the 7th century the formulas that we have just quoted would still remain linked and frequently subordinated to the arguments basing the obligation of priestly chastity on the prophetic aspect of the priesthood. It is important to stress this feature in order to be able to discern without anachronism the fundamental theological line coursing through the documents of the time concerning priestly continence in the East as well as in the West. Through and in his union to Christ the mediator, the Christian Levite is the successor of Moses, ambassador of God and entrusted with a prophetic word for the people. The mission that he carries on through the service of the "divine mysteries" remains, in the eyes of the Fathers, the essential foundation of his specific obligations, sexual abstinence being an invariable condition for access to the "holy" God and a necessary guarantee of success.[370]

---

[370] Alongside this essential motivation, we find in the writings of the Patristic period other reasons cited for requiring of the priest a perfection superior to that of the monk and consequently a perfect chastity at least comparable to that of the monk. These reasons are, notably, the duty of spiritual fatherhood (Origen), the necessity of renouncing the "flesh" so as to grow closer to the "holiness" of God, the example that the priest must give to virgins and to men who live in continence, and, to a certain extent, the priest's duty to be available for various apostolates. A very good explanation of these motivations can be found in the article by H. Crouzel, "Le célibat et la continence ecclésiastique dans l'Église primitive: leurs motivations" [The motivations for clerical celibacy and continence in the primitive Church], in J. Coppens, *Sacerdoce et célibat* (Gembloux-Louvain, 1971), pp. 333–71. To my mind, however, the author did not sufficiently emphasize the primary role played by the theology of the ministerial priesthood in the hierarchy of reasons for continence. Above all, he did not place enough stress on the priest's obligation, as intercessor and mediator in the dialogue of salvation, to make absolutely sure, by means of perfect chastity, that

Unanimously shared by the legislators of the Christian world, such a conviction explains the tenacity with which they continually endeavored to restore the discipline defeated by the vicissitudes of history or the opposition of part of the clergy. Even more than during the 3d and 4th centuries, the period under study was marked by the upheavals of invasions and political chaos. Far from enjoying propitious circumstances, the rule of continence was maintained only at the cost of ceaseless reforms. Without Caesarius of Arles—to use only one example—the provinces of Gaul would likely have collapsed under the weight of events and habits that were not favorable to priestly chastity. And the Fathers of the Council in Trullo themselves did not have an easy time when they went against the current pulling Byzantine society toward a laxity of mores. Everywhere we see persevering efforts aiming at ensuring the fidelity of Church ministers to what remains for all a tradition inherited from the apostles. There are countless documents that in one way or another intend to remain within this line of continuity. And when Constantinople contested the customs of Rome, it was also by referring to an apostolic norm. Be it temporary or perpetual, continence was never seen otherwise than from this angle, and the reformers derived from this return to the sources the energy with which they opposed the powerful forces of laxity.

None of this could have been achieved without an adjustment. The most remarkable adaptation is to be seen in the many Western regulations that, starting from St. Leo, openly authorized the higher clergy's cohabitation with their wives. This point, which previous councils had not mentioned, seems to have been clarified under the influence of the 6th pseudoapostolic canon that became known in the 5th century. The presence of a wife in the home of the bishop or priest seems more and more to be a normal thing. Conjugal love is not sacrificed but raised to the level of a spiritual intimacy reconciling the rights of affection and of chastity. The Leonian formula, *ut de carnale fiat spirituale conjugium*, inspired the decisions of the time and became the rule of life in priestly "households". From then on, continence was less synonymous with separation than with the experience of perfect chastity lived in common by the cleric and his wife. The experience was not lacking in greatness—the

---

he has met the conditions for constant and efficacious prayer. H. Crouzel failed to put sufficient emphasis on this essential point, perhaps because, while recognizing that the institution of clerical celibacy and continence has its foundation in the New Testament, he adopted Funk's thesis, repeated by R. Gryson, concerning the late origin of the vow, and he thought that the interpretation of the Pauline principle *unius uxoris virum* offered by Siricius, Innocent I, and other representatives of the Patristic period should be deemed to have been a forced interpretation ("Le célibat et la continence ecclésiastique", p. 360).

daily heroism of those couples and the quiet audacity of the laws are admirable—but the risks were not eliminated. Hence we see a multiplication of warnings: let them behave as brother and sister; let them be prudent enough not to share the same room; let them have at home another cleric or a trustworthy person able to guarantee their good behavior. Little by little, clerics are advised—even ordered—to separate the homes, and the episcopal residence becomes a monastery of sorts where a numerous clergy takes the place of a female domesticity. Any problem of cohabitation tended to be solved by the common life of the diocesan presbyterium. Even when one did not go to such extremes, one sought to preserve the future by compelling the parties to a public profession of continence. This profession had to precede ordination to the diaconate, even to the subdiaconate, and certain councils demanded a long period of probation. Often, the wife is invited to take part, her consent being indispensable for the promotion of her husband. Both must commit themselves with full knowledge, nothing dispensing them later to renege on their promise. All these measures reflect a background of complex particular situations and the increasing attention that the leaders of the Church gave to the concrete problems of couples committed to the difficult adventure of perfect chastity.

In the East, it seems, it was less easily accepted for the bishop to live in the same house as his wife. St. John Chrysostom deemed, for his part, that if this were permitted in apostolic times, given the morals of that era, it was no longer so in the Christian society that his listeners knew. More intransigent, the Code of Justinian forbade any female presence in the episcopal residence, and the Council in Trullo would adopt the imperial ordinance, making it a duty for shepherds to avoid the scandal provoked by those who were still sharing a home with their wives. Political necessities for the former and prudential reasons for the Fathers of Byzantium thus led the Eastern patriarchate to become more severe than the Roman legislation, although one can wonder whether during the 5th century and until the promulgation of the *Corpus juris civilis* the principles enunciated by the Code of Theodosius and the 6th pseudo-apostolic canon, in their places of origin, did not exercise the same influence as in the Latin provinces. It is quite probable. When it came to subdeacons, deacons, and priests, cohabitation at any rate enjoyed the official favor, its legitimacy having been recognized by the Theodosian law. Justinian himself did not change it. As to the Fathers of the Quinisext Council, they were not troubled by it because they did not demand a daily continence of such clerics. For them, common life is equivalent to a recognition of the freedom to use marital rights, contrary to what St. Leo and the Westerners may have thought. As a corollary, any cohabitation seemed suspect to them when it involved those who had made a perpetual profession of chastity, hence the prohibition concerning bishops and the reproach addressed to the priests of certain "barbarian churches" who pretended to live with their wives while abstaining from intercourse. To conclude, it seems that the situation created by the problem of clerics' wives was solved in a different way in the two parts of the Christian world: while the West accepted the risk of cohabitation for bishops and the other higher ranks of the clergy, and then progressively evolved toward a kind of monastic life, taking back what had been conceded, the East found it more difficult to accept the possibility of living chastely with one's wife and rather promptly sent the wife of the bishop away from his home, ending up with a normalization of sexual intercourse for those of the clerics who were authorized to keep their wives with them.

The canonical literature of the time repeatedly studied the case of lectors and cantors. That was a new matter compared to the previous periods. Indeed, one discerns in certain documents a tendency to extend to the lower ranks of the hierarchy the obligations of chastity that were traditional for the others. The African councils demanded from young lectors who had reached the age of puberty the choice between marriage and the definitive profession of continence; but with St. Leo and above all the Council of Chalcedon, the custom of letting anyone who was not yet a subdeacon be free to marry became generalized. The latter legislation would remain unchanged, even at the Quinisext Council.

For the subdiaconate, the development of discipline seems to follow that of the functions granted to that Order. Insofar as it became, with a specific consistency, the "fourth Order" of the ecclesiastical hierarchy, closely associated with the service at the altar, we see that it took on the same demands of chastity that the diaconate had: prohibition of marriage and perpetual continence. The East seems to have experienced a similar evolution, taking into account the margin of historical uncertainty hovering, as we have seen, over some of the documents; by the time of the Council in Trullo, the law of temporary continence had been clarified: it was also valid for subdeacons, who were, as in the West, given a status equal to that of the ministers of the liturgy.

Finally, let us point out the direct role that canon 2 of the Council of Carthage in 390 played in the disciplinary texts of that time. Inserted in the *Codex canonum Ecclesiae africanae* and then in the *Breviatio Ferrandi*, it still expressed the essence of the African Church's positions, repeating word for word the reasoning of Epigonius and his colleagues. In 691, canon 2 was used as a testimony of primary importance in the Trullan legislation, which interpreted in its own way the degree of continence demanded by the African canon, but fully endorsed the Council's claim to apostolicity and its theological preambles.

In this respect the law of 390 manifests once more the importance that we must grant to it in the history of the early centuries' discipline. Though numerous documents did not refer to it, it summarized in an excellent synthesis the feeling shared by all the legislators: the continence demanded from the Levites of the New Testament is founded on the original character of the priestly mediation and is rooted in the positive will of the apostles. Rome and Byzantium were in agreement on these essential givens. The decree voted at Carthage at the end of the 4th century conveys to us in a few sentences the message of the entire patristic period.

GENERAL CONCLUSION

One main idea constantly recurs in the whole of our study, and it is common to the parallel or competitive traditions of the various Churches in the Christian world: continence is requested from clerics working at "the service of the altar" because they exercise an original function of mediation between God and man.

In this respect the theological perspective of the Quinisext Council of 691 agrees remarkably with the previous legislation and especially with the Western viewpoint. One sentence perfectly sums up this general conception, the very same that an African uttered one day in the year 390 on behalf of his colleagues: the ministers of the divine mysteries must abstain from conjugal intercourse "so as to obtain in all simplicity what they are asking from God" (*quo possint simpliciter quod a Deo postulant impetrare*). Through such an affirmation, the ecclesiastical discipline of the early centuries was trying to harmonize with the principles posited by the New Testament, and, beyond the Gospel, to link the Christian priesthood to the Levitical institution. It is in order to appreciate better this process of continuity that we would like here, by way of conclusion, to attempt to outline several remarks.

If we first go back to the Old Testament's prescriptions concerning the sanctity of priests, we cannot help but be struck by the fact that only the sexual interdictions survived the deep mutations that put a definitive end to the rules on purity and impurity. Neither the defilement incurred by contact with a corpse; nor bodily infirmities, leprosy, or the prohibitions against certain categories of food; nor any irregularities of the old Judaic Code were retained in the law of patristic times—abolished, just like circumcision, those imperfect practices of a past Covenant! As to sexual impurities, they also had been scrutinized with discernment: it is not a physical seminal ejaculation as such that constitutes an obstacle to the exercise of the ministry, but relations with a woman, even within the framework of a legitimate marriage. While the ancient rites of purification have been erased from the Christian memory, one thing only was remembered: at the very origins of the tribe of Levi, "a tribe set apart to

429

consecrate the most holy things, . . . to burn incense in the presence of Yahweh, to serve him, and to bless his name forever" (1 Chron 23:13), the divine law demanded from priests that they abstain from conjugal intercourse in order worthily to accomplish their duties. It was the same temporary continence that all the members of the Chosen People had to observe before taking part in a sacred meal or in a military expedition (1 Sam 21:4–5; Dt 23:10), but such an observance was particularly enjoined upon the Levites when their regular turn came to serve at the rites. And the example of the priest Zechariah, returning to his wife only after having fulfilled his priestly functions in the solitude of the sanctuary, testified at the very threshold of the New Testament to the permanent character of such a specific duty. Not only did it not occur to the Fathers that this aspect of the Levitical obligations could one day become obsolete, just like all the others, but they selected it as a distinctive mark of the priesthood inaugurated by Christ and generally strengthened its scope by making conjugal abstinence a daily necessity. The Eastern tradition expressed at the Quinisext Council did the same, with this difference, that it continued to limit the obligation to the liturgical periods for all higher clerics who had not been ordained to the episcopate.

This selective attitude of the Christian Church, in preferring a sexual prohibition to all others, poses a problem. Recently it has been regarded as a late resurgence of the Judaic mentality, provoked by a movement of sacralization that tended to substitute for the "prophetic" pattern of apostolic times an archetype dominated by the "ritual" aspect. More and more defined by the "service of the altar", as minister of the *sacramenta*, the priest liberated by Jesus Christ from the old burdens of past constraints would have fallen back to the level of Old Testament servitudes resulting from the reappearance of the categories of pure and impure. The decisive factor in imposing continence, as J. P. Audet puts it, was "the encounter, within the same pastoral consciousness, of the double perception of impure and sacred, the first being present in the shadows, under the form of sexual activity, and the second, in full light, under the form of service of the *sacramenta*".[1] That perception led to a conflict between these mutually exclusive ideas, within a perspective inherited not only from Judaism but also from a more archaic depth of human consciousness, a conflict that necessarily produced a law forbidding "sacral personnel" to "defile" themselves by sexual activity. All things considered, that was a regressive phenomenon that would have sold out the radical novelty of the Christian priesthood to an invasive ritualistic image. "In the spirit of the time",

---

[1] J. P. Audet, *Mariage et célibat dans le service pastoral de l'Église, Histoire et orientation* (Paris, 1967), p. 114.

E. Schillebeeckx observes in the same vein, "this ritual image of the priest immediately brings to mind the Old Testament and ancient concepts: the exercise of sacred cult is incompatible with sexuality. The biblical mysticism of 'unsuitability for marriage because of the kingdom of heaven' remains the spirituality of monks, ascetics, and virgins; the continence of priests is, rather, within the context of 'ritual purity'."[2]

These explanations, which seem satisfactory at first glance and which certain "sacralizing" phrases of the patristic era effectively seem to authorize, do not seem, in our opinion, to explain certain facts. To speak of a revival of a Levitical pattern would lead us to suppose that before that time and at the very origins of Christianity the priestly institution had conceived itself as fundamentally independent of the Old Covenant's structures. Christ had overthrown the Temple, and with it the liturgical and cultural givens of the unfaithful people. On those ruins the young Christian community would have built a totally new organization and given to its religious leaders a fully original lifestyle and features. "None of the terms that, at the origins, described the 'service' of the 'Gospel' or the *ekklesia*, we are assured, was borrowed from the Jewish sacral universe—*apostolos, evangelistos, didaskalos, prophetes, diakonos, presbyteros, episkopos*—to mention here only the principal elements of this vocabulary . . . [all these terms] come directly from non-sacral, profane language."[3] Now, this way of looking at things does not exactly correspond to reality. Historians are today bringing to light, and rightly so, the important role played by the "Hebrews" of the Jerusalem community in the early Church. Unlike the "Hellenists" who distanced themselves from the Jewish traditions, the group of the "Hebrews" was marked by a close attachment to Mosaic customs and a regular attendance at temple worship. Far from desiring to revolutionize the ancient institutional framework, they gained sympathies among the Pharisees, thanks to what we could call a policy of integration in the Judaic system, which was their way of manifesting the deep continuity of the two Covenants. This rabbinical Christianity, whose leader was no less than James, "the brother of the Lord", exerted, more than people generally think, a preponderant importance in the young Christian communities.[4] The Twelve belonged to such an environment, and we have good reason to think that they left the same Judeo-Christian stamp on the Churches they founded after they were scattered outside of Jerusalem. Sure enough, the Christians considered

---

[2] E. Schillebeeckx, *Autour du célibat du prêtre, étude critique* (Fr. trans., Paris, 1967), p. 61.

[3] J. P. Audet, *Mariage et célibat*, p. 119.

[4] Cf. J. Danielou and H. Marrou, *Nouvelle Histoire de l'Église*, I, *Des origines à Grégoire le Grand* (Paris, 1963), pp. 36ff.

themselves the new people of God, leading a particular life and celebrating the Eucharist in private homes, but the respect they continued to manifest to the old Temple, their concern about observing the Law of Moses (even lightened by the Council of Jerusalem, the Judaic prescriptions were imposed upon the converted pagans [Acts 21:25]), shows that they were consciously the heirs of Israel, meant to perfect the Old Testament economy and not to destroy it. In other words, they spontaneously applied the fundamental principle of the Gospel: "I did not come to abolish but to perfect." Whatever their originality the Christian structures were rooted in the institutional basis of the Old Testament, and this essential relation was to give them the outlines of the future developments. As to the specific problem of the priestly functions, study of the vocabulary used by the writings of the New Testament shows that the terminology of the main ranks in the Christian hierarchy is directly borrowed from the Jewish tradition. Contrary to what J. P. Audet thought that he could affirm, the words ἀπόστολος, ἐπίσκοπος, πρεσβύτερος, διδάσκαλος, which have exact equivalents in Hebrew, refer to Jewish institutions well known by the first Christians.[5] The word διάκονος is the only one not to be rooted in the ancient background of the Old Testament, in the particular meaning we know to be its own, but the diaconal function, earlier conceived as a duplication of the tasks proper to bishop-priests, also is to be found by this bias in the line coming from Judaic antiquity.

These various remarks lead us to revise the judgment formulated by authors whom we quoted, according to which the image of the priesthood that prevailed from the 3d century on in the Christian world would have been considerably different from that which obtained during the apostolic age. If the Levitical pattern had an influence on the organization of the ecclesiastical hierarchy, it was not because of a belated regression to a pre-Christian stage, but by virtue of an internal logic of continuity that started to manifest its consequences at the very origins of Christianity.

Such a regression, which, as we have seen, does not seem to correspond to the reality of history, would be even less explicable in that the patristic consciousness constantly goes back to the tradition inherited from the apostles. On a point as important as that of the nature of the priesthood, it is quite inconceivable that after two centuries the Church would have strayed so far from the early pattern, while the Church shows a homogeneous development in other areas whenever there were essential

---

[5] See, in particular, the studies of J. Colson, *Les fonctions ecclésiales aux deux premiers siècles* (Paris, 1956); *La fonction diaconale aux origines de l'Église* (Paris, 1960).

issues at stake. And we think that it is a lack of trust in the *sensus Ecclesiae* of the third- and fourth-century Fathers, not to mention their successors, to suppose that they were capable of directing theology in a way alien to the genuinely Christian orientation.

A third point to which the above-mentioned authors do not seem to have given sufficient attention is the central importance of the mediation function in the patristic image of the Christian priesthood. It is as intercessor of the people of God, following Moses and the great prophets and leaders of Israel, that the priest is situated in a new place within the ecclesial organism. The spiritual interests of the community depend directly on his prayer in the presence of the Almighty. It is from this fundamental aspect that the responsibility of ministers is always understood, and thus also the particular statute of continence is defined. To be sure, the "ritualistic" perspective is not absent from the horizon—several formulas prove it—but it is important to see, we think, that the "service of the altar" is identified with the prophetic mission, as man approaches the "divine mysteries" only in order to enter into the sovereignly effective dialogue with the Master of history. All persons and things that concern what is divine—liturgical personnel and furnishings—receive by this very fact a sacred character, which will at times tend to take the place of the essential motivation to justify in itself the kind of sanctity necessary for the exercise of the ministry, but this upset of values is not to be found during the first seven centuries. Though they frequently speak about "sacred mysteries" and "divine sacraments", the documents of the period under study avoid falling back into the sacralizing problems of the Levitical Code by retaining the function of mediation in the first place. The reference to the priestly institution of the Old Testament does indeed make a choice among the ancient rules of purity insofar as it picks out of the heavily laden structures of Judaism the essential lode of the priesthood, the mission that places man in God's presence for salvific audiences. Again for this reason it seems inexact to us to present the patristic image of the priesthood as a purely ritualistic image, unless one gives to this word a full meaning emphasizing the mediating character of the celebrant instead of confining him, as is done only too frequently, within narrow juridical limitations. The priest of the centuries we have studied is a man who, in the exercise—and through the exercise—of sacred functions (especially the Eucharist), commits his being to the service of human history, endeavoring by the offering of himself and the weight of a pleasing prayer to gain the redemptive favors of his divine interlocutor. One could not express this truth better than by quoting the excellent commentary of the Byzantine Zonaras on canon 2 of the Council of Carthage of 390:

These are indeed intercessors between God and men who, establishing a
bond between divinity and the rest of the faithful, ask on behalf of the
whole world salvation and peace. If they thus exercise, he says, the practice
of all the virtues and hold dialogue in all confidence with God, they will
obtain immediately what they ask for. But if those men deprive themselves,
through their own fault, of their freedom of speech, how can they fulfill
their tasks as intercessors for the good of others?[6]

This means that the theology of the patristic era develops in a direct
continuity with the epistle to the Hebrews, adopting the definition in
which the anonymous author of that letter gave to the Christian priesthood, heir of the Temple, the outline of its mission: "Every high priest
has been taken out of mankind and is appointed to act for men in their
relations with God, to offer gifts and sacrifices for sin" (Heb 5:1).[7]

The perspective of our documents is thus within the theological context of the early Church, accepting and perfecting the Old Testament
pattern of priest-mediator and deriving from that traditional vision the
outlines of priestly spirituality. To imagine a solution of continuity between the Old Testament and early Christianity, on the one hand, and
between the latter and the reflection of the patristic era, on the other, is
a concept of the mind: the theological evolution was quite different, in
our opinion; in referring to the Levitical priesthood, the Fathers of the
East and of the West adopt as their own the principle that, at the very
origin of the Church, was used to graft the new image of the priest onto
the trunk of Mosaic Law, according to the living criterion of change
that Jesus himself gave as an example. As the new Moses, Christ remained
in their eyes the unique and sovereign mediator to whom all priests,
associated with his sacrificial prayer, were now to lend the help of their
intercession. It is in the last analysis the Eucharist that effects the conversion of the Old Covenant, making the salvific dialogue with God efficacious; it is the Eucharist that inaugurates and defines the theology of the
priesthood as early as the day after the Resurrection, the one that the
future centuries would endeavor to live faithfully.

---

[6]PG 138, 32c.

[7]This theological context is already that of St. Cyprian, though he never said anything
directly about the discipline of celibacy: "We must, when it comes to episcopal ordinations,
choose only leaders of intact reputation, without stain, who, offering to God worthy and
holy sacrifices, can be rewarded in the prayer they utter for the salvation of the Christian
people. Indeed, it is written: 'God does not listen to the sinner, but listens to the one who
honors God and does his will.' This is why we must, with a perfect attention and a loyal
examination, choose for the episcopate those whom we know are answered by God" (Ep.
67, 2. CSEL, 3-2, 736-37. M. Bayard, trans., Coll. "Budé", II, p. 229).

In placing the emphasis on the mediating function of the Christic priesthood, the reflection drawing on the epistle to the Hebrews logically implied the recognition of the Pauline principle of abstinence-for-prayer and its special extension to the Christians responsible for sacrificial prayer. Whatever the underlying anthropology might be in the advice given to couples not to refuse each other except by mutual consent, and then only for an agreed time, to leave themselves free for prayer (1 Cor 7:5), it is certain that the proper connection between abstention from sex and the climate of dialogue with God was stated by the apostles in terms that endorsed the Old Testament's perspective. Just as the Jewish people had to abstain from conjugal relations in certain particular circumstances, the followers of Christ are invited to manifest through the same attitude their inner freedom for the divine service. The difference is that St. Paul contents himself with moderation in proposing a general line of behavior and does not decree a precept. Nevertheless, the required fitness normally had to be more perfect in the case of a prayer whose purpose was not only the fulfillment of a "priestly" duty common to all Church members, but also the salvific intercession proper to the ministerial priesthood, thus acquiring a better chance of being heard. It is known that this *a fortiori* argument is precisely one of the favorite keystones of argumentation during patristic times. Was it already the case among the first Christian communities? Of course, it is not possible to answer with exactitude. We can, however, find that all the conditions were there for the Pauline principle to develop its effects in the framework of the young priestly institution. If we also take into account that the priestly institution was placing itself consciously in the line foreshadowed by Judaism, and that the break from the Jewish traditions occurred as a renewal and not as a flat rejection of them (Sunday replaces the Sabbath; the ecclesial assembly, the meetings at the Temple; the Eucharistic sacrifice, the animal sacrifices; and so forth), one is led more and more to wonder whether the relation of suitability established by St. Paul between prayer and chastity did not contribute effectively, as early as the beginnings of the Christian priesthood, to maintaining the Old Testament practice of conjugal abstinence and even to strengthen it by a spontaneous awareness of the necessity of a higher demand, the latter being above the former as the liturgy of intercession accomplished by the priests of Christ was above the Levitical mediation. The fact that the Apostle to the Gentiles did not think that—unlike other practices—the practice of abstinence-for-prayer prescribed by the Mosaic Law was futile would explain rather well the phenomenon of selection leading to the preference for sexual abstinence in Christianity at a time when other practices of purification were abandoned.

The question remains as to how the Christian hermeneutics of the late 4th century could read the *unius uxoris virum* of St. Paul in the way that we know it did. By affirming that the letter to Timothy aimed at recruiting monogamists *propter continentiam futuram*, and not with the afterthought of authorizing married ministers to use their marital rights, did the exegesis sanctioned by Pope Siricius find a support on scriptural bases? Was not the obvious meaning of the Pauline instruction going against such an attempt? We know that modern critics are discussing the interpretation of that passage in order to see in it either a criterion for eliminating remarried candidates or an exclusive measure against bigamists or husbands unfaithful to their wives, while agreeing, however, in not giving to Paul the intention of later compelling the men admitted to the priesthood to abstain from conjugal relations. If the commentators whom we met generally thought otherwise, would the text of the pastoral epistles provide them with indications that escape us?

It might be appropriate to welcome initially, as an indication liable one day to put research on an interesting track, the grammatical formula used by the document of Syriac origin known under the title *Testamentum Domini Nostri Jesu Christi*. Instead of the simple *unius uxoris virum*, we recall that that Eastern document of the 5th century translates the Pauline phrase by a past-tense verbal form: "*qui* fuit *unius uxoris vir*". Close to this version we have also the "*qui unam* habuerit *uxorem*" of St. Jerome in the *Adversus Vigilantium*. These authors thus solve, without ambiguity, the meaning of the scriptural verse with the help of a version that is self-explanatory. Did the Apostle speak not only of monogamists but also of men who had been *in the past* married to an only wife (or remarried) and are now free from matrimonial ties by being widowers? This is a restrictive reading when we compare it to Siricius' exegesis, as it excludes from the priesthood husbands whose wives were still alive, but it seems to have been fashionable in certain circles.

St. John Chrysostom himself knew it, though he refused to endorse it. Represented by only a small number of witnesses, this past-tense form nevertheless remains of interest to the critics. It would not be impossible, after all, that it bring us back to a lost original Greek text, more ancient perhaps than the other manuscripts. It also draws attention to a literary particularity that was not always noticed, we think, as it ought to have been. The μίας γυναικός ἀνήρ of the third chapter of the epistle to Timothy has in fact an exact counterpart in the regulation concerning widows, at the fifth chapter of the same epistle. Among the qualities required of the women to be accepted in the group of widows, St. Paul demands that they too be ἑνὸς ἀνδρός γυνή. Here, likewise, one is free to think that it might describe women who never remarried or women who had married twice but remained worthy on account of their conjugal fidelity. But in any event, they were widows, and the phrase ἑνὸς ἀνδρός γυνή, as concise as the μιᾶς γυναικός ἀνήρ of the passage related to bishops, refers obviously to a past matrimonial situation. One can easily see which remark is suggested by such a comparison. If St. Paul uses a formula of the same type in both cases, would it not mean that he had in mind similar situations? Just as he talks about women "married to only one man" and thinks about widows, it is not as strange as it might seem independently of any context to suppose that in using the phrase *unius uxoris virum* he also means, just as clearly, men whose wives' deaths freed them from conjugal obligations. The matter seems less improbable when we note the silence of the Pauline texts about the possible wife of a bishop. While he is rightly concerned about the good behavior of the children—the reputation of the shepherd being linked to theirs—it might be significant that he makes no allusion to the virtues of his wife, whose reputation is normally of greater interest to the consideration given to her husband—a mere indication that, added to the previous ones, would make quite plausible, in our opinion, the hypothesis according to which the epistle to Timothy had foreseen a preferential option for widowed monogamists. The hermeneutics developed by Siricius would thus refer to an apostolic regulation that could be traced at the level of the scriptural text; a link that could be discerned by the critics would then attach it to the foundation it claims. If the fourth-century discipline admits to the episcopate not only widowers but also monogamists whose wives are still alive, this liberal-minded evolution can be explained on the basis of the historical conjuncture. On the other hand, the opposite movement poses more problems, and it is more difficult to see how Fathers concerned with Tradition and respecting the will of the apostles could have been obstinate enough to impose a discipline of continence if it had been flatly denied by Scripture.

In the early centuries, the will of the apostles was also expressed by the examples that Peter's life and the lives of other members of the apostolic college had left in the collective memory of the Christian communities. One should never lose sight of that living norm constituted by, in addition to written or orally transmitted words, the example given by those who were the first to leave everything in order to follow Jesus and become his apostles, those to whom the Lord had entrusted the destiny of his Church. Now, as we have seen, if the Churches had not always kept a precise memory of the Twelve's family situations before their being called by Christ, they still had a common certainty that those of the apostles who could have been married had then stopped conjugal practice and observed perfect continence. Such a consensus on a particular fact from the very beginning was to play an important role in the concept the leaders of the Church held about the requirements necessary for the exercise of the priestly ministry and of the criteria for recruitment to be observed in order that the essential features of the apostles' successors' (priests and deacons) and their fellow workers' identity might be kept intact. We think that the unanimity of the Fathers' testimonies on the lifestyle of the apostles after their vocation was one of the mainstays in the transmission of the celibacy-continence discipline as a tradition of apostolic origin.

Let us also note that the motives invoked in favor of clerical continence are independent of the spiritual trend exhorting people to virginity. On the one hand, the consecration of a virgin (or a continent non-priest) appears to be a total gift of self to God "for the Kingdom of God". The virgin has to please the Divine Spouse in all things, to direct all her faculties toward him, and to surrender to him, without any reservations, her body and soul.[8] The minister of Christ, on the other hand, must be continent, less in virtue of a charismatic desire to belong totally to God (though it goes without saying that such a disposition is in keeping with his state) than in order to obtain the necessary conditions for the achievement of his specific mission, or, in other words, his functions as a mediator. Exhortations to virginity are therefore changed for the priest into compulsory canonical regulations. Independent in their motivations and in their effects, those two currents reacted on each other, of course, but their sources came from different traditions. While the call to virginity was founded in the evangelical counsels, the discipline of priestly celibacy had its origins, as we have frequently seen, in a positive will of the apostles.

It is important to stress this point, for it explains the persistence of the legislators in maintaining the obligations of chastity proper to the ministers of the altar against the many attempts constantly aiming at defeating them. We will take the liberty of pointing out once more that the history of the law on conjugal abstinence of higher clerics is not that of a slow evolution caused by the increasing influence of a movement favorable to virginity, but of a resistance by Tradition to the contrary currents that appeared at different times and places. A resistance similar to that which was to appear throughout the Church's history: let us recall, for instance, the time of the Gregorian reform or the reactions to the Protestant Reformation in the 16th century. In the same way as the

---

[8] For a good presentation of the patristic literature on virginity, see P. T. Camelot, "Les traités 'de virginitate' au 4ᵉ siècle", *Mystique et continence, Études carmélitaines* (Paris, 1952), pp. 273–92.

attitude of the Church, confronted by the protest of Luther and Calvin, would wish to be dictated by a concern for fidelity to the tradition inherited from Siricius and the African councils, Siricius' attitude and that of the African councils appear, for their part, to have been directed by a determination not to deny the inheritance of the previous centuries and especially that of the apostles.

The Augustinian principle, desiring that *"what has been kept by the entire Church and was always maintained, without having been established by the councils, [is] regarded quite rightly as having been transmitted only by the apostolic authority"*, seems to find in the discipline of celibacy-continence for the higher ranks of the clergy, as practiced during the early centuries, an adequate and justified application. The study that we have undertaken of the documents and of the historical facts demonstrates it, we think, with enough certainty. Let us conclude that the obligation demanded from married deacons, priests, and bishops to observe perfect continence with their wives is not, in the Church, the fruit of a belated development, but on the contrary, in the full meaning of the term, *an unwritten tradition of apostolic origin* that, so far as we know, found its first canonical expression in the 4th century.

"Ut quod apostoli docuerunt, et ipsa servavit antiquitas, nos quoque custodiamus"—"What the apostles taught, and what antiquity itself observed, let us endeavor also to keep." The affirmation of the Fathers of Carthage will always remain an essential link with the origins.

May it help the Churches of the East and of the West, who are both referring to it, achieve a stronger awareness of their common inheritance.

BIBLIOGRAPHY

This is a list of works dealing directly with priestly celibacy or with closely connected problems. Mention is made throughout the book of other works and articles that have been utilized.

Achelis, H. *Virgines subintroductae. Ein Beitrag zum VII. Kapitel des I. Korintherbriefs.* Leipzig, 1902.

Alexander, N. *Dissertationum ecclesiasticarum trias. Prima de divina episcoporum supra presbyteros eminentia adversus Blondellum. Altera de sacrorum ministrorum coelibatu, sive de historia Paphnutii cum Nicaeno canone concilianda. Tertia de vulgata Scripturae sacrae versione.* Paris, 1678.

Audet, J. P. *Mariage et célibat dans le service pastoral de l'Église. Histoire et orientation.* Paris, 1967.

Bardy, G., E. Jombart, et al. "Célibat des religieux et des clercs". *Catholicisme* 2:756–70.

Bauer, J. B. "Uxores circumducere (1 Kor. 9, 5)". *Biblische Zeitschrift* 3 (1959): 94–102.

Bertrams, W. "De fonte obligationis coelibatus clericorum in sacris". *Periodica de re morali canonica liturgica* 41 (1952): 107–29.

———. *Der Zölibat des Priesters. Sinngehalt und Grundlagen.* Würzburg, 1962.

Bickell, G. "Der Cölibat eine apostolische Anordnung". ZkTh 2 (1878): 26–64.

———. "Der Cölibat dennoch eine apostolische Anordnung". ZkTh 3 (1879): 792–99.

Blinzler, J. "Εἰσὶν εὐνοῦχοι Zur Auslegung von Mt 19, 12". ZntW 48 (1957): 254–70.

Bobák, J. *De coelibatu ecclesiastico deque impedimento Ordinis Sacris apud Orientales et praesertim apud Ruthenos.* Rome, 1941.

Bocquet, L. I. *Esquisse historique du célibat dans l'antiquité.* II. *Étude sur le célibat ecclésiastique jusqu'au concile de Trente.* Paris, 1894.

Boehmer, H. "Die Entstehung des Zölibates". In *Geschichtliche Studien Albert Hauck zum 70. Geburtstag dargebracht*, 6–24. Leipzig, 1916.

Boelens, M. *Die Klerikerehe in der Gesetzgebung der Kirche unter besonderer Berücksichtigung der Strafe. Eine rechtsgeschichtliche Untersuchung von den Anfängen der Kirche bis zum Jahre 1139.* Paderborn, 1968.

Calixtus, G. *De conjugio clericorum liber.* 1st ed.: Helmstadt, 1631. 2d ed.: Frankfort, 1651. 3d ed.: revised and enlarged by Henr. Phil. Conr. Henke; Helmstadt, 1873.

Carove, F. W. *Über des Cölibatgesetz des römisch-katholischen Klerus. II. Vollständige Sammlung der Cölibatgesetze für die katholischen Weltgeistlichen von den Altesten bis auf die neuesten Zeiten, mit Anmerkungen von Dr. Friedrich Wilhelm Carové.* Frankfurt am Main, 1833.

Concetti, G. *Il prete per gli Uomini d'oggi.* Rome, 1975.

Constantelos, D. "Mariage et célibat dans l'Église orthodoxe". *Concilium* 78 (1972): 29–36.

Coolen, G. "Les origines du célibat ecclésiastique". *Bulletin trimestriel de la Société académique des antiquaires de la Morinie* (Saint-Omer). 390th delivery, XX (March 1967): 545–58.

Coppens, J. *Sacerdoce et célibat. Études historiques et théologiques publiées par J. Coppens.* Bibliotheca ephemeridum theologicarum Lovaniensium, XVIII. Gembloux-Louvain, 1971.

Cross, F. L. *The Oxford Dictionary of the Christian Church*, s.v. "celibacy", 255f.

Crouzel, H. "Le célibat et la continence ecclésiastique dans l'Église primitive: leurs motivations", in *Sacerdoce et célibat. Études historiques et théologiques*, ed. J. Coppens, 333–71. Gembloux-Louvain, 1971.

Deen, H. *Le célibat des prêtres dans les premiers siècles de l'Église.* Paris, 1969.

Delhaye, P. "Brèves remarques historiques sur la législation du célibat ecclésiastique". *Studia moralia* 3 (1965): 362–96.

Denzler, G. "Zur Geschichte des Zölibats. Ehe und Ehelosigkeit der Priester bis zur Einführung des Zölibatsgesetzes im Jahre 1139". *Stimmen der Zeit* 183 (1969): 383–401.

———. "Priesterehe und Priesterzölibat in historischer Sicht". *Existenzprobleme des Priesters*, vol. 50, Münchener Akademie-Schriften, Katholische Akademie in Bayern, 13–52. München: F. Henrich, 1969.

————. *Das Papsttum und der Amtszölibat*. I: *Die Zeit bis zur Reformation*. Stuttgart, 1973.

Dortel-Claudot, M. *État de vie et rôle du prêtre*. Paris, 1971.

Duguet, J. J. "Sur le Xe canon du concile d'Ancyre touchant le célibat des ordres majeurs". In *Conférences ecclésiastiques ou Dissertations sur les auteurs, les conciles et la discipline des premiers siècles de l'Église*, II, 132–53. Cologne, 1742.

Felici, P. *Il Vaticano II e il Celibato sacerdotale*. Città del Vaticano, 1969.

Funk, F. X. "Der Cölibat keine apostolische Anordnung". TThQ 61 (1879): 208–47.

————. "Der Cölibat noch lange keine apostolische Anordnung". TThQ 62 (1880): 202–21.

————. *Real-Encyclopädie der christlichen Alterthümer* I (1880), s.v. "cölibat", 304–7.

————. "Cölibat und Priesterehe im christlichen Altertum", in *Kirchengeschichtliche Abhandlungen und Untersuchungen*, I, 121–55. Paderborn, 1897.

Galot, J. "Sacerdoce et célibat". NRTh 96 (1964): 113–36.

————. "La motivation évangélique du célibat". *Gregorianum* 52 (1972): 731–57.

Goni, C. *Coelibatus ecclesiasticus in Hispania ab Ecclesiae initiis usque ad saeculum VIII*. Pamplona, 1914.

Griffe, E. "A propos du canon 33 du concile d'Elvire". BLE 74 (1973): 142–45.

————. "Le concile d'Elvire et les origines du célibat ecclésiastique". BLE 77 (1976): 123–27.

Gryson, R. *Les origines du célibat ecclésiastique du premier au septième siècle*. Gembloux, 1970.

————. *Aux origines du célibat ecclésiastique: la continence cultuelle des clercs majeurs dans l'ancienne Église d'Occident.—Corona gratiarum. Miscellanea E. Dekkers O.S.B.*, II, 123–28. Bruges, 1975.

Hefele, C. J. "Die Entwicklung des Cölibates und die kirchliche Gesetzgebung über denselben, sowohl bei den Griechen als Lateinern", in *Beiträge zur Kirchengeschichte, Archäologie und Liturgik*, by Dr. Carl Joseph Hefele, vol. I, 122–39. Tübingen, 1864.

Houtin, A. *Courte histoire du célibat ecclésiastique*. Paris, 1929.

Jombart, E., and E. Herman. "Célibat des clercs". DDC 3:132–56, 665–72.

Jubany, M. "El celibato ecclesiastico y el canon 10 del concilio de Ancyra" (a. 314). *Analecta sacra Tarraconensia* 15 (1942): 237–56.

Klitsche, T. F. *Geschichte des Cölibats der katholischen Geistlichkeit von der Zeiten der Apostel bis zum Tode Gregor's.* Augsburg, 1830.

Knetes, C. "Ordination and Matrimony in the Eastern Orthodox Church". JTS 11 (1910): 348–400, 481–513.

Koch, H. "Tertullian und der Cölibat". TThQ 88 (1906): 406–11.

Kotting, B. *Der Zölibat in der Alten Kirche.* Münster Westf., 1970.

———. "Die Diskussion um den Zölibat". ThRev 67 (1971): 425–38.

Kottje, R. "Zur Geschichte des Zölibatsgesetzes", in *Ehelosigkeit des Priesters in Geschichte und Gegenwart,* ed. R. Kottje et al., 9–24. Regensburg, 1970.

Labriolle, P. de. "Le mariage spirituel dans l'antiquité chrétienne". *Revue historique* 46 (1921): 204–25.

Lafontaine, P. H. *Les conditions positives de l'accession aux ordres dans la première législation ecclésiastique (300–492).* Ottawa, 1963.

Lea, H. C. *The History of Sacerdotal Celibacy in the Christian Church.* London, 1867. New edition without notes or bibliography: New York: University Books USA, 1957, 1966.

Leclercq, H. "La législation conciliaire relative au célibat ecclésiastique", in C. J. Hefele and H. Leclercq, *Histoire des conciles d'après les documents originaux,* II, 2; *Appendice VI,* 1321–48. Paris, 1908.

———. "Célibat". DACL 2:2802–32.

Leinweber, W. *Der Streit um den Zölibat im 19. Jahrhundert.* Münster, 1978.

Léon-Dufour, X. "Mariage et continence selon S. Paul". In *A la rencontre de Dieu. Mémorial Albert Gelin* 8, Theological Library of Lyon, 319–29. Le Puy, 1961.

Liotta, F. *La continenza dei chierici nel pensiero canonistico classico da Graziano a Gregorio IX.* Quaderni di "Studi Senesi", 24. Milan, 1971.

Lugani, P. "Il celibato del clero nell'Occidente". *La Scuola cattolica* 32 (1904): 470–84, 566–80.

Lyonnet, S. "Le diacre 'mari d'une seule femme' (1 Tm. 3, 12)". In *Le Diacre dans l'Église et le monde d'aujourd'hui,* Unam Sanctam 59, published by P. Winninger and Y. Congar, 272–78. Paris, 1966.

Marchisano, F. "Il celibato ecclesiastico nell'insegnamento dei Sommi Pontifici e dei Concili". *Seminarium* 19 (1967): 729–63.

Moehler, J. A. "Beleuchtung der Denkschrift für die Aufhebung des den katholischen Geistlichen vorgeschriebenen Cölibates. Mit drei Actenstücken", in *J.-A. Möhler's Gessammelte Schriften und Aufsätze*. Published by Dr. Jo. Jos. Ign. Döllinger, vol. 1, 177–267. Regensburg, 1839.

Moersdorf, K. "Zölibat". LTK 10 (2d ed., 1965): 1396–1400.

Monachino, V. *La cura pastorale a Milano Cartagine e Roma nel sec. IV.* Analecta Gregoriana 41. Rome, 1947.

Pampaloni, P. "Continenza e celibato del clero. Leggi e motivi nelle fonti canonistische dei secoli IV e V". *Studia Patavina* 17 (1970): 5–9.

Papp-Szilagyi, J. *Enchiridion Juris Ecclesiae Orientalis catholicae.* 2d ed., 189–94. Magno-Varidini, 1880.

Perini, C. "Il celibato ecclesiastico nel pensiero di S. Ambrogio". *Divus Thomas* 66 (1963): 432–50.

Picard, P. *Zölibatsdiskussion im katholischen Deutschland der Aufklärungszeit. Auseinandersetzung mit der kanonischen Vorschrift im Namen der Vernunft und der Menschenrechte.* Düsseldorf, 1975.

Probst, F. *Kirchliche Disciplin in den drei ersten christlichen Jahrhunderten.* Tübingen, 1873.

Roskovany, A. de. *Coelibatus et Breviarium: duo gravissima clericorum officia, e monumentis omnium seculorum demonstrata. Accessit completa literatura.* I–IV: Pestini, 1861. V–VIII: Nitrae, 1877. IX–X: Nitrae, 1881; *Supplementa ad collectiones monumentorum et literaturae.* III–IV: Nitrae, 1888.

Scaduto, M. *Enciclopedia Cattolica* 3, s.v. "Celibato", 1261–66.

Schelkle, K. H. "Ehe und Ehelosigkeit im Neuen Testament". In *Wort und Schrift. Beiträge zur Auslegung und Auslegungsgeschichte des Neuen Testamentes,* 183–98. Düsseldorf, 1966.

Schillebeeckx, E. *Autour du célibat du prêtre, étude critique.* Paris, 1967.

Schulze, W. A. "Ein Bischof sei eines Weibes Mann . . . Zur Exeges von I. Tim. 3, 2 und Tit. 1, 6". *Kerygma und Dogma* 4 (1958): 287–300.

Segalla, G. "Il testo più antico sul celibato: Mt. 19, 11–12". *Studia Patavina* 17 (1970): 121–37.

Sloyan, G. "Motifs bibliques et patristiques du célibat des ministres de l'Église". *Concilium* 78 (1972): 13–27.

Stickler, A. M. "La continenza dei diaconi specialmente nel primo millenio della chiesa". *Salesianum* 26 (1964): 275–302.

———. "Tratti salienti nella storia del celibato". *Sacra Doctrina* 15 (1970): 585–620.

———. "Nota storica sul celibato dei chierici 'in sacris'". *L'Osservatore Romano* (March 4, 1970): 2–3.

———. "L'évolution de la discipline du célibat dans l'Église en Occident de la fin de l'âge patristique au Concile de Trente", in *Sacerdoce et célibat. Études historiques et théologiques*, published by J. Coppens, 373–442. Gembloux-Louvain, 1971.

———. "Il celibato ecclesiastico". In *L'Osservatore della Domenica*, supplement to nos. 103, 109, 115 of *L'Osservatore Romano* 6, 13. May 20, 1979.

Stiltinck, J. "An veresimile sit, S. Paphnutium se in Concilio Nicaeno opposuisse legi de continentia Sacerdotum et Diaconorum". In *Acta Sanctorum Septembris* 3, 784–87. Venice, 1761.

Theiner, J. A., and A. Theiner. *Die Einführung der erzwungenen Ehelosigkeit bei den christlichen Geistlichen und ihre Folgen. Ein Beitrag zur Kirchengeschichte.* 3 vol. Altenburg, 1828.

Thomassin, L. "Du célibat des Bénéficiers dans l'Église orientale pendant les cinq premiers siècles". Bk. II, chap. LX, in *Ancienne et nouvelle discipline de l'Église touchant les Bénéfices et les Bénéficiers.* 3 vol. in fol. Paris, 1678–79. Rev. ed., Paris, 1725. Chap LXI: "Du célibat des Bénéficiers dans l'Église latine pendant les cinq premiers siècles" (ca. 894–901).

Trautman, D. W. *The Eunuch Logion of Matthew 19:12: Historical and Exegetical Dimensions as Related to Celibacy.* Rome, 1966.

Vacandard, E. F. "Les origines du célibat ecclésiastique". In *Études de critique et d'histoire religieuse*, 1st ser., 71–120. Paris, 1905. 5th ed., Paris, 1913.

———. "Célibat ecclésiastique". DTC 2:2068–88.

Vadagnini, V. "Celibato e Sacerdozio nelle Chiese Orientali". *Ekklesia* 3/2 (1969): 120 pp.

Vernet, F. "Célibat ecclésiastique". DSp 2:385–96.

Winkelmann, F. "Paphnutios, der Bekenner und Bischof". In *Probleme der koptischen Literatur*, 1 (K2), revised by Peter Nagel, 145–53. Published by the Institut für Byzantinistik of Martin-Luther-Universität, Halle-Wittenberg. Scholarly contributions of Martin-Luther-Universität, Halle-Wittenberg. Halle (Saale), 1968.

Zaccaria, F. A. *Storia polemica del Celibato sacro da contrapporsi ad alcune detestabili opere uscite a questi tempi.* Rome, 1774.

———. *Nuova giustificazione del celibato sacro dagli inconvenienti oppostogli anche ultimamente in alcuni infamissimi libri dissertazioni quattro.* Fuligno, 1785.

INDEX